Botswana & Namibia

Victoria Falls
p183

Namibia
p215

Botswana
p44

D1053425

Anthony Ham, Trent Holden

PLAN YOUR TRIP

OSTRICH, ETOSHA
NATIONAL PARK P250

CARGE/SHUTTERSTOCK ©

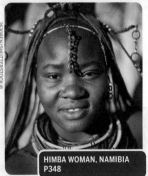

HIMBA WOMAN, NAMIBIA
P348

2630BEN/SHUTTERSTOCK ©

ON THE ROAD

Contents

WESTEND61/GETTY IMAGES ©

SAFARI IN BOTSWANA P29

SPECIAL FEATURES

Welcome to Botswana & Namibia

Ever wanted to experience the raw, wild heart of Africa? Teeming with wildlife and lush with extraordinary landscapes, Botswana and Namibia unfurl so many African dreams.

Wildlife Watching

Botswana is one of Africa's great safari destinations. There are more elephants here than in any other country on the planet. But whether it's elephants, lions, leopards, hyenas, rhinos, buffaloes, antelope or myriad other species, their numbers and variety in Botswana will quickly overwhelm your digital camera. In Namibia the series of waterholes around Etosha Pan attract astounding numbers of animals (especially in the dry season), making wildlife watching as simple as parking your car and letting the animals come to you. And if that's not up-close-and-personal enough, what about tracking highly endangered black rhinos...on foot?

Landscape

The landscapes of Namibia and Botswana will sometimes leave you wondering if you have arrived on another planet. That mighty gash hacked out of the earth's surface at Fish River Canyon is one of the great natural sights on the continent. Lonely desert roads expose you to a wilderness that will clear your mind and work its way into your soul. Humongous slabs of flat-topped granite rise out of mists of windblown sand and swirling dust – the effect is ethereal. As the road snakes into the distant horizon you may just feel as though you're driving through a coffee-table book of landscapes.

Ancient Culture

The ancestors of the San, an ancient people who have direct links back to the Stone Age, left behind extraordinary records in the form of rock paintings throughout the region. The Tsodilo Hills, Botswana's only Unesco World Heritage Site, showcase the pictorial record of this prehistoric culture, as do extensive galleries of rock art in Namibia. Also in Namibia, opportunities to interact with local cultures in the north include meeting the Himba of the Kaokoveld (a Herero subgroup who were a part of the early Bantu migrations). Himba women are famous for smearing themselves with a fragrant mixture of ochre, butter and bush herbs, which dyes their skin a burnt-orange hue.

Adventure Activities

Namibia is Southern Africa's headquarters for adrenaline-pumping fun. Fling yourself out of a plane and float back to earth, hurl yourself down a sand dune, surf the breakers on the Atlantic coast or head off into a desert sunset atop a camel. There are many ways to ensure that a visit to this region lives with you long after the desert sands recede into the distance. Swakopmund is where most of adventure activities happen, and it's worth spending a few days here if they have even the remotest appeal.

Why I Love Botswana & Namibia

By Anthony Ham, Writer

I long ago lost my heart in the waterways of the Okavango Delta, in the sands of the Central Kalahari Game Reserve, upon the hot stones of Damaraland, atop a sand dune at Deadvlei and by a waterhole in Etosha... Fabulous wildlife, soul-stirring landscapes, a true feeling of immersion in wild lands and wilderness – Botswana and Namibia have all these in abundance, and the sense of beautiful, wild places animated by just about every species of charismatic African megafauna calls me back time and again.

For more about our writers, see p408

Above: Namib Desert, Namibia

Botswana & Namibia

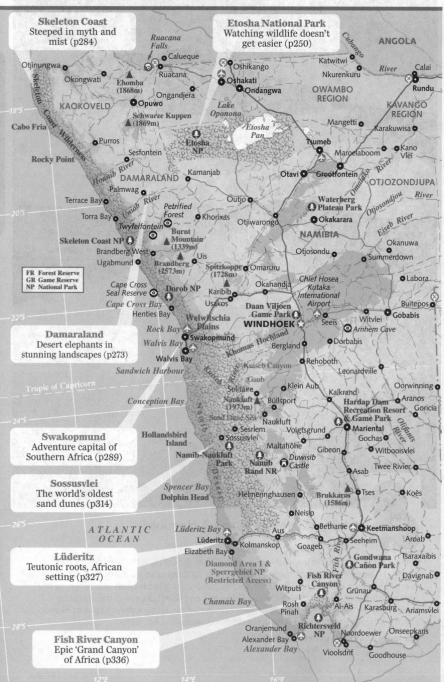

Skeleton Coast
Steeped in myth and mist (p284)

Etosha National Park
Watching wildlife doesn't get easier (p250)

Damaraland
Desert elephants in stunning landscapes (p273)

Swakopmund
Adventure capital of Southern Africa (p289)

Sossusvlei
The world's oldest sand dunes (p314)

Lüderitz
Teutonic roots, African setting (p327)

Fish River Canyon
Epic 'Grand Canyon' of Africa (p336)

FR Forest Reserve
GR Game Reserve
NP National Park

Tsodilo Hills
Ancient San rock art (p121)

Victoria Falls
The mightiest waterfall on earth (p183)

Chobe National Park
An astounding array of wildlife (p79)

Moremi Game Reserve
Botswana's wildlife central (p112)

Makgadikgadi Pans NP
Kalahari treasure of endless horizons (p75)

Okavango Delta
A watery paradise for wildlife (p93)

Central Kalahari Game Reserve (CKGR)
Iconic African wilderness (p129)

0   200 km
0   120 miles

ZAMBIA

ZIMBABWE

BOTSWANA

SOUTH AFRICA

Kalahari Desert

Okavango Delta

ELEVATION

	2000m
	1500m
	1200m
	600m
	300m
	0

Imusho
Katima Mulilo
Mpalila Island
Zambezi NP
Kasane
Livingstone
Victoria Falls
Zambezi River

Andara
Mudumu NP
Chobe River
Linyanti
Chobe FR
Kasane FR
Kazuma FR
Pandamatenga

Mahango GR
Bwabwata NP
Shakawe
Mamili NP
Savuti
Kazuma FR

Tsodilo Hills
Etsha 6
Xaa
Moremi GR
Chobe NP
Sibuyu FR

Khaudum NP
Nxaunxau
Kudumane

Tsumkwe
Gumare
Okavango Delta
Shorobe
Nxai Pan
Nxai Pan NP
Gweta
Nata
Bulawayo

Nokaneng
Maun
Matlapaneng
Nata Sanctuary
Semowane
Tutume
Plumtree

Aha Hills (1250m)
Gcwihaba (Drotsky's) Cave
Konde
Toteng
Ntwetwe Pan
Masunga
Siviya
Gwanda

Sehithwa
Makgadikgadi Pans NP
Sowa (Sua) Pan
Tlalamabele
Francistown
Matsiloje
North-East Tuli GR

Kuke
Rakops
Mopipi
Orapa
Letlhakane
Shashe River

D'kar
Ghanzi
Deception Pan
Molapo
Mmashoro
Serule
Selebi-Phikwe

Rietfontein
Central Kalahari GR
Foley
Maope
Pont Drift

Tshootsha
Okwa River
Khama Rhino Sanctuary
Palapye
Tuli Block
Mawana NR

Xanagas
Takatshwaane
Mosolotsane
Sefophe
Zanzibar
Swartwater

Kule
Lokalane
Ohe
Kodibeleng
Kalamare
Sherwood
Tom Burke

Ncojane
Kang
Tsetseng
Khutse GR
Sefare
Mahalapye
Parr's Halt

Tshane
Morwamosu
Salajwe
Takatokwane
Artesia

Sekoma
Letlhakeng
Molepolole
Mochudi

Union's End
Khakea
Jwaneng
GABORONE

Kgalagadi Transfrontier Park
Makopong
Werda
Mokolodi NR
Kanye
Otse Hill (1489m)

Vlooirskop (959m)
Phepheng
Bray
Mannyelanong GR
Lobatse
Pioneer Gate

Mata Mata
Auob River
Tshabong
Phitshane
Ramatlabama
PRETORIA

Rooiputs
Khawa
Molopo River
McCarthysrus
Mabule
Mafikeng
JOHANNESBURG

Rietfontein
Fly's Kop
Middlepits
Vryburg

Bokspits

Nakop
Spitskop NR
Upington

Augrabies Falls NP
Kimberley
Vaal River
Orange River

Botswana & Namibia's
Top 16

Okavango Delta

1 Botswana's Okavango (p8) is an astonishing, beautiful, wild place. Home to wildlife spectacles of rare power and drama, the delta changes with the seasons as flood waters ebb and flow, creating islands, river channels and pathways for animals that move this way and that at the waters' behest. Exclusive and remote lodges are an Okavango speciality but self-drivers can find outstanding campsites in the heart of Okavango's Moremi Game Reserve. No visit to the delta is complete without drifting through the waters in a traditional *mokoro* (dugout canoe).

Etosha National Park

2 There are few places in Southern Africa that can compete with the wildlife prospects in extraordinary Etosha National Park (p250). A network of waterholes dispersed among the bush and grasslands surrounding the pan – a blindingly white, flat, saline desert that stretches into the horizon – attracts enormous congregations of animals. A single waterhole can render thousands of sightings over the course of a day, with lions and rhinos the highlights. Etosha is simply one of the best places on the planet for watching wildlife.

Victoria Falls

3 The largest, most beautiful and simply the greatest waterfall in the world. As iconic to Africa as 'Dr Livingstone I presume', thunderous Victoria Falls (p183) will blow your mind and soak your shirt. It's the sheer scale of the falls that is its most impressive feature. A million litres of water a second are funnelled over the 108m drop, creating a plume of spray that can be seen for kilometres. When you're in Southern Africa this really is a sight that you should move heaven and earth to see.

Sossusvlei

4 Towering red dunes of incredibly fine sand that feels soft when it trickles through your fingers and changes iridescently with the light, Sossusvlei (p314) is an astounding place, especially given that the sands originated in the Kalahari millions of years ago. The Sossusvlei valley is dotted with hulking dunes and interspersed with unearthly dry vleis (low, open landscapes). Clambering up the face of these constantly moving giants is a uniquely Namibian experience. You survey the seemingly endless swath of nothingness that surrounds you and it feels as though time itself has slowed.

Chobe National Park

5 There are more elephants in Chobe (p79) – tens of thousands of them – than anywhere else on earth. And these are big elephants, *really* big. Then there are the iconic landscapes of Savuti with its elephant-eating lions; or Linyanti, one of the best places on the continent to see the highly endangered African wild dog; or the Chobe Riverfront where most of Africa's charismatic megafauna comes to drink. Put all of this together and it's easy to see why Chobe National Park ranks among the elite of African safari destinations.

Fish River Canyon

6 This enormous gash in the surface of the planet in the south of Namibia is an almost-implausible landscape. Seen most clearly in the morning, Fish River Canyon (p336) is desolate, immense and seemingly carved into the earth by a master builder. The exposed rock and lack of plant life is quite startling and invokes thoughtful reflection and a quiet sense of awe. Its rounded edges and sharp corners create a symphony in stone of gigantic and imposing proportions.

Central Kalahari Game Reserve

7 There is something special about the Kalahari (p129) – even the name carries more than a whiff of African magic. Perhaps it is the sheer vastness of this desert; Africa's largest protected wilderness area. The presence of black-maned Kalahari lions doesn't hurt, either. It's home to ancient river valleys, light woodland and surprising concentrations of wildlife around ts extensive network of salt pans. And then there is the silence of the Kalahari night...

MYTHO/GETTY IMAGES ©

BOBBY BRADLEY/SHUTTERSTOCK ©

The San People

8 In both Botswana and Namibia, opportunities exist to interact with the San – the original inhabitants of Southern Africa, whose presence stretches back as far as 20,000 years. In Namibia, Otjozondjupa is part of the traditional homeland of the Ju/'Hoansi-San (also known as the !Kung) and in Tsumkwe (p269), you can arrange everything from bushwalks to hunting safaris. In Botswana, villages such as D'kar offer interaction with these descendants of all our ancestors, in a way that supports the local community (p127).

A Luxury Safari

9 Botswana didn't invent the luxury safari, but it may just have perfected it. Nowhere else on earth will you find so many remote and utterly exclusive lodges and tented camps, accessible only by air or boat, where your every dream of the perfect safari comes true. Most are in the Okavango Delta, but you'll also find them in the neighbouring areas of Linyanti, Chobe National Park and the Central Kalahari Game Reserve. Picking favourites is always difficult, but we love Vumbura Plains Camp (p108).

DAVID CAYLESS/GETTY IMAGES ©

CHRIS JACKSON/GETTY IMAGES ©

Camping out on Safari

10 Sharpen your senses and heighten your awareness of Africa while sleeping under the stars (p34). This soulful experience is the antithesis of the modern world's clamour – an infinity of stars, the crackle of the campfire, the immensity of the African night. But it's not for the faint-hearted, what with wind whistling in the guy ropes, the not-so-distant roar of a lion, and the knowledge that only flimsy canvas separates you from an angry hippo. This is total immersion of the most wonderful (and sometimes scary) kind and you'll experience the African wild in a very special way.

Lüderitz

11 Namibia is a country that defies African stereotypes and this is perhaps nowhere more true than in the historic colonial town of Lüderitz (p327). Straddling the icy South Atlantic and the blazing-hot Namib Desert is this bizarre mini-Deutschland seemingly stuck in a time warp. After walking its streets and sitting down to a plate of sausages and sauerkraut with an authentic weiss beer, you'll survey the German art nouveau architecture, check the map again and shake your head in disbelief.

Skeleton Coast

12 Travel on the Skeleton Coast (p284), a treacherous stretch of shore where many ships have become graveyards, is the stuff of road-journey dreams. It's a murky region with rocky and sandy coastal shallows, where rolling fogs and swirling sandstorms encapsulate its ghostly, isolated and untamed feel. It is among the most remote and inaccessible areas in the vast country of Namibia. And it's here, in this wilderness, that you can put your favourite music on, sit back and let reality meet your imagination.

RADEK BOROVKA/SHUTTERSTOCK ©

RADEK BOROVKA/SHUTTERSTOCK ©

Makgadikgadi Pans National Park

13 Part of the world's largest network of salt pans, the endless horizons of Makgadikgadi (p75) are one of the Kalahari's least known treasures. During the rainy season zebras migrate here en masse. During the dry season, wildlife draws near to the rejuvenated Boteti River in similarly epic numbers. Meerkats are another highlight. And away across the pans, remote islands of baobabs rise from the salt like evocations of some ancient African oasis.

Rock Art

14 The Tsodilo Hills (p121), which became a Unesco World Heritage Site even before the Okavango Delta, is sometimes referred to as the 'Louvre of the Desert'. More than 4000 ancient paintings, many dating back thousands of years, adorn these caves and cliffs, which remain a sacred site for the San people. Rendered in ochre-hued natural pigments, the paintings are an invaluable chronology of the evolving relationship between humans and the natural world. And such is their remoteness, you might just have them all to yourself.

RADEK BOROVKA/SHUTTERSTOCK ©

OLEG ZNAMENSKIY/SHUTTERSTOCK ©

Damaraland

15 Damaraland (p273) is Namibia in a rather beautiful nutshell. The landscapes here, turning burnt orange and blood red with the sinking sun, would be reason enough to visit – this is one beautiful corner of the country, with bouldered mountains, snaking dry valleys, bizarrely photogenic tree shapes – but the wildlife is also a wonderful story. Tracking down the free-roaming black rhinos, desert elephants and desert lions that are such icons of the Namibian wild in such gorgeous surrounds is a wonderful way to spend your time.

The Himba & Herero

16 Culturally rich Namibia, with its colonial overtones, is best experienced in the varied communities of the Herero population, of which the Himba of the Kaokoveld (p280) are a subgroup. The characteristic Herero women's dress is derived from Victorian-era German missionaries. In contrast, Himba women are famous for smearing themselves with a fragrant mixture of ochre, butter and bush herbs, which dyes their skin a burnt-orange hue. Don't come to stare. Instead, sit alongside them for an afternoon and learn about their world.

Need to Know

For more information, see Survival Guide (p379)

Currency
Botswana pula (P)
Namibian dollars (N$)

Language
English, Setswana

Visas
Visitors to Botswana are issued a visa on arrival, valid for 30 days. Visas are not required for most nationalities visiting Namibia.

Mobile Phones
Local SIM cards can be used in Australian and European phones. Wide swaths of the country are not covered by the mobile network.

Time
Botswana is two hours ahead of GMT/UTC. There is no daylight-saving time in Botswana. In the summer months (October to April), Namibia is two hours ahead of GMT/UTC. In the winter (April to October), Namibia turns its clocks back one hour, making it only one hour ahead of GMT/UTC and one hour behind South African time.

When to Go

Desert, dry climate

Maun
• GO May–Oct

Windhoek
• GO Apr–Nov

Swakopmund
GO Apr–May, Oct–Dec

Gaborone
GO May–Oct •

•**Lüderitz**
GO Apr–Oct

High Season
(May or Jun–Oct)

➡ Dry season, warm clear days, hotter in September to October in Botswana.

➡ Best time for wildlife-watching as animals congregate around waterholes.

➡ Swakopmund and Walvis Bay can experience sandstorms June to August.

Shoulder
(Nov & Apr)

➡ A good time with fewer tourists and good wildlife viewing.

➡ The 'little rains' come in Namibia in November.

➡ By April the floodwaters have reached the upper Delta in Botswana.

Low Season
(Dec–Mar)

➡ The rainy season, so many tracks impassable but fewer tourists.

➡ From December to March it's roasting and some long hiking trails are closed.

➡ high season in parts of the Kalahari such as the Central Kalahari Game Reserve.

Useful Websites

Lonely Planet (www.lonelyplanet.com) Destination information, hotel bookings, traveller forum and more.

Botswana Tourism (www.botswanatourism.co.bw) Department of Tourism website.

Namibia Tourism (www.namibiatourism.com.na) Tourism portal for the Namibian government, with country-wide coverage.

Namibia Wildlife Resorts (www.nwr.com.na) Info and booking service for Namibia's national parks.

Cardboard Box Travel Shop (www.namibian.org) Namibia's best adventure-travel agency.

Safari Bookings (www.safaribookings.com) Fantastic resource for booking your safari, with expert and traveller reviews.

Regional Tourism Organisation of Southern Africa (www.retosa.co.za) Promotes tourism in Botswana and Namibia.

Important Numbers

Botswana

Botswana does not use area codes.

Country Code	267
International Access Code	00
Emergency	999
Ambulance	997
Fire	998
Police	999

Namibia

Namibia uses three-digit area codes.

Country Code	264
International Access Code	00
Emergency	10111

EXCHANGE RATES

		BOTSWANA	NAMIBIA
Australia	A$1	P8.03	N$10.46
Canada	C$1	P7.83	N$10.50
Europe	€1	P11.62	N$14.95
Japan	¥100	P10.05	N$12.60
New Zealand	NZ$1	P7.67	N$9.92
South Africa	R1	P0.77	N$1
UK	£1	P13.05	N$17.63
US	US$1	P10.47	N$14.17

For current exchange rates, see www.xe.com

Daily Costs

Budget: Less than US$75

➡ Dorm bed: US$10–15

➡ Campsite: US$18–30

➡ Two meals US$10–20

➡ Intercity bus: US$25–100

Midrange: US$75–150

➡ Double room in midrange hotel: US$50–150

➡ Two meals US$25–30

➡ Internal flights: US$100–200

➡ One-off scenic flight in Okavango Delta: around US$100

Top End: More than US$150

➡ Double room in top-end hotel: from US$150

➡ Per person in high-season lodge: from US$1000

➡ 4WD rental per day: from US$150

➡ Meals in top-end restaurants: US$40–50

Opening Hours

Botswana

Banks 8.30am–3.30pm Monday to Friday, 8.15am–10.45am Saturday

National parks 6am–6.30pm April to September, 5.30am–7pm October to March

Restaurants 11am–11pm Monday to Saturday; some also open the same hours on Sunday

Namibia

Banks 8am or 9am–3pm Monday–Friday, 8am–12.30pm Saturday

Post offices 8am–4.30pm Monday–Friday, 8.30–11am Saturday

Petrol stations Only a few open 24 hours; in outlying areas fuel hard to find after hours or Sunday

Arriving

OR Tambo International Airport (Johannesburg) Main gateway to the region with regular flights to Windhoek and Gaborone.

Chief Hosea Kutako International Airport (Windhoek (p218)) Taxis to the centre cost up to N$400 and take between 45 minutes and an hour.

Sir Seretse Khama International Airport (Gaborone (p177)) Taxis rarely turn up at the airport, but if you see one they cost P10 to the centre (15 to 20 minutes). The only reliable transport is the minibus operated by the top-end hotels for their guests; nonguests may be able to hitch a ride.

For much more on **getting around**, see p178 & p383

If You Like...

Big Cats

It's a fairly reliable prediction that if you dedicate any serious time to watching wildlife in Botswana and Namiba, you'll most likely see lions, leopards and cheetahs. The heart and soul of wild Africa, these apex predators will provide many of your most enduring safari memories.

Savuti Lions and leopards are commonly seen here – and these are some of Southern Africa's meanest lions. (p87)

Moremi Game Reserve There are big cats everywhere in Botswana's north (try Chobe Riverfront or deep in the Okavango Delta), and Moremi rarely disappoints. (p112)

Etosha National Park Lions on a kill at a waterhole while herds of springbok and gemsbok watch on nervously – ah, the drama of Etosha. (p250)

Okonjima Nature Reserve Track leopards and cheetahs while learning an important conservation message. (p239)

Central Kalahari Game Reserve Track down the black-maned Kalahari lions of legend. (p158)

Damaraland Desert-adapted lions roam the sand dunes, rocky mountains and dry river valleys. (p273)

Bwabwata National Park Lions are making a comeback in Namibia's far northeastern corner. (p261)

Elephants

Botswana has within its borders one-third of all African elephants left on the planet – you'll never get closer to an elephant than here – while Namibia is home to the much-famed desert elephants of the north.

Chobe National Park The world's mother lode for elephant populations, with dense congregations of very big elephants close to Chobe Riverfront. (p79)

Elephant Sands Commune with wild elephants – so close you could almost reach out and touch them – at this lodge built around a waterhole. (p69)

Moremi Game Reserve Elephants at every turn here in the Okavango Delta in Botswana's north. (p112)

Damaraland The famed desert elephants of Namibia roam the deep-red, rocky mountains of Namibia's northwest. (p273)

Etosha National Park Caked in white Etosha dust, these relatively small tuskers can look like the grey ghost-shadows of the salt pans. (p250)

Senyati Safari Camp Watch elephants at the waterhole right beneath your bar while you nurse your sundowner. (p81)

Rhinos

The increasingly precarious foothold of the rhino in Southern Africa seems to apply less in Namibia than elsewhere, although there's good news coming out of Botswana as well. Rhino tracking greatly increases your chances, but there are plenty of opportunities elsewhere too.

Palmwag Africa's largest population of free-ranging black rhinos, many with radio collars to allow tracking. (p278)

Etosha National Park Sidle up to just about any waterhole by night and wait for the rhinos to come drink and socialise. (p250)

Khama Rhino Sanctuary For decades this was Botswana's last refuge for rhinos and it's still a good place to see them. (p61)

Waterberg Plateau Park A small but growing population that can be difficult to see unless you go with the experts. (p242)

Okavango Delta Recent reintroduction efforts are bearing fruit, with some lodges and camps taking a front-row seat. (p93)

Top: Sossusvlei, Namib-Naukluft National Park
Bottom: Black rhino, Etosha National Park

Birdwatching

Botswana is a birding utopia, with almost 600 species recorded. Namibia is also a wonderful destination for birders, from the shorebirds of the coast to the desert specialists of the interior.

Okavango Panhandle A narrow strip of swampland that extends for about 100km to the Namibian border, the area is known for its fine birdwatching. (p117)

Chobe Riverfront There is extraordinary variety in the birdlife along the riverfront and overhead there's a good chance of spotting African fish-eagles. (p84)

Nata Bird Sanctuary A quarter of Botswana's birds call the sanctuary home, and it's covered in a sea of pink flamingos (and other migratory birds) during the rains. (p69)

Caprivi Strip Bwabwata and Nkasa Rupara National Parks present Namibia's best birdwatching opportunities. Nkasa Rupara has recorded more than 430 species. (p262)

Walvis Bay Lesser and greater flamingos flock in large numbers to pools along the Namib Desert coast, particularly around Walvis Bay and Lüderitz. (p306)

Central Kalahari Game Reserve Some real desert specialists inhabit the reserve, with Kalahari scrub robins, ostriches and the kori bustard particular prizes. (p158)

Etosha National Park Some of Namibia's best birding for desert-adapted species, including kori bustard and ostrich. (p250)

MARK READ/LONELY PLANET ©

MANUEL ROMARIS/GETTY IMAGES ©

Rock Art

The rock art of Botswana and Namibia is both an extraordinary chronology of an ancient people and a startling artistic form that is a link to our ancient ancestors. Dotted around in hills and caves, these are magical, sacred works of art.

Tsodilo Hills Revered by the San, this 'desert Louvre' is one of Botswana's premier sites for this pictorial form of San chronology and includes numerous fascinating panels. (p121)

Twyfelfontein One of Africa's most extensive galleries of rock art, with new examples being discovered all the time and a petrified forest nearby. (p275)

The Brandberg Fire Mountain is an extraordinarily beautiful slab of granite, containing the famous 'White Lady of the Brandberg' in its treasure chest of ancient rock paintings. (p274)

National Museum of Namibia Excellent rock-art display with some great reproductions; an ideal place to visit before seeing rock-art sites. (p220)

Landscapes

Namibia possesses an incredible array of landscapes, from soaring sand dunes and slabs of ancient granite mountains, to rock-strewn moonscapes, salt pans and endless savannah. Botswana is generally pretty flat, but even that has its own appeal and there are regions where variety abounds.

Fish River Canyon For once the clichés are true – this truly is Africa's equivalent of the Grand Canyon. (p336)

Namib-Naukluft National Park Some of the most beautiful sand dunes on the planet, plus the austerely beautiful Naukluft Mountains. (p308)

Etosha Pan Stand out on the pan and survey an empty saline nothingness that bursts into life after the rains; just behind is an artist's palette of African savannah. (p250)

Okavango Delta As desert turns into fertile land, mother nature's ebb and flow on the landscape is more apparent here – one of the world's largest inland river deltas – than anywhere in the region. (p93)

Northwestern Namibia Some of the region's most incredible landscapes include the Skeleton Coast and the Kaokoveld, with its wide-open vistas and lonely desert roads. (p273)

Makgadikgadi Pans & Nxai Pan National Parks Mesmerising and strangely beautiful, pancake-flat expanses larger than any on the planet. (p75) (p77)

Spitzkoppe The essence of Namibia's rocky mountain spine that runs for most of the length of the country. (p273)

Adventure Sports

Adventure sports thrive in Namibia with most enthusiasts zeroing in on the Atlantic coast. Here you can sandboard an ancient desert, throw yourself out of a plane, surf the Atlantic or go horse riding into a blazing sunset.

Swakopmund Namibia and indeed Southern Africa's capital of adventure sports, this is adrenaline-junkie heaven. (p289)

Rhino tracking Following black rhinos through the bush may not be considered a traditional adventure sport, but when it's on foot... (p281)

Quad biking Opportunities exist in both countries, although in Botswana it is generally limited to top-end lodges (eg in Makgadikgadi Pans). (p295)

Scenic flights Namibia's coastline, especially the Skeleton Coast, and the Okavango Delta in Botswana, both offer the chance of light-aircraft or helicopter flights over jaw-dropping scenery. (p294)

Hiking Multiday hiking opportunities exist throughout the region, although many are closed in low season. (p34)

Fly-In Safaris

Botswana is Southern Africa's top-end safari destination, and many tour operators specialise in fly-in safaris or include a fly-in element in their itineraries. It can be the only way to reach remote areas such as the north of Namibia's Skeleton Coast or Botswana's Okavango Delta.

Okavango Delta Particularly popular, the luxury lodges operating these services are some of Africa's most exclusive. (p93)

Moremi Game Reserve The only officially protected area within the Okavango Delta, so plenty of wildlife; several truly decadent lodges. (p112)

Chobe National Park Lodges here boast panoramic views across the Chobe River, and herds of elephants can be easily seen from the grounds of your accommodation. (p79)

TOBIE OOSTHUIZEN/SHUTTERSTOCK ©

African fish eagle, Botswana

Skeleton Coast Wilderness Area Remote, wild and virtually inaccessible unless you're willing to fly in. (p287)

Namibia's Northwest Corner The ultimate in isolation, located in Namibia's remote, almost trackless far northwest. (p283)

Off-Road Driving

There's plenty to challenge 4WD enthusiasts who like to get off-road. In many remote places age-old tracks (in perilous condition after the rains) are the only way to navigate the African wilderness.

Central Kalahari Game Reserve An off-roader's dream; if you're after solitude, desertscapes and the echo of lions roaring in the night, this enormous heart of the African wilderness could become your favourite place. (p129)

The Kaokoveld One of the last true wildernesses in Southern Africa, the remote and beguiling Kaokoveld is criss-crossed by sandy tracks laid down decades ago – this is a serious off-road challenge. (p280)

Khaudum National Park With virtually no signage, and navigation dependant on GPS coordinates and topographic maps, Khaudum is a wildlife-and-off-road adventure. (p260)

Makgadikgadi Pans If the notion of exploring 12,000 sq km of disorientating salt pans is your idea of adventure, then calibrate your GPS and head straight here. (p68)

Savuti The tracks that connect Savuti to the outside world are some of the sandiest in the country – make it here, and you've earned your stripes. (p87)

The Brandberg Real 4WD country out here, with gravel tracks yielding to rocky trails that you may just have to yourself. (p274)

Aha Hills This is Botswana's most remote corner, with challenging trails and a blissful sense of having dropped off the end of the earth. (p124)

Month by Month

TOP EVENTS

Windhoeker Karneval (WIKA), April

Maitisong Festival, March

Zebra migration, March–April

Late dry season wildlife, October

Oktoberfest, October

January

After a peak around Christmas and New Year (with peak rates), January is a generally quiet month, except in the Kalahari and for birdwatchers. Expect high temperatures, generally high humidity and a good chance of intermittent heavy rains.

February

February is similar to January: warm days, mild nights, and heavy if sporadic rains. Rains should ease by month's end. Birding is good in the north. High season in the Kalahari. Elsewhere expect low-season rates.

March

A big month for festivals. The rains are still around but temperatures begin to fall (it's all relative...). Most accommodation is quiet with plenty available. The zebra migration is in full swing on Botswana's salt pans.

✵ Independence Day

On 21 March, this national day is celebrated in grand style, with a parade and sports events in Windhoek. Many can still recall the day that Namibia wrestled control of its own affairs off South Africa in 1990.

✵ Maitisong Festival

Held in Gaborone over one week in March and/or April, this festival is the highlight of the Botswana calendar for lovers of local and regional music, dance and drama. The festival features an outdoor program that takes place on several stages throughout the capital. (p48)

✵ Enjando Street Festival (Mbapira)

Windhoek's biggest street party occurs in March every year. It's also a good excuse for people to dress in extravagant ethnic clothes that bring the streets to life. Expect cultural events, musical performances and much merriment. (p223)

April

Still low season (rains ending, temperatures becoming more pleasant but tourist numbers still down) except for Botswana's Kalahari and a late peak for Namibian school holidays. The zebra migration (p72) in Makgadikgadi begins the return journey west.

✵ Maun Festival

A two-day celebration with plenty of music, parades, poetry, theatre, craftwork, dance and food; visual arts also feature. The festival, held in Maun, raises funds for local schools while commemorating northwestern Botswana's rich cultural roots.

✵ Windhoek Karneval (WIKA)

Established in 1953 by a small group of German immigrants, Windhoek Karneval is now one of the highlights of Namibia's cultural calendar, culminating in the Royal Ball. (p223)

May

May is a lovely month to travel, with fine conditions and generally low-season rates (and availability) in the Okavango Delta, Etosha and elsewhere. Count on mild daytime temperatures, cooler nights and generally clear skies.

June

An excellent month to visit. June has favourable climatic conditions and is nestled nicely between local school holidays in May and the July start of high season (although high season begins now in some Okavango Delta lodges).

July

High season gets underway with limited availability, high prices and the waters of the Okavango near their peak. Expect warm, clear days and ideal conditions (apart from coastal Namibia, where sandstorms can be a problem).

August

The region's busiest month for foreign visitors, August is the high-season peak: prices are at their highest, availability is at a premium and advance bookings are essential. Lovely weather, though...

☆ Kuru Dance Festival

A worthwhile cultural festival, held near D'kar in the Kalahari Desert, with all aspects of traditional Bushman culture on display. Traditional dancing and local music feature throughout the three days of the festival.

🎊 Maherero Day

This is one of Namibia's largest festivals, falling on the weekend nearest 26 August. Dressed in traditional garb, the Red Flag Herero people gather in Okahandja for a memorial service to commemorate their chiefs killed in the Khoikhoi and German wars. (p234)

September

Temperatures are rising but it's a popular time to visit and tourist numbers remain high. Availability can be a little higher but prices remain high. Waterholes are starting to dry out so wildlife watching is generally good.

☆ /AE//Gams Arts Festival

Windhoek's main arts festival is held in September, and includes troupes of dancers, musicians, poets and performers all competing for various prizes. The best of Namibian food is also on show. (p224)

🎊 Artists Trail

Since 2007, Omaruru has played host to this dynamic festival of music and dance events over three days in September. There's

also food, wine, jewellery, photography, painting and other good things in life.

October

In the build-up to the rains, October can be very hot, especially in the north around Caprivi and the Okavango Delta. Wildlife is often concentrated around the few remaining waterholes, and delta lodges are booked out months in advance.

Oktoberfest

The end of high season, with the rains around the corner, but Windhoek is a magnet for beer drinkers and it's a popular time, especially for German tourists. Hot days and dry waterholes ensure that wildlife gravitates to water.

November

Hot and dry, November is when locals begin scanning the skies for rain. High season is over and wildlife watching is good, but the build-up to the rains can be unpleasant. Migratory birds fill the skies.

December

The rains should be in full swing. It's low season in the delta and high season in Botswana's Kalahari but there's a special peak period over Christmas and New Year, with a short, sharp influx of visitors arriving from Europe and elsewhere.

Itineraries

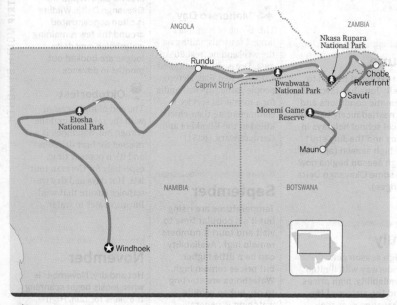

ANGOLA

ZAMBIA

Rundu

Nkasa Rupara
National Park

Caprivi Strip

Chobe
Riverfront

Bwabwata
National Park

Savuti

Moremi Game
Reserve

Etosha
National Park

Maun

NAMIBIA

BOTSWANA

Windhoek

2 WEEKS A Taste of the North

Despite the long distances, it is possible to get a taste of Botswana and Namibia's best wildlife areas in a busy two-week itinerary. To make this work, you'll need your own 4WD.

Begin in **Windhoek** and soak up its urban charms before you head out into the wilds. Spend at least three days in **Etosha National Park**, home to some of the best wildlife viewing in Southern Africa, then drive via Grootfontein to sleep on the banks of the Okavango River at steamy **Rundu**; that's Angola across the water. Track east into the Caprivi Strip for a couple of nights in **Bwabwata National Park** and the **Nkasa Rupara National Park**, before crossing into Botswana and staying along the **Chobe Riverfront** for a couple of days among big herds of big elephants. Leaving the paved road behind, make for the lion-and-leopard country of **Savuti** (two nights), then spend three days in **Moremi Game Reserve**. From there, make for **Maun** to continue your onward journey, leaving enough time for a scenic helicopter flight over the Okavango Delta with **Helicopter Horizons**.

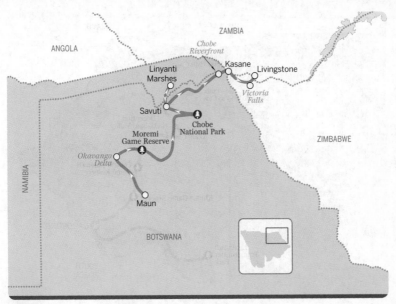

 Essential Botswana & Victoria Falls

For most of this trip you will have to be completely self-sufficient and fully confident in your navigation and survival skills. For the less adventurous, tour operators in Maun are happy to help you organise a custom safari.

Starting in **Maun**, the classic staging point for all Botswanan safaris, you can stock up on supplies before heading out to the **Okavango Delta**, either by *mokoro* (dugout canoe) or charter plane. If you're pinching your pennies, there's no shortage of budget camping trips to choose from, though it's certainly worth stretching your budget to allow for a few nights in one of the safari-chic tented camps in the wildlife-rich **Moremi Game Reserve** (try Chief's Camp if you can afford it). Containing some of the densest concentrations of wildlife on the continent, Moremi is also the only protected area of the delta.

The next stage of your bush travel is a 4WD expedition through **Chobe National Park** (known for its huge populations of massive elephants). Stop at **Savuti**, where most megafauna are resident, and which is particularly well known for sightings of predators; **Linyanti Marshes**, an extensive wetland with opportunities to see elephants, lions, wild dogs, cheetahs and leopards; and the **Chobe Riverfront**, which is the most accessible part of Chobe and has the park's largest wildlife concentration. Whether you travel by private vehicle or tour bus, the overland route through Chobe is one of the country's most spectacular and wildlife-rich journeys.

Make another supply stop in the border town of **Kasane**, at the meeting point of four countries – Botswana, Zambia, Namibia and Zimbabwe – and it's time to cross the border to visit the world-famous **Victoria Falls**. The falls are one of the seven natural wonders of the world, and a visit reveals nature at its most inspiring. Whether you base yourself in **Livingstone**, Zambia or **Victoria Falls**, Zimbabwe, it's worth exploring life on both sides of the Zambezi River. If you've got a bit of cash burning a hole in your pocket, there's no shortage of pulse-raising activities to help you get a quick adrenaline fix. Try a microlight flight over the falls for a unique perspective of this watery wonder.

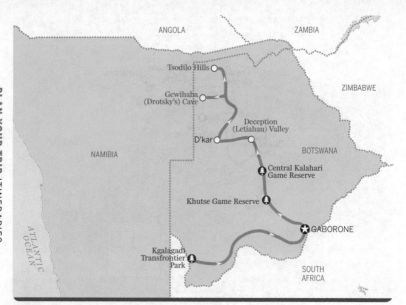

Secrets of the Kalahari

If you're looking to leave the khaki-clad tourist crowds behind, this off-the-beaten-track option takes you straight through the heart of the Kalahari.

If you're starting in Johannesburg, head west for the border where you can cross at Bokspits to enter the enormous **Kgalagadi Transfrontier Park**. The park is one of the only spots in the Kalahari where you can see shifting sand dunes, though the undisputed highlights are its pristine wilderness and low tourist volume. It's the Kalahari of your imagination, noted for its wildlife watching, including large numbers of springboks, gemsboks, elands and wildebeest as well as predators such as lions, cheetahs, leopards, wild dogs, jackals and hyenas. If you like birdwatching, you're in for a treat here too.

Head east towards Gaborone and then loop back to enter the southern gates of the utterly wild **Khutse Game Reserve**. Here are well-maintained trails and around 60 pans that once made up the largest inland lake on the continent. Leopard and lion sightings are possible wildlife highlights. From here, traverse north through some exciting 4WD territory into the adjoining **Central Kalahari Game Reserve**, where you can navigate one of the continent's most prominent topographical features. It's about the size of Denmark, so there's plenty of scope for losing yourself in Africa's raw heart. Before leaving, spend a night or two in **Deception Valley**, renowned for its rare brown hyenas. Although wildlife densities are significantly lower than in Chobe or the **Okavango Delta**, so are the number of safari vehicles.

Heading north, you'll pass through **D'kar**, where you can pick up some beautiful San crafts. If you're here in August, immerse yourself in traditional Bushman culture at the Kuru Dance Festival. Press on for the remote **Gcwihaba (Drotsky's) Cave**, renowned for its 10m-long stalagmites and stalactites, as well as Commerson's leaf-nosed bats. Finally, at the furthermost tip of the country, you'll come to the mystical **Tsodilo Hills**, which is a treasure chest of painted rock art that continues to be revered by local communities. The beautiful colours of these remote hills are striking but it's the 4000-plus prehistoric rock paintings throughout the hills that most people are here to see.

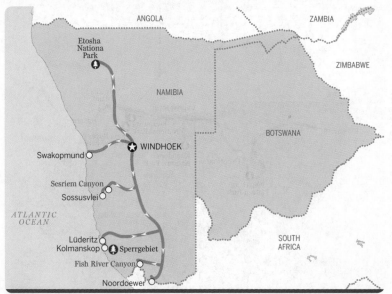

 **Namibia All Over**

This enormous itinerary meanders more than 2500km, from dusty bushveld to dramatic canyons. It combines a good dose of culture with death-defying activities, and all of it is accessible with a 2WD vehicle. There are also decent, if slow, public-transport links.

Before striking off into the desert, spend a couple of days getting your bearings in the lovely capital of **Windhoek**, which still bears architectural traces of its German colonial history. Ideally with a rental car loaded with plenty of supplies and a few friends, make a beeline north for **Etosha National Park**, one of the finest safari parks on the continent. It is possible to actually drive out onto the pan with its white saline floor stretching as far as you can see to the horizon.

Although you're going to have to backtrack, you can quickly bypass Windhoek en route to seaside **Swakopmund**, where you can take your holiday up a notch in a flurry of exciting activities, including dune boarding and quad biking. Back on the main road south, keep the heart beating during a scramble up the massive barchan dune fields of **Sossusvlei** and/or a trek through **Sesriem Canyon**. The ever-shifting dunes of the Namib Desert are particularly worth gazing upon at sunrise, when their colourful hues dance over the landscape.

Continuing the canyon theme, head south for **Fish River Canyon**, a geological wonder of monumental proportions that is one of Africa's hidden highlights. If you've packed sturdy hiking boots you could embark on a multiday hike along the canyon floor. From Fish River Canyon, detour west to marvel at the German anachronism that is **Lüderitz**. Sausages washed down with German beer are a prerequisite before embarking on your explorations. Nearby, you can stop off at the diamond-mining ghost town of **Kolmanskop** and explore the overwhelming emptiness of the **Sperrgebiet**.

Finish things off in **Noordoewer**, which sits astride the Orange River and is the jumping-off point for white-water rafting through some wild canyon country. Alternatively, head across the South African border to cosmopolitan Cape Town, which you can enjoy for a week or a weekend before setting off on the next adventure.

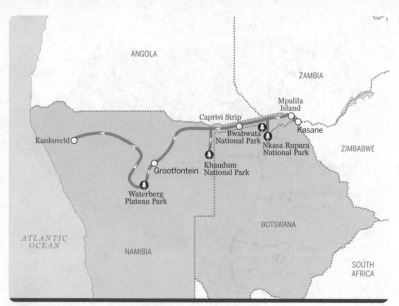

2 WEEKS Caprivi to Kaokoveld

This is not an itinerary for the faint-hearted. Many places in Namibia give you a vague sense that you've reached the end of the earth, but some of the destinations in this itinerary really are other-worldly. Getting to them, too, presents a major challenge that definitely requires determination as well as a fair bit of cash.

To do this trip as a continuous journey, you're best off starting from **Kasane** in Botswana. From here, you can charter a plane or boat to **Mpalila Island**, a luxuriously remote retreat stranded in the middle of the Zambezi River. It's where Zimbabwe, Botswana, Namibia and Zambia intersect. From here, head into Namibia's Caprivi Strip and visit the mini-Okavango of the **Nkasa Rupara National Park**, where the rains bring a delta-like feel to the forested islands that contain some of Namibia's best birdwatching. **Bwabwata National Park** is another park on the rebound with lions, wild dogs and sable antelope. Drive from here to the untamed wilderness that is **Khaudum National Park**, a serious adventure destination. Here, wandering sandy tracks lure visitors through bushland and across valleys where lions and African wild dogs can be seen.

From Khaudum the road will take you south through **Grootfontein**, from where it's worth making a short detour to the **Waterberg Plateau Park**. The park is famous as a haven for endangered species such as sable and roan antelopes and white and black rhinos, some of which you may be lucky enough to spot along one of the well-marked hiking trails. It's an unusual place in that it feels a little like a lost world on top of the plateau with its pristine bushy landscapes – take advantage of the hides at the waterholes for your best chance to spot wildlife.

North of Grootfontein the road takes you into Namibia's cultural heartland, the Owambo region, from where you can access the remote and mysterious **Kaokoveld**, homeland to the Himba – a culturally rich tribal group that has retained its striking appearance and dress – and one of the most inaccessible areas of the country.

Plan Your Trip
Planning a Safari

The unique wildlife and the landscapes they inhabit make for a magical safari experience in Botswana and Namibia. But making the most of this dream journey into the African wilds requires careful planning – here's where we show you how.

Planning Your Trip

Choosing an Operator

A good operator is the single most important variable for your safari, and it's worth spending time thoroughly researching those you're considering. At the budget level in particular, you may find operators who cut corners – be careful to go with a reputable outfit. There are many high-quality companies that have excellent track records. Operators we recommend enjoyed a good reputation at the time of writing, as do many others that couldn't be listed due to space considerations. However, we can't emphasise enough the need to check on the current situation with all of the listed companies and any others you may hear about.

Do some legwork (the internet is a good start) before coming to Botswana or Namibia. Get personal recommendations, and once in the region, talk with as many people as you can who have recently returned from a safari or trek with the company you're considering.

Be sceptical of price quotes that sound too good to be true, and don't rush into any deals, no matter how good they sound.

Also, take the time to go through the itinerary in detail, confirming what is expected and planned for each stage of the trip. Be sure that the number of wildlife drives per day and all other specifics appear in the written contract, as well as the starting and ending dates and (approximate) times.

Best...

Tips for Desert Hiking

Rise before the sun does and hike until the heat becomes oppressive. Rest through the midday heat and begin again after about 3pm. During warmer months, time your hike with the full moon so you can hike at night.

Places to Spot Wild Dogs

In Linyanti, east of the Okavango Delta in northern Botswana – one of the few healthy wild-dog populations in Africa. In Namibia, head for Bwabwata National Park.

Destinations for a Safari

In Botswana, the Okavango Delta and Chobe National Park; in Namibia, Etosha National Park.

Tips for a Self-Drive Safari

If you haven't driven in Africa before, go with someone who has. Take a satellite phone – they're easy and relatively inexpensive to hire.

Safari Style

While price can be a major determining factor in safari planning, there are other considerations that are just as important.

➡ **Ambience** Will you be staying in or near the park? (If you stay well outside the park, you'll miss the good early-morning and evening wildlife-viewing hours.) Are the surroundings atmospheric? Will you be in a large lodge or an intimate private camp?

➡ **Equipment** Mediocre vehicles and equipment can significantly detract from the overall experience. In remote areas, lack of quality equipment or vehicles and appropriate back-up arrangements can be a safety risk.

➡ **Access and activities** If you don't relish the idea of spending hours on bumpy roads, consider parks and lodges where you can fly in. To get out of the vehicle and into the bush, target areas offering walking and boat safaris.

➡ **Guides** A good driver/guide can make or break your safari.

➡ **Community commitment** Look for operators that do more than just give lip service to ecotourism principles, and that have a genuine, long-standing commitment to the communities where they work. In addition

RENTING A 4WD

There are numerous variations on the theme when it comes to 4WD rentals, but the most common vehicle models are two- or four-berth Toyota (Hilux, Land-Cruiser or Fortuner), Land Rover (Defender or Discovery, although the former is slowly disappearing) and Ford Ranger, all adapted for camping. This may mean a pop-up roof which has space to sleep two people, rooftop tents and/or ground tents, as well as all camping gear (ie bedding, although some, including Avis, don't offer sleeping bags), cooking and eating equipment, fridge/freezer and all mechanical tools necessary to get you out of a tight spot. To be sure of what you're getting, make sure you ask for a full equipment list at the time of your booking.

Prices range from US$80 to US$190 per day.

If you're looking to rent a car for exploring Botswana, we recommend booking through companies who offer specialist rental of fully equipped 4WDs with all camping equipment. Most can also arrange for pick-ups/drop-offs in Maun, Kasane, Gaborone, Windhoek, Victoria Falls, Harare or Livingstone, but remember that you'll usually pay a fee if you pick up your vehicle other than from the company's main office, or if you drop it off other than where you picked it up. Fees range between US$250 and US$650 for either service.

The following are among the better 4WD rental agencies:

Avis Safari Rentals (in South Africa ☑+27 11-387 8431; www.avis.co.za/safari-rental)

Bushlore (in South Africa ☑+27 11-312 8084; www.bushlore.com)

Travel Adventures Botswana (☑74 814 658, 686 1211; www.traveladventuresbotswana.com)

In an ever-expanding market, other 4WD-rental companies include the following:

Africamper (www.africamper.com)

Britz (in Jo'burg ☑+27 11 230 5200, in Namibia ☑+264-61-219590; www.britz.co.za) (in Namibia ☑+264-62-540242, in Jo'burg ☑+27 11-230 5200; www.britz.co.za)

If you rent directly through the rental company, you'll get just the vehicle and you'll need to make all of the other travel arrangements on your own. For most travellers, it works out more convenient to book through an operator who can also make campsite and other accommodation bookings, arrange a satellite phone and make any other necessary arrangements. For this, try the following:

Drive Botswana (p36)

Safari Drive (☑in the UK 01488 71140; www.safaridrive.com)

Self Drive Adventures (☑686 3755; www.selfdriveadventures.com)

to being more culturally responsible, they'll also be able to give you a more authentic and enjoyable experience.

➡ **Setting the agenda** Some drivers feel that they have to whisk you from one good 'sighting' to the next. If you prefer to stay in one strategic place for a while to experience the environment and see what comes by, discuss this with your driver. Going off in wild pursuit of the Big Five (lions, leopards, buffaloes, elephants and rhinos) means you'll miss the more subtle aspects of your surroundings.

➡ **Less is more** If you'll be teaming up with others to make a group, find out how many people will be in your vehicle, and try to meet your travelling companions before setting off.

➡ **Special interests** If birdwatching or other special interests are important, arrange a private safari with a specialised operator.

When to Go

Getting around is easier in the dry season (May to October), and in many parks this is when animals are easier to find around waterholes and rivers. Foliage is also less dense, making wildlife spotting simpler. However, as the dry season corresponds in part with the high-travel season, lodges and camps in some areas get crowded and accommodation prices are at a premium.

Apart from these general considerations, the ideal time to make a safari very much depends on which parks and reserves you want to visit and your particular interests. For example, the wet season is the best time for birdwatching in many areas, although some places may be inaccessible during the rains. Wildlife concentrations also vary markedly, depending on the season.

Types of Safari

As safaris become more crafted to their clientele, the typical image of khaki-clad tourists bush whacking through the scrub is becoming obsolete. These days a safari can incorporate anything from ballooning over the undulating dunes of the Namib, to scooting along the lush channels of the Okavango in a traditional *mokoro* (dugout canoe). Horse riding,

trekking, birding, fishing, night-drive and camel safaris are all on the agenda. The typical safari is now a highly sophisticated experience that reconnects with that vital sense of adventure.

Wildlife watching tops the region's list of attractions and forms the basis of most safaris, and little wonder. Etosha National Park in Namibia and Botswana's Okavango Delta and Chobe National Park (among others) are packed with animals – in fact, you'll find the greatest density and variety of wildlife in Southern Africa, and some of the best wildlife watching on the continent. The evocative topography is just the icing on the cake.

It's good to keep in mind that although there are safaris catering to most budgets, a Botswanan, and to a lesser degree Namibian, safari can be expensive. Certainly most safari experiences are skewed towards the top end of the market in Botswana.

Here we provide an overview of the factors to consider when planning a safari. There is a lot more to choose from at the higher end of the price spectrum, where ambience, safari style and the operator's overall focus are important considerations. However, good, reliable budget operators can also be found in both countries.

Fly-In Safaris

If the world is your oyster, then the sheer sexiness of taking off in a little six-seater aircraft to nip across to the next remote safari camp or designer lodge is a must. It also means you'll be able to maximise your time and cover a selection of parks and reserves, giving yourself an idea of the fantastic variety of landscapes on offer.

The biggest temptation will be to cram too much into your itinerary, leaving you rushing from place to place. Be advised, it's always better to give yourself at least three days in each camp or lodge in order to really avail yourself of the various activities on offer.

While a fly-in safari is never cheap, they are all-inclusive, including meals, drinks and activities in each camp; flight transfers often cost extra. Obviously, this all takes some planning and the earlier you can book a fly-in safari the better – many operators

32

PLAN YOUR TRIP PLANNING A SAFARI

WILD DRIVING & CAMPING IN BOTSWANA & NAMIBIA

These are road-tested tips to help you plan a safe and successful 4WD expedition.

➡ Invest in a good Global Positioning System (GPS). You should always be able to identify your location on a map, though, even if you're navigating with a GPS. We found the Tracks4Africa app to be the best.

➡ Stock up on emergency provisions, even on main highways. Fill up whenever you pass a station. For long expeditions, carry the requisite amount of fuel in metal jerry cans or reserve tanks (off-road driving burns nearly twice as much fuel as highway driving). Carry 5L of water per person per day, as well as a plenty of high-calorie, nonperishable emergency food items.

➡ You should have a tow rope, a shovel, an extra fan belt, vehicle fluids, spark plugs, bailing wire, jump leads, fuses, hoses, a good jack and a wooden plank (to use as a base in sand and salt), several spare tyres and a pump. A good Swiss Army knife or Leatherman-type tool, plus a roll of gaffer tape, can save your vehicle's life in a pinch.

➡ Essential camping equipment includes a waterproof tent, a three-season sleeping bag (or a warmer bag in the winter), a ground mat, fire-starting supplies, firewood, a basic first-aid kit and a torch (flashlight) with extra batteries.

➡ Natural water sources are vital to local people, stock and wildlife, so please don't use clear streams, springs or waterholes for washing yourself or your gear. Similarly, avoid camping near springs or waterholes lest you frighten the animals and inadvertently prevent them from drinking. You should always ask permission before entering or camping near a settlement. Remember that other travellers will pass through the region long after you've gone, so, for the sake of future tourism, please be considerate and respect the local environment and culture.

➡ Avoid camping in shady and inviting riverbeds, as large animals often use them as thoroughfares, and even when there's not a cloud in the sky, flash floods can roar down them with alarming force.

➡ In the interests of the delicate landscape and flora, keep to obvious vehicle tracks; in this dry climate, damage caused by off-road driving may be visible for hundreds of years to come.

➡ Sand tracks are least likely to bog vehicles in the cool mornings and evenings, when air spaces between sand grains are smaller. Move as quickly as possible and keep the revs up, but avoid sudden acceleration. Shift down gears before deep sandy patches or the vehicle may stall and bog.

---

advise at least six to eight months' notice if you want to pick and choose where you stay.

Fly-in safaris are particularly popular, and sometimes a necessity, in the delta region of Botswana. Given the country's profile as a top-end safari destination, many tour operators specialise in fly-in safaris or include a fly-in element in their itineraries.

Mobile Safaris

Most visitors to Botswana and Namibia will experience some sort of organised mobile safari, ranging from an all-hands-on-deck 'participation safari', where you might be expected to chip in with camp chores and supply your own sleeping bag

and drinks, all the way up to top-class, privately guided trips.

As trips at the lower end of the budget scale can vary enormously in quality, it pays to canvass opinion for good local operators. This can be done on Lonely Planet's Thorn Tree forum (http://thorntree.lonelyplanet.com), or by chatting to other travellers on the ground. Failing this, don't hesitate to ask lots of questions of your tour operator and make your priorities and budget clear from the start.

Maun is Botswana's mobile-safari HQ, while most safaris in Namibia will need to be booked out of Windhoek. For those booking through overseas tour operators, try to give as much notice as possible, especially if you want to travel in the

➡ When negotiating a straight course through rutted sand, allow the vehicle to wander along the path of least resistance. Anticipate corners and turn the wheel slightly earlier than you would on a solid surface – this allows the vehicle to skid round smoothly – then accelerate gently out of the turn.

➡ Driving in the Kalahari is often through high grass, and the seeds it disperses can quickly foul radiators and cause overheating; this is a problem especially near the end of the dry season. If the temperature gauge begins to climb, remove as much plant material as you can from the grille.

➡ Keep your tyre pressure slightly lower than on sealed roads, but don't forget to reinflate upon returning to the tarmac.

➡ Avoid travelling at night, when dust and distance may create confusing mirages.

➡ Keep to local speed limits, with a maximum of 100km/h on sealed roads, and 40 km/h off-road.

➡ Follow ruts made by other vehicles.

➡ If the road is corrugated, gradually increase your speed until you find the correct speed – it'll be obvious when the rattling stops.

➡ If you have a tyre blowout, do *not* hit the brakes or you'll lose control and the car will roll. Instead, steer straight ahead as best you can, and let the car slow itself down before you bring it to a complete stop.

➡ In rainy weather, gravel roads can turn to quagmires and desert washes may fill with water. If you're uncertain, get out and check the depth, and only cross when it's safe for the type of vehicle you're driving.

➡ Always be on the lookout for animals.

➡ Avoid swerving sharply or braking suddenly on a gravel road or you risk losing control of the vehicle. If the rear wheels begin to skid, steer gently in the direction of the skid until you regain control. If the front wheels skid, take a firm hand on the wheel and steer in the opposite direction of the skid.

➡ In dusty conditions, switch on your headlights so you can be seen more easily.

➡ Overtaking can be extremely dangerous because your view may be obscured by dust kicked up by the car ahead. Flash your high beams at the driver in front to indicate that you want to overtake. If someone behind you flashes their lights, move as far to the left as possible.

high season. This will give you a better chance of booking the camps and lodges of your choice.

Overland Safaris

Given the costs and complex logistics of arranging a big safari, many budget travellers opt for a ride on an overland expedition, run by specialists like Africa in Focus (www.africa-in-focus.com) and Dragoman (www.dragoman.com). Most of these expeditions are multicountry affairs with Namibia and Botswana featuring as part of a longer itinerary starting in either Cape Town (South Africa) or Nairobi (Kenya) and covering a combination of countries including Namibia, Botswana, Zimbabwe, Zambia, Malawi and Tanzania.

The subject of overlanding often raises passionate debate among travellers. For some the massive trucks and concentrated numbers of travellers herded together are everything that's wrong with travel. They take exception to the practice of rumbling into tiny villages to 'gawk' at the locals and then roaring off to party hard in hostels and bush camps throughout the host countries. Often the dynamics of travelling in such large groups (15 to 20 people at least) creates a surprising insularity, resulting in a rather reduced experience of the countries you're travelling through.

For others, the overland truck presents an excellent way to get around on a budget and see a variety of parks and reserves while meeting up with people from different walks of life. Whatever your view, bear in mind that you're unlikely to get the best out of any particular African country by racing through on an inflexible itinerary.

The classic overland route through Namibia and Botswana takes in Fish River Canyon, Sossusvlei, Etosha National Park, Swakopmund, the Skeleton Coast, the Caprivi Strip, the Okavango Delta and Chobe National Park and goes on to Victoria Falls in Zimbabwe.

Self-Drive Safaris

It's possible to arrange an entire safari from scratch if you hire your own vehicle. This has several advantages over an organised safari, primarily total independence and being able to choose your travelling companions. However, as far as costs go, it's generally true to say that organising your own safari will cost nearly as much as going on a cheap organised safari. Also bear in mind that it's wise to make all your campsite bookings (and pay for them) in advance, which means that you'll need to stick to your itinerary.

In addition to the cost, vehicle breakdowns, accidents, security, weather conditions and local knowledge are also major issues. It's not just about hiring a 4WD, but about having the confidence to travel through some pretty rough terrain and handle anything it throws at you. However, if all this doesn't put you off then it can be a great adventure.

Your greatest priority will be finding a properly equipped 4WD, including all the necessary tools you might need in case of a breakdown.

Note: if you're planning a self-drive safari in northeastern Namibia or northern Botswana, you'll need to watch out for the wet season (December to March) when some tracks become completely submerged and driving is particularly risky.

You can find pretty much all the camping essentials you need in major supermarket chains, which have outlets throughout Botswana and Namibia. They stock everything from tents and sleeping bags to cooking equipment and firelighters.

Walking & Hiking Safaris

At some national parks and private concessions, you can arrange walks of two to three hours in the early morning or late afternoon, with the focus on watching animals rather than covering distance. Following the walk, you'll return to the main camp or lodge.

It's also possible in Namibia to arrange safaris on foot to track black rhinos. This presents a unique opportunity to see one of Africa's most endangered animals in the wild. Such a safari usually takes place on private concessions.

Horse-Riding Safaris

Riding on horseback is a unique way to experience the landscape and its wildlife – Botswana presents numerous opportunities to canter among herds of zebras and wildebeest. The horse-riding safaris in Botswana are highly rated and there are numerous operators. You'll need to be an experienced rider, though, as most horseback safaris in Botswana don't take beginners – after all, you need to be able to get yourself out of trouble should you encounter it.

Local Tour Operators

Typically most visitors to Botswana and Namibia will book a safari with a specialist tour operator and many local operators do the bulk of their business this way. The recommendations here provide an overview of some of the best operators in Botswana and Namibia. Other agencies are listed throughout the guide.

&Beyond (www.andbeyond.com) Stunning lodge in various remote locations in Botswana plus one in Namibia, mixed with impressive conservation programs.

Capricorn Safaris (www.capricornsafaris.com) One of the largest operators in Botswana, with affiliations in Kenya and Tanzania. It has a focus on luxury tented safaris in all the main national parks. Note: groups can be quite large.

Desert & Delta Safaris (www.desertdelta.co.za) A top-notch tour operator with luxury camps and lodges located in Moremi, Chobe and the Okavango Delta. You can expect a uniformly high standard of service.

A BEGINNER'S GUIDE TO TRACKING WILDLIFE

Visitors to Africa are always amazed at the apparent ease with which professional guides locate and spot wildlife. While most of us can't hope to replicate their skills in a brief visit, a few pointers can hone your approach.

➡ **Time of day** This is possibly the most important factor for determining animal movements and behaviours. Dawn and dusk tend to be the most productive periods for mammals and many birds. They're the coolest parts of the day, and also produce the richest light for photographs. Although the middle of the day is usually too hot for much action, this is when some antelope feel less vulnerable at a watering hole, and when raptors and reptiles are most obvious.

➡ **Weather** Prevailing conditions can greatly affect your wildlife-viewing experience. For example, high winds may drive herbivores and birds into cover, so concentrate your search in sheltered areas. Summer thunderstorms are often followed by a flurry of activity as insect colonies and frogs emerge, followed by their predators. Overcast or cool days may prolong activity (such as hunting) by normally crepuscular predators, and extremely cold winter nights force nocturnal species to stay active at dawn.

➡ **Water** Most animals drink daily when water is available, so water sources are worthwhile places to invest time, particularly in the dry season. Predators and very large herbivores tend to drink early in the day or at dusk, while antelope tend to drink from the early morning to midday. On the coast, receding tides are usually followed by the appearance of wading birds and detritus feeders such as crabs.

➡ **Food sources** Knowing what the different species eat will help you decide where to spend most of your time. A flowering aloe might not hold much interest at first glance, but knowing that it is irresistible to many species of sunbirds might change your mind. Fruiting trees attract monkeys, while herds of herbivores with their young are a predator's dessert cart.

➡ **Habitat** Knowing which habitats are preferred by each species is a good beginning, but just as important is knowing where to look in those habitats. Animals aren't merely randomly dispersed within their favoured habitats. Instead, they seek out specific sites to shelter: hollows, trees, caves and high points on plains. Many predators use open grasslands but also gravitate towards available cover, such as large trees, thickets or even grass tussocks. 'Ecotones' – where one habitat merges into another – can be particularly productive because species from both habitats overlap.

➡ **Tracks and signs** Even when you don't see animals, they leave many signs of their presence. Spoor (tracks), scat (droppings), pellets, nests, scrapes and scent marks provide information about wildlife, and may even help to locate it. Check dirt and sand roads when driving – it won't take long for you to recognise interesting spoor. Elephant footprints are unmistakable and large predator tracks are fairly obvious. Also, many wild cats and dogs use roads to hunt, so look for where the tracks leave the road – often they mark the point where they began a stalk or sought out a nearby bush for shade.

➡ **Equipment** Probably the most important piece of equipment you can have is a good pair of binoculars. These help you not only to spot wildlife but also to correctly identify it (this is essential for birding). Binoculars are also useful for viewing species and behaviours where close approaches are impossible. Field guides – pocket-sized books that depict mammals, birds, flowers etc of a specific area with photos or colour illustrations – are also invaluable. These guides also provide important identification pointers and a distribution map for each species.

Drive Botswana (☑in Palapye 492 3416; www. drivebotswana.com) This excellent operator arranges 4WDs and complete-package itineraries, including maps, trip notes and bookings for campsites. We found the owner, Andy Raggett, to be outstanding and unfailingly professional.

Great Plains Conservation (www.greatplainsconservation.com) Among the elite of safari operators, combining a growing portfolio of stunning lodges with cutting-edge conservation work.

Kwando Safaris (www.kwando.com) Respected Botswanan operator of long standing, with a handful of lodges in the delta and surrounding area, as well as in Nxai Pan National Park and Central Kalahari Game Reserve (CKGR).

Mabaruli African Safaris (www.mabaruli.com) Based in Windhoek, this outfit offers cycling safaris as well as a tour that takes in Namibia (Etosha National Park), Botswana (Okavango Delta) and Zambia (Victoria Falls).

Masson Safaris (www.massonsafaris.net) A family-run outfit based in Botswana, with over 25 years' experience running mobile safaris.

Namibia Horse Safari Company (www. namibiahorsesafari.com) A range of multi-day horse-riding safari expeditions, including in the Namib Desert Damaraland in search of desert elephants; the Sperrgebiet in search of wild horses; and elsewhere as well as shorter rides.

Safari Drive (www.safaridrive.com) Expensive but professional and upmarket company with its own fleet of recent-model vehicles. Prices include all equipment, emergency backup, detailed route preparation and bookings, satellite phone and free tank of fuel.

Safaris Botswana (www.safaris-botswana.com) Specialises in budget mobile and *mokoro* trips. Safaris are practically all-inclusive but you have to bring your own sleeping bags and drinks. It also runs the friendly, no-frills Audi Camp.

UP CLOSE & PERSONAL

The threat of attack by wild animals is rare, but compliance with a number of guidelines will further diminish the chances of an unwelcome encounter. The five most dangerous animals are the Big Five: lions, leopards, buffaloes, elephants and rhinos.

➡ Always sleep inside a tent and be sure to zip it up completely. If you hear a large animal outside, lie still even if it brushes against the tent.

➡ Never pitch a tent in an open area along a riverbank – this is probably a hippo run.

➡ When camping, don't keep fresh fruit (especially oranges) in your tent, because they can attract elephants.

➡ If you encounter a lone buffalo, a lion (especially a lioness) or an elephant that detects your presence, back away slowly and quietly.

➡ Try not to make eye contact with a leopard if you encounter one while on foot.

➡ Do not run away from a lion. If you respond like a prey species, the lion will react accordingly.

➡ Elephant cows with calves should be avoided. Likewise, do not approach any elephant with visible injuries.

➡ When travelling in a boat, watch for signs of hippos and steer well away from them.

➡ When a hippo feels threatened, it heads for water – don't be in its way!

➡ Visitors should take care not to swim in rivers or waterholes where crocs or hippos are present. Always use extreme caution when tramping along any river or shoreline.

➡ Be aware that hyenas are also potentially dangerous, although they're normally just after your food.

Skeleton Coast Safaris (www.skeletoncoast-safaris.com) Conducts four- to six-day fully catered expeditions that use a combination of aircraft and 4WD vehicles to explore this wonderfully remote coastal landscape, including shipwreck sites. Some of the safaris also take in other prime Namibian destinations such as Sossusvlei and Etosha.

Uncharted Africa (p73) Multiday mobile safaris across the salt pans of northern Botswana and further afield.

Wild Dog Safaris (www.wilddog-safaris.com) This popular backpacker-oriented tour operator runs a variety of expeditions throughout Namibia.

Wilderness Safaris (www.wilderness-safaris.com) Manages an impressive array of luxury camps and lodges in Namibia, Botswana, Zimbabwe and further afield, and supports a number of commendable conservation and community projects. It even has its own airline.

Wildlife Specialists

All international companies offering safaris to Botswana and Namibia – and there are *many* of them – will most likely make wildlife-watching the centrepiece of the safari experiences they offer. But there are two UK companies in particular for whom wildlife is their raison d'être, with all of the benefits that brings:

Nature Trek (www.naturetrek.co.uk)

Wildfoot Travel (www.wildfoottravel.com)

Which Field Guide?

Field guides, apart from being damned interesting to read, can be invaluable tools for identifying animals while on safari. Our favourites:

A Field Guide to the Carnivores of the World (Luke Hunter; 2011) Wonderfully illustrated and filled with fascinating detail.

The Kingdon Field Guide to African Mammals (Jonathan Kingdon; 2nd ed, 2015) The latest edition of the classic field guide covering over 1150 species.

The Behavior Guide to African Mammals (Richard Despard Estes; 1991) Classic study of the behaviour mammal species. Estes' follow-up *The Safari Companion: A Guide to Watching African Mammals* (1993) is an excellent, slightly more accessible alternative.

Stuarts' Field Guide to Mammals of Southern Africa (Chris & Mathilde Stuart; 2014) Another excellent guide with easy identification clues and information on tracking.

Birds of Southern Africa (Ian Sinclair et al; 4th ed, 2011) Easily the best field guide to the country's birds.

Watching Wildlife: Southern Africa (Matthew Firestone & Nana Luckham; 2nd ed, 2003) Lonely Planet's very own field guide, complete with colour photographs.

Mammals of Botswana & Surrounding Areas (Veronica Roodt; 2011) Handy, well-written guide available in many lodges and bookstores around Botswana.

38

MARTIN HARVEY/GETTY IMAGES ©

1. Cheetah-Watching (p361)
The cheetah can reach speeds of up to 112km/h, but must rest for 30 minutes between hunts.

2. Okavango Delta (p93)
This watery paradise of islands and oxbow waterways sustains vast quantities of wildlife.

3. Damaraland (p273)
Laced with rivers and springs, Damaraland is one of Southern Africa's last 'unofficial' wildlife areas.

MARTIN RICHARDI/GETTY IMAGES ©

Regions at a Glance

Before exploring some of the best landscapes, wildlife-watching and cultural experiences on the continent, remember that together Botswana and Namibia make up a huge area, so making the most of your trip requires careful planning. Chobe National Park and the Okavango Delta in Botswana are the two big wildlife regions, along with Etosha National Park in Namibia's north. Incredible landscapes just seem to pop up, but Namibia's north and the Kalahari are particularly memorable, providing desertscapes, foggy coastline and flat-topped granite monoliths. Culturally, Central Namibia delivers on German heritage while the north is home to the Himba people. Both countries offer access to some of the best galleries of San rock art in Africa while the capitals, Gaborone and Windhoek, provide opportunities to delve into the region's cultural fabric.

Gaborone

Wildlife
Culture & Crafts
Food

City Parks

The nearby Mokolodi Nature Reserve (with a few retired predators) and in-town Gaborone Game Reserve (herbivores and good birdwatching only) is the best wildlife viewing that Gaborone can muster. But the Department of Wildlife and National Parks office (for paying park fees and booking some campsites) may make Gaborone an important stop.

Botswana's Story

The National Museum and the Three Dikgosi (Chiefs) Monument both have a certain run-down charm, but Gaborone's thriving cultural life includes important arts projects and tours inspired by Alexander McCall Smith's *No 1 Ladies' Detective Agency.*

A Varied Plate

Perhaps more than anywhere else in the country, Gaborone is a decent place to eat, with some excellent cafes, steakhouses and even a place serving a guinea-fowl pot.

p45

Eastern Botswana

Wildlife
Landscapes
Activities

Tuli Block & Khama Rhino Sanctuary

The main wildlife place here is Tuli Block, where you'll find healthy populations of big cats, elephants and other important species, while the Khama Rhino Sanctuary is Botswana's rhino ark.

Tswapong Hills

It's rare to find variety in Botswana's salt-pan-flat terrain, but the Tswapong Hills are a little-known pocket of dramatic canyons cutting deep into the hills that, from a distance, give no hint of the drama that lies within.

Hiking

Botswana is not known for its hiking possibilities, but the Tswapong Hills offer fine landscapes, some intriguing ruins and good birdwatching.

p58

Makgadikgadi & Nxai Pans

Landscapes
Wildlife
Lodges

Salt Pans

The largest salt pans on earth offer up views where the horizon never seems to end – an extraordinary, humbling sight. In places the pans are interrupted by baobab islands, while the Boteti River is one of the great curiosities of Botswana's natural world.

Migrations

A zebra migration that's among the largest in Africa catches most of the attention, but there are also flamingos in their massed, migratory hordes in the Nata Bird Sanctuary. The dry season's wildlife concentrations in the west, around the Boteti River, also rarely disappoint.

Luxury Lodges

Botswana's call to exclusivity is heard here, albeit on a smaller scale than the more famous Okavango or Chobe further north. There's a handful of remote and opulent lodges out on the pans here and a fine riverside option.

p68

Chobe National Park & Kasane

Wildlife
Landscape
Lodges & Campsites

Elephants & the Rest

Chobe means elephants, big elephants...more than 70,000 of them at last count. Elephants might get all the attention (rightly so, we might add), but there are also infamous lion prides, leopards, cheetahs and wild dogs, plus a full suite of antelope to keep them all happy.

Rivers, Rocks & Marshes

Chobe Riverfront is classic safari country with land- and water-based possibilities as abundant as the wildlife. Savuti has some fabulous outcrops and the intriguing Savuti Channel to its name, while the marshes of Linyanti are like a mini Okavango Delta.

Chobe Digs

From remote lodges in Linyanti, Savuti and elsewhere to riverside campsites all across the park, Chobe's accommodation choices are brilliant and perfectly located for watching the park's epic wildlife shows.

p79

Okavango Delta

Landscape
Wildlife
Activities

Water World

The Okavango is a signature African landscape, a terrain sculpted by the waters that rise and fall in time with the seasons, year after year. The combination of river, savannah, forest and all manner of variations on the themes offer a stirring backdrop of singular variety.

Greatest Wildlife Show on Earth

The Big Five have returned to the Okavango (although seeing rhinos would be a rare bonus), and the delta is otherwise like walking onto the set of a wildlife documentary. The Okavango Panhandle is especially good for birdwatching.

Land, River & Sky

Scenic flights over this breathtaking world of water are a memorable way to explore. Add to this *mokoro* (dugout-canoe) expeditions, walking safaris and wildlife drives, and the delta's exploration possibilities are endless.

p93

Kalahari

Landscapes
Wildlife
Culture

Desert

The Kalahari is a place of legend, an iconic landscape that calls to travellers to leave behind the modern world and seek out the desert's solitude. From the red dunes of the Kgalagadi to the grasslands of the Central Kalahari Game Reserve's fossilised river valleys, this is a desert unlike any other on earth.

Famous Lions

Big cats may be thinly spaced across the desert, but they remain something of a Kalahari speciality. The renowned black-maned lions of the region are one of the great sights, but there's plenty more wildlife to track down.

The San

The Kalahari is the ancestral homeland of the San, and although encounters with this ancient people are rare, many lodges and camps allow you to explore a small corner of the Kalahari with San guides, while D'kar is home to a fine San arts project.

p125

Windhoek

Architecture
Shopping
Cuisine

Colonial Gems

Neo-baroque cathedral spires, as well as, oddly, a few German castles and some lovely 20th-century colonial shells, ensure Windhoek is worth a wander. Try walking Independence Ave and Fidel Castro St up to Christuskirche, the capital's best-known landmark.

Crafts & Curios

A stroll through Post St Mall reveals lots of wooden carvings, but the place to immerse yourself in weaving, crafts, antiques and all manner of artistic ventures is the Old Breweries Craft Market.

Foodie Fare

Whether you need a pasta hit or prefer your seafood cooked Angolan style, Windhoek surprises with its international cuisine offerings. German and Namibian fare is, of course, available, but there is much more on offer in the capital.

p218

Northern Namibia

Wildlife
Off-roading
Culture

Etosha & the Waterberg

Wildlife watching reaches its pinnacle in Etosha National Park, where verdant bushland contains an extraordinary density and variety of wildlife. There are useful viewing hides to spot rare gems such as roan and sable antelope in the Waterberg.

Remote Reaches

The rawness of Africa can be experienced in the huge northern swathe of Namibia with a sturdy 4WD, navigation equipment, supplies and a sense of adventure. Places such as Damaraland, the Kaokoveld, the Skeleton Coast and the Caprivi Strip remove all obstacles between you and nature.

The Himba & the San

The Kaokoveld is the ancestral home of the Himba people, a culturally rich tribal group. The San are more difficult to encounter, but look out for their incredible rock art, especially around Damaraland, and duck into Otjozondjupa, where visits to San villages are possible.

p255

Central Namibia

Adventure Activities
Atlantic Towns
Desert

Heart-Stoppers

Namibia is Southern Africa's headquarters for adrenaline-pumping fun. Shoot down a dune on a sandboard, fling yourself out of an aircraft and float back to earth, or go camel riding into a desert sunset. The stunning landscape is just the icing on the cake.

Urban Fun

Swakopmund is something of an enigma – a German colonial relic that may be crumbling into the desert except for the influx of tourists who pour in to enjoy its raft of activities, German-style ambience, cuisine and hospitality. Walvis Bay, just a short ride away, has a developing waterfront and some great restaurants.

Shifting Sands

Namib-Naukluft Park is one of the world's largest national parks – this is desert country and the swirling sand dunes here are mesmerising. The dunes – silent, constantly shifting, gently hued in colour and ageless – are a highlight of Namibia.

p288

Southern Namibia

Landscape
Colonial Traces
Canoeing

Canyons & Desert Roads

From the moment you enter southern Namibia from South Africa, the landscapes are stunning – granite monoliths rise from the plains through mists of windblown sand and dust. The enormous gash hacked out of the planet at Fish River Canyon should not be missed – this naked symphony in stone is truly awesome.

Lüderitz & Castles

Stuck between the Namib Desert and the wind-savaged Atlantic coast, defying both the elements and logic, the time-warp town of Lüderitz makes for surreal colonial exploration. Charming hints of yesteryear, such as neo-baroque Duwisib Castle, poke their architecturally intriguing heads out of the surrounding desert.

Water Adventures

Noordoewer sits astride the Orange River, in the deep south of Namibia, and two outfits offer canoe and rafting trips that access wonderfully wild canyon country.

p320

On the Road

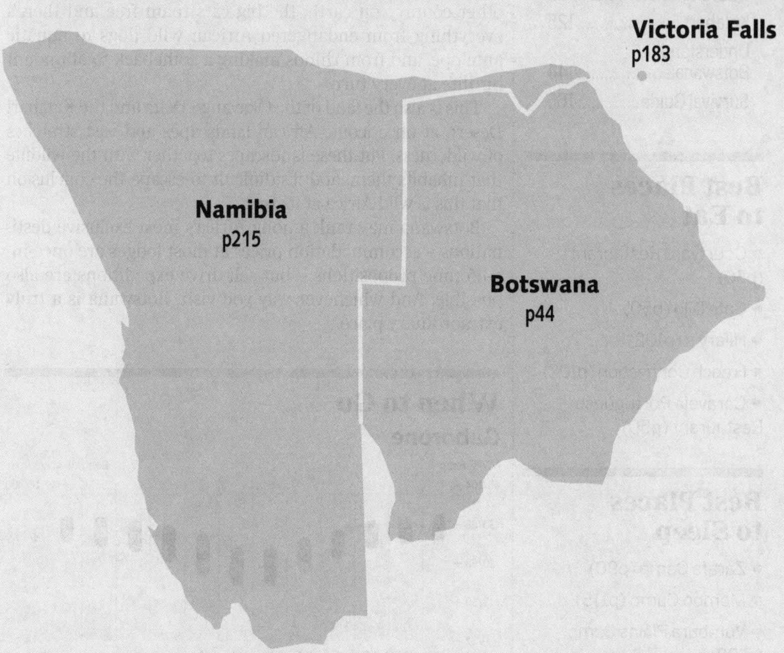

Victoria Falls
p183

Namibia
p215

Botswana
p44

Gaborone

Botswana

POP 2.183 MILLION / 🖉 27

Best Places to Eat

➜ Courtyard Restaurant (p50)

➜ Cafe Dijo (p50)

➜ Hilary's (p102)

➜ French Connection (p102)

➜ Caravela Portuguese Restaurant (p50)

Best Places to Sleep

➜ Zarafa Camp (p90)

➜ Mombo Camp (p115)

➜ Vumbura Plains Camp (p108)

➜ Sandibe Safari Lodge (p106)

➜ Selinda Camp (p91)

➜ Jao Camp (p107)

➜ Kalahari Plains Camp (p133)

Why Go?

Blessed with some of the greatest wildlife spectacles on earth, Botswana is one of the great safari destinations in Africa. There are more elephants in Botswana than any other country on earth, the big cats roam free and there's everything from endangered African wild dogs to aquatic antelope, and from rhinos making a comeback to abundant birdlife at every turn.

This is also the land of the Okavango Delta and the Kalahari Desert, at once iconic African landscapes and vast stretches of wilderness. Put these landscapes together with the wildlife that inhabits them, and it's difficult to escape the conclusion that this is wild Africa at its best.

Botswana may rank among Africa's most exclusive destinations – accommodation prices at most lodges are once-in-a-lifetime propositions – but self-drive expeditions are also possible. And whichever way you visit, Botswana is a truly extraordinary place.

When to Go
Gaborone

High Season (Jun or Jul–Oct)	Shoulder (Apr, May & Nov)	Low Season (Dec–Mar)
Warm days and mild nights, October can be oppressively hot.	A lovely, cheaper time to visit. May nights can be cold.	Rains can disrupt travel, making off-road driving difficult.

GABORONE

POP 234,500

Depending on your perspective, low-key Gaborone (or Gabs to its friends) is either terribly unexciting or one of Africa's more tranquil capital cities. There aren't that many concrete reasons to come here – it's a world of government ministries, shopping malls and a seemingly endless urban sprawl – and most travellers can fly to Maun or cross overland elsewhere. Yet, it can be an interesting place to take the pulse of the nation.

The city is largely a modern creation, with little sense of history to provide interest. Indeed, ask Batswana who were born and raised in Gaborone where they're from, and they may well tell you the name of a family village or cattle post they've never seen. So while the local Batswana may not see Gaborone as a traditional family 'home', they do see it as the place where their future, and that of their nation, is forged.

History

Archaeological evidence suggests that the banks of the nearby Notwane River have been continuously occupied since at least the middle Stone Age. However, the first modern settlement, Moshaweng, was established in the late 1880s by Chief Gaborone of the Tlokwa clan. Early European explorers and missionaries named the settlement Gaborone's Village, which was then inevitably shortened to 'Gaborones' (the 's' was dropped in 1968).

In 1895 the South African diamond magnate Cecil Rhodes used Gaborone to launch the Jameson Raid, an unsuccessful rebellion against the Boers who controlled the gold mines near Johannesburg. Rhodes was forced to resign his post as prime minister of Cape Colony, and the raid served as the catalyst for the second Boer War (1899–1902).

In 1897 the railway between South Africa and Rhodesia (now Zimbabwe) passed 4km to the west of the village, and a tiny settlement known as Gaborone's Station soon appeared alongside the railway line. As late as 1966 the greater Gaborone area was still home to fewer than 4000 inhabitants, but it was selected as the capital of independent Botswana due to its proximity to the railway line and its large water supply.

Although urban migration from elsewhere in Botswana has characterised much of Gabs' recent history, economic turmoil in Zimbabwe has sparked a wave of illegal immigration to Botswana's capital, further increasing the city's growth.

Sights

Although there's little in the way of sights, the confluence of motivated embassy staff, NGO types and ambitious Batswana makes for a fairly full calendar of events that focuses on cultural and arts-related activities.

Gaborone Game Reserve   WILDLIFE RESERVE
(☑318 4492;   adult/child/vehicle   P10/5/10; ⊙6.30am-6.30pm) This reserve was established in 1988 by the Kalahari Conservation Society to give the Gaborone public an opportunity to view Botswana's wildlife in a natural and accessible location. It seems to be working: although the reserve is only 5 sq km, it's the third busiest in the country and boasts wildebeest, elands, gemsboks, kudus, ostriches and warthogs. The birdlife, which includes kingfishers and hornbills, is particularly plentiful and easy to spot from observation areas.

The reserve also has a few picnic sites, a game hide and a small visitor-education centre. All roads in the reserve are accessible by 2WD; guided drives are not offered. The reserve is about 1km east of Broadhurst Mall and can be accessed from Limpopo Dr.

National Museum & Art Gallery   MUSEUM
(Map p52; ☑397 4616; 331 Independence Ave)
FREE Botswana's National Museum closed in mid-2016 for a much-needed overhaul. Prior to the closure, the collection itself was fairly modest, with plenty of stuffed animals alongside sections on the country's precolonial and colonial history, while the art-gallery section had a similarly unremarkable portfolio of traditional and modern African and European art.

Three Dikgosi Monument   MONUMENT
(Map p49; ☑367 4616; btwn Eastern & Western Commercial Sts; ⊙9am-6pm Tue-Fri, to 5pm Sat & Sun) It's an interesting kind of history when your nationalist heroes are three guys who argued your country should *continue* to be a protectorate of Africa's biggest imperialist power, but welcome to Botswana. The *dikgosi* (chiefs) are memorialised in imposing form at this large, badly placed (in the shadow of an office block) monument, which also includes panels featuring carvings of national virtues, including 'Botshabelo' (refuge), 'Bogaka' (heroism), 'Boitshoko' (endurance), 'Maikarabelo' (global responsibility) and 'Boipuso' (independence).

Botswana Highlights

1 Moremi Game Reserve Enjoying the ultimate safari with some of the best wildlife-watching on earth (p112).

2 Okavango Delta Gliding gently through this vast unspoiled wilderness (p93) in a wooden *mokoro* (dugout canoe).

3 Chobe National Park Getting up close and personal with Africa's largest elephant herds (p79).

4 Central Kalahari Game Reserve Looking for black-maned lions in the heart of the Kalahari Desert (p158).

5 Makgadikgadi Pans National Park Watching the wildlife gather by the banks of the Boteti River (p75).

6 Tsodilo Hills Leaving behind the crowds and searching for ancient rock art in these soulful and beautiful hills (p121).

7 Kgalagadi Transfrontier Park Exploring the Kalahari's best dune scenery in Botswana's deep south (p158).

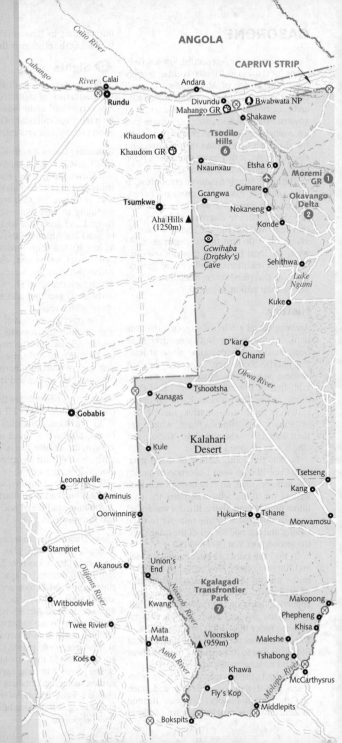

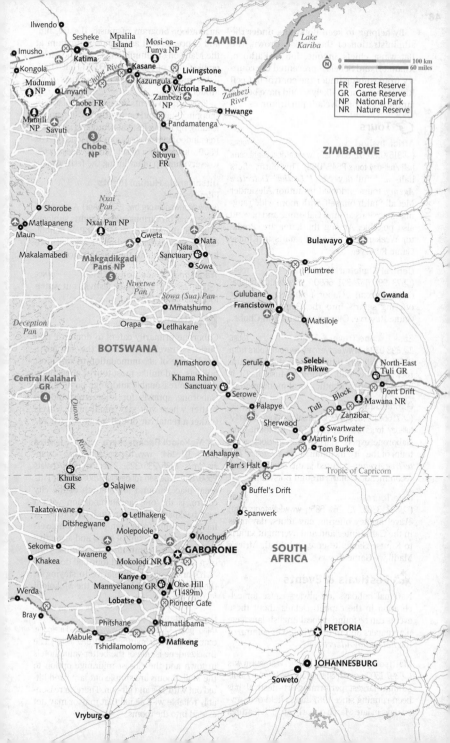

By helping to keep Botswana under the administration of the British Crown, the Batswana chiefs in question – Bathoen, Khama II and Sebele – prevented the country from coming under the control of Cecil Rhodes, who most likely would have been a far more exploitative administrator.

☞ Tours

Africa Insight
TOURS

(☑316 0180, 72 654 323; www.africainsight.com; half-/full-day tours P545/1198) This outfit offers half- and full-day *No. 1 Ladies' Detective Agency* tours endorsed by author Alexander McCall-Smith himself, with more wide-ranging excursions around Gaborone and beyond also possible. Among the latter are 'Predator Weekends' – weekend safaris to Khutse Game Reserve.

Central Khalahari Wild Tours
TOURS

(☑73 991 667, 391 6660; www.centralkhalahariwildtours.com) Gaborone-based operator offering safaris into the Central Kalahari Game Reserve, Okavango Delta and Chobe.

Easy Escape Travel & Tours
TOURS

(☑398 0394; www.easyescapebw.com; tours from P850) A full-day tour takes in the Manyana rock art, the Mall, National Museum (if it has reopened) and other local monuments.

Garcin Safaris
TOURS

(☑71 668 193, 393 6773; garcinsafaris@info.bw; half-/full-day tours from US$140/220) Resident and Gaborone expert Marilyn Garcin does great tours of the city, including a *No. 1 Ladies' Detective Agency*–focused jaunt. She also offers recommended safaris around Botswana.

Kaie Tours
TOURS

(☑397 3388, 72 261 585; www.kaietours.com) Travel agency offering city tours, day trips in the Gabs hinterland and overnight safaris to Khutse Game Reserve and South Africa's Madikwe Game Reserve.

✳ Festivals & Events

National holidays are always cause for celebration in the capital. Details about these events can be found in local English-language newspapers and in the What's On column of the *Botswana Advertiser*.

Maitisong Festival
PERFORMING ARTS

(☑397 1809; www.maitisong.org; ☺Mar-Apr) Botswana's largest performing-arts festival has been running since 1987 and is held over seven days in late March or early April. It features an outdoor program of music, theatre, film and dance, as well as an indoor program at the Maitisong Cultural Centre and the Memorable Order of Tin Hats (MOTH) Hall. Highlights include top performing artists from around Africa.

Programs to events are usually available in shopping malls and centres during the month leading up to the festival. Outdoor events are free; indoor events cost from P40 to P200. For P500 you can buy a ticket that provides access to everything on offer during the festival.

Ditshwanelo Human Rights Film Festival
FILM

(www.ditshwanelo.org.bw; ☺Mar-Apr) A series of screenings on various human rights subjects is held at the AV Centre, Maru a Pula School, during this festival, and guest speakers are invited to talk about their experiences.

Traditional Dance Competition
DANCE

(☺late Mar) Fairly low-key festival, but watch local media for details.

🛏 Sleeping

Gaborone primarily caters to domestic and business travellers. Even so, the city has a good range of accommodation to suit most budgets, and unlike most tourist areas there are some reasonable midrange possibilities. Gaborone sprawls for kilometres and no matter where you stay you'll need wheels (either a rental car or taxi) to get anywhere.

★ Mokolodi Backpackers
HOSTEL $

(☑74 111 164; www.backpackers.co.bw; camping/dm/s P135/235/325, 2-person units/chalets P550/645, 3-person rondavels P750; @🐾) This great place, around 14km south of the city centre, is the only accommodation with a real backpacker vibe around Gaborone. It has everything from comfortable rondavels (round huts with conical huts) and attractive chalets to good campsites (you can use your own tent or rent one) and four-bed dorms.

It's an excellent alternative to staying in the city centre, and handy for the Mokolodi Nature Reserve, 1km away.

Brackendene Lodge
HOTEL $

(Map p52; ☑391 2886; www.brackendenelodge.com; Tati Rd; s/d/tr from P510/570/670; ❄🐾) The Brackendene is one of the better-value hotels in town and the closest midrange option to the Mall. Rooms are simple but large and kitted out with TVs and air-con. There's a reasonably reliable wi-fi signal that may or may not extend into the rooms.

Gaborone

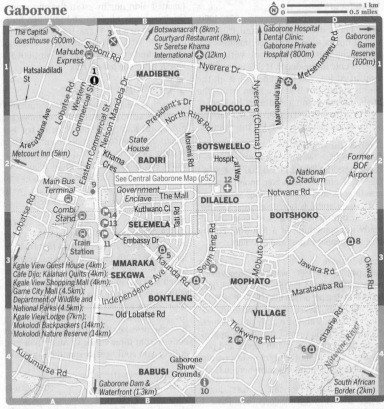

Gaborone

◎ Sights
1 Three Dikgosi Monument A1

🛏 Sleeping
2 Indaba Lodge C4

🍴 Eating
3 Bull & Bush Pub B1
Linga Longa.................................... (see 6)
Rodizio's .... (see 6)

🍷 Drinking & Nightlife
Bull & Bush Pub .... (see 3)

✪ Entertainment
4 Maitisong Cultural Centre.....................D1

🛍 Shopping
5 African Mall...B3
Exclusive Books............................. (see 6)
6 Riverwalk Mall..D4
7 South Ring Mall......................................C3
8 Thapong Visual Arts Centre D3

ℹ Information
American Express .... (see 6)
9 Immigration Office &
Passport Control A2
10 LeGaBiBo..C4
11 Namibian High Commission..................B3
12 Princess Marina Hospital......................C2
UAE Foreign Exchange .... (see 6)
13 US Embassy B3
14 Zimbabwean Embassy B3

Linville B&B **$**
(📞318 5622; www.linvillesuites.com; Plot 59865, Block 7; r/f P500/600; 🅿❄🤖🛜🏊) Extremely well-priced rooms north of the city centre are what Linville's all about. It markets itself as a boutique B&B and while that's slightly overstating things, the whole place is stylish, thoughtfully presented and friendly.

★**Metcourt Inn**   HOTEL $$
(📞363 7907; www.peermont.com; r P620-1060; ❄️🛜) Located within the Grand Palm Resort complex, this affordable business hotel has classy if smallish rooms with a hint of Afro-chic in the decor. If this is your first stop in Africa, you'll wonder what all the fuss is about, but if you've been out in the bush, it's heaven on a midrange budget.

It's on the northern side of town, around 500m northeast of the A1-A12 intersection.

Capital Guesthouse   GUESTHOUSE $$
(📞391 5905; www.thecapitalguesthouse.co.bw; 28492 Batsadi Rd, Block 3; r P950-1500; 🅿️❄️🛜🏊) One of a number of newer, more personal guesthouses and B&Bs opening up around Gabs, the Capital is quietly elegant and reasonably central. It's on a quiet street and already has something of a following among business people, expats and travellers.

Indaba Lodge   HOTEL $$
(Map p49; 📞399 9500; www.indabalodgegaborone.com; Tlokweng Rd, Plot 61916; s/d P1205/1415, buffet breakfast per person from P130; 🅿️❄️🛜) A new hotel southeast of the centre, the 84-room Indaba is aimed mainly at a business clientele, but the overall package is appealing, with moderately stylish rooms and professional staff. It's not really close to anything but, then again, neither is anywhere in Gabs.

Kgale View Guest House   GUESTHOUSE $$
(📞312 1755; www.kgaleviewlodge.com; Phase 4, Plot 222258; r incl breakfast from US$55; ❄️🛜🏊) This locally recommended guesthouse has friendly service, attractively decorated if simple rooms and a generally welcoming atmosphere. It's the sort of place that books up fast with return customers, so call ahead. The lodge is around 9km south of the city centre along the Lobatse Rd, just across the intersection from the Kgale Hill Shopping Mall.

Cresta President Hotel   HOTEL $$$
(Map p52; 📞395 3631; www.crestahotels.com; The Mall; s/d incl breakfast from P1449/1776; ❄️🛜🏊) The first luxury hotel in the city overlooks the Mall in the heart of the city. It's modern and service is helpful, and while there are no surprises, that's a pleasant enough surprise in itself.

Walmont Ambassador at the Grand Palm   HOTEL $$$
(📞363 7777; www.peermont.com/hotels/walmont; Molepolole Rd; r from P1700; ❄️🛜🏊)

Located 4km northwest of the city centre, this resolutely modern and polished hotel is situated in a Las Vegas–inspired minicity complete with restaurants, bars, a casino, cinema and spa. You'll pay to stay, but it's worth it for the pampering.

🍴 Eating

Gabs has numerous good restaurants aimed at an expat market. The upmarket hotels are another good place to try. For cheap African food, stalls near the bus station (and on the Mall during lunchtime) sell plates of traditional food, such as *mealie pap* (maize-meal porridge) and stew. For self-caterers, there are well-stocked supermarkets across the city.

★**Cafe Dijo**   CAFE $$
(📞318 0575; Kgale Hill Shopping Mall, Lobatse Rd; mains from P79; ⏱7am-4pm Mon-Fri, 8am-1pm Sat; 🛜) This classy but casual place is one of our favourite haunts in Gabs. The lunch specials change regularly, but usually include Thai chicken curry, chicken tandoori wraps and excellent salads, alongside toasted ciabatta, wraps and Botswana's best carrot cake. With free wi-fi and great coffee (from filter coffee to Australian iced coffee), you could easily spend hours here.

★**Caravela Portuguese Restaurant**   PORTUGUESE $$
(Map p52; 📞391 4284; www.thecaravela.com; Mokgosi Close, Extension 4; mains from P79; ⏱noon-2.30pm & 6-10pm) One of Gabs' most popular expat haunts, Caravela serves up assured Mediterranean cooking in a pretty garden setting. It's close to the city centre, but in a quiet residential corner, which adds to a real sense of it being for people-in-the-know. Seafood, all manner of platters and dishes such as Portuguese steaks make this a terrific place to eat.

★**Courtyard Restaurant**   AFRICAN, INTERNATIONAL $$
(📞392 2487; www.botswanacraft.bw; Western Bypass, off Airport Rd; mains P65-110; ⏱8am-5pm Mon-Sat) In the garden area out the back of Botswanacraft (p52), this tranquil spot serves up imaginative African cooking (including guinea-fowl pot), with other local staples making a rare appearance. It also serves salads and sandwiches and there's even occasional live music.

Sanitas Tea Garden   CAFE $$

(☑ 393 1358; www.sanitas.co.bw; off Samora Machel Drive, Gaborone Dam; mains from P65; ⊙ 8am-4.30pm Tue-Sun) Inhabiting a corner of Gabs' best plant nursery and close to the dam, this lovely and relaxed outdoor spot is popular with families. The food ranges from home-grown vegetables, wood-fired pizzas and light meals to made-on-site gelato.

Beef Baron   BUFFET $$

(☑ 363 7777; Grand Palm Resort; mains P75-215; ⊙ 6.30-10.30pm Mon-Sat) With a name like this, there's no mystery about the menu, with Gaborone's finest cuts of Botswana beef served in upmarket surrounds. It's inside the Grand Palm Resort complex; walk through the Walmont Ambassador lobby and you're there. Reservations are recommended, especially on weekends.

Part of the same complex are a pan-Asian restaurant and the reasonable buffet at Mokolwane's Restaurant.

Bull & Bush Pub   INTERNATIONAL $$

(Map p49; ☑ 397 5070, 71 212 233; off Sebone Rd; mains P55-126; ⊙ noon-10.30pm Mon-Fri, to 11.30pm Sat & Sun) This long-standing South African–run Gabs institution is deservedly popular with expats, tourists and locals alike. Though there's something on the menu for everyone, it's renowned for its thick steaks, pizzas and cold beers. It has some themed nights – Monday is ribs night, Thursday is pizzas – while on any given night, the outdoor beer garden is buzzing with activity.

There's a pub quiz on the last Wednesday evening of the month and menu highlights include T-bone (750g!), BBQ steak roll, rack of ribs and great burgers. To really confirm this as a place apart, there was even an Action cricket pitch under construction out the back.

Linga Longa   INTERNATIONAL $$

(Map p49; ☑ 370 0844; Riverwalk Mall; mains P48-132; ⊙ 8am-11pm) This place is a vague cross between an American sports bar and a British pub, with a menu that begins with breakfast and moves on to steaks, curries and calamari rings. Our highlight of its week is the Friday lunch 'Tswana buffet' for P50 per plate.

Mokolwane's Restaurant   AFRICAN $$$

(Grand Palm Resort; buffet P225; ⊙ 6.30-10pm) The buffet at the Grand Palm Resort serves up fairly unexciting cooking, but the salads are above average and the roasts are always a highlight. It's next to Beef Baron, inside the Grand Palm Resort.

Rodizio's   STEAK $$$

(Map p49; ☑ 392 4428; 1st fl, Riverwalk Mall; set menu from P195; ⊙ noon-3pm & 6-10.30pm Mon-Sat, 2-8pm Sun) Indulge your inner carnivore. Part of a chain of Brazilian meat houses/samba parties, Rodizio's is where waiters walk around with skewers of meat, and you hold up little flags indicating whether you want more or less. Gastrointestinal overload eventually occurs, but at least you die with a smile on your face and meat juice on your lips.

🍷 Drinking & Nightlife

When money is made in Botswana it tends to come to Gabs, which means there are a few places here to let off steam. And as it gets richer, nightclubs become more popular, though few last more than a season or two. They tend to be a cross between enormous disco-ball funhouses and Southern African shebeens (unlicenced drinking dens). Expect P50 cover charge on weekend nights.

Bull & Bush Pub   PUB

(Map p49; off Sebone Rd; ⊙ noon-10.30pm Mon-Fri, to 11.30pm Sat & Sun) The popular Bull & Bush Pub is also a centre for expat nightlife, where young (and some not-so-young) Gaborone denizens go to behave badly. The dance floor gets hot, the beer is cold and, all in all, this can be a hell of a fun place. Sundays are more mellow.

Kalahari Cocktail Lounge   COCKTAIL BAR

(Grand Palm Resort; ⊙ 7am-late) This classy venue inside the Grand Palm Resort complex (it's behind reception in the Walmont Ambassador) does a small range of cocktails (from P75) complemented by teas, coffees, smoothies and snacks. You may need to sidle up to the bar and wait for a table on weekend nights.

☆ Entertainment

To find out what's going on in Gaborone and where, check the Arts & Culture Review lift-out in the *Mmegi/Reporter* newspaper, and the What's On section of the *Botswana Advertiser*.

Maitisong Cultural Centre   PERFORMING ARTS

(Map p49; ☑ 397 1809; www.maitisong.org; Maruapula Way; ⊙ ticket office 8.30am-1pm & 2-4.30pm Mon-Fri) Maitisong (Place of Entertainment) puts on some excellent shows in its large theatre, with events ranging from Shakespearean plays to Batswana music most weeks. It's a hub of Batswana cultural life and the centrepiece of the annual Maitisong Festival (p48) in March or April.

BOTSWANA GABORONE

Central Gaborone

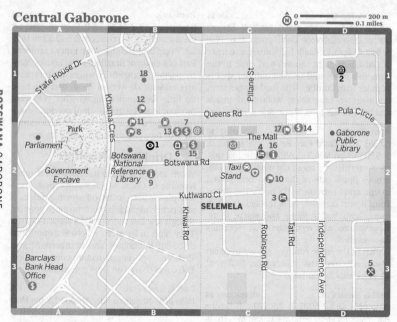

Central Gaborone

◎ **Sights**
1 Debswana House B2
2 National Museum & Art Gallery D1

🛏 **Sleeping**
3 Brackendene Lodge C2
4 Cresta President Hotel........................ C2

🍴 **Eating**
5 Caravela Portuguese
   Restaurant D3

🛍 **Shopping**
6 Botswana Book Centre B2

ℹ️ **Information**
7 Barclays Bank.................................... B2
8 British Embassy B2
9 Department of Wildlife &
   National Parks B2
10 French Embassy................................ C2
11 German Embassy................................ B1
12 South African Embassy B1
13 Standard Chartered ATM....................B2
14 Standard Chartered Bank D2
15 Standard Chartered Bank B2
16 Tourist Office.................................... C2
17 Zambian Embassy C2

ℹ️ **Transport**
18 Air Botswana B1

National Stadium STADIUM
(Map p49; ☎ 395 3449; Notwane Rd; tickets
from P10) The National Stadium plays host
to football matches between teams in the
countrywide Super League as well as the
occasional international game. Matches
start at 4pm on Saturday and Sunday and
are usually advertised and publicised in
the local English-language newspapers.

 Shopping

Botswanacraft ARTS & CRAFTS
(☎ 392 2487; www.botswanacraft.bw; Western Bypass, off Airport Rd; ⊙ 8am-6pm Mon-Fri, to 5pm Sat,
9am-1pm Sun) Botswana's largest and best craft
emporium sells traditional souvenirs, including pottery from Gabane and Thamaga, San
jewellery and baskets from across the country, at fixed prices. It also has books, jewellery,
carvings and textiles, but most of these are

from elsewhere in Africa, from Mali to the Congo. There's also the good on-site Court-yard Restaurant (p50).

Exclusive Books — BOOKS
(Map p49; ☑ 370 0130; shop 28A, Riverwalk Mall; ⊘ 9am-8pm Mon-Fri, to 5pm Sat, to 2pm Sun) Easily Gaborone's best bookshop, this large outpost of a respected South African chain has literature, nonfiction and travel books, with excellent sections focused on Africa.

Kalahari Quilts — ARTS & CRAFTS
(☑ 72 618 711; www.kalahariquilts.com; unit 7A, Kgale Hill Shopping Mall; ⊘ 9am-5pm Mon-Fri, to 2pm Sat) These stunning quilts are made by Batswana women, overseen by the engaging Jenny Healy, and are a unique craft to take home. Each one bears an individual imprint, although all do a good job at capturing the primary-colour-heavy palette that is Botswana's sensory assault.

There's a lot more than quilts: baby slings, cushion covers and the like are all for sale.

The actual shop was closed when we visited but should have reopened by the time you arrive: contact it via the website to make sure.

Riverwalk Mall — MALL
(Map p49; Tlokweng Rd) Perhaps the best of Gaborone's Western-style malls, with a good range of restaurants and shops, including Exclusive Books (p53).

Thapong Visual Arts Centre — ARTS & CRAFTS
(Map p49; ☑ 316 1771; www.transartists.org/air/thapong-visual-art-centre; Baratani Rd, The Village; ⊘ 8am-5pm Mon-Fri, 9am-5pm Sat & Sun) A small gallery of modern and contemporary local work that should be a first stop for anyone interested in buying art that goes beyond the usual African wildlife stuff and wooden masks.

Botswana Book Centre — BOOKS
(Map p52; ☑ 395 2931; The Mall; ⊘ 8.30am-5pm Mon-Fri, to 12.30pm Sat) You wouldn't cross town for it, and like the Mall it inhabits it has a neglected air, but this bookshop is worth dropping into for its excellent range of international magazines and South African newspapers. Otherwise, it's mostly stationery, religious books and school textbooks.

❶ Information

DANGERS & ANNOYANCES
Gaborone is a safe city by African standards and a welcome respite from the tension on the streets of some South African cities. Crime does happen here (mostly pickpocketing and petty theft, with occasional muggings) although most visitors encounter no problems. Even so, it pays to be careful.

➡ Always take cabs at night, especially if you're a woman or on your own.

➡ Use drivers recommended by hotels and try to keep their phone numbers, as some people have been robbed in unmarked cabs.

➡ The main Mall is fine to walk around in during the day but is best avoided after dark.

Traffic
Gridlocked traffic is becoming an increasing problem as more Batswana buy cars and start driving, often for the first time in their lives. Be extremely careful on the road during the last weekend of the month, when everyone gets paid and many people get drunk before getting behind the wheel – a toxic combination.

EMERGENCY
Central police station (Map p52; ☑ 355 1161; Botswana Rd; ⊘ 24hr)

MEDICAL SERVICES
Gaborone Hospital Dental Clinic (☑ 395 3777; Segoditshane Way) Part of the Gaborone Private Hospital.

Gaborone Private Hospital (☑ 300 1999; Segoditshane Way) For anything serious, go to this reasonably modern, but expensive, hospital, opposite Broadhurst Mall. The best facility in town.

Princess Marina Hospital (Map p49; ☑ 355 3221; Notwane Rd; ⊘ 24hr) Equipped to handle standard medical treatments and emergencies, but shouldn't be your first choice for treatment.

MONEY
Major branches of Standard Chartered and Barclays Banks have foreign-exchange facilities and ATMs and offer cash advances. The few bureaux de change around the city offer quick service at slightly better rates than the banks, but they charge up to 2.75% commission.

American Express (Map p49; shop 113, 1st fl, Riverside Mall; ⊘ 9am-5pm Mon-Fri, to 1.30pm Sat)

Barclays Bank (Map p52; The Mall; ⊘ 8.30am-3.30pm Mon-Fri, 8.15-10.45am Sat)

Barclays Bank Head Office (Map p52; Khama Cres)

Standard Chartered ATM (Map p52)

Standard Chartered Bank (Map p52; The Mall; ⊘8.30am-3.30pm Mon-Fri, 8.15-11am Sat)
Standard Chartered Bank (Map p52; The Mall)
UAE Foreign Exchange (Map p49; 1st fl, River-walk Mall; ⊘9am-5pm Mon-Fri, to 1.30pm Sat)

POST

Central post office (Map p52; The Mall; ⊘7.30am-noon & 2-4.30pm Mon-Fri, 7.30am-12.30pm Sat)

TOURIST INFORMATION

Tourist Office (Botswana Tourism; Map p52; ✎ 395 9455; www.botswanatourism.co.bw; Botswana Rd; ⊘7.30am-6pm Mon-Fri, 8am-1pm Sat) Moderately useful collection of brochures; next to the Cresta President Hotel.

ⓘ Getting There & Away

Gabs is well connected to the rest of the country by both road and air, but remember that the focus of the national public transport system is directed at locals rather than tourists – you'll find plenty of connections from Gaborone to Maun, Kasane, Francistown and Ghanzi, but little to the major national parks or other upcountry attractions.

AIR

From **Sir Seretse Khama International Airport** (p177), 14km northeast of the centre, **Air Botswana** (Map p52; ✎ 368 0900; www.airbotswana.co.bw; Matstitam Rd; ⊘ 9.30am-5pm Mon-Fri, 8.30-11.30am Sat) operates international services to Harare, Johannesburg and Lusaka, as well as domestic services to Francistown (P1406), Kasane (P2060) and Maun (P1791).

BUS

Please note that minibuses to Johannesburg drop you off in a pretty unsafe area near Park Station; try to have onward transport arranged *immediately* upon arrival.

Domestic buses leave from the **main bus terminal** (Map p49). To reach Maun or Kasane, you'll need to change in Francistown. Buses operate according to roughly fixed schedules and minibuses leave when full.

DESTINATION	FARE (P)	DURATION (HR)
Francistown	97	6
Ghanzi	155	11
Kanye	24	2
Mochudi	15	1
Palapye	60	4
Serowe	60	5
Thamaga	10	1

ⓘ Getting Around

TO/FROM THE AIRPORT

Taxis rarely turn up at Sir Seretse Khama International Airport; if you do find one, you'll pay around P100 to the centre. The only reliable transport between the airport and town are the courtesy minibuses operated by top-end hotels for their guests. If there's space, nonguests may talk the driver into a lift.

BORDER CROSSINGS: GABORONE

Gaborone's proximity to Johannesburg (280km away) makes it a decent entry/exit point for self-drivers travelling between Botswana and South Africa. The most direct route is through **Pioneer Gate** (Skilpadshek; ⊘6am-midnight), which connects Lobatse (Botswana) and Zeerust (South Africa).

Formalities on the Botswana side of the border are fairly straightforward: you'll be asked for your car's details and your vehicle may be searched for fresh meat and dairy products. On the South African side, travellers entering and departing are rarely held up for long, although if your hire vehicle is registered in South Africa, make sure you have the paper from the rental company granting permission to take the car outside the country. If travelling this route, allow longer than you expect as the succession of townships on the South African side of the border can slow you down considerably.

Other convenient border crossings:

Tlokweng Gate (Kopfontein; 6am to midnight) Another busy crossing that can work for Johannesburg and is good for Madikwe Game Reserve.

Ramotswa (Swartkopfontein; 7am to 7pm) Less frequented crossing that can also be used for Zeerust and Johannesburg.

Sikwane (Derdepoort; 6am to 7pm) For Madikwe Game Reserve.

Ramatlabama (6am to 10pm) Connects Gaborone and Johannesburg via Mafikeng.

CAR & MOTORCYCLE

Most major international car-rental companies have offices (which may not be staffed after 5pm) at the airport.

LOCAL TRANSPORT

Packed white combis (minibuses), recognisable by their blue number plates, circulate according to set routes and cost P7. They pick up and drop off only at designated lay-bys marked 'bus/taxi stop'. The main city loop passes all the major shopping centres except the Riverwalk Mall and the Kgale Centre, which are on the Tlokweng and Kgale routes respectively. Combis can be hailed either along major roads or from the combi stand.

TAXI

Taxis, which can be easily identified by their blue number plates, are surprisingly difficult to come by in Gabs. Very few cruise the streets looking for fares, and most seem to be parked around **Botswana Road** (Map p52) or near the combi stand. You're better off arranging one through your hotel. If you manage to get hold of one, fares (negotiable) are generally P50 to P80 per trip around the city.

Final Bravo Cabs (☑ 312 1785)
Speedy Cabs (☑ 390 0070)

GREATER GABORONE

Gaborone is surrounded by a few interesting day or half-day trips, although they're more for if you find yourself at a loose end than fabulous attractions in their own right. Almost all can be visited using public transport or hired taxi, though you'll get around quicker if you have your own wheels. Some can be difficult to track down under your own steam, so taking a tour with some of the operators in Gabs can be a good alternative. Options include Africa Insight (p48), Garcin Safaris (p48) and Kaie Tours (p48).

Matsieng Rock Carvings

Matsieng Rock Carvings   HISTORIC SITE
Loaded with cultural and historical significance, the Matsieng Rock Carvings are regarded by the Batswana as one of the four 'creation sites'. According to legend, the footprint and rock carvings belonged to Matsieng, one of the first Tswana ancestors who marched out of a hole followed by wild and domestic animals to inhabit the earth. There are also ancient carvings of giraffes and other plains animals.

The site lies at the end of a well-signposted 1km-long 2WD track that starts about 6km north of Pilane and close to Mochudi. There is a small information board at the gate and, on the other side of the fence from the car park, a tiny room with some explanations.

Mochudi

POP 44,815

Just off the main Gaborone–Francistown road, around 36km northeast of Gaborone, charming Mochudi is one of southern Botswana's prettiest towns, with some examples of traditional architecture, some brightly painted homes and the small **Phuthadikobo Museum** (Mochudi; ⊘ 8am-1pm Mon-Sat) FREE. As evidenced by ruined stone walls visible in the surrounding hills, Mochudi was first settled in the 1500s by the Kwena, who are one of the three most prominent lineage groups of the Batswana. In 1871, however, the Kgatla settled here after being forced from their lands by north-trekking Boers.

Other claims to fame? Michelle Obama visited here in 2011 and Mochudi was the home of Mma Ramotswe, the heroine of the *No. 1 Ladies' Detective Agency* books written by Alexander McCall Smith. Mochudi is also handy for visiting the Matsieng Rock Carvings (p55).

🔒 Shopping

Lentswe-la-Oodi Weavers   ARTS & CRAFTS
(☑ 310 2268; ⊘ 8am-4.30pm Mon-Fri, 10am-4.30pm Sat & Sun) The village of Oodi is best known for the acclaimed Lentswe-la-Oodi Weavers, a cooperative established in 1973 to provide an economic base for women from Oodi, Matebeleng and Modipane. At the workshop, wool is hand-spun then dyed using chemicals over an open fire (which creates more than 600 colours) and finally woven into spontaneous patterns invented by individual artists.

Most of the patterns depict African wildlife and aspects of rural life in Botswana. The women can also weave customised pieces based on individual pictures, drawings or stories if requested.

By car, get on the highway from Gaborone towards Francistown, and take the turn-off for Oodi village. Follow signs for another 7.5km to the workshop. Any northbound bus from Gaborone can drop you at the turn-off for

Around Gaborone

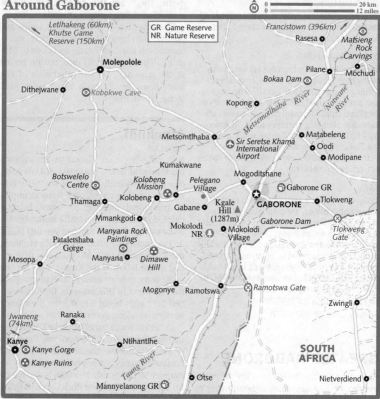

Oodi, though you will have to walk or hitch the rest of the way.

ℹ Getting There & Away

Buses to Mochudi (P32, one hour) depart from Gaborone when full. By car, head to Pilane and turn east. After 6km, turn left at the T-junction and then right just before the hospital to reach the historic village centre.

Gabane

Gabane is the quintessential Gaborone satellite town that will one day in the not-too-distant future be swallowed up by the capital's urban sprawl. A couple of minor attractions, including one of the country's best craft projects, make it worth combining with a day trip south of Gabs.

🛍 Shopping

Pelegano Village   ARTS & CRAFTS
(📞 394 7054; ⏱ workshop 8am-4.30pm Mon-Fri, craft shop 7.30am-1pm Sat, 2-4pm Sun) Pelegano Village, established in 1982, is a wonderful artisan complex that offers local crafts such as hand-fired ceramics and wine bottles recycled into dinner glasses. Run by the women of Gabane, who are often the only breadwinners in their families, this is small-scale rural development at its best. They may even let you try your hand at the potters' wheel.

ℹ Getting There & Away

Gabane village is 12km southwest of Mogoditshane and 23km from central Gaborone. Pelegano Village is 900m along a dirt road that starts at the second turn-off along the road from Mogoditshane. By public transport, take the bus towards Kanye from Gaborone (P25, 25 minutes) and walk to Pelegano Village.

Manyana

POP 3338

Manyana, 50km southwest of Gaborone, is famous for its Zimbabwean-style **rock art**, which dates back over 2000 years and feature paintings of three giraffes, an elephant and several antelope. The site is located on the southern extreme of an 8m-high rock overhang about 500m north of the village. Because the site is hard to find, it's a good idea to hire a local from the village to act as a guide.

Before leaving the area, it's also worth visiting **Dimawe Hill**, an important historical site where several groups of warriors under Chief Sechele I halted the invading forces of the Boers from South Africa in 1852. The ruins are scattered around the granite hills, not far from the roadside about 5km before Manyana. Nothing is signposted, but it's a pleasant place to wander around.

The bus from Gaborone (P34, 1½ hours) stops at the T-junction at the end of the road in Manyana village. From there, you'll need to walk to the rock art.

Thamaga

POP 19,547

The rural village of Thamaga will one day be swallowed up by Gabs' inexorable growth westward. Until this happens, Thamaga is an agreeably small town with two excellent cultural projects in town: the Botswelelo Centre and Bahurutshe Cultural Lodge.

◎ Sights

Bahurutshe Cultural Lodge CULTURAL CENTRE
(✐72 419 170; culturallodge@gmail.com; Mmankgodi) Situated about 5km east of the Botswelelo Centre, in Mmankgodi, and 2km off the Gaborone–Kanye road, is Bahurutshe Cultural Lodge, an innovative cultural village, chalet complex and camping ground (camping/chalets P100/450) where visitors can very easily access the traditional elements of Batswana music, dance and cuisine.

The comfy chalets really do up the African-hut thing, with cool stone, mud walls and rustic-smelling thatch enclosing you come the evening.

🛍 Shopping

Botswelelo Centre ARTS & CRAFTS
(✐599 9220; Molepolole Rd; tours P10; ☉8am-5pm) Thamaga is home to the Botswelelo Centre, which is also known as Thamaga Pottery. This nonprofit community project was started by missionaries in the 1970s and now sells a wide range of creations for good prices.

Tours must be booked in advance. Buses run frequently from the main bus terminal in Gaborone (P20, one hour).

❶ Getting There & Away

Most buses between Gaborone's main bus terminal and Kanye stop in Thamaga (P22, one hour), but confirm this with the driver when boarding and/or buying your ticket.

Mokolodi Nature Reserve

This 30-sq-km private **reserve** (✐316 1955; www.mokolodi.com; per vehicle per day P70, day/night wildlife drives per person P175/250, giraffe/rhino tracking P550/650; ☉7.30am-6pm, often closed Dec-Mar) was established in 1994 and is home to giraffes, elephants, zebras, baboons, warthogs, rhinos, hippos, kudus, impalas, waterbucks and klipspringers. It also protects a few retired cheetahs, leopards, honey badgers, jackals and hyenas, as well as more than 300 species of birds. The entrance to the reserve is 12km south of Gaborone. By public transport, take a bus to Lobatse and get off at the signposted turn-off. From there, it's a 1.5km walk to the entrance.

Mokolodi also operates a research facility, a breeding centre for rare and endangered species, a community-education centre and a sanctuary for orphaned, injured or confiscated birds and animals. Among the activities on offer is rhino and giraffe tracking.

It is important to note that the entire reserve often closes during the rainy season (December to March); phone ahead before you visit at this time. Visitors are permitted to drive their own vehicles around the reserve (you will need a 4WD in the rainy season), though guided tours by 4WD or on foot are available. If you're self-driving, pick up a map from the reception office.

🛏 Sleeping

**Mokolodi Nature
Reserve Campsite** CAMPGROUND $$
(camping per adult/child P150/75, chalets P680-1400) Spending the night in the reserve is a refreshing and highly recommended alternative to staying in Gaborone. The campsites are secluded and well groomed, and feature braai (barbeque) pits, thatched bush showers (with steaming-hot water) and toilets. If you want to safari in style, there are three- to eight-person chalets in the middle of the reserve; prices increase significantly on weekends.

Advance bookings are necessary. If you don't have a vehicle, staff can drive you to the campsite and accommodation areas for P10.

❶ Getting There & Away

The entrance to the reserve is 12km south of Gaborone. By public transport, take a bus to Lobatse and get off at the signposted turn-off. From there, it's a 1.5km walk to the entrance.

Otse

POP 7636

The town of Otse (*oot*-see) is known for Otse Hill (1489m), Botswana's highest point (not saying much), although the main attraction for travellers is the **Mannyelanong Game Reserve** (⊙daylight hours Sep, Oct & Feb-Apr) FREE. This reserve is an important breeding centre for the endangered Cape Griffon vulture, which nests in the cliffs. (In case you're wondering, Mannyelanong means 'where vultures defecate' in Setswana.) Loud noises can scare the birds and cause chicks and eggs to fall from the nests, so please mind the fences and be careful not to speak too loudly.

Otse village is about 45km south of Gaborone. Any Lobatse-bound bus can drop you outside the game reserve (which is obvious from the cliffs and fence).

Kanye

POP 45,196

Modern Kanye, built around the base of Kanye Hill, 91km by road southwest of Gabs, has little to recommend it. But peel back the layers of this busy provincial town and Kanye resonates with local history. The capital of the Bangwaketse people, it's home to the **Kanye Gorge**, where the entire population of the town once hid during a Ndebele raid in the 1880s. An easy 1.5km walk along the cliff face from the eastern end of Kanye Gorge will take you to **Kanye Ruins**, the remains of an early 18th-century stone-walled village.

🛏 Sleeping

Motse Lodge BUNGALOW $
(☑548 0363; Main Rd; r from P515; P❋✿)
Run by the local community, Motse Lodge has bungalows and tented rooms that look a whole better than they are. Maintenance is pretty shabby (the chances of the air-con and hot water both working for the duration of your visit seem fairly low), but there's not a whole lot of choice in Kanye.

❶ Getting There & Away

Kanye is an important regional transport hub, although it's mostly for locals travelling between Jwaneng and Lobatse or on to South Africa. Buses regularly travel between Gaborone (P55, 2½ hours) and Kanye via Thamaga. The bus station is 1.5km west of the main shopping centre.

EASTERN BOTSWANA

Eastern Botswana is the most densely populated corner of the country and it's rich in historical resonance as the heartland of the Batswana. Most travellers visit here on their way between South Africa and Botswana's north, and if you're in Botswana for a two-week safari, you're unlikely to do more than pass through.

But if you've a little more time and are keen to see a different side to the country, Botswana's east does have considerable appeal. Highlights include the country's most important rhino sanctuary, the ruins and dramatic landscapes of the Tswapong Hills, and the Tuli Block, one of Botswana's most underrated wildlife destinations.

Palapye

POP 36,211

One of the most important provincial towns in Botswana's east, Palapye, the birthplace of Festus Mogae, the country's former president, lies close to the halfway point between Gaborone and Francistown. As such it's an important crossroads town connecting the east with northern and central Botswana as well as to one of the busiest border crossings with South Africa at Martin's Drift. It's a good place to overnight if, for example, you're driving between Johannesburg and Maun.

Beyond that, and despite its name coming from the word *phalatswe*, which means 'many impalas' in Sekgalagadi or 'Large Impala' in Setswana, there's little reason to linger. This is not Botswana's most attractive town – not for nothing is Palapye known as the 'powerhouse of Botswana', thanks to the massive coal-burning power plant that operates in nearby Morupule.

🛏 Sleeping & Eating

Suitably for a crossroads town, Palapye has plenty of places to say. Some have excellent, business-style rooms, but most are way overpriced, especially considering that once you leave your room, you're only in Palapye...

The best places to eat in Palapye are the hotel restaurants. Otherwise, fast-food outlets line the main highway at the southern end of town.

Desert Sands Motel MOTEL $$
(☑ 492 4360; www.desertsandsmotel.com; Hwy A1; s/d P750/800; P ❋ 🛜) The modern business-style rooms here may lack character, but they're much better value than most others in town. The Wimpy's fast-food restaurant next door doubles as the hotel restaurant (there's even an access door direct from reception!), but aside from this Desert Sands is a good choice if you're just passing through for a night.

It's just south of the Caltex petrol station along the main road.

Majestic Five Hotel HOTEL $$
(☑ 492 1222; www.majesticfive.co.bw; Hwy A1; d/f/ste incl breakfast from P1240/1620/2760; ❋ 🛜 🛋) A few kilometres south of town on the road to Gaborone, and opened in 2011, Palapye's newest hotel has well-appointed rooms and is overall the most professionally run place in town. We still think you're paying over the odds, but standards are generally high. The evening buffet (P195 per person) is also Palapye's best place to eat.

Cresta Botsalo Hotel HOTEL $$$
(☑ 492 0245; www.crestahotels.com/cresta-botsa-lo/; Hwy A1; s/d incl breakfast P1330/1659; ❋ 🛜 🛋) This once-excellent place is living on past glories. Although marketing itself as a business hotel, not everything works, maintenance and service are patchy and if the bar's full, noise can be a problem. Thankfully the rooms remain good, with air-con, cable TV, comfy beds and bathrooms that were renovated in 2015. Even so, it's way overpriced for a three-star hotel.

The hotel is next to the Caltex petrol station, about 50m north of the junction along the highway.

ℹ Getting There & Away

Buses along the route between Gaborone (P60, four hours) and Francistown (P38, two hours) pass through Palapye and stop at the rather chaotic Engen Shopping Centre. From this shopping centre, shared taxis and combis also go to Serowe (P18, 30 minutes) and Orapa (P115, 4½ hours).

Serowe
POP 41,447

The historically significant town of Serowe is worth a detour if you're in the area – ignore the modern town centre and instead spend time in two monuments to the past.

In 1902 Chief Khama III abandoned the Bangwato capital in Phalatswe (near Palapye) and built Serowe on the ruins of an 11th-century village at the base of Thathaganyana Hill. Serowe was later immortalised by South African writer Bessie Head, who included the village in several of her works, including the renowned *Serowe – Village of the Rain Wind*. This book includes a chronicle of the Botswana Brigades Movement, which was established in 1965 at the Swaneng Hill Secondary School in Serowe and has since brought vocational education to many remote areas.

◉ Sights

Khama III Memorial Museum MUSEUM
(☑ 463 0519; ◷ 8am-5pm Tue-Fri, 10am-4.30pm Sat) FREE The Khama III Memorial Museum outlines the history of the Khama family, one of the most important dynasties in Southern Africa. The museum includes the personal effects of Chief Khama III and his descendants, as well as various artefacts illustrating Serowe's history. There are also exhibits on African insects and snakes, San culture and temporary art displays. The museum is about 800m from the central shopping area on the road towards Orapa. Donations are welcome.

Royal Cemetery CEMETERY
Before leaving Serowe, hike to the top of Thathaganyana Hill, where you'll find the Royal Cemetery, which contains the grave of Sir Seretse Khama, the founding father of modern Botswana, and Khama III; the latter is marked by a bronze duiker (a

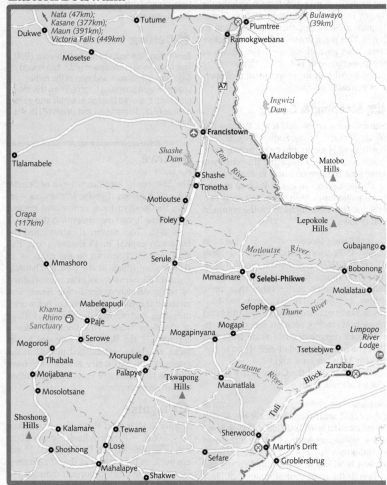

Nata (47km);
Kasane (377km);
Maun (391km);
Victoria Falls (449km)

Dukwe

Tutume

Plumtree

Bulawayo
(39km)

Ramokgwebana

Mosetse

A7

Ingwizi
Dam

Francistown

Shashe
Dam

Taii River

Madzilobge

Matobo
Hills

Tlalamabele

Shashe

Tonotha

Motloutse

Orapa
(117km)

Foley

Lepokole
Hills

Motloutse River

Gubajango

Mmashoro

Serule

Bobonong

Mmadinare

Selebi-Phikwe

Molalatau

Khama
Rhino
Sanctuary

Mabeleapudi

Paje

Sefophe

Thune River

Mogapi

Limpopo
River
Lodge

Mogorosi

Serowe

Mogapinyana

Tlhabala

Morupule

Tsetsebjwe

Moijabana

Palapye

Tswapong
Hills

Zanzibar

Mosolotsane

Maunatlala

Lotsane River

Block

Shoshong
Hills

Kalamare

Tewane

Sherwood

Tuli

Shoshong

Lose

Martin's Drift

Mahalapye

Shakwe

Sefare

Groblersbrug

small antelope), which is the Bangwato to-
tem. Be advised that police consider this a
sensitive area, so visitors need to seek permission (and possibly obtain a guide) from
the police station in the barracks house.

To reach the police station, follow the
road opposite the petrol station until you
reach the *kgotla* (traditional Batswana
community meeting place) and the surrounding barracks; one of the buildings
houses the police station.

🛏 Sleeping & Eating

There are two reasonable places to stay in Serowe, and doing so allows you to get a sense
of a provincial Batswana town far from tourist Botswana. Aside from a few cheap eateries
dotted around the town, your best bets are the
OK hotel restaurants.

Tshwaragano Hotel HOTEL **$**
(📞 463 0575; chalets P275-400; ❄ 🛜) This small
but quaint hotel with chalet-style accommodation is built on the slopes of Thathaganyana
Hill and boasts great views of the town. The

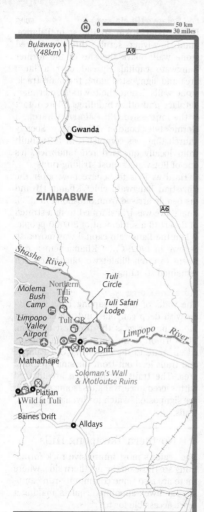

bet for a nightcap. The popular restaurant serves international fare as well as vegetarian meals.

ℹ Getting There & Away

Buses travel between Serowe and Gaborone (P60, five hours) about every hour. Alternatively, from Gabs catch a Francistown-bound bus, disembark at the turn-off to Serowe, and catch a shared taxi or combi to Serowe. Combis and shared taxis also depart for Orapa (P115, four hours) when full; this combi route passes by the entrance to the Khama Rhino Sanctuary (p61).

Khama Rhino Sanctuary

With the rhinos all but disappeared from Botswana, the residents of Serowe banded together in the early 1990s to establish the 43-sq-km **Khama Rhino Sanctuary** (☑ 463 0713; www.khamarhinosanctuary.org.bw; adult/child P79/39, vehicle under/over 5 tonnes P97/285; ⏱ 7am-7pm). Today the sanctuary protects 30 white and four black rhinos – the sanctuary was not originally set up for black rhinos, but when one wandered across the border from Zimbabwe it was the start of a beautiful relationship. Some rhinos have been released into the wild, especially in the Okavango Delta, joining imports from Botswana's regional neighbours. The sanctuary is also home to wildebeest, impalas, ostriches, brown hyenas, leopards and more than 230 bird species.

◉ Sights & Activities

The best time for spotting the rhinos is late afternoon or early morning, with Malema's Pan, Serwe Pan and the water hole at the bird hide the most wildlife-rich areas of the sanctuary; these locations are clearly marked on the sanctuary map (P10) available at the park entrance.

Two-hour day/night wildlife drives (day/night P715/836) can take up to four people. Nature walks (P275) and rhino-tracking excursions (P440) can also be arranged. If self-driving, you can also hire a guide to accompany your vehicle for P275.

🛏 Sleeping & Eating

Staying overnight inside the sanctuary at one of the well-maintained campsites or chalets means you're ideally placed to go rhino watching at the optimum times – just before sunset and just after sunrise.

attached bar-restaurant is usually the most hopping place in town – it's all relative. The hotel is above the shopping area on the road to Orapa.

Serowe Hotel   HOTEL **$$**
(☑ 463 0234; www.serowehotel.com; s/d incl breakfast P685/830; ❀ ❀) The Serowe Hotel is a terrific hotel of the kind you don't expect to find in Serowe. It's 2km southeast of town on the road to Palapye. Comfortable and well-furnished rooms ensure a quiet night's sleep, and the laid-back outdoor bar is a good

The office at the entrance sells basic non-perishable foods, cold drinks and firewood. Otherwise, bring your own supplies.

Rhino Sanctuary Trust CAMPGROUND, CHALETS $
(☏71 348 468, 73 965 655; krst@khamarhinosanctuary.org.bw; camping per adult/child 103/51, dm P440, chalets P660-880; P🐾) Shady campsites with braai pits are adjacent to clean toilets and (steaming-hot) showers, while there are also some pricey six-person dorms. For a little more comfort, there are rustic four-person chalets and six-person A-frames; both have basic kitchen facilities and private bathrooms. There's also a restaurant, bar and a swimming pool.

If you don't have a vehicle, staff can drive you to the campsite and accommodation areas for a nominal fee.

🛈 Getting There & Away

The entrance gate to the sanctuary is 26km northwest of Serowe along the Serowe–Orapa road (turn left at the poorly signed T-junction about 5km northwest of Serowe). Khama is accessible by any bus or combi heading towards Orapa, with the entrance right next to the road.

🛈 Getting Around

For self-drivers, the main roads within the sanctuary are normally accessible by 2WD in the dry season, though 4WD vehicles are required in the rainy season.

Tswapong Hills

These boulder-strewn hills east of Palapye represent some of the most dramatic landforms in Botswana. The hills watch over intriguing ruins, with steep-walled gorges that drive deep into the rocky interior, sheltering oasis-like picnic spots and important colonies of breeding Cape vultures (close to the northern limit of their range) and other birdlife.

◉ Sights

◉ Southern Tswapong Hills

The most interesting ruins in the region are scattered close to the southern Tswapong foothills.

Old Palapye (Phalatswe) RUINS
FREE About 20km southeast of Palapye, amid low-lying scrub, thinly scattered stone walls mark the site of the former Bangwato capital. Spread over a large area and signposted along the main track, stone walls denote the town's former marketplace and other buildings. More intact is the impressive **Old Palapye Church**, a Gothic-style London Missionary Society church that was completed in 1894. Built from locally quarried red mudbrick, it's one of Botswana's most striking ruins.

Hard as it is to believe now, after the Christian Bangwato chief Khama III and his people arrived from Shoshong in 1889, Phalatswe was transformed from a stretch of desert to a settlement of 30,000 people. When the Bangwato capital was moved to Serowe in 1902, Chief Khama sent a regiment to torch Phalatswe, but the church remained standing.

Motetane Gorge CANYON
The walls of the Tswapong Hills are riven with deep canyons, and the east–west Motetane Gorge is the prettiest of them. The turn-off to the gorge is well signposted en route to the church of Old Palapye and trails lead out from the small parking area. The trails in this area are littered with sacred ancestral sites, some of which are signposted. Watch for hyenas along the trails.

◉ Northern Tswapong Hills

The region's most impressive rock formations are those on the northern side, where there are also some community-run campsites and well-appointed chalets, making it more accessible for tourists.

Moremi Gorge CANYON
(Goo-Moremi Gorge; adult/child/vehicle P50/25/40) The approach to steep-walled Moremi Gorge gives little hint of what lies ahead. Once within the site, with its sheer beauty and abundant birdlife (with Cape vultures wheeling overhead or perched at their nesting sites high on the cliffs), watch for small ancestral shrines in rocky clefts and the signposted boulder that fell to the valley floor on the day that Botswana's president, Sir Seretse Khama, died on 13 July 1980.

Sleeping

Goo Moremi Gorge Campsites & Chalets CAMPGROUND, BUNGALOW $$
(☎75 988 871, 71 247 225; goomoremiresort@gmail.com; Moremi Gorge; camping per adult/child P90/51, d/q chalets P405/795) Just inside the site entrance, a track leads past nice cleared campsites with ablutions blocks and solar-heated showers. Also next to the site entrance are some lovely ensuite chalets that opened in 2012; they have fine views towards the hills from their large balconies, with state-of-the-art Alva barbecues on hand.

Getting There & Away

Accessible from both north and south, the Tswapong Hills are a popular escape for local residents with nary a tourist in sight. You'll need your own wheels – public transport is practically nonexistent.

To get to the southern side of the Tswapong Hills, take the A-1 south of Palapye for 8km then the A-141, from where there are signs to Old Palapye (Phalatswe). There is a well-signposted turn-off after the village of Lecheng.

For northern Tswapong Hills, travel 20km north of Palapye along the A-1 then take the road signposted with a number of village names, including Tamasane and Kgagodi. Later, follow the signs to Moremi; the entrance to the gorge is around 3km beyond Moremi village.

Francistown

POP 98,961

Francistown is Botswana's second-largest city and an important regional centre – there's a fair chance you'll overnight here if you're on the way north from South Africa, or driving without haste between Gaborone and Maun. There's not much to catch the eye, but there are places to stay and eat, as well as excellent supermarkets for those heading out into the wilds.

History

Unlike most Botswana cities, Francistown's history tells an interesting story. In 1867 Southern Africa's first gold rush was ignited when German Karl Mauch discovered gold along the Tati River. Two years later, a group of Australian miners, along with Englishman Daniel Francis, arrived on the scene in search of their stake. Although Francis headed for the newly discovered Kimberley diamond fields in 1870, he returned 10 years later to negotiate local mining rights with the Ndebele king Lobengula and laid out the town that now bears his name.

Sights

Supa-Ngwao Museum MUSEUM
(☎240 3088; off New Maun Rd; ⏲8am-5pm Mon-Fri, 9am-5pm Sat) FREE Housed in the 100-year-old Government Camp, the Supa-Ngwao Museum includes a prison and a police canteen, and has moderately interesting small displays about local and regional culture and history (*supa-ngwao* means 'to show culture' in Setswana). The museum also hosts temporary art exhibitions and occasional special events. Donations are suggested.

Sleeping

★ **A New Earth Guest Lodge** GUESTHOUSE $
(☎71 846 622; anewearthguestlodge@gmail.com; Bonatla St; r from P520; P❄📶≋) Out in the quiet southeastern suburbs of Francistown, this lovely little guesthouse has a family-run feel and rooms decorated in earth tones or with exposed stone walls and down-home furnishings. Patricia, your host, is a delight and reason alone to stay here. It can be a little tricky to find, so ring ahead for directions.

Grand Lodge HOTEL $
(☎241 2300; Haskins St; s/d P275/350; ❄) This is an excellent choice for budget travellers who want to stay in the city centre. Standard rooms are basic, but they're elevated above the norm by the presence of air-con, cable TV, a fridge and a hotplate.

★ **Woodlands Stop Over** CAMPGROUND, BUNGALOW $$
(☎73 325 911, 244 0131; www.woodlandscamping-bots.com; off A3, S 21°04.532', E 27°27.507'; camping per adult/child P115/95, s/d with private bathroom P725/865, with shared bathroom P415/610, q P1740; ≋) A wonderfully tranquil place, 15km north of town off the road to Maun, Woodlands is easily the pick of places to stay around Francistown if you have your own wheels. The budget chalets are tidy, the bungalows are nicely appointed and come with loads of space, while the immaculate campsites are Botswana's cleanest and a wonderful respite from dusty trails.

Anne and Mike are welcoming hosts and the grounds are filled with birdsong. There's no restaurant, but there are prepackaged meals available as well as braai packs for use on the barbecue areas.

Francistown

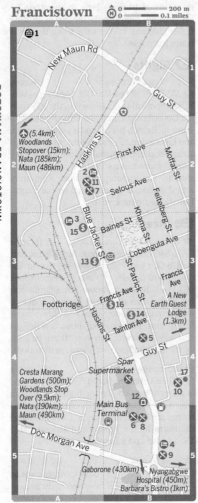

N 0 ——— 200 m
0 ——— 0.1 miles

Francistown

◎ Sights
1 Supa-Ngwao Museum..........................A1

⊟ Sleeping
2 Digger Inn...A2
3 Grand Lodge......................................A3
4 Metcourt Inn......................................B5

✖ Eating
5 Choppies...B4
6 Pie City...B5
7 Savanna..A2
8 ShopRite Supermarket.....................B5
9 Spur Steak Ranch.............................B5
10 Tandurei Restaurant.........................B4
11 Thorn Tree...A2

⊜ Shopping
12 Nswazwi Mall.....................................B4

ℹ Information
13 Barclays Bank...................................A3
   Botswana Tourism ....(see 2)
14 First National Bank...........................B4
15 FxA Bureau de Change A3
16 Standard Chartered Bank B3

ℹ Transport
17 Air Botswana.....................................B4

Metcourt Inn HOTEL **$$**
(☑ 241 1100; www.metcourt.com; Blue Jacket St; r from P1050; ✳🕾) This outpost of the Metcourt chain offers extremely comfortable, well-priced and recently renovated three-star rooms. Which is just as well, as the location (central but next to the busy road and overlooking rubbish-strewn fields at the back) is not Botswana's finest.

Tati River Lodge MOTEL **$$**
(☑ 240 6000; www.trl.co.bw; Old Gaborone Rd; s/d from P665/828; 🅿✳🕾≋) On the riverbank, this is an OK midrange option that feels like an old-school country motel. It's popular with locals and strikes a decent balance between rustic and roadside, although the pub can get a little rowdy if you're after a tranquil stay. It's on the south bank of the Tati River, southeast of the city centre.

Cresta Marang Gardens HOTEL **$$$**
(☑ 241 3991; www.crestahotels.com; Old Gaborone Rd; s/d from P1340/1639; ✳🕾≋) One of the better hotels in the Cresta chain in Botswana, this decent hotel has expansive grounds, standard rooms and some attractive thatched cottages on stilts.

Digger Inn HOTEL **$$**
(☑ 244 0544; www.diggerinn.com; St Patrick St, Village Mall; s/d P900/910, f P1000-1250; ✳🕾) At the northern end of the city centre, Diggers Inn is at once quiet, central and part of the most happening expat enclave (Village Mall) in the city. The rooms are large, if a little careworn, and the decor evokes Francistown's mining heyday. Overall, it's good value and a worthwhile alternative to the chain hotels.

Eating

Choppies SUPERMARKET $
(📋 244 1481; Blue Jacket St, The Mall; ⊗ 8am-8pm Mon-Fri, to 6pm Sat & Sun) Cheaper-than-average supermarket along the main street.

ShopRite Supermarket SUPERMARKET $
(off Blue Jacket St, Nswazwi Mall; ⊗ 8am-8pm Mon & Wed-Fri, 8.30am-8pm Tue, 8am-5pm Sat & Sun) One of the best-stocked supermarkets in this part of the country.

Spar Supermarket SUPERMARKET $
(📋 241 3820; Blue Jacket St; ⊗ 8am-7pm Mon-Fri, to 3pm Sat) Well-stocked supermarket in the city centre.

Pie City BAKERY $
(off Blue Jacket St, Nswazwi Mall; pies P11; ⊗ 8am-7pm) For a quick bite, these pies make a nice if unexciting break from the fast food that dominates things along the main road through the centre of town.

★ Barbara's Bistro INTERNATIONAL $$
(📋 241 3737; Francistown Sports Club; mains from P75; ⊗ noon-2pm & 7-10pm Mon-Sat) Located in the town's eastern outskirts in the sports club, this leafy spot is a fabulous choice. Barbara, the German owner, is a charismatic host and loves nothing better than to sit down and run through the specials. The food – German pork dishes like *eisbein* are recurring themes, while the Karoo lamb is outstanding – is easily Francistown's best.

★ Thorn Tree CAFE $$
(St Patrick St, Village Mall; breakfast P30-70, mains P55-100; ⊗ 6am-3pm Mon-Sat; 🛜) An oasis of sophistication at the northern end of Francistown, Thorn Tree (no relation to Lonely Planet's famous online bulletin board) does burgers, salads, pizza, pasta, jacket potatoes, fresh fish and great coffee. The outdoor terrace is lovely. Highly recommended.

Savanna INTERNATIONAL $$
(St Patrick St, 1st fl, Village Mall; mains P60-154; ⊗ noon-10pm Mon-Sat; 🛜) This place, upstairs in the Village Mall, serves up the town's best flame-grilled steaks, but it also does fish and chips and watch out also for the daily specials. The bar is one of few expat haunts in town.

Spur Steak Ranch STEAK $$
(📋 244 1160; Blue Jacket St; mains P60-150; ⊗ 9am-10pm Mon-Thu, to 11pm Fri & Sat, to 9pm Sun; 🛜) You've seen it before – an American-themed steakhouse in the heart of Africa with a menu that covers steaks, ribs and seafood. It's the sort of place that has very little to do with Botswana, but your kids will love you for taking them there.

Tandurei Restaurant INDIAN $$
(📋 241 2137; off St Patrick St, Galo Mall; mains P48-75; ⊗ 11.30am-10.30pm) Reasonable pan-Indian cooking in simple surrounds adds a little variety to the Francistown eating scene. Although it also does Chinese dishes, it's far better at dhal and tandoori flavours.

Drinking & Nightlife

Francistown can get lively at night and while few places rise above the pack, there's always something going on. The bars that run along the east side of the bus station along Haskins St are always packed at night, but keep your wits about you. More sedate but much less boisterous, Savanna (p65) is our pick of the in-town options.

🔒 Shopping

Nswazwi Mall MALL
(Blue Jacket St) One of Francistown's larger shopping malls.

ℹ Information

DANGERS & ANNOYANCES

Francistown is a generally a safe city to walk around by day, but always take a taxi at night, especially in the vicinity of the bus station. Keep an eye on your valuables and don't linger longer than you need to around the southern end of the bus station.

EMERGENCY

Police station (📋 241 2221, emergency 999; Haskins St; ⊗ 24hr)

MEDICAL SERVICES

Nyangabgwe Hospital (📋 211 1000, emergency 997; Marang Rd; ⊗ 24hr)

MONEY

There are plenty of banks along the main street, but most won't change money before around 10am while they wait for the day's official exchange rates from their head offices.

Barclays Bank (Blue Jacket St; ⊗ 8.30am-3.30pm Mon-Fri, 8.15-10.45am Sat)

First National Bank (⊗ 8.30am-3.30pm Mon-Fri, 8.15-10.30am Sat)

FxA Bureau de Change (Blue Jacket St; ⊗ 8.30am-4.30pm Mon-Fri, to 12.30pm Sat)

Standard Chartered Bank (Blue Jacket St; ⊗ 8.30am-4.30pm Mon, Tue, Thu & Fri, 9am-4.30pm Wed, 8.30-11am Sat)

POST
Post office (Blue Jacket St; ⊘8am-noon & 2-4.30pm Mon-Fri, 8am-noon Sat)

TOURIST INFORMATION
Tourist office (☑244 0113; www.botswana-tourism.co.bw; St Patrick St, Village Mall; ⊘7.30am-6pm Mon-Fri, 9am-2pm Sat) Moderately useful for brochures and basic local information, but little else.

❶ Getting There & Away

AIR
There's one daily **Air Botswana** (☑241 2393; www.airbotswana.co.bw; off St Patrick St, 1st fl, Galo Mall; ⊘7.30am-4.30pm Mon-Fri, 8.30-11.30am Sat) flight between Francistown and Gaborone (P1406); you may find cheaper fares online.

BUS
From the main bus terminal (Haskins St), located between the train line and Blue Jacket Plaza, buses and combis connect Francistown with the following places.

DESTINATION	FARE (P)	DURATION (HR)
Gaborone	97	6
Kasane	110	7
Maun	105	5
Nata	40	2

❶ Getting Around
Francistown's airport is 5.5km northwest of the city centre. A taxi into town shouldn't cost more than P70.

Tuli Block

Tucked into the nation's right-side pocket, the Tuli Block is one of Botswana's best-kept secrets. This 10km- to 20km-wide swath of freehold farmland extends over 300km along the Limpopo River's northern banks and is made up of a series of private properties, many with a conservation bent. The Block's northern reaches now make up the Northern Tuli Game Reserve. Wildlife is a big attraction, but so too is the landscape, which is unlike anywhere else in Botswana. With its moonscapes of muddy oranges and browns, its kopjes (hills) overlooked by deep-blue sky, it's the sort of Dalí-esque desert environment reminiscent of Arizona or Australia, yet the barren beauty belies a land rich in life. Elephants, hippos, kudu, wildebeest and impalas, as well as small numbers of lions, cheetahs, leopards and hyenas, circle each other among rocks and kopjes (hills) scattered with artefacts from the Stone Age onwards. More than 350 species of bird have been recorded.

◉ Sights
The landscape in Tuli Block is defined by its unusual rock formations. It's all beautiful, but there are a couple worth seeking out. Both sights can be explored on foot, and are accessible by 4WD from the road between the Zanzibar and Pont Drift border crossings.

Motloutse Ruins   RUINS
Near Solomon's Wall are the Motloutse Ruins, a Great Zimbabwe–era stone village that belonged to the kingdom of Mwene Mutapa. There's not a whole lot to see, but it does have a wild feel to it, as it slowly becomes swallowed up by vegetation.

Solomon's Wall   LANDMARK
Tuli Block's most famous feature is Solomon's Wall, a 30m-high basalt dyke cut naturally through the landscape on either side of the sandy riverbed.

◎ Northern Tuli Game Reserve
While the northern reaches of the region make up this reserve, in the longer term there are plans to extend its boundaries south, eventually creating a contiguous protected area across the border in Zimbabwe. Once owned by the British South Africa Company (BSAC), the land was ceded to white settlers after the railway route was shifted to the northwest. However, much of the land proved to be unsuitable for agriculture and has since been developed for tourism. As such, the potential for this region is endless.

🏃 Activities
While driving through the Tuli Block in search of its wildlife, keep in mind that it is private land – visitors are not allowed to venture off the main roads into the private concessions unless staying there or camping outside the official campsites and lodges. One advantage of visiting the Northern Tuli Game Reserve is that entrance is free. Night drives (not permitted in government-controlled parks and reserves) are also allowed, so visitors can often see nocturnal creatures, such as aardwolves, aardvarks and leopards. The best time to visit for wildlife watching is May to September,

when animals congregate around permanent water sources.

🛏 Sleeping & Eating

The office at the entrance sells basic non-perishable foods, cold drinks and firewood. Otherwise, bring your own supplies.

There's nowhere to eat in the Tuli Block other than in the camps and lodges themselves. The nearest supplies are to be had in Bobonong or, further away, Selebi-Phikwe or Palapye.

Molema Bush Camp   CAMPGROUND, CHALETS **$**
(☑264 5303; www.tulitrails.com; camping per person P125-185, chalets tw/f P500/600) Run by the owners of Tuli Safari Lodge, this campground in the Northern Tuli Game Reserve is one of few real options for self-drive visitors hoping to camp. The sites are shady and have private ablution blocks, while the simple chalets are comfy and reasonably priced.

Serolo Safari Camp   TENTED CAMP **$$**
(☑in South Africa +27 78 391 4220; www.tulitrails.com; per person self-catering/full board P1095/1595) Sitting somewhere between Tuli Safari Lodge and Molema Bush Camp (which are all owned by the same company), Serolo Safari Camp offers attractive, if simple, safari-style, ensuite tents around a water hole in the north of the Tuli Block. It's a good midrange choice.

Limpopo River Lodge   TENTED CAMP **$$**
(☑72 106 098; www.limpoporiverlodge.co.za; camping per person P122, chalets/rondavels per person P580) Consisting of a number of riverside rondavels (round, traditional-style huts) and chalets, this comfortable lodge in the southern reaches of the Tuli Block is a good choice. The brick rondavels have thatch roofs and barbecue areas, and the wildlife ticks all the right boxes. Camping is also possible, rounding out a good all-round package.

BORDER CROSSINGS: TULI BLOCK & EASTERN BOTSWANA

If you're looking for the fastest route between Johannesburg and northern Botswana, the busy border crossing at **Martin's Drift** (☑in South Africa 014-767 2929; Groblersbrug; ⊗6am-10pm) is your best bet. Entering Botswana, if you don't have any pula you will be allowed to step into the country to change money and then return; change no more than you need as exchange rates can be extremely poor. After completing all visa and customs formalities, your vehicle will be searched for fresh meat, fresh fruit and dairy products. Botswana petrol prices are generally lower than those in South Africa, and there's a petrol station just inside the border on the road to Palapye. Going the other way, South African customs may search your car (they're looking for rhino horn), but most checks are fairly cursory.

If your destination inside Botswana is the Tuli Block, avoid Martin's Drift, for two reasons. First, Martin's Drift is generally known for being stricter in its customs searches. Secondly, the gravel road that shadows the border from Martin's Drift towards the Tuli Block was awfully corrugated when we last drove it. The small **Zanzibar** (☑263 0012; ⊗8am-4pm) crossing is one option, although don't be caught out by its shorter opening hours.

Another possibility is the small post at **Platjan** (☑263 0001, in South Africa 014-767 2959; ⊗6am-6pm), which is best for the central Tuli area and the southern sections of the Northern Tuli Game Reserve. If you're coming from Johannesburg, you travel via Alldays and there are three turn-offs to Platjan. The first two involve driving along dirt roads, while the third and best, 38km beyond Alldays along a sealed road, involves around 20km on dirt roads. The crossing over the Limpopo River is on a low concrete bridge that can sometimes be impassable in the rainy season – ring ahead to the Platjan border crossing if you're unsure.

The final option, good also for the Northern Tuli Game Reserve, is **Pont Drift** (☑264 5260, in South Africa 015-575 9909; ⊗7.30am-4pm), although note that this border crossing usually requires a 4WD and can be closed when the river is too high. If you've prebooked your accommodation, you can leave your vehicle with the border police and get a transfer by vehicle (if dry) or by cable car (if the river is flooded; P50) to your lodge. If you need to arrive after 4pm, a later crossing time can be negotiated, although you'll have to ring 48 hours in advance and pay a fee (usually P80 per person, plus extra for the officers who have stayed on to let you through).

★ **Wild at Tuli**   TENTED CAMP $$$
(☑ 72 113 688; www.wildattuli.com; Kwa-Tuli Game Reserve; s/d full board US$250/400) This fabulous camp on an island in a branch of the Limpopo River is run by respected conservationists Judi Gounaris and Dr Helena Fitchat, and they bring a winning combination of warmth and conservation knowledge to the experience. Meals are home-cooked and eaten around the communal table and the tents are extremely comfortable. They'll even let you sleep in one of the hides overlooking a water hole.

Game drives on the 50-sq-km property (home to a full but often-elusive complement of predators) are included in the price. You'll need to bring your own drinks and ice.

Mashatu Game Reserve   TENTED CAMP $$$
(☑ in South Africa +27 11-442 2267; www.mashatu.com; chalets/d US$765/1020, luxury tents US$562/750; ❄ ☀) One of the largest private wildlife reserves in Southern Africa is renowned for its big cats and large elephant population. Accommodation is in enormous luxury suites decorated with impeccable taste in the main camp, while the tents are also beautifully turned out. The game reserve is close to the Pont Drift border crossing (p67).

Tuli Safari Lodge   LODGE $$$
(☑ 264 5303; www.tulilodge.com; s/d with full board & wildlife drives US$630/840; ❄ ☀) In the Northern Tuli Game Reserve, this fine lodge is set in a riverine oasis, surrounded by red-rock country that teems with wildlife. Although at the upper end of the scale for the Tuli Block, the rates are well priced compared to other exclusive private reserves in the country and the standards are high.

Be sure to have a drink at the outdoor bar built around the base of a 500-year-old *nyala* tree. The game reserve is just beyond the Pont Drift border crossing.

❶ Getting There & Away

There are daily flights between Johannesburg and the Limpopo Valley Airport at Polokwane across the border in South Africa, which is convenient for the Mashatu Game Reserve and Tuli Safari Lodge. Flights can sometimes be booked as part of a package with either reserve.

You'll need your own vehicle to reach (and explore) the Tuli Block. Once there, most roads in the Tuli Block are negotiable by 2WD, though it can get rough in places over creek beds, which occasionally flood during the rainy season.

Until it has been upgraded, avoid the deeply corrugated gravel road that runs north and roughly parallel to the South African border from Sherwood and Martin's Drift. Far better if you're coming from South Africa is to approach via the border crossings of Platjan or Pont Drift. From elsewhere in Botswana, the lodges can be accessed from the west on the paved road from Bobonong.

MAKGADIKGADI & NXAI PANS

Within striking distance of the water-drowned terrain of the Okavango Delta, Chobe River and Linyanti Marshes lies Makgadikgadi, the largest network of salt pans in the world. Here the country takes on a different hue, forsaking the blues and greens of the delta for the burnished oranges, shimmering whites and golden grasslands of this northern manifestation of the Kalahari Desert. It's as much an emptiness as a place, a land larger than Switzerland, mesmerising in scope and in beauty.

Two protected areas – Makgadikgadi and Nxai Pans – preserve large tracts of salt pans, palm islands, grasslands and savannah. Although enclosing a fraction of the pan networks, they provide a focal point for visitors: Nxai Pan has a reputation for cheetah sightings, and Makgadikgadi's west is a wildlife bonanza of wildebeest, zebras and antelope species pursued by lions. Fabulous areas exist outside park boundaries too, with iconic stands of baobab trees and beguiling landscapes.

Nata
POP 5313

The dust-bowl town of Nata serves as the eastern gateway to the Makgadikgadi Pans, as well as a convenient fuel stop if you're travelling between Kasane, Maun and/or Francistown; remember that there's no fuel in Gweta, making this an even more important place to fill up. Nata has a collection of good places to stay far out of proportion to its size, so it can be a good place to break up a long journey.

◉ Sights

Nata Bird Sanctuary WILDLIFE RESERVE
(📞71 544 342; P55; ⏱7am-7pm) This 230-sq-km community-run wildlife sanctuary was formed when local people voluntarily relocated 3500 cattle and established a network of tracks throughout the northeastern end of Sowa Pan. Although the sanctuary protects antelope, zebras, jackals, foxes, monkeys and squirrels, the principal draw is the birdlife – more than 165 species have been recorded here. It's at its best in the wet season when the sanctuary becomes a haven for Cape and Hottentot teals, white and pink-backed pelicans and greater and lesser flamingos.

Visitors should pick up a copy of the *Comprehensive Bird List & Introductory Guide* from reception at the entrance, although supplies often run short.

In the dry season (May to October), it's possible to drive around the sanctuary in a 2WD with high clearance, though it's best to enquire about the condition of the tracks before entering. During the rainy season, however, a 4WD is essential. The entrance to the sanctuary is 15km southeast of Nata.

🛏 Sleeping & Eating

Nata has good accommodation in town, but as there's nothing much in the town to detain you, don't forget the excellent options on or just off the main road south of town.

Cheap meals are available at the fast-food restaurants that cling to the petrol stations in the centre of Nata. Otherwise, bring your own supplies or eat at your hotel.

★**Elephant Sands** LODGE $
(📞73 536 473; www.elephantsands.com; camping per person P60, s/d/f safari tents & chalets from P600/810/910; 📶🏊) Some 52km north of Nata, Elephant Sands, run by Mike and Saskia, is a fabulous place to stay. Excellent and spacious safari tents, some chalets and a few campsites encircle a natural water hole that is always filled with elephants – in the bar, restaurant and pool area, you'll be as close to wild elephants as it's possible to be.

Prices are extremely reasonable and when we were last here, a pride of nine lions called the surrounding area home and a pack of wild dogs passed through regularly when we were last here. Game drives and bushwalks are possible, breakfast/dinner costs P75/140, and there's a lunchtime snack menu. It's 1.6km down a sand road off the Nata–Kasane road.

MAKGADIKGADI & NXAI PANS AT A GLANCE

Why Go? Underrated wildlife watching, especially along the pretty Boteti River and the hallucinatory, horizonless landscape of the pans. The wet-season zebra migration is one of Botswana's great spectacles.

Gateway Towns Gweta, Nata and (at a stretch) Maun.

Wildlife Nxai Pans is one of the best places in Botswana for spotting cheetahs, while both Nxai Pans and Makgadikgadi can be good for lions. There are dense concentrations of wildlife along the Boteti River in the dry season, with much wider dispersal during the wet when herbivores migrate east in large numbers.

Birdlife Around 165 bird species inhabit the Nata Bird Sanctuary (beyond the parks but part of the same pan network) in the east; flamingos and pelicans arrive in numbers in the rainy season.

When to Go Dry season (May to October) is best for driving on the pans, with big wildlife concentrations along the Boteti River later in the season. During the wet season (November to March or April), driving can be perilous but the zebra migration on the eastern pans can be quite a sight.

Budget Safaris There are few budget options, but the campgrounds and lodges of Maun and Gweta may offer affordable excursions. For self-drivers, Khumaga, South Pan, Baines' Baobab and Kubu Island campsites are excellent.

Author Tip *Always* ask about driving conditions before setting out onto the pans; failing to do so could ruin your trip.

Practicalities Fuel is only reliably available in Maun and Nata (*not* Gweta).

Maya Guest Inn
GUESTHOUSE $

(📱74 771 118; mayaguestinn5@gmail.com; r P310-410, f P610) Inhabiting a small roadside compound, this fine little inn at the southern entrance to Nata (it's just over the bridge on your right if you're coming from Francistown) has tidy rooms with the best being the cute thatched bungalows. It's easily the best value in Nata town itself, although there's no restaurant and service often goes missing.

Nata Bird Sanctuary Campsite
CAMPGROUND $

(📱71 544 342; camping per person/vehicle P75/35; 🏕) Nata Bird Sanctuary offers several serene and isolated campsites with clean pit toilets, braai pits and cold showers. All five campsites are 2WD accessible if it hasn't been raining heavily. From the campsites, it's possible to access the pan on foot (7km), though you should bring a compass, even if you're only walking a few hundred metres into the pan.

Pelican Lodge & Camping
BUNGALOW, CAMPGROUND $

(📱247 0117; www.pelicanlodge.co.bw; camping per person P80, d/tw P845/970; 🅿❄🛜❄) This promising place, just off the main highway and close to Nata Bird Sanctuary, inhabits a rather bare block where the vegetation needs a little time to mature. The lovely rock-cut swimming pool is a highlight, while the rooms are comfortable, if a little dark and unexciting.

Nata Lodge
LODGE $$

(📱620 0070; www.natalodge.com; camping per adult/child P75/45, d luxury tents/chalets US$110/138; ❄❄) Nata Lodge offers luxury wood-and-thatch chalets, stylish wood-floored

---

THE PANS IN A NUTSHELL

The Sowa (Sua), Nxai and Ntwetwe Pans together make up the 12,000-sq-km Makgadikgadi Pans. While Salar de Unyuni in Bolivia is the biggest single pan in the world, the Makgadikgadi network of parched, white dry lakes is larger. Ancient lakeshore terraces reveal that the pans were once part of a 'super lake' of more than 60,000 sq km that reached the Okavango and Chobe Rivers to the far north. However, around 10,000 years ago, climatic changes caused the huge lake to evaporate, leaving only salt behind.

---

safari tents and a good campsite all set amid a verdant oasis of monkey thorn, marula and mokolane palms. When you consider the cost of comparable places elsewhere in Botswana, this place is a steal, although remember that meals (breakfast/dinner start from P75/185) and activities cost extra to the prices quoted here.

The attempts at incorporating San and desert artwork into the general vibe of the place are subtle yet effectively accomplished. Activities include game drives onto the pans and into the bird sanctuary, as well as cultural tours of Nata village.

Northgate Lodge
LODGE $$

(📱621 1156; northgatelodge@reddysgroup.co.bw; d/f from P500/950; ❄🛜❄) In the town's heart, next to the petrol stations, Northgate Lodge is more about breaking up the journey than finding a remote base for a few days. The rooms are pleasant enough and excellent value for an overnight stay before continuing on your way elsewhere. It sits opposite the junction of roads that lead to all corners of the country.

ℹ Getting There & Away

Regular combis travelling en route to Kasane (P105, five hours), Francistown (P40, two hours) and Maun (P92, five hours) pass by Northgate Lodge.

Gweta
POP 4689

Gweta, just off the Nata–Maun highway, is a dusty and laid-back crossroads town on the edge of the pans, framed by bushveld and big skies. Given that the petrol station here has been dry for years, the only real reason to stop is to stay overnight, or as your entry point to one of Uncharted Africa's camps further south. The name of the village is derived from the croaking sound made by large bullfrogs, which, incredibly, bury themselves in the pan sand until the rains provide sufficient water for them to emerge and mate.

🛏 Sleeping & Eating

Gweta Lodge
LODGE $$

(📱76 212 220; www.gwetalodge.com; camping P80, standard/premium r P700/1100, f P1000; ❄🛜❄) In the centre of town, Gweta Lodge is a friendly place that combines a lovely bar and pool area with a range of accommodation options spread around the leafy grounds. The rooms

DRIVING SAFELY ON THE PANS

Prospective drivers should keep in mind that salt pans can have a mesmerising effect, even creating a sense of unfettered freedom. Once you drive out onto the salt, remember that direction, connection, reason and common sense appear to dissolve. Although you may be tempted to speed off with wild abandon into the white and empty distance, exercise caution and restrain yourself. You should be aware of where you are at all times by using a map and compass (GPS units are not foolproof).

As a general rule, always follow the tracks of other drivers – these tracks are a good indication that the route is dry. In addition, never venture out onto the pans unless you're absolutely sure the salty surface and the clay beneath are dry. Foul-smelling salt means a wet and potentially dangerous pan, which is very similar in appearance and texture to wet concrete. When underlying clay becomes saturated, vehicles can break through the crust and become irretrievably bogged. If you do get bogged and have a winch, anchor the spare wheel or the jack – anything to which the winch may be attached – by digging a hole and planting it firmly in the clay. Hopefully, you'll be able to anchor it better than the pan has anchored the vehicle.

It is important to stress that exploring the pans properly and independently requires more of a 4WD expedition than a casual drive. Lost travellers are frequently rescued from the pans, and there have been a number of fatalities over the years. And remember: *never* underestimate the effect the pans can have on your sense of direction.

are large and comfortable, the campsites are excellent and activities include half-day/overnight tours of Ntwetwe Pan and its human-habituated meerkats (P650/1150) and walking tours of the village (P150).

Shayna and James are welcoming hosts, and lunch and dinner are served by the pool.

Planet Baobab LODGE **$$**
(☏in South Africa +27 11-447 1605; www.unchartedafrica.com; camping per adult/child US$15/8, s/d/q huts from US$165/190/600; 🛜🌐) About 4km east of Gweta, a huge concrete aardvark marks the turn-off for Planet Baobab. This inventive lodge forsakes masks and wildlife photos, replaced by a great open-air bar-restaurant (meals P45 to P90) filled with vintage travel posters, metal seats covered in cowhide, beer-bottle chandeliers and the like. Outside, colourfully painted rondavels lie scattered over the gravel.

Staff contribute to a vibe as funky as it is friendly, while campers can pitch a tent beneath the shade of a baobab tree. There's a wide range of activities, including quad biking, spending time with some habituated meerkats and creative pan excursions of up to four nights.

❶ Getting There & Away

You're quite a distance from anywhere here: Gweta is 205km from Maun, 290km from Francistown, 416km from Kasane and 491km from Ghanzi. Hourly combis travelling to Francistown (P54, three hours) and Maun (P65, four hours) pass along the main road.

Sowa Pan

Sowa (also spelt Sua) Pan, at the eastern end of the Makgadikgadi Pans network, is mostly a single sheet of salt-encrusted mud stretching across the lowest basin in northeastern Botswana. Sowa means 'salt' in the language of the San, who once mined the pan to sell salt to the Bakalanga. Today it is mined by the Sua Pan Soda Ash Company, which sells sodium carbonate for industrial manufacturing.

Nata Delta

During the rainy season (November to May), huge flocks of water birds congregate at the Nata Delta, which is formed when the Nata River flows into the northern end of the Sowa Pan. When the rains are at their heaviest (December to February), the pan is covered with a thin film of water that reflects the sky and obliterates the horizon in a hallucinatory, perspective-challenging panorama.

The easiest place to visit the Nata delta is the Nata Bird Sanctuary (p69).

Sowa Spit

This long, slender protrusion extends into the heart of the pan and is the nexus of Botswana's lucrative soda-ash industry. Although security measures prevent public access to the plant, private vehicles can proceed as far as Sowa village on the pan's edge. Views of the pan from the village are limited, though they're better if you're travelling through the area in a 4WD.

Kubu Island

Along the southwestern edge of Sowa Pan is a ghostly, baobab-laden rock, entirely surrounded by a sea of salt. In Setswana, *kubu* means 'hippopotamus' (in ancient times this was a real island on a real lake inhabited by hippos). It's not only the name that evokes a more fertile past – the fossilised shit of water birds that once perched here overlooking the waters still adorns the boulders.

As unlikely as it may seem, given the current environment and climate, this desolate area may have been inhabited by people as recently as 500 years ago. On one shore lies an ancient crescent-shaped stone wall of unknown origin, which has yielded numerous artefacts, testament to those who lived here before the waters dried up (some think it served as a space in male initiation ceremonies).

The island (www.kubuisland.com) is now protected as a national monument, administered by the local Gaing-O-Community Trust.

🛏 Sleeping

★ **Kubu Island Campsite**　　CAMPGROUND $
(☑ 75 494 669; www.kubuisland.com; Lekhubu, S 20°53.460', E 25°49.318'; camping per adult/child P100/50) This sprawling campground has 14 sites and is one of Botswana's loveliest, with baobabs as a backdrop to most campsites, many of which also have sweeping views of the pan. There are bucket showers and pit toilets. The views from the island itself are some of the most evocative anywhere on the pans, although there's little wildlife around.

❶ Getting There & Away

Access to Kubu Island involves negotiating a maze of grassy islets and salty bays. Increased traffic has now made the route considerably clearer, but drivers still need a 4WD and a compass or Global Positioning System (GPS) equipment set with Tracks4Africa. The island can be difficult to reach after rains.

From the Nata–Maun highway, the track starts near Zoroga (GPS: S 20°10.029', E 25°56.898'), about 24km west of Nata. After about 72km, the village of Thabatshukudu (GPS: S 20°42.613', E 25°47.482') will appear on a low ridge. This track then skirts the western edge of a salt pan for 10.3km before passing through a veterinary checkpoint. Just under 2km further south, a track (17km) heads southeast to the northern end of Kubu.

From the Francistown–Rakops Rd, turn north at the junction for Letlhakane and proceed 25km until you reach Mmatshumo village. About 21km further north is a veterinary checkpoint. After another 7.5km, an 18km track heads northeast to the southern end of Kubu. This turn-off (GPS: S 20°56.012', E 25°40.032') is marked by a small cairn.

AFRICA'S UNKNOWN MIGRATION

Less known than the vast congregations of wildebeest in the Serengeti, Botswana's epic zebra migration is one of Africa's grandest and most underrated spectacles.

For much of the dry season, particularly from May or June to October, the more-than-25,000 zebras that inhabit the Makgadikgadi and Nxai Pans National Park gather together close to the only permanent water sources in the region, in the far west of the salt-pan network. In recent years that has meant along the Boteti River, which marks the western boundary of the Makgadikgadi Pans section of the park.

When the rains begin to fall in Botswana in November or December, the zebras, accompanied by smaller numbers of wildebeest, migrate east across the pans – with water now plentiful across the pans, the herds are no longer trapped in the west and can roam more freely. The rains are also usually when zebra mothers give birth – zebra foals can walk within an hour of birth, a necessary adaptation given the fact that lions, hyenas and other predators stalk the herds.

By April and into May, the herds have largely returned to the Boteti River, although some remain in the east into June.

Ntwetwe Pan

The Ntwetwe Pan was fed by the Boteti River until it was left permanently dry following the construction of the Mopipi Dam, which provides water for the diamond mines in Orapa. The waters may have returned to the river but Ntwetwe is now famous for its extraordinary lunar landscape, particularly the rocky outcrops, dunes, islets, channels and spits found along the western shore.

◉ Sights

★ **Chapman's Baobab**   LANDMARK
(S 20°29.392', E 25°14.979') About 11km south of Green's Baobab is the turn-off to the far more impressive Chapman's Baobab, which, until it crashed to the ground suddenly on 7 January 2016, had a circumference of 25m and roots that extended 1km out into the surrounding area. It was historically used as a navigation beacon and may also have been used as an early post office by passing explorers, traders and travellers, many of whom left inscriptions on its trunk.

If anything, the fallen version of the tree is even more impressive, allowing you to clamber atop and inside this vast fallen life force.

Gabatsadi Island   LANDMARK
The enormous crescent-shaped dune known as Gabatsadi Island has an expansive view from the crest that has managed to attract the likes of Prince Charles. (He went there to capture the indescribably lonely scene in watercolour, but the paints ran because it was so hot!) The island lies just west of the Gweta–Orapa track, about 48km south of Gweta.

Green's Baobab   LANDMARK
(S 20°25.543', E 25°13.859') On the Gweta–Orapa track, 27km south of Gweta, is Green's Baobab, which was inscribed by the 19th-century hunters and traders Joseph Green and Hendrik Matthys van Zyl, as well as other ruthless characters. Aside from the historical references, it's impressive primarily for the stark contrast it offers with the arid, table-flat surrounds.

☞ Tours

Uncharted Africa   TOURS
(✉ in South Africa +27 11-447 1605; www.unchartedafrica.com) The company that runs Planet Baobab and the three luxurious tented camps

SEASONS ON THE PANS

As everywhere in Botswana, seasons play an important role in determining what sort of experience you're likely to have here. In the dry season, from May to October, the great salt pans are long, low and white, curtained by an electric-blue sky and pulsing with an unstoppable glare. During the sizzling heat of the late winter (August), the stark pans take on a disorienting and ethereal austerity. Heat mirages destroy the senses as imaginary lakes shimmer and disappear, ostriches take flight, and stones turn to mountains and float in mid-air. But as the annual rains begin to fall in the late spring, depressions in the pans form temporary lakes and fringing grasses turn green with life. Herd animals arrive to partake of the bounty, while water birds flock to feed on algae and tiny crustaceans. A word of warning: wet pans make for perilous driving at this time.

on Ntwetwe Pan also organises multiday mobile safaris across the Makgadikgadi Pans area and further afield. The company has a certain cachet that's the legacy of five generations of the same family, and is lent much fame by its larger-than-life leaders, the late Jack Bousfield and son Ralph.

🛏 Sleeping & Eating

In a remote corner of Ntwetwe Pan, Uncharted Africa, the same company that manages Planet Baobab in Gweta, operates three exclusive tented camps: Camp Kalahari, Jack's Camp and San Camp. As much of the area is part of its private concession, free camping is not permitted.

Camp Kalahari   TENTED CAMP $$$
(✉ in South Africa +27 11-447 1605; www.unchartedafrica.com; s/d mid-Apr–Oct US$902/1440, per person Nov–mid-Apr US$528) The cheaper, family-friendly version of Uncharted Africa's trio of camps, Camp Kalahari is nonetheless luxurious. Beautiful safari tents brimful of old-world safari fittings (antiques, wood furnishings, thatch) and colour schemes, and a full suite of activities (quad biking, horse riding, meerkats and San nature walks) make this a fine choice.

Jack's Camp TENTED CAMP $$$
(☎ in South Africa +27 11-447 1605; www.unchartedafrica.com; all-inclusive s/d mid-Apr–Oct & last 10 days of Dec US$1945/3070, per person rest of year US$1225;) Hemingway would have loved this place. Set up for safari romantics, the whole aesthetic, complete with a classic maroon and dark-khaki colour scheme, is East African–style safaris c1940s. Regal linens, heavy wood furnishings, four-poster beds and big wooden chests furnish the canvas tents, which are romantically lit by paraffin lanterns by night (no electricity).

Inhabiting its own, oasis-like palm island that rises gently above the surrounding salt pans, Jack's Camp also has a central 'mess tent' that operates as a field museum where local guides and world-renowned experts deliver lectures and lead discussions on the area's flora and fauna against a backdrop of museum-standard exhibits (including stuffed lion and aardvark, historic paintings and bookshelves that owe far more to hard-to-find Africana and serious tomes than books left behind by travellers). There's also a separate tea tent where you can indulge in high tea while relaxing on oriental rugs and cushions.

Dry-season wildlife is scarce but you've a front-row seat for the rainy-season zebra migration. Other major highlights include a nearby brown hyena den, a couple of families of human-habituated meerkats (if you're lucky, one might use your head as a lookout post, for that ultimate safari photo opp), and there are usually lions in the area; we even saw an aardvark on one of our night drives.

In addition to wildlife drives, activities include quad biking, sundowners out on the pans, one of the more authentic 'Bushman nature walk' experiences we encountered anywhere in Botswana, and horse-riding safaris. Rates here include full board and all activities.

San Camp TENTED CAMP $$$
(☎ in South Africa +27 11-447 1605; www.unchartedafrica.com; s/d US$1665/2570; ⏲ mid-Apr–mid-Oct) This outpost of sophistication is an utterly lovely place to stay. The pristine white tents, which appear like perfectly spaced pavillions on tongues of grassland sticking out onto the salt pans, surrounded by date palms, have a lovely lightness and airiness about them. The four-poster beds and old travelling chests are offset by dazzling whites and soft tones.

There's a classy and classic-style dining tent, tea tent and activities that range from wildlife drives (the human-habituated meerkats and brown hyenas are a highlight) to horse riding and quad biking.

THE LIONS OF MAKGADIKGADI

No one knows quite how many lions inhabit the Makgadikgadi and Nxai Pans National Park – the closest that scientists come to knowing is a lower estimate of 50 and an upper limit of no more than 200. In the dry season (roughly April to October) these lions are concentrated in greatest numbers at the western limit of their range, close to the massed herds of herbivores along the Boteti River. When the rains come and the herds disperse, the lions follow suit. Thus it is that, having adapted to the meagre resources of the northern Kalahari, the Makgadikgadi lions cover far greater distances than lions elsewhere where prey is plentiful. They also live in smaller, more mobile social groups.

But perhaps their greatest adaptation is one that suggests that Makgadikgadi's lions are, it seems, rather clever. Between 1993 and 2008, the Boteti River all but dried up, prompting wildlife to cross the riverbed and enter the human-dominated world of villages and cattle posts. When the lions attacked domesticated livestock, conflict was inevitable. In response, the lions studied by one scientific project adopted a remarkably sophisticated set of strategies for avoiding human beings and their retaliation.

For a start, lions rarely moved any closer than 3km to cattle posts and whenever they killed a cow or goat, it was, on average, 4.5km from the nearest cattle post. More than that, lions avoided human-inhabited areas between 6am and 8pm – the time of the day when human beings were most likely to be out and about. Most surprising of all, the study found that lions passing through human-dominated areas moved at a normal lion speed until they reached an uncannily accurate distance of 6km from the nearest human settlement. At this point, the lions accelerated. Once past the danger, they slowed down again and continued on their way.

❶ Getting There & Away

Most travellers arrange their air transfer through Uncharted Africa when making their accommodation booking. Air fares cost around US$150 per person one way from Maun. Road transfer from Gweta costs around US$110 per person one way, and escorts (with your own 4WD) from Gweta cost US$55 per vehicle.

Makgadikgadi Pans National Park

This 3900-sq-km **park** (per day per non-resident/vehicle P120/50; ☉ 6am-6.30pm Apr-Sep, 5.30am-7pm Oct-Mar), the southern section of the Makgadikgadi and Nxai Pans National Park, extends from the Boteti River in the west to the Ntwetwe Pan in the east. The return of water to the Boteti River in recent years has drawn plenty of wildlife, particularly in the dry season from May to October, when the river, even at low levels, is the only source of permanent water in the reserve. The Boteti River has hippos a few kilometres northwest of Khumaga Campsite.

Out in the east of the park, the wildlife is less accustomed to vehicles, but watch for zebras, gemsboks and the occasional predator. Birdlife is especially rich along the Boteti River, from the plague-like red-billed queleas to much rarer African fish-eagles and wattled cranes. Out in the east, you're more likely to see vultures and birds of prey.

🛏 Sleeping

There are some great campsites, either overlooking the Boteti River or out in the remote grasslands in the park's far east. A handful of luxury lodges sit atop the western bank of the Boteti River, just outside the park's boundaries.

Khumaga Campsite CAMPGROUND **$**
(☑ 686 5365; www.sklcamps.com; S 20°27.311', E 24°30.968'; camping per adult/child US$50/25) The Khumaga Campsite sits high above the Boteti River and is an attractive site with good shade, braai pits and an excellent ablutions block with flush toilets and (usually) hot showers. Some readers have complained of night-time noise from the village across the river, but the last time we slept here all we could hear was a frog symphony.

Tree Island Campsite CAMPGROUND **$**
(S 20°29.147', E 24°55.053'; camping P30) Deliciously remote and overlooking a series of attractive small pans that are stunning around sunrise and sunset, Tree Island has three lovely sites that are slightly elevated above the surrounding grasslands and live up to their name with an oasis of shade. Site No 1 is our favourite, but it's a close-run thing. Long-drop toilets and bucket showers sit adjacent to each site.

This site is especially good in the wet season, as the zebra migration passes by. When we last visited, Tree Island was still to make an appearance on the Tracks4Africa GPS system. Ask for a paper map from the park gate when you enter, set your GPS to Njuca Hills Campsite, and follow the paper map from the Njuca Hills turn-off.

Njuca Hills Campsite CAMPGROUND **$**
(S 20°25.807', E 24°52.395') This pair of remote hilltop sites is out in the far east of the Makgadikgadi Pans section of the park. They have a neglected air, and the government occasionally closes the sites, but there's plenty of shade, the surrounding grasslands are attractive and the sense of isolation is palpable.

Meno a Kwena TENTED CAMP **$$$**
(☑ camp 71 326 089, reservations 686 0981; www.menoakwena.com; s/d US$966/1380) The name means 'Teeth of the Crocodile', and you can indeed see some down by the river from high on Meno a Kwena's riverbank perch. There are nine luxury tents with safari nostalgia furnishings – gold-plated lamps, heavy wooden chests, Persian rugs – and each faces the Boteti River valley. Excellent food is another feature, as are brilliant sunrise views.

Apart from wildlife drives, activities include 'Bushman walks' and even a floating wildlife-viewing hide when water levels are sufficiently high. Longer expeditions to the pans are also possible.

Leroo-La-Tau LODGE **$$$**
(☑ 686 1559; www.desertdelta.com; all-inclusive per person Jan-Apr US$476, s/d May-Dec US$1113/1712; ℗ ▣) Luxury East African–style canvas tents with private verandahs overlooking the Boteti River make for some of the best views in the northwestern Kalahari. The lodge is just across the river from the reserve, but game drives yield excellent wildlife viewing, especially those that range along the riverbank and riverbed, depending on water levels.

Otherwise, expect expansive rooms, wonderful facilities and professional service.

Makgadikgadi & Nxai Pans National Parks

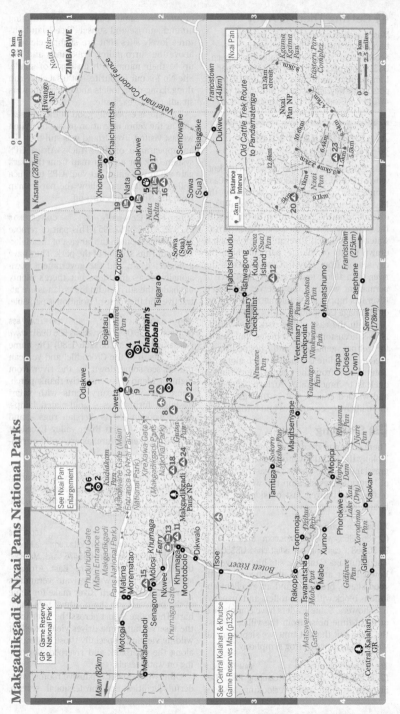

Makgadikgadi & Nxai Pans National Parks

Rates include full board, wildlife drives, bushwalks and a range of activities.

Note that you're quite a long way from pans themselves here, but the wildlife in the area can be excellent nonetheless, and sunset, when the animals come down to drink, is the time to nurse a sundowner on the veranda.

ⓘ Getting There & Away

The main entrance to the park is Phuduhudu Gate (S 20°12.439', E 24°33.346'), 141km west of Nata and 164km east of Maun, 100km south of the Gweta–Maun road.

There's another entrance, Khumaga Gate (S 20°28.333', E 24°31.056'), close to Khumaga Campsite, but you'll need to cross the river on a pontoon **ferry** (☎74 002 228; per vehicle P150; ⊙6am-6.30pm Apr-Sep, 5.30am-7pm Oct-Mar).

Otherwise, there's the little-used XireXawa Gate (S 20°25.384', E 24°7.093') in the far east of the park.

ⓘ Getting Around

A 4WD is needed to drive around the park, and the road from the main gate to the Khumaga Campsite is deep sand in places. Out in the east, the road running from Khumaga towards XireXawa is quite rutted at the beginning, but later becomes smoother as it crosses sweeping grasslands that dominate the east.

Nxai Pans National Park

This 2578-sq-km **park** (per day per non-resident/vehicle P120/50; ⊙6am-6.30pm Apr-Sep, 5.30am-7pm Oct-Mar) is one of the most accessible places to experience the salt pans that

are a Kalahari speciality, although it's more about smaller pans surrounded by grasslands and scrubby vegetation than the vast, salty wastes that you find further south. Wildlife is a highlight here, with elephants, giraffes and jackals pretty much guaranteed, and good chances to see lions and cheetahs as well. The grassy expanse of the park is interesting during the rains, when large animal herds migrate from the south and predators arrive to take advantage of the bounty, but it's also impressive when the land is dry and dust clouds migrate over the scrub and umbrella acacias.

The park also occupies an important historical area: crossing the park is the old Pandamatenga Trail, which once connected a series of bore holes and was used until the 1960s for overland cattle drives.

◎ Sights

The **main water hole** is good for elephants, jackals and other plains wildlife, while the 12km **Baobab Loop** in the park's northwest has a good combination of sheltering scrub, seasonal water holes and open grasslands. The park's eastern reaches get little traffic and feel wonderfully remote. The pans in the far northeast are often deserted.

Ask at the park entrance for the latest locations of lion and cheetah sightings.

Baines' Baobabs   LANDMARK
(S 20°06.726', E 24°46.136') In the south of the park are the famous Baines' Baobabs, which were immortalised in paintings by the artist and adventurer Thomas Baines (p78) in 1862. Baines, a self-taught naturalist, artist and cartographer, had originally been a

THOMAS BAINES

The extravagantly bearded Thomas Baines (1820–75) may not be a household name, having spent much of his life in the shadow of more famous types such as David Livingstone, but he was a distinguished explorer, botanist, artist and naturalist in his own right.

In Botswana he's known for his paintings of Baines' Baobab in what is now Nxai Pans National Park, but he actually gave his name to 17 new plant species held in the Royal Botanic Gardens in Kew, discovered a new genus of beetle that bears his name (*Bolbotritus bainesi*) and is credited with furthering our knowledge of the tstese fly. He was also the first official war artist for the British colonial authorities in South Africa. He is best known for his exploration and artistic work with colonial expeditions in outback Australia but is, sadly, most remembered for the accusations of theft levelled against him during Livingstone's expedition of Southern Africa. Livingstone's brother, who had made the accusation, later realised his mistake (but never publicly admitted it), yet Baines became the subject of ridicule in Britain. It was after his dismissal, on his subsequent journey to Namibia, that he painted many of his more famous works.

He published two books about his African travels: *Explorations in South-West Africa: being an account of a journey in the years 1861 and 1862 from Walvisch Bay, on the Western Coast, to Lake Ngami and the Victoria Falls* (1864) and *The gold regions of south eastern Africa* (1877).

member of David Livingstone's expedition up the Zambezi, but was mistakenly accused of theft by Livingstone's brother and forced to leave the party. Today, a comparison with Baines' paintings reveals that in almost 150 years, only one branch has broken off.

🛏 Sleeping

Two self-drive campsites and a luxury thatched lodge make up Nxai Pans' accommodation choice. There may not be much choice, but availability tends to be higher here than other Botswana parks, and it keeps a lid on the number of safari vehicles exploring the park at any one time.

⭐ **Baines' Baobab**   CAMPGROUND $
(📋reservations 686 2221; www.xomaesites.com; S 20°08.362', E 24°46.213'; campsing per adult/child P400/200) Just three sites sit close to the famed baobabs, and it's a wonderfully evocative site once the daytrippers go home – this is the best place to camp in the park, though wildlife is scarce. There are bucket showers and pit toilets.

South Camp   CAMPGROUND $
(📋reservations 686 2221; www.xomaesites.com; S 19°56.159', E 24°46.598'; camping per adult/child P300/150) Around 37km from the park gate along a sandy track, South Camp has 10 sites clustered quite close together behind some trees at the edge of one of the pans. There's a good ablutions block with flush toilets and solar hot-water showers, as well as braai pits.

It's at its best when things are quiet, but is a little busy for our liking when full. It's the best base in the park if wildlife is your reason for being here.

Nxai Pan Camp   TENTED CAMP $$$
(📋686 1449; www.kwando.co.bw; s/d US$620/880; ⊕) Out in the park's quiet northwestern corner, Nxai Pan Camp has eight rooms done up in an African-modern style that curve in a crescent around an open plain. Inside, smooth linens and indoor and outdoor showers do a good job of pushing the whole rustic-luxury vibe.

Some of the decor's a little dated and it's a touch below the uberluxury of some of the delta camps (but prices, too, are considerably lower). You can watch elephants, zebras and cheetahs cross the grassland from a large, polished deck, or from the comfort of a pool.

ℹ Information

Ask at the park entrance for the photocopied park map, which shows the water holes and major routes through the park.

ℹ Getting There & Away

The main entrance to the park is at Makolwane Gate, which is about 140km east of Maun and 60km west of Gweta. Some 35km north of this park gate is an additional entrance (18km north of the Baines' Baobab turn-off), where you may need to sign in.

ⓘ Getting Around

A 4WD is required to get around the national park. When we visited, the main track from Makolwane Gate to north of the Baines' Baobab turn-off consisted of deep sand and deep ruts – you're unlikely to get stuck but it's a jarring experience.

Two tracks lead from the main track to Baines' Baobabs. When we visited, the longer, northernmost of the two was much easier to traverse, but ask at the park gate.

CHOBE NATIONAL PARK

Famed for its massive elephants, and some of the world's largest herds of them, **Chobe National Park** (per day per non-resident/vehicle P120/50; ⊘ 6am-6.30pm Apr-Sep, 5.30am-7pm Oct-Mar) in Botswana's far northeastern corner is one of the great wildlife destinations of Africa. In addition to the mighty pachyderms, a full suite of predators and more than 440 recorded bird species are present; watch for roan antelope and the rare oribi antelope.

Chobe was first set aside as a wildlife reserve in the 1930s and became Botswana's first national park in 1968. It encompasses three iconic wildlife areas that all carry a whiff of safari legend: Chobe Riverfront, which supports the park's largest wildlife concentration; the newly accessible and Okavango-like Linyanti Marshes; and the remote and soulful Savuti, with wildlife to rival anywhere.

Whether you're self-driving and camping under the stars, or flying into your luxury lodge, Chobe can be enjoyed by everyone.

Kasane

Kasane lies in a riverine woodland at the meeting point of four countries – Botswana, Zambia, Namibia and Zimbabwe – and the confluence of two major rivers, the Chobe and the Zambezi. It's also the northern gateway to Chobe National Park, and the jumping-off point for excursions to Victoria Falls. Although it's nowhere near as large or developed as Maun, there's certainly no shortage of lodges and safari companies, as well as petrol stations and supermarkets for those heading out into the wilds.

About 12km east of Kasane is the tiny settlement of **Kazungula**, which serves as the border crossing between Botswana and Zimbabwe, and the landing for the Kazungula ferry, which connects Botswana and Zambia.

⊙ Sights

Kasane has little to detain you, and most people use it as a base for visiting nearby Chobe National Park.

Caracal Biodiversity Centre   ZOO
(☑ 625 2392; www.caracal.info; Airport Rd; P50; ⊘ 9am-5pm) Signposted as Biodiversity Centre, about halfway between the main highway and the Chobe Safari Lodge, this research and education centre rescues small wildlife species, then rehabilitates some into the wild and keeps the rest. It has some birds, a mongoose or two and a particularly large selection of snakes. If the latter give you frisson, this is the place to look at them through the glass.

🏃 Activities

Most lodges and campsites organise three-hour wildlife drives into Chobe National Park (from P200), three-hour boat trips along Chobe Riverfront (from P200) and full-day excursions to Victoria Falls (from P1350) across the border in Zimbabwe.

In addition to those outfits that operate out of the lodges, numerous safari companies operate out of Kasane.

Mowana Golf Course   GOLF
(http://mowanasafarilodge.net;   9/18 holes P150/280, club rental P150) Part of the Cresta Mowana Lodge complex, this nine-hole golf course is beautiful – well maintained, with plenty of water. Caddies are on hand if you think you'd benefit from a little local knowledge.

↪ Tours

Gecko   TOURS
(☑ 625 2562; www.oldhousekasane.com) Three-hour boat cruises, full-day expeditions into Chobe National Park and a Victoria Falls day trip. Canoe and fishing trips add variety to the usual game drives.

Pangolin Photography Safaris   SAFARI
(www.pangolinphoto.com; 3hr game drives or boat trips US$120) Photography tours along the Chobe Riverfront using the latest cameras with instruction thrown in; park fees cost extra. Its custom-made boats ensure that everyone has a front-row seat.

Chobe National Park

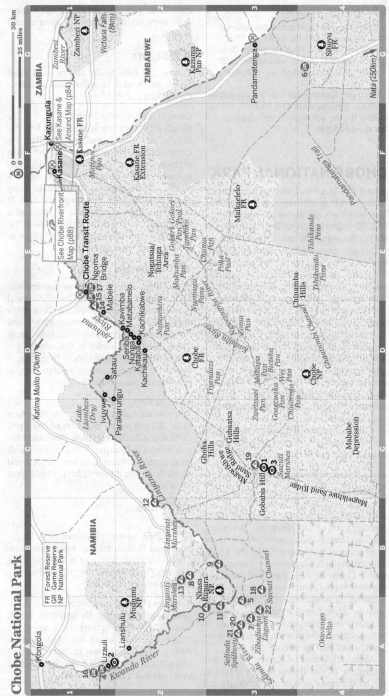

ZAMBIA

ZIMBABWE

NAMIBIA

Chobe National Park

FR   Forest Reserve
GR   Game Reserve
NP   National Park

50 km
25 miles

Zambezi NP
Zambezi River
Victoria Falls (8km)
Kazungula
Kazuma Pan NP
See Kasane & Around Map (p84)
Kasane
Kasane FR
Kasane FR Extension
Matipos Pan
Pandamatenga
Sibuyu FR
Nata (150km)
Pandamatenga Trail

Maikaelelo FR
Tshikando Pans
Tshikando Pans

Chobe Transit Route
Ngoma Bridge
Mabele
Kavimba
Matabanelo
Seriba
Nunga
Kataba
Kachikabwe
Kachikau
Satau
Ivuywe
Parakarungu
Katima Mulilo (70km)
Lake Liambezi (Dry)
Lashanu River

Nogatsaa/ Tchinga Area
Makumbu Pan
Gokori Gokori Pan Pool
Jambiko Pan
Chuma Pan
Poha Pool

Nyamashira Pan
Nyomuga Pans
Nyomuga River
Noga Pan
Chinamba Hills

Chobe FR
Chobe NP
Tripadazi Pan
Zweizwei Pan
Makapa Pan
Bietsha Pan
Geagwaba Wet Pan
Chosonga Pan

Ghaaitambi Channel
Kasabwa River
Mababe Depression

Miudumu NP
Lianshulu
Kongola
Lizauli
Linyanti Marshes
Nkasa Rupara NP
Selinda Spillway
Zibadianja Lagoon
Savuti Channel
Savuti Marshes
Gubaatsa Hills
Ghoha Hills
Gobabis Hill
Maswithwe Sand Ridge
Maswithwe Sand Ridge
Okavango Delta
Linyanti River
Linyanti River
Kwando River
Savuti River

1 2 3 4 5 6 7 8 9 10 11 12 13 16 17 18 19 20 21 22

Chobe National Park

Kalahari Holiday Tours SAFARI
(☑625 0880; www.kalaharichobe.com) Half-, full-and multiday safaris into Chobe, as well as full-day trips to Vic Falls (US$110 to US$160).

🛏 Sleeping

Kasane has good accommodation across a range of budgets, although it helps if you have your own vehicle as some of the better places are some distance away from the town centre.

SKL Booking Office ACCOMMODATION SERVICES
(www.sklcamps.com) This is the Kasane office for the company that runs the Savuti (p89), Khwai (p114), Linyanti (p91) and Khumaga (p75) campsites. Don't come here expecting to find room at any of their campsites – most are booked out months in advance.

★Senyati Safari Camp CAMPGROUND, CHALETS $$
(☑71 881 306; http://senyatisafaricampbotswana.com; off Kazungula-Nata Rd; camping per adult/child from P115/63, s/d/f chalets P450/650/800; ❄❄) Off the main highway south of Kasungula (the turn-off is well signposted 6.8km

south of Kasungula, from where it's a further 1.6km off-road), this wonderful spot has comfy chalets and some of northern Botswana's best campsites, each with their own ablutions block. The bar and some of the chalets overlook a water hole where elephants congregate in large numbers nightly.

There's a relatively new, concealed, ground-level vantage point right next to the water hole. You'll need your own wheels to reach the lodge.

Old House GUESTHOUSE $$
(☑625 2562; www.oldhousekasane.com; President Ave; s/d P940/1500; ❄❅❄) Close to the centre, with a lovely intimate feel, the Old House has attractive rooms adjacent to a quiet garden by the riverbank; rooms on the street side can be noisy with a popular bar across the road. The bar-restaurant is one of Kasane's best, and the rooms are stylish and comfortable without being overdone.

Chobe River Cottages COTTAGE $$
(☑625 2863, 75 663 152; www.choberivercottages.com; President Ave; r P1200-1320; ❄❅❄) Self-catering cottages here probably wouldn't win a style award, but they're well maintained and offer a fine alternative to hotel ambience. It can also organise a full range of activities.

Thebe River Camping LODGE, CAMPGROUND $$
(☑625 0995; www.theberiversafaris.com; Kasane-Kazungula Rd; camping P115, tent P475, tw/f P800/1200; ❄) Perched alongside the Chobe River, this leafy backpackers lodge is one of Kasane's more budget-friendly options. Well-groomed campsites are located near braai pits and a modern ablutions block with steamy showers and flush toilets. There's also a thatched bar-restaurant that serves cheap food and cold beers – come night, if there is anything going on in Kasane, it's going on here.

Toro Safari Lodge LODGE, CAMPGROUND $$
(☑625 2694; www.torosafarilodge.com; off Kasane-Kazungula Rd; camping per person P110, chalets from P780, apt P1180; ❄@❄) Down a side road off the main Kasane–Kazungula road, this excellent place has campsites beneath maturing trees, comfortable chalets (some with river view) and attractive grounds that run along the riverbank.

★Chobe Bakwena Lodge LODGE $$$
(☑625 2812; www.chobebakwena.com; s/d all inclusive May-Oct US$490/760, Nov-Apr US$410/630) Getting consistently good reviews from

CHOBE NATIONAL PARK AT A GLANCE

Why Go? Chobe is one of Botswana's most accessible and varied parks. From the relative isolation of Savuti and Linyanti to the more easily accessed and busier Chobe Riverfront, this is one of Africa's best parks for watching wildlife.

Gateway Towns Kasane (for Chobe Riverfront and Linyanti) or Maun (Savuti).

Wildlife Chobe has tens of thousands of elephants and some of the largest elephant herds in Africa. Savuti is good for predators, Linyanti for hippos and possibly African wild dogs, and Chobe Riverfront for all of the above. Watch also for roan antelope and the rare oribi antelope.

Birdlife More than 440 species of bird have been recorded here.

When to Go The best time to visit Chobe is during the dry season (April to October), when wildlife congregates around permanent water sources. Try to avoid January to March, as getting around can be difficult during the rains (although this is peak season for flying into Savuti).

Budget Safaris Most lodges and many camps in Kasane offer two- to three-hour game drives or boat safaris to Chobe Riverfront for around P200 per person.

Author Tip Be mindful of the decongestion strategy (p89) in Chobe Riverfront.

Practicalities To avoid vehicle crowding, the Chobe Riverfront section of the park has a decongestion strategy whereby self-drive daytrippers may visit the park only between 9am and 2.30pm. Visit the park gate as soon as you arrive in Kasane to line up your visit, or book a safari through your lodge or camp.

---

travellers, Bakwena is an excellent place offering the benefits of Chobe River frontage with convenient proximity to Kasane. Chalets, some right on the river, sit high on stilts and there's a prevailing sense of light and space thanks to the ample space and light colour scheme. Service is attentive, adding up to a fine package.

★**Chobe Safari Lodge**   LODGE $$$
(☑625 0336; http://underonebotswanasky.
com/camps/chobe-safari-lodge.php; President
Ave; camping per adult/child P85/60, r/f from
P1265/1675; ❈❈) One of the more affordable upmarket lodges in Kasane (or Botswana, for that matter), Chobe Safari is excellent value, especially if you're travelling with kids, with family rooms and tents available. Understated but comfortable rooms are priced according to size and location, though all feature attractive mosquito-netted beds and modern furnishings. Rates are room only, but it's still outstanding value.

Chobe Marina Lodge   LODGE $$$
(☑625 2221; www.chobe-marina-lodge.com; President Ave; s/d all-inclusive US$586/900; ❈❈❈) Occupying an attractive spot along the river, Chobe Marina Lodge is conveniently located in the centre of Kasane. The rooms blend African aesthetics and mod cons, and as a result are really rather lovely. Rates include park

fees, all meals, activities, and airport transfers. It's probably the pick of the in-town options.

Garden Lodge   LODGE $$$
(☑625 0051, 71 646 064; www.thegardenlodge.
com; President Ave; s/d incl breakfast US$400/550,
all-inclusive US$565/860; ❈❈) This simple but charming lodge is built around a tropical garden and features a number of well-furnished rooms that exude a homey atmosphere. It's a little more quirky than the average lodge in these parts, with hints of eccentricity that put it above the pack.

Kubu Lodge   LODGE $$$
(☑625 0312; www.kubulodge.net; Kasane–Kazungula Rd; s/d US$315/410; ❈❈) Located 9km east of Kasane, this riverside option lacks the stuffiness and formality found in most other top-end lodges, but is their match for quality. Rustic wooden chalets are lovingly adorned with thick rugs and wicker furniture, and scattered around an impeccably manicured lawn dotted with fig trees.

🍴 Eating

Fine dining is not a Kasane thing. With any luck, your hotel or lodge will have a half-decent restaurant. Otherwise, choices are limited. There are a number of well-stocked supermarkets for self-caterers.

Coffee & Curry INDIAN $

(625 2237; Shop 1AB, Hunters' Africa Mall, off President Ave; mains P45-70; 9am-10pm Mon-Sat, 11am-9pm Sun) Just about everything (except African!) is served at this simple Indian-run place, with a reasonable selection of curries and other Indian dishes, as well as a few pizzas and Southeast Asian–inspired dishes.

Hot Bread Shop BAKERY $

(Hunters' Africa Mall, off President Ave; 7.30am-7pm) If you're arriving from the bush and craving freshly baked bread, look no further than this fine place up behind the Shell petrol station. It also does a few cakes and pastries.

Spar Supermarket SUPERMARKET $

(Hunters' Africa Mall, off President Ave; 7.30am-7pm Mon-Fri, 8am-6pm Sat, 8am-5pm Sun) Kasane's best supermarket is right in the heart of town.

Choppies Supermarket SUPERMARKET $

(8am-8pm Mon-Fri, to 6pm Sat & Sun) Kasane's cheapest major supermarket.

★ Old House INTERNATIONAL $$

(625 2562; www.oldhousekasane.com; President Ave; breakfast P50-80, light meals P40-80, mains P50-115) This open-air bar-restaurant close to the riverbank is every bit as good as the guesthouse it inhabits. The menu contains all the usual suspects such as burgers, toasted sandwiches, salads, steaks and pizzas, with fish and chips not forgotten either. There's also a kids' menu.

Drinking & Nightlife

Kasane has plenty of local shebeens (unlicenced drinking dens) – you'll hear them before you see them. Otherwise, most hotels have agreeable bars, sometimes with river or water hole views. For the latter, Senyati Safari Camp's bar overlooks a water hole that's particularly rich in (and close to) elephants.

Shopping

African Easel Art Gallery ARTS & CRAFTS

(625 0828; President Ave, Audi Centre; 8am-1pm & 2-5pm Mon-Fri, 8.30am-12.30pm Sat) An up-market gallery exhibiting purchasable work by artists from Botswana, Namibia, Zambia and Zimbabwe, as well as woodcarvings from around the continent.

Chobe Women's Arts & Crafts ARTS & CRAFTS

(Airport Rd; 8am-5pm) This NGO-backed store sells locally woven baskets made by the women of the region. The women are often present, and are happy to demonstrate their weaving techniques. You'll find it next to the Caracal Biodiversity Centre (p79).

Kingfisher Trading Co ARTS & CRAFTS

(President Ave, Audi Centre; 8am-5pm Mon-Fri, 8.30am-1pm Sat) A simple shop selling African curios at fixed (though reasonable) prices, as well as fishing gear and a small selection of wildlife books.

Information

ENTRY & EXIT FORMALITIES

Botswana Immigration A For Kazungula Ferry to Zambia.

Botswana Immigration B For Zimbabwe.

Namibia Immigration Namibia immigration office for Mpalila Island.

Zimbabwe Immigration Zimbabwe border crossing.

MEDICAL SERVICES

Chobe Private Clinic (625 1555; President Ave) Offers 24-hour emergency services.

Kasane Hospital (625 0333; President Ave) Public hospital on the main road.

MONEY

Barclays Bank (Hunters' Africa Mall, off President Ave; 8.30am-3.30pm Mon-Fri, 8.15-10.45am Sat) Offers better exchange rates than the bureaux de change. Be sure to stock up on US dollars (post-1996) if you're heading to Zimbabwe.

Cape to Cairo Bureau de Change & Internet (Hunters' Africa Mall, off President Ave; 8.30am-5pm Mon-Fri, to 4.30pm Sat) Charges 3% commission on cash, 4% on travellers cheques.

Open Door Bureau de Change (President Ave; 8.30am-5pm Mon-Fri, 9am-4.30pm Sat) Next to Choppies Supermarket; charges 2% commission on cash, 3% on travellers cheques.

POST

Chobe Post Office (Hunters' Africa Mall, off President Ave; 9am-5pm Mon-Fri, to noon Sat)

TOURIST INFORMATION

Tourist Office (Tourist Office; 625 0555; www.botswanatourism.co.bw; Hunters' Africa Mall, off President Ave; 7.30am-6pm Mon-Fri, 9am-2pm Sat) Plenty of brochures for lodges and safari companies, and generally helpful, although you're better off visiting the park gate for information on Chobe National Park.

Department of Wildlife & National Parks (DWNP; 625 0235; Sedudu Gate) This is the place to pay for your park permit and get information on visiting Chobe National Park.

Kasane & Around

BOTSWANA CHOBE RIVERFRONT

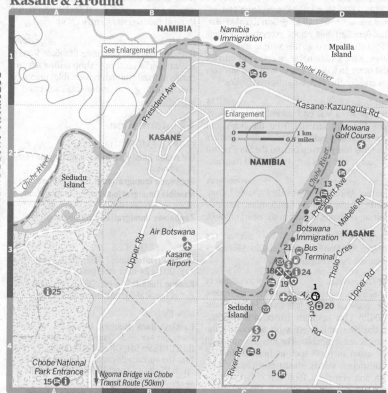

Getting There & Away

AIR

Air Botswana (📞 625 0161; www.airbotswana.co.bw) connects Kasane to Maun (P715) and Gaborone (P2060), and has an office at Kasane airport, which is near the centre of town.

LOCAL TRANSPORT

Combis heading to Francistown (P110, seven hours), Maun (P120, six hours) and Nata (P105, five hours) run when full from the Shell petrol station and bus terminal on Mabele Rd.

CAR & MOTORCYCLE

The direct route between Kasane and Maun is only accessible by 4WD, and may be impassable after heavy rains. There is nowhere along the Kasane–Maun road to buy fuel, food or drinks, or to get vehicle repairs. Most traffic between Kasane and Maun travels via Nata.

Getting Around

Combis travel regularly between Kasane and Kazungula via the ferry, and continue to the immigration posts for Zambia and Zimbabwe if requested. The standard fare for anywhere around Kasane and Kazungula is about P50.

Chobe Riverfront

The Chobe Riverfront rarely disappoints, with arguably Botswana's densest concentration of wildlife. Although animals are present along the riverfront year-round, the density of wildlife can be overwhelming during the dry season, especially in September and October. Whether you cruise along the river in a motorboat, or drive along the banks in a 4WD, you're almost guaranteed an up-close encounter with some of the largest elephants on the continent.

Kasane & Around

If you don't have your own wheels, any of the hotels and lodges in Kasane can help you organise a wildlife drive or boat cruise along the river. Two- to three-hour cruises and wildlife drives typically cost around P200, though you will also have to pay separate park fees. As always, shop around, compare prices and choose a trip that suits your needs.

🛏 Sleeping

Kasane has the region's richest concentration of places to stay. Inside the park itself, Chobe has accommodation to suit all budgets, with campsites for self-drivers in all three areas of the park (Chobe Riverfront, Linyanti Marshes and Savuti) and luxury lodges and tented camps across the park and its hinterland.

Ihaha Campsite   CAMPGROUND $
(kwalatesafari@gmail.com; S 17°50.487; E 24°52.754'; camping per adult/child P260/130) The only campsite for self-drivers inside the park along the Chobe Riverfront (p89) and a wonderful base for watching wildlife. The trees need time to mature and shade can be in short supply at some sites, but the location is excellent – it's by the water's edge 27km from the

Northern Gate. There's an ablutions block and braai areas.

Staying here gives you the run of the park without having to negotiate the decongestion strategy that restricts access for those sleeping outside the park.

Muchenje Campsite & Cottages
CAMPGROUND $

(☑75 007 327; www.muchenjecampsite.com; B334 Kachikau Road; per person camping P120, self-catering cottages P700) Some 7km from the park entrance, this good campsite has river frontage and is surrounded by an electric fence. Each campsite can sleep up to six and has braai stands, and there's an ablution block with hot showers. It's close to both Kasane and Chobe, but without the noise and bustle of the former. The cottages are spacious and comfortable.

Chobe Chilwero Lodge
LODGE $$$

(☑in South Africa +27 11-438 4650; www.sanctuarylodges.com; Airport Rd; per person low/high season from US$590/990; ❈◉❈) Chilwero

means 'place of high view' in Setswana, and indeed this exclusive lodge boasts panoramic views. Accommodation is in one of 15 elegant bungalows featuring romantic indoor and outdoor showers, private terraced gardens and colonial fixtures adorned with plush linens. The lodge is on expansive grounds that contain a pool, a spa, an outdoor bar and a well-reviewed gourmet restaurant.

The property is set back a little from the riverfront and is surrounded by a fence, meaning you can walk around safely – one big reason why families like this place.

Chobe Game Lodge
LODGE $$$

(☑625 0340, 625 1761; www.chobegamelodge.com; River Rd; s/d Jul-Oct US$1470/2370, per person Apr-Jun & Nov US$995, Jan-Mar & Dec US$795; ❈◉❈) This highly praised safari lodge is one of the best in the Chobe area. The lodge is constructed in the Moorish style and flaunts high arches, barrel-vaulted ceilings and tiled floors. The individually decorated rooms are elegant yet soothing, and some

---

BORDER CROSSINGS: KASANE & CHOBE

Kasane stands at a crossroads of countries, with Namibia, Zambia and Zimbabwe all within an hour's drive of the town centre.

Namibia The Ngoma Bridge–Kasane Gate (◷6am to 6pm) lies 57km west of Kasane and is handy for the Caprivi Strip (Namibia's Zambezi Region). As always, coming into Botswana your car will be searched for ftexresh meat, fresh fruit and dairy products (all of which will be confiscated if found), and you may be required to walk through a soda solution (and drive your car through the same) as part of measures to protect the country from foot-and-mouth disease. Otherwise, this is a relatively hassle-free border crossing.

Zambia The Kazungula–Mambova Gate (◷6am to 8pm) requires a river crossing by ferry. Don't be put off by the extraordinary queue of trucks (some of which wait up to five days to cross this border) – drive to the front of the queue. Leaving or entering Botswana should pose no special problems (save for the usual customs searches and foot-and-mouth controls). For crossing into Zambia, we recommend hiring a local fixer (agree a fee up front, never hand over money until all formalities are completed, and get your fixer's mobile-phone number and check that it works). It is possible to do it all on your own, but it will take longer and the paperwork required can be confusing. All fees into Zambia are paid in kwacha, apart from the visa fee and road-toll fee (US$48 for Botswana-registered vehicles, US$20 for Namibian or South African vehicles). Sample costs include ZMW30 council levy, ZMW150 carbon tax and ZMW487 third-party insurance.

Zimbabwe The surprisingly quiet Kazungula–Victoria Falls Gate (◷6am to 6pm) advertises that the border is open until 10pm, but we wouldn't count on it. The border is generally hassle-free. Those on day excursions to/from Victoria Falls will encounter few difficulties, while self-drivers can expect around two hours in total, with whispered requests for small 'gifts' common among customs officials on the Zimbabwean side. As long as your documents are in order and you're not in a hurry, be firm but calm and refuse all requests and you should be on your way in no time.

have views of the Chobe River and Namibian floodplains – the views from the public areas are sublime.

Service is attentive and professional, and there's a good chance you'll spot herds of elephants along the riverfront as you walk around the hotel grounds. There's also an on-site spa and gym. The lodge is about 9km west of the Northern Gate.

Ngoma Safari Lodge   LODGE **$$$**
(🖉73 747 880, 620 0109; www.africaalbidatourism.com/safari-lodges/ngoma-safari-lodge; s/d Jun-Oct US$1154/1950; ⊛ @ ⊠) At the western end of the Chobe Riverfront, close to the Ngoma Bridge border crossing between Botswana and Namibia, this lovely lodge is removed from the clamour close to Kasane. It offers eight stylishly appointed, river-facing suites with thatched roofs on a rise set back from (and high above) the riverbank.

Earth tones dominate the decor in the rooms and the service is everything you'd expect for the price.

Muchenje Safari Lodge   LODGE **$$$**
(🖉+27 170 8879, in South Africa 620 0013; www.muchenje.com; s/d Jul-Oct US$990/1390, Apr-Jun US$755/1000, per person Nov-Mar US$395; ⊛ @ ⊠) High on a hill overlooking the Chobe River at the western end of the Chobe Riverfront, Muchenje has 11 spacious rooms decorated in an attractive colonial style. There are vantage points over the river littoral from numerous points around the property, including each room's private veranda.

❶ Getting There & Away

From central Kasane, the Northern Gate is about 6km to the southwest. Unlike all other national parks operated by the DWNP, you do not need a campsite reservation to enter, though you will be expected to leave the park prior to closing if you do not have one. All tracks along the riverfront require a 4WD vehicle, and you will not be admitted into the park without one.

You can either exit the park through the Northern Gate by backtracking along the river or via the Ngoma Bridge Gate near the Namibian border. If you exit via Ngoma, you can return to Kasane via the Chobe transit route. (If you're simply bypassing Chobe en route to/from Namibia, you do not have to pay park fees to travel on this road.) Be advised that elephants frequently cross this road, so keep your speed down and do not drive at night.

CHOBE RIVERFRONT WILDLIFE

Spend even a couple of hours along the riverfront and you'll likely see elephants, giraffes, hippos, lions and possibly more elusive cheetahs and leopards along the banks. During the dry season (April to October), herds of antelope, giraffes, zebras, buffaloes and wildebeest also congregate along the river. The marshy river floodplain is also inhabited by Chobe's two trademark antelope, namely the water-loving red lechwe and the increasingly rare puku. The latter has a face like a waterbuck but can be distinguished by its notched, inward-curving horns and its small, stocky build.

The birdlife along the riverfront is extraordinarily varied. Along the river, listen for the screaming fish-eagles overhead as they make precision dives for fish.

Nogatsaa/Tchinga Area

The Nogatsaa-Tchinga area supports herds of buffaloes and elephants as well as reedbucks, gemsboks, roans and the rare oribi antelope. Located east of Linyanti and south of Chobe Riverfront, it sees far fewer tourists than the latter (and Savuti), but it also lacks the overwhelming numbers of animals found in those safari hot spots. Nogatsaa-Tchinga lacks a permanent source of water, though the pans (sometimes called 'dams') present in the area store water for months after the rains have stopped.

If you're taking the direct route between Maun and Savuti on a self-drive safari, it may be one of the more rewarding sections of the route. The area is accessible along the main Maun–Kasane track, but a 4WD is essential out here. The clay around this region is popularly known as 'black cotton', and it often defeats even the most rugged of 4WD vehicles. If you're planning on exploring the area in detail, it's best to first seek local advice, especially during the rainy season.

Savuti

Savuti's flat, wildlife-packed expanses and rocky outcrops, awash with distinctly African colours and vistas, make it one of the most rewarding safari destinations on the continent. With the exception of rhinos,

Chobe Riverfront

you'll find all of Africa's most charismatic megafauna in residence here or passing through – on one afternoon wildlife drive, we encountered 15 lions and two leopards.

The area, found in the southwestern corner of Chobe National Park, contains the remnants of the 'superlake' that once stretched across northern Botswana – the modern landscape has a distinctive harsh and empty feel to it. Because of the roughness of the terrain, the difficulty in reaching the area and the beauty you'll find when you get here, Savuti is an obligatory stop for all 4WD enthusiasts en route between Kasane and Maun.

☉ Sights

Leopard Rock   LANDMARK
The rocky monoliths that rise up from the Savuti sand provide more than welcome aesthetic relief amid the flat-as-flat plains. The outcrops' caves, rocky clefts and sometime-dense undergrowth also represent ideal habitat for leopards. The southernmost of these monoliths (the first you come to if you're driving from Maun or Moremi Game Reserve) is known as Leopard Rock and sightings of the most elusive of Africa's big cats are reasonably common here. A 1.6km-long sandy track encircles the rock.

Gobabis Hill   HILL
In the heart of Savuti, Gobabis Hill is home to several sets of 4000-year-old rock art of San origin. The best are the depictions of livestock halfway to the summit on the south side of the rock; park at S 18º35.632', E 24º04.770', from where it's an easy 150m climb up to the paintings.

Be careful, however; the area is a known haunt of leopards, and we spent one blissful morning watching a pride of lions between the paintings and the Savuti Channel just 200m away.

The paintings are signposted as 'Rock Paintings' off the main track and again at the parking place. The western edge of Gobabis Hill is guarded by a fine baobab, which is visible from the main track.

Savuti Marshes   NATURAL FEATURE
For decades since the early 1980s, this vast open area in southern Savuti consisted less of marshes than sweeping open plains, save for occasional inundations during the rainy season. But the area's name again makes sense with the return of water to the Savuti Channel. Once-dry tracks now disappear into standing water that draws predators and prey from all across the region. The marshes lie between the Savuti Channel and the main Savuti–Maun track.

If the waters allow, we recommend the **picnic spot** at S 18º36.889' E 24º04.397' as the perfect riverside place for lunch.

🛏 Sleeping

Savuti Campsite   CAMPGROUND $$
(www.sklcamps.com; S 18°34.014', E 24°03.905'; camping per adult/child US$50/20) One of the best campgrounds in Chobe, with five of the seven sites (all with braai pits) overlooking the (usually dry) river – sites one to four could do with a little more shade, while Paradise camp is our pick. The ablutions block has sit-down flush toilets and showers (usually hot).

Be careful of wandering baboons and elephants; the old Savuti Camp Site nearby was destroyed by thirsty elephants!

★ **Savute Elephant Camp**   LODGE $$$
(☑ 686 0302; www.belmondsafaris.com; s/d Jun-Oct US$4058/5680; ✳🛜🏊) The premier camp in Savuti is made up of 12 lavishly appointed East African–style linen tents on raised wooden platforms, complete with antique-replica furniture that will appeal to colonial safari nostalgics. The main tent houses a dining room, lounge and bar, and is next to a swimming pool that overlooks a pumped water hole.

★ **Savute Under Canvas**   TENTED CAMP $$$
(☑ in South Africa +27 11-809 4300; www.andbeyond.com/savute-under-canvas/; per person Jul-Oct US$725, Apr-Jun & Nov US$590, Feb & Mar US$480) This cross between a tented camp and luxury mobile safari enables you to experience the freedom of camping (sites are moved every few days) with the exclusivity that comes with having a beautifully appointed tent, butler and excellent meals served in between your game drives. Tents have bathroom facilities, including hot bucket showers. No children under 12.

As with all &Beyond operations, personal service is a hallmark to go with the high levels of comfort and carefully chosen location.

Savute Safari Lodge   LODGE $$$
(☑ 686 1559; www.desertdelta.com; s/d Jul-Oct US$1230/1890, Apr-Jun & Nov US$675, per person Dec, Jan & Mar US$535; ⊘ closed Feb) Next to the former site of the legendary Lloyd's Camp, this upmarket retreat consists of 12 large and contemporary thatched chalets with neutral tones, wooden floors and fairly standard layouts. The main safari lodge has a sitting lounge, elegant dining room, small library and cocktail bar. There's also a deck where you can watch the sunset over the bush.

Camp Savuti   TENTED CAMP $$$
(www.sklcamps.com; s/d Jul-Oct full board US$990/1320, Apr-Jun & Nov US$555, per person Dec-Mar US$465,) Given a licence to run the public campsites, cheeky SKL has also taken on the big boys with some beautifully appointed canvas tents overlooking the Savuti Channel. Prices are a touch below the longer-established camps, but the quality is pretty much on a par.

❶ Getting There & Away

Chartered flights use the airstrip several kilometres north of the lodges in Savuti. Check with your lodge regarding booking a flight.

Tracks in the Savuti area can be hard slogs – deep sand, hidden troughs to jolt the unwary, and deep corrugations. Many routes around Savuti are often unnavigable from January to March. Many travellers visit Savuti en route between Moremi Game Reserve and Linyanti. All of these routes require a 4WD vehicle.

CHOBE RIVERFRONT (DE)CONGESTION

Chobe is one of few national parks in Botswana where you may enter as a daytripper without a confirmed lodge or campsite reservation. Before you celebrate, read on.

Chobe Riverfront's proliferation of lodges and the park's proximity to Kasane and its numerous hotels and lodges means that safari trails (more specifically the main trail along the riverbank) can become overwhelmed by vehicles. Perhaps in response to complaints from exclusive lodges within the park, the park and local authorities have instituted a controversial system aimed at reducing the number of vehicles during peak times. Under the strategy, tour operators are allowed to visit the park from dawn until 9am and from 2.30pm to sunset. Self-drivers and daytrippers are left with the wholly unappealing hours of 9am to 2.30pm. That, at least, is the official position.

However, on one of our dry-season visits, we were allowed in at 3pm and permitted to stay until sunset. Confused? Enforcing the decongestion policy still seems to depend upon the discretion of the officials at the park gate – you're more likely to be allowed entry (no guarantees, though) in a single vehicle than if there are two or three vehicles in your group.

Our advice is to turn up at the Chobe Riverfront (Sedudu) gate of the park almost immediately after you arrive in Kasane to enable you to plan your visit. And unless you're in a convoy of vehicles, it's always worth trying to discuss the situation with the rangers at the gate if at first they refuse you entry.

If driving direct to Savuti from Maun, take the sealed road to Shorobe (40km), then the decent gravel road to Mababe, which is close to Mababe Gate. The road from the gate to Savuti (around 52km) is sandy and slow-going in parts.

If driving from Kasane, the sealed road goes as far as Kachikau, from where a rutted, sandy track leads 41km to Ghoha Gate. After the gate, drive 10.3km along the main track then take the road to the right labelled 'Airstrip' – it avoids the worst of the sand and loops back around onto the main track close to Savuti.

Linyanti Marshes

Hard up against the border with Namibia, the Linyanti River spreads into a 900-sq-km flooded plain that attracts stunning concentrations of wildlife during the dry season. On the Namibian side of the river, this well-watered wildlife paradise is protected by the Mudumu and Nkasa Rupara National Parks, which mirror the 7km of frontage along the northwestern edge of Chobe National Park.

Wildlife trails run along the marsh shoreline and sightings of the marshes' stable populations of elephants, lions, cheetahs and leopards are fairly common, although you'll need to be patient, especially for big cats. The Linyanti region is widely considered one of the best places in Africa for African wild dogs, but sightings are by no means guaranteed. Given that most of the luxury lodges are outside the national park, night drives are another highlight.

🛏 Sleeping

Linyanti Campsite CAMPGROUND **$**
(☑ 686 5365; www.sklcamps.com; S 18°16.228', E 23°56.163'; camping per adult/child US$50/25) Most of the sites here sit on a shady and gentle rise just up from the water's edge, with good views of the marshes costing nothing extra. There are the usual braai pits, hot showers, sit-down flush toilets and, in the dry season, lots of elephants and baboons. Expect hippos to make an awful lot of noise during the night.

★ Zarafa Camp TENTED CAMP **$$$**
(☑ in South Africa +27 87 354 6591; www. greatplainsconservation.com; s/d mid-Jun–Oct US$4133/5510, rates vary rest of year) 🍃 Make no mistake: this is one of the premier properties anywhere in Africa. As ecofriendly as it's possible to be out here, Zarafa's tented villas are utterly gorgeous – and as we've come to expect from Great Plains, the attention to detail is exemplary.

Zarafa has as its focal point a splendid ebony tree that once provided shelter for the respected wildlife-documentary film-makers Dereck and Beverley Joubert. The wildlife watching out here is like immersing yourself in a *National Geographic* wildlife film (indeed, this is where many were filmed), and the massive rooms feel like the ultimate safari experience brought to life.

SAVUTI: LION VERSUS ELEPHANT

Reports of lions preying on elephants have for decades emerged from the Botswana wilds, but because most attacks took place at night in national parks where night driving was prohibited, no one could say for sure. That was until the early 1990s when filmmakers Dereck and Beverley Joubert finally captured on film one of wild Africa's most epic contests. The resulting documentary, *Ultimate Enemies,* which was filmed in the Savuti region of Chobe National Park, is as confronting as it is extraordinary.

Male lions weigh on average 190kg, while females weigh 126kg. Although there have been isolated cases of large lion prides killing rhinos or hippos, the preferred prey size of lions is, on average, around 350kg. Elephants, on the other hand, weigh between 4 and 6 tonnes. When lions kill elephants, it is the largest predator-to-prey weight ratio known among terrestrial mammals. Taking place in the dry season of August to November (with a peak in October), the hunts observed by the Jouberts were only successful at night, and only when less than five elephants and 27 or more lions were present (the pride's overall size was 30). Surprisingly, no infant elephants were killed by lions, probably due to high levels of maternal vigilance and protection – most elephants killed were between four and 11 years old.

Reports of lions attacking elephants have tapered off somewhat in recent years as the pride filmed by the Jouberts has divided and groups have gone their separate ways. And lions killing elephants is now more common across the region, especially towards the end of the dry season. But the reputation for strength and ferocity that these exploits have earned the lions of Savuti remains very much in place.

★**Duma Tau** TENTED CAMP $$$
(📶686 0086; www.wilderness-safaris.com; s/d
high season US$2050/3450, rates vary rest of year;
✳️☃️) 🍃 This 10-room camp was rebuilt
completely in 2012 with a commitment to
sustainability; all of the camp's power comes
from solar energy, and waste disposal is
state of the art. The raised tents overlook
the hippo-filled Zibadianja Lagoon from a
mangosteen grove.

The lagoon can be explored by boat when
the water levels are high, or you can kick
back in a luxury tent under thatch.

The tents are, as you'd expect, large and
luxurious and, like the public areas that
extend out over the water, make maximum
use of the location – you can lie in bed and
look out over the waters of the delta without
moving. The look is understated safari chic,
with plenty of replica safari nostalgia to go
with the soothing earth tones and linens.

When it comes to wildlife, there's a decent
chance you'll see the big cats here (Duma
Tau means 'Roar of the Lion'). You'll certain-
ly see elephants, and red lechwe and African
wild dogs are also possible here.

Hyena Pan TENTED CAMP $$$
(www.hyenapan.com; s/d all-inclusive high season
US$604/930, low season US$448/690) This quietly elegant and relatively affordable camp,
an hour's drive from the Khwai airstrip, is an
excellent choice. Appealing if simple tents
sit close to a water hole that's popular with
elephants. All the region's wildlife is possible
on the wildlife drives, but a real highlight is
the 'Elephant Song' walking trail that takes
you up close to the local elephants.

King's Pool Camp TENTED CAMP $$$
(📶686 0086; www.wilderness-safaris.com; s/d
Jun-Oct US$2700/4700, rates vary rest of year;
✳️☃️) Occupying a magical setting on a
Linyanti River oxbow overlooking a lagoon,
this nine-room camp, part of Wilderness Sa-
faris' Premier collection, is one of the most
luxurious properties in Linyanti, with pri-
vate plunge pools in the very large rooms.
Accommodation is in private thatched
chalets with modern four-poster beds and
there's fabulous wildlife in the area.

This place almost prides itself on being
noisy – you will almost certainly be woken
up by the nearby hippos, elephants, baboons
and lions. Night drives are a highlight, as is
the in-camp birding, while a sundowner on
the two-tiered, colonial-style *Queen Sylvia*
barge is the height of sophistication. There
are no bad choices here...

Lebala Camp TENTED CAMP $$$
(📶686 1449; www.kwando.co.bw; s/d Jul-Oct
US$1619/2608, Apr-Jun & Nov US$770/1120, per
person Dec-Mar US$560; ☃️) The name means
'Open Plains', which is what you get in terms
of a view, along with dense game concentrations, a commitment to multiple game
drives and excellent bushwalks. The grasslands eventually give way to the marshlands of Linyanti, which conceal abundant
birdlife. The eight rooms, with open-air
bathrooms, are large and arguably the best
in the Kwando portfolio.

Wildlife watching here is truly exceptional, with wild dogs and sitatungas the possible highlights among many.

Savuti Camp TENTED CAMP $$$
(www.wilderness-safaris.com; s/d Jun-Oct all-in-
clusive US$1820/3000, rates vary rest of year;
☃️) Part of Wilderness Safaris' classic port-
folio, Savuti has all the hallmarks of the
Wilderness camps: friendly staff, luxurious
tents (with soaring thatched roofs) and a
prime wildlife-viewing location on the Lin-
yanti Concession. Rooms nicely combine
wood floors and antique furnishings with
artfully chosen Afro-chic decor. Elephants,
big cats and even wild dogs and roan or
sable antelope are all possibilities.

In wooded country and overlooking the
water between Savuti and Linyanti, this
wonderfully remote small camp has large
and luxurious tents. The perennial water
hole it overlooks attracts large concentra-
tions of wildlife during the dry season.

Selinda Camp TENTED CAMP $$$
(📶in South Africa +27 11-807 1800; www.wilder-
ness-safaris.com; s/d mid-Jun–Oct US$2535/3380,
rates vary rest of year; ✳️☃️) This East African
vintage-style nine-person camp is the one of
the flagship properties for Great Plains Conservation, which took it over from Wilderness
Safaris. The tented rooms are luxurious by
any stretch of the imagination and the wildlife is outstanding. It inhabits the 1300-sq-km
Selinda Reserve, a hunting preserve turned
wildlife refuge in the heart of Linyanti. As
such, it stands at the heart of this excellent
organisation's conservation efforts.

Camp Linyanti TENTED CAMP $$$
(📶686 5365; www.sklcamps.com; S 18°16.228', E
23°56.163'; s/d Jul-Oct full board US$835/1270,
Apr-Jun & Nov US$685/1070, per person Dec-Mar
US$450) Just as it has in Savuti (p89), SKL
has set up a luxury tented camp within
earshot of the cheaper public sites. The

THE SAVUTI CHANNEL

Northern Botswana contains a bounty of odd hydrographic phenomena. For instance, the Selinda Spillway passes water back and forth between the Okavango Delta and Linyanti Marshes. Just as odd, when the Zambezi River is particularly high, the Chobe River reverses the direction of its flow, causing it to spill into the area around Lake Liambezi. Historically, there was also a channel between the Khwai River system in the Okavango Delta and the Savuti Marshes.

But the strangest phenomenon of all is perhaps the Savuti Channel, which links the Savuti Marshes with the Linyanti Marshes and – via the Selinda Spillway – the Okavango Delta. Most confounding is the seeming complete lack of rhyme or reason to the flow of the channel. At times it will stop flowing for years at a stretch (eg from 1888 to 1957, 1966 to 1967 and 1982 until 2008). As of 2016 the Savuti Channel was again dry and the Savuti Marshes likewise.

When flowing, the channel changes the entire ecosystem, creating an oasis that provides water for thirsty wildlife herds and acts as a magnet for a profusion of water birds. Between flows, the end of the channel recedes from the marshes back towards the Chobe River, while at other times the Savuti Marshes flood and expand; as a result, many of the trails shown on many maps were impassable at the time of writing. What's more, the flow of the channel appears to be unrelated to the water level of the Linyanti–Chobe River system itself. In 1925, when the river experienced record flooding levels, the Savuti Channel remained dry.

According to the only feasible explanation thus far put forward, the phenomenon may be attributed to tectonics. The ongoing northward shift of the Zambezi River and the frequent low-intensity earthquakes in the region reveal that the underlying geology is tectonically unstable. The flow of the Savuti Channel must be governed by an imperceptible flexing of the surface crust. The minimum change required to open or close the channel would be at least 9m, and there's evidence that this has happened at least five times in the past 100 years.

camps are supremely comfortable without being overdone, and with prices less than their near neighbours, they're well worth considering.

Lagoon Camp
TENTED CAMP $$$
(☑ 686 1449; www.kwando.co.bw; s/d Jul-Oct US$1619/2608, Apr-Jun & Nov US$770/1120, per person Dec-Mar US$560; ☀) This series of luxury tents looks out over floodplains and river tracks (that's Namibia's Mudumu National Park across the water) thick with wild dogs, lions and buffaloes. Fishing trips and evening boat cruises are available. There are fine views from many vantage points, not least some of the free-standing bath-tubs.

The vast rooms are extremely comfortable, although they perhaps lack the polish of others in the area. The wildlife area here is, however, one of the best in the delta, with wild dogs frequently sighted, as well as a full suite of predators and prey.

Selinda Explorers Camp
TENTED CAMP
(www.greatplainsconservation.com; s/d mid-Jun–Oct US$1643/2190, per person rest of year US$720-750) With just four luxury tents and being one of just two camps in the entire 1300-sq-km private Selinda Reserve, there is a palpable sense of blissful isolation and very personal service out here. This is some of the best wildlife-watching country in Africa, with big cats, big elephants, wild dogs, sable and roan antelope all possible highlights among many. The tents have that whole bush-experience-in-utter-comfort vibe down pat, and there's a recurring feeling that this is your own private corner of Africa.

❶ Getting There & Away

From the south, the track from Savuti is a hard slog of deep sand. The track running east towards Kachikau (where it meets the sealed road to Kasane) is only slightly better.

Most guests choose to fly into their camp on a chartered flight from Maun or Kasane. Flights tend to be cheaper from Maun.

OKAVANGO DELTA

Welcome to one of Africa's most extraordinary places. There is something elemental about the Unesco World Heritage–listed Okavango Delta: the rising and falling of its waters; the daily drama of its wildlife encounters; its soundtrack of lions roaring, saw-throated leopard barks and the crazy whoop of a running hyena; and the mysteries concealed by its papyrus reeds swaying gently in the evening breeze. Viewed from above on a flight from Maun, the Okavango is a watery paradise of islands and oxbow waterways. At ground level, the silhouettes of dead trees in the dry season give the delta a hint of the apocalypse.

The stirring counterpoint to Botswana's Kalahari Desert, the Okavango is one of the world's largest inland deltas. The up-to-18,000-sq-km expansion and expiration of the Okavango River means that this mother of waters sustains vast quantities of wildlife that shift with the seasons in this mother of waters.

Maun

POP 60,263

As the main gateway to the Okavango Delta, Maun (mau-uunn) is Botswana's primary tourism hub. With good accommodation and a reliably mad mix of bush pilots, tourists, campers, volunteers and luxury-safari-philes, it's a decent-enough base for a day or two. That said, if your only business in Botswana involves staying in the lodges and tented camps of the delta, you may do little more than hang around the airport. No great loss: the town itself has little going for it – it's strung out over kilometres with not much of a discernible centre – but some of the hotels and camps have riverside vantage points.

Despite extending more than 15km away from the city centre, Matlapaneng, an outlier of Maun northeast of the centre and along the east bank of the river, is generally considered part of Maun itself.

◉ Sights

Nhabe Museum　　　MUSEUM
(Map p98, C2; ☑ 686 1346; Sir Seretse Khama Rd; ⊙ 9am-4.30pm Mon-Sat) FREE This neglected museum is in a historic building built by the British military in 1939 and used during WWII as a surveillance post keeping tabs on German Namibia. The museum offers a few displays about the history of the Ngamiland district and some dusty exhibitions of photography, basket weaving and art. Donations are welcome. The museum also houses a centre for local artists.

🏃 Activities

Flying over the delta in a light plane or helicopter is the experience of a lifetime. Yes, prices can be steep, but the views are unforgettable.

To join a scenic flight you can either contact a charter company or simply ask at the front desk at your accommodation. But plan ahead, as it's unlikely that you'll be able to contact a charter company and join a scenic flight on the same day. Prices can depend on the length of your flight (usually 45 minutes or one hour) and the number of people on board (planes are generally of the three-, five- or seven-seat variety). Sample prices start from P2900/3600 per plane for a 45-/60-minute flight. One alternative to the fixed-wing flights, and one that many travellers prefer since they take the doors off, is a scenic helicopter flight with Helicopter Horizons.

The offices for all air-charter companies in Maun are either in or next to the airport. Bring your passport when making a booking.

Helicopter Horizons　　SCENIC FLIGHTS
(Map p98, B1; ☑ 680 1186; www.helicopterhorizons.com; per person from US$150, min 3 people) A range of helicopter options, all with the passenger doors removed to aid photography. If you're willing to drive out to the buffalo fence and take your flight from there, the 22-minute flight will be almost entirely over the delta, rather than wasting time and money flying there. You may need to combine this option with a *mokoro* excursion.

Wilderness Air　　SCENIC FLIGHTS
(Map p98, B1; ☑ 686 0778; www.sefofane.com) Part of Wilderness Safaris. Offers scenic flights and flies in guests to Wilderness Safaris lodges and camps.

Mack Air　　SCENIC FLIGHTS
(Map p98, B1; ☑ 686 0675; www.mackair.co.bw; Mathiba I St) Offers scenic flights; located around the corner from Wilderness Safaris. It costs P2900/3600 for the whole plane for 45/60 minutes – how much you pay depends on how many people.

Major Blue Air　　SCENIC FLIGHTS
(Map p98, C1; ☑ 686 5671; www.majorblueair.com; Mathiba I St) One of the better operators for scenic flights.

Air Shakawe
SCENIC FLIGHTS

(Map p98, C1; ☑686 3620; www.airshakawe.com; Airport Ave; per person for 45/60min flight P720/830, per plane P2900/3400) Scenic-flight operator.

Delta Air
SCENIC FLIGHTS

(Map p98, C1; ☑686 0044; www.okavango.bw/air; Mathiba I St) Near the Bushman Craft Shop inside the airport gate.

☞ Tours

Audi Camp Safaris
SAFARI

(Map p100, C1; ☑686 0599; www.audisafaris. com; Shorobe Rd, Matlapaneng) Well-run safaris into the delta and further afield out of the popular Audi Camp.

Ker & Downey
SAFARI

(Map p98; C1; ☑686 0570; www.kerdowney.com; Mathiba I St) One of Africa's most exclusive tour operators, Ker & Downey is all about pampering and luxury lodges.

Lelobu Safaris
SAFARI

(☑74 511 600; www.botswanabudgetsafaris.com) A flexible and professional operation (the name means 'Chameleon' in Setswana) run by Rebecca and Anton, Lelobu organises excellent custom-designed itineraries with a focus on getting you out into the delta, especially around Chief's Island, with reasonable price tags attached.

Old Bridge Backpackers
SAFARI

(Map p100, C2; ☑686 2406; www.maun-backpackers.com; Shorobe Rd, Matlapaneng) This experienced budget operation is run from the Old Bridge Backpackers and we're yet to hear a bad word about its expeditions.

The Booking Company
SAFARI

(Map p98; C1; ☑686 1797; www.thebookingcompany.net; Mathiba I St) A good place to start organising your safari.

Via Origins
SAFARI

(Map p98; C1; ☑76 823 146, 72 688 141) Operating out of Wax Apple Cafe and with the same switched-on vibe, LGBT-friendly Via Origins offers mobile tented safaris across a range of budgets. It also caters specially for families, and includes some novel safari themes: visual arts and photography, local communities, interspecies communication and a 'back-to-origins' option with guidance on bird language and tracking. It's also a good one-stop shop for information on Maun and wider Botswana activities.

Wild Lands Safaris
SAFARI

(☑686 0570; www.kerdowney.com; Mathiba I St☑72 302 489; www.wildlandsafaris.com) A reliable operator with a good customer-service record and camping safaris to suit a range of budgets.

Wilderness Safaris
SAFARI

(Map p98, B1; ☑686 0086; www.wilderness-safaris.com; Mathiba I St) Near the airport, this operator specialises in upmarket safaris and owns many of Botswana's best camps.

Wilmot Safaris
SAFARI

(☑686 2615; www.wilmotsafaris.com) Run by the legendary Lloyd Wilmot, who used to operate Lloyd's Camp in Savuti, with adventurous mobile safaris for families and small groups.

African Animal Adventures
SAFARI

(☑733 66 461; www.africananimaladventures.com) A highly recommended outfit that does horse safaris into the delta and the salt pans of Makgadikgadi. Can also be contacted through the Old Bridge Backpackers and Gweta Lodge (p70). The emphasis is generally more on birding and the riding rather than spotting wildlife.

African Secrets
SAFARI

(Map p100, C1; ☑686 0300; www.africansecrets.net; Mathiba I St, Matlapaneng) This excellent operation is run out of the Island Safari Lodge.

Afro-Trek
SAFARI

(Map p100, A2; ☑686 2574; www.afrotrek.com; Shorobe Rd, Matlapaneng) This company specialises in midmarket safaris and has an office in the Sedia Hotel.

Birding Botswana
BIRDWATCHING

(☑72 191 472; www.birdingbotswana.com) Bird-watching specialist.

Crocodile Camp Safaris
SAFARI

(Map p100, D1; ☑686 0222; www.crocodilecamp.com; Shorobe Rd, Matlapaneng) This budget operator is at the Crocodile Camp.

Liquid Giraffe Travel Shop
SAFARI

(Map p100, D2; ☑680 1054; www.liquidgiraffe.com; Shorobe Rd) Recommended agency in the Motsana Arts Centre that organises safaris, scenic flights, lodge bookings and just about anything else, with a focus on budget travellers.

OKAVANGO DELTA AT A GLANCE

Why Go? Quite simply, the Okavango is one of the greatest wildlife-watching destinations on earth, with a full complement of African megafauna and stunning scenery that is never the same from one season to the next.

Gateway Towns Maun

Wildlife A full complement of herbivores (including large elephant herds and numerous antelope species) inhabit the delta. Most commonly sighted are hippos, which are submerged throughout most of the day, only to emerge in the late afternoon and evening to graze on the riverbanks. Hippos are easily startled and prone to attack – keep your distance. The delta also supports a stable population of predators, including lions, cheetahs, leopards and hyenas. At the canine end of the spectrum, Moremi is home to 30% of the world's remaining African wild dogs. A handful of reintroduced rhinos also roam around the delta's islands.

Birdlife The Okavango is a world-class birding destination, with charismatic species such as African fish-eagles, oft-heard Pel's fishing owl and an abundance of water-bird species. The Okavango Panhandle in particular is known for its birdwatching.

When to Go Generally, the best time to visit the delta is from July to September or October, when the water levels are high and the weather is dry. Tracks can get extremely muddy and trails are often washed out during and after the rains. From January to March, the Moremi Game Reserve can be inaccessible, even with a state-of-the-art 4WD. Bear in mind that several lodges close down for part or all of the rainy season, but others revel in the abundant birdlife. Mosquitoes are prevalent, especially in the wet season (November to March).

Budget Safaris Maun is the best place to join a mobile safari into the delta, although in most cases you'll waste precious time if you arrive in town without a reservation. Most of the backpackers places and riverside lodges and camps organise reliable and well-priced safaris. The Eastern Delta's proximity to Maun makes it one of the more accessible regions of the delta.

Author Tips Allocate as much time as you can to the delta to experience a mix of iconic experiences, from exclusive fly-in lodges to *mokoro* (dugout canoe) trips and self-driving excursions.

Practicalities Although a few visitors arrive from Chobe National Park and Kasane, Maun is where you'll have the most choice when it comes to organising safaris. Charter flights into the lodges and camps of the delta from Maun are considerably cheaper than those from Kasane.

Meyhu Adventure Safaris SAFARI
(☑72 609 968; info@meyhu.com) This small operator prides itself on offering safaris for everyone from budget to top-end travellers.

Naga Safaris SAFARI
(☑680 0587; www.nagasafaris.com) Flexible, custom-made itineraries make this operator stand out.

Nxuma Adventure Safaris WILDLIFE
(☑76 462 829; nxumu@hotmail.com) *Mokoro* and other boat trips in the Okavango, as well as San-guided walks; ask for Oscar.

Okavango River Lodge SAFARI
(Map p100, D1; ☑686 3707; www.okavango-river-lodge.com; Shorobe Rd, Matlapaneng) Reliable safaris run out of the Okavango River Lodge.

🎊 Festivals & Events

Maun Festival CULTURAL
A two-day celebration with plenty of music, parades, poetry, theatre, craftwork, dance and food; visual arts also feature. The festival raises funds for local schools while commemorating northwestern Botswana's rich cultural roots.

Okavango Delta

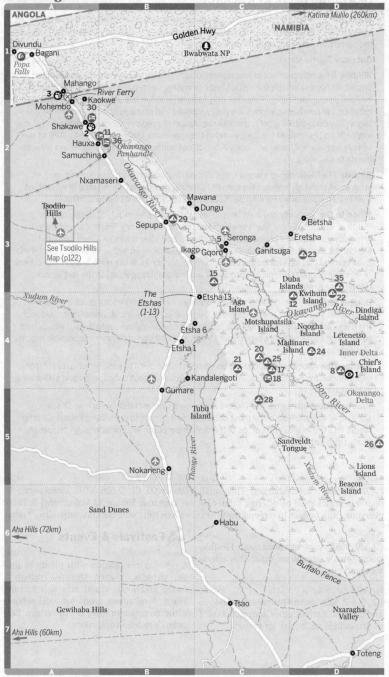

ANGOLA

NAMIBIA

Katima Mulilo (260km)

Golden Hwy

Bwabwata NP

Divundu
Bagani
Popa Falls
Mahango
River Ferry
Kaokwe
Mohembo
30
Shakawe
2
11
Hauxa
36
Samuchina
Okavango Panhandle
Nxamaseri

Tsodilo Hills
See Tsodilo Hills Map (p122)

Okavango River

Mawana
Dungu
Sepupa
29
Seronga
Betsha
Eretsha
Ikago
Gqoro
5
Ganitsuga
23

Xudum River

15
Duba Islands
35
Etsha 13
Kwihum Island
22
12
Okavango River
Dindiga Island
The Etshas (1-13)
Aga Island
Motshupatsila Island
Nqogha Island
Letenetso Island
Inner Delta
Etsha 6
Etsha 1
Madinare Island
24
Chief's Island
21
20
25
8
1
Kandalengoti
17
18
Okavango Delta
Gumare
28
Tubu Island
Boro River
Thaoge River
Sandveldt Tongue
26
Nokaneng
Lions Island
Beacon Island
Xudum River

Sand Dunes

Habu

Buffalo Fence

Aha Hills (72km)

Gcwihaba Hills
Tsao
Nxaragha Valley

Aha Hills (60km)
Toteng

BOTSWANA MAUN

Okavango Delta

◎ Sights

⊕ Activities, Courses & Tours

⊟ Sleeping

⊟ Shopping

ⓘ Information

Maun

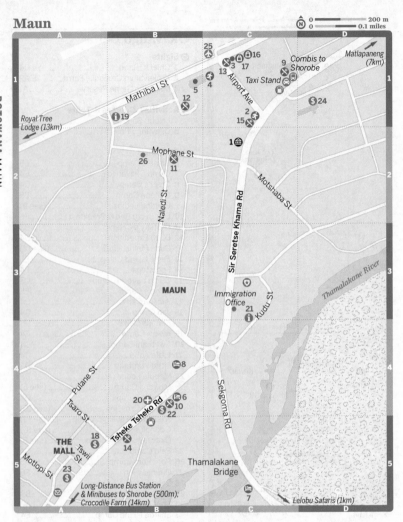

🛏 Sleeping

Most campsites, hotels and lodges – except Riley's – are in either Sedie or Matlapaneng. The attraction of the latter is that the camps and lodges are quiet, secluded and pleasantly located along Thamalakane River (although the effect is limited somewhat when water levels are low). The downside is that they can be up to 10km from central Maun. Many are accessible by public transport, however, and most offer transfers to/from Maun daily, sometimes for a small fee. Most campsites, hotels and lodges also have a decent restaurant and bar.

★**Old Bridge Backpackers** CAMPGROUND $
(Map p100, C2; ☑686 2406; www.maun-back-packers.com; Hippo Pools, Old Matlapaneng Bridge; camping P80, dm P150, s/d tents without bathroom P330/400, s/d tents with bathroom P480/580; @⊠) One of the great boltholes on Southern African overland trails, 'the Bridge' has a great bar-at-the-end-of-the-world kind of vibe. Accommodation ranges from dome tents by the riverbank, to well-appointed campsites and some more private tents.

Here, bush pilots and backpackers chat each other up, families take a break from the rigours of life on the African road, and

Maun

a semiregular cast of drunks keeps the bar propped up.

A good range of *mokoro* trips and the like is on offer. In short, this is a place that understands travel and doesn't make you pay over the odds for it.

Audi Camp   CAMPGROUND $
(Map p100, C1; ☑686 0599; www.audisafaris.com/audi-camps; Matlapaneng; camping from P70, s/d tents without bathroom from P160/190, with bathroom P630/760; @ ⊚ 🎿) Off Shorobe Rd, Audi Camp is a fantastic campsite that's become increasingly popular with families, although independent overlanders will also feel welcome. Management is friendly and helpful, and there's a wide range of safari activities. The restaurant does a mean steak. If you don't have your own tent, the preerected tents complete with fan are a rustically luxurious option.

Okavango River Lodge CAMPGROUND, CHALET $
(Map p100, D1; ☑686 3707; www.okavango-river-lodge.com; Matlapaneng; camping P100, s/d tents P180/300, s/d/f chalets P330/460/600) This down-to-earth spot off Shorobe Rd has a lovely setting on the riverbank. The owners are friendly and unpretentious, and pride themselves on giving travellers useful (and independent) information on trips

through the delta. Between this spot and the Old Bridge Backpackers, you'll find most of Maun's tourist and expat-oriented nightlife.

On that note, we've got to give the owners credit for the excellent name of their boat: *Sir Rosis of the River*.

Crocodile Camp   CAMPGROUND, CHALET $
(Map p100, D1; ☑680 0222; www.crocodilecamp.com; Matlapaneng; camping per person P70, chalets per person incl breakfast P450; 🎿) 'Croc Camp' occupies a superb spot right on the river and is a quieter place for those not needing shots of presafari sambuca (not that it doesn't serve sambuca...). Off Shorobe Rd, the campsite is excellent and secure and there are also thatched riverside chalets with bathrooms.

Maun Rest Camp   CAMPGROUND $
(Map p100, B1; ☑686 3472; http://maunrestcamp.com; Shorobe Rd, Matlapaneng; camping P70-90, s/d tents P225/350) This no-frills rest camp off Shorobe Rd is spotless and boasts what justifiably may be 'the cleanest ablution blocks in Maun'. A recent change of ownership has seen it fall under the sway of Old Bridge Backpackers, but it promised to maintain the camp's motto of 'Clean, Quiet, Comfortable'. Accommodation is in tidy, well-kept tents.

Matlapaneng

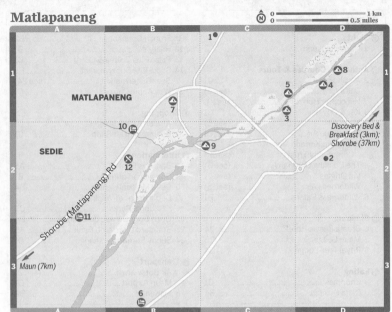

Maun (7km)

Discovery Bed & Breakfast (3km); Shorobe (37km)

Queness Inn APARTMENT $
(Map p96, F6; ☑74 319 384, 684 1000; www.que-nessinn.com; Disaneng Rd; d/f P660/1070; ❄️🛜) These mini, self-catering apartments aren't really close to anything, but they're large, nicely kept and generally quiet – perfect if you have your own set of wheels. The rooms don't have a lot of character, but it's still an excellent and reliable midrange option.

Rivernest Boutique Cottages COTTAGE $
(Map p100, B2; ☑684 0400; www.rivernestcot-tages.com; along Sedie - Matlapana Rd; s/d/tw/f P710/750/780/1300; ❄️🛜🏊) These excellent self-catering cottages have bright colour schemes, excellent apartment-style rooms with plenty of space and free wi-fi. There's a swimming pool, too, as well as a lovely garden setting that's not immediately apparent from the road.

★**Kraal Lodging** GUESTHOUSE $$
(Map p100, B3; ☑72 320 090; http://thekraallo-dgingbotswana.com; exit 6, Disaneng Rd; r P1200-2000; 🅿️❄️🛜🏊) Run by respected film-makers June and Tim Liversedge, the Kraal is a terrific place to stay. The attractive thatched rondavels are beautifully appointed with just the right blend of safari prints, earth tones and African handicrafts and artwork.

There's a pool, free wi-fi and a barbecue area, and the owners are a mine of informa-tion on the region.

The same owners run African Arts & Im-ages (p103) next to the airport.

Discovery Bed & Breakfast B&B $$
(Map p96, F6; ☑72 448 298; www.discovery-bedandbreakfast.com; Matlapaneng; s/d from US$60/80; 🏊) Dutch-run Discovery does a cool job of creating an African-village vibe in the midst of Maun – the owners strive for 'affordable accommodation with a traditional touch'. The thatched, rondavel-style housing looks pretty bush from the outside and feels as posh as a nice hotel on the inside.

A pretty garden connects the dusty grounds, and there's a good communal fire pit for safari stories with fellow travellers.

Island Safari Lodge CAMPGROUND, CHALET $$
(Map p100, C1; ☑686 0300; www.islmaun.com; Matlapaneng; camping per person P90, s/d US$75/115; 🛜🏊) One of the original lodg-es in Maun, Island Safari is still one of the best, with a range of accommodation set along a nice stretch of riverbank. The campsites have ablutions blocks and give access to the lodge's pool, restaurant and bar. The chalets are excellent value. The

Matlapaneng

riverside location is ideal on lazy afternoons and the restaurant is excellent.

It also runs a professional, well-established series of safaris.

Maun Lodge   LODGE $$
(Map p98, C5; ☏ 686 3939; www.maunlodge.com; Sekgoma Rd; s/d P1200/1400, chalets P1050; ❄ 🗙) This upmarket option is just south of the town centre and boasts all the luxuries you'd expect at this price. It's certainly a comfortable option, though it's lacking in personality and atmosphere, especially if you're coming from (or going to) any of the luxury lodges in the delta.

Sedia Riverside Hotel   HOTEL $$
(Map p100, A2; ☏ 686 2574; www.sedia-hotel.com; Shorobe Rd, Sedie; campsite per person P60, s/d P865/955, cottages from P1170; ❄ 🗙) If you feel most comfortable in a hotel-style environment, the Sedia is a good option. This resort-like complex features an outdoor bar, a continental-inspired restaurant and a huge swimming pool. You can choose from a number of rooms and self-contained chalets, or simply pitch a tent and take advantage of all the hotel facilities.

Royal Tree Lodge   LODGE $$$
(Map p98, B4; ☏ 680 0757; www.royaltreelodge. com; s/d Jun-Oct from US$425/700, per person Nov-May full board US$285; ❄ @ 🗙) This pri-

vate farm-reserve, about 13km west of the airport, is a lovely luxury option that maintains a good crew of regular visitors. These returnees are probably impressed by the resident wandering giraffes, kudus and ostriches, the large, beautifully decked-out private cabins and the utter sense of calm and quiet far from Maun's bustle.

Thamalakane Lodge   LODGE $$$
(Map p96, F6; ☏ 72 506 184; www.thamalakane-lodge.com; Shorobe Rd; d/f chalets US$238/345; ❄ @ 🗙) With a beautiful setting on a sun-drenched curve of the Thamalakane River, overlooking wading hippos and waving reeds (when there's enough water), Thamalakane wins in the location stakes, at least for Maun. It has beautiful little stone chalets stuffed with modern amenities and dressed up in safari-chic tones. The lodge is 19km northeast of Maun, off the road to Shorobe.

The lodge has a kitchen cranking out some of the best food in Maun.

Tshima Bush Camp   TENTED CAMP $$$
(Map p96, E7; ☏ 75 342 225; www.tshimabush-camp.com; Ghanzi-Maun Rd; s/d incl with half board P1450/1900) Set in 30 hectares of bushland along the Nhabe River 30km west of Maun along the road to Ghanzi, Dutch-run Tshima is a lovely bush alternative to sleeping in Maun. There are just four classic safari tents, but they're immaculately maintained and a steal when compared to tented accommodation in the delta's luxury camps. Plenty of birdlife inhabits the camp.

Cresta Riley's Hotel   HOTEL $$$
(Map p98, B4; ☏ 686 0204; www.crestahotels.com; Tsheke Tsheko Rd; s/d from P1096/1437; ❄ 🗑 🗙) Riley's is the only hotel or lodge in central Maun and it has a long pedigree: it's been here since before tourists began arriving, although it's barely recognisable these days, especially since the Cresta chain made it one of its landmark properties. It offers comfortable rooms in a convenient setting in leafy grounds – just don't expect a lodge/wilderness experience.

🍴 Eating

Maun is not one of the culinary capitals of the world, but that's not to say you can't get a decent meal – some camps have accomplished kitchens. Away from the camps and lodges, there's a handful of good restaurants, especially in the area around the airport. Otherwise, Maun has versions of every peri peri–obsessed fast-food chain in Southern Africa, and there are excellent supermarkets.

French Connection
FRENCH $
(Map p98, B2; Mophane St; breakfast P40-75, mains P40-95; ⊙8.30am-5pm Mon-Fri, to 2pm Sat) Close to the airport, but on a quiet backstreet, this fine place serves up fresh tastes that might include Turkish pide, Moroccan lamb or Creole fish cakes; the meze platter is especially good. Run by a delightful French owner and driven by a far-ranging passion for new tastes, it's a lovely spot to eat with a shady garden setting.

Wax Apple Cafe
CAFE $
(Map p98, C1; ☑72 703 663; Airport Ave; breakfast P20-45, light meals P30-45; ⊙7.30am-5pm Mon-Fri, to 2pm Sat; 🖭) Handy for the airport (a 100m walk away) and with a lovely casual atmosphere, Wax Apple is a wonderful addition to Maun's eating scene. Apart from great teas and coffees, it serves tasty baguettes and wraps, with the odd local dish on the short-but-sweet menu. There's also a gift shop with some nice jewellery and paintings and free wi-fi.

Delta Deli
DELI $
(Map p98, B4; ☑686 1413; Tsheke Tsheko Rd; ⊙8am-5.30pm Mon-Fri, to 1.30pm Sat) Ask anyone in Maun the best place to buy meat in town for your next barbecue or camping expedition and they're likely to send you here. Part of the Riley's Garage service station set-up, it has easily the most appealing meat selection we found in Botswana – terrific steaks, marinated cuts and excellent sausages.

Choppies
SUPERMARKET $
(Map p98, C1; ☑686 2063; www.choppies.co.bw; off Sir Seretse Khama Rd; ⊙8am-8pm Mon-Fri, to 6pm Sat & Sun) One of the cheaper supermarkets in Maun. It has slightly less choice than some of the others and we'd buy our meat elsewhere, but you'll save quite a bit if you stock up here on cans and packet food.

Shop-Rite Supermarket
SUPERMARKET $
(Map p98, B5; ☑686 0497; Tsheke Tsheko Rd; ⊙8am-6pm Mon-Fri, to 5pm Sat) Shop-Rite is astoundingly well stocked, selling fresh meat, fruit and vegetables, and a bakery that sells fresh bread, sandwiches and takeaway salads.

Spar Supermarket
SUPERMARKET $
(Map p98, D1; Mokoro Shopping Centre; ⊙8am-7.30pm Mon-Fri, to 5pm Sat, to 3pm Sun) Well-stocked supermarket.

★Hilary's
INTERNATIONAL $$
(Map p98, B1; breakfast P16-92, light meals P46-56, mains P82; ⊙8am-4pm Mon-Fri, 8.30am-noon Sat; 🍴) This homey place offers a choice of wonderfully earthy meals, including homemade bread, homemade lemonade, filter coffee, baked potatoes, soups and sandwiches. It's ideal for vegetarians and anyone sick of greasy sausages and soggy chips. We're just sorry it doesn't open in the evenings.

Motsana Arts Cafe
CAFE $$
(Map p100, D2; Piano Cafe; ☑684 0405; Shorobe Rd, Matlapaneng; meals P40-85; ⊙8am-4pm Fri-Wed, to 7pm Thu; 🖭) Housed in an arts complex northeast of town on the road to Shorobe, this casual cafe serves up steaks, salads, Thai curries and good breakfasts, with real coffee and free wi-fi thrown in.

Sports Bar & Restaurant
INTERNATIONAL $$
(Map p100, B2; ☑686 2676; Shorobe Rd, Matlapaneng; meals P70-135; ⊙5-10pm) Bucking the trend by only opening for dinner, Sports Bar does the usual pasta and pizza suspects with occasional curries and some excellent Botswana-bred steaks, ribs and honey-marinated chicken. You'll need a taxi (P60 from the city centre) or your own wheels to get here.

When the kitchen closes, the place morphs into an expat-filled bar with music you can dance to on Fridays and Saturdays, and sport on the big screen other nights.

Pizza Plus Coffee & Curry
INTERNATIONAL $$
(Map p98, C1; cnr Airport Ave & Mathiba I St; mains P60-85; ⊙8am-10pm) We suspect that this place is usually full not because of the quality of its food (which is reasonable, rather than exciting) but rather for its position facing the airport gate – people waiting for their flights don't have to go far. Then again, perhaps it's the variety on offer – there are more than 200 menu items. Dishes range from Italian (pizza) to Chinese, but it's in Indian cooking that it's at its best.

🍷 Drinking & Nightlife

Most lodges have their own bar, most of which are fairly sedate. If you're after a more overland and expat scene, try the Old Bridge Backpackers or Okavango River Lodge. Of the restaurants, Sports Bar has the best and liveliest bar. For a more African vibe, there are, of course, numerous shebeen (unlicenced drinking dens) serving home-brewed sorghum beer to a local crowd; the staff at your hotel or lodge can point you in the right direction for this sort of off-licence fun.

Shopping

Maun's best curio and gift shops are all close to the airport. Don't miss the jewellery and paintings at Wax Apple Cafe (p102).

African Arts & Images   ARTS & CRAFTS
(Map p98, C1; www.juneliversedge.com; Mathiba I St; ◎8am-5pm Mon-Fri, 9am-5pm Sat & Sun) Next to the Bushman Craft Shop on the road near the airport terminal, this upmarket shop has an impressive range of books about Botswana and high-quality photographic prints by owner June Liversedge.

Bushman Craft Shop   ARTS & CRAFTS
(Map p98, C1; Mathiba I St; ◎8am-5pm) Although it caters more to travellers who need a last-minute souvenir before catching a flight out of town, this small shop near the airport has a decent range of books, textiles and woodcarvings.

ℹ Information

DANGERS & ANNOYANCES

Maun is an extremely safe destination in which to travel. Petty theft (usually from cars or campsites, but rarely with violence) was an issue until a police crackdown a few years ago. These days you're unlikely to have a problem, but it still pays to be careful – don't leave valuables or bags in parked cars in the city centre and lock them away if you're sleeping in a tent at one of the campsites.

Emergency
Police station (☑686 0223; Sir Seretse Khama Rd)
MedRescue (☑390 1601, 680 0598, 992; www.mri.co.bw) For evacuations in the bush.

ENTRY & EXIT FORMALITIES
Immigration (◎9am-4pm Mon-Fri)

MEDICAL SERVICES
Delta Medical Centre (☑686 1411; Tsheke Tsheko Rd) Along the main road; this is the best medical facility in Maun. It offers a 24-hour emergency service.
Maun General Hospital (☑686 0661; Shorobe Rd) About 1km southwest of the town centre.

MONEY
Barclays Bank (Map p98, A5; Tsheke Tsheko Rd; ◎8.30am-3.30pm Mon-Fri, 8.15-10.45am Sat) Has foreign-exchange facilities and of-fers better rates than the bureaux de change.

Barclays charges 2.5% commission for cash/travellers cheques, but no commission for cash advances with Visa and MasterCard.
Open Door Bureau de Change (Map p98, B4; Tsheke Tsheko Rd; ◎7.30am-6pm Mon-Fri, 8am-4pm Sat, 9am-4pm Sun)
Standard Chartered Bank (Map p98, A5; Tsheke Tsheko Rd; ◎8.30am-3.30pm Mon-Fri, 8.15-11am Sat) Has foreign-exchange facilities and offers better rates than the bureaux de change. Standard Chartered charges 3% commission for cash and travellers cheques, but isn't as well set up as Barclays Bank.
Sunny Bureau de Change (Map p98, D1; Sir Seretse Khama Rd, Ngami Centre; ◎8am-6pm) Although you will get less favourable exchange rates than at the banks, this is a convenient option if the lines at the banks are particularly long.

POST
Post office (◎9am-5pm Mon-Fri, to noon Sat) Near the Mall.

TOURIST INFORMATION
Department of Wildlife & National Parks (DWNP; Map p98, C3; ☑686 1265; Kudu St; ◎7.30am-4.30pm Mon-Fri, 7.30am-12.45pm & 1.45-4.30pm Sat, 7.30am-12.45pm Sun) To

---

BOOKING A SAFARI IN MAUN

Most visitors to Maun have their safaris organised long before they arrive in town, but in case you haven't, Maun is brimful of travel agencies and safari companies. It can be a little daunting at first, but if you take your time and keep a few simple rules in mind, you shouldn't have too many problems.

First of all, it helps to know that most delta lodges are affiliated with specific agencies, so it pays to shop around and talk to a few different tour operators. Second, if you're planning an extended trip into the delta, or intend to stay at a luxury lodge, contact one or more recommended agencies or operators *before* you arrive if possible. While the cheaper lodges can usually accommodate guests at the drop of a hat, don't come to Maun and expect to jump on a plane to a safari lodge, or embark on an overland safari the next day.

pay national park entry fees and book park campsites not in private hands.

Tourist office (Map p98, B1; ☑ 686 1056; off Mathiba I St; ⊙ 7.30am-6pm Mon-Fri, 9am-2pm Sat) Provides information on Maun's many tour companies and lodges.

ⓘ Getting There & Away

AIR

Air Botswana (☑ 686 0391; www.airbotswana.co.bw) has flights to Gaborone (from P1791) and Kasane (from P715). There are also international flights between Maun and Johannesburg (South Africa), Victoria Falls (Zimbabwe) and Livingstone (Zambia).

BUS

The **bus station** (Tsheke Tsheko Rd) for long-distance buses and combis is southwest of the centre. For Gaborone, you'll need to change in Ghanzi or Francistown. Combis to Shorobe leave from Sir Seretse Khama Rd near the taxi stand.

DESTINATION	FARE (P)	DURATION (HR)
D'kar	55	4
Francistown	105	5
Ghanzi	75	5
Gweta	65	4
Kasane	120	6
Nata	92	5
Shakawe	130	7

CAR & MOTORCYCLE

The direct route between Kasane and Maun is only accessible by 4WD and may be almost impassable after heavy rain. There is nowhere along the Kasane–Maun road to buy fuel, food or drinks, or to get vehicle repairs. All other traffic between Kasane and Maun travels via Nata – this route is sealed all the way.

BOOKING A MOKORO TRIP

A day trip from Maun into the Eastern Delta usually includes a two- to three-hour return drive in a 4WD to the departure point, two to three hours (perhaps longer each day on a two- or three-day trip) in a *mokoro* (dugout canoe), and two to three hours' hiking. At the start of a *mokoro* trip, ask the poler what he has in mind, and agree to the length of time spent per day in the *mokoro*, out hiking and relaxing at the campsite – bear in mind that travelling by *mokoro* is tiring for the poler.

One of the most refreshing things about booking *mokoro* trips is the absence of touts wandering the streets of Maun. That's because all polers operating *mokoro* trips out of Maun are represented by the **Okavango Kopano Mokoro Community Trust** (☑ 686 4806; www.okmct.org.bw; off Mathiba 1 St; ⊙ 8am-5pm Mon-Fri, to noon Sat). This trust sets daily rates for the polers (P180 per poler per day, plus a P68 daily membership fee for the trust) by which all safari operators have to abide. Other costs include a guide (P200 per day) and a camping fee (P50 per person per night) if your expedition involves an overnight component.

In terms of pricing, catering is an important distinction. 'Self-catering' means you must bring your own food as well as cooking, sleeping and camping equipment. This option is a good way to shave a bit off the price, though most travellers prefer catered trips. It's also easier to get a lower price if you're booking as part of a group or are planning a multiday tour.

A few other things to remember:

➡ Ask the booking agency if you're expected to provide food for the poler (usually you're not, but polers appreciate any leftover cooked or uncooked food).

➡ Bring good walking shoes and long trousers for hiking, a hat and plenty of sunscreen and water.

➡ Water from the delta (despite its unpleasant colour) can be drunk if boiled or purified.

➡ Most campsites are natural, so take out all litter and burn toilet paper.

➡ Bring warm clothes for the evening between about May and September.

➡ Wildlife can be dangerous, so make sure to never swim anywhere without checking with the poler first.

❶ Getting Around

TO/FROM THE AIRPORT
Maun airport (MUB; ☎ 686 1559) is close to the town centre, so taxis rarely bother hanging around the terminal when planes arrive. If you've prebooked accommodation at an upmarket hotel or lodge in Maun or the Okavango Delta, make sure it provides a (free) courtesy minibus. Otherwise, walk about 300m down Airport Rd to Sir Seretse Khama Rd and catch a combi (around P40 to P50 for the camps in the Matlapaneng or Sedie districts northeast of the city).

CAR & MOTORCYCLE
Renting a car in Maun can be expensive (expect to pay around P600 per day for a small vehicle for getting around town). If you do arrive without a reservation, there are a number of car-rental agencies opposite the airport on Mathiba I St.

McKenzie (☎ 686 1875; www.mckenzie4x4.com; Mophane St) is a Maun-based, family-run 4WD rental outfit with a small fleet of cars.

Other companies use McKenzie mechanics, so your car is likely to be in good nick. It can also make lodge and campsite bookings on your behalf, and it's also a good option if you need a sat phone, even if you're not renting a vehicle with the company.

LOCAL TRANSPORT
Combis marked 'Maun Route 1' or 'Sedie Route 1' travel every few minutes during daylight hours between the station in town and a stop near Crocodile Camp in Matlapaneng. The standard fare for all local trips is P10.

Taxis also ply the main road and are the only form of transport in the evening. They also hang around a stand along Pulane St in the town centre. A typical fare from central Maun to Matlapaneng is about P20/60 in a shared/private taxi. To prebook a taxi, ask your hotel or campsite for a recommendation.

Shorobe

Around 40km north of Maun along the road to Kasane, Moremi or Savuti, Shorobe has little to detain you. The main reason for stopping is to shop for traditional baskets at the **Shorobe Baskets Cooperative** (Shorobe; ☉vary). The cooperative draws together around 70 local women who produce Ngamiland-style baskets with beautiful and elaborate patterns. It's right next to the main road through town and signposted. If it's closed, ask around (at the nearby shop, for example) and someone should be able to track down the key. A small number of buses leave daily for Shorobe (P12, one hour) from the main bus station in Maun.

If you're driving, the sealed road ends soon after Shorobe and is one of the most rutted, washboard roads in Botswana – pray that it has been upgraded by the time you arrive.

Eastern Delta

The Eastern Delta includes the wetlands between the southern boundary of Moremi Game Reserve and the buffalo fence that crosses the Boro and Santandabie Rivers, north of Matlapaneng. If you're short of time and/or money, this part of the Okavango Delta remains an affordable and accessible option. From Maun it's easy to arrange a day trip on a *mokoro*, or a two- or three-night *mokoro* trip combined with bush camping.

Then again, the Chitabe concession and surrounding area has been quietly building a reputation as one of the wildlife hotspots of recent times, and a luxury experience is very much a possibility here as well.

🛏 Sleeping

Although most excursions through the Eastern Delta are budget trips that involve bush camping, two tented camps and one lodge in the area rank among the most sought after anywhere in the delta.

★**Chitabe Lediba** TENTED CAMP $$$
(☎ 686 0086; www.wilderness-safaris.com; s/d Jun-Oct US$1950/3280, rates vary rest of year; ❄ ❄) One of the more intimate camps run by Wilderness Safaris, Chitabe Lediba has just five tents (including two family ones) and a warm and intimate atmosphere. The larger-than-usual tents here are supremely comfortable, and the whole place is also distinguished by the warm service and brilliant game drives.

Nice touches in the tents include fine black-and-white photographic prints, antique African maps, alongside classic safari furnishings, although such is the size of the tents that they never feel overdone; and yes, there are the usual indoor and outdoor shower options. The broad private terraces are the place to watch as passing elephants or buffaloes wander past.

Chitabe concession, which this camp shares with Chitabe, is prime wildlife country – we saw lion cubs and leopards here, with wild dogs sometimes a possibility – but the landscapes too are exceptionally beautiful here, from the acacia woodlands to the ghostly forests of dead leadwood trees on the way in from the air strip.

★ **Sandibe Safari Lodge**　　LODGE $$$
(✉ in South Africa +27 11-809 4300; www.andbe-yondafrica.com; per person Jun-Oct US$2350, rates vary rest of year; 🛜 🛏) This riverine forest retreat is the architectural jewel of the Okavango Delta, as well as one of the premier safari camps anywhere in Southern Africa. Service is warm and welcoming, the accommodation is exceptional in its style and comfort, and the location (next to the famed Chitabe concession) is one of the best anywhere in the delta.

The newly built main lodge building rises from the water's edge like an apparition. Built to resemble a pangolin in pine and cedar, its effect is utterly breathtaking, feeling at once a part of the surrounding woodland (the main building is open-sided and a magnificent place to relax). When we had dinner here, a spotted hyena wandered past just metres from where we sat. Attached to the main building is one of the delta's best gift shops. There's also a spa and massage area, and a gym.

The rooms, too, have a style all their own. Built to resemble golden weaver nests, they are curvaceous things of beauty. Open fires are just the ticket in winter, and everything is beautifully designed – we loved the copper washbasins and playful sense of perspective. Expansive private terraces with plunge pools overlook the water, and there's plenty of space to spend an afternoon just taking it all in while your private butler brings you the drink of your choice...yes, every room has its own designated 'butler' who will cater to your every whim. This sense of elevated levels of very personal service is something of an &Beyond hallmark.

The wildlife watching here is first-rate – we saw lions and leopards alone on just an overnight stay. There's also wi-fi in both communal areas and the rooms.

Chitabe Camp　　TENTED CAMP $$$
(✉ 686 0086; www.wilderness-safaris.com; s/d Jun-Oct US$1950/3280, rates vary rest of year; ❄) Near the Santandadibe River, at the southern edge of Moremi Game Reserve, Chitabe is an island oasis (only accessible by boat or plane). Accommodation at Chitabe Camp is in East African–style luxury tents, which have bathrooms and are built on wooden decks and sheltered beneath the shade of a lush canopy.

Chitabe is renowned for the presence of African wild dogs and other iconic wildlife, including leopards, lions and cheetahs – the Chitabe concession is widely considered among the elite delta safari destinations. It's this combination of stunning wildlife and supremely comfortable places to sleep, as well as the usual high standards of service we've come to expect from Wilderness, that make this a brilliant choice.

ⓘ Getting There & Away

If you're on a *mokoro* day trip or a multiday bush-camping expedition from Maun, you will be

---

OKAVANGO DELTA SEASONS

The Okavango Delta varies greatly with the seasons and understanding how the delta changes over time is important for planning your visit.

November–December Rains begin to fall in the highlands of Angola, in the catchment areas of the Cubango and Cuito Rivers. Down in the delta, waters are receding, despite rains falling in the delta itself and surrounding area. By December, the waters have begun to flow down these two rivers towards Botswana.

January–February The waters of the Cubango flow more quickly and near the Okavango River, arriving before the waters of the Cuito. Water levels in the delta remain low.

March–April Continuing rainfall (in good years) adds to the growing volume of water that flows southeast through the Okavango Panhandle and begins to enter the delta proper.

May–June The flooding of the Okavango Delta begins in earnest, and water levels rise across the delta. Depending on the year and its rains, waters may reach further into the southeast via the Boteti River and Selinda Spillway.

July–September The flooding of the delta peaks and the waters reach their southeast-ernmost limits, a point that can vary considerably from one year to the next.

October Having reached their limits some time in September, the waters begin to evaporate and disappear, and water levels recede towards the northwest.

transported to/from the Eastern Delta by 4WD. Transport into the lodges is usually by charter flight and then 4WD and/or *mokoro*.

As with elsewhere in the delta, Wilderness Safaris' camps are serviced by Wilderness Air (p93), with Mack Air (p93) the other most popular charter company. Enquire with your lodge.

Inner Delta

Welcome to the heart of the Okavango, a world inaccessible by roads and inhabited by some of the richest wildlife concentrations on earth. Not surprisingly, these are some of the most exclusive patches of real estate in Botswana, with luxury lodges and tented camps inhabiting some of the delta's prettiest corners. If for whatever reason you can't stay here, take a scenic flight or, better still, a helicopter sightseeing flight from Maun with Helicopter Horizons (p93).

Roughly defined, the Inner Delta occupies the areas west of Chief's Island and between Chief's Island and the base of the Okavango Panhandle. Most of the water-based camps of the Inner Delta offer *mokoro* trips through the Inner Delta (roughly from June to October or November), with game drives also a possibility. Some lodges that inhabit islands also offer that rare travel experience of arriving by boat (usually after a short 4WD transfer from the nearest airstrip).

🛌 Sleeping

Although budget trips are possible in some areas, particularly at the eastern reaches close to the Okavango Panhandle, they're most likely to be brief forays around the fringes, rather than deep immersion in the delta's heart. The quintessential delta experience is staying in one of the fly-in luxury lodges or camps – if you're going to make a splash with your money in Botswana, make it here. Given the choice that's on offer, take your time to research which camp is for you – each has its own special features and wildlife experiences vary considerably.

★ Jao Camp   LODGE $$$
(☑ 686 0086; www.wilderness-safaris.com; s/d Jun-Oct US$2700/4700, rates vary rest of year; 🛜 🐘)
Part of Wilderness Safaris' portfolio of premier camps, Jao is a special place that combines Asian style (the public areas and the rooms were inspired by a Balinese longhouse) with a very African feel (jackalberry and mangosteen trees, liberal use of thatch). Rooms

are uberluxurious and the staff are extremely professional and attentive to your every need.

This place is an experience as much as it is a lodge and it does things that no other lodges do – it has a first-class wine cellar you're welcome to browse, a small gym, arguably the best gift shop we saw in the delta, a real tree-house feel that comes from an award-winning design that incorporates elevated walkways, and a high vantage point overlooking the water.

The rooms, with perfectly sited outdoor day beds on the long terraces, feel like your own extremely large delta hideaway. Wooden furnishings, nightly hot-water bottles placed in your bed while you're at dinner, marvellous beds, yoga mats, a mini library in your room – this is one place where you'll almost certainly want to spend an afternoon or morning in camp. If you do so, you might be really lucky and have the elusive Pel's fishing owl perch right outside your window.

Calling you out are the activities, from *mokoro* or motorboat excursions on the skein of waterways, to wildlife drives led by expert guides in search of lions, leopards and even sitatungas, not to mention rich birdlife.

Unusually, there is a small entertainment room with wi-fi connectivity for those who really must stay in touch with the outside world.

★ Kwetsani Camp   TENTED CAMP $$$
(☑ 686 0086; www.wilderness-safaris.com; s/d Jun-Oct US$1820/3000, rates vary rest of year; 🐘) This highly recommended camp has the usual high levels of comfort, but there are some very special selling points. First, the recently overhauled rooms, elevated high above the water, are simply stunning, while the camp manager, Dan Myburg, is a top-class photographer who can help elevate your photography above the usual even in just a few days.

The five rooms sport a striking, contemporary look, with whites and steely greys making a refreshing change from wood and wicker. Of all the camps in Wilderness Safaris' classic portfolio, those here come the closest to getting an upgrade into the premium class.

The public areas sport a modern bar alongside the wooden terrace, and safari prints and throws beneath the shady sausage tree. Like the rooms, these public areas are places to linger. The pool sits down at floodplain level, while Dan can proffer

ZONES OF THE OKAVANGO

The Okavango Delta is a complex and unique ecosystem, but its scope can be daunting. It is, however, easier to plan a trip through the region than you might imagine, especially if you think of the delta as having four distinct areas.

Eastern Delta This part of the delta is relatively accessible (and therefore cheaper to reach) from Maun compared to the Inner Delta and Moremi. You can easily base yourself in Maun and arrange a day trip by *mokoro* (dugout canoe), or an overnight bush-camping trip for far less than the cost of staying in (and getting to) a lodge or campsite in the Inner Delta or Moremi.

Inner Delta The area west and north of Moremi is classic delta scenery where you can truly be seduced by the calming spell of the region. Accommodation is mostly in top-end luxury lodges, almost all of which are only accessible by expensive chartered flights.

Moremi Game Reserve This region includes Chief's Island and the Moremi Tongue, and is one of the most popular destinations within the delta. The Moremi Game Reserve is the only officially protected area within the delta, and wildlife is plentiful. Moremi has a few campsites as well as several truly decadent lodges with prices to match. The reserve is accessible by 4WD from Maun or Chobe, as well as by charter flight.

Okavango Panhandle This swampy extension of the Inner Delta stretches northwest towards the Namibian border. Although this area does not offer the classic delta experience, it is growing in popularity among budget travellers due to its ease of accessibility by public transport or 2WD. As a general rule, this is prime birdwatching and fishing terrain, rather than the domain of wildlife safaris.

advice on photographic techniques or post-processing down in his studio. You'll also find a good mix here of water- and land-based activities.

★**Vumbura Plains Camp**   TENTED CAMP $$$
(✆686 0086; www.wilderness-safaris.com; s/d Jun-Oct US$2810/4890, rates vary rest of year; ☒) One of Wilderness Safaris' flagship properties, this regally luxurious twin camp is on the Duba Plains in the transition zone between the savannahs and swamps north of the delta. Although divided into north and south sections, with separate eating and other common areas, this is essentially a single lodge. It inhabits the Kwedi Concession and the wildlife viewing is superlative.

The rooms, arrayed along the shores of an expansive floodplain that has water for most of the year, are supremely luxurious and represent a refreshing change from the traditional safari look – everything here has a stylish contemporary feel and the massive, split-level rooms are simply gorgeous. They are some of the largest rooms in the delta. Gloriously comfortable beds, open-sided showers (as well as outdoor showers), wooden floors, a sunken sitting area with plush cushions and wildlife field guides, and large terraces right by the water are just some of the highlights. Floor-to-ceiling glass on three sides creates a wonderful sense of light and space without compromising on privacy. Rooms also have their own private plunge pools.

This is one of few camps to offer both full water-based activities (including *mokoros* and motorboats, although availability depends on water levels) and wildlife drives. When it comes to the latter, there are good chances of sighting leopards, lions, African wild dogs, red lechwes and abundant birdlife over the course of your stay. Other activities include scenic helicopter flights (30/45/60 minutes per person US$445/565/695) and hot-air balloon rides (one hour US$430 per person). The public areas – the restaurant, bar and cushioned seating areas – face the setting sun across the water, and even the 'public' loo has a view.

Whenever you visit, and whichever part of the camp you find yourself in, you may never want to leave.

★**Duba Expedition Camp**   TENTED CAMP $$$
(✆in South Africa +27 87 354 6591; www.greatplainsconservation.com; s/d mid-Jun–Oct US$2700/3600, rates vary rest of year) Opened in 2016, this wonderful camp has six tents that are immaculate, large and the sort of canvas home you'll struggle to tear yourself away from. But do so you must, for the

wildlife here is some of the best in Africa – this is the homebase area for Dereck and Beverley Joubert and their marvellous wildlife films.

Everything is thought of, the location is perfect and it gets just right the sense of being out in the African wilds with not the slightest compromise on comfort.

It's the latest addition to the terrific portfolio of Great Plains Conservation.

★ Gunn's Camp
TENTED CAMP $$$

(✉ 686 0023; www.underonebotswanasky.com; s/d Jul-Oct US$900/1480, per person Apr-Jun US$560, Nov-Mar US$405) A beautiful option for those wanting the amenities of a high-end safari – expertly cooked meals, attentive service and wonderful views over its island location in the delta – with a more rugged sense of place. The elegant tented rooms are large, lovely and as comfy as you'll find anywhere, but there's more of a feeling of being engaged with the wilderness.

What with the hippos, warthogs and even elephants that occasionally wander through the grounds, the abundance of water, and the great wildlife in the vicinity, this is a real delta experience and, compared with prices elsewhere, Gunn's represents fabulous value.

★ Nxabega Okavango Camp
TENTED CAMP $$$

(✉ in South Africa +27 11-809 4300; www.andbeyond.com; per person Jun-Oct US$1665, rest of year US$755-1035; ☎ ✉) In a grove of ebony trees on the flats near the Boro River, this exquisitely designed tented camp has sweeping views of the delta floodplains. The rooms are magnificent – the private terraces in each are large with lovely swing chairs, each built around water's-edge termite mounds or trees, lending a real sense of intimacy with the landscape.

Inside the nine tents, every comfort is catered for, while the standards of service here are as exemplary as we have come to expect from &Beyond's camps. The rooms are also designed so that you wake up and you're instantly immersed in the landscape.

The main lodge area, which includes the bar, restaurant, sitting area and swimming pool, is undergoing a major overhaul as of early 2017. Unlike the rooms, which sport a daring contemporary look, the main lodge will remain old-school, classic-safari in aesthetics. There's also wi-fi in communal

areas and, unlike other lodges around the delta, meals are taken at your own table, not communally with other guests.

The whole property overlooks a wide floodplain – classic Okavango views – that is home to a resident hippo and is a precursor to excellent game drives. Like all of &Beyond's camps, your vehicle will have both a driver and a tracker, and on a single afternoon's drive here, we drew near to a pride of nine lions and a coalition of five cheetahs.

Duba Plains
TENTED CAMP $$$

(✉ 087 354 6591; www.greatplainsconservation.com; from US$1250; ✉) North of the Moremi Game Reserve, Duba Plains is one of the delta's most remote camps. It was recently taken over by Great Plains Conservation and, when we last visited, was being totally dismantled. A new camp, built on entirely green foundations and principles, has since reopened in 2017.

Eagle Island Camp
TENTED CAMP $$$

(✉ in South Africa +27 21-483 1600; www.belmondsafaris.com; s/d Jun-Oct US$4604/6460, rates vary rest of year) Eagle Island occupies a stunning concession deep in the waters. The silk-soft tents are suitably luxurious with private plunge pools and vantage points over the delta's waterways at every turn. The copper bedheads are a nod to Botswana's mining history. Helicopter and *mokoro* safaris are part of your stay, plus the usual range of wildlife drives, walks and lavish meals.

Jacana Camp
TENTED CAMP $$$

(✉ 686 0086; www.wilderness-safaris.com; s/d Jun-Oct US$1570/2580, rates vary rest of year) Arriving here by boat is just the start of your enjoyable island-camp experience. There are just five tents, and the look is decidedly rustic. The tents are classic safari canvas, perhaps a little simpler than others in the Wilderness portfolio, and the sycamore tree around which the communal dining and bar area is built is a pleasing feature.

Game drives are possible here, but it's the *mokoro* and motorboat excursions that are the main event – fabulous birdlife, elephants, hippos and great sunsets are highlights of this watery world.

Rooms have the usual outdoor/indoor showers, while tent 1 is often used for honeymooners because of its copper, claw-foot bath overlooking the water.

The 'public' toilet is a place to linger with its fine views, and there are plans to go fully solar within a couple of years.

Kanana Camp   TENTED CAMP $$$
(☑ 686 0375; www.kerdowneybotswana.com; s/d Jun-Oct US$1420/1860, rates vary rest of year; ☒) This classy retreat occupies a watery site in a maze of grass- and palm-covered islands on the Xudum River. It was overhauled in 2016 and is an excellent base for wildlife viewing by *mokoro* around Chief's Island, or fishing in the surrounding waterways. The birding, too, is outstanding. Accommodation is in eight well-furnished linen tents shaded by towering riverine forest.

Little Tubu   TENTED CAMP $$$
(☑ 686 0086; www.wilderness-safaris.com; s/d Jun-Oct US$1950/3280, rates vary rest of year) This adjunct to Wilderness Safaris' Tubu Tree Camp (p110) promises one of the delta's more intimate experiences – there are just three tents and you're treated like family. It shares Hunde Island with Tubu Tree and the leopard viewing is consistently good. The tents are wonderfully uncluttered, with an emphasis on letting in as much light and air as possible.

Pelo Camp   TENTED CAMP $$$
(☑ 686 0086; www.wilderness-safaris.com; s/d Jun-Oct US$910/1380, rates vary rest of year; ☒) Billed as an 'adventure' camp in the Wilderness Safaris portfolio, Pelo was rebuilt in 2015 to fit a more classic mould, though prices remain as low as you'll find for this kind of comfort and experience in Botswana. Built on an island, and offering only waterborne activities (*mokoro* and motorboat excursions), Pelo is perhaps the delta's most relaxed such place.

There's an inviting swimming pool, excellent birding (including in 2016 *two* resident pairs of Pel's fishing owls), a resident elephant and 100% solar power, while the tents are conventional in design with an attractive contemporary look. Unless you need your dose of big cats and game drives, Pelo is a fine overall package.

Seba Camp   TENTED CAMP $$$
(☑ 686 0086; www.wilderness-safaris.com; s/d Jun-Oct US$1741/2858, rates vary rest of year; ☒) Seba, a lovely Setswana word meaning 'Whisper', is set in an equally lovely riverine forest. While it offers many of the same aristocratic offerings as other top-end safa-

ri lodges, what sets it apart is the emphasis on family service – unlike other properties, this one really welcomes children.

Youngsters (and oldsters) can pass their days watching researchers study nearby elephants that have been released into the wild from captivity.

It's not the delta's most prolific wildlife area, but the birding is terrific, the woodland setting gorgeous and the rooms and service are top-notch.

Tubu Tree Camp   TENTED CAMP $$$
(☑ 686 0086; www.wilderness-safaris.com; s/d Jun-Oct US$1950/3280, rates vary rest of year; ☒) Get your khaki and pith-helmet fix from the gorgeous tilted accommodation that hovers over this pretty little corner of the Okavango. Verandas look out from your accommodation over one of the delta's largest consistently dry areas, which often teems with a good variety of wildlife – it prides itself on leopard sightings. Rooms are lovely without being overdone.

Xigera Camp   TENTED CAMP $$$
(☑ 686 0086; www.wilderness-safaris.com; s/d Jun-Oct US$1310/2170, rates vary rest of year; ☒) Pronounced 'kee-*jera*', this isolated spot is deep in the heart of the Inner Delta and is renowned for its rich birdlife. It's predominantly a water camp, but game drives are possible. The area surrounding the camp is permanent wetland, which gives Xigera a lush and tropical atmosphere. Accommodation is in eight rather lovely tent-chalets.

The tents (including one family tent) have a wonderful sense of privacy, they are well furnished and get the whole safari-tent-in-the-wilderness thing spot on without compromising on comfort – we would happily spend a day sitting on one of the ample triangular terraces contemplating the delta's waters. Wooden floors are offset by straw mats and modern desks that lighten the feel.

Elephants and hippos are often seen around camp, and a leopard even wandered across the bridge and along the walkways to the tents when we were last in camp. Vervet monkeys also inhabit the island. On the game drives, leopards are possible year-round, with lions and wild dogs only possible in the dry season when water levels drop. We spent a most pleasurable morning with a leopard family, including a cub that decided to eat our vehicle's tyres, out in the lovely game-drive area west of camp where the palm trees, wild sage and termite mounds look for all the world like a plain filled with Burmese pagodas. *Mokoro* or motorboat excursions are good for birdlife (we saw a Pel's fishing owl here), as well as elephants and hippos.

Eminently reasonable prices by delta standards are another reason to choose Xigera as your base in the delta. Most transfers from the airstrip involve 4WD then a boat into camp.

Xudum Lodge
LODGE $$$

(📶 in South Africa +27 11-809 4300; www.andbeyond. com; per person Jun-Oct US$1770, rates vary rest of year; 🛜) Style and stellar service are recurring themes at all &Beyond properties and Xudum, in the northern Okavango Delta, is no exception. The rooms here have a lovely mix of safari chic and contemporary style with light wood fittings. Abundant use of glass gives a real sense of oneness with the elements and the rooms are perfectly proportioned.

Wildlife watching is excellent – this is the delta, after all.

Footsteps
TENTED CAMP $$$

(📶 686 0375; www.kerdowneybotswana.com; s/d Jun-Oct US$995/1580, rates vary rest of year) This relatively new program, run by Ker & Downey, places an emphasis on walking and *mokoro* safaris across the delta floodplains. It's the sort of thing that rewards fit travellers, but with that said, the rest camps are still impressively posh – the theme is old Africa exploration, but we doubt Livingstone ever laid his bushy beard on these soft sheets.

Family safaris, too, are an important part of the Ker & Downey package.

Mapula Lodge
TENTED CAMP $$$

(📶 686 3369; www.mapula-lodge.com; s/d Jul-Oct US$1010/1550, per person rest of year US$440-650; 🛬) Located on the fringe of the Moremi Game Reserve, this lodge has a style all its own and is one of few independent lodges in the delta. African hardwoods dominate the decor, with adobe walls and zinc bath-tubs adding a more rustic, *Out of Africa* feel without compromising on comfort. It offers a good mix of land- and water-based activities.

Moremi Crossing
TENTED CAMP $$$

(📶 686 0023; www.underonebotswanasky.com; s/d Jul-Oct US$750/1180, per person rest of year US$365-520; 🛬) This well-priced collection of lovely chalets flanks a simply gorgeous (and enormous) thatched dining and bar area that overlooks a long floodplain where you can often see wandering giraffes and elephants.

Rooms are simpler than many in the delta, but prices, too, are more modest. *Mokoro* trips and wildlife drives are the main activities.

The camp is to be commended for pioneering a plumbing system that minimises environmental impact (it's also quite a feat of engineering – ask to see how it all works).

It's part of the well-regarded portfolio of Under One Botswana Sky.

Oddball's
TENTED CAMP $$$

(📶 686 1154; www.oddballscamp.com; s/d Jun-Oct US$580/890, per person rest of year US$295-360) For years, Oddball's was a well-regarded budget lodge and something of a delta institution, but although it's still way below lodge prices elsewhere in the delta,

---

THE BEST OF THE DELTA ON DVD

Dereck and Beverley Joubert, *National Geographic* 'Explorers in Residence', have spent almost 30 years visiting the Okavango Delta and documenting its wildlife, especially the big cats. The result is an extraordinary portfolio of DVDs that captures the spirit of the delta and the daily dramas of its wildlife. Jeremy Irons' narration on many of the stories adds gravitas, if any were needed.

➡ **The Last Lions** (2011) Follows a lioness and her cubs as they struggle to survive around Duba Island in the heart of the delta (narrated by Jeremy Irons).

➡ **Living with Big Cats** (2007) An intimate portrait of the film-makers, the delta and the animals that take centre stage in their films.

➡ **Eye of the Leopard** (2006) A remarkable chronicle of two years in the life of a leopard mother and her cub in the delta.

➡ **Ultimate Enemies** (2003–06) Three-part series documenting the enduring rivalry of lions with buffaloes, hyenas and elephants.

we reckon it's asking too much considering you're still staying in budget dome tents. It occupies less-than-exciting woodland beside an airstrip, but is within walking distance of some classic delta scenery.

Pom Pom Camp   TENTED CAMP $$$
(📞686 4436; www.underonebotswanasky.com; s/d Jul-Oct US$1100/1880, Apr-Jun US$780/1280, per person Dec-Mar US$485; ☒) This intimate camp was one of the delta's original luxury retreats, though frequent renovations have kept it up to speed with recent properties. Six linen tents, rather standard in design, are skilfully placed around a scenic lagoon, which contributes to the tranquil and soothing atmosphere. Some of the tents could be a little larger.

There's good wildlife in the area – we saw cheetahs and lions on our last visit to the concession.

Little Vumbura   TENTED CAMP
(📞686 0086; www.wilderness-safaris.com; s/d Jun-Oct US$2050/3450, rates vary rest of year) Little Vumbura has a stunning island setting: this is one camp where you can only arrive by boat (after a short vehicle ride from the airstrip) for much of the year. With just six tents (including one family tent), the whole place has an intimate feel and is one of the more personal delta-camp experiences.

The island is a haven of birdsong, and all of the safari tents face onto the water. The look in the tents is the perfect blend of traditional safari aesthetics (wooden floors and furnishings, including the obligatory, water-facing writing desk, as well as free-standing claw-foot bath-tubs) with lighter colour schemes and a real sense of space. We love the hammocks, while honeymooning couples will want tent number 6 with its outdoor bath-tub. Pretty communal areas and welcoming staff round out a fine package.

It's the sister camp to Wilderness Safaris' showpiece Vumbura Plains Camp (p108).

ℹ️ Getting There & Away

The only way into and out of the Inner Delta for most visitors is by air. This is an expensive extra, but the pain is alleviated if you look at it as two scenic flights. Chartered flights to the lodges typically cost about US$200 per leg. A *mokoro* or 4WD vehicle will meet your plane and take you to the lodge.

If you're flying into one of the camps operated by Wilderness Safaris, Wilderness Air (p93) will be your carrier. For other camps, Mack Air (p93)

is one of the most reliable operators. It is possible to book directly with the air-charter company, but it usually makes more sense to make a booking through the safari or lodge company as part of your accommodation booking, not least because it sometimes works out cheaper that way.

Moremi Game Reserve

Moremi Game Reserve, which covers one-third of the Okavango Delta, is home to some of Africa's densest concentrations of wildlife. It's also one of the most accessible corners of the Okavango, with well-maintained trails and accommodation that ranges from luxury lodges to public campsites for self-drivers.

Moremi has a distinctly dual personality, with large areas of dry land rising between vast wetlands. The most prominent 'islands' are Chief's Island, accessible by *mokoro* from the Inner Delta lodges, and Moremi Tongue at the eastern end of the reserve, which is mostly accessible by 4WD. Habitats range from mopane (woodland) and thorn scrub to dry savannah, riparian woodland, grassland, floodplain, marsh and permanent waterways, lagoons and islands.

With the recent reintroduction of rhinos, Moremi is now home to the Big Five (lions, leopards, buffaloes, elephants and rhinos), and notably Africa's largest population of red lechwe. The reserve also protects one of the largest remaining populations of endangered African wild dogs.

History

Moremi is unusual because it's the only part of the Okavango Delta that is officially cordoned off for the preservation of wildlife. It was set aside as a reserve in 1963 when it became apparent that poaching was decimating wildlife populations. Named after the Batawana chief Moremi III, the reserve has been extended over the years and now encompasses almost 5000 sq km.

👁 Sights & Activities

Moremi is the launching point for some wonderful boat excursions into the delta. Although *mokoro* trips may be possible, most of what's on offer is in open-sided motor-propelled boats. More jetties spring up with each passing year, but at the time of writing there were two in the Xakanaxa area, with a further site at the Mboma boat station on

Mboma Island. Prices start at P650/750/825 per hour for an eight-/12-/16-seater craft.

Chief's Island   ISLAND
The largest island in the Okavango Delta, Chief's Island (70km long and 15km wide) is so named because it was once the sole hunting preserve of the local chief. Raised above the water level by tectonic activity, it's here that so much of the delta's wildlife retreats as water levels rise. As such, the island is home to what could be the richest concentration of wildlife in Botswana. It's the Okavango Delta as you've always imagined it.

The combination of reed-fringed waters, grasslands and light woodlands makes for game viewing that can feel like a BBC wildlife documentary brought to life. Not surprisingly, the island is home to some of the most exclusive lodges and tented camps in Africa.

Mboma Island   ISLAND
The grassy savannah of this 100-sq-km island, a long extension of the Moremi Tongue, contrasts sharply with the surrounding landscapes and provides some excellent dry-season wildlife watching – cheetah, lion and buffalo sightings are reasonably common. The 32km sandy Mboma Loop starts about 2km west of Third Bridge (p113) and is a pleasant side trip. Boat trips from the Mboma boat station on the island's northwestern tip are highly recommended.

Paradise Pools   LAKE
One of the prettiest corners of Moremi, the area known as Paradise Pools is as lovely as the name suggests. In the dry season, trails lead past forests of dead trees and among the perimeter of reed-filled swamps, while impala and other antelope species drink nervously at the receding shoreline of water holes. When we were last here, there were lion and leopard sightings in the area.

Xakanaxa Lediba   LAKE
(Xakanaxa Lagoon) With one of Africa's largest heronries, Xakanaxa Lediba is renowned as a birdwatchers' paradise. In addition to herons, potential sightings here include storks, egrets and ibises. The area also supports an array of wildlife and large numbers of fish. There are myriad trails around the Xakanaxa backwaters – the *Shell Map of the Moremi Game Reserve* is the most detailed resource.

Dombo Hippo Pools   LAKE
The drive between North Gate (including Khwai) and Xakanaxa Lediba follows one of Botswana's more scenic tracks, although the exact route changes with the years, depending on flood levels. A worthwhile stop en route, Dombo Hippo Pool (about 14km southwest of North Gate) is where hippos crowd along the shore. Their shenanigans can be enjoyed in relative safety from an elevated observation post.

Fourth Bridge   BRIDGE
Quite a long, wooden crossing on the trail between Third Bridge and Xakanaxa.

Third Bridge   BRIDGE
Literally the third log bridge after entering the reserve at South Gate (although First Bridge and Second Bridge were, at the time of writing, easy to bypass in the dry season along parallel tracks), this ramshackle bridge spans a reed-filled, tannin-coloured pool on the Sekiri River. The neighbouring campsite is one of our favourites in the Okavango. Don't even think of going for a swim here – it's a favourite haunt for crocs and hippos, and lions often use the bridge.

First Bridge   BRIDGE
Blink and you'll miss it. First Bridge is more useful than interesting – depending on its state of repair, an alternative track alongside may serve the same purpose.

Second Bridge   BRIDGE
Not long before Mboma if you're coming from Maun. In fairly poor condition last time we visited.

🛏 Sleeping

There are four public campsites in Moremi, but they're often booked well in advance, especially during South African school holidays (mid-April, July, September, and December to January) – book as early as possible. Each site has an ablutions block with sit-down flush toilets, running water (which needs to be boiled or purified for drinking), picnic tables and braai pits.

In the Khwai area, the **Khwai Development Trust** (📞 686 2361; khwai@botsnet.bw) operates three community-run campsites – Magotho, Matswere and Sable Alley – just across the river from Khwai Campsite.

MOREMI GAME RESERVE AT A GLANCE

Why Go? Some of Southern Africa's best wildlife watching with even the Big Five (lions, leopards, buffaloes, elephants and rhinos) possible. The backdrop to all this abundance is a full range of Okavango Delta landscapes.

Gateway Towns Maun

Wildlife With the recent reintroduction of rhinos, Moremi is now home to the Big Five, and notably Africa's largest population of red lechwe. The reserve also protects one of the largest remaining populations of endangered African wild dogs.

Birdlife Birding in Moremi is incredibly varied and rich, and it's arguably the best place in Africa to view the rare and secretive Pel's fishing owl.

When to Go The best time to see wildlife in Moremi is the late dry season (July to October), when animals are forced to congregate around permanent water sources, which are accessible to wildlife (and humans). September and October are optimum times for spotting wildlife and birdlife, but these are also the hottest two months. January and February are normally very wet, and as tracks in the reserve are mostly clay, they are frequently impassable during these months.

Budget Safaris Organise your visit through one of the backpacker or overland lodges in Maun. Otherwise, get a group of four together, rent a 4WD and stay in the game reserve's campsites.

Practicalities The village of Khwai has a couple of shops that sell basic supplies. Otherwise, petrol and supplies are only available in Kasane and Maun. If you're self-driving, you'll need to book your campsites many months in advance.

Entry fees to the reserve should be paid for in advance at the DWNP office in Maun (p103), though they can be paid at the gate if you have no other choice. Self-drivers will, however, only be allowed entry to the reserve if they have a confirmed reservation at one of the four public campsites.

★**Xakanaxa Campsite** CAMPGROUND $
(Xakanaxa Lediba; kwalatesafari@gmail.com; S 19°10.991', E 23°24.937'; camping per adult/child P260/130) A favourite Moremi campground, Xakanaxa occupies a narrow strip of land surrounded by marshes and lagoons. It's no coincidence that many upmarket lodges are located nearby – the wildlife in the area can be prolific and campers are frequently woken by elephants or serenaded by hippo grunts. Be warned: a young boy was tragically killed by hyenas here in 2000.

Boat journeys onto the lagoon are also possible.

Third Bridge Campsite CAMPGROUND $
(www.xomaesites.com; Third Bridge; S 19°14.340', E 23°21.276'; per adult/child P400/200) The favourite campsite for many self-drivers, Third Bridge has sites away from the main track – set on the edge of a lagoon (watch out for hippos and crocs), it's a beautiful place to pitch. Be wary of baboons and avoid walking on the bridge or sleeping in

the open because wildlife – especially lions – uses the bridge as a thoroughfare.

South Gate Camp Site CAMPGROUND $
(Maqwee Camp Site; kwalatesafari@gmail.com; GPS: S 19°25.526', E 23°38.654'; camping per adult/child P260/130) This campsite is quite reasonably developed, but its distance from the main wildlife-watching areas would make it our last choice of the public campsites. Alternatively, it's a good option if you don't think you can reach Third Bridge or Xakanaxa by nightfall. Be careful not to leave any food lying about, as the baboons here are aggressive and ill-tempered.

Khwai Campsite CAMPGROUND $$
(www.sklcamps.com; camping per adult/child US$50/25) The campsites at this expansive campground are shady and well developed, with some lovely sites close to the riverbank; others are a little further inland. There's an ablutions block and good wildlife watching in the area. In July 2012 there was a nonfatal leopard attack on a

lone camper; always drive to the ablutions block from your campsite after dark.

There are a couple of small shops in Khwai village on the other side of the river selling food and other supplies.

★**Mombo Camp**　　　TENTED CAMP **$$$**
(✆686 0086; www.wilderness-safaris.com; s/d Jun-Oct US$3564/5736, rates vary rest of year; ✵) Ask anyone in Botswana for the country's most exclusive camp and they're likely to nominate Mombo. The surrounding delta scenery is some of the finest in the Okavango and the wildlife watching is almost unrivalled. The rooms are enormous and the entire package – from the service to the comfort levels and attention to detail – never misses a beat. It's situated (with its sister camp, Little Mombo) on the northwest corner of Chief's Island.

★**Baine's Camp**　　　TENTED CAMP **$$$**
(✆in South Africa +27 11-438 4650; www.sanctuary-retreats.com; per person US$750-1530) Five elevated suites overlook a tree line that conceals (but not too much) great wildlife viewing in a shady, woodsy area of the delta close to the southern end of Chief's Island; the outdoor bath tubs are pure indulgence.

There's a very private, world-in-its-infancy sense of fresh beauty in the place; you'd be forgiven for thinking a naked couple arguing over an apple were about to emerge from the landscape.

★**Xaranna Camp**　　　TENTED CAMP **$$$**
(✆in South Africa +27 11-809 4300; www.andbeyond.com; per person Jun-Oct US$1770, rates vary rest of year; ✿✵) Xaranna is a worthy member of the elite group of camps run by &Beyond, which mixes daringly designed luxury accommodation with serious conservation work. Xaranna's large rooms have expansive terraces, private pools and as little to separate you from the delta surrounds as is possible. The food is excellent and the service first-rate.

You're on your own island here, and helicopter flights are possible, as are wildlife drives on which big cats are a real possibility.

Camp Okavango　　　TENTED CAMP **$$$**
(✆686 1559; www.desertdelta.com; s/d Jul-Oct US$1230/1890, per person Apr-Jun & Nov US$675, Dec, Jan & Mar US$535; ⊘closed Feb; ✵) Set amid sausage and jackalberry trees

on Nxaragha Island, just outside Moremi, this charming lodge is elegant, and the staff are known for their meticulous attention to detail. If you want Okavango served up with silver tea service, this could be the place for you.

Chief's Camp　　　TENTED CAMP **$$$**
(✆in South Africa +27 11-438 4650; www.sanctuaryretreats.com; per person US$1160-2430; ✵) Considered by many to be one of the premier camps in the delta, Chief's blends into its marshy surroundings like a hunter in a duck blind. With a front-row seat to some of the finest wildlife on the delta from 12 pretty incredible luxury 'bush pavilions', who are we to argue?

Sango Safari Camp　　　TENTED CAMP **$$$**
(✆683 0230; www.sangosafaricamp.com; per person Jun-Oct US$680, Nov-May US$350) On the north side of the Khwai River, not far from the village, Sango's is somewhat less pretentious than some other Moremi camps, but nonetheless maintains an air of quiet exclusivity. Handcrafted furnishings are a nice touch, while game drives generally go where other lodges don't.

It's also unusual in offering cheaper rates for those driving their own vehicles and not looking to join the game drives.

Shinde Island Camp　　　TENTED CAMP **$$$**
(✆686 0375; www.kerdowneybotswana.com; s/d Jun-Oct US$1265/1900, rates vary rest of year) This lagoonside camp sits just north of Moremi, between the savannah and the delta, and is one of the delta's oldest camps, but a 2015 renovation has helped keep everything fresh, with stunning rooms sporting a classic wood-and-canvas aesthetic.

Xugana Island Lodge　　　LODGE **$$$**
(✆686 1559; www.desertdelta.com; s/d Jul-Oct US$1230/1890, per person Apr-Jun & Nov US$675, Dec, Jan & Mar US$535; ✵) Set on a pristine lagoon just north of Moremi, this lodge offers superb birdwatching and fishing. Accommodation is in beautiful thatched chalets with wood furnishings, large, water-facing private decks and a good mix of safari nostalgia and modern comforts.

This area was historically frequented by ancient San hunters, and Xugana means 'kneel down to drink' – a reference to the welcome sight of perennial water after a long hunt.

Moremi Tongue

Moremi Tongue

◉ Sights
1 Dombo Hippo Pools	C1
2 Mboma Island	A2
3 Moremi Game Reserve	C2
4 Xakanaxa Lediba	A1

◎ Sleeping
5 Camp Moremi	A1
6 Camp Xakanaxa	A1
7 Khwai Campsite	D1
8 Khwai River Lodge	D1
9 Sandibe Safari Lodge	A3
10 Sango Safari Camp	D1
11 South Gate Camp Site	C3
12 Third Bridge Campsite	A2
Xakanaxa Campsite	(see 6)

ⓘ Information
13 North (Khwai) Gate & Park Headquarters	D1

Camp Moremi TENTED CAMP $$$
(☑686 1559; www.desertdelta.com; s/d Jul-Oct US$1230/1890, per person Apr-Jun & Nov US$675, Dec, Jan & Mar US$535; ⊘closed Feb; ≋) This long-standing wilderness retreat sits amid giant ebony trees next to the heronry at Xakanaxa Lediba and is surrounded by wildlife-rich grasslands. Accommodation is in East African–style linen tents that are attractively furnished with wooden fixtures.

Camp Xakanaxa TENTED CAMP $$$
(☑686 1559; www.desertdelta.com; s/d Jul-Oct US$1230/1890, per person Apr-Jun & Nov US$675, Dec, Jan & Mar US$535; ⊘closed Feb) This camp, of longer standing than most, offers a pleasant mix of delta and savannah habitat, and teems with huge herds of elephants and other wildlife. However, it's most famous for its legendary birdwatching, especially along the shores of the nearby Xakanaxa Lediba. It's very good at providing the luxury safari experience.

Khwai River Lodge LODGE $$$
(☑686 1244; www.belmondsafaris.com; per person Jun-Oct from US$1200, rates vary rest of year; ☎≋) Perched on the northern shores of the Khwai River, this opulent lodge overlooks the Moremi Game Reserve and is frequently visited by large numbers of hippos and elephants. Accommodation is in 15 wonderful luxury tents.

Stanley's Camp TENTED CAMP $$$
(☑in South Africa +27 11-438 4650; www.sanctuaryretreats.com; s/d Jun-Oct US$1800/2560, rates vary rest of year) Although less ostentatious than other lodges in Moremi, Stanley's, located near the Boro River near the southern

end of Chief's Island, lacks the formality and pretence commonly found in this corner of the country. The eight tents are simple but spacious, and elephant sightings in particular are almost guaranteed in the camp's vicinity, with wild dogs also a possibility.

Kwara Camp TENTED CAMP **$$$**
(🖄686 1449; www.kwando.co.bw; s/d Jul-Oct US$1373/2116, Apr-Jun & Nov US$924/1428, per person Dec-Mar US$602) This island camp lies in an area of subterranean springs that attract flocks of pelicans (*kwara* means 'where the pelicans feed'). These pools also attract heavy concentrations of wildlife, which is a major drawcard for the lodge. Although the place is semiluxurious and more modest than many other Moremi options, guests enjoy the informal and relaxed atmosphere and lower prices.

ℹ Information

North (Khwai) Gate & Park Headquarters
Pick up your photocopied map of the reserve (they sometimes run out) and pay your park fees here.

ℹ Getting There & Away

Chartered flights (and/or 4WD) are usually the only way to reach the luxury lodges of Moremi, with the Khwai River and Xakanaxa strips being regularly used.

If you're driving from Maun, the reserve entrance is at South (Maqwee) Gate, about 99km north of Maun via Shorobe. Take the sealed road to Shorobe, where the road turns into awfully corrugated gravel. Once inside the park, it's about 52km (two hours) from South Gate to Third Bridge along a reasonable track, en route passing through beautiful, wildlife-rich country.

It's about 25km (one hour) from Third Bridge to Xakanaxa Lediba, and another 45km (1½ hours) from there to North Gate.

From Kasane and the east, a track links Chobe National Park with the other gate at North (Khwai) Gate.

Check the road conditions with the DWNP offices in Gaborone (p164) or Maun (p103), and/or with other drivers, before attempting to drive into Moremi during the wet season; some tracks can even be impassable well into the dry season.

Okavango Panhandle

The main attractions of the Okavango Panhandle, a narrow strip of swampland that extends for about 100km from Etsha 13 to the Namibian border, are birdwatching and fishing. In the panhandle, the waters spread across the valley on either side to form vast reed beds and papyrus-choked lagoons. You may see other wildlife, but don't count on it, as it's more elusive and thinly spread.

As the rest of the delta grows more expensive, the Okavango Panhandle is booming as a result of local cooperatives that offer affordable accommodation and *mokoro* trips. Although it is arguably not the 'real' delta, the panhandle is the main population centre in the region and it has permanent water year-round, which means it's always possible to organise a *mokoro* trip.

◉ Sights

Krokavango Crocodile Farm ZOO
(🖄72 306 200; willeroxl@gmail.com; adult/child P40/20; ⏱8.30am-4pm Mon-Sat) It's difficult to know what to make of this place, not far south of Drotsky's Cabins (the turn-off from the main Sehithwa–Shakawe road is at GPS

THE CARNIVORE CHAIN OF COMMAND

By far the largest African carnivore, the lion sits pretty much unchallenged at the top of the pecking order and is usually able to kill anything it can get hold of, including other predators. Adult lions usually only worry about other lions, though large hyena clans occasionally kill injured or adolescent lions, and they're certainly able to drive small prides from their kills.

Hyenas also trail after other predators in the hopes of getting a free meal. At Moremi, it's fairly common to see spotted hyena clans trailing African wild dogs on the hunt. Again, strength in numbers is a key factor: a few hyenas can lord over an entire pack of wild dogs, though a single hyena is easily harassed into retreating. Coincidentally, both hyena clans and wild-dog packs dominate leopards, but individuals do so at their peril as leopards will occasionally bring down a lone hyena or wild dog.

At the very bottom of the hierarchy is the world's fastest land predator, the cheetah. By sacrificing brute force for incredible speed, cheetahs are simply unable to overpower other predators. Nor can they afford the risk of injury, and invariably give way to other superpredators, regardless of numbers.

ⓘ PANHANDLE PRACTICALITIES

Along the road between Sehithwa and Shakawe, there are petrol stations in Sehithwa, Gumare, Etsha 6 and Shakawe, but fill up whenever you can as supplies can run dry. Shakawe has a supermarket and a Barclays ATM.

S 18°26.363', E 21°53.114'). Partly a refuge for rescued crocodiles from the panhandle (those that have acquired a taste for livestock), it has some extraordinary specimens up to 5m long. Meanwhile, it also breeds crocodiles for the lucrative crocodile-skin market (think purses, belts etc) and there are almost 8000 captive-bred crocs on-site.

Feeding time is at 11am on Tuesdays and Fridays. There's a shop, and a visit to the farm is by guided tour.

🏃 Activities

The most popular leisure activity in the panhandle is fishing. Anglers from around the world flock here to hook tigerfish, pike, barbel (catfish) and bream. Tigerfish season is from September to June, while barbel are present from mid-September to December.

Most lodges and campsites along the panhandle arrange fishing trips, and hire out gear.

👉 Tours

Okavango Polers Trust BOATING
(☏687 6861; www.okavangodelta.co.bw) Established in 1998 by the people of Seronga, the Okavango Polers Trust provides cheaper and more accessible *mokoro* trips and accommodation for visitors. As no travel agency or safari operator is involved, the

THE PANHANDLE'S NATURAL & HUMAN WORLD

A geological curiosity, the panhandle is the result of a 15km-wide geological fault that constricts the meandering river until it's released into the main delta. Here a cosmopolitan mix of people (Mbukushu, Yei, Tswana, Herero, European and San, as well as Angolan refugees) occupy clusters of fishing villages and extract their livelihoods from the rich waters.

cooperative can afford to charge reasonable prices for *mokoro* trips.

Since the collective is run entirely by the village, all profits are shared by the nearly 100 workers, invested into the trust and used to provide the community with better facilities. Although it's not uncommon to pay upwards of US$200 per day for a *mokoro* trip out of Maun, the trust charges around P750 per day for *two* people. Keep in mind, however, that you must self-cater (ie bring your own food, water and, if necessary, camping and cooking equipment).

🛌 Sleeping

Panhandle camps are mostly (and refreshingly) midrange in price, and have until recently catered mainly for the sport-fishing crowd. However, this is changing with the recent increase in travellers looking for affordable delta trips. Camping is also available at most lodges.

★ **Shakawe River Lodge** LODGE $
(☏684 0403, 73 254 408; www.shakawelodge.com; camping per adult/child P200/130, dome tents P400, chalets P1290) Stylish rooms on slightly elevated wooden decks have a refreshingly contemporary look that you just don't expect to find in this dusty, nondescript border town. Many overlook the small river channel (as do the campsites). It also has comfortable, elevated dome tents for those without their own camping equipment.

The whole place is an excellent choice and is something of an oasis for those travelling between Namibia and Botswana.

Mbiroba Camp CAMPGROUND $
(☏687 6861; www.okavangodelta.co.bw; camping P130, rondavels P225, chalets from P375) This camp is run by the Okavango Polers Trust and is the usual launching point for *mokoro* trips into the delta. Sadly, like so many community projects, the camp has gone downhill in recent years and the campsites, bar, traditional restaurant and two-storey chalets have all seen better days. Mbiroba is 3km from Seronga village.

★ **Guma Lagoon Camp** CAMPGROUND $$
(☏687 4626; www.guma-lagoon.com; camping P135, 2-person cabins P1016) This lovely spot at the panhandle's lower end is a fantastic place. Each of the shady campsites has its own shower and toilet, and the tranquil setting continues with a lovely public area where

you can order drinks and also use the kitchen. Most of the chalets overlook the water. It can also arrange everything from boat hire and fishing trips to night drives and three-day *mokoro* trips.

If you're driving, the trail is well signposted from Etsha 13. Transfer to or from Etsha 13/Seronga costs P112/1232.

Sepupa Swamp Stop CAMPGROUND **$$**
(☑ 75 670 252; Sepupa; camping from P120, tents/chalets from P250/800; ☒) This laid-back riverside campsite is secluded, handy to Sepupa village, very affordable and accessible (3km) from the Maun–Shakawe road. The lodge can arrange *mokoro* trips through the Okavango Polers Trust and transfers to Sepupa, as well as boat trips that start at P325/1900 per hour/day.

Most *mokoro* trips from here require a boat transfer as the waters here are usually too deep for poling.

★**Drotsky's Cabins** LODGE, CAMPGROUND **$$$**
(☑ 683 0226; https://drotskys.com; camping per person P160, chalets & A-frames from P1500; ☒☎☒) This lovely, welcoming lodge lies beside a channel of the Okavango River. The chalets have air-con; the A-frames are fan only. Boats can be rented and the bar-restaurant serves breakfast/lunch/dinner for P150/180/220. The campsite is similarly attractive and there's a boat to take you to the restaurant in the evening.

The lodge is about 5km southeast of Shakawe and around 4km east of the main road. Set amid a thick riverine forest, it's very secluded, with fabulous birdwatching and fine views across the reeds and papyrus.

Okavango Houseboats HOUSEBOAT **$$$**
(☑ 686 0802; www.okavangohouseboats.com; houseboats per day P8500) Floating down the river in one of these houseboats, which vaguely resemble Mississippi steamboats that got lost somewhere in Angola, gives a new, aquatic twist to the 'mobile safari' experience. The craft depart from Seronga, and should be booked well in advance. Expect some amazing birding and riverside wildlife viewing. The boats accommodate six to 20 people.

Petrol and food costs extra but a crew is included; check the website.

Xaro Lodge LODGE **$$$**
(☑ 683 0226; http://drotskys.com/xaro-lodge.html; luxury tents P1500; ☒) Run by the son of the

---

BORDER CROSSING: THE OKAVANGO PANHANDLE

The **Mohembo–Shakawe Gate** (⊙ 6am to 6pm) is generally hassle-free, but remember when calculating the border post's opening hours that Namibia is one hour behind Botswana from late May to the end of August. As always, coming into Botswana your car will be searched for fresh meat, fresh fruit and dairy products (all of which will be confiscated if found), and you may be required to walk through a soda solution (and drive your car through the same) as part of measures to protect the country from foot-and-mouth disease.

---

owners of Drotsky's Cabins, this lodge is remote – about 10km downstream from Drotsky's – but serene and extremely picturesque. Accommodation is in several clean and tidy 'luxury' tents that surround a modest bar-restaurant. The main activity is fishing, though the lodge also makes for a great retreat and there's good birdwatching in the vicinity.

Boat transfers from Drotsky's Cabins cost P40 per person.

ⓘ Getting There & Away

The road between Maun and Shakawe, via Sehithwa, is sealed (if potholed in places) and continues into Namibia. You'll need a 4WD for the tracks into most lodges and campsites; most will arrange pick-ups (for a fee) from the nearest town.

To reach Sepupa, catch a bus towards Shakawe from Maun, disembark at the turn-off to the village (P115, six hours) and hitch a lift or walk (about 3km) into Sepupa. To get to Seronga, there are several options: ask Sepupa Swamp Stop about a boat transfer (P275 per person, minimum of six people), or wait for the public boat (P80 per person, two hours), which leaves Sepupa more frequently in the afternoon. Alternatively, catch the bus all the way from Maun to Shakawe (P130, seven hours); jump on a combi (P15, 30 minutes) up to Mohembo; take the free car ferry (45 minutes, 6.30am to 6.30pm) across the river; and then hitch (which is usually easy enough) along the good sandy road (accessible by 2WD) to Seronga. Otherwise, drive via Shakawe and Mohembo, or fly to Seronga from Maun – try Mack Air (p93).

Northwestern Botswana

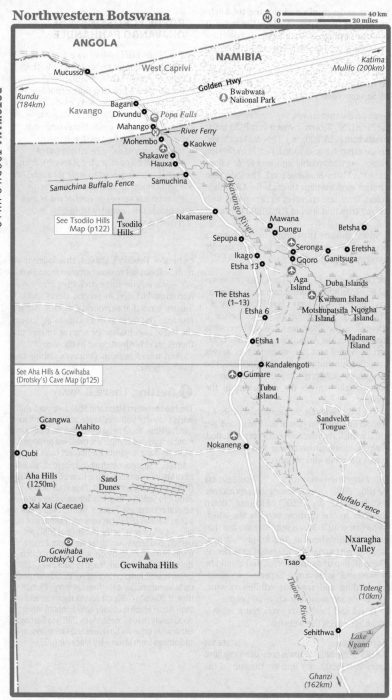

N

| 0 | 40 km |
| 0 | 20 miles |

ANGOLA

NAMIBIA

Katima
Mulilo (200km)

West Caprivi

Golden Hwy

Bwabwata
National Park

Mucusso

Rundu
(184km)

Kavango

Bagani

Divundu

Popa Falls

Mahango

River Ferry

Mohembo

Kaokwe

Shakawe

Hauxa

Samuchina Buffalo Fence

Samuchina

Okavango River

See Tsodilo Hills
Map (p122)

Tsodilo
Hills

Nxamasere

Mawana

Dungu

Betsha

Sepupa

Seronga

Eretsha

Ikago

Gqoro

Ganitsuga

Etsha 13

Aga
Island

Duba Islands

The Etshas
(1–13)

Kwihum Island

Etsha 6

Motshupatsila
Island

Nqogha
Island

Etsha 1

Madinare
Island

Kandalengoti

See Aha Hills & Gcwihaba
(Drotsky's) Cave Map (p125)

Gumare

Tubu
Island

Gcangwa

Mahito

Sandveldt
Tongue

Qubi

Nokaneng

Aha Hills
(1250m)

Sand
Dunes

Xai Xai (Caecae)

Buffalo Fence

Gcwihaba
(Drotsky's) Cave

Gcwihaba Hills

Nxaragha
Valley

Tsao

Thaoge River

Toteng
(10km)

Sehithwa

Lake
Ngami

Ghanzi
(162km)

NORTHWESTERN BOTSWANA

The far northwest of Botswana, outside of the Okavango Delta, is a wild and remote border space of small towns and cattle posts separated by long, windy stretches of yellow grass and bleached thornbush. You make your own adventures out here. Elsewhere are marshy outflows wrapped in reeds, the latter used in the construction of some of the country's prettiest crafts. Scattered throughout are rocky outcrops, their sides daubed with pigments and ancient paintings from the San and their relatives. The San, many of them still living traditional lives unlike elsewhere in the Kalahari, inhabit the area, with plenty of villages here and across the border in Namibia.

Tourism infrastructure remains essentially undeveloped and very few visitors make it out here – you may have the 'desert Louvre' of the Tsodilo Hills, for example, almost completely to yourself.

Tsodilo Hills

The Unesco World Heritage–listed Tsodilo Hills rise abruptly from the northwestern Kalahari, west of the Okavango Panhandle. Rare outposts of vertical variety in this extremely flat country, these lonely chunks of quartzite schist are dramatic and beautiful, distinguished by streaks of vivid natural hues – mauve, orange, yellow, turquoise and lavender. The hills are also a site of huge spiritual significance for the region's original inhabitants, the San. The major drawcards are more than 4000 prehistoric rock paintings spread over 200 sites throughout the hills.

Excavations of flaked stone tools indicate that Bantu people arrived as early as AD 500, but layers of superimposed rock art and other archaeological remnants suggest that ancestors of the San have been here for up to 30,000 years.

⊙ Sights

The Tsodilo Hills and their incredible rock art are now a national monument, and fall under the auspices of the National Museum in Gaborone. All visitors must report to the headquarters at the Main (Rhino) Camp (p123), about 2.5km north of the airstrip (admission to the hills is free).

Zebra Painting   HISTORIC SITE

One of the most fascinating paintings is the zebra painting on a small outcrop north of Female Hill. This stylised equine figure is now used as the logo of Botswana National Museum and Monuments. It lies beyond the main trails.

Divuyu Village Remains   RUINS

An adjunct to the Rhino Trail (p123) is a short but hazardously rocky climb along what is sometimes called the Divuyu Trail, leading to the scattered remains of Divuyu village.

TSODILO LEGENDS

The Tsodilo Hills are imbued with myth, legend and spiritual significance for the original San inhabitants. Most significantly, the San believe the Tsodilo Hills are the site of the first Creation, and the Mbukushu claim that the gods lowered the people and their cattle onto Female Hill.

Four main chunks of rock make up the Tsodilo Hills – Male Hill, Female Hill, Child Hill and a distant hillock known as North Hill, which remained nameless until recently – and each of them has a story attached. According to one San legend, for example, Male Hill sent away North Hill (a wife of Male Hill) for being too argumentative. The hollows within some of the hills are also believed to represent animal footprints.

Visitors from the outside world are not immune to the Hills' magic. The Tsodilo Hills were the 'Slippery Hills' described by Sir Laurens van der Post in his 1958 classic *The Lost World of the Kalahari*. Hoping to make a documentary film of the hills, his cameras inexplicably jammed, his tape recorders ceased functioning and his group was attacked by swarms of bees on three consecutive mornings. When he learned that two members of his party had ignored a warning from his San guide by killing a warthog and steenbok while approaching the sacred hills, van der Post buried a note of apology beneath the panel of paintings that now bears his name.

Tsodilo Hills

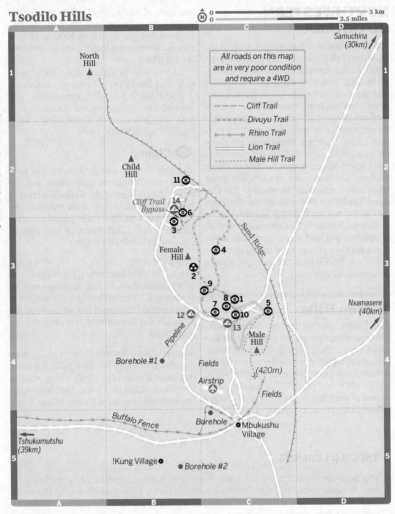

All roads on this map are in very poor condition and require a 4WD

- - - - Cliff Trail
.... Divuyu Trail
+—+—+ Rhino Trail
——— Lion Trail
- - - - Male Hill Trail

Museum   MUSEUM

(Main (Rhino) Camp; ☉ sunrise-sunset) **FREE**
There is a small, dusty museum at Main (Rhino) Camp with a handful of ethnographic exhibits and wall-sized quotes about the rock art.

🏃 Activities

The hills can be explored along any of five walking trails. Although there are some signposts, most trails require a guide (expect to pay around P75 to P100 for a two- to three-hour hike, or P150 per day), which can be arranged at the Main (Rhino) Camp (p123).

Early morning is the best time to walk the hills, followed by late afternoon.

Cliff Trail   WALKING
The partially marked Cliff Trail goes past the unassuming '**Origin of Sex**' painting, around the northern end of Female Hill and into a deep and mysterious hidden valley. This trail also passes an amazing natural **cistern** (in a rock grotto near the northwestern corner of Female Hill) that has held water year-round for as long as anyone can remember.

The San believe this natural tank is inhabited by a great serpent with twisted horns,

Tsodilo Hills

so visitors should warn the occupant of their approach by tossing a small stone into the water. This impressive feature is also flanked by rock art.

Rhino Trail   WALKING
From the Main (Rhino) Camp, the steep and signposted Rhino Trail is probably the most interesting of the trails, taking you as it does to some of the best-loved (and most beautiful) paintings anywhere in the Tsodilo Hills.

The trail climbs past several distinctive paintings to a water pit where dragonflies and butterflies flit around a slimy green puddle. Near this site is an odd tree, once described to Laurens van der Post as the **Tree of True Knowledge** by the San guide who led him there. According to the guide, the greatest spirit knelt beside this fetid pool on the day of Creation. In the rocks beyond this pool are several 'hoof prints', which the Mbukushu believe were made by the cattle lowered onto the hill by the god Ngambe.

The Rhino Trail continues over the crest of a hill into a bizarre grassy valley flanked by peaks that seem a bit like an alternative universe. The route passes several rocky outcrops and some rock art, and then descends into the prominent hollow in the southeastern side of Female Hill. Inside the hollow is a **rhino painting**, which also includes a 'forgery' of a buffalo that was created more recently. Directly across the hollow, one of the few Tsodilo paintings containing

human figures depicts a dancing crowd of sexually excited male figures – Alec Campbell, the foremost expert on the hills and their paintings, has amusingly dubbed it the **'Dancing Penises'**.

On the southeast corner of Female Hill, look for the amazing **whale and penguin paintings** that suggest an intriguing link between the early San and the Namibian coast. Around the corner and to the west, the **rhino and giraffe painting** portrays a rhino family and an authentic-looking giraffe.

Divuyu Trail   WALKING
An adjunct to the Rhino Trail is a short but hazardously rocky climb along what is sometimes called the Divuyu Trail, leading to **Laurens van der Post's Panel**, which contains elands and giraffes. This trail also leads to the Divuyu Village remains (p121).

Male Hill Trail   WALKING
The summit of Male Hill is accessible along this trail, climbing from the hill's base near a painting of a **solitary male lion** on the northern face of the hill. The route is rough, rocky and plagued by false crests, but the view from the summit may well be the finest in the Kalahari.

Lion Trail   WALKING
Between Male and Female Hills, the Lion Trail crosses the flat valley between the hills and links the Male Hill Trail with the Rhino Trail. And therein lies the trail's main appeal, as it doesn't pass anything particularly interesting.

🛏 Sleeping

Unofficial camping is possible anywhere, but be wary of wild animals, and please be respectful of local people.

The main campsites are run by the National Museum and services are basic. Camping is free at all the sites, although you usually have to register at the Main (Rhino) Camp. The staff's presence rarely amounts to much more than an attendant on duty at the Main Camp.

Malatso Camp Site   CAMPGROUND
FREE On the north side of Female Hill, Malatso is rarely full and is a lovely bush campsite, albeit with no facilities.

Main (Rhino) Camp   CAMPGROUND
FREE Tsodilo Hills' main campsite has a simple ablutions block with sit-down toilets

and cold-water showers; staff sometimes lock the block in the evening. The campsite is rarely full and it shouldn't be too hard to find a shady corner, although the sites are close together and dusty rather than green. The camp is the closest to the trailheads for the Rhino and Divuyu Trails.

Makoba Woods Camp Site CAMPGROUND

FREE Slightly away from the main park headquarters and busier campsite, Makoba Woods sits beneath the southern edge of Female Hill and is quieter, has decent shade and pit toilets.

❶ Getting There & Away

CAR & MOTORCYCLE

Although numerous routes connect the Sehithwa–Shakawe road with the Tsodilo Hills, the good gravel track is the only one worth recommending. It's well signposted off the main road just south of Nxamasere village; it's around 35km from the main road to the entrance to the site.

MOBILE SAFARIS

Although it might be possible to arrange a mobile safari to the Tsodilo Hills through one of the operators in Maun, you'll need a group to avoid skyrocketing costs.

Lake Ngami

Arriving at the shores of Lake Ngami in 1849, Dr David Livingstone witnessed a magnificent expanse of water teeming with animals and birdlife. However, for reasons not completely known, the lake disappeared entirely a few years later, reappearing briefly towards the end of the 19th century, a pattern that has continued.

Lake Ngami lacks an outflow and can only be filled by an overflow from the Okavango Delta down the Nhabe River. Following heavy rains in 1962, the lake reappeared once more, covering an area of 250 sq km. Although the lake was present for nearly 20 years, it mysteriously disappeared again in 1982, only to reappear once more in 2000. Since then, heavy rains have kept the lake partially filled at various times, though it's anyone's guess when it will dry up again.

Following heavy rains, the lake attracts flocks of water birds, among them flamingos, ibises, pelicans, eagles, storks, terns, gulls and kingfishers.

All (unsigned) tracks heading south from the sealed road between Toteng and Sehithwa lead to the lake. You'll need a 4WD to reach and explore the lakeshore.

Aha Hills

Straddling the Botswana–Namibia border, the 700-million-year-old limestone and dolomite Aha Hills rise 300m from the flat, thorny Kalahari scrub. Due to the almost total absence of water, there's an eerie dearth of animal life – there are few birds and only the occasional insect. However, the main attraction of the Aha Hills is their solitude and isolation. When night falls, the characteristic sounds of Southern Africa are conspicuously absent, though the resulting stillness is near perfect.

With precious few reliable maps, the Aha Hills present the perfect opportunity to put the guidebook down and explore a region that very few tourists visit.

You'll need a 4WD vehicle to get here and to explore the hills, which are located about 33km south of Gcangwa and about 12km north of Xai Xai. Travelling onward, you can reach Gcwihaba (Drotsky's) Cave.

Gcwihaba (Drotsky's Cave)

In 1932 a group of San showed Gcwihaba (meaning 'Hyena's Hole') to a farmer named Martinus Drotsky, who humbly decided to name the cave after himself. Legend also has it that the fabulously wealthy Hendrik Matthys van Zyl stashed a portion of his fortune here in the late 1800s; the treasure has never been found. The cave interior is famous for its 10m-long stalagmites and stalactites, which were formed by dripping water that seeped through and dissolved the dolomite rock.

The cave (S 20°01.302′, E 21°21.275′) is home to large colonies of Commerson's leaf-nosed bats (which have a wingspan of up to 60cm) and common slit-faced bats (distinguished by their long ears), which, although harmless, can make your expedition a hair-raising experience.

Gcwihaba (Drotsky's) Cave is not developed for tourism: the interior of the cave is completely dark, and there are no lights or route markings. It is possible to walk (about 1km) through the cave from one entrance to the other, but venturing far inside is only for those with some experience, confidence and proper lighting – carry strong flashlights, as well as emergency light sources such as matches and cigarette lighters. The main entrance is signposted from the end of the track, and is near

Aha Hills & Gcwihaba (Drotsky's) Cave

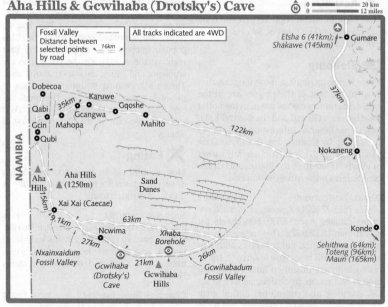

a noticeboard. The cave is permanently open and there's no admission charge.

Unofficial camping is possible beneath the thorn trees. A fully equipped 4WD with high clearance is essential for visiting the cave, which lies around 100km west of the main Maun–Shakawe highway, from where the caves are signposted.

KALAHARI

The parched alter ego of the Okavango Delta, the Kalahari is a primeval landscape, recalling in stone, thorns and brush the earliest memories of the human experience. This impression of a land where time began finds voice in the hot winds and the snap of thorn bush under a San tracker's feet in the Kalahari. It is the timeless roar of a Kalahari lion resonating across the still desert air. It is a valley that cuts through the desert's heart and follows the path left by ancient rivers that long ago disappeared into the dust. This is indeed dry, parched country. It's no surprise that the Tswana call this the Kgalagadi: Land of Thirst.

The Kalahari's 1.2-million-sq-km basin stretches across parts of the Democratic Republic of Congo, Angola, Zambia, Namibia, Botswana, Zimbabwe and South Africa, and in Botswana it also includes places such as the Tsodilo Hills and Makgadikgadi Pans.

Ghanzi

POP 12,267

The 'capital of the Kalahari' isn't much more than a break in the dust, although it's a growing town with good accommodation options and a handful of petrol stations and supermarkets. The town itself is a place of few attractions, but its appeal lies in its statistics: Ghanzi is 275km from Maun, 540km from Windhoek and 636km from Gaborone. Spend any time in the country's west and you're likely to spend some time here, whether to fill your petrol tank, stock up on supplies or get a good night's sleep.

It may be difficult to understand how a town could prosper in such inhospitable terrain, but it helps that Ghanzi sits atop a 500km-long low limestone ridge containing vast amounts of artesian water. Interestingly enough, the name 'Ghanzi' comes from the San word for a one-stringed musical instrument with a gourd soundbox, and *not* the Setswana word *gantsi* (flies), though this would arguably be more appropriate.

🏃 Activities

Most accommodation options here can hook you up with wildlife drives, San cultural activities and the like.

🛌 Sleeping

There is one intriguing in-town option, but most of the rest of the choices are in the vast, arid country east of town, in the buffer zone between Ghanzi and the Central Kalahari Game Reserve. Interesting alternatives to staying in Ghanzi are the Dqãe Qare San Lodge (p127), which is slightly closer to nearby D'kar than to Ghanzi, and Grassland Safari Lodge (p128), 60km east.

Ghanzi Trailblazers CAMPGROUND $
(☑659 7525, 72 102 868; www.ghanzitrailblazers. co.bw; camping from US$10, huts/chalets per person from US$20/72) This relaxed place offers horse riding, guided walks with San guides who will teach you about San tracking techniques, Bushmen huts and simple motel-style rooms in chalets, as well as an OK campsite and communal dining area. The turn-off is around 10km south of town along the road to Kang; from the turn-off it's 5km down a sandy track.

Other activities include swimming at an abandoned local quarry and traditional San dancing performances.

Kalahari Arms Hotel HOTEL $$
(☑659 6298; www.kalahariarmshotel.com; Henry Jankie Dr; camping per person P60, s/d/f P690/800/860; ❄☎❄) This Ghanzi institution has modern (if slightly tired) rooms with air-con and cable TV, though the campsite is cramped, can be noisy and feel like someone's backyard. The rooms in rondavels in the garden by the pool are nicest and cost the same as other accommodation.

Tautona Lodge LODGE $$
(☑659 7499; www.tautonalodge.com; camping per person P145, safari tents per person P258, s/d P850/1100, s/d chalets from P870/1132; ❄❄) This reasonable lodge has expansive grounds featuring two swimming pools and a watering hole that's frequented by antelope. Spacious rooms in Batswana-style thatched buildings have air-con and cable TV, and are decorated with traditional spreads, although they're more comfortable than luxurious. It also has a range of chalets and family suites. The ensuite safari tents are a steal. It's 5km northeast of Ghanzi.

Thakadu Bush Camp CAMPGROUND $$
(☑72 120 695; www.thakadubushcamp.com; camping per person P110, s P610-1070, d P650-850, s/d cottages with shared bathroom P270/360; ❄) This popular campsite is a fun place to stop for a night or three, enjoying the boozy, friendly ambience and letting the stars soar overhead. There's a refreshing swimming pool and a pub-style restaurant and bar. The rough access road is just passable to low-slung 2WD vehicles – use caution. It's 6km southwest of Ghanzi.

🍴 Eating

Most visitors eat in their accommodation or survive on snacks from petrol stations as they pass through town.

Spar Supermarket SUPERMARKET $
(☑659 7873; Henry Jankie Dr; ☺8am-8pm Mon-Sat, 8.30am-8pm Sun) Ghanzi's best-stocked supermarket, Spar is in the heart of town, across from Gantsi Craft and the Kalahari Arms Hotel.

Choppies Supermarket SUPERMARKET $
(☑659 7082; ☺8am-8pm Mon-Fri, to 6pm Sat & Sun) Ghanzi's cheapest supermarket is in the centre of town.

R66 FAST FOOD $
(off A3; mains P15-40; ☺6am-11pm) The fact that we include this place should be read as a statement about the lack of choice in Ghanzi more than as a recommendation of quality. Wilted burgers, soggy chips and toasted sandwiches are the staples.

Kalahari Arms Hotel INTERNATIONAL $$
(Henry Jankie Dr; mains P62-120; ☺11.30am-1.45pm & 7-9.45pm) The dining room at the Kalahari Arms is Ghanzi's only real sit-down restaurant, and you won't exactly be spoiled for choice. The menu has all the usual suspects of steak, chips and pasta, as well as a few local Setswana dishes. The T-bones are the stuff of lore in Kalahari travel, not least because they are huge.

🛍 Shopping

Gantsi Craft ARTS & CRAFTS
(☑659 6241, 72 792 954; www.kuru.co.bw/Gantsi_Craft.html; Henry Jankie Dr; ☺8am-12.30pm & 2-5pm Mon-Fri, 8am-noon Sat) This cooperative was established in 1983 as a craft outlet and training centre for the San. It's an excellent place to shop for traditional San crafts, including hand-dyed textiles, decorated bags,

leather aprons, bows and arrows, musical instruments and woven mats. Prices are 30% to 50% lower than in Maun or Gaborone. All proceeds go to artists from 15 San settlements across the western and southern Kalahari. There's a small museum at the back of the shop.

ℹ Information

MONEY

Bank of Gaborone (⊘8.30am-4pm Mon-Fri, to noon Sat)

Barclays Bank (Henry Jankie Dr; ⊘8.30am-3.30pm Mon-Fri, 8.15-10.45am Sat)

FNB (off Trans-Kalahari Hwy (A3); ⊘8.30am-4pm Mon-Fri, to noon Sat)

TOURIST INFORMATION

Botswana Tourism (www.botswanatourism.co.bw; Trans-Kalahari Hwy (A3); ⊘7.30am-4.30pm Mon-Fri, 9am-2pm Sat) In the Shoprite Shopping Mall. Useful for brochures.

ℹ Getting There & Away

From the bus terminal behind the BP petrol station along Kgosi Sebele Way, there are buses to Maun (P75, five hours, two daily) via D'Kar (P18, one hour), and to Gaborone (P155, 11 hours, three daily).

A combi leaves most mornings for the Namibian border at Mamuno (P43, three hours), but there are no cross-border services.

D'kar

POP 2000

This small village just north of Ghanzi is home to a large community of Ncoakhoe San who operate an art gallery, cultural centre and wildlife ranch. The ranch is run under the auspices of the Kuru Family of Organisations (www.kuru.co.bw), an affiliated group of NGOs working towards the empowerment of the indigenous peoples of Southern Africa.

◉ Sights

★ Kuru Art Project ARTS CENTRE
(⌨72 898 407; www.kuruart.com; ⊘8am-12.30pm & 2-5pm Mon-Fri) FREE This fabulous art project provides opportunities for local artists (14 at last count) to create and sell paintings and other artwork; it's worth spending an hour or two leafing through the various folios of artworks. Some of the artists here are well known around the world and their works hang in some of the world's most prestigious art spaces, including the Smith-

sonian Institute. It's well signposted along D'kar's only road, close to the turn-off to the Ghanzi–Maun highway.

There's also a small but well-stocked curio shop and there's sometimes a chance to sit down and watch the artists at work.

Museum MUSEUM
(⊘8am-12.30pm & 2-5pm Mon-Fri) FREE This dusty little museum adjacent to Kuru Art Project is well worth half an hour of your time, with some interesting displays and an informative timeline of San history.

🛏 Sleeping

Although there's nowhere to stay in the village itself, members of the local San community run two excellent accommodation choices in the town's hinterland.

Dqãe Qare San Lodge CAMPGROUND $$
(⌨72 527 321; www.dqae.org; camping per person P75, lodge rooms per person with/without half board P655/425) This excellent lodge/guesthouse/campground run by the local San community is a terrific place to stay. Accommodation is simple, but there's a real authenticity about the place. It lies just 7km off the A3 in the Dqãe Qare Game Farm, a 75-sq-km private reserve where visitors can participate in traditional activities.

Possibilities include guided nature walks (P75), fire-making (P240 per group), rope-making and trap setting (P240), craft-making (P240), San storytelling (P240)

ℹ BORDER CROSSING: NAMIBIA

The **Buitepost–Mamuno Gate** (⊘7am to midnight) is convenient for travelling between Windhoek and Gaborone, the Kalahari or Maun. Like most such crossings, it is for the most part hassle-free, but remember when calculating the border crossing's opening hours that Namibia is one hour behind Botswana from late May until the end of August. As always, coming into Botswana your car will be searched for fresh meat, fresh fruit and dairy products (these will be confiscated if found), and you may be required to walk through a soda solution (and drive your car through the same) as part of measures to protect the country from foot-and-mouth disease.

Southern Kalahari

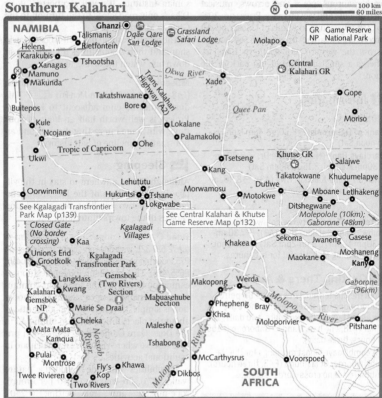

and a star talk (P75). Deeper immersion activities include traditional dance performances (P1100 per group) or the 24-hour 'San experience' (P2970 per group). Money spent at the farm is invested in the community. Although it's possible to drop by for an hour or two, spending a night either camping or in one of the San huts is a great opportunity to meet locals in a relaxed setting.

The ranch is only accessible in a high-clearance vehicle. Alternatively, transfers are possible from Ghanzi/D'Kar for P155/280 per four-passenger vehicle to the farm.

Grassland Safari Lodge LODGE $$$
(📞 72 104 270; www.grasslandlodge.com; camping P175, chalets per person Nov-May US$308, Jun-Oct US$358) Highly recommended by readers, Grassland Safari Lodge is well off the beaten track, about 70km from the main Ghanzi–Maun road. This admirable lodge, with

comfortable chalet accommodation and its own water hole, runs a predator-protection program that temporarily houses lions, cheetahs, leopards and wild dogs, which are often shot by farmers protecting their livestock.

It also conducts wildlife drives and horse safaris, and hosts excellent cultural activities with local San. Grassland's owner, Nelltjie Bowers, can speak the clicking Naro language and is a mine of information on the local area. Contact the lodge in advance for directions to the property.

ℹ️ Getting There & Away

Buses, minibuses and shared taxis between Maun and Ghanzi sometimes take the short detour off the highway into D'Kar, but always check with the driver before boarding the bus. Otherwise, you might find a few dedicated shared taxis every day leaving for D'Kar (P18) from the Ghanzi bus station, but expect a long wait for the seats to fill, especially on weekends.

Central Kalahari Game Reserve

The dry heart of the dry south of a dry continent, the Central Kalahari Game Reserve (CKGR) is an awesome place. If remoteness, desert silences and the sound of lions roaring in the night are your thing, this could become one of your favourite places in Africa. Covering 52,800 sq km (about the size of Denmark), it's also one of Africa's largest protected areas. This is big-sky country, home to black-maned Kalahari lions, a full suite of predators and an utterly wonderful sense of the remote.

◉ Sights

Ask for the free photocopied map at the park's entrance gates, although note that it only covers the northern half of the CKGR. Khutse Game Reserve is served by a similar map, available at the Khutse Gate. For everything in between, make sure you have Tracks4Africa loaded onto your GPS and carry the latest edition of Tracks4Africa's paper *Botswana* map (1:1,000,000).

There are artificially filled water holes at various points throughout the CKGR, including at Letiahau, Pipers, Sunday, Passarge and Motopi.

◉ Deception Valley

The CKGR is perhaps best known for Deception Valley, the site of Mark and Delia Owens' 1974–81 study of brown hyenas and lions, which is described in their cult-classic book *Cry of the Kalahari*. Deception Valley's appeal also owes much to the variety of its landscapes. This broad valley, lined on its eastern and western fringes by light woodland climbing gentle hills, is all about swaying grasslands, tight clusters of trees and roaming gemsboks, springboks and the occasional predator. It's a beautiful spot around sunrise or sunset, while Deception Pan, at the southern end of the valley, can feel like the end of the earth at midday.

Deception is one of four fossil valleys in the Central Kalahari – the others are the Okwa, the Quoxo (Meratswe) and the Passarge – that were carved out by ancient rivers, bringing topographical relief to the virtually featureless expanses. The rivers themselves ceased flowing more than 16,000 years ago.

◉ Passarge Valley

Passarge Valley is far quieter than Deception Valley – we spent an entire afternoon driving along its length one July and saw not one other vehicle. On the said afternoon, we did, however, see a male lion, a cheetah, gemsboks, bat-eared foxes and a honey badger. There is a water hole (artificially pumped to provide water for animals throughout the dry season) at the southwestern end of the valley.

◉ Northern CKGR

The 39km from the Passarge Valley water hole to Motopi Pan takes you through classic Kalahari country with rolling dune-hills covered in thorn scrub, acacias and light woodland, with some lovely views out across the plains

---

THE KALAHARI CONSERVATION SOCIETY

The Kalahari Conservation Society (KCS) is a nongovernmental organisation (NGO) that was established in 1982 by former president of Botswana Sir Ketumile Masire. KCS was formed in recognition of the pressures on Botswana's wildlife and has spent the last three decades actively collaborating with other NGOs and government departments to help conserve the country's environment and natural resources. To date, the organisation has been involved in more than 50 conservation projects in the Kalahari, Chobe National Park, Moremi Game Reserve and the Okavango Delta.

The KCS aims to promote knowledge of Botswana's rich wildlife resources and its environment through education and publicity; to encourage and finance research into issues affecting these resources and their conservation; and to promote and support policies of conservation towards wildlife and its habitat. To achieve these objectives, the KCS relies on private donations and memberships. For more information, visit www.kcs.org.bw.

en route. Motopi Pan itself is a lovely spot late in the afternoon, with the water hole regularly visited by gemsboks, giraffes and ostriches, with lions never far away. The low hills that separate the three Motopi campsites include some of the CKGR's more varied topography and on one visit we spent an entire morning with a pride of lions around here before another vehicle appeared over the horizon.

⊙ The Western Pans

Some 26km southwest of the main loop through the central section of the reserve, Piper Pans is well worth a visit; you'll pass through here if you enter the reserve at Xade Gate and plan to head towards Deception Valley, or if you're completing a north–south (or vice-versa) crossing. The appeal here is a series of interlocking pans encircled by good trails, lightly wooded surrounds and the last of the good wildlife watching if you're heading south.

We've seen cheetahs and kudus around here, have heard reports of lions, and you're almost guaranteed to see wildebeest and good birdlife around the water hole, even in the heat of the day.

Tau Pan is, as the name suggests (*tau* means 'lion' in Setswana), reasonable for lion sightings, while we also saw cheetahs and aardwolves when we were last here. San Pan and Phokoje Pan are similar, with bat-eared foxes, gemsboks and hartebeests all possible.

⊙ The Far South

You're a long way from anywhere down here. Xade Gate and its campsites inhabit the site of the old San settlement that was based around Xade Pan, although nothing remains in evidence. Wildlife is generally scarce all across the south, although a pride of lions with cubs was centred upon the Xaxa water hole when we visited. The landscapes here are generally flat with golden grasslands, fewer salt pans than further north and thinly scattered vegetation such as the acacia thorn and Kalahari apple-leaf everywhere.

The main campsites are Xade, Xaxa and Bape. And as far as the trails are concerned, remember that they involve some of the more challenging conditions in the CKGR. Due to its remoteness and the fact that only a trickle of traffic passes through here (you may travel a whole day or two without seeing another vehicle), the trails aren't as well maintained as some others, with plenty of overhanging branches grabbing at your vehicle as you pass. The stretch between Xade Gate and the turn-off to Xaxa water hole is deep sand in parts, particularly at the western end, and you may need to reduce tyre pressure to avoid getting stuck. As always, driving in the early morning when the sand is colder and less loose tends to make for easier going.

🏃 Activities

Wildlife drives are the main (and often the only) event here. The only exceptions are the Bushmen nature walks offered by the luxury lodges, and quad biking with Haina Kalahari Lodge.

Most lodges and tour operators in Maun can organise mobile safaris around the CKGR. Trips can cost anywhere from US$150 to US$250 per day, though prices can vary greatly according to the season and the number of people in the party. It's easier to get a lower price if you're booking as part of a group.

🛏 Sleeping

There are campsites dotted around the reserve and camping is only allowed at designated campsites, which must be booked in advance. Many of the more remote campsites lack any facilities at all, but most campsites have a braai pit, bucket showers and a pit toilet. Ask at the park gate where you enter for a list of all the campsites and their GPS coordinates, although if you're travelling with Tracks4Africa on your GPS, you shouldn't have too many difficulties.

The expensive lodges within the CKGR (and those just beyond the reserve boundaries) are usually accessed by charter flight, but can be reached by self-drivers.

★ **Passarge Valley**
Campsites CAMPGROUND $
(☑ 395 3360; www.bigfoottours.co.bw; camping per adult/child P200/100) These three campsites have no facilities, but their location on the valley floor (some kilometres apart) is among the best in the Kalahari. Site No 2 (S 21°26.847', E 23°47.694'), under a shady stand of trees in the centre of the valley floor, is simply wonderful and the world is yours and yours alone.

Site No 3 (S 21°13.466', E 23°32.154') would be our second choice, lying as it does in the heart of the valley, while No 1 (S 21°24.599', E 23°59.122') is at the northeastern end, close to where you enter Passarge if you're coming from Deception Valley.

CENTRAL KALAHARI GAME RESERVE AT A GLANCE

Why Go? The solitude of Southern Africa's largest desert, fine wildlife watching without the crowds and a sense of inhabiting one of the last great wilderness regions in Africa.

Gateway Towns Ghanzi, Rakops and (at a stretch) Maun.

Wildlife Estimates by scientists suggested minimum 2016 predator populations (including the contiguous Khutse Game Reserve) at around 800 brown hyenas, 500 lions, 300 leopards, 150 African wild dogs, 100 cheetahs and 100 spotted hyenas. Watch also for gemsboks, springboks and bat-eared foxes.

Birdlife Birds are numerous around the ancient river valleys, with sightings of larger species such as ostriches and kori bustards (the world's heaviest flying bird) almost guaranteed. Desert-adapted species are other drawcards, with the Kalahari scrub robin, a common visitor to campsites, a much-sought-after prize for twitchers.

When to Go The park is most easily accessible during the dry season (May to September) when tracks are sandy but easily negotiated by 4WD vehicles. Nights can be bitterly cold at this time and daytime temperatures are relatively mild. During the rainy season (November to March or April), tracks can be muddy and nearly impassable for inexperienced drivers. Watch for grass seeds clogging engines and searing temperatures in October.

Budget Safaris Maun is the best place to join a mobile safari into the CKGR – any of the safari operators there can arrange multiday excursions to the reserve, although in most cases you'll waste precious time if you arrive in town without a reservation.

Author Tips Ask for the free photocopied map at the park's entrance gates.

Water holes in some areas in the northern part of the reserve – Letiahau, Pipers, Sunday, Passarge and Motopi – are artificially pumped to provide water for animals and are good places to watch and wait.

Practicalities You will not be permitted into the park without a campsite reservation. Collecting firewood is banned in the CKGR, so bring your own.

★**Piper Pan Campsites**   CAMPGROUND $
(☑ 395 3360; www.bigfoottours.co.bw; camping per adult/child P200/100) Slightly removed from the main circuit, the two Piper Pan sites have a wonderfully remote feel and wildlife watching is good thanks to a water hole. The pans are 26km southwest off the main Letiahau track. Site No 1 (S 21°76.827', E 23°19.843'), overlooking the main pan, is probably our favourite, but No 2 (S 21°76.827', E 23°19.843') is also excellent. The sites have pit toilets, bucket showers and braai pits.

Bape Campsite   CAMPGROUND $
(☑ 318 0775; dwnp@gov.bw; S 22°40.802', E 24°10.185'; camping per person P30) Welcome to one of the more remote campsites in Botswana. There are no facilities, but this site has plenty of shade, sometimes-pretty views of the surrounding countryside and an utterly delicious sense of the remote. It's 149km southwest of Xade Gate and around

89km north of Khutse Game Reserve, with not a whole lot in between.

Kori Campsites   CAMPGROUND $
(☑ 381 0774; dwnp@gov.bw; camping per person P30) The four campsites known as Kori sit on the hill that rises gently from the western edge of Deception Valley. There's plenty of shade and some have partial views of the valley, making any of them a wonderful base. There are braai pits and pit toilets. The GPS coordinates for the four sites are as follows: No 1 (S 21°42.774', E 23°79.829'), No 2 (S 21°42.314', E 23°79.579'), No 3 (S 21°42.140', E 23°79.236') and No 4 (S 21°41.683', E 23°79.036').

Motopi Campsites   CAMPGROUND $
(☑ 395 3360; www.bigfoottours.co.bw; camping per adult/child P200/100) In the northwestern corner of the reserve, these three campsites are wonderfully isolated from the rest of the reserve. Nearby Motopi Pan is great for wildlife,

Central Kalahari & Khutse Game Reserves

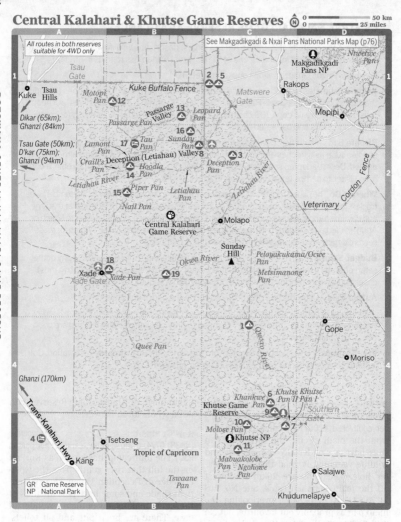

Central Kalahari & Khutse Game Reserves

Sleeping

1 Bape Campsite	C4
2 Brakah Campsite	C1
Deception Valley Lodge	(see 2)
Haina Kalahari Lodge	(see 2)
3 Kalahari Plains Camp	C2
4 Kalahari Rest	A5
5 Kaziikini Campsite	C1
6 Khankhe Pan Campsites	C4
7 Khutse Pan Campsites	C5
8 Kori Campsites	B2
9 Mahurushele Pan Campsites	C4
10 Molose Pan Campsites	C5
11 Moreswe Pan Campsites	C5
12 Motopi Campsites	B1
13 Passarge Valley Campsites	B1
14 Phokoje Campsite	B2
15 Piper Pan Campsites	B2
16 Sunday Pan Campsites	B2
17 Tau Pan Camp	B2
18 Xade Campsites	B3
19 Xaxa Campsite	B3

and lions are common in the surrounding area – we spent hours with one pride here without seeing another vehicle.

When we visited, the Tracks4Africa satellite-navigation program was incorrect for the three sites, which are some distance off the main track. While that may have been rectified since, just in case the GPS coordinates for the sites are: campsite 1 (S 21°10.581', E 23°04.811'), campsite 2 (S 21°08.074', E 23°04.444') and campsite 3 (S 21°09.927', E 23°06.097').

Xade Campsites   CAMPGROUND $
(☑318 0774; dwnp@gov.bw; camping per person P30) Ignore the three sites by Xade Gate (but do use their hot-water showers), and head for Xade Wilderness Campsite (booking code CKWIL-05), 9km east along the main (sandy) track from the park gate towards Xaxa and the heart of the park. It's a lovely spot, and while it has no facilities, the openness of the surrounding country more than compensates.

The GPS coordinates are S 22°34.136', E 23°10.412'.

Brakah Campsite   CAMPGROUND $
(www.hainakalaharilodge.com; S 20°59.310', E 23°41.905'; camping per adult/vehicle US$27/11) Sharing the private concession with (and run by the same owners as) Haina Kalahari Lodge (p134), Brakah has five appealing sites, with plenty of shade, braai pits and an ablutions block with flush toilets and hot-water showers.

Kaziikini Campsite   CAMPGROUND $
(☑680 0664; www.kaziikinicampsite.com; camping P190, self-catering bungalows with shared bathroom P240, s/d self-catering tents P640/980, s/d from P1495/2300) This community-run campsite has a range of accommodation, from campsites and simple straw huts to more luxurious safari tents that come in a range of packages. Adjacent to the camp is Shandereka Cultural Village, which hosts cultural events and displays from the local Sankuyo community. Kaziikini is just outside the northeastern corner of the CKGR and is accessible from Rakops.

Phokoje Campsite   CAMPGROUND $
(☑318 0774; dwnp@gov.bw; camping per person P30) Although the long, north–south-running Phokoje Pan is itself quite attractive, this campsite feels a little enclosed behind high grasses and thus doesn't take full advantage of the location. There's a pit toilet,

braai pit and plenty of birdlife. The GPS coordinates are S 21°59.187', E 23°22.231'.

Sunday Pan Campsites   CAMPGROUND $
(☑395 3360; www.bigfoottours.co.bw; camping per adult/child P200/100) Just off the main track between the eastern ends of Deception and Passarge Valleys, Sunday Pan has three sites dotted around a pan that's good for wildlife. GPS coordinates are as follows: site No 1 (S 21°29.220', E 23°70.908'), No 2 (S 21°35.107', E 23°67.187') and No 3 (S 21°33.196', E 23°68.810').

★Kalahari Plains Camp   TENTED CAMP $$$
(☑in South Africa +27 11-807 1800; www.wilderness-safaris.com; per person mid-Jan–May US$965, Nov–mid-Jan US$935, Jun-Oct US$650; ▧) If we could choose one place to stay in the CKGR, this would be it. These lovely solar-powered tents inhabit a gorgeous location southeast of Deception Valley and face the setting sun with stunning views. The spacious tents have wooden floors, extremely comfortable beds, 24-hour electricity, yoga mats and a roof terrace (for those wishing to sleep under the stars).

Activities include excellent San nature walks (an estimated 90% of staff come from the area) and wildlife drives on which the chances of seeing lions, leopards or cheetahs are good; there were two lion prides in the area when we were last here.

The food is excellent, Mama B is the perfect camp host, the gift shop is rather lovely and the whole camp is oriented towards vast Kalahari views across the grasslands. Nights can be cold, which is why you'll appreciate the hot-water bottles that are placed in your bed while you're at dinner – don't, as one tourist did in a similar camp, mistake it for an animal and stab it with a knife... And when it's high season in the Okavango Delta, it's usually low season down here, enabling a nice break from crowds and high-season prices.

To get here if you're driving, you can either follow the fence line south from Matswere Gate and arrange for a guide to meet you, or drive through the heart of the reserve en route. If doing the latter, the Tracks4Africa GPS system was strangely unhelpful when we visited, so we suggest you do the following. From Matswere Gate, follow the sandy track all the way into the CKGR to Deception Valley (37km). Turn left (south) and drive along the valley for 12.7km, ignoring all turn-offs along the way. After the last turn-off to the left to Deception Pan, an unsigned track leaves the main track, heading east. Some 11.5km after taking this track, another track joins from the left – ignore it and veer right. After another 7.2km, you will reach another junction at the entrance to a large grassy pan – take the right fork and follow the track for 6km into camp.

★ **Deception Valley Lodge** LODGE $$$
(www.dvl.co.za; S 20°59.12', E 23°39.47'; s/d/f all-inclusive Jun-Oct US$789/1214/1821, Nov-May US$660/1016/1525; ✹) Just outside the CKGR's northeastern boundary, this exclusive bush retreat inhabits 150 sq km of privately owned Kalahari bush and has a much more personal feel than many of Botswana's luxury lodges. The eight large chalets (two can be combined into family accommodation) are swathed in lovely earthen hues, while the food is as memorable as the warm, attentive service.

The soothing rooms blend Victorian and African design elements, which are never overdone, and feature a private lounge and outdoor shower. There's also a swimming pool. Activities, which are included in the room rates, include wildlife drives both into the CKGR and the private concession (because this is private land, not within the game-reserve boundaries, night drives are possible) and excellent Bushmen walks. The surrounding concession is known for being particularly good for lions. Travellers rave about their experience here.

The lodge is about 120km south of Maun, and most visitors fly into the airstrip from Maun. If driving, you'll need a 4WD and the lodge's detailed directions from its website.

Haina Kalahari Lodge TENTED CAMP $$$
(🖉683 0238; www.hainakalaharilodge.com; S 21°00.006', E 23°41.085'; s/d incl full board Jul-Oct from US$795/1060, Nov-Jun US$654/872, children 3-12yr US$218-347; 🖀✹) As the CKGR grows in popularity, places like this come into their own for those looking for a quieter Kalahari experience. Set on a 110-sq-km private concession just beyond the fence on the CKGR's northeastern boundary, it has nine solar-powered, supremely comfortable tents and excellent facilities in the main lodge, including a swimming pool, gym and spa.

The standard luxury tents have lovely wooden decks and slatted canopies on the outside and a stylish combination of wood, linen and canvas within. The three, more expensive superior tents have thatched roofs, free-standing bath-tubs and a heightened sense of privacy. Activities include Bushmen walks and wildlife drives; day trips into the CKGR and quad-bike excursions cost extra. It gets consistently good reviews from travellers and there's wi-fi in the main public area.

It also runs the well-maintained Brakah Campsite (p133), 1.5km away.

CRY OF THE KALAHARI

In 1974 Mark and Delia Owens set out for Botswana with very little money and a dream of studying wildlife in an area barely touched by human settlements and encroachment. They would spend the next seven years living in the Central Kalahari Game Reserve's (CKGR) Deception Valley. Back then, there were very few paved roads in Botswana (the road from Maun to Nata was a quagmire) and tourists were almost nonexistent in the CKGR. In the course of their research, they made some important findings – that, for example, the Kalahari's lions lived in quite fluid social groups and moved easily between prides – and made some of the earliest studies of the brown hyena. They were forced from Botswana in 1981 after their very public international campaign against government-built fences and their devastating impact upon migrating wildlife. Their experiences (in fact, all but the reasons for their sudden departure from the Kalahari) are beautifully told in their memoir, *Cry of the Kalahari* (1985).

The Owens later moved to North Luangwa National Park in Zambia, and controversy followed them – they were later expelled from Zambia, either for exposing corruption in the government, or for an overly robust approach to antipoaching activities, depending on who you believe. The Owens' version of the story is told in their books *The Eye of the Elephant* (1993) and *Secrets of the Savannah* (2007). The other side has been told in articles published by the *New Yorker* and the *Atlantic* in the US.

Back in the Kalahari, echoes remain of the Owens' time, not least in the popularity of Deception Valley and the shady site where the Owens once made their camp. And when we were last in the CKGR, we came across two male lions who moved southwest after being born in the Deception Valley area and who locals call 'the Owens Boys'.

Tau Pan Camp LODGE $$$
(📱 686 1449; www.kwando.co.bw; s/d Jul-Oct from US$1373/2116, Apr-Jun & Nov US$924/1428, per person Jan-Mar US$608; 🐘) 🍴 The first camp to be opened within the CKGR and the only one out in the park's west, this solar-powered luxury lodge overlooks magnificent Tau Pan from a rugged sand ridge with fabulous Kalahari views. The thatched rooms are massive and extremely comfortable, with both indoor and outdoor showers and fine decks from which to take in the view.

Wildlife drives (with San trackers as well as your guide) and San-led bushwalks are the order of the day, and neither disappoint, especially when the rains hit and this becomes one of Southern Africa's best wildlife-viewing locations. During the dry season, lions are always a possibility, and we saw cheetahs and an aardwolf on a game drive here. Day excursions to Deception Valley are also possible. The whole place is starting to show its age a little, but it's still impressive.

Xaxa Campsite CAMPGROUND
(S 22°28.634', E 23°58.282') Although this site is in need of some tender loving care from park authorities – sadly, not all visitors clean up after themselves and the site's remoteness means authorities don't always visit as often as they otherwise might – it does sit adjacent to the only water hole for hundred of kilometres in any direction. There are no facilities here of any kind.

One group of travellers who camped here told us they were kept up all night by a pride of roaring lions.

ℹ️ Getting There & Away

Airstrips (for chartered flights only) are located near Xade, Xaka and Deception Pan.

A 4WD is essential to get around the reserve, and a compass (or GPS equipment) and petrol reserves are also recommended. Several 4WD tracks lead into the CKGR, but not all are official entrances. Accessible gates:

Matswere Gate (S 21°09.047', E 24°00.445') The main gate, signposted off the sealed B300 just northwest of Rakops.

Southern Gate (S 23°21.388', E 24°36.470') The main gate to Khutse Game Reserve (which abuts the CKGR to the south, with no fence between the two), which is most easily reached via Letlhakeng, 100km to the southeast.

Tsau Gate (S 21°00.081', E 24°47.845') In the reserve's far northwest and the most accessible gate from Maun.

Xade Gate (S 22°20.268', E 23°00.577') The tracks to the gate start near D'kar or Ghanzi and are signposted.

ℹ️ Getting Around

Unless you're staying at an upmarket lodge in which game drives are included, or have organised your visit on a mobile safari from Maun, you'll need your own fully equipped 4WD to get around.

Khutse Game Reserve

The 2500-sq-km **Khutse Game Reserve** (📱 596 0013; per day per non-resident/vehicle P120/50; ⏰6am-6.30pm Apr-Sep, 5.30am-7pm Oct-Mar), which is an extension of the southern boundary of the CKGR, is a popular weekend excursion for residents of Gaborone, but it's still deliciously remote and crowds are rare, especially from Sunday to Thursday. It has all the attractions of the Kalahari, including good (if low-density) wildlife watching, well-maintained trails and around 60 mineralised clay pans that once belonged to Africa's largest inland lake. Leopard and lion sightings in particular are possible, while gemsboks and giraffes are also commonly seen.

The name Khutse, which means 'Where One Kneels to Drink' in Sekwena (the local dialect of Setswana), indicates that the area once had water, though today the reserve experiences continual droughts.

👁️ Sights

The major pan networks should guide your exploration of the reserve. Khutse Pan and the surrounding area sees the most visitors, while the northern pans and, out in the west, Moreswe and Molose Pans are all quieter, with good wildlife-watching possibilities.

👁️ Moreswe & Molose Pans

The pans at the western end of the reserve provide good wildlife watching thanks to the artificially supplied water holes, one at each pan. **Moreswe Pan** is delightfully remote and stands in the heart of some pretty Kalahari grasslands-and-pans country. We were kept awake all night by roaring lions on one visit here... **Molose Waterhole** is busier, but still good for wildlife.

The most direct (but least interesting) trail from the reserve's entrance gate to Moreswe is 62km in length (one way), but the longer (72km one way) northern loop takes you past a series of pans and is much better for wildlife. If taking the northern route (ie via Mahurushele Pan), you'll pass a sign marking the **Tropic of Capricorn**.

◉ The Northern Pans

A series of pans – Galalabadimo, Sutswane, Khutse 2, Motailane, Tshilwane, Mahurushele, Sekushwe and Khankhe – lines the main northern trail from the entrance gate all the way northwest to where the trails forge on north into the heart of the Kalahari. In fact, much of what is called Khutse, including the last three pans mentioned above, actually lies within the CKGR, although it is administered as part of the Khutse Game Reserve. **Khankhe Pan**, 26km northwest of Khutse Pan, sees very few visitors beyond those heading north into the CKGR and is well worth exploring for a bit of Kalahari immersion.

◉ Khutse Pan

The crowds of visitors, such as they are, tend to congregate around the **Khutse Pan** network close to the park entrance. There's an artificial water hole here, just a few hundred metres before the turn-off to the Khutse Pan campsites, where we've seen leopards, giraffes and gemsboks. A 7km **loop** skirts the southern sections of this pan (it's signposted to the left as you approach Khutse Pan, and before you reach the water hole) and, unusually, has some elevations that allow for fabulous views close to sunrise and sunset.

🛏 Sleeping

Khutse boasts several superbly located campsites, all of which are administered by **Big Foot Tours** (☑ 395 3360; www.bigfoottours. co.bw; camping per adult/child P200/100).

Moreswe Pan Campsites   CAMPGROUND $
(☑ 395 3360; www.bigfoottours.co.bw; camping per adult/child P200/100) Our pick of the campsites in Khutse, these four sites far from civilisation are fine places to rest, and some have terrific, sweeping views over the pan, with the water hole nearby. Each site has a braai pit, bucket showers and a pit toilet. We've stayed in site No 2 and thought it one of the loveliest campsites in the country.

Khankhe Pan Campsites   CAMPGROUND $
(☑ 395 3360; www.bigfoottours.co.bw; camping per adult/child P200/100) Well inside the boundaries of the CKGR (although administered as part of Khutse Game Reserve), and just north of the Tropic of Capricorn, Khwankwe Pan has four lovely sites (No 1 is our favourite, sitting on a gentle rise overlooking the main pan). Wildlife here is less used to vehicles than elsewhere in the reserve, but sites are much quieter.

Khutse Pan Campsites   CAMPGROUND $
(☑ 395 3360; www.bigfoottours.co.bw; camping per adult/child P200/100) The closest campsites to the park entrance, the 10 Khutse Pan sites are the busiest in the reserve, although they should be fairly quiet from Sunday night to Friday lunchtime. All have pit toilets, bucket showers and braai pits. Our pick of the sites is No 10.

Mahurushele Pan Campsites   CAMPGROUND $
(☑ 395 3360; www.bigfoottours.co.bw; camping per adult/child P200/100) There's rarely an issue finding space at one of Mahurushele Pan's three sites, which are 11km northwest of Khutse Pan (or 24km from the park entrance), but you will have semiregular vehicles passing by within earshot on their way elsewhere during daylight hours.

Molose Pan Campsites   CAMPGROUND $
(☑ 395 3360; www.bigfoottours.co.bw; camping per adult/child P200/100) The busiest of the camping areas in the reserve's west (the four sites here are 24km closer to the entrance gate than those at Moreswe), these sites are nonetheless excellent, with a nearby water hole maintained by the park authorities and open plains country offering good wildlife visibility.

ℹ Information

Pick up the free photocopied map of the reserve from the park entrance.

ℹ Getting There & Away

The entrance gate and park office are 210km from Gaborone. To Kang it's 363km via Lethlhakeng, or 285km if you take the short cut that heads southwest from Salajwe; only take the latter route if you have sufficient fuel to get you all the way to Kang. From Letlhakeng to the park entrance (100km), the road is graded gravel that is generally fine for 2WD vehicles.

THE SAN & THE CKGR

The Central Kalahari Game Reserve (CKGR) was originally established in 1961 as a private reservation for the San in order to protect them from the encroachments of the modern world and to protect their ancestral homelands. But the government of Botswana later changed its mind (primarily, critics say, because diamonds were found within the park's boundaries), and although the southern and western parts of the CKGR are still home to small populations of San, a wave of forced relocations has greatly reduced the population. The future of the San is now one of the biggest political issues for Botswana's government.

Nearly all of Botswana's and Namibia's San were relocated from their ancestral lands to new government settlements such as New Xade, just outside the CKGR. In 2006 this re-settlement program earned the government a reprimand from the UN's Committee on the Elimination of Racial Discrimination. The Botswanan government maintains that its relocation policies have the San's best interests at heart. Development, education and modernisation are its buzzwords. The trouble is, many San actively rejected the government's version of modernisation if it meant giving up their ancestral lands and traditions.

After South Africa's highest court found in favour of the Richtersveld people (relatives of the San) of Northern Cape Province in 2003 – for the first time, the court recognised that indigenous people have both communal land ownership and mineral rights over their territory – the San of Botswana launched a similar appeal. The court case brought by the First People of the Kalahari (FPK) against the government's relocation policies was concluded in May 2006, and approximately 1000 San attached their names to the effort. During the proceedings many San tried to return home to the CKGR, but most were forced off the grounds of the reserve. In December 2006 the high court ruled that the eviction of the San was 'unlawful and unconstitutional'. One justice went so far as to say that not allowing the San to hunt in their homeland 'was tantamount to condemning the residents of the CKGR to death by starvation.'

In 2007 DeBeers sold its stake in the Ghaghoo (formerly Gope) Diamond Mine in the far east of the CKGR to Gem Diamonds, and the mine began production in September 2014.

A few San have been allowed back into the reserve, although the government continues to drag its heels in fully implementing the court ruling, more than a decade after it was handed down.

❶ Getting Around

A 4WD vehicle is necessary for exploring the reserve.

Kang

POP 5985

The small settlement of Kang, 277km southeast of Ghanzi, sits at the turn-off to the Kgalagadi Transfrontier Park. As such, it's an important crossroads town for those travelling between Namibia, South Africa and Botswana (at some places in town you can pay in the currencies of any of the three countries). Kang wouldn't win a beauty contest, but it has reliable petrol stations as well as affordable places to eat and sleep.

🛏 Sleeping

Compared to other provincial Botswana towns, Kang is well served by small hotels and guesthouses.

★ Kalahari Rest
LODGE $

(☑ 72 386 548, 73 774 009; www.kalaharirest. com; Trans Kalahari Hwy/A2; camping P110, d/chalets/tr P730/815/970; ❋ 🛜 ⛄) One of the more attractive options in the southern Kalahari, this private game lodge, 25km northwest of Kang along the Trans Kalahari Hwy, combines a lovely sense of Kalahari isolation with the comforts of home. The overall look is ochre, wood and thatch, with rooms at once stylish and quirky.

There's a good restaurant for guests, and it offers game drives into the surrounding arid country.

Kang Ultra Stop
MOTEL $

(☑ 651 7294; www.kangultrastop.com; camping per person from P60, r P410-820, f P1620; ❋ 🛜 ⛄) At the main petrol station, close to where the Hukunsti/Kgalagadi road branches off the Trans Kalahari Highway (A2), Kang Ultra Stop aims to meet all of your needs in one. The motel-style rooms are simple but reasonably priced, well-maintained and span a range of budgets.

There's also a restaurant, petrol station, general store, a curio shop, the tourist office and a bar that can get rowdy in the evenings, all as part of the complex.

Kang Echo Lodge
MOTEL $

(🗹 651 7094; echolodgereception@btcmail.co.bw; d/f from P630/780; 🅿 ❄ 🛜) Don't be fooled by the thatched roofs – Kang Echo Lodge has comfortable if uninspiring motel-style rooms set back a little from the highway. There's a simple restaurant and the facilities of Kang Ultra Stop, including restaurant and small grocery store, are a short walk away.

Kang Lodge
MOTEL $

(🗹 651 8050; www.kanglodge.com; Trans Kalahari/A2; camping P100, s/d/ste P399/569/689; ❄ 🛜) Just out of town along the road to Gaborone, Kang Lodge is similar to other places in town, although, like most, its bare surrounds and rather depressing concrete budget rooms hardly make you want to stay longer than a night. The more expensive rooms are better and it's all a little quieter than those places that surround the petrol stations.

There's an OK (if often deserted) restaurant attached.

Nkisi Guesthouse
GUESTHOUSE $$

(🗹 651 7374; www.nkisiguesthouse.com; d/tw/f from P670/770/910; ❄ 🛜 ☒) Nkisi has far and away the most character of Kang's accommodation options – many rooms have exposed stone floors and soothing earth tones, and the grounds are shady and appealing. Some rooms are suitable for families, with bunks in addition to double beds. There's a good restaurant (mains P70 to P125) and small swimming pool. It's just a shame the service often goes missing...

✖ Eating

Gourmands probably won't remember their visit to Kang with any great fondness, but neither will you leave hungry – basic roadside fare is readily available and there's also a supermarket for those heading out into the wilds.

Kang Ultra Stop
INTERNATIONAL $

(mains from P45) The restaurant connected to the petrol station and motel (p137) of the same name is a fairly simple place serving up uninspiring but filling meals such as chicken schnitzel or pizza. If you're just after takeaway, it's quicker to order from the counter inside the general store.

ShopRite
SUPERMARKET $

(🗹 393 6994; Main Rd, Goo Monyamane Ward; ⊙8am-8pm Mon & Wed-Fri, 8.30am-8pm Tue, 8am-5pm Sat & Sun) One of the best supermarkets in the whole southern Kalahari region. It's in the main town, 3km off the highway.

🛈 Information

MONEY

Bank of Gaborone (🗹 651 7190; www.bank-gaborone.co.bw; Trans Kalahari Hwy/A2; ⊙8.30am-4pm Mon-Fri, to noon Sat) Kang's most reliable bank for foreign exchange, conveniently close to the petrol stations along the main highway south of town.

TOURIST INFORMATION

Botswana Tourism (🗹 651 7070; www.botswanatourism.co.bw; Trans Kalahari Hwy/A2; ⊙7.30am-4.30pm Mon-Fri, 9am-2pm Sat) Part of the whole one-stop Kang Ultra Stop experience, this tourist office is, surprisingly given its provincial-town location, one of the best-stocked such offices in the country when it comes to brochures.

Kang Wildlife Office (🗹 651 7036; off Trans Kalahari Hwy/A2; ⊙7.30am-12.45pm & 1.45-4.30pm) We strongly recommend that you make your campsite bookings for Kgalagadi Transfrontier Park long before you make it this far, but stop by at this office if you haven't, or if you need to pay for the campsites, or otherwise find out more.

It's in the town centre, 3.7km off the A2; look for the signpost just east of the intersection between the Hukuntsi road and the A2.

🛈 Getting There & Away

Buses between Ghanzi and Gaborone pass through Kang, as does onward transport headed for Hukuntsi, although there's no public transport into the Kgalagadi Transfrontier Park – you'll need your own wheels or be prepared to hitch.

Kgalagadi Transfrontier Park

In 2000 the former Mabuasehube-Gemsbok National Park was combined with South Africa's former Kalahari Gemsbok National Park to create the new Kgalagadi Transfrontier Park. The result is a 28,400-sq-km bi-national park that is one of the largest and most pristine arid wilderness areas on the continent. The park is also the only place in

Kgalagadi Transfrontier Park

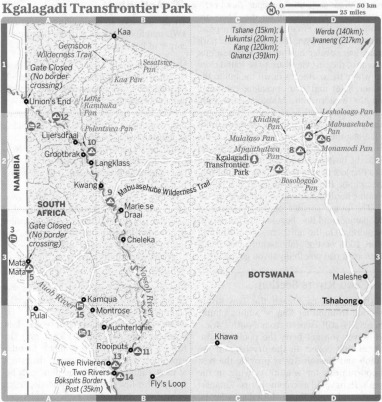

Kgalagadi Transfrontier Park

Sleeping

1 !Xaus	A4	
2 Gharagab Wilderness Camp	A2	
3 Kalahari Game Lodge	A3	
4 Mabuasehube Pan Camp Sites	D2	
5 Mata Mata Rest Camp	A3	
6 Monamodi Campsites	D2	
7 Motopi Campsites	C2	
8 Mpayathutlwa Pan Campsites	D2
9 Nossob Rest Camp	B2
10 Polentswa	A2
11 Rooiputs	B4
12 Swart Pan	A2
13 Twee Rivieren Rest Camp	B4
14 Two Rivers	B4
15 Urikaruus Wilderness Camp	A4

Botswana where you'll see the shifting sand dunes that many mistakenly believe to be typical of the Kalahari. This is true desert; in the summer it can reach 45°C, and at night it can drop to -10°C.

☉ Sights

◉ Mabuasehube Section

The eastern Mabuasehube section covers 1800 sq km and is the easiest area of the park to access from the Botswana side of the border. Here, a series of salt pans, separated by classic Kalahari scrub vegetation, makes this section of the park a worthwhile destination in its own right. That said, if you restrict yourself to Mabuasehube and surrounding pans alone, you'll miss the exceptional breadth of Kalahari landscapes that is a feature of this park.

The two largest pans, Mpayathutlwa and Mabuasehube, are also the most beautiful, surrounded as they are by low hills from where there are some gorgeous views early in the morning or late in the day. There are 4WD trails that circumnavigate both pans. **Mpayathutlwa Pan**, 12km west of the park gate, has a water hole at the northern end (some of the best views are to be found close to where the trail leads down the hill to the water hole) and two appealing campsites on the western side. **Mabuasehube Pan**, around 10km north of Mpayathutlwa, is similarly superb, with marvellous views from all along the southern edge and parts of the eastern and western sides; the trail heads off into the bush at the northern end, but there is a fine lookout around halfway around. Mabuasehube Pan is used as a salt lick by migrating herds in late winter and early spring.

The other, smaller pans – Lesholoago, Monamodi and Bosobogolo – are also worth exploring. On the northern side of **Khiding Pan**, 11km west of Mabuasehube Pan, meerkats are a real possibility if you go quietly.

Two Rivers Section

Although you can reach the Two Rivers section from either Kaa or Mabuasehube, access is still easiest from South Africa. However you get here, the pools of rainwater that collect in the dry beds of the Auob and Nossob Rivers provide the best opportunities for wildlife viewing in the park. Here you'll also come across Kalahari dunes and camel thorn–dotted grasslands.

We recommend spending at least three days in this area of the park, slowly making your way back and forth along the riverbanks and dipping down to the river's edge where possible, but allowing time also for watching and waiting from the shadows as wildlife comes and goes. Look up also into the trees for horizontal branches that might just provide a vantage point for a sleeping leopard.

There's a lot of ground to cover – it's 161km from Two Rivers to Nossob, and a further 61km to Polentswa and this section offers the best wildlife watching – and that's just along the **Nossob River**. Over on the **Auob River**, it's 121km from Two Rivers to Mata Mata, which will take around 2½ hours, or even longer if you stop along the way, as you will in all likelihood. And don't neglect the trails that connect the two rivers – it is a little-known fact that lion prides thrive close to river confluences, and this is classic Kalahari lion country.

Activities

There are several challenging wilderness 4WD and hiking tracks through this remote corner of Botswana.

!Xerry Wilderness Trail HIKING
(Swartbas Wilderness Trail; ☑ in South Africa +27 54-561 2050; www.sanparks.org/parks/kgalagadi/tourism/swartbas.php; ⊘ departs 11.30am Wed Apr-Oct, closed Nov-Mar) The !Xerry or Swartbas Wilderness Trail is a two-day hiking expedition with basic camping facilities. You'll be transported via 4WD from Nossob to the base camp in a park 4WD, and from there you take morning and afternoon hikes.

You'll need to bring all of your own food, water, firewood, tents and anything else you think you'll need; a single trailer is provided for three to eight people. You return to Nossob at noon on Friday.

Prices were under review at the time of writing.

Nossob 4x4 Eco Trail SCENIC DRIVE
(☑ in South Africa 054 561 2000; www.sanparks.org/parks/kgalagadi/tourism/nossob4x4.php; ⊘ 9am Mon, closed two weeks over Christmas & New Year) The Nossob Eco Trail is a three-night, four-day expedition, entirely self-catered, that stops at basic campsites across the dune hills between Twee Riverien and Nossob, departing from Twee Riverien in even months and Nossob in odd months. You'll need to bring everything (food, water, firewood, camping equipment) with you.

Hand-held radios are provided for the journey, which requires a minimum of two and a maximum of five vehicles. No children under 12 and no trailers.

Sleeping

Camping in the park is only allowed at designated campsites, and those on the Botswana side of the frontier must be booked at the DWNP office in Gaborone (p164) or Maun (p103). Bookings for huts and chalets on the South African side are recommended from June to September and during all weekends and public and school holidays. Contact the National Parks Board (p143).

Mabuasehube Section

There are campsites at Lesholoago Pan, Khiding Pan, Mabuasehube Pan, Mpayathutlwa

KGALAGADI TRANSFRONTIER PARK AT A GLANCE

Why Go? This, at last, is the Kalahari of your imagination, with red sand dunes, arid savannah and good wildlife watching.

Gateway Towns Kang, Hukuntsi

Wildlife Kgalagadi is home to large herds of springboks, gemsboks, elands and wildebeest, as well as a full complement of predators, including lions (official estimates put the lion population of the park at around 450), cheetahs, leopards, wild dogs, jackals and hyenas. More than 250 bird species are present, including several endemic species of larks and bustards.

Birdlife More than 250 bird species are present, including several endemic species of larks and bustards.

When to Go The best time to visit is from December to May, although the park can be visited year-round. From June to October or November, night-time temperatures can be extremely cold (as low as -10°C) and daytime temperatures are relatively mild. Although October can be very hot (45°C), the best wildlife watching is from October onwards.

Budget Safaris If you're on a really tight budget, Kgalagadi Transfrontier Park can be difficult. Your best bet is to get a group of four together, rent a 4WD and self-drive, but it can still be expensive.

Author Tip Book your campsite as early as possible, especially if your visit coincides with South African school or public holidays.

Practicalities

➡ Campers staying at the Polentswa and Rooiputs campsites can pick up firewood at Two Rivers campsite (Botswana), while petrol and basic food supplies are available at Twee Rivieren (South Africa).

➡ In Botswana there are reliable petrol supplies at Hukuntsi and Kang.

➡ Maps of the park are available at the park gates.

➡ The only mobile-phone reception in the park is at Twee Rivierien.

Pan, Monamodi Pan and Bosobogolo Pan. Facilities at most are limited to pit toilets and braai pits, but most have water holes for viewing wildlife. Most also have A-frame shelters. There are also three campsites close to Mabuasehube Gate, but these are to be avoided unless everywhere else is full – by night you can hear the sounds coming from the park's staff village. There are two further campsites on the public 4WD track between Bosobogolo Pan and Nossob.

On the road between Mabuasehube and the Two Rivers section of the park you'll find Motopi 1 and Motopi 2 campsites, which are 11km apart. The former is 95km west of Mabuasehube Gate and 96km from Nossob, while Motopi 2 is 84km from Mabuasehube Gate and 107km from Nossob.

★ Mabuasehube Pan
Camp Sites
CAMPGROUND $

(✎ bookings 318 0774; dwnp@gov.bw; camping per person P30) The four campsites that sit above or close to the southern end of Mabuasehube Pan are among the loveliest in the Kalahari, with fabulous, sweeping views of the pan, for the most part uninterrupted. They're all terrific (and have showers and toilets) but Sites No 2 and 3 are our pick – the only, minor drawback here is that they're quite close to one another.

Mpayathutlwa Pan Campsites CAMPGROUND $
(✎ bookings 318 0774; dwnp@gov.bw; camping per person P30) It's a close-run thing for us to choose between these lovely sites and those of Mabuasehube, around 10km to the north. The Mpayathutlwa sites, on the west side of the pan some 12km west of the park

entrance gate, have fine views from their shady, elevated vantage point.

Site No 2 has a shower and distant views of the water hole, but both sites are first-rate.

Motopi Campsites
CAMPGROUND $

(📞 bookings 318 0774; dwnp@gov.bw; camping per person P30) On the road between Mabuase-hube and the Two Rivers section of the park you'll find Motopi 1 and Motopi 2 campsites, which are 11km apart. While there can be a little passing traffic during the day, the sites' remoteness is magnificent at night.

Motopi 1 is 95km west of Mabuasehube Gate and 96km from Nossob, while Motopi 2 is 84km from Mabuasehube Gate and 107km from Nossob.

Monamodi Campsites
CAMPGROUND $

(📞 bookings 318 0774; dwnp@gov.bw; camping per person P30) Very much in the second tier of campsites in the Mabuasehube area, Mona-modi's two sites sit above the pan of the same name, a few kilometres north of the park entrance gate. Neither site has views and they're quite enclosed by the surrounding vegetation.

Site No 2 is slightly more open and has a bucket shower and pit toilet, while site No 1 only has a tap and pit toilet. Then again, the tap can bring surprising results. The last time we camped here, we ran the tap briefly and birds appeared from nowhere, among them a Kalahari scrub robin, red headed finch, African red-eyed bulbul and the exquisite violet-eared waxbill – pure magic!

Two Rivers Section

In the western area of the Botswana section of the park, campsites are found along the Nossob Valley at Two Rivers. Although within Botswana territory, these campsites must be accessed from the South African side of the border.

On the South African side of the border, huts and chalets are all equipped with bedding and cooking equipment. Each place has a shop that sells basic supplies, such as food, drinks (including alcohol) and usually petrol. For more information, check out http://sanparks.org.za/parks/kgalagadi/tourism/accommodation.php.

KGALAGADI VILLAGES

Hukuntsi, Tshane, Lokgwabe and Lehututu are collectively known as the Kgalagadi Villages, and were one of the most remote areas in Botswana prior to the sealing of the road leading to Kang. For travellers, the villages serve as the jumping-off point for Kgalagadi Transfrontier Park, but with the wonderful landscapes of the park and the proliferation of roadside guesthouses in Kang close by, there are few reasons to linger.

Hukuntsi is 114km southwest along a sealed road from Kang and 271km north of Tshabong along a sandy 4WD track – it's the best place to fill up on petrol.

Buses and minibuses run to Hukuntsi via Kang from Ghanzi and Gaborone, but there's very little onward transport from there – you'll need a 4WD to go any further.

If you're just heading from Kang to Kgalagadi Transfrontier Park, your most likely route is to take the sealed road to Hukuntsi (108km), the potholed road to Lokgwabe and then the graded track towards the Mabuasehube Gate (126km). If you're heading for Kaa Gate, continue through Hukuntsi and then 59km on to Zutshwa, then a further 72km on to the gate.

Hukuntsi Along the route from Hukuntsi to Tshatswa (about 60km to the southwest) are sparkling-white **salt pans** that fill with water during the rainy season and support large populations of gemsboks, ostriches and hartebeests.

Lokgwabe Lokgwabe, which lies 11km south of the commercial centre of Hukuntsi, was settled by the Nama leader Simon Kooper, who sought British protection in Be-chuanaland after leading the 1904 Nama rebellion in Namibia. He was subsequently pursued across the Kalahari by German troops and 800 camels. German detritus, including empty tins of corned beef, still litters the route.

Tshane Tshane, 12km east of Hukuntsi, has a **colonial police station** dating from the early 1900s.

Lehututu Named after the sound made by ground hornbills, Lehututu, 10km north-west of Tshane, was once a major trading post but is now little more than a spot in the desert.

Twee Riverien Rest Camp CAMPGROUND $
(www.sanparks.org; camping R265, 2-person cottages from R1045, family cottages/chalets R1275/1635; ☒) The most accessible and popular rest camp on either side of the river, Twee Rivieren features a swimming pool and, unusually for this area, an outdoor bar-restaurant. Rustic chalets have modern amenities, including air-con, hot showers and a full kitchen. This is the only one of the Kgalagadi camps to have 24-hour electricity and a relatively strong mobile phone (cellphone) signal.

Nossob Rest Camp CAMPGROUND, CHALET $
(camping R305, chalets R995, 4-bed guesthouses R1615) This fairly basic rest camp is attractively situated alongside the Nossob River, just 3½ hours' drive from Twee Rivieren. There's generator electricity for 18 hours every day and the area is known for its predators.

Polentswa CAMPGROUND $
(DWNP; ☎ 318 0774; dwnp@gov.bw; campsite per person P30) This simple campsite has shade and latrines but no running water. The location is everything – in the heart of some of Kgalagadi's richest wildlife-watching areas.

Rooiputs CAMPGROUND $
(DWNP; ☎ 318 0774; dwnp@gov.bw; campsite per person P30) A good site with shade and basic ablution blocks about 30km from Two Rivers.

Two Rivers CAMPGROUND $
(DWNP; ☎ 318 0774; dwnp@gov.bw; camping per person P30) This site has cold showers and sit-down flush toilets, and may be accessible from north of Bokspits in Botswana without having to go into South Africa first; check when making your booking.

Swart Pan CAMPGROUND $
(DWNP; ☎ 318 0774; dwnp@gov.bw; camping per person P30) A simple campsite, but it can be convenient if you're entering the park through the Kaa Gate (84km away) and aren't arriving until late afternoon.

Mata Mata Rest Camp CAMPGROUND $$
(www.sanparks.org; camping per site R305, chalets R945-2615; ☒) A pretty basic rest camp, Mata Mata sits alongside the scenic Auob River near the Namibian border, a 2½- to three-hour drive from Twee Rivieren. There's generator electricity for 18 hours every day and giraffes are frequent camp visitors.

★ **!Xaus** LODGE $$$
(www.xauslodge.co.za; s/d all-inclusive R5707/8780; @☒) If you're after Kgalagadi's most luxurious experience, book a night here. Owned and operated by the local San community, the lodge is a dry, dreamy fantasy in ochre, decorated with wall hangings made by a local women's sewing collective and overlooking an evocative circular pan.

There's an on-site pool and the San staff, cultural activities (including wilderness walks) and excellent wildlife drives round out a fine package.

Gharagab Wilderness Camp CABIN $$$
(www.sanparks.org; 2-bed cabins R1495) Blending into the wiry bush of the northern portion of the park, Gharagab is a dusty, surreally beautiful spot for watching sunsets over the local water hole with sand dunes and thorn savannah all around. You'll need a 4WD to reach the camp, and accommodation is in log cabins with solar-powered electricity and hot water.

Urikaruus Wilderness Camp CABIN $$$
(☎ in South Africa +27 12-428 9111; www.sanparks.org; 2-bed cabins R1630-1845) A stilted camp hidden amid camel thorn trees that has good wildlife viewing near its dry riverbed and water hole. The cabins are connected by an elevated walkway, and have kitchens and solar power. Check in at Twee Rivieren, 72km or two hours' drive away.

ℹ️ Information

South African National Parks (☎ in South Africa +27 12-428 9111, in South Africa +27 82-233 9111; www.sanparks.org) Your starting point for information and reservations for the South African side of Kgalagadi Transfrontier Park.

ℹ️ Getting There & Away

There is no public transport to the park. The park gates are located in the following places:
➡ Twee Rivieren (South Africa)
➡ Two Rivers (Botswana)
➡ Mabuasehube (Botswana)
➡ Kaa (Botswana)

AIR
Airstrips (for chartered flights only) are located at Ghanzi, Tshabong, Twee Rivieren and Nossob Camp.

CAR & MOTORCYCLE

The Two Rivers Section is accessible from the south via Two Rivers and Twee Riverien, and from the north via Kaa. Access to the Kalahari Gemsbok National Park is via Twee Rivieren. Both are about 53km north of the Bokspits border crossing. The border crossings to Namibia at Union's End and Mata Mata are closed because traffic disturbs the wildlife.

To get to Mabuasehube Gate, most travellers coming from the Botswana side take the sealed road from Kang, southwest to Hukuntsi (108km). Just before Hukuntsi, a potholed road branches left (south) to Lokgwabe (11km). From Lokgwabe, an unsealed road (which was regraded in 2016 but remains sandy in patches) runs south, then east, then south again for 136km to Mabuasehube Gate. The gate is signposted at various points along the way from Lokgwabe. Allow for three hours' driving from Kang to the gate.

To reach Kaa Gate from the Botswana side, make your way to Hukuntsi, pass through the town and take the reasonable unsealed road heading southwest. From Hukuntsi, it's 59km to the small settlement of Zutshwa then a further 73km to the gate. Mabuasehube section is possible from the south (via Tshabong), north (via Tshane) and east (via Werda).

ⓘ Getting Around

You'll need your own 4WD vehicle for getting around the park, although some of the camps are accessible by 2WD.

Two 4WD trails connect the Two Rivers and Mabuasehube sections of the park, but only the southernmost of the two (which connects Nossob and Bosobogolo Pan, 171km away and 20km southwest of Mabuasehube Gate) is open to the public. The northern Mabuasehube Wilderness 4x4 Trail (155km) must be prebooked through the DWNP in Gaborone (p164) or Maun (p103).

UNDERSTAND BOTSWANA

Botswana Today

Botswana hasn't changed much in recent years and that is, for the most part, a very good thing. This is a country with much to envy: a stable, democratic political system, a relatively prosperous economy and a wealth of natural resources. Botswana isn't perfect, but 50 years after winning its independence, it's still one of the best places in Africa in which to live.

The Unhappiest Place on Earth?

We've always found people in Botswana to be a pretty welcoming and cheerful lot, and their booming economy suggests that there is much for them to be happy about. But not everyone agrees. In 2012 the New Economics Foundation (www.neweconomics.org) surveyed people in 151 countries in order to create the latest version of its Happy Planet Index. Contrary to popular reporting in Botswana in the wake of the survey, the index doesn't measure people's day-to-day happiness. Instead, it reveals the efficiency with which countries convert their natural resources into long and happy lives for their citizens while maintaining a small ecological footprint. In other words, the countries that do well are those where people achieve long, happy lives without overstretching the earth's natural resources. Having languished in the lower regions since the index was created in 2006, in 2012 Botswana came in... *last*. Thankfully, things have improved in the years since – Botswana rose to a better, if still rather disappointing, 126th out of 140 countries in 2016.

Resource Rich

By any standards, Botswana's recent history is a lesson to other African countries. Instead of suffering from Africa's oft-seen resource curse, Botswana has used the ongoing windfall from its diamond mines to build a stable and, for the most part, egalitarian country, one whose economic growth rates have, for decades, been among the highest on earth. This is a place where things work, where education, health and environmental protection are government priorities. Even when faced with one of the most serious challenges confronting Africa in the 20th century – HIV/AIDS – the government broke new ground in making antiretroviral treatment available to all.

The country's dependence on diamonds is, however, also a major concern when looking into Botswana's future; diamonds make up 85% of the country's export earnings and one third of government revenues. As such, the economy remains vulnerable to a fluctuating world economy – in 2015 the economy grew by just 1% (which is very low by the country's recent, albeit lofty standards) and unemployment sits at a worrying 20%, prompting the government to announce an economic stimulus package in 2016. Tourism is the big growth industry as the country attempts to diversify an economy that remains, despite some leaner times, one of the strongest in Southern Africa.

Fifty & Proud

On 30 September 2016, Botswana celebrated 50 years as an independent country. We were fortunate enough to join in the celebrations and the outpouring of national pride made it clear that this is one of Africa's most enduring success stories. Yes, much of it wouldn't have been possible without diamonds – the country would be unrecognisable to those who were around 50 years before – but Botswana has used its resources to make a better life for its people, something that can be said about few other resource-rich African nations. But there's more to it than simple good economic management, because this country is very much united. Despite considerable diversity, the project of building a cohesive and peaceful nation has been similarly successful – people here identify themselves

first and foremost as Botswanans, with tribal affiliation very much in second place. If this sounds like a given, again, a quick scan of other countries on the continent serves as a reminder that this is so special that it fully deserves the slogan that accompanied the anniversary celebrations – 'Botswana: United and Proud'.

Political Stability

In many African countries, an 11th straight election victory for the ruling party – in this case, the Botswana Democratic Party (BDP) – would be a signal that all is not well. But in Botswana, the opposite applies. The government was reelected in 2014, with President Ian Khama and his BDP taking just under 50% of the vote, winning an absolute majority in parliament; for the first time, more voters chose opposition presidential candidates than the president himself. The opposition mounted a strong campaign and the electoral process was judged by international observers to be

DIAMONDS: A COUNTRY'S BEST FRIEND

In the 1960s Botswana ranked as one of the world's poorest countries, with GDP per capita at less than US$200. Educational facilities were minimal, with fewer than 2% of the population having completed primary school and fewer than 100 students enrolled in university. In the entire country there was only one, 12km-long, paved road.

Then, in 1967, everything changed with the discovery of diamonds at Orapa. Two other major mines followed at Letlhakane in 1977 and Jwaneng in 1982, making Botswana the world's leading producer of gem-quality stones – Botswana still extracts around one-quarter of the world's diamond supply. With the exception of the Lerala and Ghaghoo mines, the country's diamond industry is run by Debswana, a joint venture between the Botswanan government and South African company De Beers.

Where other African countries have squandered the proceeds of bountiful natural resources or have descended into conflict in what has become known as the 'resource curse', Botswana has bucked the trend. The government has spread this wealth throughout Botswana's small population fairly equitably, and diamond dollars have been ploughed into infrastructure, education (adult literacy stands at 84.4%) and health. Private business has been allowed to grow and foreign investment has been welcomed. In 1994 Botswana became the first country in the world to graduate from the UN's Least Developed Country Status, a league table of development based around key economic, social and quality-of-life indicators. From 1966 to 2005 Botswana's economy grew faster than any other in the world. In 2015 Botswana ranked 28th out of 168 countries on Transparency International's Corruption Perception Index, the highest ranking of any country in Africa. In the same year, Botswana's GDP per capita was a respectable US$16,400, compared with US$2100 in Zimbabwe, US$3900 in Zambia, US$11,400 in Namibia and US$13,200 in South Africa.

Conscious of the need to develop alternative revenue streams, Botswana's government is desperately trying to diversify into manufacturing, light engineering, food processing and textiles. Tourism, too, is set to play a major role in the country's future, although the challenge remains to increase revenue without adversely affecting the environment and local communities.

free and fair. In the aftermath, there were no complaints over electoral fraud, and a robust political debate prevails thanks to a free press and a marked lack of authoritarianism. In Botswana, it seems, voters keep reelecting the government thanks to a widespread perception that the government is doing a decent job. The fact that Botswana's past presidents have, for the most part, stepped off the political stage voluntarily, offers further credence to the idea that Botswana's governance, though far from perfect, is less about personal aggrandisement for its rulers than it is a reflection of the society it represents.

A Fragile Environment

Botswana inhabits one of the driest regions on earth, and not just because the Kalahari sweeps across much of the country's territory. In 2016 Botswana, along with the rest of Southern Africa, suffered its fourth successive year of drought, causing massive problems for the country's agricultural and cattle-farming sectors. Drinking water, particularly in the country's northwest from D'Kar to Maun, has become increasingly scarce, prompting concerns for the long-term sustainability of entire communities.

Despite low water levels in places like the Boteti River and the drying up once again of the Savuti Channel and neighbouring marshlands, wildlife tends to be surviving the crisis a little better than the country's human population, but poaching in the region remains a concern – despite promising news compared to the rest of Africa, the fact remains that Botswana has lost 15% of its elephants since 2010. Hunting, too, is a fraught issue, with the country's ban on commercial or trophy hunting in 2014 winning both praise and criticism from conservationists. The worldwide clamour for change in the hunting industry after the killing of Cecil the lion in neighbouring Zimbabwe in 2015 makes it unlikely that the government will change tack any time soon.

History

First Footprints

To understand Botswana, one must look deep into the past. Here, history extends back through the millenniums to the earliest presence of humanity on the planet, when humans took their first footsteps on the savannahs of southern and eastern Africa. Developing rudimentary tools, these people hunted and gathered across the abundant plains, moving seasonally over grassland and scrub in and around the extensive wetlands that once covered the north of the country.

By the Middle Stone Age, which lasted until 20,000 years ago, the Boskop, the primary human group in Southern Africa, had progressed into an organised hunting and gathering society. They are thought to be the ancestors of the modern-day San.

Archaeological evidence and rock art found in the Tsodilo Hills place these hunter-gatherers in shelters and caves throughout the region from around 17,000 BC. The paintings that gave expression to the natural world in which they lived attest to their increasing level of sophistication – clumsy stone tools gave way to bone, wood and, eventually, iron implements. Better tools meant more efficient hunting, which allowed time for further innovation, personal adornment and artistic pursuits such as the emerging craft of pottery.

Such progress prompted many of these hunter-gatherers to adopt a pastoral lifestyle – sowing crops and grazing livestock on the exposed pastures of the Okavango Delta and the Makgadikgadi lakes. Some migrated west into central Namibia, and by 70 BC some had even reached the Cape of Good Hope.

Settlement

Following the fragmented trail of ancient pottery, archaeologists and anthropologists have been able to piece together the complex, criss-crossing migration of different ethnic groups into Southern Africa. From AD 200 to 500, Bantu-speaking farmers began to appear on the southern landscape from the north and east. To begin with, relations between the San and Khoekhoen appear to have been cordial, and the groups mixed freely, traded and intermarried. After all, there was much to learn from each other. The farmers brought with them new political systems, and superior agricultural and metalworking skills. In the Tswapong Hills, near Palapye, there's evidence of an early iron-smelting furnace that dates back to AD 190. One of the earliest and most powerful Bantu groups to settle in the region was the Sotho-Tswana, who consisted of three distinct entities: the Northern Basotho (or

Pedi), who settled in the Transvaal of South Africa; the Southern Basotho of Lesotho; and the Western Basotho (or Batswana), who migrated north into Botswana.

Cattle herders began arriving from Zimbabwe around AD 600, and in the 13th century most of eastern Botswana came within the sphere of influence of Great Zimbabwe, one of Africa's most legendary ancient kingdoms. Between the 13th and 15th centuries, Great Zimbabwe incorporated many chiefdoms of northeastern Botswana, and the region was still part of Zimbabwe-based dynasties several hundred years later.

The only other significant migrations into Botswana were those of the Herero in the late 19th century. Faced with German aggression in Namibia, they fled eastward, settling in the northwestern extremes of Botswana.

Rise of the Tswana

One of the most significant developments in Botswana's human history was the evolution of the three main branches of the Tswana ethnic group during the 14th century. It's a typical tale of family discord, where three brothers – Kwena, Ngwaketse and Ngwato – broke away from their father, Chief Malope, to establish their own followings in Molepolole, Kanye and Serowe respectively. These fractures probably occurred in response to drought and expanding populations eager to strike out in search of new pastures and arable land.

The Ngwato clan split further in the late 18th century, following a quarrel between Chief Khama I and his brother Tawana, who subsequently left Serowe and established his chiefdom in the area around Maun. The four major present-day Batswana groups – the Batawana, Bakwena, Bangwaketse and Bangwato – trace their ancestry to these splits and Botswana's demographic make-up owes much to the dispersal of the various groups.

The Difaqane

As people fanned out across Southern Africa, marking out their territories of trade and commerce, the peaceful fragmentation of the past became increasingly difficult. By the 1700s villages were no longer small, open affairs but fortified settlements situated on strategic, defensive hilltops. This antagonistic mood was exacerbated by the increasing trade in ivory, cattle and slaves, which prompted raids and counterraids between powerful tribes eager to gain control over these lucrative resources.

The most prominent aggressor was the Zulu warlord Shaka, the new chief of the Zulu confederation. From his base in Natal he launched a series of ruthless campaigns aimed at forcibly amalgamating or destroying all tribes and settlements in his way. By 1830 the Bakwena and Bangwato areas had been overrun, and survivors had started the *difaqane* (literally 'the scattering' or exodus). In Shaka's wake came his equally ruthless Ndebele general, Mzilikazi, who continued to send raiding parties into the villages of Botswana and forced villagers to flee as far as Ghanzi and Tshane in the heart of the Kalahari. His troops also defeated the Bangwaketse, who fled into the desert, finally settling near Letlhakeng.

The Tswana states of Ngwaketse, Kwena and Ngwato were only reconstituted in the 1840s after the ravages of the *difaqane* had passed. Realising from their experience that their divided nation was vulnerable to attack, they began to regroup under the aegis of King Segkoma I.

These new states were then organised into wards under their own chiefs, who then paid tribute (based on labour and cattle) to the king. Botswana may have begun to unite, but the states were also highly competitive, vying with each other for the increasing trade in ivory and ostrich feathers being carried down new roads to the Cape Colony in the south. Those roads also brought Christian missionaries into Botswana for the first time and enabled the Boer trekkers to begin their migrations further north.

The Boers & the British

While Mzilikazi was wreaking havoc on the Batswana and missionaries were busy trying to convert the survivors to Christianity, the Boers were feeling pressured by their British neighbours in the Cape. The Boers were farmers from the eastern Cape in Southern Africa, the descendants of Dutch-speaking settlers. In 1836 around 20,000 Boers set out on the Great Trek across the Vaal River into Batswana and Zulu territory and proceeded to set up their own free state ruling the Transvaal – a move ratified by the British in the Sand River Convention of 1852. Effectively, this placed the Batswana under the rule of the so-called new South

African Republic, and a period of rebellion and heavy-handed oppression ensued. Following heavy human and territorial losses, the Batswana chiefs petitioned the British government for protection from the Boers.

But Britain had its hands full in Southern Africa and was in no hurry to take on and support a country of uncertain profitability. Instead, it offered to act as arbitrator in the dispute. By 1877, however, animosity against the Boers had escalated to such a dangerous level that the British conceded and annexed the Transvaal – thereby starting the first Boer War. The war continued until the Pretoria Convention of 1881, when the British withdrew from the Transvaal in exchange for Boer allegiance to the British Crown.

With the British out of their way, the Boers once again looked northward into Batswana territory. In 1882 the Boers managed to subdue the towns of Taung and Mafikeng, and proclaimed them the republics of Stellaland and Goshen. They might have gone much further had it not been for the annexation of South West Africa (modern-day Namibia) by the Germans in the 1890s.

With the potential threat of a German-Boer alliance across the Kalahari, which would have put paid to their dreams of expansion into mineral-rich Rhodesia (Zimbabwe), the British started to look seriously at the Batswana petitions for protection. In 1885 they proclaimed a protectorate over their Tswana allies, known as the British Crown Colony of Bechuanaland.

Cecil John Rhodes

British expansion in Southern Africa came in the form of a private venture under the auspices of the British South Africa Company (BSAC), owned by millionaire businessman Cecil John Rhodes.

By 1889 Rhodes already had a hand in the diamond-mining industry in Kimberley (South Africa), and he was convinced that other African countries had similar mineral deposits just waiting to be exploited. He aimed to do this through the land concessions that companies could obtain privately in order to colonise new land for the Crown. The system was easily exploited by Rhodes, who fraudulently obtained large tracts of land from local chiefs by passing off contracts as treaties. The British turned a blind eye, as they eventually hoped to transfer the entire Bechuanaland protectorate to the BSAC and relieve themselves of the expense of colonial administration.

Realising the implications of Rhodes' aspirations, three Batswana chiefs – Bathoen, Khama III and Sebele – accompanied by a sympathetic missionary, WC Willoughby, sailed to England to appeal directly to the British parliament for continued government control of Bechuanaland. Instead of taking action, the colonial minister, Joseph Chamberlain, advised them to contact Rhodes directly and work things out among themselves.

Naturally, Rhodes was immovable, so the delegation approached the London Missionary Society (LMS), who in turn took the matter to the British public. Fearing that the BSAC would allow alcohol in Bechuanaland, the LMS and other Christian groups backed the devoutly Christian Khama and his entourage. The British public in general felt that the Crown should be administering the Empire, rather than the controversial Rhodes. Public pressure rose to such a level that the government was forced to concede to the chiefs. Chamberlain agreed to continue British administration of Bechuanaland, ceding only a small strip of the southeast (now known as the Tuli Block) to the BSAC for the construction of a railway line to Rhodesia.

Colonial Years

By 1899 Britain had decided it was time to consolidate the Southern African states, and it declared war on the Transvaal. The Boers were overcome in 1902, and in 1910 the Union of South Africa was created.

By selling cattle, draught oxen and grain to the Europeans streaming north in search of farming land and minerals, Bechuanaland enjoyed an initial degree of economic independence. However, the construction of the railway through Bechuanaland to Rhodesia and a serious outbreak of foot-and-mouth disease in the 1890s destroyed the transit trade. This new economic vulnerability, combined with a series of droughts and the need to raise cash to pay British taxes, sent many Batswana to South Africa to look for work on farms and in mines. Up to 25% of Botswana's male population was abroad at any one time. This accelerated the breakdown of traditional land-use patterns and eroded the chiefs' powers.

The British government continued to regard the protectorate as a temporary expedient until it could be handed over to

Rhodesia or the new Union of South Africa. Accordingly, investment and administrative development within the territory were kept to a bare minimum. Even when there were moves in the 1930s to reform administration or initiate agricultural and mining development, these were hotly disputed by leading Tswana chiefs on the grounds that they would only enhance colonial control. So the territory remained divided into eight largely self-administering 'tribal' reserves and five white settler farm blocks, with the remainder classified as 'Crown' (ie State) land. Similarly, the administrative capital, Mafikeng, which was situated outside the protectorate's border, in South Africa, remained where it was until 1964.

Independence

The extent to which the British subordinated Botswanan interests to those of South Africa during this period became clear in 1950. In a case that caused political controversy in Britain and across the Empire, the British government banned Seretse Khama from the chieftainship of the Ngwato and exiled him for six years. This, as secret documents have since revealed, was in order to appease the South African government, which objected to Khama's marriage to a British woman at a time when racial segregation was enforced in South Africa.

This only increased growing political agitation, and throughout the 1950s and '60s Botswanan political parties started to surface and promote the idea of independence, at the precise historical moment when African colonies elsewhere were seeking their freedom. Following the Sharpeville Massacre in 1960, South African refugees Motsamai Mpho, of the African National Congress (ANC), and Philip Matante, a Johannesburg preacher affiliated with the Pan-African Congress, joined with KT Motsete, a teacher from Malawi, to form the Bechuanaland People's Party (BPP). Its immediate goal was independence.

In 1962 Seretse Khama and Kanye farmer Ketumile 'Quett' Masire formed the moderate Bechuanaland Democratic Party (BDP). The BDP formulated a schedule for independence, drawing on support from local chiefs such as Bathoen II of the Bangwaketse, and traditional Batswana. The BDP also called for the transfer of the capital into Botswana (ie from Mafikeng to Gaborone) and a new nonracial constitution.

The British gratefully accepted the BDP's peaceful plan for a transfer of power, and Khama was elected president when general elections were held in 1965. On 30 September 1966, the country – now called the Republic of Botswana – was granted full independence.

In contrast to the situation in so many other newly independent African states, Seretse Khama wisely steered Botswana

BOOKS ABOUT BOTSWANA'S HISTORY

History of Botswana (Thomas Tlou & Alec Campbell; 1984) Essentially a school textbook, this is still one of the best resources on Botswana's past from the Stone Age to independence.

Missionary Travels (David Livingstone; 1857) Enjoy the drama of discovery in this evocative classic of travel literature. Janet Wagner Parsons' biography The Livingstones at Kolobeng (1997) is another good read.

Seretse Khama: 1921–1980 (Neil Parsons, Willie Henderson & Thomas Tlou; 1995) The definitive biography of the country's first president.

Seretse and Ruth: Botswana's Love Story (Wilf & Trish Mbanga; 2005) An insider's account of one of the most dramatic love stories and political scandals of its time. In 2016, the story became a film, A United Kingdom.

Building of a Nation: A History of Botswana from 1800 to 1910 (Jeff Ramsay, Barry Morton & Part Themba Mgadla; 1996) Arguably the best account of Botswana's colonial history.

Botswana: The Road to Independence (Peter Fawcus; 2000) An erudite history by two of Britain's most senior administrators during the protectorate period.

Diamonds, Dispossession and Democracy in Botswana (Kenneth Good; 2008) A searing critique of modern Botswana's rulers and its treatment of the San.

through its first 14 years of independence. He guaranteed continued freehold over land held by white ranchers, and adopted a strictly neutral stance (at least until near the end of his presidency) towards South Africa and Rhodesia. The reason, of course, was Botswana's economic dependence on the giant to the south, but, that said, Khama refused to exchange ambassadors with South Africa and officially disapproved of apartheid in international circles.

Modern Politics

Sir Seretse Khama died in 1980 (not long after Zimbabwean independence), but his Botswana Democratic Party (BDP), formerly the Bechuanaland Democratic Party, continues to command a substantial majority in the Botswana parliament. Sir Ketumile 'Quett' Masire, who succeeded Khama as president from 1980 to 1998, followed the path laid down by his predecessor and continued to cautiously follow pro-Western policies.

In 1998 President Masire did something very few African leaders seem to manage – he retired in keeping with new constitutional provisions and stepped gracefully off the political stage. His successor and former vice-president, Festus Mogae, became president and his position was confirmed in elections the following year. With the country in the grip of an HIV/AIDS catastrophe – Botswana had the highest infection rate of any country in the world – Mogae won international acclaim by announcing in 2001 that treatment drugs for HIV/AIDS patients were to be distributed free of charge. Mogae was reelected president in a landslide in 2004.

Festus Mogae handed over the presidency to vicepresident Ian Khama (son of Sir Seretse Khama) on 1 April 2008. Mogae is lauded in global circles for the move. Whatever the international community thought of Mogae, his decision to make Khama president generated concern at home as Khama had not yet been elected as president.

Since assuming power, Khama has cracked down on drinking, demanding earlier curfews at bars (sometimes enforced, sometimes not). In addition, Khama, a former commander of the Botswana Defence Force, has appointed military and law-enforcement colleagues to government posts traditionally held by civilians, which has caused some concern in civil society. Nonetheless, the BDP with Khama at the helm easily won elections in October 2009.

Khama also generated controversy with his government's policies that continue to make life difficult for the San who want to return to the CKGR (p137) and with his decision to ban all commercial hunting in Botswana from 2014. Even so, he remains popular and he was reelected as president for a second term in 2014. At the same time, the BDP won a clear majority of parliamentary seats and the BDP, which has controlled Botswana's politics since independence, looked likely to remain in power for some years to come.

People of Botswana

Botswana's population is made up of eight major tribal groupings, although within this broader framework there are 26 tribal groups in all. The Tswana are the most populous, and all citizens of Botswana – regardless of colour, ancestry or tribal affiliation – are known as Batswana (plural) or Motswana (singular). Almost everyone, including members of non-Tswana tribes, communicates in Setswana, a native language, rather than the official language of English.

Tswana

Botswana means 'land of the Tswana' and about 80% of the country's population claims Tswana heritage. The origins of the Tswana are simple enough. As land-owning agriculturalists, the Tswana ethnic group has clearly defined areas of influence. The Bangwato are centred on the Serowe area, the Bakwena in and around Molepolole, and the Bangwaketse near Kanye. A later split in the Bangwato resulted in a fourth group, the Batawana, who are concentrated near Maun in the northwest.

Known for being proud, conservative, resourceful and respectful, the Batswana have an ingrained feeling of national identity and an impressive belief in their country. Their history – a series of clever manoeuvres that meant they avoided the worst aspects of colonisation – has nurtured a confidence that is rare in postcolonial Africa.

The importance of the family in Batswana society has made the crisis caused by the HIV/AIDS pandemic particularly damaging. At last count, the country had more than 60,000 AIDS orphans (down from more than 90,000 in 2011), a staggering 2.7% of the population. How the country reacts to this breakdown of traditional family networks is one of the greatest challenges facing its people.

TRADITIONAL TSWANA CULTURE

In Batswana society, traditional culture acts as a sort of societal glue. Villages grew up around reliable water sources and developed into complex settlements with *kgosi* (chiefs) ultimately responsible for the affairs of the community. Respect for one's elders, firmly held religious beliefs, traditional gender roles and the tradition of the *kgotla* – a specially designated meeting place in each village where social and judicial affairs are discussed and dealt with – created a well-defined social structure with some stiff mores at its core. At a family level, in Batswana village life each family was entitled to land, and traditional homesteads were social places, consisting of communal eating places and separate huts for sleeping, sometimes for several family members.

Even today, as mudbrick architecture gives way to breeze blocks, and villages grow into busy towns and cities, most homes retain traditional features and life is still a very social affair. The atmosphere in family compounds is busy and convivial, although everything is done at a leisurely pace. Likewise, in shops and businesses people spend a huge amount of time greeting and agreeing with each other, and checking up on each other's welfare.

Historically, the Batswana are farmers and cattle herders. Cattle, and to a lesser extent goats and sheep are still, in many ways, the measure of a family's status.

Bakalanga

Botswana's second-largest ethnic group, at around 11% of the population, the Bakalanga is a powerful land-owning group whose members are thought to descend from the Rozwi empire – the culture responsible for building Great Zimbabwe. In the colonial reshuffle, the Bakalanga were split in two and now some 75% of them live in western Zimbabwe. In Botswana, they are based mainly, although not exclusively, around Francistown.

Herero

The Herero probably originated from eastern or central Africa and migrated across the Okavango River into northeastern Namibia in the early 16th century. In 1884 the Germans took possession of German South West Africa (Namibia) and systematically appropriated Herero grazing lands. The ensuing conflict between the Germans and the Herero was to last for years, only ending in a calculated act of genocide that saw the remaining members of the tribe flee across the border into Botswana.

The refugees settled among the Batawana and were initially subjugated but eventually regained their herds and independence. These days the Herero are among the wealthiest herders in Botswana.

Basubiya & Wayeyi

The Basubiya, Wayeyi (Bayei) and Mbukushu are all riverine tribes scattered around the Chobe and Linyanti Rivers and across the Okavango Panhandle. Their histories and migrations are a textbook example of the ebb and flow of power and influence. For a long time, the Basubiya were the dominant force, pushing the Wayeyi away from the Chobe River and into the Okavango after a little spat over a lion skin, so tradition says. The Basubiya were agriculturists and as such proved easy prey for the growing Lozi empire (from modern Zambia), which in turn collapsed in 1865. They still live in the Chobe district.

Originally from the same areas in Namibia and Angola as the Mbukushu, the Wayeyi moved south from the Chobe River into the Okavango Delta in the mid-18th century to avoid the growing conflict with the Basubiya. They established themselves around Lake Ngami and eventually dispersed into the Okavango Delta. At the same time, the Bangwato (a Batswana offshoot) were pushing northward and came into contact with the Wayeyi. Over time this relationship became a form of clientship, which many Wayeyi still feel resentful about today.

In 1948 and 1962 the Wayeyi made efforts to free themselves of Batswana rule, but neither attempt succeeded. In 1995 these efforts were renewed in a more concerted manner with the establishment of the Kamanakao Association, which aims to develop and protect Wayeyi culture and language. Following this, the Wayeyi decided to revive their chieftainship and on 24 April 1999 they elected Calvin Diile Kamanakao as Chief Kamanakao I and recommended him for inclusion in the House of Chiefs. The government rejected this proposal, so in 2001 the Wayeyi took the matter to the

BOOKS ABOUT THE SAN

The Lost World of the Kalahari (Laurens van der Post; 1958) Classic study of the San people, including a haunting section on the Tsodilo Hills.

Hunter and Habitat in the Central Kalahari (George B Silberbauer; 1981) Definitive anthropological study of the CKGR San in the late 1950s and early 1960s prior to their expulsion.

The Harmless People (Elizabeth Marshall Thomas; 1989) A 1950s anthropological study of the Botswana San, with updates from the 1980s.

Voices of the San (Willemien Le Roux & Alison White (eds); 2004) Fascinating collection of oral histories from ordinary San people.

The Healing Land (Rupert Isaacson; 2004) Generous and nuanced journey through the lands of the San in modern Southern Africa.

Tears for my Land (Kuela Kiema; 2010) Polemical and compelling treatise on San rights and dispossession.

High Court, which passed judgement that chiefs elected by their own tribes should be admitted to the house. In 2008 the Wayeyi chief Shikati Fish Matepe Ozoo was appointed to the House of Chiefs by former president Festus Mogae. In the meantime, the United Nations High Commissioner for Refugees (UNHCR) has pointed out that most Wayeyi children cannot speak their ancestral tongue, one of the keys to maintaining a distinct ethnic identity.

Mbukushu

The Mbukushu (or Hambukushu), who now inhabit the Ngamiland area around the Okavango Delta, were originally refugees from the Caprivi Strip in northeastern Namibia. They were forced to flee south in the late 18th century after being dislodged by the forces of Chief Ngombela's Lozi empire. The Mbukushu carried on to southeastern Angola, just north of present-day Andara (Namibia). There, they encountered Portuguese and African traders, who began purchasing Mbukushu commoners from the tribal leadership to be used and resold as slaves. To escape, some

Mbukushu headed back to the Okavango Panhandle, where they mixed and intermarried with the Batawana. Many remain in and around the villages of Shakawe and Sepupa.

San

The San are Botswana's first inhabitants: they were living in the Kalahari and Tsodilo Hills as far back as 30,000 years ago, as archaeological finds in the Kalahari have demonstrated. Some linguists even credit them with the invention of language. Unlike most other African countries, where the San have perished or disappeared through war and interbreeding, Botswana, along with Namibia, retains the remnants of its San communities – barely 100,000 individuals in total, which may include many with mixed San ancestry. Of these, around 60% live in Botswana (the !Kung, G//ana, G/wi and !xo being the largest groups), where they make up just 3% of Botswana's population, and 35% in Namibia (the Naro, !Xukwe, Hei//kom and Ju/'hoansi), with the remainder scattered throughout South Africa, Angola, Zimbabwe and Zambia.

For a window on the life of the San, join local hunter !Nqate in Craig and Damon Foster's film *The Great Dance* (2000), an inspiring collaborative project that involved the local community at every stage of the filming and editing.

And a word on terminology: in Botswana you'll often hear the term 'Basarwa' being used to describe the San, but this is considered by the San to be pejorative as it literally means 'people of the sticks'.

THE PAST

Traditionally the San were nomadic hunter-gatherers who travelled in small family bands (usually between around 25 and 35 people) within well-defined territories. They had no chiefs or hierarchy of leadership and decisions were reached by group consensus. With no animals, crops or possessions, the San were highly mobile. Everything that they needed for their daily existence they carried with them.

Initially, the San's social flexibility enabled them to evade conquest and control. But as other powerful tribes with big herds of livestock and farming ambitions moved into the area, inevitable disputes arose over the land. The San's wide-ranging, nomadic lifestyle (some territories extended over 1000 sq km) was utterly at odds with the settled world of the farmers and soon became a source of bitter conflict. This situation was rapidly accelerated by European colonists, who arrived in the area during the mid-17th century. The early Boers pursued an extermination campaign that lasted for 200 years and killed as many as 200,000 indigenous people. Such territorial disputes, combined with modern policies on wildlife conservation, have seen the San increasingly disenfranchised and dispossessed. What's more, in the modern world their disparate social structure has made it exceedingly difficult for them to organise pressure groups to defend their rights and land as other groups have done. Even so, they have enjoyed a measure of success in fighting their expulsion from the Central Kalahari Game Reserve (CKGR).

THE FUTURE

Like so many indigenous peoples the world over, the San are largely impoverished. Many work on farms and cattle posts or live in squalid, handout-dependent and alcohol-plagued settlements centred on boreholes in western Botswana and northeastern Namibia, as debate rages around them as to their 'place' in modern African society. As such, the outlook for the San is uncertain.

Tourism provides some measure of economic opportunity for the San, who are often employed in Ghanzi- and Kalahari-based lodges as wildlife guides and trackers. But it is also argued that for this race to survive into the 21st century, they require not only self-sufficiency and international support but institutional support and recognition from within the Gaborone government.

For more on the San and the challenges they face in modern Botswana, contact the grassroots bodies such as South African San Institute (www.san.org.za) or Survival International (www.survivalinternational.org).

Religion

Batswana society is imbued with spirituality, whether that be Christianity or local indigenous belief systems. For most Batswana, religion is a vital part of life, substan-

tiating human existence in the universe as well as providing a social framework.

Tribal Chiefs

Botswana's early tribal belief systems were primarily cults centred on ancestor worship. For the Batswana, this meant the worship of Modimo, a supreme being who created the world and represented the ancestors. Other ethnic groups may have differing cosmologies, but the majority of belief systems revolve around the worship of an omnipotent power (for the San it is N!odima and for the Herero it is Ndjambi) and the enactment of rituals to appease the ancestors, who are believed to play an active role in everyday life.

Introduction of Christianity

By the 19th century, Christian missionaries had begun to arrive, bringing with them an entirely new set of ideas that dislodged many indigenous traditions and practices. They established the first schools and as a result the Christian message began to spread.

Religion Today

Today about 30% of Batswana adhere to mainstream Christian faiths (the majority are either Catholic or Anglican), while around 60% adhere to the practices of what is known as the African Religion, an indigenous religion that integrates Christian liturgy with the more ritualistic elements of traditional ancestor worship. It comprises a variety of churches (the Healing Church of Botswana, the Zionist Christian Church and the Apostolic Faith Mission), and is extremely popular in rural areas.

Arts & Crafts

Traditional arts and crafts lie at the heart of Botswana's historical cultural life – Botswana's earliest artists were the San, who painted the world they lived in on the rock walls of their shelters, and they were master craftspeople, producing tools, musical instruments and material crafts from wood, leather and ostrich eggshells. Traditional dance and architecture are also enjoying something of a revival, while Botswana has a small but dynamic contemporary music and literary scene.

Traditional Arts & Crafts

Handwoven baskets and the traditional crafts of the San are the best of a fairly modest collection of locally made traditional handicrafts. There are some impressive woodcarvings and textiles in Botswana, but very few are produced here – most come from West Africa (Mali in particular) or the Democratic Republic of Congo. One exception is Lentswe-la-Oodi Weavers (p55), close to Gaborone.

BASKET WEAVING

Botswana is most famous for the basketry produced in the northwestern regions of the Okavango Delta by Wayeyi and Mbukushu women. Like most material arts in Africa, they have a practical purpose, but their intricate construction and evocative designs – with names like Tears of the Giraffe or Flight of the Swallows – are anything but.

In the watery environs of the delta, the baskets serve as watertight containers for grains and seeds. The weaving is so tight on some that they were also used as beer kegs. All the baskets are made from the leaf fibre of the real fan palm (mokolane) and colours are derived from soaking the fibres in natural plant dyes. The work is incredibly skilful and provides one of the most important sources of income for rural families.

One of the best places to purchase the work is the Shorobe Baskets Cooperative (p105) in Shorobe, north of Maun. While it is always better to buy craftwork in the area in which it is produced (you tend to get better prices and the proceeds go directly to the community in question), another good place to browse for high-quality crafts is Botswanacraft (p52) in Gaborone.

SAN CRAFTS

Traditional San crafts include ostrich-eggshell jewellery, leather aprons and bags, and strands of seeds and nuts (you may not be allowed to import these into some countries).

In recent years, traditional San painting has been experiencing something of a revival, with traditional themes wedded to contemporary techniques. The following are the best places to see San art and handicrafts:

➡ Botswanacraft Marketing (p52), Gaborone

➡ Gantsi Craft (p126), Ghanzi

➡ Kuru Art Project (p127), D'kar

Architecture

Traditional Botswana architecture is compact and beautiful, and blends well with the landscape. A typical village would have been a large, sprawling and densely populated affair, comprising hundreds of round mudbrick houses (ntlo or rondavel) topped with neat thatched roofs of motshikiri (thatching grass).

The mudbricks used for construction are ideally made from the concrete-like earth of the termite mound, and then plastered with a mixture of soil and cow dung. Often, the exterior is then decorated with a paint made from a mixture of cow dung and different coloured soils. The paint is spread by hand using the unique lekgapho designs (designs made entirely using the fingers), which are lovely and quite fanciful.

The thatch on the roofs is also an intricate business. Roof poles are taken from strong solid trees, lashed together with flexible branches and covered with tightly packed grass. When it's finished, the thatch is coated with oil and ash to discourage infestation by termites. Barring bad weather, a good thatching job can last five to 15 years and a rondavel can last 30 years or more.

These days, cement is the building material of choice, so the traditional home with its colourful designs may eventually die out. Decorated Homes in Botswana (1995), by Sandy and Elinah Grant, is an attempt to capture just some of the wonderful examples of traditional architecture and promote the art of home decorating.

One interesting and accessible village where visitors can see traditional Botswanan architecture is Mochudi, near Gaborone.

Dance

In traditional tribal societies, dance has an important symbolic role in expressing social values and marking the different stages of life. It is also a key component of traditional medicine and ancestor worship, where dance is a medium of communication with the spiritual realm. In a world without TV, it's also a great excuse for a community knees-up.

The best-documented dances in popular travel literature such as *The Healing Land* (Rupert Isaacson; 2001) and films such as *The Great Dance* (2001) are those of the San, whose traditional dances have many different meanings. They were a way to thank the gods for a successful hunt and plentiful rains, to cure the sick and to celebrate a girl's transition into womanhood. Implements used in San dancing include decorated dancing sticks, fly whisks created from wildebeest tails, and dancing rattles, which are leather strings through cocoons full of tiny stones or broken ostrich eggshells.

One of the more interesting dances is the *ndazula* dance, a rain dance used to thank the gods for a plentiful harvest. Another is *borankana,* which originated in southern Botswana but is now enjoyed all over the country. It features in dance and music competitions and exhibitions, and is practiced by school groups across Botswana. *Borankana,* which is Setswana for 'traditional entertainment', includes the unique *setlhako* and *sephumuso* rhythms, which feature in music by artists such as Nick Nkosanah Ndaba.

Most visitors will encounter traditional dancing in the rather staged displays at top-end safari camps. While they may lack the passion and spontaneity of traditional performances, such performances are important in preserving traditions that might otherwise be lost. A more genuine and less affected arena is the Maitisong Festival (p48), Botswana's biggest arts festival, held at the end of March in Gaborone.

Literature

The first work to be published in Setswana was the Holy Bible (completed by 1857), shortly followed by *The Pilgrim's Progress.* As you may gather from this, Botswana had little literary tradition to speak of until well into the 20th century.

Botswana's most famous modern literary figure was South African–born Bessie Head

---

BEST BOTSWANA READS

Fiction

The No. 1 Ladies' Detective Agency (Alexander McCall Smith; 1998) The book that created a phenomenon.

Jamestown Blues (Caitlin Davies; 1996) Set in a poor salt-mining town, it explores the disparities between expatriate and local life through the eyes of a young Motswana girl.

Whites (Norman Rush; 1986) A collection of short stories on expatriate life.

Mating (Norman Rush; 1991) A prize-winning comedy of manners featuring two Americans in 1980s Botswana.

Far and Beyon' (Unity Dow; 2000) Well-told chronicle of a family struggling with the often-contradictory pull of modern and traditional Botswana life.

Nonfiction

The Lost World of the Kalahari (Laurens van der Post; 1958) A classic and often eulogistic account of the disappearing culture of the San in the 1950s.

Cry of the Kalahari (Mark & Delia Owens; 1984) A wonderfully written tale of seven years spent living among the wildlife of the Kalahari.

Botswana Time (Will Randall; 2005) An endearing story of the author's time spent travelling with his school football team.

Twenty Chickens for a Saddle (Robyn Scott; 2008) Funny yet enlightening retelling of a childhood in eastern Botswana, including the Tuli Block.

Place of Reeds (Caitlin Davies; 2005) Fascinating story of life as a Motswana wife and mother.

Serowe: Village of the Rain Wind (Bessie Head; 1981) An intriguing cultural study of life in Serowe in eastern Botswana.

THE NO. 1 LADIES' DETECTIVE AGENCY & ITS AUTHOR

Gaborone may once have been one of the world's lesser known capitals, but Alexander McCall Smith's runaway international success *The No. 1 Ladies' Detective Agency* changed that forever. Based around the exploits of the Motswana Mma Precious Ramotswe, Botswana's first female detective, the book spawned a whole series of novels with names like *Morality for Beautiful Girls* (2001), *The Kalahari Typing School for Men* (2002) and *The Double Comfort Safari Club* (2010). This is crime writing without a hard edge, a delightfully whimsical and almost gentle series of tales that seems to fit perfectly within Botswana's relatively peaceful society.

The author was born in Rhodesia (now Zimbabwe) in 1948 and went on to become a leading international expert in medical law. Before turning his hand to crime fiction, he wrote a number of children's books, among them *The White Hippo* (1980) and *Akimbo and the Lion* (1992). He lectured at the University of Botswana from 1981 to 1984, but it was not until 1999 that *The No. 1 Ladies' Detective Agency* was published, changing his life forever and putting Botswana on the literary map. Although he lives in Scotland, he has sponsored a number of projects in Botswana. And if you're a fan of the series, don't miss one of the themed tours of Gaborone and be sure to visit the author's website (www.alexandermccallsmith.co.uk).

(1937–86), who fled apartheid in South Africa and settled in Sir Seretse Khama's village of Serowe. Her writings, many of which are set in Serowe, reflect the harshness and beauty of African village life and the physical attributes of Botswana itself. Her most widely read works include *Serowe – Village of the Rain Wind* (1981), *When Rain Clouds Gather* (1968), *Maru* (1971), *A Question of Power* (1973), *The Cardinals* (1993), *A Bewitched Crossroad* (1984), and *The Collector of Treasures* (1977), which is an anthology of short stories.

Since the 1980s Setswana novel writing has had something of a revival with the publication in English of novels like Andrew Sesinyi's *Love on the Rocks* (1983) and Gaele Sobott-Mogwe's haunting collection of short stories, *Colour Me Blue* (1995), which blends fantasy and reality with the everyday grit of African life.

Other novels that lend insight into contemporary Batswana life are *Jamestown Blues* (1997) and *Place of Reeds* (2005) by Caitlin Davies, who was married to a Motswana and lived in Botswana for 12 years.

Unity Dow, Botswana's first female high-court judge, also writes novels dealing with contemporary social issues in the country; we recommend *Far and Beyon'* (2002).

Poetry

Like many African cultures, Botswana has a rich oral tradition of poetry, and much of Botswana's literary heritage, its ancient myths and poetry, is still unavailable in translation. One of the few books that is available is *Bayeyi & Hambukushu: Tales from the Okavango* (1994), edited by Thomas J Larson, which is a primary source of oral poetry and stories from the Okavango Panhandle region.

Botswana's best-known poet is probably Barolong Seboni, who, in 1993, was poet in residence at the Scottish Poetry Library in Edinburgh. He has written several books of poems, including the short volume *Love Songs* (1994) and *Windsongs of the Kgalagadi* (1995), which details some of the Batswana traditions, myths and history that have been recited for centuries.

More modern poetry tends to highlight current issues. For example, *The Silent Bomb* aimed to promote awareness of HIV/AIDS. It was written by AIDS activist Billy Mosedame (1968–2004), who himself succumbed to the virus.

Music

Musical traditions run deeply through Botswana's cultural traditions, and have done so ever since the earliest San societies where men gathered around their campfires playing their thumb pianos (*mbira*) accompanied by music bows. Compact discs and cassettes of traditional San music are available in D'kar and at Botswanacraft (p52) in Gaborone.

Jazz, reggae, gospel and hip hop are the most popular forms of modern music, and almost nothing else features on Batswana radio or is played live in nightclubs and bars.

One reliable measure of local talent is *My African Dream,* Botswana's version of *Pop Idol.* The show is faithfully watched across the country and, as these things are wont to do, has plucked at the musical dreams of many a Gaborone-bound Motswana youth.

Jazz & Reggae

Bojazz is the colloquial term for a form of music called Botswana jazz. It has been immortalised by Nick Nkosanah Ndaba, among others, who recently released *Dawn of Bojazz* (2007), the first bojazz album to be produced in Botswana.

Another popular artist is Ras Baxton, a Rastafarian who plays what he calls 'tswana reggae', but he, like many other Batswana artists, has to go to South Africa to make a living. Banjo Mosele is huge all around the nation, while Bonjour Keipidile is perhaps the greatest living guitarist in Botswana.

Jazz performances are staged every few weeks in the winter (dry season) in and around Gaborone. Details are advertised in the English-language newspapers.

Fusion & Hip Hop

Gumba-gumba is a modern blend of Zulu and Tswana music mixed with a dose of traditional jazz – the word comes from the township slang for 'party'. Alfredo Mos is the father of *rumba kwasa,* that African bum-gyrating jive that foreigners have so much trouble emulating. Hot on his heels is *kwasa kwasa* king Franco, one of the most successful artists in Botswana at the moment, alongside the Wizards, Vee and Jeff Matheatau.

Wildly popular is Botswana's version of hip hop, championed by the Wizards, who fuse the style with ragga and R&B. It's nearly always been the case that talented Batswana musicians have had to move to South Africa to make a living, but as of this writing there was still some decent talent here, including Kast, Scar, Vee and Stagga Don Dada. Kwaito music, the South African township fusion of hip hop, house and all things that make booties shake, is also hugely popular.

Botswana Cuisine

Botswana's local cuisine may not be Africa's most exciting, but that doesn't mean you won't eat well. Many of the country's lodges have made excellence in the kitchen part of their appeal, and the major towns have some excellent restaurants from which to choose. If you're self-catering, well-stocked supermarkets inhabit most major towns and for atmosphere there's nothing quite like cooking your meal over a campfire out in the wilderness.

The Basics

Local Batswana cooking is, for the most part, aimed more at sustenance than exciting tastes. Forming the centre of most Batswana meals nowadays is *mabele* (sorghum) or *bogobe* (porridge made from sorghum), but these staples are rapidly being replaced by imported maize mealies, sometimes known by the Afrikaans name *mealie pap,* or just plain *pap.* This provides the base for an array of meat and vegetable sauces such as *seswaa* (shredded goat or lamb), *morogo* (wild spinach) or *leputshe* (wild pumpkin). For breakfast, you might be able to try *pathata* (sort of like an English muffin) or *megunya,* also known as fat cakes. These are little balls of fried dough that are kind of like doughnuts minus the hole and, depending on your taste, the flavour.

Sadly, most travellers rarely encounter local dishes, not least because locals generally eat at home and foreign self-drivers are usually also self-caterers. Some top-end safari lodges do make variations on some of the more conventional Batswana meat and vegetable recipes. In general, however, you'll be dining on international fare, some of which is quite sumptuous considering the logistical problems of getting food in and out of remote locations. One plate where local and international tastes converge is in the local obsession with steaks – Botswana's cattle industry is well regarded and its steaks are available in restaurants in most cities and larger towns.

Gaborone's Courtyard Restaurant (p50) is a rare and welcome exception to the separation of international clientele from local dishes – it serves guinea-fowl stew among other local dishes.

Otherwise, many hotels offer buffets, and there's always a good range of fruit and vegetables. In larger towns you'll even find a selection of Indian and Chinese restaurants.

Local Dishes

When it comes to local dishes, there's one you may find to be an acquired taste: mopane worms. These fat suckers are pulled off mopane trees and fried into little delicacies – they're tasty and a good source of protein. You might be able to buy some from ladies selling them by the bag in the Main Mall in Gaborone; otherwise, they're pretty common up in Francistown.

Kalahari Cooking

The more challenging environment of the Kalahari means that the San have an extraordinary pantry, including desert plants such as *morama,* which produces leguminous pods that contain edible beans. There is also an immense tuber that contains large quantities of water. Other desert delectables include marula fruit, wild plums, berries, tsama melons, wild cucumbers and honey. There's also a type of edible fungus *(grewia flava)* related to the European truffle but now presented by marketing people as the 'Kalahari truffle'.

Drinks

Decent locally made beers include Castle Lager (made under licence from the South African brewery), St Louis Special Light and Lion Lager. Also available are the excellent Windhoek Lager (from Namibia) and Zambezi Lager (from Zimbabwe).

Traditional drinks are plentiful. Legal home brews include the common *bojalwa,* an inexpensive sprouted-sorghum beer that is brewed commercially as Chibuku. Another serious drink is made from fermented marula fruit. Light and nonintoxicating *mageu* is made from mealies or sorghum mash. Another is *madila,* a thickened sour milk that is used as a relish or drunk ('eaten' would be a more appropriate term) plain.

Mosukujane tea and *lengane* tea are used to treat headaches/nausea and arthritis respectively. They're a bit strong in flavour, but locals faithfully tout their remedial properties.

Environment

Botswana's environment stands front and centre to any visit to the country, from its stirring natural attributes of desert and delta to the wildlife that populates these extreme landscapes. Endangered species and species protection are among the most important environmental issues facing the country, but so, too, are the fraught problems of water scarcity; creeping desertification; managing the difficult balance between the lucrative livestock and tourism sectors; and the emotive issue of commercial or trophy hunting.

The Land

Botswana is the geographic heart of sub-Saharan Africa, extending over 1100km from north to south and 960km from east to west, an area of 582,000 sq km that's equivalent in size to France. The country is entirely landlocked, and is bordered to the south and southeast by South Africa, across the Limpopo and Molopo Rivers; to the northeast by Zimbabwe; and to the north and west by Namibia.

THE KALAHARI

Around 100 million years ago the supercontinent Gondwanaland dramatically broke up. As the land mass ripped apart, the edges of the African continent rose up, forming the mountain ranges of Southern and central Africa. Over the millennium, water and wind weathered these highlands, carrying the fine dust inland to the Kalahari Basin. At 2.5 million sq km, it's the earth's largest unbroken tract of sand, stretching from northern South Africa to eastern Namibia and Angola, and to Zambia and Zimbabwe in the west.

Depending on who you believe, between 68% and 85% of the country, including the entire central and southwestern regions, is taken up by the Kalahari. The shifting sand dunes that compose a traditional desert are found only in the far southwest, in the Kgalagadi Transfrontier Park. In the northeast are the great salty deserts of the Makgadikgadi Pans; in ancient times part of a vast superlake, they're now the largest (about 12,000 sq km) complex of salt pans in the world and considered to be part of the Kalahari.

In Botswana, large tracts of the Kalahari are protected, with at least five protected areas (listed from north to south):

➡ Nxai Pans National Park (p77)

➡ Makgadikgadi Pans National Park (p75)

➡ Central Kalahari Game Reserve (p129)

➡ Khutse Game Reserve (p135)

➡ Kgalagadi Transfrontier Park (p138)

OKAVANGO DELTA

The Okavango Delta is one of Africa's most extraordinary landscapes, not to mention the antidote to the Kalahari's endless sea of sand. Covering between 13,000 and 18,000 sq km, it snakes into the country from Angola to form a watery paradise of convoluted channels and islands that appear and disappear depending on the water levels. The delta is home to more than 2000 plant species, 450 bird species and 65 fish species, not to mention an estimated 200,000 large mammals.

The delta owes its existence to a tectonic trough in the Kalahari basin, a topographical depression that ensures that the waters of the Okavango River evaporate or are drunk by plants without ever reaching the sea; the delta is extremely flat with no more than a 2m variation in the land's altitude, which means that the waters simply come to a halt. The delta's waters surge and subside at the behest of the rains in far-off Angola, and every year around 11 cu km of water flood into the delta. The flooding is seasonal, beginning in the Angolan highlands in January and February, the waters travelling approximately 1200km in a month. Having reached the delta, the waters disperse across it from March to June, before peaking in July and August – during these months, the water surface area of the delta can be three times that of the nonflooding periods.

MOUNTAINS

Botswana could be one of the flattest countries on earth, but there are a few sites of topographical interest. The country's highest point above sea level is the rather modest Otse Hill (1489m), which lies around 45km south of Gaborone.

Of far greater interest are the Tsodilo Hills in the country's far northwest, with dramatic scenery and prehistoric rock art; the Tswapong Hills, a range of low, flat-topped hills cut through with vertiginous canyons, good for hiking and birdwatching; and the Tuli Block, shadowing the Limpopo River in Botswana's far east, with otherworldy kopjes (hills) rising up from the riverine plains.

Wildlife

Botswana is home to anywhere between 160 and 500 different mammal species, 593 recorded bird species, 150 different reptiles, over 8000 insect and spider species, and more than 3100 types of plants and trees.

LIONS

Lions may be the easiest of the big cats to spot – leopards are notoriously secretive and largely keep to the undergrowth, while cheetahs live in populations of much lower density and can be extremely shy. But don't let appearances fool you: the lion is under threat.

Scientists such as the peak cat conservation body Panthera (www.panthera.org) estimate that fewer than 20,000 lions remain in Africa. Only six lion populations in Africa – the Okavango Delta is one of these – are sufficiently protected to hold at least 1000 lions, the conservation gold standard that Panthera applies for guaranteeing the long-term survival of the species. The most recent estimates for Botswana suggest a population of around 2700 lions (or roughly 14% of all lions left in Africa). Of these, the most important populations are the 1750 lions in the Okavango Delta and northern savannah woodlands (including Chobe and Savuti), around 300 in the CKGR, and approximately 500 in the Kgalagadi Transfrontier Park (of which 350 are thought to reside on the Botswana side of the border). As such, Botswana is one of the lion population's most important strongholds.

Like lions elsewhere, lions in Botswana are facing threats from poisoning, either in retaliation for killing livestock or encroaching onto farming lands, bush-meat poaching and habitat loss.

ELEPHANTS

According to the results of the Great Elephant Census (www.greatelephantcensus.com), published in 2016, Botswana has more elephants within its borders than any other country on earth – an estimated 130,451 out of 352,271, which represents more than a third of African elephants left on the planet. According to the same continent-wide survey, Africa's elephant population fell by a staggering 30% in the preceding seven years. By these standards, Botswana – which has lost 15% of its elephant population since 2010 – is doing better than other countries, although the figures are still deeply concerning; some 7% of elephants seen from the air in Botswana during the census were carcasses.

Botswana's elephants overwhelmingly inhabit the country's north, spread across the Okavango Delta and Chobe National Park. The Chobe population in particular, which may number more than 70,000 elephants, represents the densest concentration of elephants on the planet.

BOTSWANA ENVIRONMENT

RHINOS

Rhinoceroses were once plentiful across Botswana, particularly in the north, with black rhinos concentrated around the Chobe River and white rhinos more widely spread across Chobe, Moremi and elsewhere in the Okavango Delta. But the poaching holocaust in the 1970s and 1980s that sent numbers of both black and white rhinos plummeting across Africa saw the rhino all but disappear from Botswana. By 1992 the black rhino was considered extinct in Botswana, with just 19 white rhinos remaining in the country.

At around the same time, the 4300-hectare Khama Rhino Sanctuary was established, and all remaining rhinos were shut away in the sanctuary in a bid to save the species. The sanctuary has been something of a success story, now protecting around 30 white rhinos and four blacks.

Better still, in 2001 the Botswana Rhino Reintroduction Project, a collaboration between the government, conservation groups and tourism operators (among them &Beyond, Wilderness Safaris and Great Plains Conservation), began the process of sending rhinos once more out into the Botswana wild. At the time of writing, official estimates put Botswana's wild rhino population (mostly in Moremi Game Reserve and elsewhere in the Okavango Delta) at between 77 and 100. In 2015, airlifts of rhinos from overcrowded or imperilled South African parks began, and over 100 white rhinos and 42 black rhinos have since been translocated. The goal is to have at least 250 white rhinos and 80 black rhinos in the wild in Botswana by 2020.

FENCES: A HISTORY OF CONFLICT

Fences are a big issue in Botswana. At its core, the issue is simple: wildlife populations and the country's lucrative livestock herds don't mix, and so the government has built fences stretching for thousands of kilometres to separate them. In practice, it's all a bit more complicated than that.

The main problem with Botswana's fences are that many prevent wild animals from migrating to water sources along age-old seasonal routes; national parks often enclose only part of their migratory routes. As a result, Botswana's wildebeest population has declined by 99% over the past 20 years and all remaining buffaloes and zebras are stranded and in decline because of the fences.

The worst disaster occurred in the drought of 1983, in which the Kuke Fence barred herds of wildebeests heading for the Okavango waters, resulting in the death of 65,000 animals. The final section of Mark and Delia Owens' *Cry of the Kalahari* (1984) chronicles another heartbreaking example, with wildebeest from the southern Kalahari suddenly barred from their grazing grounds around Lake Xau. The Owens' publicising of the issue ultimately led to their expulsion from the country.

The 80km-long Northern Buffalo Fence (a fence designed to separate wild buffalo herds from domestic livestock populations north of the Okavango Delta) has opened a vast expanse of wildlife-rich – but as yet unprotected – territory to cattle ranching. Safari operators wanted the fence set as far north as possible to protect the seasonally flooded Selinda Spillway; prospective cattle ranchers wanted it set as far south as possible, maximising new grazing lands. The government sided with the ranchers and the fence opened up to 20% of the Okavango Delta to commercial ranching.

In 2003 the controversy started up again with the proposal of a new cordon fence around the Makgadikgadi Pans. When (or if) completed, the fence will extend for 480km and is intended to limit predator-livestock conflict along the Boteti River. However, on the completion of the western section of the fence, the Environmental Investigation Agency (www.eia-international.org) found that the alignment failed to adhere to the suggestions of the Department of Wildlife & National Parks Environmental Appraisal, and as a result the majority of the Boteti River now lies outside the park, cutting off the animals within.

The net effect was immediately felt: in early 2005 some 300 zebras died trying to reach the river. In addition, the cattle fence around the Okavango Delta has already been damaged by roving elephant herds. The issue has been largely frozen in time since then and the fence has been allowed to deteriorate to such an extent that elephants and other wildlife now routinely cross the Boteti River unimpeded.

A recent upsurge in rhino poaching – rhino horn had an estimated black-market value of US$60,000 per kilo in 2016 – has seen the number of rhinos killed in neighbouring South Africa rise from 13 in 2007 to as many as 1338 in 2015; with approximately 18,000 rhinos, South Africa is home to an estimated 90% of the world white rhinoceros population.

AFRICAN WILD DOGS

One of Botswana's most charismatic creatures, the African wild dog (also known as the Cape hunting dog) is under serious threat. Where once half a million wild dogs roamed 39 African countries, today only 3000 to 5300 remain in the wild in just 14 countries.

African wild dogs live in packs of up to 28 animals, which may account for the fact that they have one of the highest hunting success rates (as high as 70%) of all carnivores – that and their maximum speed of 66km/h. Their preferred prey includes impala, red lechwe, wildebeest, steenbok and warthog.

Moremi Game Reserve is believed to be home to 30% of the world's population, with the Linyanti Marshes one of the best places to spot wild dog packs. Numbers are lower, but the species also persists in the CKGR and the Tuli Block.

REPTILES & AMPHIBIANS

Botswana's dry lands are home to over 150 species of reptile. These include 72 species of snake, such as the poisonous Mozambique spitting cobra, Egyptian cobra and black mamba. Although about 80% of snakes in Botswana are not venomous, watch out for the deadly puff adder, much more frequently seen than the cobras and mamba. Tree snakes, known as boomslangs, are also common in the delta.

Lizards are everywhere; the largest are *leguaans* (water monitors), docile creatures that reach over 2m in length. Smaller versions, savannah *leguaans*, inhabit small hills and drier areas. Also present in large numbers are geckos, chameleons and rock-plated lizards.

Although Nile crocodiles are threatened elsewhere in Southern Africa, the Okavango Delta is full of them. You will hear rather than see them while gliding through the channels in a *mokoro* (traditional dugout canoe).

Frogs of every imaginable shape, size and colour are more delightful; they jump from reeds to a *mokoro* and back again, and provide an echoing chorus throughout the delta (and elsewhere such as the Boteti River in Makgadikgadi Pans National Park) at night.

INSECTS & SPIDERS

Botswana boasts about 8000 insect and spider species. The most colourful butterflies can be found along the Okavango Panhandle (the northwestern extension of the delta), and include African monarchs and citrus swallowtails. Other insects of note include stick insects, expertly camouflaged among the reeds of the Okavango Delta; large, scary but harmless button spiders; and sac spiders, which look harmless but are poisonous (although rarely fatal) and live mainly in rural homes. The delta is also home to grasshoppers, mopane worms and locusts, as well as mosquitoes and tsetse flies in increasing and potentially dangerous numbers.

Scorpions are not uncommon in the Kalahari; although their sting is not fatal, it can be painful.

BIRDS

Botswana is not only a big wildlife country but also a birding paradise. Between September and March, when the delta is flush with water, you should be able to train the lenses of your binoculars on any number of Botswana's 593 recorded species, including the delta's famous African skimmers, the endangered wattled crane, slaty egrets, African jacanas, bee-eaters, pygmy geese and the shy Pel's fishing owl. You can still see many bird species in the dry season, when it's often easier to spot them around the few remaining water sources.

Most of Botswana's best birding is concentrated in the north of the country around the Okavango Delta, including the Okavango Panhandle, the Chobe Riverfront, the CKGR, Khama Rhino Sanctuary, and the Tuli Block, especially around the Limpopo River.

One especially good site is the Nata Bird Sanctuary; home to over a quarter of Botswana's birds. The sanctuary is covered in a sea of pink flamingos and other migratory birds, during the rainy season (November to March).

Inevitably, the birdlife in Botswana is under threat from overgrazing, urban sprawl and insecticides that are used to tackle the scourge of tsetse flies that sometimes plague the delta.

Endangered among Botswana's birds are wattled cranes and African skimmers. Cape Griffon vultures, which are protected in the Mannyelanong Game Reserve in Otse, also have important breeding colonies in the Moremi Gorge in the Tswapong Hills in Botswana's east.

USEFUL RESOURCES

Birding Botswana (p94) is a Maun-based operator specialising in birdwatching safaris.

BirdLife Botswana (✆ 319 0540; www. birdlifebotswana.org.bw) is BirdLife International's local chapter and is actively involved in conservation projects, such as building observation posts, and organising birdwatching trips.

PLANTS

More than 2500 species of plant and 650 species of tree have been recorded in Botswana.

The Okavango Delta enjoys a riparian environment dominated by marsh grasses, water lilies, reeds and papyrus, and is dotted with well-vegetated islands thick with palms, acacias, leadwood and sausage trees. At the other extreme, the Kalahari is characterised by all sorts of savannah, including bush savannah with acacia thorn trees, grass savannah and arid shrub savannah in the southwest.

The country's only deciduous mopane forests are in the north, where six forest reserves harbour stands of commercial timber, as well as both *mongonga* and marula trees. Also common around Botswana are camel thorn trees, which some animals find tasty and which the San use for firewood and medicinal purposes; and *motlopi* trees, also called shepherd's tree, which have edible roots.

For more on the plant life of the Okavango, pick up a copy of *Common Wildflowers of the Okavango Delta* (1998) and *Trees & Shrubs of the Okavango Delta* (1998) by Veronica Roodt. Both have informative descriptions accompanied by useful paintings and drawings.

Environmental Issues

As a relatively large country with a very low population density, Botswana is one of Africa's most unpolluted and pristine regions. Botswana faces most of the ecological problems experienced elsewhere in Africa, such as land degradation and desertification, deforestation (around 21% of the country is covered by forests), water scarcity and urban sprawl. In addition to these, some major ecological and conservation issues continue to affect the country's deserts, wetlands and savannahs.

THE FENCE DILEMMA

If you've been stopped at a veterinary checkpoint, or visited the eastern Okavango Delta, you'll be familiar with the country's 3000km of 1.5m-high 'buffalo fence', officially called the Veterinary Cordon Fence. It's not a single fence but a series of high-tensile steel-wire barriers that run cross-country through some of Botswana's wildest terrain.

The fences were first erected in 1954 to segregate wild buffalo herds from domestic free-range cattle in order to thwart the spread of foot-and-mouth disease. Botswana's beef-farming industry is one of the most important in the country, both economically and in terms of the status conferred by cattle upon their owners in Batswana society. At the same time, wildlife tourism is a major money-earner and the country's international reputation is often tied to its perceived willingness to protect the country's wildlife. Balancing these two significant yet sometimes-conflicting industries is one of the most complicated challenges facing Botswana's government.

DANGERS THREATENING THE DELTA

Despite its status as a biodiversity hot spot, Unesco World Heritage–listed site and the largest Ramsar Wetland Site on the planet, the Okavango Delta has no international protection (apart from the Moremi Game Reserve), despite the fact that many prominent conservationists consider it to be under threat.

Wetland ecosystems are disappearing globally at an alarming rate, partly due to climate change and partly due to mismanagement and unsustainable development, and the Okavango Delta is no exception. Already a survey team from the DWNP

BOTSWANA'S ENDANGERED SPECIES

According to the International Union for the Conservation of Nature (IUCN), species which are listed as Vulnerable in Botswana include the cheetah, black-footed cat, lion and hippo. In greater trouble and listed as Endangered is the African wild dog, while the black rhino is considered Critically Endangered.

THE HUNTING DEBATE

In 2012 Botswana announced to the world that it would ban all commercial or trophy hunting within its borders from 2014. The hunting industry, previously an important money-earner for the country with numerous private hunting concessions across the country's north, was aghast, while many conservationists applauded the ban. But the ban remains controversial, including within Botswana, and the issue is far more more complicated than it may first appear.

While abhorrent to many conservationists, some recognise that controlled hunting can play an important part in preserving species. If we can distil the conservation argument in favour of hunting to its essence, it would be as follows. Tourism revenues (whether national park fees or lodge revenues) have too often failed to reach local communities, reinforcing a perception that wildlife belongs to the government. Hunting on private concessions, however, generally attracts massive fees (lion licences in Southern Africa can sell for US$20,000), of which, the theory goes, a significant proportion is fed back into local community projects, thereby giving wildlife a tangible economic value for local people. Hunting, the argument goes, also makes productive use of land which is considered unsuitable for photographic tourism, either because of its remoteness or infrastructure. If controlled strictly – through the use of quotas and killing only a limited number of solitary male lions who are past their prime, for example – hunting can, according to its proponents, play a part in saving species from extinction.

At the same time, opponents of hunting argue that the whole debate is premised on the failure of governments and private operators to fairly redistribute their revenues from non lethal forms of tourism – why, they ask, should we expect that hunting be any different? They also argue that the solution lies in a fairer distribution of tourism revenues and greater community involvement in conservation rather than in killing the very animals upon which tourism depends. And finally, some critics point to the double standards of arresting and imprisoning locals who hunt wildlife (whether for commercial or subsistence reasons), while permitting rich (and usually white) hunters to shoot animals during short visits to the continent. Among the biggest critics of the hunting industry is respected wildlife film-maker Dereck Joubert, who, along with Great Plains Conservation (www.greatplainsconservation.com), has transformed Botswana's Selinda Concession from a hunting concession into one of the most exclusive wildlife experiences – wildlife has returned in great numbers and the economic model seems to be working.

The debate continues.

and BirdLife Botswana has concluded that the delta is shrinking. The Kubango River – originating in the highlands of Angola – carries less water and floods the delta for a shorter period of the year.

Other key threats include overgrazing, which is already resulting in accelerated land and soil degradation, commercial gill netting and illegal fire lighting, unplanned developments in Angola as post-civil-war resettlement occurs, and pressure for new and increased abstraction of water for mining, domestic use, agriculture and tourism. Most worrying of these is the proposed extraction of water from the Okavango River to supply the growing needs of Namibia. One such proposal is the construction of a 1250km-long pipeline from the Okavango River to Namibia's capital, Windhoek, which first reared its head in 1997 and has grown and faltered in fits and starts since.

In 1994 Botswana, Namibia and Angola signed the Okavango River Basin Commission (www.okacom.org), aimed at coordinating the sustainable management of the delta's waters. Although the commission has high principles, the practicalities on the ground are far from simple and the process of moving towards a sustainable management plan and eventual treaty has been very slow. As Angola, the basin state where 95% of the water flow originates, settles into its first period of peace in some 30 years, it is hoped that the pace will accelerate.

POACHING

Poaching is not common in Botswana due to its relatively stable economy, which makes such a risky and illegal undertaking unnecessary and unattractive. Also, transporting hides and tusks overland from remote areas of Botswana to ports hundreds of kilometres away in other countries is well nigh impossible, especially considering Botswana's well-patrolled borders, which are monitored by the Botswana Defence Force (BDF). What little poaching there is seems to be 'for the pot' – local people supplementing their diets by hunting wild animals – rather than large-scale commercial enterprises.

National Parks & Reserves

Around one-third of Botswana's land mass is officially protected, representing one of the highest proportions of protected areas on earth. According to the United Nations Environment Program (UNEP), the figure is 30.2%. Government sources put it at around 17% of the country locked away in parks or game reserves, with another 20% in 'wildlife management areas' (WMA). Most parks in Botswana are characterised by vast open spaces with a few private safari concessions, next to no infrastructure and limited amenities.

Visiting National Parks

All public national parks and reserves in Botswana are run by the **Department of Wildlife & National Parks** (DWNP; Map p52; 381 0774; dwnp@gov.bw; 7.30am-4.30pm Mon-Fri, 7.30am-12.45pm & 1.45-4.30pm Sat, 7.30am-12.45pm Sun). There are other park offices in Maun (p103) and Kasane (p83), as well as a rarely visited outpost in Kang (p138).

NATIONAL PARKS – BEST OF BOTSWANA

PARK	FEATURES	ACTIVITIES	BEST TIME
Central Kalahari Game Reserve (CKGR)	52,800 sq km; one of the largest protected areas in the world; semi-arid grassland	wildlife viewing; walking; visiting San villages	year-round
Chobe National Park	11,700 sq km; mosaic of grassland and woodland; high elephant population	wildlife viewing; birdwatching; fishing	Jun-Oct
Kgalagadi Transfrontier Park	38,000 sq km; straddles the South African border; semi-arid grassland	wildlife viewing; birdwatching	year-round
Khama Rhino Sanctuary	43 sq km; last refuge of Botswana's rhinos	wildlife viewing; birdwatching	May-Oct
Khutse Game Reserve	2590 sq km; adjoins Central Kalahari Game Reserve; same features	wildlife viewing; walking; visiting San villages	year-round
Makgadikgadi & Nxai Pans NPs	7300 sq km; largest salt pans in the world; migratory zebras and wildebeest; flamingos	wildlife viewing; trekking with San; quad biking	Mar-Jul
Moremi Game Reserve	3800 sq km; grassland, flood plains and swamps; huge wildlife density	wildlife viewing; walking; scenic flights; boating	Jun-Oct
Northern Tuli Game Reserve	collection of private reserves; unique rock formations	wildlife viewing; horse riding; walking; night drives	May-Sep

There are a few things worth remembering about visiting Botswana's national parks and reserves:

➡ Park fees have long been slated for a significant rise – we thought it would have happened by now, but don't be surprised if they're significantly above those listed here by the time you arrive.

➡ Although there are exceptions (such as the Chobe Riverfront section of Chobe National Park) and it may be possible on rare occasions to get park rangers to bend the rules, no one is allowed into a national park or reserve without an accommodation booking for that park.

➡ It is possible to pay park entrance fees at park entrance gates, after a spell in which places had to be reserved and fees paid in advance at DWNP offices in Gaborone, Maun or Kasane (you'll still see some signs around Botswana to that effect). Even so, you should always try to book and pay in advance.

➡ The gates for each DWNP park are open from 6am to 6.30pm (1 April to 30 September) and from 5.30am to 7pm (1 October to 31 March). It is vital that all visitors be out of the park, or settled into their campsite, outside of these hours. Driving after dark is strictly forbidden (although it is permitted in private concessions).

CAMPING & BOOKING

The Department of Wildlife & National Parks runs a small number of campsites (especially in the Central Kalahari Game Reserve and Kgalagadi Transfrontier Park), and reservations for any DWNP campsite can be made up to 12 months in advance at the DWNP offices in Maun (p103) or Gaborone (p164); Chobe National Park bookings are also possible at the Kasane DWNP office (p83). It's at these offices that you can also pay the park entry fees (upon presenting proof of a confirmed campsite reservation).

We recommend that, wherever possible, you make the bookings in person or arrange for someone to do so on your behalf. In theory, the DWNP also allows you to make bookings over the phone or via email, but in practice getting anyone to answer the phone or reply to emails is far more challenging than it should be. If you do manage to make a phone or email booking, insist on receiving (either by fax, email or letter) a receipt with a refer-

ence number on it that you must keep and quote if you need to change your reservation.

When making the reservation, you need to tell the DWNP:

➡ the name of the preferred campsite(s) within the park – in order of preference if listing more than one

➡ the number of nights required, and the date of your arrival at and departure from the park and campsite

➡ the number of adults and children camping

➡ the vehicle's number plates and also the country in which the vehicle is registered (this may be waived if you don't yet have a vehicle)

➡ proof of your status if you are not paying 'foreigner' rates.

Once you have booked it is difficult to change anything, so make sure to plan your trip well and allow enough time to get there and look around. A refund (less a 10% administration charge) is only possible with more than 30 days' notice.

COSTS

Infants and children up to the age of seven are entitled to free entry into the national parks.

	COST FOR FOREIGNERS
adult	P120
child (8-17)	P60
camping	P50
vehicles <3500kg	P50

SURVIVAL GUIDE

ℹ Directory A–Z

ACCOMMODATION

Botswana's accommodation is a story of extremes. At one end, there are fabulously located campsites for self-drivers (the closest the country comes to budget accommodation outside the main towns). At the other, there are top-end lodges where prices can be eye-wateringly high. In between, you will find some midrange options in the major towns and places such as the Okavango Panhandle, but elsewhere there's very little for the midrange (and nothing for the noncamping budget) traveller.

Bed Levy & Government Tax

Note that all hotels, lodges, campsites and other forms of accommodation are required by the government to charge a P10 bed levy per person per night. This levy is rarely, if ever, included in quoted accommodation rates.

In addition to the levy, a 12% government tax is levied on hotels and lodges (but not all campsites) and, unlike the levy, *is* usually included in prices.

Seasons

While most budget and midrange options tend to have a standard room price, many top-end places change their prices according to season. High season is usually from June to November (and may also apply to Christmas, New Year and Easter, depending on the lodge), low season corresponds to the rains (December to March or April) and the shoulder is a short April and May window. The only exception is the Kalahari, where June to November is generally considered to be low season.

Camping

Just about everywhere of interest, including all major national parks, has a campsite. Once the domain of the Department of Wildlife and National Parks (DWNP), many of the campsites are now privately run.

The change in ownership has seen prices rise considerably. In some cases, the companies in question have upgraded the ablutions blocks to have hot and cold showers and flush toilets, and they generally make sure the sites are in good nick. Others do little to maintain their sites, offer cold bucket showers and pit toilets and run inefficient booking systems. All campsites have braai (barbecue) pits. The prices we've given are per person and per night unless otherwise stated.

All campsites *must* be booked in advance and they fill up fast in busy periods, such as during South African school holidays. It is very important to remember that you will not be allowed into almost every park run by the DWNP without a reservation for a campsite.

Camping areas are usually small, often with only two or three places to pitch a tent and/or park a vehicle.

SLEEPING PRICE RANGES

The following price ranges refer to a double room with bathroom. Unless otherwise stated, breakfast is included in the price. Upmarket places tend to price in US dollars rather than pula.

$ less than P800 (US$75)

$$ P800-1600 (US$75-150)

$$$ more than P1600 (US$150)

Outside of the parks and reserves, some hotels and lodges also provide camping areas. Most private and hotel/lodge campsites have sit-down toilets, showers (often hot), braai pits and washing areas. One definite attraction is that campers can use the hotel bars and restaurants and splash around the hotel swimming pool for free.

Other places where camping is possible include the Tsodilo Hills and Khama Rhino Sanctuary.

Elsewhere, camping in the wild is permitted outside national parks, reserves, private land and away from government freehold areas. If you want to camp near a village, obtain permission from the village leader or police station and enquire about a suitable site.

Hotels

Every major town has at least one hotel, and the larger towns and tourist areas, such as Gaborone, Maun, Francistown and Kasane, offer several in different price ranges. In general, midrange and top-end travellers are well looked after, but budget travellers will struggle to find anything as cheap as the budget accommodation in Namibia (the really cheap places in Botswana often double as brothels). There's a relatively high demand for hotel rooms in Gaborone, in particular from business travellers, so it pays to book ahead here and also elsewhere in the high season.

The range of hotel accommodation available includes rondavels, which are detached rooms or cottages with a private bathroom; B&B-type places, often with a shared bathroom (mostly in Gaborone); motel-style units with a private bathroom and, sometimes, cooking facilities, usually along the highways of eastern Botswana; and luxury hotels in major towns.

Lodges & Tented Camps

Botswana's claim to being Africa's most exclusive destination is built around its luxury lodges (sometimes called 'camps'). You'll find them where there are decent concentrations of wildlife, most notably in Chobe National Park, the Tuli Block, Moremi Game Reserve, all over the Okavango Delta and, to a lesser extent, the parks and reserves of the Kalahari. It's impossible to generalise about them, other than to say that most pride themselves on their isolation, exclusivity, luxury and impeccable service. Most feature permanent or semipermanent luxury tents, a communal dining area overlooking a water hole or other important geographical feature, and a swimming pool.

For many visitors, they're once-in-a-lifetime places with accommodation rates to match – some start at around US$1000/1500 per person per night in the low/high season, but many cost considerably more than that. Usually included in these rates are all meals, some drinks and most wildlife drives and other activities. Most places are only

WHAT NOT TO EXPECT FROM YOUR LUXURY LODGE

The experience of staying in a remote safari lodge invariably involves high levels of service and comfort, but there are some things that, it may surprise you to learn, your rather large nightly rate does not necessarily entitle you to (although there is considerable variety in what's on offer):

➡ **24-hour electricity** Some camps have it, some don't.

➡ **In-room electricity** Some have power points in your room or tent, others have an area where you can charge your phone, laptop or camera batteries in the main communal area. In some camps, candlelight and gas lanterns provide the only lights in your tent.

➡ **Wi-fi** Very few lodges have wi-fi, even in communal areas. Although most will have some way of communicating with the outside world in case of emergency, these are not generally available to guests. Check with the company in question when making your booking.

➡ **Private game drives** In most lodges you'll be partnered with other guests with whom you will share a boat or game-drive vehicle. If you want a private vehicle and guide, you must usually pay extra. On most occasions, the shared nature causes few problems, but it may be less than ideal if you have a particular interest (eg birdwatching) or desire to spend longer out on the trail or watching that pride of lions sleep under a tree.

accessible by 4WD transfer or air; the latter will cost an extra US$150 to US$200 per leg.

ACTIVITIES

Such is the nature of travelling in Botswana that even the most tranquil holidays will involve some form of activities, from rugged 4WD excursions to poling gently along the Okavango Delta's waterways in a traditional *mokoro* (dugout canoe). Beyond these activities there are few options, and most activities that are possible are organised as part of lodge packages rather than designed for individual travellers.

Hiking

Botswana lags behind neighbours Namibia and Zambia as a hiking destination, although a number of treks are possible.

Walking safaris in the company of an armed guard form part of the available activities at many lodges, and leaving the safety of your vehicle will sharpen your senses and your awareness of your surroundings. Places where such hiking excursions along nature trails are possible include the Okavango Delta, the Central Kalahari Game Reserve (CKGR) and the Makgadikgadi Pans. The treks run out of the luxury lodges of the Makgadikgadi Pans or the CKGR, for example, are a fascinating opportunity to explore the arid environs with San guides, who can point out the hidden details of the landscape and its specially adapted flora and fauna.

You don't need to be staying at a luxury lodge or tented camp to explore a small corner of the delta on foot, as many of the *mokoro* expeditions organised from Maun include walking components. Also, a small but growing number of mobile safaris in the delta and Moremi Game Reserve, organised from Maun, involve multiday hikes.

Options are limited for more free-range trekking, but the Tsodilo Hills, where trails lead up to thousands of rock-art sites, is undoubtedly the premier spot. Guides are available from the main campsite in the region. Another possibility is the Tswapong Hills in the country's east, which sees very few tourists. For both, you'll need to be entirely self-sufficient.

Horse Riding

Cantering among herds of zebras and wildebeest is an unforgettable experience, and the horse-riding safaris in Botswana are second to none. You'll need to be an experienced rider as most horseback safaris in Botswana don't take beginners – after all, you need to be able to get yourself out of trouble should you encounter it.

Places where such safaris are possible:

African Animal Adventures (p94) Expeditions from Maun.

Grassland Safari Lodge (p128) Safaris into the Central Kalahari Game Reserve.

Mashatu Game Reserve (p68) In the Tuli Block.

Ride Botswana (📞71 671 608, 72 484 354; www.ridebotswana.com) Based in Maun, with expeditions to the delta and Kalahari.

Uncharted Africa (p73) Out onto the salt pans of Makgadikgadi.

Mokoro Trips

Travelling around the channels of the Okavango Delta in a *mokoro* is a wonderful experience that is not to be missed. The *mokoro* is poled along the waterways by a skilled poler, much like an African gondola. Although you won't be spotting much wildlife from such a low viewpoint, it's a great way to appreciate the delta's birdlife and gain an appreciation, hopefully from a distance, of the formidable bulk of hippos.

Motorboat & Fishing Trips

The only two places where motorboats can operate for wildlife cruises and fishing trips are along the Okavango and Chobe Rivers.

For fishing, the only stretches of water to consider are the deep and fast-flowing waters of the Okavango Panhandle. The most popular form of freshwater fishing is fly-fishing for tigerfish, although pike, barbel (catfish) and bream are also plentiful. Tigerfish season runs from September to June, while barbel are present from mid-September to December.

Quad Bikes

Some lodges in the Makgadikgadi Pans area in northeastern Botswana offer trips across the expansive salt pans on four-wheeled quad bikes, also called ATVs (all-terrain vehicles). These are safe to drive, require no experience, do not need a car or motorbike licence and are great fun. Most operators are reputable, but sadly in recent years some travellers have begun to bring their own quad bikes to Botswana, where they criss-cross the pans with little concern for the wildlife or fragile ecosystems of the area.

Scenic Flights

A scenic flight of fancy in a light aircraft or helicopter high above the Okavango Delta is a thrilling activity. These can be arranged either in Maun directly with the operator or through your accommodation.

---

24 HOURS IN A SAFARI CAMP

All of the fly-in, luxury lodges and safari camps in the Okavango Delta and elsewhere follow a remarkably similar formula when it comes to your daily program.

Wake-up This usually takes place at 6am, but can be as early as 5.30am or as late as 6.30am. You can, of course, ask for a lie-in, but unless you have a private game drive organised (and paid for), this will most often mean missing the morning activity. Sometimes a staff member will bring you tea, coffee or juice, though more often it's a firm but discreet 'good morning!' from outside your tent or room. Once they hear a response and know you're awake, they'll leave.

Breakfast This happens around half an hour after your wake-up call.

Morning activity Whether it's a game drive, nature walk or a *mokoro* (dugout canoe) trip, this usually begins around 7am, though a 6.30am departure is generally preferable to make the most of the morning's best light.

Brunch/lunch Unless your activity involves being out all day (in which case, you'll have lunch somewhere out on the trail), you'll most often return to camp around 10.30am or 11am. You'll be given time to return to your room and freshen up before brunch or lunch is served, usually around half an hour after your return to camp (11.30am is the most common time).

Relax After brunch/lunch you're free to return to your room or tent for a siesta, go for a swim in the swimming pool, or hang out in the bar – this is free time and how you spend it is usually up to you.

High tea This old, colonial-era institution is alive and well. At around 3.30pm or 4pm, guests are served afternoon tea, which in some lodges can be quite lavish and large, and more simple in others. It usually involves coffee and tea, while you may be offered something a little stronger.

Afternoon activity At around 4pm or 4.30pm, you'll head out on a game drive, boat activity or nature walk. Guides will usually make sure that you are somewhere special for that perfect safari sunset experience – the sundowner. At the better camps, they will ask you for your sundowner drink of choice before setting out from camp. Drinks are often accompanied by nibbles.

Dinner Returning to camp after sunset, you'll again be given time to return to your room or tent if you wish. In almost every safari camp or lodge, you must be accompanied by a staff member as you go to and from your tents after dark, due to the dangers of wandering wildlife. Dinner is usually served around 7pm and is sometimes accompanied by some form of entertainment, such as a dance performance or a predinner nature lecture.

CHILDREN

Botswana can be a challenging destination for families travelling with children. That's primarily because the distances here can be epic and long days in the vehicle on bumpy trails will test the patience of most kids. It's also worth remembering that many upmarket lodges and safari companies won't accept children under a certain age (sometimes seven, more often 12), and those that do will probably require you to book separate game drives.

On the other hand, if you can keep the kids entertained on the long drives (bring lots of activity books, CDs and games), camping out in the wilds can be a wonderful family experience. It may require eternal vigilance – almost no private or public campsite in the country has enough fencing to keep animals out and children in, and there are the additional hazards of campfires, mosquitoes, snakes and biting/stinging insects. But long distances and these basic rules of camping life aside, a self-driving camping safari is something your kids will remember forever.

The best piece of advice we can give to get the most out of Botswana's abundant attractions is to not be too ambitious. Instead of trying to cover the whole country, concentrate on really getting to know just one or two places over the course of a week or 10 days, thereby cutting travel times. Wildlife densities are at their highest in the north, especially in the Okavango Delta, Moremi Game Reserve and Chobe National Park. As a result, you shouldn't need to spend too long in the car before tracking down elephants or lions.

There are lodges and safari operators that do offer family packages that can be worth checking out. Some offer specialist children's guides and imaginative activity programs, which might include things like making paper from elephant dung! One of the better ones is Young Explorers offered by Great Plains Conservation (http://greatplainsconservation.com/young-explorers), an outstanding three-day program for children. From the Wilderness Safaris portfolio, Seba Camp (p110) is considered particularly good for families.

Most lodges and tented camps also have swimming pools, which provide a fine reward for long hours spent in the car.

Although the following activities are rarely aimed at a young audience, older kids will get a kick out of quad biking in the Makgadikgadi Pans, horse-riding safaris, *mokoro* trips in the reedy waters of the delta or even scenic flights high above the delta. Fishing in the Okavango Panhandle might also appeal.

Practicalities

Unless you're planning to be in Botswana for the long haul, we advise you to bring everything with you that you think you'll need. For invaluable general advice on taking the family abroad, see Lonely Planet's *Travel with Children*.

➡ **Babysitting** Many lodges make a point of saying they are not babysitting agencies (in other words, your kids are your responsibility), and such agencies are otherwise extremely rare.

➡ **Car seats** These may be available from car-rental firms, but you'd be better off bringing your own; there are no car seats in safari vehicles.

➡ **Changing facilities** Almost unheard of.

➡ **Cots** Rarely available in hotels or lodges.

➡ **Health** A check-up with your doctor back home is a good idea before setting out for Botswana, but this is a comparatively safe country and medical facilities are good.

➡ **High chairs** Almost nonexistent in restaurants.

➡ **Mosquito repellent** Check with your doctor before setting out, as some mosquito repellents with high levels of DEET may be unsuitable for young children. Some lodges have mosquito nets; if you're camping, consider bringing your own.

➡ **Nappies and baby food** These are available from supermarkets in larger towns, but they may not be the brands you're used to and you don't want to find yourself in trouble if you're in town on a Sunday or public holiday.

➡ **National park entry fees** Free for children under eight and half-price for those aged from eight to 17 years of age.

CUSTOMS REGULATIONS

Most items from elsewhere in the Southern African Customs Union (SACU) – Namibia, South Africa, Lesotho and Swaziland – may be imported duty free. You may be asked to declare new laptops and cameras, but this is very rarely enforced.

Visitors may bring into Botswana the following amounts of duty-free items: up to 400 cigarettes, 50 cigars or 250g of tobacco; 2L of wine or 1L of beer or spirits; and 50mL of perfume or 250mL of eau de cologne.

The most rigorous searches at customs posts are for fresh meat products – don't buy succulent steaks in South Africa for your camping barbecue and expect them to be allowed in.

There is no restriction on currency, though you may need to declare any pula or foreign currency you have on you when entering or leaving the country. This depends on the border crossing and who is on duty.

DANGERS & ANNOYANCES

Botswana is modern and developed, and most things work. You can safely drink the tap water in the towns and cities, and you do not need protection against cholera or yellow fever.

HIV/AIDS is a serious issue but, unless you fail to take common-sense precautions, there should be no undue risk. In fact, the greatest danger to the traveller is posed by wildlife and the risks of driving in the bush.

Crime

Crime is rarely a problem in Botswana, and doesn't usually extend beyond occasional pickpocketing and theft from parked cars. Gaborone is one of Africa's safer cities, but it still pays to take a taxi after dark.

Police & Military

Although police and veterinary roadblocks, bureaucracy and bored officials may be tiresome, they're mostly harmless. Careful scrutiny is rare, but you may have to unpack your luggage for closer inspection at a border or veterinary checkpoint.

The Botswana Defence Force (BDF), on the other hand, takes its duties seriously and is best not crossed. The most sensitive base, which is operated jointly with the US government, lies in a remote area off the Lobatse road, southwest of Gaborone. Don't stumble upon it accidentally! Also avoid State House, the official residence of the president in Gaborone, especially after dark. It's located near the government enclave, where there's not much else going on in the evening, so anyone caught 'hanging around' is viewed suspiciously.

Road Safety

Although vehicle traffic is light on most roads outside of the major towns and cities, the most significant concern for most travellers is road safety. Botswana has one of the highest accident rates per capita in the world, and drunk and reckless driving are common, especially at month's end (wage day). Cattle, goats, sheep, donkeys and even elephants are deadly hazards on the road, especially at dusk and after dark when visibility is poor. Never drive at night unless you absolutely have to.

HIV & AIDS: A NATIONAL CATASTROPHE

Botswana's HIV prevalence is the second worst in the world. According to UNAIDS and the World Health Organization, 22.2% of all adult Batswana (around 340,000 people) were HIV positive in 2015, and women represent over half of those cases. Things are, however, improving – at least in some areas.

Botswana symbolises the tremendous challenge that HIV/AIDS poses to African development in the 21st century. It is blessed with sizeable diamond reserves that have fuelled rapid economic growth since independence and have raised incomes for thousands of its citizens to world-class standards. Yet almost 3200 people died of HIV/AIDS here in 2015 (just over half the figure of four years earlier) and life expectancy (55.97 years for men, 52.33 years for women) is far lower than it should be in a country with Botswana's impressive economic profile. It's estimated that without the scourge of AIDS, life expectancy in Botswana would now be on a par with the USA. In 2001 former president Festus Mogae lamented that, unless the epidemic was reversed, his country faced 'blank extinction'. Some economic experts also fear that AIDS will make Botswana poorer by the day, as the virus tends to hit people in their most productive years.

In the midst of all the gloom, Botswana has taken some of the most admirable steps of any sub-Saharan African nation in reversing the damaging trends wrought by AIDS. In 2001 Botswana became the first African country to trial antiretroviral (ARV) drug therapy on a national scale, for which it earned international praise. And it is one of just a handful of countries worldwide that have committed to providing ARV treatment free to all of its HIV-positive citizens. In addition, it has committed itself to reversing the epidemic.

These policies are already bearing some fruit. Life expectancy has reached current levels from an appalling low of 35 years in 2005, although it has fallen slightly in the past four years. In 2012 transmission of the disease from mother to child was down from between 20% and 40% to around 2%. But issues remain and the overall figures remain appalling.

To keep up with the effects of HIV/AIDS on sub-Saharan countries, log on to www.unaids.org, www.avert.org and www.who.int.

DISCOUNT CARDS

There is no uniformly accepted discount-card scheme in Botswana, but a residence permit entitles you to claim favourable residents' rates at hotels. Hostel cards are of little use, but student cards score a discount (usually around 15%) on some buses. Seniors over 60, with proof of age, also receive a discount on some buses and airfares.

EMBASSIES & HIGH COMMISIONS

Most diplomatic missions are in Gaborone. Many more countries (such as Australia and New Zealand) have embassies or consulates in South Africa.

France (Map p52; ☑ 368 0800; www.amba-france-bw.org; 761 Robinson Rd, Gaborone; ☺ 8am-4pm Mon-Fri)

Germany (Map p52; ☑ 395 3143; www.gabo-rone.diplo.de; Queens Rd, Gaborone; ☺ 9am-noon Mon-Fri)

Namibia (Map p49; ☑ 390 2181; namibhc@info.bw; Plot 186, Morara Close, Gaborone; ☺ 7.30am-1pm & 2-4.30pm Mon-Fri)

South Africa (Map p52; ☑ 390 4800; sahcgabs@botsnet.bw; 29 Queens Rd, Gaborone; ☺ 8am-noon & 1.30-4.30pm Mon-Fri)

UK (Map p52; ☑ 395 2841; www.gov.uk/government/world/botswana; Queens Rd, Gaborone; ☺ 8am-4.30pm Mon-Thu, to 1pm Fri)

US (Map p49; ☑ 395 3982; http://botswana.usembassy.gov; Embassy Dr, Government Enclave, Gaborone; ☺ 7.30am-5pm Mon-Thu, to 1.30pm Fri)

Zambia (Map p52; ☑ 395 1951; zamhico@work.co.bw; Plot No 1118 Queens Rd, The Mall, Gaborone; ☺ 8.30am-12.30pm & 2-4.30pm Mon-Fri)

Zimbabwe (Map p49; ☑ 391 4495; www.zimgaborone.gov.zw; Plot 8850, Orapa Close, Government Enclave, Gaborone; ☺ 8am-1pm & 2-4.30pm Mon-Fri)

LGBT TRAVELLERS

Homosexuality, both gay and lesbian, is illegal in Botswana. Article 164 of Botswana's Penal Code prescribes a maximum seven-year prison term for 'carnal knowledge...against the order of nature'. While arrests are rare, Botswana's High Court ruled on a case involving two gay men in July 2003. The court found that 'the time has not yet arrived to decriminalise homosexual practices even between consenting adult males in private'.

Intolerance has increased in the region over the last few years due to the homophobic statements of leaders in neighbouring Namibia and Zimbabwe. When asked in 2011 about a plan to distribute condoms to prisoners engaged in same-sex sexual activity, the deputy speaker of the Botswana National Assembly,

GOVERNMENT TRAVEL ADVICE

The following government websites offer travel advisories and information for travellers.

Australian Department of Foreign Affairs & Trade (www.smartraveller.gov.au)

Canadian Department of Foreign Affairs & International Trade (www.voyage.gc.ca)

French Ministère des Affaires Étrangères et Européennes (www.diplomatie.gouv.fr/fr/conseils-aux-voyageurs)

Italian Ministero degli Affari Esteri (www.viaggiaresicuri.mae.aci.it)

New Zealand Ministry of Foreign Affairs & Trade (www.safetravel.govt.nz)

UK Foreign & Commonwealth Office (www.gov.uk/foreign-travel-advice)

US Department of State (www.travel.state.gov)

Pono Moatlhodi, suggested that were he to have the power, he would have homosexuals killed.

And yet the situation is more nuanced than it may first appear. Botswana's employment laws forbid workplace discrimination or dismissal on the basis of a person's sexual orientation, while Botswana's former president, Festus Mogae, told the BBC in 2011 that prejudice against gays and lesbians was harming the country's fight against HIV/AIDS. He also said that he had, while in office, directed police to neither harass nor arrest gays and lesbians. Gay and lesbian people with whom we spoke in Botswana suggested that the situation, at least in Gaborone, is relatively relaxed and that they were able live quite openly as gays and lesbians.

Even so, given the sensitivity of the subject and the strongly held views of many Batswana, it is advisable to refrain from any overt displays of affection in public.

Organisations

In 1998 a group of lesbians, gays and bisexuals established the advocacy and support group **LeGaBiBo** (Lesbians, Gays and Bisexuals of Botswana; Map p49; ☑ 393 2516; http://legabibo.wordpress.com; 5062 Medical Mews, Fairgrounds). The first thing it did was to publish a human-rights charter under the auspices of Ditshwanelo, the Botswana Centre for Human Rights, and it has since run safe-sex workshops to highlight the risks of HIV/AIDS. Ditshwanelo continues to advocate and lobby for the decriminalisation of homosexuality.

The government registrar twice refused to register LeGaBiBo, on the grounds that the group was engaged in illegal activities and posed a threat to order in Botswana society. The decision mattered because without such registration, it would be extremely difficult for LeGaBiBo to raise money. In 2013 members of LeGaBiBo sued the Botswana government and, a year later, won the case before the High Court, which ruled that LeGaBiBo must be registered. The government appealed and in 2016 the Court of Appeal ruled in favour of LeGaBiBo on the basis that any refusal to register the group was unconstitutional.

Useful Resources

Afriboyz (www.afriboyz.com/Homosexuality-in-Africa.html) Links to gay topics in an African context.

African Horizons (www.africanhorizons.com) Gay-friendly tour operator that offers trips to Southern Africa, including Botswana.

David Tours (www.davidtravel.com) Can arrange seven- and 12-day trips to northern Botswana, all with a gay focus.

Global Gayz (www.globalgayz.com/africa/botswana) Links to gay issues in Botswana and other African countries.

Via Origins (p94) A LGBT-friendly safari operator who is also a good one-stop shop for information on Maun and wider Botswana activities.

INSURANCE

Two words: get some! A travel-insurance policy to cover theft, loss and medical problems is a very sensible precaution. Worldwide travel insurance is available at www.lonelyplanet.com/travel-insurance. You can buy, extend and claim online anytime – even if you're already on the road.

Medical cover is the most vital element of any policy, but make sure you check the small print.

Some policies specifically exclude 'dangerous activities', which can even include motorcycling and trekking. If such activities are on your agenda you'll need a fully comprehensive policy, which may be more expensive. Using a locally acquired motorcycle licence may not be valid under your policy.

You may prefer a policy that pays doctors or hospitals direct rather than you having to pay on the spot and claim later. If you have to claim later, make sure you keep all documentation.

Some policies ask you to call back (reverse charges) to a centre in your home country, where an immediate assessment of your problem is made.

Check that the policy covers ambulances or an emergency flight home.

INTERNET ACCESS

Cyber cafes Common in large and medium-sized towns; connection speeds fluctuate wildly.

Post offices Some post offices, including in Kasane, have a few internet-enabled PCs.

Wireless Reasonably common in midrange and top-end hotels in towns, but very rarely available in safari lodges.

MAPS

The best paper map of Botswana is the *Botswana* (1:1,000,000) map published by Tracks4Africa (www.tracks4africa.co.za). Updated every couple of years using detailed traveller feedback, the map is printed on tear-free, waterproof paper and includes distances *and* estimated travel times. Used in conjunction with Tracks4Africa's unrivalled GPS maps, it's far and away the best mapping product on the market. Even so, be aware that, particularly in the Okavango Delta, last year's trails may this year be underwater, depending on water levels, so these maps should never be a substitute for expert local knowledge.

If for some reason you are unable to get hold of the Tracks4Africa map, the only other maps that we recommend are those published by Shell Oil Botswana and Veronica Roodt. The *Shell Tourist Map of Botswana* (1:1,750,000) is available at major bookshops in Botswana and South Africa.

Probably of more interest are Shell's zoomed-in maps (with varying scales) of the various reserves and other popular areas. These include numerous GPS coordinates for important landmarks and the tracks are superimposed onto satellite images of the area in question. Some are a little out of date, but they're still excellent. Titles include *Okavango Delta, Chobe National Park, Moremi Game Reserve* and *Kgalagadi Transfrontier Park*.

MONEY

There are ATMs in major towns. Credit cards are accepted in most top-end hotels, but lodges and tour operators require advance payment by bank transfer. Otherwise, bring US dollars in cash.

ATMs

Credit cards can be used in ATMs displaying the appropriate sign, or to obtain cash advances over the counter in many banks – Visa and

MasterCard are among the most widely recognised. Transaction fees can be prohibitive and usually apply per transaction rather than by the amount you're withdrawing – take out as much as you can each time. Check also with your bank before leaving home to see if some banks have agreements with your home bank that work out cheaper than others.

You'll find ATMs at all the main bank branches throughout Botswana, including in Gaborone, Maun, Francistown and Kasane, and this is undoubtedly the simplest (and safest) way to handle your money while travelling.

Cash

The unit of currency is the Botswanan pula (P). Pula means 'blessings' or 'rain', the latter of which is as precious as money in this largely desert country. Notes come in denominations of P10, P20, P50 and P100, and coins (thebe, or 'shield') are in denominations of 5t, 10t, 25t, 50t, P1, P2 and P5.

Most common foreign currencies can be exchanged, but not every branch of every bank will do so. Therefore it's best to stick to US dollars, euros, UK pounds and South African rand, which are all easy to change.

Foreign currency, typically US dollars, is also accepted by a number of midrange and top-end hotels, lodges and tour operators. South African rand can also be used on Botswana combis (minibuses) and buses going to/from South Africa, and to pay for Botswanan vehicle taxes at South Africa–Botswana borders.

Most banks and foreign-exchange offices won't touch Zambian kwacha and (sometimes) Namibian dollars; in border areas you can sometimes pay at some businesses with the latter. To make sure you don't get caught out, buy/sell these currencies at or near the respective borders.

There are five commercial banks in the country with branches in all the main towns and major villages. Although you will get less favourable rates at a bureau de change, they are a convenient option if the lines at the banks are particularly long.

There is no black market in Botswana. Anyone offering to exchange money on the street is doing so illegally and is probably setting you up for a scam, the exception being the guys who change pula for South African rand in front of South Africa–bound minibuses – locals use their services, so they can be trusted.

For current exchange rates, log on to www.xe.com.

Credit/Debit Cards

All major credit cards, especially Visa and MasterCard, but also American Express and Diners Club, are widely accepted in most shops,

restaurants and hotels (but only in *some* petrol stations).

Major branches of Barclays Bank and Standard Chartered Bank also deal with cash advances over the counter and don't charge commissions for Visa and MasterCard. Almost every town has at least one branch of Barclays and/or Standard Chartered that offers foreign-exchange facilities, but not all have the authority or technology for cash advances.

Exchange Rates

AUSTRALIA	A$1	P8.03
CANADA	C$1	P7.83
EUROPE	€1	P11.62
JAPAN	¥100	P10.05
NEW ZEALAND	NZ$1	P7.67
SOUTH AFRICA	R1	P0.77
UK	£1	P13.05
US	US$1	P10.47

For current exchange rates, see www.xe.com.

Tipping

While tipping isn't obligatory, the government's official policy of promoting upmarket tourism has raised expectations in many hotels and restaurants. A service charge may be added as a matter of course, in which case there's no need to leave a tip. If there is no service charge and the service has been good, leave around 10%.

It is also a good idea to tip the men who watch your car in public car parks and the attendants at service stations who wash your windscreens. A tip of around P10 is appropriate.

Guides and drivers of safari vehicles will also expect a tip, especially if you've spent a number of days under their care.

Most safari companies suggest the following as a rule of thumb:

➡ guides/drivers – US$10 per person per day
➡ *mokoro* trackers and polers – US$5 each per person per day
➡ camp or lodge staff – US$10 per guest per day (usually placed in a communal box)
➡ transfer drivers and porters – US$3

EATING PRICE RANGES

The following price ranges refer to a main course.

$ less than P50 (US$5)
$$ P50-100 (US$5–10)
$$$ more than P100 (US$10)

CHANGING MONEY AT THE BORDER

A word of warning: if you're changing money at or near border crossings and not doing so through the banks, be aware that local businesses (sometimes bureaux de change, sometimes just shops with a sideline in currencies so that arriving travellers can pay their customs duties) usually have *abysmal* rates. Change the minimum that you're likely to need and change the rest at a bank or bureau de change in the nearest large town.

Travellers Cheques

Travellers cheques can be cashed at most banks and exchange offices. American Express (Amex), Thomas Cook and Visa are the most widely accepted brands. Banks charge anywhere between 2% and 3% commission to change the cheques; Barclays usually offers the most efficient service and charges 2.5% commission for most brands.

As a general rule, it is preferable to buy travellers cheques in US dollars, euros or UK pounds. Get most of the cheques in largish denominations to save on per-cheque commissions.

You must take your passport with you when cashing cheques.

OPENING HOURS

The whole country practically closes down on Sunday.

Banks 8.30am–3.30pm Monday to Friday, 8.15am–10.45am Saturday

National parks 6am–6.30pm April to September, 5.30am–7pm October to March

Post offices 9am–5pm Monday to Friday, 9am–noon Saturday, or 7.30am–noon and 2pm–4.30pm Monday to Friday, 7.30am–12.30pm Saturday

Restaurants 11am–11pm Monday to Saturday; some also open the same hours on Sunday

PHOTOGRAPHY

While many Batswana enjoy being photographed, others do not. The main point is that you should always ask permission and respect the wishes of the person in question. You should also avoid taking pictures of bridges, dams, airports, military equipment, government buildings and anything that could be considered strategic.

Digital memory cards, CDs and the like can be purchased in Gaborone in large malls such as Game City. They're a bit harder to find in Maun and Kasane, but it's possible.

POST

Botswana Post (www.botspost.co.bw) is generally reliable, although it can be slow, so allow at least two weeks for delivery to or from any overseas address.

To send parcels, go to the parcel office at the Central Post Office in Gaborone, fill out the customs forms and pay the duties (if required). Parcels may be plastered with all the sticky tape you like, but they must also be tied up with string and sealing wax, so bring matches to seal knots with the red wax provided.

PUBLIC HOLIDAYS

During official public holidays, all banks, government offices and major businesses are closed. However, hotels, restaurants, bars, smaller shops, petrol stations, museums and national parks and reserves stay open, while border crossings and public transport continue operating as normal. Government offices, banks and some businesses also take the day off after New Year's Day, President's Day, Botswana/Independence Day and Boxing Day.

New Year's Day 1 January

Easter Good Friday, Easter Saturday and Easter Monday (March/April)

Labour Day 1 May

Ascension Day May/June, 40 days after Easter Sunday

Sir Seretse Khama Day 1 July

President's Day Third Friday in July

Botswana/Independence Day 30 September

Christmas Day 25 December

Boxing Day 26 December

TELEPHONE

The operator of Botswana's fixed-line telephone service is Botswana Telecom (BTC; www.btc.bw). Local and domestic calls at peak times start at P40 per minute and rise according to the distance. When deciding when to call, remember that prices drop by up to one-third for local and domestic calls, and 20% for international calls, from 8pm to 7am Monday to Friday, 1pm to midnight Saturday and all day Sunday. These discounts don't apply if you use the operator.

There are no internal area codes in Botswana. The country code for Botswana is ☏267, and the international access code is ☏00.

Mobile Phones

Botswana has two main mobile-phone networks, Mascom Wireless (www.mascom.bw) and Orange Botswana (www.orange.co.bw), of which Mascom is the largest provider. All providers have dealers in most large and medium-sized towns, where you can buy phones, SIM cards and top up your credit. Government-run Botswana Telecommunications Corporation (www.btc.bw) runs the beMobile network, but its future was uncertain at the time of writing.

The coverage map for the two main providers is improving with each passing year, but when deciding whether to get a local SIM card, remember that there's simply no mobile coverage across large parts of the country (including much of the Kalahari and Okavango Delta). That said, the main highway system is generally covered.

Most Botswana mobile numbers begin with 71, 72 or 73.

Phonecards

Telephone booths can be used for local, domestic and international calls, and can be found in and outside all BTC offices, outside all post offices and around all shopping centres and malls. Blue booths (with the English and Setswana words 'coin' and *madi*) take coins, and the green booths (with the words 'card' and *karata*) use phonecards.

Phonecards can be bought at BTC offices, post offices and some small grocery shops. Local and long-distance telephone calls can also be made from private telephone agencies, often called 'phone shops'.

TIME

Botswana is two hours ahead of GMT/UTC, so when it's noon in Botswana, it's 10am in London, 5am in New York, 2am in Los Angeles and 8pm in Sydney (not taking into account daylight-saving time in these countries). There is no daylight-saving time in Botswana.

TOURIST INFORMATION

The Department of Tourism, rebranded in the public sphere as Botswana Tourism (www.botswanatourism.co.bw), has an excellent website and a growing portfolio of tourist offices around the country. These tourist offices don't always have their finger on the pulse, but they can be an extremely useful source of brochures from local hotels, tour operators and other tourist services.

For information on national parks, you're better off contacting the Department of Wildlife and National Parks (p164).

Another useful resource is the Regional Tourism Organisation of Southern Africa (in South Africa 011-315 2420; www.retosa.co.za), which promotes tourism throughout Southern Africa, including Botswana.

There are tourist offices in the following places:

➡ Gaborone (p54)
➡ Maun (p104)
➡ Kasane (p83)
➡ Francistown (p66)
➡ Kang (p138)

TRAVELLERS WITH DISABILITIES

People with limited mobility will have a difficult time travelling around Botswana – although there are many disabled people living in the country, facilities are very few and much of the country can be an obstacle course. Along streets and footpaths, kerbs and uneven surfaces will often present problems for wheelchair users, and only a very few upmarket hotels/lodges and restaurants have installed ramps and railings. Also, getting to and around any of the major lodges or camps in the national wildlife parks will be extremely difficult, given their remote and wild locations.

❶ ESSENTIAL DOCUMENTS

Travellers with children should be aware of recent changes regarding the documents you must carry with you while travelling through the region. The law requires that all parents arriving, transiting and departing South Africa, Namibia and Botswana must produce an unabridged birth certificate for their children, and the birth certificate must state the names of both parents. Families not in possession of these documents will be refused travel.

If one parent is travelling alone with their children, the travelling parent must carry with them an affidavit from the other (ie nontravelling) parent who is listed on the birth certificate granting their consent for the travel to take place in their absence. Where this is not possible, either a court order granting full parental responsibilities and rights, or a death certificate of the other parent, must be produced.

We have travelled across the borders of all three countries with our children on numerous occasions and although we were not always asked for these documents, we were asked for each of them at least once. Travel without them at your peril.

Make sure to choose the areas you visit carefully, and clearly explain your requirements to the lodge and/or safari operator when making your original enquiry. The swampy environs of the Okavango Delta will be particularly challenging for people who have special needs, although the lodges in the Kalahari and the Makgadikgadi Pans are relatively accessible, providing you are travelling with an able-bodied companion. It is also worth bearing in mind that almost any destination in Botswana will require a long trip in a 4WD and/or a small plane.

Download Lonely Planet's free Accessible Travel guide from http://lptravel.to/AccessibleTravel.

VISAS

Most visitors can obtain tourist visas at the international airports and borders (and the nearest police stations in lieu of an immigration official at remote border crossings). Visas on arrival are valid for 30 days – and possibly up to 90 days if requested at the time of entry – and are available for free to passport holders from most Commonwealth countries (but not Ghana, India, Nigeria, Pakistan and Sri Lanka), all EU countries, the USA and countries in the Southern African Customs Union (SACU), ie South Africa, Namibia, Lesotho and Swaziland.

If you hold a passport from any other country, apply for a 30-day tourist visa at an overseas Botswanan embassy or consulate. Where there is no Botswanan representation, try going to a British embassy or consulate.

Tourists are allowed to stay in Botswana for a maximum of 90 days every 12 months, so a 30-day visa may be extended twice. Visas can be extended for free at immigration offices in Gaborone, Francistown, Maun and Kasane. Whether you're required to show an onward ticket and/or sufficient funds at this time depends on the official(s).

Anyone travelling to Botswana from an area infected with yellow fever needs proof of vaccination before they can enter the country.

VOLUNTEERING

There are very few volunteering opportunities in Botswana. The community and conservation projects that exist are usually small, focused grassroots projects that simply aren't set up for drop-in volunteers. Another factor is that Botswana is a pretty well-organised, wealthy country and the need for volunteer projects simply doesn't exist, with the exception of NGOs working with HIV/AIDS sufferers.

Botswana Projects

Specific volunteering opportunities within Botswana at the time of writing:

Frontier Conservation Expeditions

(www.frontier.ac.uk) Teaching and wildlife conservation.

Project Trust (www.projecttrust.org.uk) School teaching near Maun.

WOMEN TRAVELLERS

In general, travelling around Botswana poses no particular difficulties for women travellers. For the most part, men are polite and respectful, and women can often meet and communicate with local men without their intentions necessarily being misconstrued. However, unaccompanied women should be cautious in nightclubs or bars, as generally most instances of hassle tend to be the advances of men who have had one too many drinks.

The threat of sexual assault isn't any greater in Botswana than in Europe, but women should still avoid walking alone in city parks and backstreets, especially at night. Don't hitch alone or at night and, if you can, find a companion for trips through sparsely populated areas. Use common sense and things should go well.

Dress modestly. Short sleeves are fine, and baggy shorts and loose T-shirts are acceptable where foreigners are common, but in villages and rural areas try to cover up as much as possible.

ⓘ Getting There & Away

Botswana is not the easiest or cheapest place in the world to reach by air, and some travellers prefer to enter the country overland from South Africa or, more recently, Namibia as part of a longer safari.

Flights, tours and rail tickets can be booked online at www.lonelyplanet.com/bookings.

ENTERING BOTSWANA

Entering Botswana is usually straightforward provided you are carrying a valid passport. Visas are available on arrival for most nationalities and are issued in no time. If you're crossing into the country overland and in your own (or rented) vehicle, expect to endure (sometimes quite cursory, sometimes strict) searches for fresh meat, fresh fruit and dairy products, most of which will be confiscated if found. For vehicles rented in South Africa, Namibia or other regional countries, you will need to show a letter from the owner that you have permission to drive the car into Botswana, in addition to all other registration documents.

At all border crossings you must pay P120 (a combination of road levy and third-party insurance) if you're driving your own vehicle. Hassles from officialdom are rare.

For a moderately useful list of the government's entry requirements, see www.botswanatourism.co.bw/entryFormalities.php. The Tracks4Africa *Botswana* map has opening hours for all border crossings.

Passport

All visitors entering Botswana must hold a passport that is valid for at least six months. Also, allow a few empty pages for stamp-happy immigration officials, especially if you plan on crossing over to Zimbabwe and/or Zambia to Victoria Falls.

AIR

The only scheduled flights to Botswana come from Johannesburg and Cape Town (South Africa), Victoria Falls and Harare (Zimbabwe), Lusaka and Livingstone (Zambia) and Windhoek (Namibia). No European or North American airline flies directly into Botswana, and most travellers fly into either Jo'burg or Cape Town (both of which are served by an array of international and domestic carriers) and hop on a connecting flight.

Airports & Airlines

Botswana's main airport, **Sir Seretse Khama International Airport** (GBE; ☑ 391 4401; www.caab.co.bw), is located 11km north of Gaborone. Although it's well served with flights from Jo'burg and Harare, it's seldom used by tourists as an entry point into the country.

Other, more popular entry points are **Kasane Airport** (BBK; ☑ 625 0133, 368 8200) and Maun Airport (p105).

The national carrier is **Air Botswana** (BP; ☑ 390 5500; www.airbotswana.co.bw), which flies routes within Southern Africa. Air Botswana has offices in Gaborone, Francistown, Maun, Kasane and Victoria Falls (Zimbabwe). It's generally cheaper to book Air Botswana tickets online than through one of its offices.

In addition to **Air Namibia** (☑ in Maun 686 0391; www.airnamibia.com) and **South African Airways** (☑ in Gaborone 397 2397; www.flysaa.com), which do fly into Botswana, the country is served by a number of special charter flights.

LAND

Botswana has a well-developed road network with easy access from neighbouring countries. All borders are open daily. It is advisable to try to reach the crossings as early in the day as possible to allow time for any potential delays. Remember also that despite the official opening hours, immigration posts at some smaller border crossings sometimes close for lunch between 12.30pm and 1.45pm. At remote

border crossings on the Botswanan side, you may need to get your visa at the nearest police station in lieu of an immigration post.

Border Crossings to/from Namibia

There are five border crossings between Botswana and Namibia:

Gcangwa–Tsumkwe Little-used crossing along a 4WD-only track close to Botswana's Tsodilo Hills.

Kasane–Mpalila Island Crossing this border is only possible for guests who have prebooked accommodation at upmarket lodges on the island.

Mamuno Remote but busy crossing on the road between Ghanzi and Windhoek.

Mohembo Connects Shakawe, Maun and the Okavango Panhandle with northeastern Namibia.

Ngoma Bridge East of Kasane, connecting to Namibia's Caprivi Strip.

Bus

The public-transport options between the two countries are few. Going to Namibia, one option is to catch the daily combi (minibus) from Ghanzi to Mamuno (three hours) and then to cross the border on foot, bearing in mind that this crossing is about 1km long. You will then have to hitch a ride from the Namibian side at least to Gobabis, where you can catch a train or other transport to Windhoek. It's time-consuming and unreliable at best.

Tok Tokkie Shuttle (☑ in Namibia 061 300 743; www.shuttlesnamibia.com) makes the 12-hour Windhoek–Gaborone run, departing Windhoek at 6pm on Wednesday and Friday, and from Gaborone at 1pm on Thursday and Saturday. One-way fares cost N\$500 and there's free wi-fi and air-con on board.

Car & Motorcycle

Drivers crossing the border at Mohembo must secure an entry permit for Mahango Game Reserve. This is free if you're transiting, or N\$100 per person per day plus N\$50 per vehicle per day if you want to drive around the reserve (which is possible in a 2WD).

From Divundu, turn west towards Rundu and then southwest for Windhoek, or east towards Katima Mulilo (Namibia), Kasane (Botswana) and Victoria Falls (Zimbabwe), or take the ferry to Zambia.

Border Crossings to/from South Africa

Gaborone is only 280km as the crow flies from Jo'burg along a good road link.

There are 14 border crossings between South Africa and Botswana. Five of these provide access of sorts from the South African side of the

Kgalagadi Transfrontier Park, five are handy for Gaborone, and the remaining four are good for eastern Botswana and the Tuli Block.

The major crossings are:

Bokspits The best South African access to the Kgalagadi Transfontier Park.

Martin's Drift, Zanzibar, Platjan & Pont Drift Eastern Botswana and the Tuli Block from the Northern Transvaal.

Pioneer Gate Connects Gaborone (via Lobatse and Zeerust) with Jo'burg.

Ramatlabama Connects Gaborone with Mafikeng.

Tlokweng Connects Gaborone and Jo'burg via the Madikwe Game Reserve in South Africa.

Bus

Intercape Mainliner (☑ 397 4294, in South Africa 021-380 4400; www.intercape.co.za) runs a service from Jo'burg to Gaborone (from SAR420, 6½ hours, one daily); while you need to get off the bus to sort out any necessary visa formalities, you'll rarely be held up for too long at the border. From Gaborone, the Intercape Mainliner runs from the petrol station beside the Mall and tickets should be booked a week or so in advance; this can be done online.

The **Mahube Express** (Map p49; ☑ 396 0488, 7423 6441; www.mahubeexpress.com) runs twice-daily services from Gaborone to Johannesburg's OR Tambo International Air-

port, leaving the Square Mart close to the city centre at 7am and 2pm. Tickets cost P300.

You can also travel between South Africa and Botswana by combi. From the far (back) end of the bus station in Gaborone, combis leave when full to a number of South African destinations, including Jo'burg (P310/R4100, six to seven hours). Be warned that you'll be dropped in Jo'burg's Park Station, which is *not* a safe place to linger. Combis also travel from Selebi-Phikwe to the border at Martin's Drift (P52, two hours).

Public transport between the two countries bears South African number plates and/or signs on the door marked 'ZA Cross Border Transport'.

Car & Motorcycle

Most border crossings are clearly marked, but it is vital to note that some crossings over the Limpopo and Molopo Rivers (the latter is in Botswana's south) are drifts (river fords) that cannot be crossed by 2WD in wet weather. In times of very high water, these crossings may be closed to all traffic.

Border Crossings to/from Zimbabwe

There are three land border crossings between Botswana and Zimbabwe.

Kazungula The main crossing point from Kasane to Victoria Falls.

Pandamatenga A little-used backroads crossing off the road between Kasane and Nata.

Ramokgweban–Plumtree Connects Francistown with Bulawayo and Harare.

Bus

Incredibly, there is *no* public transport between Kasane, the gateway to one of Botswana's major attractions (Chobe National Park), and Victoria Falls. Other than hitching, the only cross-border options are the 'tourist shuttle' minibuses that about one hour and can be arranged through most hotels, camps and tour operators in Kasane. There is little or no coordination between combi companies in either town, so combis often return from Victoria Falls to Kasane empty. Most combis won't leave Kasane unless they have at least two passengers.

Some hotels and lodges in Kasane also offer private transfers to Livingstone/Victoria Falls (from P1450, two hours). They usually pick up booked passengers from their hotels at around 10am.

From the Zimbabwean side of the border, try Backpackers Bazaar in Victoria Falls. Some hotels and hostels in Zimbabwe will arrange for your transport from the border, but you need to contact them beforehand.

RENTING A 4WD IN SOUTH AFRICA

Renting a 4WD in South Africa sometimes works out cheaper than doing so in Botswana. You'll also need to factor in the extra distance and time you'll need to drive just to get into Botswana. Most South African rental companies will usually let you pick up the vehicle within Botswana itself, but this will, of course, cost extra.

Recommended South African companies include the following:

Around About Cars (☑ 0860 422 4022; www.aroundaboutcars.com)

Britz (☑ in South Africa 011-230 5200; www.britz.co.za)

Bushlore (☑ in South Africa 011-312 8084; www.bushlore.com)

Avis Safari Rentals (☑ in South Africa 011-387 8431; www.avisvanrental.co.za/avis-safari-rental.aspx)

Elsewhere, buses leave early to mid-afternoon from the bus station in Francistown bound for Bulawayo (P80, two hours) and Harare (P150, five hours). For anywhere else in western Zimbabwe, get a connection in Bulawayo.

To/From Zambia

River

Botswana and Zambia share one of the world's shortest international borders: about 750m across the Zambezi River. The only way across the river is by ferry from Kazungula.

At the time of writing there was no cross-border public transport. A combi from Kasane to the border crossing at Kasungula should cost no more than P50. Once there, you'll need to complete the formalities and take the ferry on foot. There is no regular public transport from the Zambian side of the river, although there is one combi that goes to Dambwa, 3km west of Livingstone. If you don't have a vehicle, ask for a lift to Livingstone, Lusaka or points beyond at the ferry terminal or on the ferry itself.

Visas into Zambia cost US$50 per person for most nationalities, while you'll also have to pay the Zambian road toll (US$48), carbon tax (ZMW150) and third-party vehicle insurance (ZMW487, valid for one month and payable even if you already have insurance) if you are taking a vehicle into Zambia.

If you're heading to Liuwa National Park and other places in Zambia's far west, consider crossing into Namibia at Ngoma and driving around 70km to the Namibia–Zambia border at Katima Mulilo – although it involves an extra crossing, the roads are much better on the Zambian side.

❶ Getting Around

Botswana's public-transport network is limited.
Car Hiring a vehicle is the best and most practical option.
Air Although domestic air services are fairly frequent and usually reliable, Air Botswana (and charter flights) is not cheap and only a handful of towns are regularly served.
Bus & Combi Public buses and combis (minibuses) are also cheap and reasonably frequent, but are confined to sealed roads between towns.

AIR

Air Botswana (p177) operates a limited number of domestic routes. It's usually much cheaper to purchase tickets online through the Air Botswana website than in person at

one of its offices. Sample one-way fares at the time of writing:
Gaborone–Francistown P1406
Gaborone–Kasane P2060
Gaborone–Maun P1791
Kasane–Maun P715

Children aged under two, sitting on the lap of an adult, are charged 10% of the fare and children aged between two and 12 are charged 50% of the fare. Passengers are allowed 20kg of luggage (unofficially, a little more is often permitted if the flight is not full).

Charter Flights

Charter flights are often the best – and sometimes the only – way to reach remote lodges, but they are an expensive extra cost; fares are not usually included in the quoted rates for most lodges.

On average, a one-way fare between Maun and a remote lodge in the Okavango Delta will set you back around US$150 to US$250. These services are now highly regulated and flights must be booked as part of a safari package with a mandatory reservation at one of the lodges. This is essential as you can't simply turn up in these remote locations and expect to find a bed for the night, as many lodges are very small. Likewise, you are not permitted to book accommodation at a remote lodge in the delta without also booking a return airfare at the same time. Packages can be booked through agencies in Maun. Wilderness Air (p93) and Mack Air (p93) are the main companies.

It is very important to note that passengers on charter flights are only allowed 10kg to 15kg (and rarely 20kg) of luggage each; check the exact amount when booking. However, if you have an extra 2kg to 3kg, the pilot will usually only mind if the plane is full of passengers.

If you can't stretch the budget to staying in a remote lodge, you can still book a flight over the delta with one of the scenic flight or helicopter companies in Maun (p93).

BICYCLE

Botswana is largely flat – and that's about the only concession it makes to cyclists. Unless you're an experienced cyclist and equipped for the extreme conditions, abandon any ideas you may have about a Botswanan bicycle adventure. Distances are great; the climate and landscapes are hot and dry; and, even along major routes, water is scarce and villages are widely spaced. Also bear in mind that bicycles are not permitted in Botswana's national parks and reserves, and cyclists may encounter potentially dangerous wildlife while pedalling along any highway or road.

BUS & COMBI

Buses and combis regularly travel to all major towns and villages throughout Botswana, but are less frequent in sparsely populated areas such as western Botswana and the Kalahari. Public transport to smaller villages is often nonexistent, unless the village is along a major route.

The extent and frequency of buses and combis also depends on the quantity and quality of roads. For example, there is no public transport along the direct route between Maun and Kasane (ie through Chobe National Park), and services elsewhere can be suspended if roads are flooded. Also bear in mind that there are very few long-distance services, so most people travelling between Gaborone and Kasane or Maun, for example, will need a connection in Francistown.

Buses are usually comfortable and normally leave at a set time, regardless of whether they're full. Finding out the departure times for buses is a matter of asking around the bus station, because schedules are not posted anywhere. Combis leave when full, usually from the same station as buses. Tickets for all public buses and combis cannot be bought in advance; they can only be purchased on board.

CAR & MOTORCYCLE

The best way to travel around Botswana is to hire a vehicle. With your own car you can avoid public transport and organised tours. Remember, however, that distances are long.

You cannot hire motorbikes in Botswana and motorbikes are *not* permitted in national parks and reserves for safety reasons.

Driving Licences

Your home driving licence is valid for six months in Botswana, but if it isn't written in English you must provide a certified translation. In any case, it is advisable to obtain an International Driving Permit (IDP). Your national automobile association can issue this and it is valid for 12 months.

Fuel & Spare Parts

The cost of fuel is relatively expensive in Botswana – at the time of writing it was P7.62 for petrol and P7.35 for diesel – but prices vary according to the remoteness of the petrol station. Petrol stations are open 24 hours in Gaborone, Francistown, Maun, Mahalapye and Palapye; elsewhere, they open from about 7am to 7pm daily.

Hire

To rent a car you must be aged at least 21 (some companies require drivers to be over 25) and have been a licenced driver in your home country for at least two years (sometimes five). For further information on types of vehicles and rental companies, see the Planning a Safari chapter (p30).

TRACKS4AFRICA ERRORS

We're huge fans of the Tracks4Africa (T4A) paper and GPS maps. We simply couldn't travel around Botswana without them, or at least can't imagine doing so without getting lost. But, of course, nothing is perfect, and we noticed a number of errors on our most recent trip – they may or may not have been corrected by the time you read this.

Another issue can sometimes be routes that appear more direct but actually take longer. For example, T4A prefers to send you via the Khumaga Ferry or across the pans if you're travelling from somewhere like Jack's Camp or Tree Island Campsite to the Central Kalahari Game Reserve (CKGR), when, in fact, the quickest route involves returning to the Gweta–Maun road and taking the sealed-road options from there. If this happens, or if you suspect that T4A may not be suggesting the best route, set a waystation (eg Gweta in the above example) and then recalibrate as you go.

In each of the following cases, we have provided detailed driving instructions to compensate for T4A errors:

➡ **Motopi Campsites, CKGR** (p131) The T4A locations for the three campsites remain incorrect.

➡ **Tree Island Campsite, Makgadikgadi Pans National Park** (p75) Makes no appearance on the T4A GPS system.

➡ **Kalahari Plains Camp, CKGR** (p133) The quickest trail from Deception Valley does not appear on the T4A GPS – it'll have you taking an impossibly indirect route.

Accessories

Most 4WD vehicles from reputable companies come fully equipped with all the necessary tools and camping equipment. This should include, as a bare minimum, all kitchen and cooking equipment, gas stove, shower, bedding, GPS with Tracks4Africa loaded and a fridge/freezer. These should be included in the rental price, but always ask.

Other things worth asking for (at an additional cost) include a satellite phone and an inverter (to allow you to charge your batteries – always ask which plug is required). Some companies may also expect you to request the GPS as an extra, although this is considered standard with most rentals.

Insurance

Insurance is *strongly* recommended. No matter who you hire your car from, make sure you understand what is included in the price (such as unlimited kilometres, tax and so on) and what your liabilities are. Most local insurance policies do not include cover for damage to windscreens and tyres.

Third-party motor insurance is a minimum requirement in Botswana. However, it is also advisable to take Damage (Collision) Waiver, which costs around P150 extra per day for a 2WD and about P300 per day for a 4WD. Loss (Theft) Waiver is also an extra worth having. For both types of insurance, the excess liability is about P5000 for a 2WD and P10,000 for a 4WD. If you're only going for a short period of time, it may be worth taking out the Super Collision Waiver, which covers absolutely everything, albeit at a price.

Road Conditions

Good sealed roads link most major population centres. The most notable exception is the direct route between Kasane and Maun – a horribly corrugated gravel track – meaning that you'll need to take the long way around via Gweta and Nata. The road from Maun to Shakawe past the Okavango Panhandle is generally reasonable, but beware of potholes.

Tracks with sand, mud, gravel and rocks (and sometimes all four) – normally accessible by 2WD except during exceptional rains – connect most villages and cross a few national parks.

Most other 'roads' are poorly defined – and badly mapped – and should only be attempted by 4WD. In the worst of the wet season (December to February), 4WDs should carry a winch on some tracks (eg through Chobe or Moremi National Parks). A compass or, better, GPS unit with the Tracks4Africa maps loaded is essential for driving by 4WD around the salt

A JERRYCAN TRICK

If you're carrying extra fuel in a jerrycan – which we strongly advise you to do in more remote areas, including the Central Kalahari Game Reserve – there is a simple solution for getting the fuel into your tank without a funnel. Take a plastic bottle of soft drink, cut off the base with a knife and wash and dry it thoroughly. When you're ready to fill your tank, insert the drinking end of the plastic bottle into the tank and pour away. And one final thing: a 20L jerrycan filled with fuel can be very heavy, so ideally have two people holding the jerrycan while you pour.

pans of the Kalahari or northern Botswana at any time.

Road Rules

To drive a car in Botswana, you must be at least 18 years old. Like most other Southern African countries, traffic keeps to the left side of the road. The national speed limit is 60km/h up to 120km/h on sealed roads; when passing through towns and villages, assume a speed limit of 60km/h, even in the absence of any signs. Mobile police units routinely set up speed cameras along major roads, particularly between Gaborone and Francistown and between Maun and Gweta – on-the-spot fines operate on a sliding scale, but can go as high as P500 if you're 30km/h over the limit and you'll may be asked to pay on the spot. On gravel roads, limits are set at 60km/h to 80km/h, while it's 40km/h in all national parks and reserves.

Other road rules to be aware of:
➤ Sitting on the roof of a moving vehicle is illegal.
➤ Wearing seatbelts (where installed) is compulsory in the front (but not back) seats.
➤ Drink-driving is against the law, and your insurance policy will be invalid if you have an accident while drunk.
➤ Driving without a licence is a serious offence.
➤ If you have an accident causing injury, it must be reported to the authorities within 48 hours. If vehicles have sustained only minor damage and there are no injuries – and all parties agree – you can exchange names and

addresses and sort it out later through your insurance companies.

➡ In theory, owners are responsible for keeping their livestock off the road, but in practice animals wander wherever they want. If you hit a domestic animal, your distress (and possible vehicle damage) will be compounded by trying to find the owner and the red tape involved when filing a claim.

➡ Wild animals, including elephants and the estimated three million wild donkeys in Botswana, are a hazard, even along the highways. The Maun–Nata and Nata–Kasane roads are frequently traversed by elephants. The chances of hitting a wild or domestic animal is far, far greater after dark, so driving at night is definitely not recommended.

➡ One common, but minor, annoyance are the so-called 'buffalo fences' (officially called Veterinary Cordon Fences). These are set up to stop the spread of disease from wild animals to livestock. In most cases your vehicle may be searched (they're looking for fresh meat or dairy products) and you may have to walk (and put additional pairs of shoes) through a soda solution and drive your car through soda-treated water.

HITCHING

Hitching in Botswana is an accepted way to get around, given that public transport is sometimes erratic, or nonexistent, in remote areas. Travellers who decide to hitch, however, should understand that they are taking a small but potentially serious risk. People who do choose to hitch will be safer if they travel in pairs and let someone know where they are planning to go.

The equivalent of a bus fare will frequently be requested in exchange for a lift, but to prevent uncomfortable situations at the end of the ride, determine a price before climbing in.

It is totally inadvisable to hitch along backroads, for example through the Tuli Block or from Maun to Kasane through Chobe National Park. This is because traffic along these roads is virtually nonexistent; in fact, vehicles may only come past a few times a day, leaving the hopeful hitchhiker at risk of exposure or, even worse, running out of water. One way to circumvent this problem is to arrange a lift in advance at a nearby lodge.

LOCAL TRANSPORT

Public transport in Botswana is geared towards the needs of the local populace and is confined to main roads between major population centres. Although cheap and reliable, it is of little use to the traveller as most of Botswana's tourist attractions lie off the beaten track.

Combi

Combis, recognisable by their blue number plates, circulate according to set routes around major towns; ie Gaborone, Kasane, Maun, Ghanzi, Molepolole, Mahalapye, Palapye, Francistown, Selebi-Phikwe, Lobatse and Kanye. They are very frequent, inexpensive and generally reliable. However, they aren't terribly safe (most drive too fast), especially on long journeys, and they only serve the major towns. They can also be crowded.

Taxi

Licensed taxis are recognisable by their blue number plates. They rarely bother hanging around the airports at Gaborone, Francistown, Kasane and Maun, so the only reliable transport from the airports is usually a courtesy bus operated by a top-end hotel or lodge. These are free for guests, but anyone else can normally negotiate a fare with the bus driver. Taxis are always available *to* the airports, however.

It is not normal for taxis to cruise the streets for fares, even in Gaborone. If you need one, telephone a taxi company to arrange a pick up or go to a taxi stand (usually near the bus or train stations). Taxi companies in Gaborone include Speedy Cabs (p55) and Final Bravo Cabs (p55). Fares for taxis are negotiable, but fares for occasional shared taxis are fixed. Taxis can be chartered – about P400 to P600 per day, although this is negotiable depending on how far you want to go.

Train

The Botswana Railways system no longer takes passengers. In case passenger services do resume, services are likely to be limited to one line running along eastern Botswana from Ramokgwebana on the Zimbabwean border to Ramatlabama on the South African border.

Victoria Falls

Best Places to Eat

➡ Cafe Zambezi (p93)

➡ Lola's Tapas & Carnivore Restaurant (p98)

➡ Olga's Italian Corner (p93)

➡ Lookout Cafe (p97)

➡ Boma (p98)

Best Places to Sleep

➡ Victoria Falls Hotel (p97)

➡ Jollyboys Backpackers (p91)

➡ Stanley Safari Lodge (p93)

➡ Victoria Falls Backpackers (p97)

Why Go?

Taking its place alongside the Pyramids and the Serengeti, Victoria Falls (*Mosi-oa-Tunya* – the 'smoke that thunders') is one of Africa's original blockbusters. And although Zimbabwe and Zambia share it, Victoria Falls is a place all of its own.

As a magnet for tourists of all descriptions – backpackers, tour groups, thrill seekers, families, honeymooners – Victoria Falls is one of Earth's great spectacles. View it directly as a raging mile-long curtain of water, in all its glory, from a helicopter ride or peek precariously over its edge from Devil's Pools; the sheer power and force of the falls is something that simply does not disappoint.

Whether you're here purely to take in the sight of a natural wonder of the world, or for a serious hit of adrenalin via rafting or bungee jumping into the Zambezi, Victoria Falls is a place where you're sure to tick off numerous items from that bucket list.

When to Go

There are two main reasons to go to Victoria Falls – to view the falls, and to experience the outdoor activities – and each has its season.

July to December is the season for white-water rafting, especially August for hard-core rapids.

From February to June you'll experience the falls at their full force, so don't forget your raincoat.

From July to September you'll get the best views of the falls, combined with lovely weather and all activities to keep you busy.

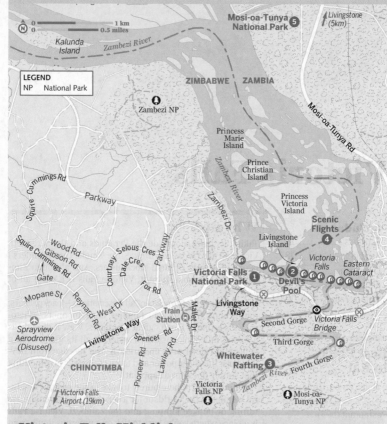

Victoria Falls Highlights

1 **Victoria Falls National Park** (p95) Taking in the full force of the falls with unobstructed views.

2 **Devil's Pool** (p90) Experiencing the world's most extreme infinity pool.

3 **Whitewater rafting** (p87) Taming Grade-5 rapids along the Zambezi.

4 **Scenic flights** (p88) Taking the 'flight of the angels' helicopter ride over Victoria Falls.

5 **Mosi-oa-Tunya National Park** (p90) Tracking white rhino on foot on a walking safari.

SEVENTH NATURAL WONDER OF THE WORLD

Victoria Falls is the largest, most beautiful and most majestic waterfall on the planet, and is the Seventh Natural Wonder of the World as well as a Unesco World Heritage Site. A trip to Southern Africa would not be complete without visiting this unforgettable place.

Up to one million litres of water fall – per second – down a 108m drop along a 1.7km wide strip in the Zambezi Gorge; it's an awe-some sight. Victoria Falls can be seen, heard, tasted and touched; it is a treat that few other places in the world can offer, a 'must see before you die' spot.

Victoria Falls is spectacular at any time of year, yet varies in the experiences it offers.

🏃 Activities

While it's the falls that lures travellers to the region, its awesome outdoor adventure scene is what makes them hang around. From world-class whitewater rafting, bungee jumping and high-adrenalin activities, to scenic flights and walking with rhinos, Victoria Falls is undoubtedly one of the world's premier adventure destinations.

Abseiling

Strap on a helmet, grab a rope and spend the day rappelling down the 54m sheer drop cliff face of Batoka Gorge from US$55.

Birdwatching

Twitchers will want to bring binoculars to check out 470 species of bird that inhabit the region, including Schalow's turaco, Taita falcon, African finfoot and half-collared kingfisher. Spot them on foot in the parks or on a canoe trip along the Zambezi.

Bridge Walk

For those not interested in bungee jumping off the bridge, walking along it is a good alternative. Strapped in with a harness, the guided tours take the walkways running just beneath the Victoria Falls Bridge, and offer a good way to learn about this engineering marvel, as well as fantastic photo ops. It's US$65 per person. Don't forget your passport.

Bungee Jumping & Bridge Swinging

One of the most famous bungee jumps in the world, the leap here is from atop of the iconic Victoria Falls bridge, plunging 111m into the Zambezi River. It's a long way down, but man it's a lot of fun. It costs US$160 per person.

Otherwise there's the bridge swing where you jump feet first, and free fall for four seconds; you'll end up swinging, but not upside down. There are two main spots: one right off the Victoria Falls Bridge, and the other a bit further along the Batoka Gorge. Costs for single/tandem are US$160/240.

Combine bungee with a bridge swing and bridge slide, and it'll cost US$210.

Canoeing & Kayaking

If whitewater rafting isn't for you, there's more relaxed guided canoe trips along the Upper Zambezi River on two-person inflatable canoes. Options include half (US$110) or whole day (US$125 to US$155) trips, and overnight jaunts (US$250 to US$285) and longer trips are available.

There's even more relaxed three-hour guided sunset river float trips where you can kick back and let someone else do the paddling for US$100, including refreshments.

On the Zambian side, take on the Zambezi's raging rapids in an inflatable kayak on a full-day trip (US$155).

Crocodile Cage Diving

On the Zimbabwe side of the falls, bring along your bathers for a close encounter with a Nile croc, where you plunge within the safety of a cage into a croc-filled enclosure wearing a mask and breathing apparatus. It costs US$70

Cultural Activities

Spend an hour in the evening by a campfire drumming under the African sky, which includes a traditional meal, for US$25. On the Zimbabwe side you can visit a local's home for lunch (US$23) or dinner (US$25)

Hiking

There's a good choice of guided walks in the area. One of the most popular treks is the trek down Batoka Gorge to the Boiling Pot (US$48) where you can get up close and personal with Victoria Falls. You can only do this from late August to December.

Horse Riding

Indulge in a bit of wildlife spotting from horseback along the Zambezi. Rides for 2½ hours cost US$100, and full-day trips for experienced riders are US$155.

Jet Boating

This hair-raising trip costs US$120, and is combined with a cable-car ride down into the Batoka Gorge.

Quadbiking

Discover the spectacular landscape surrounding Livingstone, Zambia, and the Batoka Gorge, spotting wildlife as you go on all-terrain quad bikes. Trips vary from ecotrail riding at Batoka Land to longer-range cultural trips in the African bush. Trips are one hour (US$95) or 2½ hours (US$165).

Rafting

This is one of the best white-water rafting destinations in the world, both for experienced rafters and newbies. Rafting can be done on either side of the Zambezi River, so it doesn't matter what side of the border you're on – you'll find Grade 5 rapids. Expect very long rides with huge drops and big kicks; it's not for the faint-hearted.

The best time for rafting is between July and mid-February (low water season); peak season is around August to October. Day trips run between rapids 1 and 21 (to rapid 25 on the Zambian side), covering a distance of around 25km.

The river fills up between mid-February and July (high water season), when day trips move downstream from rapids 11 to 25, covering a distance of around 18km. Only half-day trips are offered during this time. The river will usually close for its 'off season' around April or May, depending on the rain pattern for the year.

Trips are cheaper on the Zimbabwe side, costing about US$120 (versus US$160 in Zambia), but Zambia has the benefit of the cable car (and a few additional rapids) as opposed to the steep climb out on the Zimbabwe side.

Overnight and multiday jaunts can also be arranged.

An add-on activity to rafting is river-boarding, which is basically lying on a boogie board and careering down the rapids. A package including rafting for a half/full day is US$170/190. Otherwise get in touch with **Bundu Adventures** (☑0213-324406, 0978-203988; www.bunduadventures.com; 1364 Kabompo Rd, Gemstone Restaurant) about its **hydrospeed surfing** trips, where you can ride rapid number 2 on an Anvil board for US$70 for three hours.

River Cruises

River cruises along the Zambezi range from breakfast cruises to civilised jaunts on the grand *African Queen* and all-you-can-drink sunset booze cruises. Prices range from US$48 to US$85, excluding park fees. They're great for spotting wildlife, though some tourists get just as much enjoyment out of the bottomless drinks. Highly recommended.

Scenic Flights

Just when you thought the falls couldn't get any more spectacular, discover the 'flight of angels' helicopter ride that flies you right by the drama for the undisputed best views available. Rides aren't cheap, but they're worth it. **Zambezi Helicopter Company** (☑013-43569; www.zambezihelicopters. com; flights 13-/25-min US$150/284, plus US$12 govt fee) and **Bonisair** (☑0776 497888; www. bonisair.com; 15-/22-/25-mins US$150/235/277) in Zimbabwe, and **United Air Charter** (☑0955 204282, 0213-323095; www.uaczam. com; Baobab Ridge, Livingstone; 15/20/30min US$165/235/330) and **Batoka Sky** (☑0213-323589; www.seasonsinafrica.com; 15-min flights from US$155) in Zambia all offer flights. Flights cost from US$150 for 15 minutes over the falls, with longer trips available to take in the surrounding area.

On the Zambian side you can take a microlight flight with Batoka Sky, which offers another way to get fabulous aerial views.

Steam Train Journeys

To take in the romance of yesteryear, book yourself a ride on a historical steam train on the **Bushtracks Express** (☑013-45176; www.gotothevictoriafalls.com; 205 Courtney Selous Cr),

THE FALLS VIEWING SEASONS

Though spectacular at any time of year, the falls has a wet and dry season and each brings a distinct experience.

When the river is higher and the falls fuller it's the Wet, and when the river is lower and the falls aren't smothered in spray it's the Dry. Broadly speaking, you can expect the following conditions during the year:

January to April The beginning of the rainy season sees the falls begin their transitional period from low to high water, which should give you decent views, combined with experiencing its famous spray.

May to June Don't forget your raincoat, as you're gonna get drenched! While the falls will be hard to see through the mist, it'll give you a true sense of its power as 500 million litres of water plummets over the edge. The mist during this time can be seen from 50km away. If you want views, don't despair, this is the best time for aerial views with a chopper flight taking you up and over this incredible sight.

July to October The most popular time to visit, as the mist dissipates to unveil the best views and photography options from directly across the falls, while the volume maintains its rage to give you an idea of its sheer force – but only from the Zimbabwe side. However, those on the Zambian side will be able to experience Devil's Pool, which is accessible from August.

November to January The least popular time to visit, as temperatures rise and the falls are at their lowest flow. But they're impressive nevertheless, as the curtain of water divides into sections. The advantage of this time of year is you're able to swim right up to the edge of Devil's Pool on the Zambian side.

a 1953 class 14A Garratt steam train that will take you over the iconic Victoria Falls bridge at sunset with gourmet canapés and unlimited drinks. It's US$125 (including transfers, alcohol and snacks), with departures on Tuesday and Friday either at 5pm or 5.30pm; check the website for the latest schedule. Even if you're not booked on a trip it's worth getting along to the station to watch the drama of its departure.

The **Royal Livingstone Express** (☑ 0213-4699300; www.royal-living stone-express.com; Mosi-oa-Tunya Rd; US$180 incl dinner, drinks & transfers; ⊙ 4.30pm Wed & Sat) in Zambia takes you on a 3½-hour ride including five-course dinner and drinks on a 1924 10th-class or 12th-class steam engine. The journey takes you to through Mosi-oa-Tunya National Park on plush leather couches, en route to the Victoria Falls Bridge for a sundowner. It's priced at $180 per person, including return transfers within Livingstone.

Wildlife Safaris

There are plenty of options for wildlife watching in the area, both in the national park in the immediate area and further afield, as well as private game reserves.

In Zambia the game reserve section of Mosi-oa-Tunya National Park is home to white rhino, and hence a popular spot to tick off that last member from the big five in the wild. You're able to track them on foot for US$80 per person (including park fees), but you can only do this as part of a walking tour. Get in touch with Livingstone Rhino Walks (p91) or Savannah Southern Safaris (p90) for bookings; note that you need to be over 12 years of age.

The Zambezi National Park in Zimbabwe is much bigger in scale and has a greater diversity of wildlife (including a few cats) and some wonderful lodges and campsites along the Zambezi.

On both sides of the border river cruises (from US$48) along the Zambezi River are another popular way to see various wildlife including elephants, hippos and plenty of birdlife.

Another convenient option, only 15km from Victoria Falls town, is the Stanley and Livingstone Private Game Reserve. Set on a 4000-hectare private reserve here you can track the Big Five, including black rhino that have been translocated from Hwange National Park. A standard three-hour game drive costs US$100, or you can do a night drive and a bush dinner (US$137).

Hwange National Park (www.zimparks. org; national parks accommodation per day guests/ nonguests US$10/20; ⊙ main gate 6am-6pm) in Zimbabwe is the other option, with one of the largest number of elephants in the world, as well as good sightings of predators. A day trip will cost around US$220 (minimum four people), or otherwise it's a two-hour bus ride away.

You can travel further afield, with operators arranging day trips to Chobe National Park in Botswana for US$160 (excluding visas). It's only a one-hour drive from Victoria Falls, and includes a breakfast boat cruise, a game drive in Chobe National Park, lunch and transfer back to Victoria Falls by 5pm. Wildlife viewing is excellent: lions, elephants, wild dogs, cheetahs, buffaloes and plenty of antelopes.

Zipline, Flying Fox & Gorge Swings

Glide at 106km/h along a zipline (single/ tandem US$69/111), or soar like a superhero from one country to another (from Zim to Zam) on the 'bridge slide' as you whiz over Batoka Gorge (single/tandem US$45/70). Other similar options are flying-fox rides (US$42).

A *slightly* less terrifying variation of the bungee jump is the gorge swing (US$95), where you take the plunge foot first before swinging across the gorge like a human pendulum.

❶ Information

Hands down the best independent advice is from **Backpackers Bazaar** (☑ 013-45828, 013-44511, 013-42208; www.backpackersba zaarvicfalls. com; off Parkway, Shop 5, Bata Bldg; ⊙ 8am-5pm Mon-Fri, 9am-4pm Sat & Sun) in the town of Victoria Falls, run by the passionate owner, Joy, who has a wealth of info and advice for Victoria Falls and beyond. In Livingstone, the folks at Jollyboys Backpackers (p91) are also extremely knowledgeable on all the latest happenings. Both are good places to book activities and onward travel.

ZAMBIA

☑ 260

As Zambia continues to ride the wave of tourism generated by the falls, it manages to keep itself grounded, offering a wonderfully low-key destination. The waterfront straddling the falls continues its rapid development and is fast becoming one of the most exclusive destinations in Southern Africa.

Livingstone

POP 136,897 / 0213

The relaxed and friendly town of Livingstone, set just 11km from Victoria Falls, is a fantastic base for visiting the Zambian side of the natural world wonder. It attracts travellers not only to experience the falls but also to tackle the thrilling adventure scene, and has taken on the role of a backpacking mecca. Its main thoroughfare, Mosi-oa-Tunya Rd, leads south to a wonderful stretch of the Zambezi River around 7km from town.

◉ Sights

★ Victoria Falls World Heritage National Monument Site

WATERFALL

(Mosi-au-Tunya National Park; adult/child/guide US$20/10/10; ⊙ 6am-6pm) This is what you're here for. The mighty Victoria Falls is part of the Mosi-oa-Tunya National Park, located 11km outside town before the Zambia border. From the centre, a network of paths leads through thick vegetation to various viewpoints.

For close-up views of the **Eastern Cataract**, nothing beats the hair-raising (and hair-wetting) walk across the footbridge, through swirling clouds of mist, to a sheer buttress called the **Knife Edge**.

★ Devil's Pool

VIEWPOINT

(www.devilspool.net; Livingstone Island; from US$90) One of the most thrilling experiences – not only at the falls but in all of Africa – is the hair-raising journey to **Livingstone Island**. Here you will bathe in Devil's Pool – nature's ultimate infinity pool, set directly on the edge of Victoria Falls. You can leap into the pool and then poke your head over the edge to get an extraordinary view of the 100m drop. Here also you'll see the plaque marking the spot where David Livingstone first sighted the falls.

Mosi-oa-Tunya National Park

NATIONAL PARK

(adult/child US$15/7.50; ⊙ 6am-6pm) This park is divided into two sections: the Victoria Falls area and the wildlife sector. The latter is only 3km southwest of Livingstone, and most famous for its population of white rhino, which you can track on foot. For their protection, the rhino are accompanied by anti-poaching rangers round-the-clock. You can only see them as part of a pre-booked tour (US$80 per person, inclusive of park fees and hotel

transfer), booked through Livingstone Rhino Walks or Savannah Southern Safaris.

Livingstone Museum

MUSEUM

(0213-324429; www.museumszambia.org; Mosi-oa-Tunya Rd; adult/child US$ 5/3; ⊙ 9am-4.30pm) The excellent Livingstone Museum is the oldest, largest and best museum in the country. It's divided into sections covering archaeology, history, ethnography and natural history. Highlights include its collection of original David Livingstone memorabilia (including signed letters), tribal artefacts (from bark cloth to witchcraft exhibits), a life-sized model of an African village, taxidermy displays and coverage of modern-day Zambian history.

ⓖ Tours

Savannah Southern Safaris

WILDLIFE, WALKING

(0973 471486; www.savannah-southern-safaris.com) Offers a range of nature tours, but it's best known for its walks to see white rhino in Mosi-au-Tunya National Park. For two or more people it's US$70, or US$80 for individuals, inclusive of transport and park fees. Note you need to be over 12 years of age.

There are also tours to visit local communities, as well as Livingstone walking tours.

Livingstone Rhino Walks   SAFARI
(☑ 0213-322267; www.livingstonerhinosafaris.com; per person US$80) This Livingstone-based tour operator specialises in walking safaris to see white rhino in Mosi-au-Tunya National Park. Visitors must be over 12 years of age. The price is inclusive of park entry fees and transfers in the Livingstone area.

🛏 Sleeping

★**Jollyboys**
Backpackers   HOSTEL, CAMPGROUND **$**
(☑ 0213-324229; www.backpackzambia.com; 34 Kanyanta Rd; campsite per person US$9, dm US$12-15, d from US$65, d/tr/q with shared bathroom US$45/50/80; ✳@🔊☎) 🍴 The clued-in owner knows exactly what backpackers want, making Jollyboys popular for good reason. From its friendly staff, social bar and restaurant to the sunken reading lounge and sparkling pool, it's a great place to hang out. Dorms and bathrooms are spotless (with a flashpacker option, too), while the private rooms comprise A-frame garden cottages or very comfortable rooms with air-con and attached bathroom.

Rose Rabbit
Zambezi River Bushcamp   TENTED CAMP **$**
(☑ in Zimbabwe 0784 007283, 0773 368608; www.facebook.com/theroserabbit; Rapid 21, Lower Zambezi River; per person campsite/dm/tented camping/treehouse US$10/15/20/40) This riverside beach camp is one for independent travellers looking for a different scene. Right on rapid 21 of the Lower Zambezi, it will suit not only rafting enthusiasts but also a more free-spirited crowd who are into bonfire jamborees, swimming and hanging out by the beach. As well as campsites, there are dorms, tented camps and A-frame treehouse digs.

Livingstone
Backpackers   HOSTEL, CAMPGROUND **$**
(☑ 0213-324730; www.livingstonebackpackers.com; 559 Mokambo Rd; campsite US$7, dm from US$12, d US$45, with shared bathroom US$65; 🔊☎) Resembling the *Big Brother* household, this place can be a bit 'party central', particularly when the Gen Y volunteer brigade is on holiday. You'll find them lounging by the pool, in the hot tub, at the bar, or in the sandy outdoor cabana, swinging in hammocks, cooking barbecues or tackling the rock-climbing wall. There is also an open-air kitchen and living room. Very friendly staff.

Fawlty Towers   BACKPACKERS, LODGE **$**
(☑ 0213-323432; www.adventure-africa.com; 216 Mosi-oa-Tunya Rd; dm US$12, r from US$50, with shared bathroom US$45; ✳@🔊☎) As well as some of the nicest and most spacious dorms we've seen, things have been spruced up here into a guesthouse full of upmarket touches – no longer catering exclusively to backpackers. There's free wi-fi, large well-maintained lawns, a great pool, a bar, a homely lounge, free pancakes for afternoon tea, a self-catering kitchen, and no Basil or Manuel in sight.

Olga's Guesthouse   GUESTHOUSE **$$**
(☑ 0213-324160; www.olgasproject.com; cnr Mosi-oa-Tunya & Nakatindi Rds; s/d/f incl breakfast US$40/60/80; ✳🔊) 🍴 With a good location

---

ZIM OR ZAM?

Victoria Falls straddles the border between Zimbabwe and Zambia, and is easily accessible from both countries. However, the big question for most travellers is: do I visit the falls from the town of Victoria Falls, Zimbabwe, or from Livingstone, Zambia? The answer is simple: visit the falls from both sides and, if possible, stay in both towns. You'll need to pay for extra visas, but you've come this far so it's worth it.

From the Zimbabwean side, you're further from the falls, though the overall views are much, much better. From the Zambian side, for daring souls you can literally stand on top of the falls from Devil's Pool, though from here your perspective is narrowed.

The town of Victoria Falls was built for tourists, so it's easily walkable and located right next to the entrance to the Falls. It has a natural African bush beauty. As for whether it's safe given Zimbabwe's ongoing political issues, the answer is a resolute 'yes'.

Livingstone is an attractive town with a relaxed ambience and a proud, historic air. Since the town of Victoria Falls was the main tourist centre for so many years, Livingstone feels more authentic, perhaps because locals earn their livelihood through means other than tourism. Livingstone is bustling with travellers year-round, though the town is fairly spread out, and is located 11km from the falls.

Livingstone

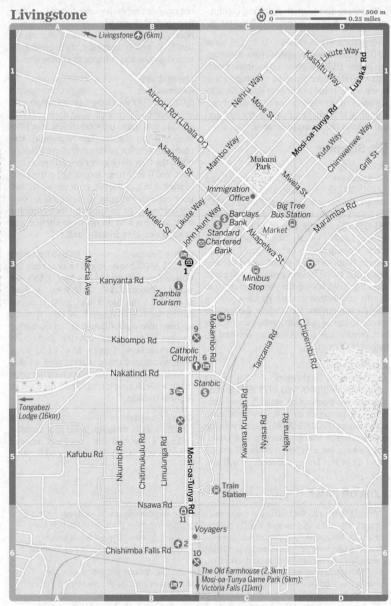

N
0 ──────────── 500 m
0 ──────────── 0.25 miles

Livingstone ✈ (6km)

Kashitu Way

Likute Way

Lusaka Rd

Nehru Way

Mose St

Airport Rd (Libala Dr)

Mambo Way

Mosi-oa-Tunya Rd

Kuta Way

Chimwemwe Way

Grill St

Akapelwa St

Mukuni Park

Mwela St

Maramba Rd

Mutelo St

Likute Way

John Hunt Way

Immigration Office

Barclays Bank

Big Tree Bus Station

Standard Chartered Bank

Market

Akapelwa St

Macha Ave

4 🏨 🏛 1

Kanyanta Rd

Minibus Stop

ℹ

Zambia Tourism

5

9 ✕

Mokambo Rd

Kabompo Rd

Catholic Church

6

Tanzania Rd

Chipembi Rd

Nakatindi Rd

Stanbic

3 🏨

Kwama Krumah Rd

Nyasa Rd

Ngama Rd

8 ✕

Kafubu Rd

Nkumbi Rd

Chitimukulu Rd

Limulunga Rd

Mosi-oa-Tunya Rd

Train Station

Nsawa Rd

11

Voyagers

2

Chishimba Falls Rd

10 ✕

The Old Farmhouse (2.3km);
Mosi-oa-Tunya Game Park (6km);
Victoria Falls (11km)

7

Tongabezi Lodge (16km)

---

in the centre of town, Olga's offers clean, spacious rooms with cool tiled floors, teak furniture and slick bathrooms just a few feet away. Profits go towards helping an organisation supporting local youth. Another bonus is its on-site Italian restaurant, Olga's Italian Corner.

ZigZag GUESTHOUSE $$
(☎0213-322814; www.zigzagzambia.com; 693 Linda Rd, off Mosi-oa-Tunya Rd; s/d/tr incl breakfast

Livingstone

US$50/70/90; P✱@☎🐾) Don't be deceived by the motel-meets-caravan-park exterior: the rooms here are more boutique B&B with loving touches throughout. Rooms are spotless, and set on a sprawling garden property with an assortment of fruit trees, picnic tables, a plush pool and a playground for kids. Its great restaurant is another drawcard, too.

Victoria Falls Waterfront
LODGE, CAMPGROUND $$
(☑0213-320606; www.thevictoriafallswaterfront.com; Sichango Dr; campsite per person US$13, s/d tented camping US$36/48, s/d incl breakfast chalet from US$165/215; ✱☎🐾) Sharing space with the luxury resorts along the banks of the Zambezi, this is the only waterfront lodge that caters to budget travellers. For this reason it's a popular place, with a wilderness charm (crocs inhabit a small creek on the property), and a choice of camping, domed tents or alluring riverside chalets. Its pool with decking and bar overlooking the river is unsurprisingly popular at sunset.

★ Stanley Safari Lodge
LODGE $$$
(☑in Malawi 0265-1794491; www.stanleysafaris.com; Stanley Rd; per person with full board & activities from US$510; @☎🐾) Intimate and indulgent, Stanley is a 10km drive from the falls in a peaceful spot surrounded by mopane (woodland). Rooms scattered among the landscaped bush garden are as plush as can be expected at these prices; the standouts are the rustic open-air suites where you can soak up nature from your own private plunge pool. When you tire of that, curl up by the fire in the open-air lounge. Rates are all-inclusive.

Tongabezi Lodge
LODGE $$$
(☑0979 312766, 0213-327468; www.tongabezi.com; cottage/house per person incl full board & activities from US$775/875; ✱☎🐾) Has sumptuous, spacious cottages, open-faced 'treehouses'

and private dining decks. The houses are good for families and have private plunge pools. Guests are invited to spend an evening on nearby Sindabezi Island (from US$595 per person), a luxurious, rustic getaway.

✕ Eating

★ Da Canton
GELATERIA $
(Mosi-Oa-Tunya Rd; gelato small/large cup ZMW8/24, pizza from ZMW19; ☺9am-11pm) While all the Italian food here is tasty and authentic, it's the homemade gelato that has locals raving. The Italian owner makes all 18 flavours, including all the classics and some original concoctions.

★ Cafe Zambezi
AFRICAN $$
(☑0978 978578; www.facebook.com/cafezambezi; 217 Mosi-oa-Tunya Rd; mains US$6-10; ☺7.15am-midnight; ☎🍴) Head straight through to the courtyard, sunny by day and candlelit by night. Bursting with local flavour, the broad menu covers local favourites of goat meat, smoky crocodile tail and mopane (woodland) caterpillars. Authentic wood-fired pizzas are a winner or sink your teeth into impala or eggplant-and-haloumi burgers.

★ Olga's Italian Corner
ITALIAN $$
(www.olgasproject.con; cnr Mosi-oa-Tunya & Nakatindi Rds; pizza & pasta ZMW35-88; ☺7am-10pm; ☎🍴) Olga's does authentic wood-fired thin-crust pizzas, as well as delicious homemade pasta classics all served under a large thatched roof. Great options for vegetarians include the lasagne with its crispy blackened edge served in the dish. All profits go to a community centre to help disadvantaged youth.

Golden Leaf
INDIAN $$
(☑0213-321266; 1174 Mosi-Oa-Tunya Rd; mains ZMW54-95; ☺12.30-10pm) As soon as those aromas hit you upon arrival you'll realise Golden Leaf is the real deal when it comes to authentic

Indian food. It's a good option for vegetarians with a lot of choices including house-made paneer dishes, creamy North Indian curries and tandoori dishes in the evenings.

ZigZag CAFE **$$**
(Mango Tree Cafe; www.zigzagzambia.com/the-mango-tree-cafe; 693 Linda Rd, off Mosi-oa-Tunya Rd; mains from ZMW25-62; ☉7am-9pm; 🛜) Zig-Zag does drool-inducing homemade muffins, excellent Zambian coffee and smoothies using fresh fruit from the garden. Its changing menu of comfort food is all made from scratch, and you can expect anything from drop scones (pikelets) with bacon and maple syrup to thin-crust pizzas and burgers.

Drinking & Nightlife

The Sundeck BAR
(http://royal-livingstone.anantara.com/the-sundecks; Mosi-au-Tunya Rd; cocktail from ZMW40; ☉10.30am-7pm; 🛜) Just the spot for a sundowner, this open-air bar within the Royal Livingstone Hotel overlooks a dramatic stretch of the Zambezi. As well as the usual bar drinks there's a choice of old-fashioned cocktails such as the Manhattan, Americano and champagne cocktail. There's also decent burgers, mezze platters and salads. From here it's a 15-minute walk to the falls.

Shopping

Wayawaya FASHION & ACCESSORIES
(www.wayawaya.no; Mosi-oa-Tunya Rd; ☉9am-5pm) 🖉 A social enterprise founded by two Norwegian girls, Wayawaya sells quality, contemporary handmade bags put together by local women. Its principles are based on the slow fashion movement, and you can meet all the ladies when visiting. Get in touch if you want to volunteer.

ℹ️ Information

DANGERS & ANNOYANCES
Don't walk from town to the falls as there have been a number of muggings along this stretch of road – even tourists on bicycles have been targeted. It's a long and not terribly interesting walk anyway, and simply not worth the risk (especially given there are elephants around). Take a taxi or free shuttle from your guesthouse. While Livingstone is generally a very safe town, avoid walking around town once it becomes dark.

IMMIGRATION
Immigration Office (☎0213-3320648; www.zambiaimmigration.gov.zm; Mosi-oa-Tunya Rd; ☉8am-1pm & 2-5pm Mon-Fri)

MEDICAL SERVICES
SES-Zambia (www.ses-zambia.com; Mosi-au-Tunya Rd, AVANI Victoria Falls Resort; ☉8am-5pm) The best medical facility in the area, both for emergency services and general medicine. It's within the **AVANI resort** (☎0978 777044; www.minorhotels.com/en/avani; Mosi-oa-Tunya Rd).

MONEY
The following banks accept MasterCard and Visa, but can occasionally go offline during power outages.
Barclays in town (cnr Mosi-oa-Tunya Rd & Akapelwa St) and at the AVANI resort.
Standard Chartered Bank (Mosi-oa-Tunya Rd) In town.
Stanbic (Mosi-oa-Tunya Rd) In town.

POLICE
Police (☎0213-320116, 0213-323575; Maramba Rd)

POST
Post Office (Mosi-oa-Tunya Rd) Has a poste restante service.

TOURIST INFORMATION
Tourist Centre (☎0213-321404; www.zambiatourism.com; Mosi-oa-Tunya Rd; ☉8am-5pm Mon-Fri, 8am-noon Sat) Mildly useful and can help with booking tours and accommodation, but Jollyboys and Fawlty Towers have all the information you need.

ℹ️ Getting There & Away

AIR
Livingstone's newly renovated airport – officially known as Harry Mwanga Nkumbula International Airport – is located 6km northwest of town. It has an ATM and free wi-fi. It's around a US$5 taxi ride into town, or US$8 to the waterfront hotels.
South African Airways (☎0213-323031; www.flysaa.com) and **British Airways** (Comair; ☎in South Africa +27 10-3440130; www.britishairways.com) have daily flights to and from Johannesburg (1¾ hours); the cheapest economy fare starts at around US$270 return.
Proflight Zambia (☎0977 335563, in Lusaka 0211-252452; www.proflight-zambia.com) flies daily from Livingstone to Lusaka for around US$210 one way (1¼ hours).

BUS & MINIBUS
Plenty of minibuses and shared taxis ply the route from the Big Tree Bus Station at Livingstone's town market along Senanga Rd in Livingstone. Note that plans are in place to relocate the bus terminal to Nakatindi Rd. As muggings have been reported, it is best to take a taxi if you arrive at night.

CAR & MOTORCYCLE

If you're driving a rented car or motorcycle, be sure to carefully check all info regarding insurance, and that you have all the necessary papers for checks and border crossings such as 'owners' and 'permission to drive' documents, insurance papers and a copy of the carbon tax receipt. Expect to pay around US$100 in various fees when crossing the border into Zimbabwe.

TRAIN

While the bus is a much quicker way to get around, the train to Lusaka is for lovers of slow travel or trains. The operative word here is *slow*, taking anywhere from 15 to 20 hours for the trip to Lusaka (economy/business/1st-class sleeper ZMW 70/90/135), via Choma, departing 8pm on Monday and Friday. Bring your own food. Reservations are available at the **train station** (☑ 0961 195353), which is signed off Mosi-oa-Tunya Rd.

❶ Getting Around

CAR & MOTORCYCLE

Hemingways (☑ 0213-323097; www.heming wayszambia.com) in Livingstone has new 4WD Toyota Hiluxes for around US$225 per day. Vehicles are fully kitted out with everything you need, including cooking and camping equipment. Drivers must be over 25.

Voyagers (☑ 0213-320517, 0213-323259; www. voyagerszambia.com; 163 Mosi-oa-Tunya Rd) Zambian operator affiliated with Europcar has reasonably priced 4WDs for around US$100 per day.

TAXIS

Minibuses run regularly along Mosi-oa-Tunya Rd to Victoria Falls and the Zambian border (ZMW5,15 minutes). Blue taxis cost ZMW60 to ZMW80 from the border to Livingstone. Coming from the border, shared taxis are parked just over from the waiting taxis, and depart when full. The going rate for one day's taxi hire around Livingstone and the falls is about US$25.

ZIMBABWE

☑ 263

There may still be a long way to go, but finally things seem to be looking up for Zimbabwe. All the bad news that has kept it in the glare of the spotlight – rampant land reform, hyperinflation and food shortages – fortunately now seem to be a thing of the past. In reality, safety has never been a concern for travellers here and, even during the worst of it, tourists were never targets for political violence. Word of this seems to have spread, as tourists stream back to the Zim side of the falls.

Victoria Falls

POP 33,360 / ☑ 013

A genuine bucket-list destination, Victoria Falls remains one of Africa's most famous tourist towns. Not only does it offer the best views of the iconic falls, but it also has a world-class adventure-tourism scene and wildlife safaris.

It's home to the country's tourism industry, and despite Zimbabwe's political issues, it's always been a safe spot for tourists; locals are exceptionally friendly. While for a few years it felt like a resort in off-season, there's no mistake about it now – it's officially reopened for business.

Though built specifically for tourism, it retains a relaxed local feel, and has neat, walkable streets (though not at dark, because of the wild animals) lined with hotels, bars and some of the best crafts you'll find anywhere in Southern Africa.

◉ Sights

★**Victoria Falls National Park**   WATERFALL
(US$30; ⊙ 6am-6pm) Here on the Zimbabwe side of the falls you're in for a real treat. Some two-thirds of Victoria Falls are located here, including the main falls themselves, which flow spectacularly year-round. The walk is along the top of the gorge, following a path with various viewing points that open up to extraordinary front-on panoramas of these world-famous waterfalls.

★**Jafuta Heritage Centre**   CULTURAL CENTRE
(www.elephantswalk.com/heritage.htm;   Adam Stander Dr, Elephant's Walk; admission by donation; ⊙ 8am-5pm) **FREE** This impressive little museum details the cultural heritage of Zimbabwe's indigenous ethnic groups. There's good background information on the Shona, Ndebele, Tonga and Lozi people, as well as fascinating artefacts, jewellery and costumes.

Zambezi National Park   NATIONAL PARK
(☑ 013-42294; www.zimparks.org; day/overnight US$15/23; ⊙ 6am-6pm) Just 5km from the town centre is this vastly underrated national park, comprising 40km of Zambezi River frontage and a spread of wildlife-rich mopane (woodland) and savannah. It's best known for its herds of sable, elephant, giraffe, zebra and buffalo, plus the occasional (rarely spotted) lion, leopard and cheetah. It's easily accessible by 2WD vehicle.

Victoria Falls

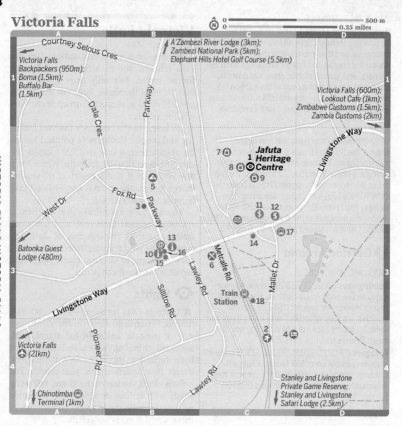

Victoria Falls

Stanley and Livingstone
Private Game Reserve WILDLIFE RESERVE
(Victoria Falls Private Game Reserve; ☑013-44571; www.stanleyandlivingstone.com/activities) This private 4000-hectare game reserve 12km from town has the Big Five, including the critically endangered black rhino, which you're almost guaranteed to see. Game drives are US$100, US$135 for a night drive with a bush dinner.

🛏 Sleeping

★ Victoria Falls
Backpackers HOSTEL, CAMPGROUND $
(☑013-42209; www.victoriafallsbackpackers.com; 357 Gibson Rd; camping/dm per person US$10/18, d US$60, with shared bathroom US$50; @🛜🏊) One of the best budget choices in town, this long-standing backpackers received a much-needed revamp when the original owners returned. The eclectic mix of rooms are scattered among the well-tended garden property full of quirky touches. Other notable features are its bar, small inviting pool, games room and TV lounge, plus self-catering kitchen, massage and fish spa.

Victoria Falls
Restcamp & Lodges CAMPGROUND, LODGE $
(☑013-40509; www.vicfallsrestcamp.com; cnr Parkway & West Dr; camping/dm US$16/20, s/d dome tents from US$29/40, s/d chalets without bathroom US$35/46, cottages from US$127; 🌀🛜🏊) A great alternative for independent travellers, it has a relaxed holiday-camp feel, within secure grassy grounds, with a choice of no-frills dorms, lodge-style rooms (or pricier air-con rooms with bathroom) and safari tents. There's a lovely pool and fantastic open-air restaurant, In Da Belly. Wi-fi available (for a fee).

Zambezi National
Park Lodge CHALETS, CAMPGROUND $$
(☑013-42294; www.zimparks.org; camping $17, cottage $138; 🌀) These wonderful two-bedroom cottages are right on the Zambezi river. You'll need to bring your own food, but all come with fridges, full kitchen, couches, TV, bathtubs and even air-con. There's an outdoor barbecue area too. Further into the park are basic bush campsites (firewood US$5), but with no water or ablutions.

★ Victoria Falls Hotel LUXURY HOTEL $$$
(☑0772 132175, 013-44751; www.victoriafalls hotel.com; 1 Mallet Dr; s/d incl breakfast from US$423/455; 🌀🛜🏊) Built in 1904, this historic hotel (the oldest in Zimbabwe) oozes elegance and sophistication. It occupies an impossibly scenic location, looking across manicured lawns (with roaming warthogs) to the gorge and bridge. You can't see the falls as such, but you do see the spray from some rooms. Taking high tea here at Stanley's Terrace is an institution.

Stanley and Livingstone
Safari Lodge LODGE $$$
(☑013-44571; www.stanleyandlivingstone.com; Stanley & Livingstone Private Game Reserve; r per person incl full board & activities US$436; 🌀🛜🏊) Set on a private game reserve 15km from Victoria Falls, this luxury lodge will suit visitors without the time to visit a national park but who want to be surrounded by wildlife. Rooms on the luxurious grounds feature all the modern comforts combined with Victorian-style bathrooms featuring claw-foot tubs, lounge suite and patio.

Batonka Guest Lodge GUESTHOUSE $$$
(☑013-47189/90; www.batonkaguestlodge.com; Reynard Rd; s/d incl breakfast US$195/300; 🌀🛜🏊) 🍃 Mixing modern comforts with colonial charm, Batonka is an excellent choice for those not wanting a large-scale resort. It has a relaxed ambience, with rooms overlooking a landscaped lawn and inviting pool. Rooms have stylish bathrooms, cable TV and filter coffee. The reception/bar/restaurant is in a homestead-style building with wraparound veranda and a boutique interior design with original artwork throughout.

Elephant Camp LODGE $$$
(☑013-44571; www.theelephantcamp.com; s/d incl full board US$838/1118; @🛜🏊) One of the best spots to splash out; the luxurious 'tents' have a classic lodge feel and are set on a private concession within the Victoria Falls National Park. Each room has its own outdoor private plunge pool and balcony decking to spot grazing animals or the spray of the falls. You might get to meet Sylvester, the resident cheetah.

🍴 Eating

★ Lookout Cafe CAFE $$
(☑0782 745112; www.wildhorizons.co.za/the-lookout-cafe; Batoka Gorge; mains US$12-15; ⏰8am-7pm; 🛜) A stunning location overlooking Batoka Gorge. Enjoy views of the bridge and the Zambezi river while tucking into a burger or crocodile kebab, or a cold drink on its open-air deck or grassy lawn terrace. It's operated by **Wild Horizons** (☑013-44571, 0712 213721; www.wildhorizons. co.za; 310 Parkway Dr), so you'll get the added

Victoria Falls & Mosi-oa-Tunya National Parks

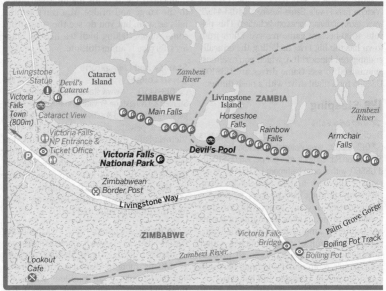

entertainment of watching daredevils take the plunge or soar across the gorge.

⭐**Lola's Tapas & Carnivore Restaurant** SPANISH, AFRICAN **$$**
(📞013-42994; 8B Landela Complex; dishes US$8-20; ⏰8am-10pm; 🛜) Run by welcoming host Lola from Barcelona, this popular eatery combines a menu of Mediterranean cuisine with local game meats, with anything from crocodile ravioli to paella with kudu. Other items include zebra burgers, impala meatballs, and more traditional tapas dishes. There's also a full spread of all-you-can-eat game meat for US$30.

⭐**Boma** AFRICAN **$$**
(📞013-43211; www.victoria-falls-safari-lodge.com; Squire Cummings Rd, Victoria Falls Safari Lodge; buffet US$40; ⏰dinner 7pm, cafe from 7am) Enjoy a taste of Africa at this buffet restaurant set under a massive thatched roof. Here you can dine on smoked crocodile tail, BBQ warthog, guinea fowl stew and wood-fired spit roasts; and the more adventurous can try a mopane worm (you'll get a certificate from the chef for your efforts). There's also traditional dancing (8pm), interactive drumming (8.45pm) and fortune telling by a witch doctor. Bookings essential.

Africa Café CAFE **$$**
(www.elephantswalk.com/africa_cafe.htm; Adam Stander Dr, Elephant's Walk; breakfast/burgers US$7/11; ⏰8am-5pm; 🛜🚭) This appealing outdoor cafe does the best coffee in Victoria Falls, made by expert baristas using beans sourced from Zimbabwe's eastern highlands. There's plenty of seating scattered about to enjoy big breakfasts, burgers, vegetarian dishes and desserts such as its signature baobab-powder cheese cake. There's a bar, too.

In Da Belly Restaurant AFRICAN, INTERNATIONAL **$$**
(📞013-332077; Parkway, Victoria Falls Restcamp & Lodges; meals US$5-15; ⏰7am-9.30pm) Under a large thatched hut, looking out to a sparkling pool, this relaxed open-air eatery has a menu of warthog schnitzel, crocodile curry and impala burgers, as well as one of the best breakfast menus in town. The name is a play on Ndebele, one of the two major population tribes in Zimbabwe.

🍷 Drinking & Nightlife

⭐**Stanley's Terrace** HIGH TEA
(📞013-44751; www.victoriafallshotel.com/stanleys-terrace; Mallet Dr, Victoria Falls Hotel; high tea for 1-/2-people US$15/30; ⏰high tea 3-6pm; 🛜) The Terrace at the stately Victoria Falls Hotel just

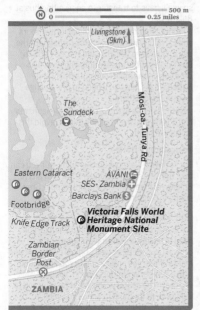

brims with English colonial ambience. High tea is served to a postcard-perfect backdrop of the gardens and Victoria Falls Bridge, with polished silverware, decadent cakes and three-tiered trays of finger sandwiches. (Cucumber? Why yes, of course.) A jug of Pimms makes perfect sense on summer day at US$24. The only thing missing is croquet.

Buffalo Bar   BAR
(www.victoria-falls-safari-lodge.com; Squire Cummings Rd, Victoria Falls Safari Lodge; ⊙7am-10pm) Unquestionably the best sundowner spot in town; enjoy a gin-and-tonic on its outdoor terrace overlooking distant animals on the plains of Zambezi National Park. Part of the Victoria Falls Safari Lodge, it's a good pre-dinner spot if you've got a booking at the hotel's Boma restaurant. Otherwise come during the day for the 1pm vulture feeding.

🛍 Shopping

★**Elephant's Walk Shopping**
& Artist Village   SHOPPING CENTRE
(🖉0772 254552; www.elephantswalk.com; Adam Stander Dr; ⊙9am-5pm) A must for those in the market for quality Zimbabwean and African craft, this shopping village is home to boutique stores and galleries owned by a

collective that aims to promote and set up local artists.

At the back of Elephant's Walk Village you'll find local vendors at **Big Curio Open Market** (Adam Stander Dr), and the **Tshaka's Den Complex** (⊙7.30am-6pm), both of which sell locally made handicraft and Shona sculpture.

Matsimela   COSMETICS
(www.matsimela.co.za; Adam Stander Dr, Elephant's Walk; ⊙8am-5pm) South African body-care brand Matsimela has set up shop here with an enticing aroma of natural scented soaps, body scrubs and bath bombs (anything from rose and lychee to baobab-seed oil). They also offer massage treatments (from US$30), manicures and pedicures.

Prime Art Gallery   ART
(🖉0772 239805; www.primeart-gallery.com; Adam Stander Dr, Elephant's Walk; ⊙8am-5pm) This quality gallery, run by two friendly brothers, represents more than 40 local artists, most notably it has original pieces by Dominic Benhura, Zimbabwe's pre-eminent current-day Shona sculptor whose worked has been exhibited around the world.

Ndau Collection   JEWELLERY
(🖉013-386221; www.ndaucollectionstore.com; Adam Stander Dr, Elephant's Walk; ⊙8am-6pm) This upmarket showroom stocks handmade individual pieces, including silver bracelets, rings and necklaces, made at its on-site studio. They also sell exquisite antique African trade beads to be incorporated into custom-made jewellery. Its range of organic fragrances made using local ingredients is also popular, as are its croc-skin purses and briefcases.

ℹ Information

DANGERS & ANNOYANCES
Mugging is not such a problem any more, but at dawn and dusk wild animals such as elephants and warthogs do roam the streets away from the town centre, so take taxis at these times. Although it's perfectly safe to walk to and from the falls, it's advisable to stick to the more touristed areas.

INTERNET ACCESS
Most lodges and restaurants offer wi-fi; otherwise there are a few internet cafes about town, including **Econet** (Park Way; per 30min/1hr US$1/2; ⊙8am-5pm Mon-Fri, to 1pm Sat & Sun).

VICTORIA FALLS VICTORIA FALLS

MONEY
Barclays Bank (off Livingstone Way)
Standard Chartered Bank (off Livingstone Way)

POST
Post Office (off Livingstone Way)

TOURIST INFORMATION
Backpackers Bazaar (p89) Definitive place for all tourist info and bookings.
Zimbabwe Tourism Authority (☑0772 225427, 013-44202; zta@vicfalls.ztazim.co.zw; Park Way; ⊙8am-6pm) A few brochures, but not very useful.

❶ Getting There & Away

AIR
Victoria Falls Airport is located 18km southeast of town. Its new international terminal opened in late 2015.

While nothing compared to the heydays of the 1980s and '90s, there's still no shortage of flights arriving at Victoria Falls. Most come from Johannesburg (US$150 to US$500 return). There are also regular flights from Harare with FastJet and Air Zimbabwe for as little as US$20.

Check out www.flightsite.co.za or www.travelstart.co.za, where you can search all the airlines including low-cost carriers (and car-hire companies) for the cheapest flights and then book yourself.
Air Namibia (☑0774 011320, 0771 401918; www.airnamibia.com)
Air Zimbabwe (☑0712 212121, 013-443168, 013-44665; www.airzimbabwe.aero)
British Airways (☑013-2053; www.britishairways.com)
FastJet (☑86 7700 6060; www.fastjet.com/zw; cnr Livingstone Way and Parkway Dr; ⊙9am-4pm Mon-Fri, to 1pm Sat)
South African Airways (☑04-702702; www.flysaa.com)

BUS & SHARED TAXI
Though its standards have dropped in recent years, **Intercape Pathfinder** (☑0778 888880; www.intercapepathfinder.com) easily remains the safest and most comfortable bus company in Zimbabwe.

To Bulawayo & Harare
Intercape Pathfinder has departures for Hwange National Park (US$10, two hours), Bulawayo (US$15, six hours) and Harare (US$35, 12 hours) on Wednesday, Friday and Sunday at 7.30am from outside the Kingdom Hotel. You can book tickets online. If you're heading to Hwange National Park, you'll need to tell the driver beforehand as it only stops there on request. There's no direct bus to Harare,

so you'll have to transfer to an awaiting bus at Bulawayo.

From Chinotimba Bus Terminal, Bravo Tours and Extra City have departures throughout the day to Bulawayo (US$13) and Harare (US$25). Buy tickets at the bus station. They can also drop you on the main road outside Hwange National Park, but you'll need to pre-arrange transport from there.

Note that, due to the prevalence of elephants and donkeys on the road, it's best to avoid this journey at night.

To Johannesburg
These days it's almost quicker to fly, but you can take the Intercape Pathfinder from Vic Falls to Bulawayo, then connect with Intercaper Greyhound to Johannesburg.

CAR & MOTORCYCLE
If you're driving a rented car into Zambia, you need to make sure you have insurance and carbon tax papers, as well original owner documents. When you enter Zambia you are issued with a Temporary Import Permit, valid for while you are in the country. This must be returned to immigration for them to acquit the vehicle.

TRAIN
A popular way of getting to/from Victoria Falls is by the overnight *Mosi-oa-Tunya* train that leaves Victoria Falls daily at 7pm for Bulawayo (economy/2nd/1st class US$8/10/12, 12 hours). First class (comprising two-berth compartments) is the only way to go. Be aware that delays of several hours aren't uncommon, and you'll need to bring your own food. Make reservations at the **ticket office** (⊙7am-noon & 2-7pm) inside the train station.

The luxurious **Rovos Rail** (☑in South Africa 012-315 8242; www.rovos.com; from US$1650) to Pretoria also departs from here.

❶ Getting Around

CAR & MOTORCYCLE
Zimbabwe Car Hire (☑0783 496253, 09-230306; www.zimbabwecarhire.com; Victoria Falls Airport) gets positive reviews for its good rates, and is a good place for 4WDs. All the big name companies, such as **Hertz** (☑013-47012; www.hertz.co.za; 1 Bata Bldg, Parkway; ⊙8am-5pm Mon-Fri), **Avis** (☑091 2511128; www.avis.com; 251 Livingstone Way) and **Europcar** (☑013-43466; Victoria Falls Airport), have offices in town and at the airport.

TAXI
A taxi around town costs about US$10, or slightly more after dark.

Wildlife

by David Lukas

Despite Botswana being mostly covered in sand, and Namibia being one of the driest places on earth, huge numbers of wildlife still wander their ancestral routes. In fact Botswana and Namibia both offer superb wildlife-viewing opportunities, particularly in the north where the Chobe and Okavango Rivers create one of the world's premier wetland ecosystems.

Running giraffes, Okavango Delta (p93)

DOUG McKINLAY/GETTY IMAGES ©

Cats

Excellent vision and keen hearing make Botswana and Namibia's cats superb hunters. Some of Africa's most stunning scenes are big cats making their kills.

Caracal

1 *Weight 8–19kg; length 80–120cm* A tawny cat with long, pointy tufted ears and jacked up hind legs, enabling it to make vertical leaps of 3m to swat birds. Best seen: Okavango Delta, Nkasa Rupara National Park (NP).

Leopard

2 *Weight 30–60kg (female), 40–90kg (male); length 170–300cm* Leopards rely on expert camouflage to stay hidden. During the day you might only spot one reclining in a tree, but at night there is no mistaking its bone-chilling groans. Best seen: Okavango Delta, Moremi Game Reserve (GR), Okonjima Nature Reserve (NR), Erindi Private Game Reserve (GR), Chobe National Park (NP).

Lion

3 *Weight 120–150kg (female), 150–225kg (male); length 210–275cm (female), 240–350cm (male)* Africa's most feared predators, lions are equipped with teeth that tear effortlessly through bone and tendon; taking down an animal as large as a bull giraffe. Each pride is based around generations of females that do the majority of hunting. Best seen: Chobe NP, Etosha NP, Moremi GR, Central Kalahari Game Reserve (GR).

Cheetah

4 *Weight 40–60kg; length 200–220cm* A world-class sprinter, reaching speeds of 112km/h, the cheetah runs out of steam after 300m and must cool down for 30 minutes before hunting again. So adapted for hunting, it lacks the strength and teeth to defend its prey from attack by larger predators. Best seen: Etosha NP, Nxai Pans NP, Central Kalahari GR.

Black-Footed Cat

5 *Weight 1–2kg; length 40–60cm* This pint-sized predator is one of the smallest cats in the world. Though only 25cm high, this nocturnal cat is a fearsome hunter that can leap six times its height. Best seen: Okavango Delta, Moremi GR.

Wildcat

6 *Weight 3–6.5kg; length 65–100cm* Found near villages, the wildcat looks like a common tabby and is the direct ancestor of our domesticated house cats. It's best identified by its unmarked rufous ears and longish legs. Best seen: Okavango Delta, Moremi GR, Okonjima NR.

Primates

Botswana and Namibia are home to a mere three species of primates. Of these, only the Chacma baboon is common and widespread, but they are so fascinating to watch that they make up for the absence of other primates.

Vervet Monkey

1 *Weight 4–8kg; length 90–140cm* Found in northern Botswana and Namibia, vervets spend a lot of time on the ground, but always near to trees where they can escape from predators. Each troop is composed of females, while males fight each other for bragging rights and access to females. Best seen: Moremi GR, Okavango Delta, Etosha NP.

Lesser Galago

2 *Weight 100–250g; length 40cm* The nocturnal lesser galago (commonly called 'bushbaby') is phenomenally agile and acrobatic, making 5m-long leaps between trees and even leaping into the air to catch flying prey. In Botswana and Namibia they are only found in lush forested woodlands along the rivers of the north. Best seen: Okavango Delta, Moremi GR, Nkasa Rupara NP.

Chacma Baboon

3 *Weight 12–30kg (female), 25–45kg (male); length 100–200cm* Chacma baboons are worth watching because they have exceedingly complex social dynamics. See if you can spot signs of friendship, deception or deal-making within a troop. Best seen: Moremi GR, Linyanti, Bwabwata NP.

SOUPYSUE/GETTY IMAGES ©

Cud-Chewing Mammals

Many of Africa's ungulates (hoofed mammals) live in groups to protect themselves. Ungulates that chew cud and have horns are called bovines. Antelopes are particularly numerous, with over a dozen species in Botswana and Namibia.

Hartebeest

1 *Weight 120–220kg; length 190–285cm* The long face allows this short-necked antelope to reach down and graze while still looking up for predators. Best seen: Etosha NP, CKGR, Okavango Delta.

Gemsbok

2 *Weight 180–240kg; length 230cm* With straight 1m-long horns, this desert antelope can survive for months on scant water, derived from plants, and withstands temperatures that would kill other animals. Best seen: Central Kalahari GR, Khutse GR, Etosha NP, Namib-Naukluft NP.

African Buffalo (Cape Buffalo)

3 *Weight 250–850kg; length 220–420cm* The African buffalo is similar to a cow on steroids, with a fearsome set of curling horns. They're usually docile, but if angry or injured can be extremely dangerous. Best seen: Moremi GR, Okavango Delta, Chobe NP, Bwabwata NP.

Impala

4 *Weight 40–80kg; length 150–200cm* Their prodigious capacity to reproduce means impalas reach great numbers quickly, outstripping predators' ability to eat them all. Best seen: Namibia's Etosha NP to see the unique black-faced impala, Okavango Delta, Moremi GR.

Wildebeest

5 *Weight 140–290kg; length 230–340cm* The wildebeest of northern Botswana are sedentary creatures, moving only when conditions fluctuate seasonally. Because they favour expansive views, wildebeest are in turn easily viewed themselves. Best seen: Etosha NP, Moremi GR, Okonjima NR.

Large Mammals

Apart from giraffes, these ungulates are not ruminants and can be seen over a much broader range of habitats than bovines. They have been in Africa for millions of years and are among the most successful mammals on the continent.

Black Rhinoceros

1 *Weight 700–1400kg; length 350–450cm* Once widespread and abundant, the rhino has been poached to the brink of extinction for its horn, worth more than gold. Best seen: Damaraland, Etosha NP Okaukuejo waterhole, Khama Rhino Sanctuary.

Mountain Zebra

2 *Weight 230–380kg; length 260–300cm* The unique mountain zebras of central Namibia differ from their savannah relatives in having unstriped bellies and rusty muzzles. Best seen: Erongo Mountains, Naukluft Mountains, Fish River Canyon.

African Elephant

3 *Weight 2200–3500kg (female), 4000–6300kg (male); height 2.4–3.4m (female), 3–4m (male)* Elephants are abundant at Chobe NP, where up to 55,000 congregate in the lush wetlands. Even more interesting are the unique desert-loving elephants of Namibia. Best seen: Chobe NP, Okavango Delta, Moremi GR, Nkasa Rupara NP, Bwabwata NP, Damaraland.

Hippopotamus

4 *Weight 510–3200kg; length 320–400cm* Hippos spend all their time in or very near water, and are tremendously ferocious and strong if provoked. Best seen: Okavango Delta, Moremi GR, Chobe NP, Bwabwat NP.

Giraffe

5 *Weight 450–1200kg (female), 1800–2000kg (male); height 3.5–5.2m* The 5m-tall giraffe does such a good job reaching up to high branches that stretching down to get a drink of water is difficult. Though they stroll along casually, they can outrun any predator. Best seen: Chobe NP, Etosha NP, Okavango Delta.

Carnivores

As well as the cats, Botswana and Namibia are home to a couple of dozen carnivores, ranging from slinky mongoose to highly social hunting dogs. All are linked in having 'carnassial' (slicing) teeth, but visitors may be more interested in witnessing their hunting prowess.

Bat-Eared Fox

1 *Weight 3–5kg; length 70–100cm* This animal has huge ears that it swivels in all directions to pick up the sounds of subterranean food like termites. Monogamous pairs of these social foxes will often mingle with other pairs and families when hunting. Best seen: Central Kalahari GR, Etosha NP, Khutse GR.

Meerkat

2 *Weight 0.5–1kg; length 50cm* The area's several species of mongoose may be best represented by the meerkat (also known as a suricate). Spending much of their time standing up, if threatened they all spit and jump up and down together. Best seen: Makgadikgadi Pans, Kgalagadi Transfrontier Park.

African Wild Dog

3 *Weight 20–35kg; length 100–150cm* Uniquely patterned, hunting dogs run in packs of 20 to 60. These highly social but endangered canids are incredibly efficient hunters. Best seen: Moremi GR, Linyanti, Okavango Delta, Bwabwata NP.

Cape Fur Seal

4 *Weight 80kg (female), 350kg (male); length 120–200cm* Several giant breeding colonies of seals are located on Namibia's Skeleton Coast. Forced to gather in dense numbers as protection against marauding hyenas, these colonies are turbulent, noisy and exciting to watch. Best seen: Cape Cross Seal Reserve.

Spotted Hyena

5 *Weight 40–90kg; length 125–215cm* Living in packs ruled by females, these savage fighters use their bone-crushing jaws to disembowel prey or to do battle with lions. Best seen: Okavango Delta, Etosha NP, Moremi GR, Damaraland.

Birds of Prey

Botswana and Namibia are home to about 70 species of hawk, eagle, vulture and owl, so you are likely to see an incredible variety of birds of prey here. Look for them perching on trees, soaring high overhead or gathered around a carcass.

Lappet-Faced Vulture

1 *Length 115cm* Vultures mingle with predators around carcasses in Botswana and Namibia. Through sheer numbers, they compete for scraps of flesh and bone. The monstrous lappet-faced vulture gets its fill before other vultures move in. Best seen: Makgadigadi NP, Okavango Delta, Chobe NP.

Pale Chanting Goshawk

2 *Length 55cm* Small clusters of these slim grey raptors with red beaks and legs often perch low on bushes. Look closely because they are probably following some other small hunter like a honey badger. Best seen: Moremi GR, Etosha NP, Okavango Panhandle.

Bateleur

3 *Length 60cm* French for 'tightrope-walker', the name refers to its distinctive low-flying aerial acrobatics. In flight, look for its white wings and tailless appearance; at close range look for the bold colour pattern and scarlet face. Best seen: Okavango Delta, Kgalagadi Transfrontier Park, Moremi GR.

African Fish Eagle

4 *Length 75cm* With a wingspan over 2m, this replica of the American bald eagle hunts for fish around water, but it is most familiar for its loud ringing vocalisations that have become known as 'the voice of Africa'. Best seen: Okavango Delta, Nkasa Rupara NP, Moremi GR, Bwabwata NP.

Secretary Bird

5 *Length 100cm* With the body of an eagle and the legs of a crane, the secretary bird towers 1.3m tall and walks up to 20km a day across the savannah in search of vipers, cobras and other snakes that it kills with lightning speed and agility. Best seen: Moremi GR, CKGR, Etosha NP.

Other Birds

Come to Botswana and Namibia prepared to see an astounding number of birds in every shape and colour. You may find them a pleasant diversion after a couple of days of staring at sleeping lions.

Lilac-Breasted Roller

1 *Length 40cm* This gorgeously coloured bird gets its name from the tendency to 'roll' from side to side in flight as a way of showing off its iridescent blues, purples and greens. Best seen: Everywhere! Okavango Panhandle, Moremi GR, Etosha NP, Chobe NP.

Cape Gannet

2 *Length 85cm* These crisply marked seabirds congregate by the thousands to catch fish with high-speed dives into the waves. Best seen: Cape Cross Seal Reserve, Skeleton Coast Park, Dorob NP.

Lesser Flamingo

3 *Length 100cm* Deep rose pink and gathering by the hundreds of thousands on shimmering salt lakes, the lesser flamingo creates one of Africa's most dramatic wildlife spectacles. Best seen: Walvis Bay.

Ostrich

4 *Length 200–270cm* Weighing upwards of 130kg, these flightless birds escape predators by running away at 70km/h or lying flat on the ground to resemble a pile of dirt. Wild ostriches are still found in the Kalahari Desert. Best seen: CKGR, Etosha NP, Kgalagadi Transfrontier Park.

African Penguin

5 *Length 60cm* The African penguin got its former moniker (the jackass penguin) for its donkey-like call, part of the courtship displays given by the males. Some penguin colonies are ridiculously tame. Best seen: Namibian coast and on offshore islands.

Hamerkop

6 *Length 60cm* The hamerkop is a stork relative with an oddly crested, woodpecker-like head. Nicknamed the 'hammerhead', it is frequently observed hunting frogs and fish at the water's edge. Look for its massive 2m-wide nests in nearby trees. Best seen: Okavango Panhandle, Moremi GR, Caprivi Strip.

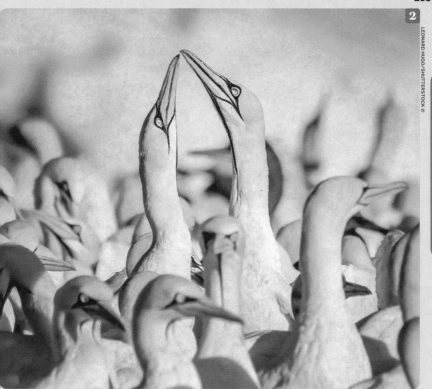

Namibia

POP 2.4 MILLION / ☎ 264

Best Places to Eat

➡ Leo's (p227)
➡ Purple Fig Bistro (p247)
➡ Raft (p308)
➡ Anchor @ The Jetty (p307)
➡ Sam's Giardino Hotel (p298)

Best Places to Sleep

➡ Serra Cafema Camp (p284)
➡ Sossusvlei Desert Lodge (p319)
➡ Little Kulala (p317)
➡ Hoanib Skeleton Coast Camp (p288)
➡ Erongo Wilderness Lodge (p236)
➡ Inchingo Chobe River Lodge (p266)

Why Go?

Namibia has some of the most stunning landscapes in Africa, and a trip through the country is one of the great road adventures. Natural wonders such as that mighty gash in the earth at Fish River Canyon and the wildlife utopia of Etosha National Park enthral, but it's the lonely desert roads, where mighty slabs of granite rise out of swirling desert sands, that will sear themselves in your mind. It's like a coffee-table book come to life as sand dunes in the world's oldest desert meet the crashing rollers along the wild Atlantic coast.

Among all this is a German legacy, evident in the cuisine and art nouveau–architecture and in festivals such as Windhoek's legendary Oktoberfest. Namibia is also the headquarters of adventure activities in the region, so whether you're a dreamer or love hearing the crunch of earth under your boots, travel in Namibia will stay with you long after the desert vistas fade.

When to Go
Windhoek

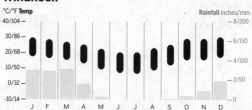

High Season (Jun–Oct)	Shoulder Season (May & Nov)	Low Season (Dec–Apr)
Temperatures soar in September.	Heavy rains in November. May is mild.	Rains begin in earnest in December.

Namibia Highlights

❶ Etosha National Park (p250) Crouching by a waterhole in one of the world's premier wildlife venues.

❷ Sossusvlei (p314) Watching the sun rise from the top of fiery-coloured dunes.

❸ Fish River Canyon (p336) Hiking through one of Africa's greatest natural wonders.

❹ Twyfelfontein (p276) Admiring the ancient petroglyphs of the San people.

❺ Kaokoveld (p280) Getting off the beaten track (and the sealed road) in a true African wilderness.

❻ Caprivi Strip (p261) Exploring fabulous wildlife reserves while they're still quiet.

❼ Waterberg Plateau (p242) Hiking to the top for breathtaking views, while keeping an eye out for rare sable and roan.

❽ Swakopmund (p289) Fulfilling your need for adrenaline at the extreme-sports capital of Namibia.

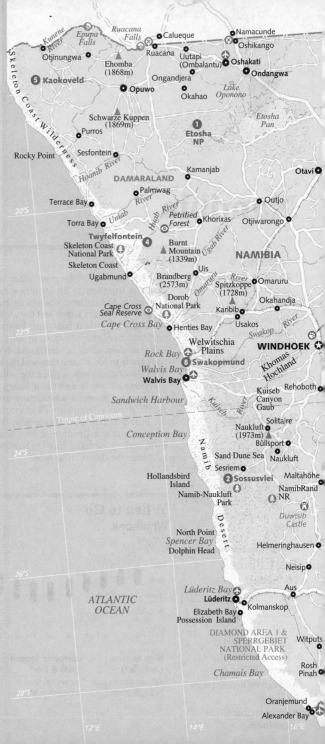

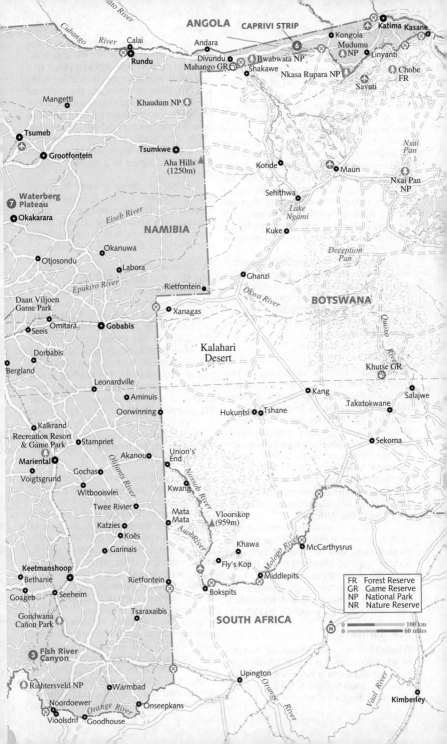

WINDHOEK

POP 325,860 / 📞 061

If Namibia is Africa for beginners, then Windhoek is very much its capital in more than name only. It's the sort of place that divides travellers, with those who love it for the respite it offers from the rigours of life on the African road facing off against those who find it a little too 'Western' for their African tastes. And they're both right: Windhoek is a modern, well-groomed city where office workers lounge around Zoo Park at lunchtime, tourists funnel through Post St Mall admiring African curios and taxis whizz around honking at potential customers. Neo-baroque cathedral spires, as well as a few seemingly misplaced German castles, punctuate the skyline, and complement the steel-and-glass high-rises.

Such apparent incongruities aside, Windhoek makes a great place to begin or break a journey through Namibia or rest at journey's end. The accommodation choices, food variety, cultural sights, shopping and African urban buzz give it an edge not found anywhere else in Namibia.

History

The city of Windhoek has existed for just over a century, but its history is as diverse as its population. During the German colonial occupation, it became the headquarters for the German Schutztruppe (Imperial Army), which was ostensibly charged with brokering peace between the warring Herero and Nama in exchange for whatever lands their efforts would gain for German occupation. For over 10 years at the turn of the 20th century, Windhoek served as the administrative capital of German South West Africa.

In 1902, a narrow-gauge railway was built to connect Windhoek to the coast at Swakopmund, and the city experienced a sudden spurt of growth. During this period, Windhoek began to evolve into the business, commercial and administrative centre of the country, although the modern city wasn't officially founded until 1965.

◎ Sights

Windhoek is not really known for its tourist attractions, but it is one of Africa's more agreeable cities and if you're here for a few days and have time to kill, it's an easy and interesting city for a stroll.

Zoo Park   PARK

(Map p222; ☉ dawn-dusk) **FREE** Although this leafy park served as a public zoo until 1962, today it functions primarily as a picnic spot and shady retreat for lunching office workers. Five thousand years ago the park was the site of a Stone Age elephant hunt, as evidenced by the remains of two elephants and several quartz tools found here in the early 1960s. This prehistoric event is honoured by the park's prominent **elephant column** (Map p222), designed by Namibian sculptor Dörthe Berner.

A rather anachronous mate to the elephant column is the Kriegerdenkmal, topped by a rather frightening golden imperial eagle, which was dedicated in 1987 to the memory of German Schutztruppe soldiers who died in the Nama wars of 1893–94.

★ Christuskirche   CHURCH

(Map p222; Fidel Castro St) **FREE** Windhoek's best-recognised landmark, and something of an unofficial symbol of the city, this German Lutheran church stands on a traffic island and lords it over the city centre. An unusual building, it was constructed from local sandstone in 1907 and designed by architect Gottlieb Redecker in conflicting neo-Gothic and art-nouveau styles. The resulting design looks strangely edible, and is somewhat reminiscent of a whimsical gingerbread house. The altarpiece, the *Resurrection of Lazarus,* is a copy of the renowned work by Rubens.

To view the interior, pick up the key during business hours from the nearby church office on Peter Müller St.

Daan Viljoen Game Park   WILDLIFE RESERVE

(📞 061-232393; per person/vehicle N$40/10; ☉ sunrise-sunset) This beautiful wildlife park sits in the Khomas Hochland about 18km west of Windhoek. You can walk to your heart's content through lovely wildlife-rich desert hills, and spot gemsbok, kudu, mountain zebra, springbok, hartebeest, warthog and eland. Daan Viljoen is also known for its birdlife and over 200 species have been recorded, including the rare green-backed heron and pin-tailed whydah. Daan Viljoen's hills are covered with open thorn-scrub vegetation that allows excellent wildlife viewing, and three walking tracks have been laid out. There's also an onsite luxury lodge (p226).

The 3km Wag-'n-Bietjie Trail follows a dry riverbed from near the park office to Stengel Dam. A 9km circuit, the Rooibos

Windhoek

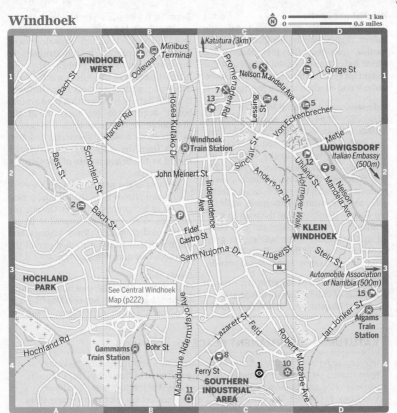

Windhoek

◎ Sights
1 Showground..................................... C4

🛏 Sleeping
2 Haus Ol-Ga.. A2
3 Hotel Thule....................................... D1
4 Olive Grove...................................... C1
5 Roof of Africa.................................. D1

🍴 Eating
6 Joe's Beerhouse.............................. C1
7 Social.. C1

🍷 Drinking & Nightlife
8 Club London..................................... C4
Joe's Beer House.......................... (see 6)

9 Pharaoh Lounge.............................. D2

✪ Entertainment
10 Ster Kinekor.................................... C4

🛍 Shopping
Cape Union Mart......................... (see 10)
11 Safari Den.. B4

ℹ Information
12 Botswanan Embassy....................... D2
13 French Embassy.............................. C1
14 Rhino Park Private Hospital........... B1
15 South African High
Commission.................................. D3

Trail crosses hills and ridges and affords great views back to Windhoek in the distance. The 34km Sweet-Thorn Trail circuits the empty eastern reaches of the reserve.

To get to Daan Viljoen, take the C28 west from Windhoek; Daan Viljoen is clearly signposted off the Bosua Pass Hwy, about 18km from the city.

Heinitzburg Castle
CASTLE

(Map p222; 22 Heinitzburg St) FREE Uphill from Robert Mugabe Ave are the three Windhoek 'castles', including the 1914 Heinitzburg, which today houses a hotel (p226) and fine restaurant (p227). The other castles, Schwerinsburg and Sanderburg, are nearby.

Independence Memorial Museum
MUSEUM

(Map p222; ☎061-302236; www.museums.com. na; Robert Mugabe Ave; ⊙9am-5pm Mon-Fri, 10am-5pm Sat & Sun) FREE Opened in 2014, this museum is dedicated to the country's anti-colonial and independence struggle. The first floor tells the story of Namibia under colonial rule, with the next floor up shifting gears to the resistance movement, while the top floor is dominated by the road to independence. Don't miss taking the glass elevator up the outside of the building for great views out over Windhoek. There's a statue of founding president Sam Nujoma outside.

National Museum of Namibia
MUSEUM

(Map p222; ☎061-302230; www.museums.com. na; Robert Mugabe Ave; ⊙9am-6pm Mon-Fri, 3-6pm Sat & Sun) FREE The excellent display on Namibia's independence at the country's historical museum provides some enlightening context to the struggles of this young country. But probably the most interesting part of the museum is the rock-art display, with some great reproductions; it would definitely be worth a nose around before heading to see rock art at the Brandberg or Twyfelfontein. It's housed in Windhoek's oldest surviving building, dating from the early 1890s; it originally served as the headquarters of the German Schutztruppe.

The rest of the museum contains memorabilia and photos from the colonial period as well as indigenous artefacts. Outside the museum, don't miss the somewhat incongruous collection of railway engines and coaches, which together formed one of the country's first narrow-gauge trains.

Owela Museum
MUSEUM

(State Museum; Map p222; www.museums.com.na; 4 Robert Mugabe Ave; ⊙9am-6pm Mon-Fri, 3-6pm Sat & Sun) FREE Part of the National Museum

KATUTURA – A PERMANENT PLACE?

In 1912, during the days of the South African mandate – and apartheid – the Windhoek town council set aside two 'locations', which were open to settlement by black Africans working in the city: the Main Location, which was west of the city centre, and Klein Windhoek, to the east. The following year, people were forcibly relocated to these areas, which effectively became haphazard settlements. In the early 1930s, streets were laid out in the Main Location and the area was divided into regions. Each subdivision within these regions was assigned to an ethnic group and referred to by that name (eg Herero, Nama, Owambo, Damara), followed by a soulless numerical reference.

In the 1950s, the Windhoek municipal council, with encouragement from the South African government (which regarded Namibia as a province of South Africa), decided to 'take back' Klein Windhoek and consolidate all 'location' residents into a single settlement northwest of the main city. There was strong opposition to the move, and in early December 1959 a group of Herero women launched a protest march and boycott against the city government. On 10 December, unrest escalated into a confrontation with the police, resulting in 11 deaths and 44 serious injuries. Frightened, the roughly 4000 residents of the Main Location submitted and moved to the new settlement, which was ultimately named 'Katutura'. In Herero the name means 'we have no permanent place', though it can also be translated as 'the place we do not want to settle'.

Today in independent Namibia, Katutura is a vibrant Windhoek suburb – Namibia's Soweto – where poverty and affluence brush elbows. The town council has extended municipal water, power and telephone services to most areas of Katutura, and has also established the colourful and perpetually busy Soweto Market, where traders sell just about anything imaginable. Unlike its South African counterparts, Katutura is relatively safe by day, assuming you can find a trustworthy local who can act as a guide.

The tourist office can book township tours but even better is **Katu Tours**, which offers guided tours by bike. You get a good taste of township life and the chance to meet plenty of locals; it also includes dropping into Penduka, where local women produce a range of handicrafts and textiles. Tours depart at 8am from Katutura and take 3½ hours.

of Namibia, located about 600m from the main building, exhibits at the Owela Museum focus on Namibia's natural and cultural history; note it may sometimes close early.

Trans-Namib Transport Museum   MUSEUM
(Map p222; ☑ 061-2982624; www.museums.com.na; N$5; ⊙ 8am-1pm & 2-5pm Mon-Fri) Windhoek's beautiful old Cape Dutch–style train station on Bahnhof St was constructed by the Germans in 1912, and was expanded in 1929 by the South African administration. Across the driveway from the entrance is the German steam locomotive *Poor Old Joe*, which was shipped to Swakopmund in 1899 and reassembled for the treacherous journey across the desert to Windhoek. Upstairs in the train station is the small but worthwhile Trans-Namib Transport Museum outlining Namibian transport history, with a focus on rail transport.

Gathemann's Complex   HISTORIC BUILDING
(Map p222; Independence Ave) FREE Along Independence Ave are three colonial-era buildings, all designed by the famous architect Willi Sander. The one furthest south was built in 1902 as the Kronprinz Hotel, which later joined Gathemann House (now home to a gourmet restaurant) to function as a private business. The most notable of the three is the Erkrath Building, which was constructed in 1910 as a private home and business.

Kaiserliche Realschule   HISTORIC BUILDING
(Map p222; Robert Mugabe Ave) FREE Windhoek's first German primary school was built in 1908, and opened the following year with a class size of 74 students. Notice the curious turret with wooden slats, which was designed to provide ventilation for European children unaccustomed to the African heat. The building later housed Windhoek's first German high school and an English middle school, and today it's the administrative headquarters of the National Museum of Namibia.

National Art Gallery   GALLERY
(Map p222; cnr Robert Mugabe Ave & John Meinert St; Mon-Fri free, Sat N$20; ⊙ 8am-5pm Tue-Fri, 9am-2pm Sat) This art gallery contains a permanent collection of works reflecting Namibia's historical and natural heritage. The collection displays works by Muafangejo – Namibia's first black artist to gain international acclaim. His linocuts depict the liberation struggle from a religious and narrative perspective.

Owambo Campaign Memorial   MONUMENT
(Map p222; Bahnhof St) At the entry to the train station parking area, you'll see the Owambo Campaign Memorial, which was erected in 1919 to commemorate the 1917 British and South African campaign against Chief Mandume of the Kwanyama Owambo. Heavily outmatched by the colonial armies, the chief depleted all of his firepower and committed suicide rather than surrendering.

Tintenpalast   NOTABLE BUILDING
(Map p222; ☑ 061-2889111; www.parliament.gov.na; ⊙ tours 9am-noon & 2-4pm Mon-Fri) FREE The former administrative headquarters of German South West Africa have been given a new mandate as the Namibian parliament building. As a fitting homage to the bureaucracy of government, the name of the building means 'Ink Palace', in honour of all the ink spent on typically excessive official paperwork. The building is remarkable mainly for its construction from indigenous materials.

The surrounding gardens, which were laid out in the 1930s, include an olive grove and a bowling green. In the front, have a look at Namibia's first post-independence monument, a bronze-cast statue of the Herero chief Hosea Kutako, who was best known for his vehement opposition to South African rule.

Turnhalle   HISTORIC BUILDING
(Map p222; Bahnhof St) The Turnhalle was built in 1909 as a training hall for the Windhoek Gymnastic Club, though in 1975 it was modernised and turned into a conference hall. On 1 September of that year, it served as the venue for the first Constitutional Conference on Independence for South West Africa, which subsequently – and more conveniently – came to be called the Turnhalle Conference. During the 1980s, the building hosted several political summits and debates that paved the way to Namibian independence.

It now houses a tribunal for the Southern Africa Development Community (SADC).

☞ Tours

Katu Tours   TOUR
(☑ 081 303 2856; www.katutours.com; tours per person N$450) Cycling tours in Katutura, one of Windhoek's most dynamic (and historically, poverty-stricken) neighbourhoods.

NAMIBIA WINDHOEK

Central Windhoek

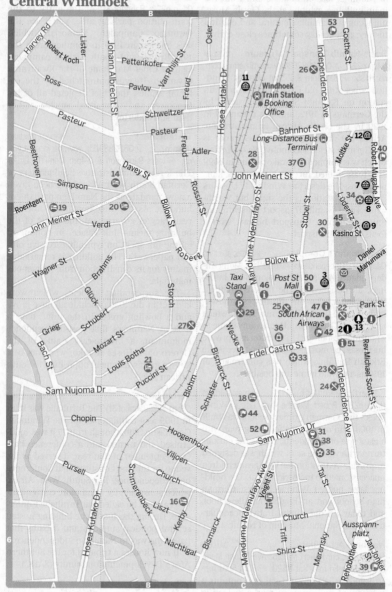

★ **Cardboard Box Travel Shop** TOURS
(Map p222; ☑ 061-256580; www.namibian.org; Johann Albrecht St) Attached to the hostel of the same name, this recommended travel agency can arrange both budget and upmarket bookings all over the country. Great website, too.

★ **Chameleon Safaris** SAFARI
(Map p222; ☑ 061-247668; www.chameleonsafaris. com; Voight St) This travel agency, attached to the backpacker hostel of the same name, is recommended for all types of safaris around the country.

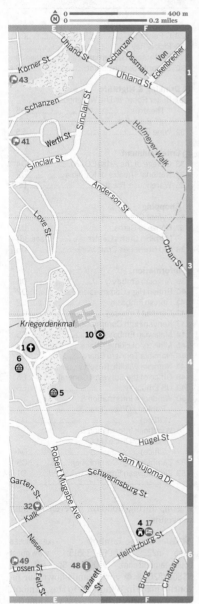

Kaokohimba Safaris   CULTURAL TOUR
(📞065-695106; koos.cuneneiway.na) Kaokohimba organises cultural tours through Kaokoveld and Damaraland, and wildlife-viewing trips in Etosha National Park.

Magic Bus Safaris   BUS
(📞081 129 8093, 061-259485; magicbus@iafrica.com.na) This small company runs budget trips from Windhoek to Sossusvlei, Etosha and other destinations.

Muramba Bushman Trails   CULTURAL TOUR
(📞067-220659; bushman@natron.net) This popular company, owned by Reinhard Friedrich in Tsumeb, provides a unique introduction to the Heikum San people.

Wild Dog Safaris   ADVENTURE
(📞061-257642; www.wilddog-safaris.com) This friendly operation runs Northern Namibia Adventures and Southern Swings, Etosha or Sossusvlei circuits, as well as longer participation camping safaris and accommodated excursions.

★ Festivals & Events

Bank Windhoek Arts Festival   ART
(www.bankwindhoek.com.na; ⊘Feb-Sep) This is the largest arts festival in the country, with events running from February to September.

Mbapira/Enjando Street Festival   CARNIVAL
(⊘Mar) Windhoek's big annual bash is held around the city centre. It features colourful gatherings of dancers, musicians and people in ethnic dress.

Oktoberfest   BEER
(www.windhoekoktoberfest.com; ⊘Oct) True to its partially Teutonic background, Windhoek stages this festival towards the end of October – beer lovers should not miss it.

Independence Day   PARADE
(⊘21 Mar) This national day is celebrated in grand style, with a parade and sports events.

Wild Cinema Festival   FILM
An annual international film festival that takes place in late spring and early summer.

Windhoek Karneval (WIKA)   CARNIVAL
(windhoek-karneval.org/en/; ⊘Apr) This German-style carnival takes place in late April and features music performances, a masked ball and a parade down Independence Ave.

Windhoek Show   AGRICULTURE
(www.windhoek-show.com; ⊘Sep-Oct) In late September or early October the city holds this agricultural show, on the showgrounds (Map p219) near the corner of Jan Jonker and Centaurus Sts.

NAMIBIA WINDHOEK

Central Windhoek

◎ Sights
1 Christuskirche E4
2 Elephant Column D4
3 Gathemann's Complex D3
4 Heinitzburg Castle....................................F6
5 Independence Memorial Museum E4
6 Kaiserliche Realschule E4
7 National Art Gallery D2
8 National Museum of Namibia D2
Owambo Campaign
Memorial ....(see 11)
9 Owela Museum D3
10 Tintenpalast E4
11 Trans-Namib Transport
Museum...C1
12 Turnhalle D2
13 Zoo Park D4

❶ Activities, Courses & Tours
Cardboard Box Travel Shop .... (see 14)
Chameleon Safaris .... (see 15)

⬛ Sleeping
14 Cardboard Box Backpackers B2
15 Chameleon Backpackers Lodge
& Guesthouse C6
16 Guesthouse Tamboti................................B6
17 Hotel Heinitzburg F6
18 Hotel-Pension Steiner C5
19 Rivendell Guest House A3
20 Villa Verdi B3
21 Vondelhof Guesthouse B4

❷ Eating
22 Café Balalaika D4
23 Checkers D4
24 Crafter's Kitchen D4
25 Gourmet C4
26 La Marmite..D1
Leo's ....(see 17)
Namibia Crafts Cafe ....(see 38)
27 Nice... B4

28 O Pensador C2
29 Pick & Pay..C4
Restaurant Gathemann .... (see 3)
30 Shoprite Supermarket...........................D3

❸ Drinking & Nightlife
31 Boiler Room @ The Warehouse
Theatre..D5
Café Balalaika .... (see 22)
32 Wine Bar... E5

❹ Entertainment
33 College of the Arts (COTA)...................D4
34 National Theatre of Namibia D2
35 Warehouse Theatre D5

❺ Shopping
36 Cymot Greensport C4
37 House of Gems D2
Namibia Crafts Centre................ (see 38)
38 Old Breweries Craft Market..................D5

❻ Information
39 Angolan Embassy D6
40 British High Commission......................D2
41 Finnish Embassy E2
42 German Embassy D4
43 Kenyan High Commission E1
44 Malawian Embassy C5
45 Ministry of Home Affairs......................D3
46 Namibia Tourism Board C3
47 Namibia Wildlife Resorts D4
48 Office of the Surveyor General.............E6
49 US Embassy E6
50 Windhoek Information &
Publicity Office (Branch
Office) D3
51 Windhoek Information &
Publicity Office (Main
Office) D4
52 Zambian High Commission...................C5
53 Zimbabwean Embassy D1

/AE//Gams Arts Festival ART
(www.facebook.com/AeGamsArtsandCulturalFestival/; ☉ Oct) Highlighting Namibian artwork, it's held in venues around Windhoek.

🛏 Sleeping

Whether you bed down in a bunkhouse or a historic castle, Windhoek has no shortage of appealing accommodation options. Compared to the rest of the country, prices in the capital are relatively high, though you can usually be assured of a corresponding level of quality. Note that in a city this small, space is limited, so consider booking your bed well in advance, especially in high

season, during holidays or even on busy weekends.

★ **Guesthouse Tamboti** GUESTHOUSE $
(Map p222; ☎ 061-235515; www.guest house-tamboti.com; 9 Kerby St; s/d from N$560/820; ❋ @ 🛜 ⛱) Hands-down our favourite place in Windhoek to stay, Tamboti is very well-priced, has a great vibe and terrific hosts who will go out of their way to ensure you are comfortable (such as driving you to the airport if you have a flight to catch). The rooms here are spacious and well set up – it's situated on a small hill just above the city centre. Book ahead as it's popular.

★ **Cardboard Box Backpackers**   HOSTEL $
(Map p222; ☑ 061-228994; www.cardboard
box.com.na; 15 Johann Albrecht St; camping/dm
N$90/150, r/tr/q N$450/550/660; @☎☲)
Hostels are hard to come by in this country
but 'The Box' has been doing it for years,
with a rep as one of Windhoek's better backpackers. It has a fully stocked bar and swimming pool to cool off in, and travellers have
a tough time leaving. Rates include free
coffee and pancakes in the morning and
there are free pick-ups from the Intercape
bus stop.

If you do decide to motivate yourself, the
city centre is just a short walk away, and
the excellent on-site travel shop gives useful information and can help sort out your
future travel plans.

Chameleon Backpackers
Lodge & Guesthouse   HOSTEL $
(Map p222; ☑ 061-244347; www.chameleonback-
packers.com; 5-7 Voight St; dm/s/d incl breakfast
from N$170/280/350; @☎☲) With a chilled
vibe and a considerable range of accommodation options, this Backpackers offers
decent-sized, luxurious African-chic rooms
and spick-and-span dorms at shoestring prices. There are also three self-catering flats if
you're in town for an extended period. The
on-site safari centre offers some of the most
affordable trips in Namibia.

Haus Ol-Ga   GUESTHOUSE $
(Map p219; ☑ 061-235853; www.olga-namibia.
de; 91 Bach St; s/d N$450/650) The name of
this German-oriented place is derived from
the owners' names: Gesa Oldach and Erno
Gauerke, who go out of their way to provide
a good measure of Deutsch hospitality here
in Namibia. Haus Ol-Ga enjoys a nice, quiet garden atmosphere in Windhoek West,
and is a good choice if you're looking for accommodation that is more reminiscent of
a homestay. It's like staying at your grandma's. Rooms are simple, neat and unfussy.

Hotel-Pension Steiner   HOTEL $
(Map p222; ☑ 061-222898; www.natron.net/
tour/steiner/main.html; 11 Wecke St; s/d from
N$660/1020; ☎☲) Although it has an excel-
lent city-centre location just a few minutes'
walk from Independence Ave, this small
hotel-pension is sheltered from the hustle
and bustle of the street scene. Simple but
comfortable rooms open to a thatched bar
and swimming pool, where you can quickly
unwind.

Rivendell Guest House   GUESTHOUSE $
(Map p222; ☑ 061-250006; www.rivendell-
namibia.com; 40 Beethoven St; s N$290-700, d
N$570-1000; ☎☲) This homey set-up gets
good reviews from travellers. It's a very relaxed guesthouse located in a shady suburb
within easy walking distance of the city
centre. Bright and airy rooms open to a
lush garden and a sparkling pool; cheaper
rooms have shared bathrooms. It's a good
place to try if everywhere is full as the owner will try and help with alternative accommodation. Rates do not include breakfast.

Roof of Africa   HOTEL $$
(Map p219; ☑ 061-254708; www.roofofafrica.com;
124-126 Nelson Mandela Ave; s N$960-1300, d
N$1250-1590; ❈@☎☲) A pleasant haven locat-
ed about 30 minutes by foot from the city
centre, Roof of Africa has a rustic barnyard
feel, offering well-designed rooms of varying
price, size and comfort that attract laid-back
travellers looking for a quiet retreat from
the city. It's worth shelling out a few more
Namibian dollars for the luxury rooms.

The better rooms come with far more
space, sink-in-and-smile beds and modern
bathrooms; ask to see a few though, as they
do vary.

Vondelhof Guesthouse   GUESTHOUSE $$
(Map p222; ☑ 061-248320; www.vondelhof.com; 2
Puccini St; s/d/tr N$830/1190/1440; ❈@☎☲)
This rather grand-looking affair has great-
sized rooms; the very friendly staff have a
good attitude towards hospitality and serve
a decent breakfast. Ask to have a look at a
few rooms but we try to snare No 8, which is
a beauty. Don't let the horrible green colour
on the outside of the building put you off;
the interior is far more palatable.

Casa Blanca   BOUTIQUE HOTEL $$
(☑ 061-249623; s/d N$1038/1496; ☎☲) Styling
itself as a boutique hotel, the long-standing
White House has good if unexciting rooms –
those opening onto the garden are the nicest.
They've recently added a nice Moroccan-style
teahouse and Jacuzzi near the pool. Street
noise can be a problem.

Hotel Thule   HOTEL $$
(Map p219; ☑ 061-371950; www.hotelthule.com;
1 Gorge St; s/d from N$1285/1785; ❈@☎☲)
Perched on a hilltop in Eros Park, akin to
the Beverly Hills of Windhoek, Hotel Thule
commands some of the most impressive
views of any hotel in the capital. Cavernous
rooms with a touch of European elegance

are complemented by a classy restaurant and wraparound sundowner bar where you can sip a cocktail while watching the twinkling lights of the city switch on for the night.

Email the hotel for better rates than listed here.

Belvedere Boutique Hotel   BOUTIQUE HOTEL $$
(☑ 061-258867; www.belvedere-boutiquehotel.com; 76 Dr Kwame Nkrumah St; r/ste from N$1650/1875; ✳ 🖭 🖬) Highly recommended by travellers, the Belvedere has classically styled rooms, quiet grounds and professional service. It's the sort of place that will appeal equally to business travellers and those seeking calm in the big city before heading out into the Namibian wilds.

★ **Hotel Heinitzburg**   HOTEL $$$
(Map p222; ☑ 061-249597; www.heinitzburg.com; 22 Heinitzburg St; s/d from N$2137/3154; ✳ @ 🖬) Inside Heinitzburg Castle, which was commissioned in 1914 by Count von Schwerin for his fiancée, Margarethe von Heinitz, Hotel Heinitzburg is a member of the prestigious Relais & Chateaux hotel group, and far and above the most personable upmarket accommodation in Windhoek. Rooms have been updated for the 21st century with satellite TV and air-con.

Another highlight of the hotel is the palatial dining room, which offers excellent gourmet cuisine and an extensive wine dungeon.

★ **Olive Grove**   BOUTIQUE HOTEL $$$
(Map p219; ☑ 061-302640; www.olivegrove-namibia.com; 20 Promenaden St; s/d standard N$995/1610, luxury N$1319/2370; ✳ @ 🖬) Refined elegance is the order of the day at this boutique hotel in Klein Windhoek, which features 10 individually decorated rooms and two suites awash in fine linens, hand-crafted furniture and all-around good taste. Guests in need of some pampering can indulge in a massage, or warm their toes on a cold Windhoek night in front of the crackling fire.

If the package here isn't high-end enough for you, check out its exclusive lodging next door.

Villa Verdi   BOUTIQUE HOTEL $$$
(Map p222; ☑ 061-221994; 4 Verdi St; s/d budget N$860/1400, standard N$1280/2200; ✳ 🖬 🖬) This unique Mediterranean-African hybrid features whimsically decorated rooms complete with original paintings and arty touches. Straddling the divide between midrange and top-end properties, Villa Verdi competes in opulence and class with the bigger hitters on the block, yet offers more affordably priced rooms by targeting the boutique market rather than the tour-group crowd.

Daan Viljoen Lodge   LODGE $$$
(☑ 061-232393; www.sunkarros.com; camping N$260, s/d chalet from N$1774/2818; @) Daan Viljoen Lodge provides luxury accommodation within Daan Viljoen Game Park – a refreshing alternative for those who can't handle city life. Chalets have captivating views and private barbecues or you can take advantage of the well-stocked restaurant. Wildlife drives are also available.

✗ Eating

Namibia's multicultural capital provides a range of restaurants. It's worth stretching your budget and indulging the gourmand lifestyle while you're in town. Be advised that reservations are a very good idea on Friday and Saturday nights.

Namibia Crafts Cafe   CAFE $
(Map p222; Old Breweries Complex, cnr Garten & Tal Sts; mains N$35-90; ⊙ 9am-6pm Mon-Fri, to 3.30pm Sat & Sun) This cafe-restaurant-bar is a great spot to perch yourself above Tal St, checking out the local action and taking in the breeze from the outside deck. The extensive drinks menu includes health shakes and freshly squeezed juices. Meals in the way of salads, large pitas, cold-meat platters, open sandwiches and healthy (or just filling) breakfasts hit the spot.

Checkers   SUPERMARKET $
(Map p222; Gustav Voigts Centre; ⊙ 8am-7pm Mon-Fri, 8am-6pm Sat, 8am-3pm Sun) If you're keeping a tight budget, Windhoek is a grocery paradise for self-caterers.

Crafter's Kitchen   CAFE $
(Map p222; 109 Independence Ave; mains N$30-55; ⊙ 8am-2pm Mon-Sat) You can shop for handicrafts here and get a bite at the same time from the busy little kitchen which churns out decent fuel, such as toasties, burgers and soups, for locals and tourists alike. Takeaway is available; consider dropping in for the cake and coffee too.

★ **Joe's Beerhouse**   PUB FOOD $$
(Map p219; ☑ 061-232457; www.joesbeerhouse. com; 160 Nelson Mandela Ave; mains N$74-179; ⊙ 4.30-11pm Mon-Thu, 11am-11pm Fri-Sun) A legendary Windhoek institution, this is where

you can indulge (albeit with a little guilt...) in flame-broiled fillets of all those amazing animals you've seen on safari! Seriously. We're talking huge cuts of zebra tenderloin served with garlic butter, ostrich skewers, peppered springbok steak, oryx sirloin, crocodile on a hotplate and marinated kudu steak.

★**Stellenbosch**
Wine Bar & Bistro BISTRO $$
(☑061-309141; www.thestellenboschwinebar.com; 320 Sam Nujoma Dr; mains N$81-169; ⊙noon-10pm) When well-to-do locals want an enjoyable night out with the guarantee of good food, this is their No.1 pick. With a classy outdoor-indoor setting and thoughtfully conceived international food – beef burger with camembert, Bangladeshi lamb curry, crispy pork belly, baked vanilla cheesecake – and excellent service, we can't think of a single good reason not to join them.

La Marmite AFRICAN $$
(Map p222; ☑061-240306; 383 Independence Ave; mains N$100; ⊙noon-2pm & 6-10pm) Commanding a veritable legion of devoted followers, this humble West African eatery deserves its long-garnered popularity. Here you can sample wonderful North and West African cuisine, including Algerian, Senegalese, Ivorian, Cameroonian (try the curry) and Nigerian dishes, all of which are prepared with the finesse of the finest French haute cuisine. The jolof rice is particularly good.

Café Balalaika CAFE $$
(Map p222; ☑061-233479, 081 648 8577; Zoo Park, Independence Ave; sushi N$80, mains N$80-100; ⊙11am-2am; ☎) This sheltered spot beneath a giant rubber tree with an outdoor terrace on the edge of Zoo Park is just lovely for a cappuccino accompanied by a sushi plate. With some decent beer on tap and a large menu covering pizza, salads and meat dishes, it's a great spot to while away an afternoon. It also morphs into a bar-club in the evening but keeps serving food until the wee hours.

Gourmet INTERNATIONAL $$
(Map p222; ☑061-232360; www.thegourmet-restaurant.com; Kaiserkrone Centre, Post St Mall; mains N$65-215; ⊙7.30am-10pm Mon-Fri, 8am-10pm Sat) Tucked away in a peaceful courtyard just off Post St Mall, this alfresco bistro has one of the most comprehensive menus you'll find. The unifying trend is the use of gourmet ingredients to create a blend of Namibian, German, French and Italian dishes

that are as innovative as they are delicious. The word on the street is that it's not what it was, but make up your own mind.

Nice INTERNATIONAL $$
(Map p222; ☑061-300710; cnr Mozart St & Hosea Kutako Dr; mains N$65-130; ⊙noon-2.30pm Mon-Fri, 6-9pm daily) The Namibia Institute of Culinary Education – or 'nice' for short – operates this wonderfully conceived 'living classroom' where apprentice chefs can field test their cooking skills. Spanning several indoor rooms and a beautiful outdoor courtyard, the restaurant itself is more akin to a stylish gallery (think white tablecloths and clinking wine glasses too). The menu is short and targeted (seafood and game meats feature regularly) and service is very good.

O Pensador ANGOLAN, SEAFOOD $$
(Map p222; ☑061-221223; cnr Mandume Ndemufayo Ave & John Meinert St; mains N$130-225; ⊙6.30-10pm) A quality seafood restaurant with a twist of Angolan here and a hint of Portuguese there; the food may not be squirming on your plate but our overall impression was one of freshness, tasty morsels and attentive service.

Shoprite Supermarket SUPERMARKET $
(Map p222; Independence Ave; ⊙9am-6pm Mon-Fri, 9am-2pm Sat, 9am-1pm Sun) One of Windhoek's best supermarkets.

Pick & Pay SUPERMARKET $
(Map p222; Wernhill Park Centre; ⊙9am-6pm Mon-Fri, 9am-2pm Sat, 9am-1pm Sun) Good supermarket in the Wernhil Park Centre

★**Leo's** INTERNATIONAL $$$
(Map p222; ☑061-249597; www.heinitzburg.com; 22 Heinitzburg St; mains N$250; ⊙noon-3pm & 6.30-9pm) Leo's takes its regal setting in Heinitzburg Castle to heart by welcoming diners into a banquet hall that previously served the likes of royalty. The formal settings of bone china and polished crystal glassware are almost as extravagant as the food itself, which spans cuisines and continents, land and sea.

★**Restaurant Gathemann** NAMIBIAN $$$
(Map p222; ☑061-223853; 179 Independence Ave; mains N$90-250; ⊙noon-10pm) Located in a prominent colonial building overlooking Independence Ave, this splash-out spot serves gourmet Namibian cuisine that fully utilises the country's unique list of ingredients. From Kalahari truffles and Owamboland legumes

to tender cuts of game meat and Walvis Bay oysters, Restaurant Gathemann satisfies the pickiest of appetites.

Social INTERNATIONAL $$$
(Map p219; ☑061-252946; www.facebook.com/thesocialnamibia/; Liliencron St; mains N$110-230) A relative newcomer to the Windhoek dining scene, Social already has a loyal following for its contemporary setting and great food – we enjoyed the steak tartare and oryx loin, but we left longing to try the guinea fowl linguine... Service is friendly and they get the mix of classy and casual without seeming to try too hard.

🍷 Drinking & Nightlife

There are a few perennially popular spots where you can enjoy a few drinks and maybe even a bit of dancing. Many restaurants also double as late-night watering holes, particularly tourist-friendly establishments such as Nice (p227), which is also a great spot for a drink. While the nightlife scene in Windhoek is relaxed and generally trouble-free, you should always travel by taxi when heading to and from establishments.

★ Boiler Room @ The Warehouse Theatre BAR
(Map p222; ☑061-402253; www.warehousetheatre.com.na; 48 Tal St; ⊙9pm-late) From after-work drinks to live music and a crowd that likes to dance, the Boiler Room at the Warehouse is one of the coolest and most versatile places in town – the latter quality makes us think it might just last the distance.

★ Joe's Beer House PUB
(Map p219; ☑061-232457; www.joesbeerhouse.com; 160 Nelson Mandela Ave; ⊙noon-11pm) True to its moniker, Joe's stocks a wide assortment of Namibian and German beers, and you can count on prolonged drinking here until early in the morning. It's the favoured drinking hole of Afrikaners and something of a Windhoek institution.

Wine Bar WINE BAR
(Map p222; ☑061-226514; www.thewinebarshop.com; 3 Garten St; ⊙4-10.30pm Mon-Thu, 4-11.30pm Fri, 5-10.30pm Sat) In a lovely historic mansion that actually used to store the town's water supply, but now houses the city's premium wine selection, staff here have an excellent knowledge of their products, pairing an admirable South African wine selection with Mediterranean-style tapas and small snacks. It's a beautiful spot for a glass of wine and a fiery African sunset. There's a wine shop here too.

Café Balalaika BAR
(Map p222; ☑061-223479; Zoo Park, Independence Ave; ⊙9am-late) This spot, cafe by day, bar by night, features a terrace with the capital's largest rubber tree. There's live music and karaoke and a cool bar scene with some great beer on tap.

Pharaoh Lounge BAR
(Map p219; 22 Nelson Mandela Ave) Good for a cocktail and a dance or just a chill out in lounge chairs, this bar is located on the corner of Nelson Mandela and Sam Nujoma Aves.

Club London CLUB
(Map p219; ☑063-225466; Southern Industrial Area, 4 Nasmith St; ⊙7pm-late Wed-Sat) Formerly La Dee Da's, this relocated club has undergone a makeover. Check out the Facebook page to see whether it's a foam party, glow-stick event or some other inventive idea enticing patrons to show their moves. At other times you can dance to Angolan *kizomba* (fast-paced Portuguese-African music), hip-hop, rave, traditional African, rock and commercial pop accompanied by special effects.

☆ Entertainment

Warehouse Theatre THEATRE
(Map p222; ☑061-402253; www.warehousetheatre.com.na; Old South-West Brewery Bldg, 48 Tal St) This place used to be a warehouse for the breweries but has been converted into a full-scale, state-of-the-art theatre. The industrial interior and versatility of its design makes the Warehouse ideal for staging live African and European music and theatre productions. There's also a permanent exhibition space and an internet cafe.

College of the Arts (COTA) CLASSICAL MUSIC
(Map p222; ☑061-374100; 41 Fidel Castro St) The conservatorium in this college occasionally holds classical concerts.

National Theatre of Namibia THEATRE
(Map p222; ☑061-234633; www.ntn.org.na; Robert Mugabe Ave) Located south of the National Art Gallery (p221), the national theatre stages infrequent theatrical performances; for information see the *Namibian* newspaper.

Ster Kinekor CINEMA
(Map p219; ☑083 330 0360; Maerua Park Centre; ⊙9am-8.45pm Sun-Thu, 9am-11pm Fri & Sat) Off

Robert Mugabe Ave, this place shows recent films and has half-price admission on Tuesday.

 Shopping

The handicrafts sold in Post St Mall are largely imported from neighbouring countries, though there is still an excellent selection of woodcarvings, baskets and other African curios on offer. You're going to have to bargain hard if you want to secure a good price, though maintain your cool and always flash a smile – you'll win out with politeness in the end! Another spot with a good range of curios is along Fidel Castro St, near the corner of Independence, snaking up the hill towards Christuskirche.

Mall culture is alive and well in Windhoek, and you'll find them scattered throughout the city centre and out in the 'burbs. Most of the stores are South African standards, which generally offer high-quality goods at a fraction of the price back home. Katutura's **Soweto Market** is more reminiscent of a traditional African market, though it's best to visit either with a local or as part of an organised tour.

You can find gear for 4WD expeditions at **Safari Den** (Map p219; ☑061-2909294; www.agra.com.na/safari-den/; 20 Bessemer St; ☺9am-5pm Mon-Fri, 9am-2pm Sat, 9am-noon Sun).

★**Namibia Crafts Centre**   ARTS & CRAFTS
(Map p222; ☑061-242222; Old Breweries Craft Market, 40 Tal St; ☺9am-5.30pm Mon-Fri, to 3.30pm Sat & Sun) This crafts centre is an outlet for heaps of wonderful Namibian inspiration – leatherwork, basketry, pottery, jewellery, needlework, hand-painted textiles and other material arts – and the artist and origin of each piece is documented. We like the root carvings.

★**Penduka**   ARTS & CRAFTS
(☑061-257210; www.penduka.com; Goreangab Dam; ☺8am-5pm) Penduka, which means 'wake up', operates a non-profit women's needlework project at Goreangab Dam, 8km northwest of the city centre. You can purchase needlework, baskets, carvings and fabric creations for fair prices and be assured that all proceeds go to the producers. Ask about their places to stay as an alternative to the city's hotels.

To get here, take the Western Bypass north and turn left on Monte Cristo Rd, left on Otjomuise Rd, right on Eveline St and right again on Green Mountain Dam Rd. Then follow the signs to Goreangab Dam/Penduka.

Old Breweries Craft Market   ARTS & CRAFTS
(Map p222; cnr Garten & Tal Sts; ☺9am-5pm Mon-Fri, 9am-2pm Sat) This hive of tourist shopping euphoria contains a heap of small and large shops with a range of African arts and crafts on offer. A couple of our favourite shops are **Woven Arts of Africa**, with some wonderfully fine weavings in the form of wall-hangings and rugs; and **ArtiSan**, a small pokey shop with genuine Bushmen crafts.

Cymot Greensport   SPORTS & OUTDOORS
(Map p222; ☑061-234131; 60 Mandume Ndemufayo St; ☺8am-6pm Mon-Fri, 8am-1pm Sat) This is the place to head for supplies before you head off into the Namibian wilds – it's good for air compressors, a vital accessory. It is also a supplier of quality camping, hiking, cycling and vehicle-outfitting equipment.

House of Gems   JEWELLERY
(Map p222; ☑061-225202; www.namrocks.com; 131 Werner List St; ☺9am-5pm Mon-Sat, 9am-1pm Sun) A reputable shop in Windhoek for buying both raw and polished minerals and gemstones.

RARE GEMS

The former owner of **House of Gems**, Sid Pieters, who died in 2003, was once Namibia's foremost gem expert. In 1974, along the Namib coast, Pieters uncovered 45 crystals of jeremejevite, a sea-blue tourmaline containing boron – the rarest gem on earth. His discovery was only the second ever; the first was in Siberia in the mid-19th century. Another of his finds was the marvellously streaky 'crocidolite pietersite' (named for Pieters himself), from near Outjo in North-Central Namibia. Pietersite, a beautiful form of jasper shot through with asbestos fibres, is certainly one of the world's most beautiful and unusual minerals, and some believe that it has special energy and consciousness-promoting qualities. Other New Age practitioners maintain that it holds the 'keys to the kingdom of heaven'; stare at it long enough and perhaps you'll agree.

Post St Mall MALL
(Map p222; ☑ 061-257210; ⊗ 8am-5pm Mon-Sat)
The throbbing heart of the Windhoek shopping district is the bizarrely colourful Post St
Mall, an elevated pedestrian walkway lined
with vendors selling curios, artwork, clothing and practically anything else that may
be of interest to tourists.

Scattered around the centre of the mall is
a display of meteorites from the Gibeon meteor shower, which some time in the distant
past deposited upwards of 21 tonnes of mostly ferrous extraterrestrial boulders around
the town of Gibeon in southern Namibia.

Cape Union Mart SPORTS & OUTDOORS
(Map p219; www.capeunionmart.co.za; Maerua Park
Centre; ⊗ 9am-5.30pm Mon-Fri, 9am-2pm Sat,
9am-1pm Sun) Cape Union Mart, an outpost
of the South African chain, has camping,
hiking, cycling and vehicle-outfitting gear.

ℹ Information

DANGERS & ANNOYANCES

Staying alert Central Windhoek is quite relaxed
and hassle free. As long as you stay alert, walk
with confidence, keep a hand on your wallet and
avoid wearing anything too flashy, you should
encounter nothing worse than a few persistent
touts and the odd con artist.

Carrying bags However, you do need to be
especially wary when walking with any kind
of bag, particularly on backstreets. Most
importantly, don't use bumbags or carry
swanky camera or video totes – they're all
prime targets.

Thieves One popular con is for would-be-
thieves to play on the conscience of white
tourists and get their attention by posing the
question 'why won't you talk to a black man?'.
Ignore this and keep walking. As an extra
precaution, always travel by taxi at night,
even in the wealthy suburbs. The streets in
Windhoek are ominously quiet once the sun
goes down, which sadly means that foreign
tourists quickly become easy targets.

Theft The most likely annoyance for travellers
is petty theft, which more often than not occurs
at budget hotels and hostels around the city.
As a general rule, you should take advantage of
the hotel safe, and never leave your valuables
out in the open.

Parking If you're driving, avoid parking on the
street, and never leave anything of value visible in your vehicle. Also, never leave your car
doors unlocked, even if you're still in the car:
a common ploy is for someone to distract you
while someone else opens of the other doors,
grabs a bag and does a runner.

During the day, the safest and most convenient
parking is the underground lot beneath the
Wernhill Park Centre. At night, you should stay
at accommodation that provides off-street
secure parking.

Neighbourhoods The township of Katutura
and the northwestern industrial suburbs of
Goreangab, Wanaheda and Hakahana are not as
dangerous as their counterparts in South Africa,
and are reasonably safe during the daytime.
However, if you do visit these neighbourhoods,
it's best to either go with a local contact or as
part of an organised tour.

MAPS

Office of the Surveyor General (Map p222;
☑ 061-245055; cnr Robert Mugabe Ave & Korn
St) You can purchase topographic sheets of
much of Namibia for around US$4 from the map
section of the Office of the Surveyor General.

MEDICAL SERVICES

Rhino Park Private Hospital (Map p219;
☑ 061-375000, 061-225434; www.hospital.
com.na; Sauer St) Provides excellent care and
service, but patients must pay up front.

Mediclinic Windhoek (☑ 061-4331000; Helio-
door St, Eros; ⊗ 24hr) Emergency centre and a
range of medical services.

POLICE

Ministry of Home Affairs (Map p222; ☑ 061-
2922111; www.mha.gov.na; cnr Kasino St &
Independence Ave; ⊗ 8am-1pm Mon-Fri)

POST

Main Post Office (Map p222; Independence
Ave; ⊗ 8am-4.30pm Mon-Fri, 8-11.30am Sat)
The modern main post office can readily handle
overseas post. It also has telephone boxes in
the lobby.

TELEPHONE

Telecommunications Office (Map p222;
Independence Ave; ⊗ 8am-4.30pm Mon-Fri,
8am-11.30am Sat) Next door to the main post
office is the Telecommunications Office, where
you can make international calls and send or
receive faxes.

TOURIST INFORMATION

Namibia Tourism Board (Map p222; ☑ 061-
2906000; www.namibiatourism.com.na; 1st fl,
Channel Life Towers, 39 Post St Mall; ⊗ 8am-
1pm & 2-5pm Mon-Fri, 8am-1pm Sat & Sun) The
national tourist office can provide information
for all over the country.

Namibia Wildlife Resorts (NWR; Map p222;
☑ 061-2857200; www.nwr.com.na; Independence Ave) The semiprivate Namibia Wildlife
Resorts in Windhoek manages a large number
of rest camps, campsites and resorts within
the national parks. If you haven't prebooked

(eg if you're pulling into a national park area on a whim), there's a good chance you'll find something available on the spot, but have a contingency plan just in case. This is not advised for Etosha or Sossusvlei, which are always busy.

Windhoek Information & Publicity Office (Main Office) (Map p222; ☎ 061-2902092, 061-2902596; www.cityofwindhoek.org.na; Independence Ave; ⊙7.30am-4.30pm) The friendly staff at this office are on hand to answer questions and distribute local publications and leaflets, including *What's On in Windhoek* and useful city maps. There's another branch (Map p222; Post St Mall; ⊙7.30am-noon & 1-4.30pm) in the Post St Mall that is open the same hours but closes from noon to 1pm.

ℹ Transport

GETTING THERE & AWAY
Air

Chief Hosea Kutako International Airport (p373), which is about 40km east of the city centre, serves most international flights into and out of Windhoek. **Air Namibia** (p374) operates flights daily between Windhoek and Cape Town and Johannesburg, as well as daily flights to and from Frankfurt. Direct services to Amsterdam are also due to begin. Several airlines including Air Namibia also offer international services to and from Maun, Botswana, and Victoria Falls, Zimbabwe.

Eros Airport (p374), immediately south of the city centre, serves most domestic flights into and out of Windhoek. Air Namibia offers around three weekly flights to and from Katima Mulilo, Ondangwa, Rundu and Swakopmund/Walvis Bay.

Coming from Windhoek, make sure that your taxi driver knows which airport you need to go to.

Bus

From the main long-distance **bus terminal** (Map p222; cnr Independence Ave & Bahnhof Sts), the **Intercape Mainliner** (p375) runs to and from Cape Town, Johannesburg, Victoria Falls and Swakopmund, serving a variety of local destinations along the way. Tickets can be purchased either though your accommodation, from the Intercape Mainliner office at the bus terminal or online – given the popularity of these routes, advance reservations are recommended.

There are some useful shuttle services out to Swakopmund and Walvis Bay such as the **Town Hoppers** (☎ 064-407223, 081 210 3062; www.namibiashuttle.com), departing daily at 2pm (N$270, 4½ hours), and returning in the morning to Windhoek.

Local combis (minibuses) leave when full from the **Rhino Park petrol station** (Map p219), Katutura (get there very early in the morning) and can get you to most urban centres in central and southern Namibia. For northern destinations such as Tsumeb, Grootfontein and Rundu, you need to go to the local minibus station opposite the hospital on Independence Ave, Katutura.

Generally, combi routes do not serve the vast majority of Namibia's tourist destinations, which are located well beyond major population centres. Still, they're a fine way to travel if you want to visit some of the country's smaller towns and cities, and it's great fun to roll up your sleeves and jump into the bus with the locals.

Car & Motorcycle

Windhoek is literally the crossroads of Namibia – the point where the main north–south route (the B1) and east–west routes (B2 and B6) cross – and all approaches to the city are extremely scenic, passing through beautiful desert hills. Roads are clearly signposted; those travelling between northern and southern Namibia can avoid the city centre by taking the Western Bypass.

Train

Windhoek train station has a **booking office** (Map p222; ☎ 061-2982175; ⊙7.30am-4pm Mon-Fri) where you are able to reserve seats on any of the country's public rail lines. Routes are varied, and include overnight trains to Keetmanshoop, Tsumeb and Swakopmund, though irregular schedules, lengthy travel times and far better bus connections make train travel of little interest for the majority of overseas travellers.

GETTING AROUND

Collective taxis from the main ranks at Wernhill Park Centre follow set routes to Khomasdal and Katutura, and if your destination is along the way, you'll pay around N$10 to N$25. With taxis from the main bus terminals or by radio dispatch, fares are either metered or are calculated on a per-kilometre basis, but you may be able to negotiate a set fare per journey. Plan on N$70 anywhere around the city.

If you're arriving at Chief Hosea Kutako International Airport, taxis typically wait outside the arrivals area. It's a long drive into the city, so you can expect to pay anywhere from N$350 to N$400 depending on your destination. For Eros Airport, fares are much more modest at around N$70. In the city there are always reliable taxis that hang around the tourist office on Independence Ave. If you flag one down off the streets just be aware there are plenty of cowboys around and often not much English is spoken.

NAMIBIA WINDHOEK

NORTH-CENTRAL NAMIBIA

When you have little more than a car window separating you from the surrounding white plains, and with a thermos of early morning coffee and cameras ready, there are few places that can match the wildlife prospects of dawn in Etosha National Park. Home to a network of artificial waterholes and naturally up-welling springs, the southern boundary of the Etosha Pan harbours enormous congregations of African animals. Just one day of wildlife watching at a single waterhole can produce literally thousands of sightings, which has justifiably earned Etosha the reputation as one of the best reserves in the world.

Unlike the vast majority of safari parks in Africa, all roads inside Etosha are 2WD accessible and open to private vehicles. This, of course, means that if you've been fortunate enough to rent your own vehicle, you're in for one of the most memorable safaris of your life. Anyone can tell their friends and family back home how quickly their guide spotted a pride of lions, but how many people can say that they drove on the edges of a salt pan while tracking herds of zebra in the distance?

The crown jewel in Namibia's rich treasure trove of protected areas, Etosha dominates the tourism circuit in North-Central Namibia. However, there are plenty of worthwhile opportunities here for hiking and exploring, and there's a good chance that the tourist crowds will be elsewhere. If you have the time to spare, don't overlook the region's other highlights, which run the gamut from lofty plateaus and art-laden caves to hulking meteorites and dino footprints.

East to Botswana

The seemingly never-ending B6 runs east from Windhoek to the Botswana border, passing through the heart of one of Namibia's most important ranching centres. Together, the 970 farms of the Omaheke region cover nearly 50,000 sq km, and provide over one-third of Namibia's beef. While passionate carnivores can certainly rejoice at these numbers, the road east to the Botswana border is a long and monotonous slog – fortunately it is sealed, flat and in excellent condition.

Gobabis

POP 19,100 / ☑ 062

Gobabis is situated on the Wit-Nossob River, 120km from the Botswana border at Buitepos. The name was meant to be Khoikhoi for 'place of strife', but a slight misspelling (Goabbis) renders it 'place of elephants', which locals seem to prefer, despite its obvious shortage of elephants.

Although Gobabis is the main service centre of the Namibian Kalahari, there isn't a lot to look at and, let's face it, noone ever fell in love with Gobabis. The town's only historic building is the old military hospital, the Lazarett, which once served as a town museum. It's not officially open, but it's more interesting from the outside anyway.

🛏 Sleeping

Roadside rest stops offer basic but passable accommodation and meals – they're all signposted along the main highway. There are some more interesting options in the hinterland.

Zelda Game & Guest Farm   LODGE $

(☑ 062-560427; www.zeldaguestfarm.com; camping N$70, s/d N$570/920; 🛜🏊) The rooms here are a mix of safari chic (think zebra rugs) and grandma decor (chintzy knick-knacks and floral prints); the eclectic blend of styles won't be to everyone's taste. But this is one of the cheaper options in the area and it's all very comfortable. Activities include Bushman walks, and cheetah and leopard feeding.

Harnas Wildlife Foundation & Guest Farm   FARMSTAY $$

(☑ 061-228545, 081 140 3322; www.harnas.org; camping N$270, s/d igloos N$1520/2500, s/d cottages N$1900/3100, self-catering units from N$1800; ⊙6am-6pm) The Harnas Wildlife Foundation & Guest Farm is a rural development project that likens itself to Noah's Ark. Here you can see wildlife close up, including rescued cheetahs, leopards and lions. A wide range of accommodation is available, including options for full board, and there are plenty of activities here to keep you amused for a couple of days – kids will love it.

Many of the animals here are caged and there's not much that's wild, but since most animals were either orphaned or injured, they would be unable to survive were it not for the foundation. Activities include an afternoon wander through the various enclosures (you'll join the feeding of the mongooses, play with baby cheetahs...), a morning game drive to watch as lions, leopards, cheetahs, African wild dogs and other species are fed, and a lion's-roar sundowner – quite an experience.

To get here, turn north on the C22 past Gobabis and continue for 45km, then drive east on the D1668 for another 45km (following the signs).

Kalahari Bush Breaks   LODGE $$
(☑ 062-568936; www.kalaharibushbreaks.com; s/d N$900/1630; ✳ 🛜 🏊) Some 26km into Namibia west of the Mamuno border post, and 85km east of Gobabis, Kalahari Bush Breaks is a lovely spot run by Elsabe and Ronnie who bring much warmth to the experience of chilling in the Kalahari. The eight rooms are warm and lovingly appointed, four with fabulous views out into the eternity of the Kalahari. There's a stunning swimming pool, good restaurant, and a campsite.

There are some excellent walks on the 50 sq km farm, some ancient rock engravings and you might see one of the free-roaming cheetahs if you're lucky on the 4WD trail.

Kalahari Game Lodge   LODGE $$$
(Map p139; ☑ in South Africa 27-21-880 9870; www.kalaharigamelodge.com.na; s/d with half board N$1250/2050; ✳ 🛜 🏊) In a remote corner of the Namibian Kalahari, just across the border from the Kgalagadi Transfrontier Park shared between Botswana and South Africa, Kalahari Game Lodge has eight lovely chalets and an excellent camping area. Rooms have the whole 'wood, linen and colourful throws thing' down pat, while there's a fine restaurant and bar, too. Scenic game drives, lion tracking and night drives are highlights here, and there's a self-guided 4WD trail.

SanDüne Lodge   LODGE $$$
(☑ 061-259293; www.namibiareservations.com/sanduene_lodge_b.html; C22; s N$850-1250, d N$1700-2500) Part of a 46 sq km farm, SanDüne Lodge has luxury Meru-style safari tents and comfortable standard rooms in the main lodge building. Although quite pricey by Namibian standards, they're a steal when compared with similar places in Botswana.

ℹ Getting There & Away

Public transport is unreliable along this route, and it's recommended that you head east from Windhoek in a private vehicle. If you're planning on crossing into Botswana in a rental car, be sure in advance that all of your paperwork is in order.

Buitepos
☑ 062
Buitepos, a wide spot in the desert at the Namibia–Botswana border crossing, is little more than a petrol station and customs and immigration post. The border opens from 7am to midnight, though you should try to cross with plenty of daylight since it's a long drive to Ghanzi, the next settlement of major size along the Trans-Kalahari Hwy in Botswana.

🛏 Sleeping

**East Gate Service
Station & Rest Camp**   CAMPGROUND $$
(☑ 062-560405; www.eastgate-namibia.com; Trans-Kalahari Hwy; camping N$120, cabins without bathroom per person N$180, 2-person bungalows N$750-1400; ✳ 🏊) The East Gate Service Station & Rest Camp rises from the desert like a mirage, and is a decent enough place to crash if you're not particularly fussy. The restaurant serves simple roadside fare such as burgers, but you'll appreciate it as it's the only place on either side of the border for a square meal.

ℹ Getting There & Away

There is no cross-border public transport. You may find buses or combis travelling between here and Gobabis or (at a stretch) Windhoek. To cross the border, you'll need to walk or hitch, and catch onward transport once in Botswana.

North to Etosha
The immaculate B1 heads north from Windhoek, and provides access to Outjo as well as Tsumeb and Grootfontein. Prominent towns in their own right, together they serve as the launching point for excursions into nearby Etosha National Park. While it's very tempting to strike north with safari fever, it's definitely worth slowing down and taking a bit of time to explore the quirky sights of this comparatively untouristed section of North-Central Namibia.

Okahandja
☑ 062
Okahandja is a busy little place, but not as busy as Windhoek – it's far more manageable than the capital and it makes a great alternative staging post, especially for forays further north to Etosha and west to Swakopmund.

Okahandja

Okahandja Country Hotel (2km)

Okahandja

⊙ **Sights**
1 Friedenskirche B3
2 Moordkoppie A2

🛏 **Sleeping**
3 Sylvanette Guest House A2

🍴 **Eating**
4 Bäckerei Dekker & Café B3

From the mid-19th century to the early 20th century, the town served as a German-run mission and a colonial administrative centre, remnants of which still dot the town centre.

⊙ Sights

Friedenskirche   CHURCH
(Church of Peace; Kerk St; ⊙ dawn-dusk) In the churchyard and across the road from the 1876 Friedenskirche are the graves of several historical figures, including Herero leader Willem Maherero, Nama leader Jan Jonker Afrikaner and Hosea Kutako, the 'father of Namibian independence', who was the first politician to petition the UN against the South African occupation of Namibia.

German Fort   HISTORIC BUILDING
The German fort was built in the 19th century and is an important local landmark.

Moordkoppie   HISTORIC SITE
The historical animosity between the Nama and the Herero had its most emphatic expression at the Battle of Moordkoppie (Afrikaans for 'Murder Hill') on 23 August 1850. During the battle, 700 Herero under the command of chief Katjihene were massacred by Nama forces. Half of the victims were women and children, whose bodies were dismembered for the copper bangles on their arms and legs. The scene of this tragedy was a small rocky hill near the centre of town between the B2 and the railway line, 500m north of the Gross Barmen turn-off.

🎆 Festivals & Events

Maherero Day   CULTURAL
(⊙ Aug) On the weekend nearest 26 August is Maherero Day, which is when the Red Flag Herero people meet in traditional dress in memory of their fallen chiefs, killed in battles with the Nama and the Germans. A similar event is held by the Mbanderu, or Green Flag Herero, on the weekend nearest 11 June.

🛏 Sleeping & Eating

Sylvanette Guest House   GUESTHOUSE $
(📞 062-505550; www.sylvanette.com; Anderson St; s/d from N$480/700; ❉ @ 🛜 ⊠) This cosy guesthouse is located in a quiet, garden-like suburban setting and centred on a refreshing swimming pool surrounded by all manner of potted plants. Well-priced rooms pay tribute to the wilds of Namibia with ample animal prints, although the proliferation of zebra stripes in some rooms can start to do your head in after a while...

Okahandja Country Hotel   HOTEL $$
(📞 062-504299; www.okahandjahotel.com; camping N$140, s/d N$885/1520) This big old stalwart is a great bastion of hospitality. The stone buildings with sweeping thatched roofs stay cool in summer and have plenty of room. The rooms are a little old-fashioned but large and comfortable, while the grounds are a green oasis in an otherwise dusty setting, it's 2km north of town, opposite the D2110 turnoff.

Bäckerei Dekker & Café   BAKERY $
(Martin Neib St; meals & snacks N$25-50; ⊙ 6.30am-3.30pm Mon-Fri, to noon Sat) This

German cafe and bakery serves tasty break-fasts and lunches including toasties, bread rolls, sandwiches, salads, freshly made pies, a cold platter and game steaks, along with hot and cold drinks.

❶ Getting There & Away

BUS

Intercape Mainliner (p375) buses make the trip between Windhoek and Okahandja (from N$342, one hour, one to two daily). Book your tickets in advance online as this service continues on to Victoria Falls and fills up quickly.

Okahandja is a minor public-transport hub, serving various regional destinations by combi (minibus). Combis also run up and down the B1 with fairly regular frequency, and a ride between Windhoek and Okahandja shouldn't cost more than N$160.

CAR

Okahandja is 70km north of Windhoek on the B1, the country's main north–south highway.

TRAIN

Trans-Namib (p378) operates trains between Windhoek and Okahandja (from N$155, two hours, daily except Saturday), though the limited early-morning and late-night departures are inconvenient for most.

Erongo Mountains (Erongoberg)

📞 064

The volcanic Erongo Mountains, often referred to as the Erongoberg, rise as a 2216m massif north of Karibib and Usakos and they're among the most beautiful and accessible of Namibia's mountain areas. The Erongo range is best known for its caves and rock art, particularly the 50m-deep Phillips Cave.

Black rhinos and the rare black-nosed impala have also been released into the Erongo Conservancy, a 30-farm area in the heart of the range, although both can be difficult to spot. For more information on the rhino, contact the **Erongo Mountain Rhino Sanctuary Trust** (EMRST; www. foerderverein-emrst.de).

History

After the original period of volcanism here, some 150 million years ago, the volcano collapsed on its magma chamber, allowing the basin to fill with slow-cooling igneous material. The result is a hard granite-like core, which withstood the erosion that washed away the surrounding rock. Much later in prehistory, the site was occupied by the San, who left behind a rich legacy of cave paintings and rock art that has weathered remarkably well throughout the ages.

◉ Sights

Phillips Cave   CAVE

(day permit N$50) This cave, 3km off the road, contains the famous humpbacked white elephant painting. Superimposed on the elephant is a large humpbacked antelope (perhaps an eland), and around it frolic ostriches and giraffes. The Ameib paintings were brought to attention in the book *Phillips Cave* by prehistorian Abbè Breuil, but his speculations about their Mediterranean origins have now been discounted. The site is open to day hikers via Ameib Gästehaus.

The Ameib picnic site is backed up by outcrops of stacked boulders, one of which, the notable Bull's Party, resembles a circle of gossiping bovines. Other formations that are often photographed include one resembling an elephant's head and another that recalls a Herero woman in traditional dress, standing with two children.

The path to the cave is fairly rugged – it should take around 45 minutes to an hour uphill and around 30 minutes coming back down.

▥ Sleeping

There aren't many places to stay in the area, but what there is does a good job of spanning budgets – there's camping up to a luxury lodge.

Erongo Plateau Camp   CAMPGROUND $

(📞 064-570837; www.erongo.iway.na/camp/camp. html; camping N$120) This appealing campsite has four sites with fine views out over the plains and mountains. Sites have hot and cold showers, toilets, fireplaces (firewood costs N$25 a bundle) and a tap. Hiking trails and excursions to nearby rock-art sites are highlights.

Ameib Gästehaus   GUESTHOUSE $$

(📞 081 857 4639; www.ameib.com; camping N$150, s/d from N$750/1400; ▦) At the base of the Erongo foothills, this historic guest farm offers accommodation in the farmhouse, adjacent to a landscaped pool, a *lapa* (a circular area with a fire pit, used for socialising) and the well-maintained campsite. Ameib Gästehaus owns the concessions on Phillips Cave, and issues permits for the sight in addition to guided hikes and day tours.

The 'Green Hill' Ranch was established in 1864 as a Rhenish mission station.

Camp Mara CAMPGROUND, GUESTHOUSE **$$**
(☑ 064-571190; www.campmara.com; camping N$150, s/d with half board N$1025/1750) This lovely spot by a (usually dry) riverbed has shady, well-tended campsites, as well as eclectic but extremely comfortable rooms with whitewashed walls and creative use of wood in the decor. Activities include day tours into the mountains and Bushman activities.

★ Erongo Wilderness Lodge LODGE **$$$**
(☑ 061-239199, 064-570537; www.erongowilderness-namibia.com; tented bungalows incl full board s/d from N$2975/5000; ❄ @ 중) This highly acclaimed wilderness retreat combines spectacular mountain scenery, wildlife viewing, bird-watching and environmentally sensitive architecture to create one of Namibia's most memorable lodges. Accommodation is in one of 10 tented bungalows, which are built on wooden stilts among towering granite pillars crawling with rock hyrax. The restaurant overlooks a waterhole where you might see kudu or genet.

When you're not lounging in front of the fireplace in the main lodge, you can take a guided walk (cost included in the full-board price) or a nature drive (N$485). Birders will enjoy the fact that rosy-faced lovebirds, Hartlaub's francolin and freckled nightjars are often seen in the area.

To get to the lodge, go to Omaruru, turn west on the D2315 (off the Karibib road 2km south of town) and continue for 10km.

ℹ Getting There & Away

North of Ameib, the D1935 skirts the Erongo Mountains before heading north into Damaraland. Alternatively, you can head east towards Omaruru on the D1937. This route virtually encircles the Erongo massif and provides access to minor 4WD roads into the heart of the mountains.

Omaruru

POP 6300 / ☑ 064

Omaruru's dry and dusty setting beside the shady Omaruru riverbed lends it a real outback feel and it sits in the heart of some interesting country between Erongo and Okonjima. The town has a growing reputation as an arts-and-crafts centre and in recent years has become home to the Artist Trail (p236), an annual arts event in September; you can pick up a free copy of the program of events around town.

The town itself is a welcoming little oasis with some great accommodation options, good food and one of the very few wineries in the country – there's little as surreal as enjoying a platter of meats and cheeses under trees while wine tasting in the Namibian outback.

◉ Sights

Kristall Kellerei Winery WINERY
(☑ 064-570083; www.kristallkellerei.com; D2328; ⏲ 8am-4.30pm Mon-Fri, 8am-12.30pm Sat) One of very few wineries in Namibia, this is a lovely spot to come for lunch. In the afternoon you can enjoy light meals – cheese and cold-meat platters – while tasting their wines and other products, and take a tour of the gardens. Apart from schnapps, the winery produces Colombard, a white wine, and Paradise Flycatcher, a red blend of ruby cabernet, cabernet sauvignon and Tinta Barocca. The winery is 4km east of Omaruru on the D2328.

Franke Tower HISTORIC SITE
In January 1904 Omaruru was attacked by Herero forces under chief Manassa. German captain Victor Franke, who had been engaged in suppressing an uprising in southern Namibia, petitioned Governor Leutwein for permission to march north and relieve the besieged town. After a 20-day, 900km march, Franke arrived in Omaruru and led the cavalry charge, which defeated the Herero attack. For his efforts, Franke received the highest German military honours, and in 1908 the grateful German residents of Omaruru erected the Franke Tower in his honour.

The tower, which was declared a national monument in 1963, holds a historical plaque and affords a view over the town. It's normally locked, though if you want to climb it you can pick up a key at the Central Hotel.

★ Festivals & Events

Artist Trail ART
(www.facebook.com/omaruruartisttrail/; ⏲ Sep) Omaruru has been home to the Artists Trail since 2007, marking it as Namibia's artist town. Music and dance events feature over three days in September, along with food and wine, jewellery, photography and painting.

White Flag Herero Day CULTURAL
(⏲ Oct) Each year on the weekend nearest to 10 October the White Flag Herero people

hold a procession from the Ozonde suburb to the graveyard, opposite the mission station, where their chief Wilhelm Zeraua was buried after his defeat in the German-Herero wars.

🛏 Sleeping

Central Hotel Omaruru   HOTEL $

(☑ 064-570030; www.centralhotelomaruru.com; Wilhelm Zeraua St; s/d from N$600/900; ❄ ☀) This place is the town's focal point for eating and drinking and has rondavels in the huge garden – they are simple concrete setups with small beds, clean linen and good bathrooms. The dining room may well be the only show in town in the evening for dinner. Fortunately, the standard of food is pretty good for a remote pub – there are German favourites plus local game dishes (mains N$80).

Kashana Hotel   HOTEL $

(☑ 064-571434; www.kashana-namibia.com; Dr I Scheepers St; r per person from N$480; ❄ 🛜 ☀) Offering a swag of accommodation, upmarket Kashana has luxury bungalows and spare but nicely furnished rooms set around a large shady courtyard. In the main building is a bar and restaurant. Also based here is a goldsmith and a shop selling herbal products.

River Guesthouse   GUESTHOUSE $$

(☑ 064-570274;   www.river-guesthouse.com; 134 Dr I Scheepers St; campsites N$120, s/d/f N$530/830/1050; 🛜 ☀) The camping here is the best in town with some great shady trees to pitch a tent under and excellent facilities including fireplaces and power outlets. You may just have the family dogs keeping you company as well. The rooms are tidy and comfortable and surround a shady courtyard well set up for relaxing.

🍴 Eating

Omaruru

Souvenirs & Kaffestube   CAFE, SOUVENIRS $

(☑ 064-570230; Wilhelm Zeraua St; meals N$20-55) The building housing this intimate cafe dates from 1907. This place is a good choice for a strong cup of coffee and traditional German baked goods, as well as for a cold pint of Hansa and some pub grub in the outdoor beer garden. The pies are especially good.

★ Main Street Cafe   CAFE $$

(☑ 064-570303; Wilhelm Zeraua St; mains from N$35; ⊙ 8am-3pm; 🛜) Quiche, hazelnut cheesecake, white-wood furniture...what's

not to like about this fine little lunch and breakfast spot that makes a priority of fresh ingredients and friendly service? Oh, and there's great coffee, art on the walls, free wi-fi and so much more.

🛍 Shopping

CmArte Gallery   ARTS & CRAFTS

(☑ 064-570017; Wilhelm Zeraua St; ⊙ 9am-5pm) This arts-and-crafts outlet has some really good crafts, including some from local artists, alongside imported antiques from both Angola and the DRC. It's worth sticking your nose in here and having a good rummage around, as you just may find a gem. We like some of the black-and-white wildlife sketches, both framed and unframed.

ℹ Getting There & Away

With your own vehicle, the paved C33 passes through Omaruru, and provides the quickest route between Swakopmund and Etosha.

Uis

POP 3600 / ☑ 064

Just over an hour's drive from Omaruru, Uis is a small, dusty settlement that's at a handy crossroads for those heading north through Damaraland, or southwest to the Skeleton Coast or Swakopmund.

🛏 Sleeping

White Lady B&B   B&B $

(☑ 064-504102;   uiswhiteladyguesthouse.com; camping N$100, s/d incl breakfast N$702/1042; 🛜 ☀) At the welcoming White Lady B&B, simple, well-kept rooms are a good size, and the small orderly campsite has some shady trees. Dinner is also available.

**Brandberg
Rest Camp**   CAMPGROUND, GUESTHOUSE $

(☑ 064-504038; www.brandbergrestcamp.com; camping N$100, dm/s/d N$200/600/900) A fairly basic in-town choice that could serve as a base for visiting the Brandberg, this rest camp has fairly standard accommodation that won't win any style awards but is clean and ample for a night. The campsites lack any sense of being out in the Namibian wilds, but are otherwise fine.

ℹ Getting There & Away

There's no public transport to/from Uis – you'll need your own vehicle to get here and to explore the surrounding area.

Kalkfeld

POP 5000 / ☑ 067

Around 200 million years ago, Namibia was covered in a shallow sea, which gradually filled with wind-blown sand and eroded silt. Near the tiny town of Kalkfeld, these sandstone layers bear the evidence of a 25m-long dinosaur stroll – quite a sight.

◉ Sights

Dinosaur Footprints   HISTORIC SITE
(N$20) The 170-million-year-old dinosaur footprints were made in what was then soft clay by a three-toed dinosaur that walked on its hind legs – probably a forerunner of modern birds. The footprints, which were declared a national monument in 1951, are on a farm 29km from Kalkfeld, just off route D2414.

⌁ Sleeping

Otjihaenamparero Farm   FARMSTAY $
(☑ 067-290153; www.dinosaurstracks.com/home.html; camping N$100, s/d N$440/760) Aside from hosting the dinosaur tracks, Otjihaenamparero Farm has a three-room guesthouse offering B&B; dinner can be organised for an additional cost (N$180). There's also a small campground.

Mt Etjo Safari Lodge   LODGE $$$
(☑ 067-290173; www.mount-etjo.com; 4-person campsite N$420, per person r/ste/villa N$1665/1800/3178; ❋ @ ☀) The Mt Etjo Safari Lodge, in the heart of the private Okonjati Game Reserve, provides access to a small set of dinosaur tracks, which are located on the edge of the appropriately named Dinosaur Campsite. Accommodation is either in the main safari lodge, an upmarket affair that benefits from the beauty of the surrounding nature, or in the expensive but entirely private campsite, a few kilometres down the road.

'Mt Etjo' means place of refuge, and refers to the nearby table mountain. It could also refer to the rescued lions and cheetahs that inhabit the farm – watching them being fed is one of the activities here. Other possibilities include rhino tracking and visits to a local school.

Mt Etjo's place in history was sealed in April 1989 when the Mt Etjo Peace Agreement was signed, ending the South-West African People's Organisation's (Swapo) liberation struggle and setting the stage for Namibian independence the following March.

The lodge is 35km from Kalkfeld via the D2414 and the D2483 – just follow the brightly painted signs.

❶ Getting There & Away

Kalkfeld is just off the C33, approximately halfway between Omaruru and Otjiwarongo.

Erindi Private Game Reserve

☑ 064

It may lack the scale of Etosha National Park, but many travellers rank **Erindi** (☑ 064-570800, 081 145 0000; www.erindi.com) as their most memorable wildlife-watching experience in Namibia. With over 700 sq km of savannah grasslands and rocky mountains, Erindi lacks the zoo-like feel of many smaller private reserves in the country and lacks for nothing when it comes to wildlife – you can reliably expect to see elephants and giraffes, with lions, leopards, cheetahs, African wild dogs and black rhinos all reasonable possibilities. Night drives, too, open up a whole new world of nocturnal species. Throw in guided bush walks, visits to a San village and rock-art excursions, and it's not difficult to see why Erindi is fast attracting a growing army of devotees and return visitors.

⌁ Sleeping

★ **Camp Elephant**   CAMPGROUND, CHALET $$$
(☑ 083 333 1111; www.erindi.com; camping per site N$712, s/d chalet N$1095/2190) In the heart of Erindi, Camp Elephant has 15 excellent self-catering chalets that overlook a waterhole that's floodlit at night, while the 30 campsites have some lovely greenery and plenty of shade, not to mention good facilities.

★ **Old Traders Lodge**   LODGE $$$
(☑ 083 330 1111; www.erindi.com; s with half board N$3090-4090, d with half board N$5380-7180; 🛜 ☀) Erindi's main lodge has 48 luxury rooms that combine the safari feel (thatched roofs and earth tones) with classic wood-and-four-poster-bed interiors. It's never pretentious, and although it can get a little frenetic when the lodge is full, it's a terrific place to stay on a terrific reserve.

❶ Getting There & Away

Erindi lies west of Omaruru, northwest of Okahandja and southwest of Otjiwarongo. There are four entrance gates. To reach the main gate, travel 48km north of Okahandja or 124km south of Otjiwarongo along the B1, then turn west onto the D2414, a decent gravel road, for 40km.

Okonjima Nature Reserve

📱 067

The 200-sq-km Okonjima Nature Reserve is the epicentre of one of Namibia's most impressive conservation programs. Home of the AfriCat Foundation, it protects cheetahs and other carnivores rescued from human-wildlife conflict situations across the country, and gives them room to move. Aside from excellent accommodation and fascinating education programs, Okonjima offers the chance to track wild leopards, as well as cheetahs, African wild dogs and (coming soon) lions within the reserve. There are also self-guided walks, first-rate guides and the chance to be a part of something that makes a genuine difference.

Day visitors are welcome, but we recommend staying here for a minimum of two nights to take full advantage of the activities on offer.

🏃 Activities

Only those staying overnight at the lodges or campsites can take part in most of the activities, which include cheetah and leopard tracking. There are also a number of self-guided walks, with maps available from the AfriCat Day Visitors Centre, lodges, or camp manager.

Activities are not included in the room rates, and cost N$670/340 per adult/child for leopard or cheetah tracking, or N$450/225 per adult/child for guided Bushman nature trails.

AfriCat Foundation WILDLIFE
(📱 067-687032; www.africat.org; ⊘10am-4pm) This foundation runs education programmes and activities within Okonjima Nature Reserve. Day visitors can join the tours that leave from the AfriCat Day Centre at 10.30am and 12.30pm from April to August, and 11am and 1pm from September to March.

The tours take you to AfriCat Care Centre – where you'll learn about the AfriCat story and the foundation's programs, as well as visit a large enclosure where cheetahs are held awaiting their return to the wild. You'll also receive a light lunch as part of the tours which cost N$385/285 per adult/child; children under 7 are free.

🛏 Sleeping & Eating

Within the reserve's boundaries, you'll find a range of outstanding lodge accommodation and a handful of excellent campsites. Campers must check in at the AfriCat Day Centre.

⭐Omboroko Campsite CAMPGROUND $
(www.okonjima.com; Okonjima Nature Reserve; per adult/child N$330/165; ⊛) These are some of the best campsites in Namibia. There's plenty of shade, firewood is provided, there's a (freezing!) swimming pool, hot showers and flush toilets, and the five sites are beautifully maintained in the shadow of one of the large rocky outcrops that dominates the reserve's core. You're also within the 20-sq-km fenced zone and, hence, unlikely to be surprised by wandering predators.

⭐Okonjima Plains Camp LODGE $$$
(📱 067-687032; www.okonjima.com; s/d standard rooms with half board N$2830/4050, view rooms with half board N$3955/6300; ⊛🛜⊛) With 10 'view' and 14 'standard' rooms, these newly built lodgings open out onto the Okonjima grasslands, with the ample terraces and abundant glass taking full advantage of the wildlife-rich views. The view rooms in particular are supremely comfortable, spacious and stylish, decorated with a pleasing mix of soothing earth tones and bold colours, as well as plenty of stunning photographs of Okonjima's wildlife.

Okonjima Bush Camp & Suites LODGE $$$
(📱 067-687032; www.okonjima.com; s/d with half board N$5700/9900, ste N$8800-14,400; 🛜⊛) Removed from the main lodge area and hence quieter and more discreet, the Bush Camp and nearby Bush Suites are beautifully turned out. The camp rooms are nicely spaced to ensure maximum privacy and actually have two small adobe bungalows, one for sleeping, the other with a lovely sitting area. The split-level suites are even more beautiful.

AfriCat Day Centre CAFE $
(light meals from N$40; ⊘11.30am-2.30pm) The day centre serves a few simple meal choices at lunchtimes from a menu that changes regularly. There are fine views from the back terrace.

ℹ Getting There & Away

Unless you visit Okonjima as part of an organised tour, you'll need your own vehicle to visit. The signpost is impossible to miss, 49km south of Otjiwarongo and 130km north of Okahandja along the B1. After taking the turn-off, you pass through a series of gates and the main lodge is 10km off the main road, along a well-graded gravel track.

Otjiwarongo

POP 28,250 / ☑ 067

Handy as a jumping-off point for Etosha, and particularly the Waterberg Plateau, Otjiwarongo is especially pleasant in September and October when the town explodes with the vivid colours of blooming jacaranda and bougainvillea. Beyond that, it's a place to refuel, stock up on supplies and break up the journey.

⊙ Sights

Crocodile Farm FARM
(cnr Zingel & Hospital Sts; N$50; ⊙ 8am-5pm Mon-Fri, 8am-3pm Sat, 9am-3pm Sun) Otjiwarongo is home to Namibia's first crocodile ranch. This ranch produces skins for export, and you can do a worthwhile tour. There's a shop which has mainly wooden carvings with some jewellery and metalwork, though not much in the way of croc-skin products. The restaurant has a full-blown menu for breakfast and lunch – try any number of croc delicacies, such as a croc wrap or kebabs.

Locomotive No 41 MONUMENT
At the train station stands Locomotive No 41, which was manufactured in 1912 by the Henschel company of Kassel, Germany, and then brought all the way to Namibia to haul ore between the Tsumeb mines and the port at Swakopmund. It was retired from service in 1960 when the 0.6m narrow gauge was replaced with the wider 1.067m gauge.

🛏 Sleeping & Eating

There's a **Spar Supermarket** (9 Hage Geingob St; ⊙ 8am-8pm Mon-Fri, 8am-noon Sat, 8am-7pm Sun) in the centre of town.

★ Bush Pillow GUESTHOUSE $$
(☑ 067-303885; bushpillow.co.za; 47 Sonn Rd; s/d incl breakfast N$650/850; 🛜🕸) This great little guesthouse styles itself as 'executive accommodation' by targeting the business market, but with comfortable modern rooms and wi-fi connectivity throughout, it also makes an ideal pit stop for travellers. The seven rooms include a couple set up for families – the kids will love the pool. There's a lovely restaurant as well.

★ Hadassa Guest House GUESTHOUSE $
(☑ 067-307505; www.hadassaguesthouse.com; Lang St; s/d N$640/800; 🛜🕸) Overseen by the welcoming French owners Orlane and Emmanuel, this fine little guesthouse has the intimate feel of a B&B and the quality of a small, personalised boutique hotel. Rooms are immaculate, the meals are beautifully prepared and service is excellent.

Casa Forno Country Hotel HOTEL $
(☑ 067-304504; www.casaforno.com; Ramblers Rd; s/d from N$820/920; 🅿🕸🛜) Large and semi-luxurious, Casa Forno is decorated in classic Cape Dutch style and it's far enough away from the main street to ensure a quiet night's sleep. The excellent restaurant serves pasta, steaks and other international staples in an agreeable setting.

C'est Si Bon Hotel HOTEL $
(☑ 067-301240; www.cestsibonhotel.com; Swembad Rd; s/d from N$720/820; 🕸🕸) Named after a common French expression that translates to 'it is good', this charmer of a hotel takes its moniker to heart, blending Namibian design with European flourishes. After a few laps in the pool, a cappuccino on the sundeck and a glass of wine in the bar, you'll probably agree that everything is indeed *c'est si bon*.

Out of Africa Town Lodge LODGE $
(☑ 067-302230; www.out-of-afrika.com; Long St; s/d from N$680/780; 🕸🕸) This attractive whitewashed, colonial-style lodge is a nice place to break up the drive to Etosha. Lofty, sometimes cavernous rooms retain their historical accents, although frequent renovations have kept them in sync with the times.

ℹ Getting There & Away

There are buses at least daily between Otjiwarongo and Windhoek (from N$288, 3½ hours) with **Intercape Mainliner** (061-227847; www.intercape.co.za). Minibuses travelling between Windhoek and the north stop at the Engen petrol station. All train services between Tsumeb and Windhoek or Walvis Bay (via Swakopmund) also pass through.

Outjo

POP 8450 / ☑ 067

Given the tourist traffic through this small town, it has retained a surprisingly country, low-key feel. Although it has few attractions, it serves as an increasingly appealing place to rest on your way to/from Etosha. If you're coming from the south, Outjo is the last major rest stop before reaching Okaukuejo, the administrative headquarters of and western gateway to Etosha.

⊙ Sights

Outjo Museum MUSEUM
(Herholt Rd; N$10; ⊙8am-1pm & 2-5pm Mon-Fri) Originally called the Kliphuis or stone house, Franke House is one of Outjo's earliest buildings and now houses the town's museum. It was constructed in 1899 by order of Major von Estorff as a residence for himself and subsequent German commanders. It was later occupied by Major Franke, who posthumously gave it his name, though the current focus of the museum is political and natural history. It's worth a quick look, nothing more.

Naulila Monument MONUMENT
This monument commemorates the 19 October 1914 massacre of German soldiers and officials by the Portuguese near Fort Naulila on the Kunene River in Angola. It also commemorates soldiers killed on 18 December 1914, under Major Franke, who was sent to avenge earlier losses.

🛏 Sleeping

Sophienhof Lodge LODGE $
(☑067-312999; www.sophienhof-lodge.com; off C39; camping/dm N$200/300, r per person N$440-1650; ☎🐾🏊) This place just off the C39, 12km southwest of Outjo, gets consistently good reviews from travellers. Accomodation are in good, grassy campsites, sturdy bungalows or the appealing farmhouse; there's even a dorm for budget travellers. In addition to guided walking tours, you can also watch the feeding of rescued cheetahs and ostriches.

Etotongwe Lodge LODGE $
(☑067-313333; www.etotongwelodge.com; camping N$120, s/d N$580/960; ☎) This refreshing, professionally run place on the way to Etosha, just outside of town, feels like an unlikely oasis of green. Its neat appearance and trim lawns break up the concrete, stone and thatched roofs spun around an attractive area. Rooms are fairly bare inside, but have some nice African touches and are neat as a pin and very roomy.

Probably the best feature is the small front veranda with chairs and table.

Farmhouse GUESTHOUSE $
(☑067-313444; www.farmhouse-outjo.com; Hage Geingob Ave; s/d N$390/600) Better known for its downstairs restaurant, the Farmhouse also has a single and three double rooms on offer, all of a very comfortable standard. Rooms are either nicely sized or cavernous and devoid of furnishings, depending on your perspective.

Etosha Garden Hotel HOTEL $
(☑067-313130; www.etosha-garden-hotel.com; s/d incl breakfast N$450/700; ❄🏊) Just a short walk from the town centre, this friendly old place gets mixed reviews and features curio-filled rooms surrounding plush greenery and a swimming pool. It's looking a bit rundown these days and is pretty disorganised, but it's worth dropping by to see if they will give you a decent walk-in rate.

🍴 Eating

Topaz Bistro Culinarium INTERNATIONAL $
(☑067-313244; Sam Nujoma Dr; mains from N$55; ⊙7am-4pm; ☎) Set up as a catch-all tourist centre, this unusual place has a restaurant, tourist information centre, curio shop and a model Himba village. It hasn't quite worked out what it wants to be and lacks a little soul as a result, but it's still worth stopping by, if only to try the mix of Namibian and international dishes and the free wi-fi while you make up your own mind.

★ Outjo Bakery BAKERY, CAFE $$
(☑067-313055, 081 141 3839; Hage Geingob Ave; breakfast N$48-120, mains N$65-160; ⊙7am-4.30pm Mon-Fri, 7am-1.30pm Sat; ☎) Opened in 2016, this stylish place wouldn't look out of place in Windhoek or urban South Africa. All of the international staples are here – pasta, steaks, burgers and open sandwiches – but it's the clean lines, tempting array of bakery items and all-round sophistication of everything from the food to the service that make this place a winner.

Farmhouse INTERNATIONAL $$
(www.farmhouse-outjo.com; Hage Geingob Ave; mains N$45-105; ⊙7am-9pm; ☎) This all-rounder is the centre of food and drink in town, serving meals all day every day. Its pleasant beer garden is a great spot to reconnect with social media. Burgers, pies, grills (including game such as kudu, eland and oryx), wraps, pizza, salads and ever-changing daily specials are on offer, as are tempting cakes. It also serves the best coffee in town.

It might not pull off the farmhouse feel, but it does have rustic overtones inside.

ℹ Getting There & Away

Combis (minibuses) run between the OK Supermarket in Outjo to towns and cities around North-Central Namibia, though there is no public transport leading up to Okakuejo and the Andersson Gate of Etosha National Park. If you're driving, however, the paved route continues north as far as the park gate.

Self-drivers can top up at **Puma** (⊙7am-10pm).

Waterberg Plateau Park

⌨ 067

The wild Waterberg is highly recommended – there is nothing quite like it in Namibia. It takes in a 50km-long, 16km-wide sandstone plateau, looming 150m above the desert plains. It doesn't have the traditional big wildlife attractions (such as lions or elephants). What it does have are some rare and threatened species, including sable and roan antelope, and little-known populations of white and black rhinos. Most animals here have been introduced and after breeding successfully some are moved to other parks. That said, all of these species can prove difficult to see – most are skittish and the bush is very thick.

History

While Waterberg is known among tourists as a unique safari park, the plateau has played a prominent role in Namibian history.

In 1873 a Rhenish mission station was established at Waterberg, but it was destroyed in 1880 during the Herero-Nama wars. In 1904 it was the site of the decisive Battle of the Waterberg between German colonial forces and the Herero resistance. Due to superior weaponry and communications, the Germans prevailed and the remaining Herero were forced to flee east into the Kalahari. The final death blow was dealt by German soldiers, who were sent ahead to refuse the retreating Herero access to the region's few waterholes.

🏃 Activities

Waterberg Unguided Hiking Trail   HIKING
(per person N$100; ⊙9am Wed;) A four-day, 42km unguided hike around a figure-eight track begins at 9am every Wednesday from April to November. It costs N$100 per person, and groups are limited to between three and 10 people. Book through Namibia Wildlife Resorts (p230) in Windhoek. Hikers stay in basic shelters and don't need to carry a tent but must otherwise be self-sufficient. Shelters have drinking water, but you'll need to carry enough to last you between times – plan on drinking at least 3L to 4L per day.

The first day begins at the visitor centre (which is the Waterberg Camp, and follows the escarpment for 13km to Otjozongombe shelter. The second day's walk to Otjomapenda shelter is just a three-hour, 7km walk.

WATERBERG PLATEAU PARK AT A GLANCE

Why Go?
Fabulous hiking, excellent if hard-won wildlife-watching, terrific accommodation and superlative views.

Gateway Towns
Otjiwarongo

When to Go
May to October is the best time to visit, although year-round is possible. Avoid hiking in the heat of the day from December to February in particular.

Budget Safaris
Waterberg is an excellent budget destination – hiking permits are cheap and there's good budget accommodation.

Practicalities
Waterberg Plateau Park is accessible by private vehicle, though visitors must explore the plateau either on foot or as part of an official wildlife drive conducted by NWR (p230). With the exception of walking trails around the Waterberg Resort, both unguided and guided hiking routes in Waterberg must be booked well in advance through Namibia Wildlife Resorts in Windhoek.

Waterberg Plateau Park

The third day consists of an 8km route that loops back to Otjomapenda for the third night. The fourth and final day is a six-hour, 14km return to the visitor centre.

Waterberg Wilderness Trail   HIKING

(per person N$220; ⊘2pm Thu) From April to November the four-day, guided Waterberg Wilderness Trail operates every Thursday. The walks, which are led by armed guides, need a minimum of two people. They begin at 2pm on Thursday from the visitor centre and end early on Sunday afternoon. They cost N$220 per person and also must be prebooked through NWR (p230) in Windhoek. There's no set route, and the itinerary is left to the whims of the guide. Accommodation is in simple huts, but participants must carry their own food and sleeping bags.

Wildlife Drive   WILDLIFE WATCHING

(incl breakfast pack N$600; ⊘6am or 3pm) If you're not doing a hike, wildlife drives are the only way to get onto the plateau to spot the animals (self-drives are not allowed). The four-hour drive takes you to hides cleverly hidden around waterholes. Antelope, including eland, sable, roan and red hartebeest are the ones you're most likely to spot.

Leopards, cheetahs and brown hyenas are around but rarely seen.

Resort Walking Trails   HIKING

Around the pink-sandstone-enclosed rest camp are nine short walking tracks, including one up to the plateau rim at Mountain View. They're great for a pleasant day of easy walking, but watch for snakes, which sun themselves on rocks and even on the tracks themselves. No reservations are required for these trails.

🛏 Sleeping

★Waterberg
Wilderness Lodge   LODGE, CAMPGROUND $$

(☑067-687018; www.waterberg-wilderness.com; off D2512; camping N$170, tented room N$690, r with half board N$1150-1480; ❈🛜🏊) Waterberg Wilderness occupies a vast private concession within the park and is a wonderful upmarket choice. The Rust family has painstakingly transformed the property (formerly a cattle farm) by repopulating game animals and allowing nature to return to its pre-grazed state. The main lodge rests in a sun-drenched, jacaranda-strewn meadow at the end of a valley, where you'll find red-sandstone chalets adorned with rich hardwood furniture.

Waterberg Plateau Unguided Hiking Trail

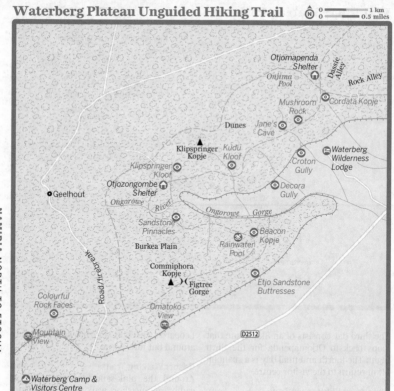

Otjomapenda Shelter
Onjima Pool
Dassie Alley
Rock Alley
Mushroom Rock
Cordata Kopje
Dunes
Jane's Cave
Klipspringer Kopje
Kudu Kloof
Klipspringer Kloof
Croton Gully
Waterberg Wilderness Lodge
Otjozongombe Shelter
Decora Gully
Geelhout
Ongorowe River
Ongorowe Gorge
Sandstone Pinnacles
Burkea Plain
Beacon Kopje
Rainwater Pool
Commiphora Kopje
Figtree Gorge
Etjo Sandstone Buttresses
Road/firebreak
Colourful Rock Faces
Omatoko View
D2512
Mountain View
Waterberg Camp & Visitors Centre

NAMIBIA NORTH TO ETOSHA

But there's so much more here. Arrive before 3pm so as to join the rhino wildlife drives. It has other accommodation around the valley: Plateau Camp (a handful of more secluded chalets perched high on a rock terrace deeper in the concession), a tented camp (Meru-style safari tents facing down the valley with fine views), or you can pitch your own tent in the high-lying Andersson Camp.

To reach Waterberg Wilderness Lodge, take the D2512 gravel road around 100km from Otjiwarongo and follow the signs.

Waterberg Camp   CAMPGROUND, LODGE $$

(067-305001; www.nwr.com.na; camping N$160, s/d bush chalets N$810/1320) Together with its sibling properties in Etosha, the Waterberg Camp is part of NWR's Classic Collection. At Waterberg, campers can pitch a tent in any number of scattered sites around braai (barbecue) pits and picnic tables. Campsites benefit from space, views of the plateau and

the plains beyond, and well-kept amenities. The lodge rooms and bush chalets are unexciting but nicely kept and well-priced for what you get.

Campers can pick up firewood, alcohol, basic groceries and other supplies from the shop, while others can sink their teeth into a fine oryx steak at the restaurant (a rather grand stone building up the hill from the campsite – it's a bit of a slog on foot – complete with old pics and chandeliers) and wash it down with a glass of South African Pinotage from the bar. A word of warning, though: Waterberg is overrun with crafty baboons, so keep your tents zipped and your doors closed, and watch where you leave your food.

Wabi Lodge   LODGE $$$

(067-306500; www.wabi.ch; s/d from N$1185/2170;) Wabi is a private luxury set-up almost 30km from Waterberg Plateau on the D2512. The Swiss owners have imparted their heritage on the design and furnishings of the eight bungalows and in the well-prepared food. It runs its own wildlife drives including night drives where you've a chance to see honey badgers, caracals, genets, brown hyenas, and even cheetahs and leopards.

ℹ Getting There & Away

Waterberg Plateau Park is only accessible by private car – motorcycles are not permitted anywhere within the park boundaries. From Otjiwarongo it's about 90km to the park gate via the B1, C22 and the gravel D512. While this route is passable to 2WD vehicles, go slow in the final stretches as the road can be in bad shape after the rainy season. An alternative route is the D2512, which runs between Waterberg and Grootfontein – this route is OK during winter but can be terrible during summer, the rainy season, when it requires a high-clearance 4WD.

Grootfontein

POP 23,790 / 📞 067

With a pronounced colonial feel, Grootfontein (Afrikaans for Big Spring) has an air of uprightness and respectability, with local limestone constructions and honour guards of jacaranda trees that bloom in the autumn. The springboard for excursions out to Khaudum National Park and the San villages in Otjozondjupa or a way station on your way to/from Etosha's east, Grootfontein can be the last town of any real significance that you see before heading out into the deep, deep bush.

History

It was the town's eponymous spring that managed to attract Grootfontein's earliest travellers, and in 1885 the Dorsland (Afrikaans for 'Thirst Land') trekkers set up the short-lived Republic of Upingtonia. By 1887 the settlement was gone, but six years later Grootfontein became the headquarters for the German South-West Africa Company, thanks to the area's abundant mineral wealth. In 1896 the German Schutztruppe constructed a fort using local labour, and Grootfontein became a heavily fortified garrison town. The fort and nearby colonial cemetery are still local landmarks.

◉ Sights

German Fort & Museum   FORT
(adult/child N$25/15; ⊙ 8.30am-4.30pm Mon-Fri) Historical settler history is depicted here through some fascinating black-and-white photos. The Himba, Kavango and Mbanderu collections of artefacts and photographs are also interesting, as is the history of research into the area's rock art. It's a huge museum; put a couple of hours aside at least.

The 1896 fort in which the museum is housed was enlarged several times in the

NAMIBIA NORTH TO ETOSHA

THE RED LINE

Between Grootfontein and Rundu, and Tsumeb and Ondangwa, the B8 and B1 cross the 'Red Line', the Animal Disease Control Checkpoint veterinary control fence separating the commercial cattle ranches of the south from the communal subsistence lands to the north. Since the 1960s, this fence has barred the north–south movement of animals as a precaution against foot-and-mouth disease and rinderpest. Animals bred north of this line have not been allowed to be sold to the south or exported to overseas markets.

As a result, the Red Line has effectively marked the boundary between the developed and developing world. The landscape south of the line is characterised by a dry, scrubby bushveld (open grassland) of vast ranches, which are home only to cattle and a few scattered ranchers. North of the Animal Disease Control Checkpoint, travellers enter a landscape of dense bush, baobab trees, mopane scrub and small kraals (huts), where the majority of individuals struggle to maintain subsistence lifestyles.

This impasse may soon be resolved, however. In 2012, and again in 2014, the Namibian government publicly stepped up its efforts to have much of the existing 'protected' area internationally recognised as being free of livestock disease. If successful, this could see the Red Line shifted up as far as the western boundary of Bwabwata National Park (the Caprivi Strip is still regarded as a high-risk zone for foot-and-mouth disease), or possibly even as far as the Angolan border. But until this complicated issue is resolved in such a way that the line can be shifted without threatening Namibia's lucrative export market, even for a short time, expect the line to stay in place.

Grootfontein

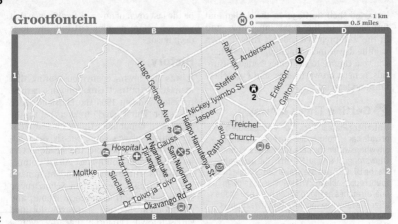

Grootfontein

early 20th century and in 1922 a large limestone extension was added.

Later the building served as a boarding school, but in 1968 it fell into disuse.

Hoba Meteorite NATURAL FEATURE

(adult/child N$20/10; ⊙ dawn-dusk) Near the Hoba Farm, the world's largest meteorite was discovered in 1920 by hunter Jacobus Brits. This cuboid bit of space debris is composed of 82% iron, 16% nickel and 0.8% cobalt, along with traces of other metals. No one knows when it fell to earth (it's thought to have been around 80,000 years ago), but since it weighs around 54,000kg, it must have made one hell of a thump.

In 1955, after souvenir hunters began hacking off bits to take home, the site was declared a national monument. There's now a visitors information board, a short nature trail and a shady picnic area. Unless you have a specialised interest, however, it's

worth a quick stop only, and its size is not all that impressive.

From Grootfontein, follow the C42 towards Tsumeb. After 500m, turn west on the D2859 and continue 22km; then follow the clearly marked signs until you reach the complex.

Cemetery CEMETERY

In the town cemetery, off Okavango Rd, you can wander the graves of several Schutztruppe soldiers who died in combat with local forces around the turn of the century.

🛏 Sleeping & Eating

Stone House Lodge GUESTHOUSE $

(☑ 067-242842; www.stonehouse.iway.na; 10 Toenessen St; s/d N$450/650; ❄ 🔊 🛏) Probably the best of the in-town options, Stone House has six attractive rooms overseen by Boet and Magda. This guesthouse has a welcoming, family feel to it.

Courtyard Guesthouse GUESTHOUSE $

(☑ 067-240027; 2 Gauss St; s/d N$430/660; ❄ @ 🔊 🛏) The top spot in Grootfontein is modest by any standard, but its truly enormous rooms (not all – ask to see a few) leave you plenty of space to unpack your bag and take stock of your gear. If you're about to embark on a bush outing, spend the afternoon poolside and bask in comfort while you can. The restaurant (mains N$60 to N$100, open 7am to 10pm) serves fish, salads, pastas and grills dabbling in a bit of everything.

Roy's Rest Camp CAMPGROUND, BUNGALOW $$

(☑ 067-240302; www.roysrestcamp.com; camping N$110, s/d N$865/1470; 🛏) Accommodation in this recommended place looks like a fairytale illustration – the handmade wooden furnishings are all fabulously original, while the thatched bungalows sit tranquilly beneath towering trees. Possible activities include a 2.5km hiking trail, drives around the large farm on which the camp is set, and a day trip to a traditional San village. Roy's is located 55km from Grootfontein on the road towards Rundu.

★ **Purple Fig Bistro**   INTERNATIONAL **$$**
(📞 081 124 2802; www.facebook.com/purplefigbis tro; 19 Hage Geingob St; mains N$40-120; ⊙7am-9pm) In the heart of town, the Purple Fig gets good reviews from travellers. Eat under the eponymous fig or in the cafe. Light meals take the form of salads, wraps and toasted sandwiches, but there are also burgers, steaks and pancakes. Servings are large, staff are friendly and it's easily the most pleasant place to eat in Grootfontein.

🛈 Getting There & Away

Minibuses leave for **Rundu and Oshakati** from one stop along Okavango Rd, with others to **Tsumeb and Windhoek** from another; all depart when full. The **Intercape Mainliner** (p375) bus that departs Windhoek for Victoria Falls also passes through Grootfontein (from N$772, six hours) on Monday, Wednesday and Friday; going the other way they pass through on Monday, Thursday and Saturday.

If you're heading out to Tsumkwe, you will need a private vehicle. The gravel road into town is accessible by 2WD if you take it slow, but you will need a high-clearance vehicle to reach the various villages in Otjozondjupa, and a 4WD might be necessary in the rainy season. If you're heading to Khaudum, a sturdy 4WD is a requirement, as is travelling as part of a well-equipped convoy.

Tsumeb
POP 19,280 / 📞 067

Tsumeb is one Namibian town worth a poke around, especially if you are trying to get a feel for the country's urban side. The streets are very pleasant to wander, made more so by the plentiful shady trees, it's reasonably compact, and there's usually a smile or two drifting your way on the busy streets. There are a few attractions to guide your visit, but it's more about getting a window on the world of an appealing northern Namibian town.

⊙ Sights

St Barbara's Church   CHURCH
(cnr Main St & Sam Nujoma Dr) Tsumeb's distinctive Roman Catholic church was consecrated

---

MIGHTY MINERALS, WORLDLY WONDERS

The prosperity of Tsumeb is based on the presence of 184 known minerals, including 10 that are unique to this area. Its deposits of copper ore and a phenomenal range of other metals and minerals (lead, silver, germanium, cadmium and many others), brought to the surface in a volcanic pipe – as well as Africa's most productive lead mine – give it the distinction of being a metallurgical and mineralogical wonder of the world. Tsumeb specimens have found their way into museum collections around the globe, but you'll also see a respectable assembly of the region's mineralogical largesse and historical data in the town museum.

---

in 1914 and dedicated to St Barbara, the patron saint of mineworkers. It contains some fine colonial murals and an odd tower, which makes it look less like a church than a municipal building in some small German town.

Tsumeb Mining Museum   MUSEUM
(📞 067-220447; cnr Main St & 8th Rd; adult/child N$40/10; ⊙9am-5pm Mon-Fri, 9am-noon Sat) If you normally skip museums, make an exception here. Tsumeb's story is told in this museum, which is housed in a 1915 colonial building that once served as both a school and a hospital for German troops. In addition to outstanding mineral displays (you've never seen anything like psitticinite!), the museum also houses mining machinery, stuffed birds, Himba and Herero artefacts, and weapons recovered from Lake Otjikoto.

There is also a large collection of militaria, which was dumped here by German troops prior to their surrender to the South Africans in 1915.

Helvi Mpingana Kondombolo Cultural Village   MUSEUM
(📞 067-220787; N$60; ⊙8am-4pm Mon-Fri, to 1pm Sat & Sun) This complex, located 3km outside the town on the road to Grootfontein, showcases examples of housing styles, cultural demonstrations and artefacts from all major Namibian traditions. It's a little rundown and staff don't really illuminate the place with their enthusiasm but it's a worthwhile detour.

Tsumeb

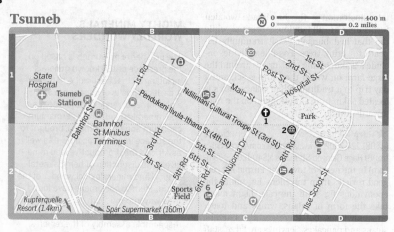

Tsumeb

◉ Sights
1 St Barbara's Church C1
2 Tsumeb Mining Museum C2

🛏 Sleeping
3 Makalani Hotel C1
4 Mousebird Backpackers & Safaris C2
5 Olive Tree Court D2
6 Travel North Namibia Guesthouse C2

🛍 Shopping
7 Tsumeb Arts & Crafts Centre B1

ℹ Information
Travel North Namibia Tourist Office .... (see 6)

🛏 Sleeping & Eating

Mousebird Backpackers & Safaris
HOSTEL $

(☑ 067-221777; cnr of 533 Pendukeni Iivula-Itha-na St/4th St; camping N$120, dm/tw N$160/460; @) Tsumeb's long-standing backpacker spot continues to stay true to its roots, offering economical accommodation without sacrificing personality or character – there's a really good feel to this place. It's a small house-style set-up with decent communal areas, including a kitchen. The best twin rooms share a bathroom inside the house although the twin outside does have its own bathroom. The four-bed dorm is also very good.

Olive Tree Court
APARTMENT $

(☑ 081 122 5846; www.facebook.com/olivetreetsb/; apt from N$650) The modern rooms and spacious living areas and kitchen make for an excellent bolthole for those passing through Tsumeb. Relatively new and well-run, Olive Tree Court amplifies Tsumeb's claims to being the best place to overnight on your way between eastern Etosha and Caprivi.

Kupferquelle Resort
RESORT $$

(☑ 067-220139; www.kupferquelle.com; Kupfer St; camping N$115, s/d N$1110/1530; ☀) This modern, resort-style place has lovely, contemporary rooms with high ceilings, quiet terraces and a real sense of space, style and light. Some have kitchens, and all have modern art on the walls. There's an onsite swimming pool and ample grounds. An excellent choice.

Makalani Hotel
HOTEL $$

(☑ 067-221051; www.makalanihotel.com; cnr of Ndilimani Cultural Troupe St/3rd St; s/d/f from N$590/870/1200; ❋ 🕏 ☀) Situated in the town centre, the upmarket Makalani Hotel is a rather garish-looking place that markets itself as both a small hotel and almost a mini-resort complete with casino. But it can't have it both ways and it sits uncomfortably between the two. What it does have is excellent rooms – if you prefer slightly more comfy, hotel-like options, then this place is for you.

Travel North Namibia Guesthouse
GUESTHOUSE $

(☑ 067-220728; www.travelnorthguesthouse.com/index.htm; Sam Nujoma Dr; s/d N$450/580; ❋ @ 🕏) This budget guesthouse is a wonderful spot if you're counting your Nam dollars.

It's a fantastically friendly place delivering decent, good-value accommodation. Rooms are a bit old-fashioned but they're enhanced by splashes of colour that update things considerably. The smallish beds still have enough life left to ensure a good night's snooze.

Spar SUPERMARKET
(☑067-222840; Hage Geingob Dr; ⊘8am-6pm Mon-Sat) is Tsumeb's best supermarket.

Shopping

Tsumeb Arts & Crafts Centre ARTS & CRAFTS
(☑067-220257; 18 Main St; ⊘9am-5pm Mon-Fri, 9am-1pm Sat) This craft centre markets Caprivian woodwork, San arts, Owambo basketry (also some great basketry from the San), European-Namibian leatherwork, karakul weavings, and other traditional northern Namibian arts and crafts. There's a very helpful, jolly lady overseeing what is a small but interesting selection.

🛈 Information

Travel North Namibia Tourist Office
(☑067-220728; 1551 Sam Nujoma Dr; 🛜)
Inside the guesthouse of the same name.

Provides nationwide information, arranges accommodation, transport, car hire and Etosha bookings, and has internet access. No maps available.

🛈 Getting There & Away

BUS

Intercape Mainliner (p375) buses make the trip between Windhoek and Tsumeb (from N$340, 5½ hours, twice weekly). It is recommended to book your tickets in advance online as this service continues on to Victoria Falls and fills up quickly.

Combis also run up and down the B1 with fairly regular frequency, and a ride between Windhoek and Tsumeb shouldn't cost more than N$280. If you're continuing on to Etosha National Park, be advised that there is no public transport serving this route.

CAR

Tsumeb is an easy day's drive from Windhoek along paved roads and serves as the jumping-off point for Namutoni and the Von Lindequist Gate of Etosha National Park. The paved route continues north as far as the park gate, though keep your speed under control as wildlife is frequently seen along the sides of the highway.

NAMIBIA NORTH TO ETOSHA

LAKE OTJIKOTO

In May 1851, explorers Charles John Andersson and Francis Galton stumbled across the unusual **Lake Otjikoto** (N$25; ⊘8am-6pm summer, to 5pm winter). The name of the lake is Herero for 'deep hole', and its waters fill a limestone sinkhole measuring 100m by 150m, reaching depths of 55m. Interestingly, Lake Otjikoto and nearby Lake Guinas are the only natural lakes in Namibia, and they're also the only known habitats of the unusual mouth-brooding cichlid fish.

These fish are psychedelic in appearance – ranging from dark green to bright red, yellow and blue – and are believed by biologists to eschew camouflage due to the absence of predators in this isolated environment. It's thought that these fish evolved from tilapia (bream) washed into the lake by ancient floods.

In 1915 the retreating German army dumped weaponry and ammunition into the lake to prevent it from falling into South African hands. It's rumoured that they jettisoned five cannons, 10 cannon bases, three Gatling guns and between 300 and 400 wagonloads of ammunition. Some of this stuff was salvaged in 1916 at great cost and effort by the South African army, the Tsumeb Corporation and the National Museum of Namibia. In 1970, divers discovered a Krupp ammunition wagon 41m below the surface; it's on display at the Owela Museum (p220) in Windhoek. In 1977 and 1983, two more ammunition carriers were salvaged as well as a large cannon, and are now on display at the Tsumeb Mining Museum (p247).

Although the site is undeveloped, there is a ticket booth, an adjacent car park and several small kiosks selling cold drinks and small snacks, as well as quite a bit of shade. While treasure seekers have been known to don scuba gear and search the lake under cover of night, diving (and swimming for that matter) is presently forbidden.

Lake Otjikoto lies 25km north of Tsumeb along the B1, and there are signs marking the turn-off. Note that the entry to the lake is just past the sign for it (about 100m) coming from Etosha.

Etosha National Park

🎵 067

Etosha National Park (per person per day N$80, per vehicle N$10; ☉ sunrise-sunset), covering more than 20,000 sq km, is one of the world's great wildlife-viewing venues. Unlike other parks in Africa, where you can spend days looking for animals, Etosha's charm lies in its ability to bring the animals to you. Just park your car next to one of the many waterholes, then wait and watch while a host of animals – lions, elephants, springboks, gemsboks etc – come not two by two but by the hundreds.

Etosha's essence is the vast Etosha Pan, an immense, flat, saline desert that, for a few days each year, is converted by rain into a shallow lagoon teeming with flamingos and pelicans. In contrast, late in the dry season, everything, from the elephants to the once-golden grasslands seems cast, spectre-like, in Etosha's white, chalky dust. And what wildlife there is! Even if you've had a taste of African wildlife watching previously, you are likely to be mesmerised by it here.

History

The first Europeans in Etosha were traders and explorers Charles John Andersson and Francis Galton, who arrived by wagon at Namutoni in 1851. They were later followed in 1876 by an American trader, G McKeirnan, who observed: 'All the menageries in the world turned loose would not compare to the sight I saw that day'.

However, Etosha didn't attract the interest of tourists or conservationists until after the turn of the 20th century, when the governor of German South West Africa, Dr von Lindequist, became concerned about diminishing animal numbers and founded a 99,526-sq-km reserve, which included Etosha Pan.

At the time, the land was still unfenced and animals could follow their normal migration routes. In subsequent years, however, the park boundaries were altered a few times, and by 1970 Etosha had been reduced to its present size.

🏃 Activities

Etosha's most widespread vegetation type is mopane woodland, which fringes the pan and constitutes about 80% of the vegetation. The park also has umbrella-thorn acacias and other trees that are favoured by browsing animals, and from December to March this sparse bush country has a pleasant green hue.

Depending on the season, you may observe elephants, giraffes, Burchell's zebras, springboks, red hartebeests, blue wildebeest, gemsboks, elands, kudus, roans, ostriches, jackals, hyenas, lions and even cheetahs and leopards. Among the endangered animal species are the black-faced impala and the black rhinoceros.

Etosha is Namibia's most important stronghold for lions, with more than half of the country's wild lions – 450 to 500 according to the last estimate by peak conservation NGO Panthera (www.panthera.org).

The park's wildlife density varies with the local ecology. As its Afrikaans name would suggest, Oliphantsbad (near Okaukuejo) is attractive to elephants, but for rhinos you couldn't do better than the floodlit waterhole at Okaukuejo. We've also seen them by night at the waterhole at Olifantsrus and Halali. In general, the further east you go in the park, the more wildebeest, kudus and impalas join the springboks and gemsboks. The area around Namutoni, which averages 443mm of rain annually (compared with 412mm at Okaukuejo), is the best place to see the black-faced impala and the Damara dik-dik, Africa's smallest antelope. Etosha is also home to numerous smaller species, including both yellow and slender mongoose, honey badgers and *leguaans* (water-monitor lizards).

In the dry winter season, wildlife clusters around waterholes, while in the hot, wet summer months, animals disperse and spend the days sheltering in the bush. In the afternoon, even in the dry season, look carefully for animals resting beneath the trees, especially prides of lions lazing about. Summer temperatures can reach 44°C, which isn't fun when you're confined to a vehicle, but this is the calving season, and you may catch a glimpse of tiny zebra foals and fragile newborn springboks.

Birdlife is also profuse. Yellow-billed hornbills are common, and on the ground you should look for the huge kori bustard, which weighs 15kg and seldom flies – it's the world's heaviest flying bird. You may also observe ostriches, korhaans, marabous, white-backed vultures and many smaller species.

The best time for wildlife drives is at first light and late in the evening, though visitors aren't permitted outside the camps after dark. While self-drivers should definitely wake up at twilight, when animals are most active, guided night drives (N$600 per person) can

Etosha National Park

20 km
12 miles

Von Lindequist Gate
Twee Palms
Aroe
Namutoni Rest Camp
Mokuti Lodge (2km); Tsumeb (88km)
Klein Namutoni
Dikdik Drive
Kameeldoring
Mushara
Fischer's Pan
King Nehale Waterhole (dry)
Tsam
Tsumcor Windmill
Groot Okevi
Klein Okevi
Koinachas
Chudob
Kalkheuwel
Andoni Plain
Stinkwater
Andoni
Springbokfontein
Batia
Dungariespomp
Onkoshi Camp
Leeunes (dry)
Okerfontein
Ngobib
Kawaseb
Koinseb
Eland Drive
Poacher's Point
Goas
Noniams
Etosha Pan
Etosha Lookout
Nuamses
Helio Windmill
Halali Rest Camp
Tsumasa Kopje
Rhino Drive
Rietfontein
Charitsaub
Salvadora
Sueda
Gonob
Homob
Ondongab
Aus
Oshigambo River
Ekuma River
Okondeka
Wolfsnes (dry)
Kapupuhedi Pan
Gaseb (dry)
Gemsbokvlakte Windmill
Olifantsbad Windmill
Ombika
Game Fence
Outjo (102km)
Andersson Gate
Ongava Lodge
Okaukuejo Rest Camp
Natukanaoka Pan
Okakuana Pan
Adamax (dry)
Nacto (dry)
Haunted Forest
Grünewald (dry)
Ozonjuitji m Bari Windmill
Dolomite Camp (130km); Galton Gate (144km)
Ondundozonananandana Mountains
D1998

be booked through any of the main camps and are your best chance to see lions hunting, as well as the various nocturnal species. Each of the camps also has a visitor register, which describes any recent sightings in the vicinity.

🛏 Sleeping

The main camps inside the park are open year-round and have restaurants, bars, shops, swimming pools, picnic sites, petrol stations, kiosks and floodlit watering holes that attract game throughout the night. Al-

though fees are normally prepaid through NWR in Windhoek (p230), it is sometimes possible to reserve accommodation at any of the gates. However, be advised that the park can get very busy on weekends, especially during the dry season – if you can manage it, prebooking is strongly recommended.

🛏 In the Park

Olifantsrus Rest Camp   CAMPGROUND $
(☑061-2857200; www.nwr.com.na; camping N$280) The newest of Etosha's rest camps,

---

ETOSHA NATIONAL PARK AT A GLANCE

Why Go?

Let's talk numbers: Etosha is home to 114 mammal species as well as 340 bird species, 16 reptile and amphibian species, one fish species and countless insects. Or landscapes: the desolate nature of the pan, the low-cut landscapes and (of course) the waterholes, means wildlife viewing is some of the easiest and most productive on the continent. It's also one of the best places to spot the highly endangered black rhino in Southern Africa.

Gateway Towns

Most people call in at Outjo, if approaching from the south – it's about 100km to Etosha from here on a smooth sealed road. Outjo is a fine place to stock up on supplies at the supermarket, use the internet and indulge in some good food. If you're heading straight to the eastern side of the park (if you're coming from the Caprivi Strip or Rundu, for example) you'll go via Tsumeb, another handy launching point for the park; it's about 110km from Von Lindequist Gate.

Wildlife

The opportunity to see black rhinos is a big draw here; they are usually very difficult to spot, but as they come to some of the waterholes around the camps by night, it couldn't be easier! There's also lions, cheetahs, elephants, black-backed jackals, giraffes, gemsboks, ostriches and all manner of antelope species.

Author Tip

➡ If you're self-catering, bring your own supplies into the park, as the food selection in the park's shops is abysmal.

➡ At the camps, try hanging around the floodlit waterholes late, after most folk have gone to bed. We did just that at Halali and Okaukuejo and had two of the best wildlife encounters – watching black rhinos – we have had in Africa.

Budget Safaris

Getting together a group is one way to save costs on vehicle rental. Otherwise, either join a budget safari (Swakpmund is one place to ask around), or camp at the park's campsites and join the game drives organised by the park authorities.

Practicalities

➡ You'll find maps of Etosha National Park across the country and at the shops at most of the park gates. **NWR** (p230)'s reliable English-German *Map of Etosha* (from N$40) is the best and is also the most widely available. It has the added bonus of park information and quite extensive mammal and bird identification sheets.

➡ Etosha's four main entry gates are Von Lindequist (Namutoni), west of Tsumeb; King Nehale, southeast of Ondangwa; Andersson (Okaukuejo), north of Outjo; and Galton, northwest of Kamanjab.

out in the recently opened-to-the-public western reaches of the park, fenced Olifantsrus occupies an old elephant culling site with some of the gruesome paraphernalia still on show. There's a small kiosk, decent sites and a marvellous elevated hide overlooking a waterhole.

At the waterhole in the morning, expect wildlife and flocks of Namaqua sand grouse, while we've seen black rhinos drinking here by night.

Halali Rest Camp LODGE, CAMPGROUND $

(☑ 067-229400, 061-2857200; www.nwr.com.na; campsites N$250, plus per person N$150, s/d chalets from N$1150/2040, s/d chalets from N$1530/2800; ✳ ✉) Etosha's middle camp, Halali, nestles between several incongruous dolomite outcrops. The best feature at Halali is its floodlit waterhole, which is a 10-minute walk from the rest camp and is sheltered by a glen of trees with huge boulders strewn about. There is a very well-serviced campsite here, in addition to a fine collection of semi-luxurious chalets.

The short Tsumasa hiking track leads up Tsumasa Kopje, the hill nearest the rest camp, from where you can snap wonderful panoramic shots of the park. While it's not as dramatic in scope as Okaukuejo, the waterhole here is a wonderfully intimate setting to savour a glass of wine in peace, all the while scanning the bush for rhinos and lions, which frequently stop by to drink in the late-evening hours.

Day/night drives cost an additional N$500/600 per person and the latter in particular should be booked in advance.

Namutoni Rest Camp LODGE, CAMPGROUND $$

(☑ 067-229300, 061-2857200; www.nwr.com.na; campsites N$200, plus per person N$110, s/d from N$850/1500, s/d chalets from N$1000/1800; ✳ ✉) Etosha's easternmost camp is defined by its landmark whitewashed German fort. Namutoni offers an immaculate campsite (the only campsite in the park with grass) in addition to a few luxury chalets on the edge of the bush – the use of whitewashed walls, dark woods and Afro-chic decor make these some of NWR's more attractive in-park rooms.

Beside the fort is a lovely freshwater limestone spring and the floodlit King Nehale waterhole, which is filled with reed beds and some extremely vociferous frogs. The viewing benches are nice for lunch or watching the pleasant riverbank scene, but the spot attracts surprisingly few thirsty animals. Day/

night drives cost an additional N$500/600 per person. Make sure to book well ahead for night drives.

Wildlife is scarcer than at other camps.

★Onkoshi Camp LODGE $$$

(☑ 067-687362, 061-2857200; www.nwr.com.na; per person with half-board incl transfers from Namutoni N$2750; ✳ ✉) Upon arrival at Onkoshi (from Namutoni), you'll be chauffeured to a secluded peninsula on the pan's rim, and given the keys to one of 15 thatch-and-canvas chalets resting on elevated wooden decks and occupying exclusive locations well beyond the standard tourist route. The opulent interiors blend rich hardwoods, delicate bamboo, elaborate metal flourishing, finely crafted furniture, hand-painted artwork and fine porcelain fixtures.

While the temptation certainly exists to spend your days lounging about such regal settings, guests are treated to personalised wildlife drives (from N$500 per person) conducted by Etosha's finest guides, and dinners are multi-course affairs illuminated by candlelight.

Okaukuejo Rest Camp LODGE, CAMPGROUND $$$

(☑ 067-229800, 061-2857200; www.nwr.com.na; campsites N$250, plus per person N$150, s/d N$1400/2540, s/d chalets from N$1470/2680; P ✳ ✉) Pronounced 'o-ka-kui-yo', this is the site of the Etosha Research Station, and it also functions as the official park headquarters and main visitor centre. The Okaukuejo waterhole is probably Etosha's best rhino-viewing venue, particularly between 8pm and 10pm. Okaukuejo's campsite can get very crowded, but the shared facilities (washing stations, braai pits and bathrooms with hot water) are excellent.

The self-contained accommodation includes older but refurbished rooms alongside stand-alone chalets. The luxury 'waterhole chalet' is a stunning two-storey affair complete with a furnished centre-stage balcony boasting views of animals lining up to drink – the only drawback is the large number of people walking to and from the waterhole just metres from your door until late at night.

Day/night drives cost an additional N$500/600 per person. Book night drives in advance.

Dolomite Camp LODGE $$$

(☑ 061-2857200, 065-685119; www.nwr.com.na; s/d with half-board from N$2040/3580; ✳ ✉)

Recently opened in a previously restricted area in western Etosha, Dolomite Camp is beautifully carved into its rocky surrounds. Accommodation is in thatched chalets (actually luxury tents), including a couple with their own plunge pool. The views of surrounding plains are wonderful and there's even a waterhole at the camp, so spotting wildlife doesn't mean moving far from bed.

When you do get out and about, the wildlife viewing is superb as the area has been free from human activity for half a century. Guided three-hour day/night wildlife drives cost an extra N$500/650.

Outside the Park

Toshari
LODGE $$

(☏ 067-333440; www.etoshagateway-toshari.com; camping N$125, s/d N$900/1320; ⏱⚐) This convenient alternative to staying in the park is 25km from Etosha, right on the C38. It has cubicle-type chalets that are rather ugly, but forgiven for their comfort and bushy setting. The campsites (only three) are excellent, and all have that unusual feature in Namibia – grass. Each also has its own bathroom, braai, stone bench and shade.

When camping, you can use the lodge facilities, including free tea and coffee, a well-stocked bar and relaxing communal area complete with pet mongoose.

Mokuti Lodge
LODGE $$

(☏ 061-2075360; www.mokutietoshalodge.com; per person incl breakfast N$1065; ✳@⏱⚐) This sprawling lodge, located just 2km from Von Lindequist Gate, has rooms, chalets and luxurious suites, as well as several swimming pools, spa and tennis courts, though the low-profile buildings create an illusion of intimacy. The accommodation mixes contemporary fittings with African style, creating a fine blend. Chalets have comfy sofas and welcome platters.

The lodge seeks to create an informal, relaxed atmosphere (there's a boma with fire pit and nightly storytelling), which makes this a good choice if you're travelling with the little ones. Don't miss the attached reptile park and its resident snake collection, which features locals captured, somewhat ominously, around the lodge property.

★Ongava Lodge
LODGE $$$

(☏ 061-225178; www.wilderness-safaris.com; s/d half board N$4771/7632; ✳@⚐) One of the more exclusive luxury lodges in the Etosha area, Ongava Lodge is not far south of Andersson Gate. Ongava is actually divided into two properties: the main Ongava Lodge is a collection of safari-chic chalets surrounding a small waterhole, while the Ongava Tented Camp has eight East African–style canvas tents situated a bit deeper in the bush.

It's part of Ongava Game Reserve, which protects several prides of lions, a few black and white rhinos and your standard assortment of herd animals. There are also two other accommodation options in the reserve.

Onguma Etosha Aoba Lodge
LODGE $$$

(☏ 067-229100; www.etosha-aoba-lodge.com; s/d with half board from N$2020/3340; ✳@⚐) Part of the 70-sq-km private Onguma Game Reserve, 10km east of Von Lindequist Gate, this tranquil lodge is located in tamboti forest next to a dry riverbed. The property comprises 10 cottages that blend effortlessly into their riverine environment. The atmosphere is peaceful and relaxing, and the main lodge is conducive to unwinding with other guests after a long day on safari.

Other affiliated lodges inhabit the reserve, as well as a number of excellent campsites (per person from N$220). Some, such as Tamboti Luxury Campsite, have private facilities, a restaurant and a swimming pool. For more information, check out www.onguma.com.

Taleni Etosha Village
TENTED CAMP $$$

(☏ 067-333413, in South Africa 27-21-930 4564; www.taleni-africa.com; camping N$150, s/d full board high season N$1951/2928; ✳⏱) This little hideaway, just a couple of kilometres outside Etosha, has self-catering safari tents (half- and full-board options available) with outdoor seating area, braai (barbecue), wooden floors, power points and other little luxuries. The tents are nestled into bushland among mopane trees, and the friendly staff can also organise food if you're self-catering. Etosha Village is 2km before the Andersson Gate.

There are also some good campsites here, although there's little shade.

Mushara Lodge
LODGE $$$

(☏ 061-241880; www.mushara-lodge.com; s/d from N$1850/3700; ⏱⚐) Part of the elegant and varied Mushara Collection, which includes three other fine properties, this lodge is impeccably attired in wood, thatch and wicker in the large and extremely comfortable rooms.

Epacha Game Lodge & Spa   LODGE **$$$**
(☑061-375300; www.epacha.com; s/d full board N$3500/5800) Superb rooms are a hallmark of this beautiful lodge on the private 21 sq km Epacha Game Reserve. Night drives, great views from its elevated hillside position and a pervasive sense of quiet sophistication are all well and good, but where else in Etosha can you practise your clay-pigeon shooting? There's also a tented lodge and exclusive private villa on the reserve.

Emanya Lodge   LODGE **$$$**
(☑061-222954; www.emanya.com; s/d N$1730/3068; ☎🛏) Boutique elegance and an air of exclusivity dominate this unusually modern lodge. Soothing earth tones and clean lines give the rooms their considerable appeal, while some unusual features, such as the well-stocked wine cellar and foot spa, are welcome deviations from the Etosha norm.

Etosha Safari Camp   CAMPGROUND, LODGE **$$$**
(☑061-230066; www.gondwana-collection.com; camping N$175, s/d chalet N$1211/2264; ❄☎🛏) Excellent grassed campsites spill over a large area here, so there's a good chance you'll get a pitch even if you haven't booked. This whole place is set up like a small village, complete with shebeen bar; be warned there is plenty of kitsch, including a shop in a railway carriage. Safari drives into Etosha are available.

It's 9km from the park on the C38, just off the road and well signed. **Etosha Safari Lodge** next door is also owned by the Gondwana group.

Hobatere Lodge   LODGE **$$$**
(☑061-228104, 067-330118; www.hobatere-lodge.com; s/d half board N$1944/3240; ☎🛏) Close to Etosha's western boundary, 65km northwest of Kamanjab, Hobatere inhabits an 88 sq km private concession where you could see all three big cats as well as elephants and all the usual plains wildlife. The lodge works closely with the local community, both day and night game drives are available and the renovated thatch-roof chalets are well turned out.

❶ Getting There & Away

There's no public transport into and around the park, which means that you must visit either in a private vehicle or as part of an organised tour.

The vast majority of roads in Etosha are passable to 2WD vehicles. The park speed limit is set at 60km/h both to protect wildlife and keep down the dust.

The park road between Namutoni and Okaukuejo skirts Etosha Pan, providing great views of its vast spaces. Driving isn't permitted on the pan, but a network of gravel roads threads through the surrounding savannah and mopane woodland and even extends out to a viewing site, the Etosha Lookout, in the middle of the salt desert.

NORTHERN NAMIBIA

The country's most densely populated region, and undeniably its cultural heartland, northern Namibia is a place for some serious African adventure. It is where endless skies meet distant horizons in an expanse that will make you truly wonder if this could be your greatest road trip of all time. There is space out here to think, and you may just find yourself belting down a dirt road hunched over the steering wheel, pondering in detail whatever's on your mind...for many hours. It's the place for serious problem solving, all induced by that unforgettable landscape.

Northern Namibia takes form and identity from the Caprivi Strip, where, alongside traditional villages, a collection of national parks are being repopulated with wildlife after many decades of war and conflict. At the time of independence, these parks had been virtually depleted by poachers, though years of progressive wildlife management have firmly placed the region back on the safari circuit.

The North

The regions of Omusati, Oshana, Ohangwena and Otjikoto comprise the homeland of the Owambo people, Namibia's largest population group. Although there's little in terms of tourist attractions in this region, Owambo country is home to a healthy and prosperous rural society that buzzes with activity. It's also a good place to stock up on the region's high-quality basketry and sugar-cane work, which is often sold at roadside stalls. Designs are simple and graceful, usually incorporating a brown geometric pattern woven into the pale-yellow reed.

Ondangwa

POP 22,822 / ☑065
The second-largest Owambo town is known as a minor transport hub, with combis fanning out from here to other cities and towns in the north. Its large number of warehouses provide stock to the 6000 tiny *cuca* shops

(small bush shops named after the brand of Angolan beer they once sold) that serve the area's rural residents. As this description of the town implies, Ondangwa is more necessary as a transit town on your way elsewhere than desirable as a destination in itself.

◉ Sights

Lake Oponono   LAKE
The main attraction in the area is Lake Oponono, a large wetland fed by the Culevai *oshanas* (underground river channels). After a heavy rainy season, the lakeshores attract a variety of birdlife, including saddle-billed storks, crowned cranes, flamingos and pelicans. The edge of the lake is 27km south of Ondangwa.

Nakambale Museum   MUSEUM
(N$15; ◷8am-1pm & 2-5pm Mon-Fri, 8am-1pm Sat, noon-5pm Sun) Nakambale, which was built in the late 1870s by Finnish missionary Martti Rauttanen, is believed to be the oldest building in northern Namibia. It now houses a small museum on Owambo history and culture. Nakambale is part of Olukonda village, which is 20km south of Ondangwa on the D3629.

🛌 Sleeping

Nakambale Campsite   CAMPGROUND $
(☑065-245668; campsites N$50, huts per person N$100) Here's your opportunity to sleep in a basic hut that historically would have been used by an Owambo chief or one of his wives – high on novelty, if a little short on comfort. Nakambale lies on the outskirts of Olukonda village, 20km south of Ondangwa on the D3629.

★Protea Hotel Ondangwa   HOTEL $$
(☑065-241900; www.marriott.com/hotels/travel/ondon-protea-hotel-ondangwa; s/d from N$1038/1215; ❉🛜🛆) What a Marriott hotel is doing out here in Ondangwa is anyone's guess, but whatever the reason, this plush business hotel features bright rooms decorated with tasteful artwork as well as modern furnishings. The attached Chatters restaurant serves decent European-inspired cuisine, and there's also a small espresso shop and takeaway in the lobby.

❶ Getting There & Away

AIR
Air Namibia flies to and from Windhoek's Eros Airport daily. Note that the airstrip in Oshakati

is for private charters only, which means that Ondangwa serves as the main access point in the north for air travellers.

BUS
Combis run up and down the B1 with fairly regular frequency, and a ride between Windhoek and Ondangwa shouldn't cost more than N$200. From Ondangwa, a complex network of combi routes serves population centres throughout the north, with fares typically costing less than N$40 a ride.

CAR
The B1 is sealed all the way from Windhoek to Ondangwa and out to Oshakati.

The Oshikango border crossing to Santa Clara in Angola is 60km north of Ondangwa; to travel further north, you'll need an Angolan visa that allows overland travel.

Oshakati
POP 36,541 / ☑065
The Owambo capital is an uninspiring commercial centre that is little more than a strip of characterless development along the highway. But it's worth spending an hour or so at the large covered market, which proffers everything from clothing and baskets to mopane worms and glasses of freshly brewed *tambo* (beer).

🛌 Sleeping

Oshakati Guest House   GUESTHOUSE $
(☑065-224659; www.oshakatiguesthouse.com; Sam Nujoma Rd; r N$400-700; ❉) Simple but nicely turned out en-suite rooms make this appealing guesthouse an excellent base in the area. There's also a rather noisy restaurant.

Oshandira Lodge   LODGE $
(☑065-220443; oshandira@iway.na; s/d N$550/800; ❉) If you get stuck here for the night, Oshandira Lodge, next to the airstrip, offers simple but spacious rooms that surround a landscaped pool and a thatched open-air restaurant serving local staples. The rooms are fine for the night, but that's about it.

Oshakati Country Lodge   LODGE $$
(☑065-222380; Robert Mugabe Rd; s/d from N$880/1320; ❉@🛆) The Oshakati Country Lodge is a favourite of visiting government dignitaries and businesspeople. It's your best bet if you're a slave to modern comforts.

❶ Information
If you're looking to apply for an Angolan visa, the **Angola Consulate** (☑065-221799; Dr Agostinho

Neto Rd) is currently the best place to submit an application.

ℹ️ Getting There & Away

From the bus terminal at the market, combis leave frequently for destinations in the north.

Uutapi (Ombalantu) & Around

♪ 065

The area around Uutapi (also known as Ombalantu), which lies on the C46 between Oshakati and Ruacana, is home to a revered national heritage site, and warrants a quick visit if you've got your own wheels and are passing through the area.

👁 Sights

Fort FORT

The most famous attraction in Uutapi is the former South African Defence Force (SADF) base, which is dominated by an enormous baobab tree. This tree, known locally as *omukwa*, was once used to shelter cattle from invaders, and later used as a turret from which to ambush invading tribes. It didn't work with the South African forces, however, who invaded and used the tree for everything from a chapel to a coffee shop.

To reach the fort, turn left at the police station 350m south of the petrol station and look for an obscure grassy track winding between desultory buildings towards the conspicuous baobab.

Ongulumbashe TOWN

The town of Ongulumbashe is regarded, not without reason, as the birthplace of modern Namibia. On 26 August 1966 the first shots of the war for Namibian independence were fired from this patch of scrubland. The site is also where the People's Liberation Army of Namibia enjoyed its first victory over the South African troops, who had been charged with rooting out and quelling potential guerrilla activities. At the site, you can still see some reconstructed bunkers and the 'needle' monument marking the battle. An etching on the reverse side honours the Pistolet-Pulemyot Shpagina (PPSh), the Russian-made automatic rifle that played a major role in the conflict.

Be advised that this area is considered politically sensitive – you will need permission to visit the site from the Swapo office (♪ 065 251 038) in Uutapi.

Ongandjera TOWN

If you're feeling especially patriotic (in a Namibian sense), you can visit the town of Ongandjera, which is the birthplace of former president Sam Nujoma. The rose-coloured *kraal* (hut) that was his boyhood home is now a national shrine, and is distinguished from its neighbours by a prominent Swapo flag hung in a tree. It's fine to look from a distance, but the *kraal* remains a private home and isn't open to the public.

Ruacana

POP 2985 / ♪ 065

The tiny Kunene River town of Ruacana (from the Herero words *orua hakahana* – 'the rapids') is the jumping-off point for visiting the Ruacana Falls. Here the Kunene River splits into several channels before plunging 85m over a dramatic escarpment and through a 2km-long gorge of its own making. Ruacana was built as a company town to serve the 320-megawatt underground Ruacana hydroelectric project, which now supplies over half of Namibia's power requirements.

👁 Sights

Ruacana Falls WATERFALL

At one time, Ruacana Falls was a guaranteed wonder, though all that changed thanks to Angola's Calueque Dam, 20km upstream, and NamPower's Ruacana power plant. On the rare occasion when there's a surfeit of water, Ruacana returns to its former glory. In wetter years, it's no exaggeration to say it rivals Victoria Falls – if you hear that it's flowing, you certainly won't regret a trip to see it (and it may be the closest you ever get to Angola).

At all other times, the little water that makes it past the first barrage is collected by an intake weir, 1km above the falls, which ushers it into the hydroelectric plant to turn the turbines.

To reach the falls, turn north 15km west of Ruacana and follow the signs towards the border crossing. To visit the gorge, visitors must temporarily exit Namibia by signing the immigration register. From the Namibian border crossing, bear left (to the right lies the decrepit Angolan border crossing) to the end of the road. There you can look around the ruins of the old power station, which was destroyed by Namibian liberation forces. The buildings are pockmarked with scars from mortar rounds and gunfire, providing a stark contrast to the otherwise peaceful scene.

🛏 Sleeping

Hippo Pools Camp Site
CAMPGROUND **$**

(📞065-270120; camping N$60) Also known as Otjipahuriro, this community-run campsite sits alongside the river and has a good measure of shade and privacy. There are also braai (barbecue) pits, hot showers and environmentally friendly pit toilets. Local community members can organise trips to Ruacana Falls or nearby Himba villages for a small fee.

Ruacana Eha Lodge
LODGE **$$**

(📞065-271500; www.ruacanaehalodge.com.na; Springbom Ave; camping N$90, huts per person N$250, s/d N$775/1100; ❄@🐝) This upmarket lodge appeals to travellers of all budgets by offering manicured campsites and rustic A-frame huts alongside its polished rooms. An attractive oasis in the middle of Ruacana, the Eha Lodge is highlighted by its lush gardens and refreshing plunge pool. It can also arrange excursions to local Himba villages and Ruacana Falls.

❶ Getting There & Away

Ruacana is near the junction of roads between Opuwo, Owambo country and the rough 4WD route along the Kunene River to Swartbooi's Drift. Note that mileage signs along the C46 confuse Ruacana town and the power plant, which are 15km apart. Both are signposted 'Ruacana'.

For westbound travellers, the 24-hour petrol station is the last before the Atlantic. It's also the terminal for afternoon minibuses to and from Oshakati and Ondangwa, costing around N$40.

Kavango Region

The heavily wooded and gently rolling Kavango region is dominated by the Okavango River and its broad flood plains. Most people visit here in conjunction with time spent in the Caprivi or Zambezi region, and Khaudum National Park. Along with the re-emergence of the Caprivi national parks as wildlife destinations, this is increasingly one of Namibia's most rewarding wildlife regions.

The rich soil and fishing grounds up here support large communities of Mbukushu, Sambiyu and Caprivi peoples, who are renowned for their high-quality woodcarvings – animal figures, masks, wooden beer mugs, walking sticks and boxes are carved in the light *dolfhout* (wild teak) hardwood and make excellent souvenirs.

Rundu

POP 63,430 / 📞066

Rundu, a sultry tropical outpost on the bluffs above the Okavango River, is a major centre of activity for Namibia's growing Angolan community. Although the town has little of specific interest for tourists, the area is home to a number of wonderful lodges where you can laze along the riverside, and spot crocs and hippos doing pretty much the same. As such, it's a fine place to break up the journey between the Caprivi Strip and Grootfontein or Etosha.

BORDER CROSSING: RUNDU–ANGOLA

The border crossing here is almost one-way traffic, with plenty of Angolans coming into Namibia to purchase goods from the shops, seek medical help and visit relatives; however, we heard reports of Namibians getting a lot of hassle when they try to enter Angola. As for tourists, they are seen as easy pickings for the Angolan authorities, and you may be asked for a bribe or even arrested. Basic Portuguese-language skills would be a huge bonus, as English is not widely spoken. Getting an Angolan visa (US$100) in Windhoek is *very* difficult, and you need time and patience (one traveller we heard about waited for months with no success). It may just depend on who you deal with at the Angolan embassy and, of course, your nationality. For one thing, you need a letter of invitation from somebody in Angola as part of your visa application, as well as a copy of their ID. At the time of writing, Oshakati in Namibia was the best place to try and lodge an Angolan visa application.

There are a few travel agents running basic organised trips into Angola, which consist of you and your guide, your vehicle and all your own camping equipment; Namib-i (p303) in Swakopmund is a good place to make enquiries. The bonus here is that they will organise your visa, including the letter of invitation.

Some lodges, such as N'Kwazi Lodge in Rundu, run boat trips along the Okavango River and will dock on the Angolan side to give you a chance to get some Angolan soil on the soles of your shoes.

📖 Sleeping

Lodges in Rundu and the surrounding region offer a variety of excursions, including sunset cruises, canoeing and fishing.

★ N'Kwazi Lodge   LODGE $

(☎ 081 242 4897; www.nkwazilodge.com; camping per adult/child N$100/50, s/d N$600/1000) On the banks of the Okavango, about 20km from Rundu's town centre, this is a tranquil and good-value riverside retreat where relaxation is a by-product of the owners' laid-back approach. The entire property blends naturally into the surrounding riverine forest, while the rooms are beautifully laid out, with personal touches; there's a great camp-site, although it's sometimes overrun by safari trucks. The lodge represents incredibly good value with no surcharge for singles and a justifiably famous buffet dinner for N$260 at night.

The lodge's owners, Valerie and Weynand Peyper, are active in promoting responsible travel and work closely with the local community. They also have many other ongoing projects, including supporting orphans in the area. Guests can visit local villages (N$50 for a village walk).

Sarasungu River Lodge   LODGE $

(☎ 066-255161; camping N$170, r from N$996; ❄🛜🍽) Sarasunga River Lodge is situated in a secluded riverine clearing 4km from the town centre. It has attractive thatched chalets that surround a landscaped pool, and a decent-sized grassed camping area with basic amenities and beautiful sunsets. There is also a bar-restaurant on-site. The river excursions don't always happen and they aim more for the local conference market than tourists, but it's still a good place.

Tambuti Lodge   LODGE $

(☎ 066-255711; www.tambuti.com.na; N$100, s/d incl breakfast N$700/900; 🛜🍽) An old place that has been around for a while, Tambuti leaks faded grandeur from its stone walls and flagstone floors. Less than a kilometre from town, it feels like a forgotten resort, which gives it an allure all of its own. Rooms are large, and come with a big free-standing bathtub, mosquito nets and small verandas. The lodge also arranges boat trips on the Okavango River.

Hakusembe Lodge   LODGE $$

(☎ 061-427200, 066-257010; www.gondwana-collection.com; camping N$140, chalets per per-

Rundu

son with half board from N$1450; ❄🍽) Now part of the well-regarded Gondwana Collection chain, this secluded hideaway sits amid lush riverside gardens, and comprises luxury chalets (one of which is floating) decked out in safari prints, wood floors and locally crafted furniture. Activities centre on the river and include birdwatching, croc-spotting and rather lovely sundowner cruises. It's located 17km down the Nkurenkuru Rd, then 2km north to the riverbank.

Taranga Safari Lodge   LODGE $$

(☎ 066-257010; www.taranganamibia.com; off B10; camping N$250, chalet N$1400-1750; ❄🛜🍽) With just six tented chalets (two deluxe, four luxury), Taranga is a relatively new and intimate addition to the Kavango accommodation scene. Most rooms have free-standing bathtubs, four-poster beds, wooden floors and plenty of space. It's around 35km west of Runu, past Kapako and just off the B10 on the riverbank.

🛍 Shopping

Covered Market   MARKET

Take a stroll around this large market, which is one of Namibia's most sophisticated informal sales outlets. From July to

September, don't miss the fresh papayas sold straight from the trees.

Ncumcara Community Forestry Craft Centre
ARTS & CRAFTS

(B8; ☺ Mon-Sat, after church Sun) Very reasonably priced woodcarvings from a sustainable source are on offer at Ncumcara Community Forestry Craft Centre, a neighbourhood craft shop. The carvings are high quality with proceeds going back to the local community. It's 35km south of Rundu; if the shop is unattended, just wait for someone to show up and open the gate.

❶ Getting There & Away

BUS
Several weekly **Intercape Mainliner** (p375) buses make the seven-hour trip between Windhoek and Rundu (fares from N$780). Book your tickets in advance online, as this service continues on to Victoria Falls and fills up quickly.

Combis connect Windhoek and Rundu with fairly regular frequency, and a ride shouldn't cost more than N$600. From Rundu, routes fan out to various towns and cities in the north, with fares costing less than N$60 a ride. Both buses and combis depart and drop off at the Engen petrol station.

CAR & MOTORCYCLE
Drivers will need to be patient on the road (B8) to Rundu from Grootfontein. It's in good condition but passes by many schools where the speed limit drops suddenly – fertile ground for speed cameras.

Khaudum National Park

Exploring the largely undeveloped 3840 sq km **Khaudum National Park** (adult/child/vehicle N$80/free/10; ☺ sunrise-sunset) is an intense wilderness challenge. Meandering sand tracks lure you through pristine bush and across *omiramba* (fossil river valleys), which run parallel to the east–west-oriented Kalahari dunes. As there is virtually no signage, and navigation is largely based on GPS coordinates and topographic maps, visitors are few, which is precisely why Khaudum is worth exploring – Khaudum is home to one of Namibia's most important populations of lions and African wild dogs, although both can be difficult to see.

In addition to African wild dogs and lions, the park protects large populations of elephants, zebras, giraffes, wildebeest, kudus, oryxes and tsessebes, and there's a good chance you'll be able to spot large herds of roan antelope here. If you're an avid birder, Khaudum supports 320 different species,

---

KHAUDUM NATIONAL PARK AT A GLANCE

Why Go?
One of Southern Africa's most underrated experiences; lions and African wild dogs; wild country that sees few visitors.

Gateway Towns
Rundu and Tsumkwe

When to Go
Wildlife viewing is best from June to October, when herds congregate around the waterholes and along the *omiramba*. November to April is the richest time to visit for birdwatchers, though you will have to be prepared for a difficult slog through muddy tracks.

Budget Safaris
Given the need for a high-clearance 4WD and total self-sufficiency when it comes to food and equipment, budget travel is near impossible here. Getting a group of other travellers together could help bring costs down.

Practicalities
Take a satellite phone with you. The park authorities usually require a minimum of two vehicles for exploring the park. Pick up the *Kavango-Zambezi National Parks* map, which is available at some lodges or online via www.thinkafricadesign.com. There's little detail but the GPS coordinates for the major track intersections could save your life. The nearest fuel is at Rundu, Divundu and (sometimes) Tsumkwe.

including summer migratory birds such as storks, crakes, bitterns, orioles, eagles and falcons.

🛌 Sleeping

Namibia Wildlife Resorts (NWR) used to administer two official campsites in the park – one in the north, the other in the south – but after one too many episodes of elephants gone wild, it decided to close up shop. You can still camp here but the two sites have been neglected for a long time – if you are planning to stay at either one, keep your expectations low.

Khaudum Camp   CAMPGROUND
(GPS: S 18°30.234', E 20°45.180') FREE Khaudum Camp is somewhat akin to the Kalahari in miniature, but this is true wilderness camping – shade can be meagre and facilities are non-existent. The sunsets here are the stuff of legend.

Sikereti Camp   CAMPGROUND
(GPS: S 19°06.267', E 20°42.300') FREE 'Cigarette' camp, in the south of the park, inhabits a shady grove of terminalia trees, though full appreciation of this place requires sensitivity to its subtle charms, namely isolation and silence. This is true wilderness camping with no facilities whatsoever.

❶ Getting There & Away

From the north, take the sandy track from Katere on the B8 (signposted 'Khaudum'), 120km east of Rundu. After 45km you'll reach the Cwibadom Omuramba, where you should turn east into the park.

From the south, you can reach Sikereti Camp via Tsumkwe. From Tsumkwe, it's 20km to Groote Döbe and another 15km from there to the Dorslandboom turning. It's then 25km north to Sikereti Camp.

The Caprivi Strip

Namibia's spindly northeastern appendage, the Caprivi Strip (now officially known as Namibia's Zambezi region, although the name is taking time to catch on...) is typified by expanses of mopane and terminalia broadleaf forest, and punctuated by *shonas* or fossilised parallel dunes that are the remnants of a drier climate. For most travellers, the Caprivi serves as the easiest access route connecting the main body of Namibia with Victoria Falls and Botswana's Chobe National Park.

THE FIGHT FOR CAPRIVI

The Caprivi has only recently found its way to peace. On 2 August 1999, rebels – mainly members of Namibia's Lozi minority letd by Mishake Muyongo, a former vice president of Swapo and a long-time proponent of Caprivian independence – attempted to seize Katima Mulilo. However, the poorly trained perpetrators failed to capture any of their intended targets, and after only a few hours, they were summarily put down by the Namibian Defence Force (NDF).

Later that year, Nujoma committed troops from the NDF to support the Angolan government in its civil war against Unita rebels – an act that triggered years of strife for the inhabitants of the Caprivi Strip, where fighting and lawlessness spilled over the border. When a family of French tourists was robbed and murdered while driving between Kongola and Divundu, the issue exploded in the international press, causing tourist numbers to plummet. Continuing reports of fighting, attacks on civilians and land-mine detonations caused a huge exodus of people from the region, and kept tourists firmly away until the cessation of the conflict in 2002.

But Caprivi is also one of Southern Africa's wildlife destinations to watch. After decades of poaching, the region's wildlife is returning and visitors with time and patience can get off the beaten path here, exploring such emerging wildlife gems as Nkasa Rupara and Bwabwata National Parks.

Bwabwata National Park
🎵 066
Only recently recognised as a national park, Bwabwata (per person per day N$10, per vehicle N$10; ☺ sunrise-sunset) was established to rehabilitate local wildlife populations. Prior to the 2002 Angolan ceasefire, this area saw almost no visitors, and wildlife populations had been virtually wiped out by rampant poaching instigated by ongoing conflict. But the guns have been silent now for well over a decade and the wildlife is making a slow but spectacular comeback. If you come here expecting Etosha, you'll be disappointed. But you might very well see lions, elephants, African wild

Bwabwata NP (Western Section)

dogs, perhaps even sable antelope and some fabulous birdlife – and you might just have them all to yourself.

Sights

Mahango Game Reserve
WILDLIFE RESERVE
(Map p96; per person/vehicle N$40/10; ☺sunrise-sunset) This small but diverse 25-sq-km reserve occupies a broad flood plain north of the Botswana border and west of the Okavango River. It attracts large concentrations of thirsty elephants and herd animals, particularly in the dry season. It's particularly nice to stop beside the river in the afternoon and watch the elephants swimming and drinking among hippos and crocodiles.

With a 2WD vehicle, you can either zip through on the Mahango transit route or follow the Scenic Loop Drive past Kwetche picnic site, east of the main road. With a 4WD you can also explore the 20km Circular Drive Loop, which follows the *omiramba* (fossil river valleys) and offers the best wildlife viewing.

Popa Falls
WATERFALL
(per person/vehicle N$80/10; ☺sunrise-sunset) Near Bagani, the Okavango River plunges down a broad series of cascades known

as Popa Falls. The falls are nothing to get steamed up about, especially if Victoria Falls lies in your sights. In fact, the falls are actually little more than large rapids, though periods of low water do expose a drop of 4m. Aside from the 'falls', there are good opportunities here for hiking and birdwatching. Swimming is definitely not safe as there are hungry crocs about.

Sleeping

While private concessions here handle their own bookings, the campsite at Popa Falls is run by NWR (p230) and must be prebooked through its main office in Windhoek. Also at the eastern end of the park are several accommodation options. Otherwise, there's a growing population of lodges and campsites along the east bank of the Kwando River, across the water from the Kwando Core Area.

Ngepi Camp
LODGE $
(☏066-259903; www.ngepicamp.com; camping N$140, bush or tree huts per person from N$770) One of Namibia's top backpacker lodges that appeals beyond the budget market, Ngepi makes a great base for the area. Crash for the night in a bush hut or tree hut, or pitch a tent on grass right by the river's edge and let the sounds of hippos splashing about ease you into a restful sleep; we love the outdoor bathtubs.

Laze about in lovely green, shady common areas during the day and find a chat partner at the happening bar in the evening. There's also a wide range of inexpensive excursions, including Mahango wildlife drives (N$420, three hours), canoe trips, booze cruises and *mokoro* (traditional dugout canoe) trips in the Okavango Panhandle. Or try a local village walk. The camp is 4km off the main road, though the sandy access can prove difficult without a high-clearance vehicle. Phone the lodge if you need a lift from Divundu.

Mavunje Campsite
CAMPGROUND $
(☏081 461 9608; mashiriversafaris.com/campsites.html; camping N$185, tented camp per person N$400) Excellent campsites just across the Kwando River from the Kwando Core Area of Bwabwata National Park. Sites have private shower and toilet, there's a kitchen and covered dining area, and elephants are known to wander through camp. There are also some simple safari-style tents on the site.

Mukolo Campsite CAMPGROUND $
(☑ 081 124 7542, 081 124 0403; mukolocamp@
mtcmobile.com.na; camping N$150; ☒) This
simple campsite overlooks a channel of the
Kwando River and is an excellent base for
excursions in the area; fishing trips can be
arranged here. Three of the sites sit right
on the water, and all have electricity and an
ablutions block with flush toilets and hot
water. The turn-off to the campsite is 8.6km
south of Kongola along the C49, from where
it's 1.3km to camp.

There are also plans for self-catering
cabins.

Nunda River Lodge LODGE $
(☑ 066-259093; www.nundaonline.com; camping/
safari tents per person N$150/780, chalets N$875)
This very welcoming lodge has an appealing aesthetic comprising stone buildings
with thatched roofs and wooden decks on
the river's edge. It's really well set up, with
relaxing common areas overlooking the
water where you can catch the breeze. The
campsites are excellent, with sites 6 and 7
the best; all have power, braai (barbecue)
plates and bins.

Safari tents are also on the riverbank,
with a small table and chair on the deck
out the front to enjoy the water views. Chalets are set up in a similar way to the safari
tents but are roomier and have bigger bathrooms – but if it's the views you're after, go
for a safari tent. Rates are often reduced if
they're not busy.

★ **Nambwa**
Tented Lodge LODGE, CAMPGROUND $$$
(www.africanmonarchlodges.com/nambwa-
luxury-tented-lodge; camping N$195, s/d Jul-Oct
N$6415/9930, Apr-Jun & Nov N$5045/7790, Dec-
Mar N$3195/6390; ☏) Nambwa, 14km south
of Kongola, is one of the very few places in
the park itself, and it combines an excellent
campsite with a luxury lodge, replete with
elevated walkways, stunning interiors (tree
trunks and antique chandeliers anyone?)
and glorious views out over the flood plains.
Some of Bwabwata's best wildlife areas are
close by, and the lodge overlooks a waterhole
that's especially popular with animals late in
the dry season.

Elephants are perhaps the most frequent
visitors. To reach the lodge, follow the 4WD
track south along the western bank of the
Kwando River. Transfers can be arranged
from Kongola and elsewhere.

Namashashe Lodge LODGE $$$
(Map p80; ☑ 061-427200; http://www.gondwa-
na-collection.com/the-zambezi-experience/ac-
commodation/namushasha-river-lodge/; s/d incl
breakfast N$1710/2748; ☒) Part of the upmarket
Gondwana Collection chain, Namashashe sits

BWABWATA NATIONAL PARK AT A GLANCE

Why Go?
Growing wildlife populations, still very small visitor numbers and the chance to see one
of Southern Africa's emerging wildlife destinations before the word really gets out.

Gateway Towns
Divundu, Kongola, Katima Mulilo

When to Go
Our favourite time to visit is from May to August – September and October are also good,
although the build up to the rains brings oppressive heat. The rains usually fall from November to March – getting around can be difficult, but this is also the best time for birdwatching.

Budget Safaris
Budget travel is not really possible here, but if you've already rented a vehicle, you could
well camp outside the park and make day-trip forays inside.

Practicalities
The nearest airport is at Katima Mulilo, while access to the park by road is via Divundu,
Kongola and Katima Mulilo. The park's distinct areas, with the best wildlife at the far
eastern and western extremities of the park, mean that it's necessary to plan ahead. The
Mahango Game Reserve and Kwando Core Area are, for the moment at least, the most
rewarding choices.

ZONES OF BWABWATA

Bwabwata includes a number of zones: the Divundu area, the West Caprivi Triangle, the Mahango Game Reserve, Popa Falls, former West Caprivi Game Reserve and the Kwando Core Area. The Mahango Game Reserve (p262) presently has the largest concentrations of wildlife, while the Kwando Core Area is where the repopulation of carnivores is really taking off.

Divundu, with two (nominally) 24-hour petrol stations and a relatively well-stocked supermarket, is merely a product of the road junction. The real population centres are the neighbouring villages of Mukwe, Andara and Bagani. Divundu is marked as Bagani on some maps and road signs, though technically they're separate places about 2km apart.

The West Caprivi Triangle, the wedge bounded by Angola to the north, Botswana to the south and the Kwando River to the east, was formerly the richest wildlife area in the Caprivi. Poaching, bush clearing, burning and human settlement have greatly reduced wildlife, though you can still access the area via the road along the western bank of the Kwando River near Kongola.

Finally, the Golden Hwy between Rundu and Katima Mulilo traverses the former West Caprivi Game Reserve. Although this was once a haven for large herds of elephants, it served as a pantry for local hunters and poachers for decades, and was for too long largely devoid of wildlife. But this zone is becoming an important corridor for wildlife from northern Botswana and the Caprivi Strip and the hitherto-threatened wildlife of southeastern Angola.

just across the river from Bwabwata National Park with all the wildlife possibilities that brings. It's also particularly good for birdlife and hippos, and the whole property takes full advantage of the Kwando River frontage. The large and lovely rooms have slate-tiled floors, which cool things down nicely when the weather starts to become uncomfortably hot.

Camp Kwando   LODGE $$$
(Map p80; ☏ 081 206 1514; www.camp kwando.cc.na; camping N$150, s with half board N$1130-1840, d half-board N$2020-2520; ▣) This gorgeous property has luxury thatch-and-canvas chalets that each overlook the Kwando River in all its glory. Elephants and abundant birdlife are frequent visitors, while soaring ceilings, prolific use of wood and four-poster beds are all stunningly put together. There's also a grassy and shady campsite.

ⓘ Getting There & Away

The paved Trans-Caprivi Highway between Rundu and Katima Mulilo is perfectly suited to 2WD vehicles, as is the gravel road between Divundu and Mohembo (on the Botswana border). Drivers may transit the park without charge, but be aware that you will incur national park entry fees if you use the loop drive through the park.

Katima Mulilo

POP 28,360 / ☏ 066
Out on a limb at the eastern end of the Caprivi Strip, remote Katima Mulilo is as far from Windhoek (1200km) as you can get and still be in Namibia. Once known for the elephants that marched through the village streets, Katima is a sprawling town these days, one that thrives as a border town – Zambia's border is just 4km away, while Botswana is less than 100km away to the southeast – and minor commercial centre.

🛏 Sleeping

Mukusi Cabins   CABIN $
(☏ 066-253255; www.mukusi.com; Engen petrol station, off B8; campsites N$120, s incl breakfast N$28-460, d incl breakfast N$400-640; ▣) Although Mukusi Cabins lacks the riverside location of other properties in the area, this oasis behind the Engen petrol station has a good selection of accommodation, from simple rooms with fans to small but comfortable air-con cabins. The lovely bar-restaurant dishes up a range of unexpected options – including calamari, snails and kingklip – as well as steak and chicken standbys.

Caprivi Houseboat
Safari Lodge   HOUSEBOAT, LODGE **$$**
([☎]066-252287; www.zambezisafaris.com; off Ngoma Rd; s/d from N$750/1100) Rustic en-suite chalet accommodation with mosquito nets, ceiling fans and reed provide a lovely sense of being close to nature, but it's the houseboats that are the real novelty here. These aren't luxury houseboats, but the fun value is extremely high and it's certainly a wonderful experience to spend a night actually *on* the Zambezi...As you'd expect in this part of the world, the birdwatching is a highlight.

Caprivi River Lodge   LODGE **$$**
([☎]066-252288; www.capriviriverlodge.com; Ngoma Rd; s N$480-1250, d N$780-1600; ✳✲) This diverse lodge offers options to suit travellers of all budgets, from rustic cabins with shared bathrooms to luxurious chalets facing the Zambezi River. It also offers a decent variety of activities, including boating, fishing and wildlife drives in the various Caprivi parks. The lodge is 5km from town along Ngoma Rd.

★Protea Hotel Zambezi Lodge   LODGE **$$$**
([☎]066-251500; www.marriott.com/hotels/travel/mpapr-protea-hotel-zambezi-river-lodge/; Ngoma Rd; camping N$100, r from N$1058; ✳@✲) This stunning riverside lodge is perched on the banks of the Zambezi and features a floating bar where you can watch the crocs and hippos below. The campsite is amid a flowery garden, while accommodation is in well-equipped modern rooms that open up to small verandas and ample views.

Shopping

Caprivi Arts Centre   ARTS & CRAFTS
(⊙8am-5.30pm) Run by the Caprivi Art & Cultural Association, the centre is a good place to look for local curios and crafts, including elephant and hippo woodcarvings, baskets, bowls, kitchen implements, and traditional knives and spears.

ℹ Getting There & Away

AIR
Air Namibia (www.airnamibia.com.na) has several weekly departures between Windhoek's Eros Airport and Katima's Mpacha Airport, located 18km southwest of town.

BUS & MINIBUS
Three weekly **Intercape Mainliner** (p375) buses make the 16-hour run between Windhoek and Katima Mulilo. Book your tickets (fares from

N$530) in advance online, as this service continues on to Victoria Falls and fills up quickly.

Combis connect Windhoek and Katima with fairly regular frequency, and a ride shouldn't cost more than N$280. From Katima, routes fan out to various towns and cities in the north.

CAR
The paved Golden Hwy runs between Katima Mulilo and Rundu, and is in excellent condition, accessible to all 2WD vehicles.

Mpalila Island
[☎]066

Mpalila (Impalilia) Island, a wedge driven between the Chobe and Zambezi Rivers, represents Namibia's outer limits at the 'four-corners meeting' of Zimbabwe, Botswana, Namibia and Zambia. The island itself, which is within easy reach by boat from Chobe National Park, is home to a handful of exclusive lodges catering to upmarket tourists in search of luxurious isolation.

🛏 Sleeping

Prebooking is essential for all accommodation on the island. All lodges offer a variety

---

BORDER CROSSING: MAHANGO–MOHEMBO

About 12km before the **Mahango–Mohembo** border (6am to 6pm) with Botswana is the entry point to the Mahango Game Reserve. If you're transiting to the border there is no fee payable – just fill out the register at the entrance gate, indicating that you have entered the area. At the border, formalities are straightforward – on the Namibian side, fill in a departure card and get your passport stamped at the immigration desk. On your way to the Botswana side, you need to stop at the exit gate, enter a small office and fill out the registration book (you'll need your licence and vehicle details). It's a fairly quiet border post – very few trucks pass this way – so you should be on your way in no time at all.

On the Botswana side, fill in the registration book for your vehicle, the entry card and get your passport stamped. Pay P140 (or N$190) for a road permit and insurance (payment accepted in either currency). Welcome to Botswana.

of activities for guests, including cruises on the Chobe River, guided wildlife drives, fishing expeditions, island walks and *mokoro* (dugout canoe) trips. Rates include full board and transfers.

★ **Chobe Savannah Lodge** LODGE $$$
(Map p84; ☑ in South Africa 021-4241037; www.desertdelta.co.za; Jan-Apr/Jun-Dec US$410/650; ❋ ☎) The most famous spot on the island, Chobe Savannah Lodge is one of Desert & Delta's flagship properties and is renowned for its panoramic views of the wildlife-rich Puku Flats. Each stylishly decorated room has a private veranda from where you can spot animals without ever having to change out of your pyjamas.

★ **Inchingo Chobe River Lodge** LODGE $$$
(Map p84; ☑ in South Africa 27-21-715 2412; www.zqcollection.com/ichingo-lp; two-night all-incl packages s US$559-780, d US$860-1200) Right by the water and rich in birdsong, Inchingo has an exclusive, alluring feel to it. Air-conditioned safari tents (from where you can hear the Chobe River flowing by) have wood floors, plenty of space and catch refreshing riverine breezes. Great food, stellar birdwatching and plenty of big-game wildlife nearby make for a wonderful place to spend some time; minimum two-night stay.

Kaza Safari Lodge LODGE $$$
(☑ 061-401047; s/d from US$550/740; ❋ ☎) Overlooking the impressive Mombova rapids, Kaza Safari Lodge (formerly Impalila Island Lodge) is a stylish retreat of eight luxury chalets built of wood on elevated decks at the water's edge. The centrepiece of the lodge is a pair of ancient baobab trees, which tower majestically over the grounds.

❶ Getting There & Away

Access to Mpalila Island is either by charter flight or by boat from Kasane (Botswana), though lodges will organise all transport for their booked guests.

Mudumu National Park
☑ 066

Mudumu National Park has a tragic history of environmental abuse and neglect. Although it was once one of Namibia's most stunning wildlife habitats, by the late 1980s the park had become an unofficial hunting concession gone mad. In under a decade, the wildlife was decimated by trophy hunters, which prompted the Ministry of Environment and Tourism (MET) to gazette Mudumu National Park in a last-ditch effort to rescue the area from total devastation. Of all the parks in the Caprivi region, Mudumu is the one that is taking the longest to recover, surrounded as it is by burgeoning human populations. While Mudumu's wildlife has begun to return, it will take years of wise policy making and community awareness before the area returns to its former glory.

◉ Sights

Lizauli Traditional Village VILLAGE
(Map p80; per person N$40; ⊙ 9am-5pm Mon-Sat) The culmination of a joint partnership between the owners of a one-time local lodge (Lianshulu, now closed), MET, private benefactors and the Lizauli community, the Lizauli Traditional Village was established to educate visitors about traditional Caprivian lifestyles, and to provide insight into the local diet, fishing and farming methods, village politics, music, games, traditional medicine, basketry and tool making. After the guided tour, visitors can shop for good-value local handicrafts without the sales pressure.

The aforementioned partnership has also enabled the recruitment of Mudumu game scouts from Lizauli and other villages, and was given responsibility for community conservation and antipoaching education. Most importantly, the project provides a forum in which locals can interact with tourists, and benefit both economically and culturally from the adoption of a strict policy of environmental protection.

❶ Getting There & Away

Access to the park is from the C49, between Lianshulu and Lizauli, which cuts through the eastern section of the park. Tracks within the park can become impassable after rains, thanks to the black-cotton soils close to the Kwando riverfront.

Nkasa Rupara National Park

📞 066
Watch this space – this is one of Namibia's, perhaps Southern Africa's most exciting **national parks** (per person/vehicle N$40/10). In years of good rains, this wild and seldom-visited national park (formerly called Mamili National Park) becomes Namibia's equivalent of Botswana's Okavango Delta. Forested islands fringed by

NAMIBIA THE CAPRIVI STRIP

BORDER CROSSINGS: EASTERN CAPRIVI STRIP

Zambia–Victoria Falls

The border crossing between Zambia and Namibia (7am to 6pm) can take a couple of hours if you're heading into Zambia, far less if going the other way – the Namibian side of things is generally quick and easy but Zambian formalities can take a little longer.

Visa fees into Zambia cost US$50 per person for most nationalities, and you'll also have to pay the Zambian road toll (US$48), carbon tax (ZMK150), third party vehicle insurance (ZMK487, valid for one month and payable even if you already have insurance). There is a bank next to the border post. Changing money at the bank is preferable to the young men who will approach your vehicle with wads of kwacha. If you arrive outside banking hours and are left with no choice, make sure you know the current exchange rates, count your money carefully and don't let them hurry you into a quick exchange that will rarely be to your benefit.

If you're heading to Liuwa National Park and other places in Zambia's far west, an excellent paved road runs from the border all the way to Mongu and Kalabo, at the entrance to Liuwa National Park.

If you're on your way to Livingstone, the road is paved but not in great condition. It is, however, accessible in a 2WD and provides access to Livingstone and other destinations in Zambia.

Botswana–Kasane & Chobe

With a private vehicle, the **Ngoma Bridge** (8am to 6pm) border crossing enables you to access Chobe National Park (Botswana) and Kasane (Botswana) in just a couple of hours. Border crossings are straightforward on both sides – assuming that all of your paperwork is in order. Unless you get stuck behind a tour bus, you should be through both sides in well under an hour.

Once in Botswana, if you stick to the Chobe National Park Transit Route, you're excused from paying Botswana park fees, but that would only be worth it if you're in a hurry to get elsewhere.

reed and papyrus marshes foster some of the country's richest birdwatching, with more than 430 recorded species to count. Poaching has taken a toll on Nkasa Rupara's wildlife, though – as recently as 2013, the park's largest lion pride was wiped out in retaliation for livestock lost to predators. Since then, things are on the up, thanks to human-wildlife conflict mitigation programs by Panthera (www.panthera.org), and lions are returning to the area; sightings of wild dogs across the water on the Botswana side are also possible while semi-iaquatic species such as hippos, crocodiles, pukus, red lechwes, sitatungas and otters, will impress.

🛏 Sleeping

There are two officially designated camping areas in the park: Liadura, beside the Kwando River, and Mparamura. They're often deserted and facilities are extremely basic.

★ **Livingstone's Camp** CAMPGROUND $
(Map p80; ☑ 081 033 2853, 066-686208; www.livingstonescamp.com; camping Nov-Mar/Apr-Oct N$200/250) Overlooking the wetlands and marketing itself as an exclusive campsite, Livingstone's has just five sites, each with their own shower and toilets and all with front-row seats to the water. It can also or-

ganise wildlife drives into Nkasa Rupara National Park and *mokoro* (dug out canoe) trips on the Kwando river network.

Jackalberry Tented Camp TENTED CAMP $$$
(Map p80; ☑ 081 147 7798; www.jbcamp.com; r N$8600) Run by the same people who brought you Nkasa Lupala Lodge, Jackalberry has just four luxury tents close to the water's edge near the entrance for Nkasa Rupara National Park. With such a small number of tents, the feel is much more intimate and exclusive than most in the area.

★ **Nkasa Lupala Lodge** TENTED CAMP, LODGE $$
(Map p80; ☑ 081 147 7798; www.nkasalupala lodge.com; r per person N$1930) Located 30km from Mudumu, and just outside the entrance to Nkasa Rupara National Park, this remote luxury, Italian-run lodge sits on the banks of the Kwando–Linyanti River system. The lodge gets rave reviews from travellers and offers activities such as game drives in both national parks, including night drives. Accommodation is in tents on stilts, from where you may just spot elephants trooping past your deck.

The lodge is around 12km beyond Sangwali village, with plenty of signposts along the way.

NKASA RUPARA NATIONAL PARK AT A GLANCE

Why Go?
A wildlife area on the upswing, with wildlife similar to Botswana's Okavango Delta and Linyanti regions just across the border, but without the crowds.

Gateway Towns
Katima Mulilo, Kongola and Sangwali

When to Go
Birding is best from December to March, though the vast majority of the park is inaccessible during this time. Wildlife viewing is best from June to August, and is especially good on Nkasa and Lupala islands. It can be oppressively hot from October through to March or April.

Budget Safaris
Safaris don't come cheap out in this corner of Namibia. Get a group together to keep down the per-person costs of visiting.

Practicalities
You must bring everything with you, including your own water, and be prepared for extremely rough road conditions. Although there is generally a ranger to collect park fees at the entrance gate, you're all alone once inside. The simple but handy *Kavango-Zambezi National Parks* map includes a high-level overview of Nkasa Rupara National Park. It's available at Nkasa Lupala Lodge or online via www.thinkafricadesign.com.

Nkasa Rupara National Park

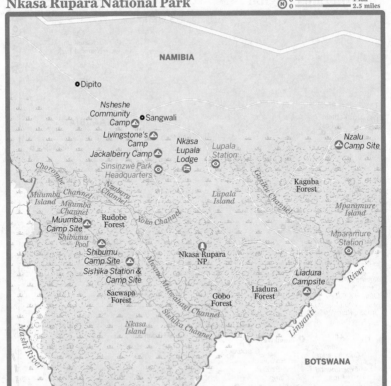

ⓘ Getting There & Away

Nkasa Lupala Lodge is approximately 75km from Kongola and 130km from Katima Mulilo. Take the C49 (a maintained gravel road from Kongola and tarred from Katima Mulilo) to Sangwali. From Sangwali, head to the Nkasa Rupara National Park – you'll need a high-clearance 4WD.

Otjozondjupa

Out in Namibia's northeast, where the horizon shimmers in the heat haze of the Kalahari, is the land of the Ju/'Hoansi–San. The Nyae Nyae Conservancy (☏061-244011; ◷8am-5pm Mon-Fri) stands at the heart of this remote land where San villages offer a fraught, if fascinating insight into the lives of Southern Africa's longest-standing inhabitants.

With interest in Kalahari cultures growing around the world, tourist traffic has increased throughout the region, though any expectations you might have of witnessing an entirely self-sufficient hunter-gatherer society will, sadly, not be met here. Hunting is forbidden, and most communities have abandoned foraging in favour of cheap, high-calorie foods such as pap (corn meal) and rice, which are purchased in bulk from shops. Try instead to look beyond the dire realities of the San's economic situation, and attempt to use the experience as a rare opportunity to the modern-day descendants of perhaps all of our ancestors.

Tsumkwe
☏067

Tsumkwe is the only real permanent settlement in the whole of Otjozondjupa, though it's merely a wide spot in the sand that consists of a few rust-covered buildings. Originally constructed as the regional

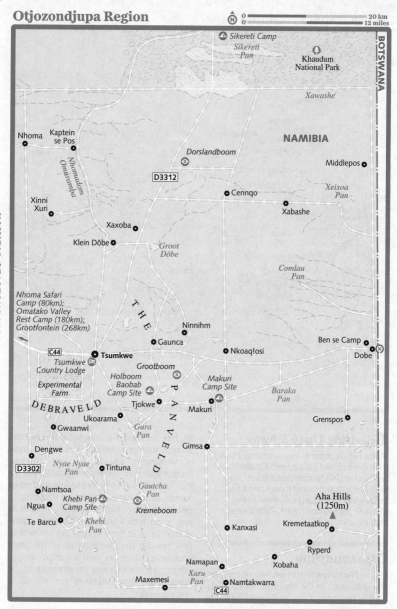

BOTSWANA

0 20 km
0 12 miles

NAMIBIA

Sikereti Camp
Sikereti Pan
Khaudum National Park

Xawashe

Nhoma   Kaptein se Pos
Nhomadom Omuramba
Dorslandboom
D3312
Middlepos
Xeixoa Pan

Xinni Xuri
Cennqo
Xabashe

Xaxoba
Klein Döbe
Groot Döbe
Comlau Pan

Nhoma Safari Camp (80km); Omatako Valley Rest Camp (180km); Grootfontein (268km);

THE

Ninnihm
Gaunca
Nkoaq!osi
Ben se Camp
Dobe

C44
Tsumkwe
Tsumkwe Country Lodge
Grootboom
Makuri Camp Site
Baraka Pan

Experimental Farm
Holboom Baobab Camp Site
Tjokwe
Makuri

DEBRAVELD
Ukoarama
Gura Pan
P
Gwaanwi
A
Grenspos

Dengwe
N
Gimsa
D3302
Nyae Nyae Pan
Tintuna
V
E
Namtsoa
Gautcha Pan
L
Aha Hills (1250m)
Khebi Pan Camp Site
D
Ngua
Te Barcu
Khebi Pan
Kremeboom
Kanxasi
Kremetaatkop

Ryperd
Namapan
Xobaha
Maxemesi
Xaru Pan
Namtakwarra
C44

headquarters of the South African Defence Force (SADF), Tsumkwe was then given a mandate as the administrative centre of the Ju/'Hoansi–San community, and is home to the Nyae Nyae Conservancy office. While organised tourism in the region is still something of a work in progress, Tsumkwe is where you can arrange everything from bush walks to hunting safaris, and inject some much-needed cash into the local community.

⊙ Sights

Foraging and recreated hunting trips are the highlight of any visit to Otjozondjupa. Traditional gear, namely a bow with poisoned arrows for men, and a digging stick and sling for women, is used. In the past, men would be gone for several days at a time in pursuit of herds, so you shouldn't expect to see any big game on an afternoon excursion. But it's fascinating to see trackers in pursuit of their quarry, and you're likely to come across spoor and maybe even an antelope or two.

Foraging is very likely to turn up edible roots and tubers, wild fruits and nuts, and even medicinal plants. At the end of your excursion, the women will be more than happy to slice up a bush potato for you, which tastes particularly wonderful when roasted over a bed of hot coals. Baobab fruit is also surprisingly sweet and tangy, while protein-rich nuts are an exotic yet nutritious desert treat.

While stereotypes of the San abound from misleading Hollywood cinematic representations to misconstrued notions of a primitive people living in the bush, San society is extremely complex. Before visiting a San village, take some time to read up on their wonderfully rich cultural heritage – doing so will not only provide some context to your visit but also help you better engage your hosts.

Living Hunter's Museum of the *Ju*/Hoansi   MUSEUM
(D3315; ☉ sunrise-sunset) About 25km out of Tsumkwe, heading towards Khaudum National Park, is the Living Hunter's Museum of the *Ju*/'Hoansi, which is run and managed independently by the San. A lot of effort has gone into representing the old San hunter-gather culture as authentically as possible. Cultural interactions on offer include hunting trips (N$250 per person) with San hunters using traditional methods and equipment. There are also bush walks (N$150) and singing/dancing shows.

Aha Hills   HILLS
Up against the Botswana border, the flat landscape is broken only by the arid Aha

NAMIBIA OTJOZONDJUPA

THE SHAPE OF THINGS PAST

The Caprivi Strip's notably odd shape is a story in itself. When Germany laid claim to British-administered Zanzibar in 1890, Britain naturally objected, and soon after the Berlin Conference was called to settle the dispute. In the end, Britain kept Zanzibar, but Germany was offered a vast strip of land from the British-administered Bechuanaland protectorate (now Botswana). Named the Caprivi Strip after German chancellor General Count Georg Leo von Caprivi di Caprara di Montecuccoli, this vital tract of land provided Germany with access to the Zambezi River.

For the Germans, the motivation for this swap was to ultimately create a colonial empire that spanned from the south Atlantic Coast to Tanganyika (now Tanzania) and the Indian Ocean. Unfortunately for them, the British colonisation of Rhodesia (now Zimbabwe) stopped the Germans well upstream of Victoria Falls, which proved a considerable barrier to navigation on the Zambezi.

Interestingly enough, the absorption of the Caprivi Strip into German South West Africa didn't make world news, and it was nearly 20 years before some of its population discovered that they were under German control. In 1908 the German government finally dispatched one Hauptmann Streitwolf to oversee local administration, a move that prompted the Lozi tribe to round up all the cattle – including those belonging to rival tribes – and drive them out of the area. The cattle were eventually returned to their rightful owners, but most of the Lozi people chose to remain in Zambia and Angola rather than submit to German rule.

On 4 August 1914 Britain declared war on Germany and, just over a month later, the German administrative seat at Schuckmannsburg was attacked by the British from their base at Sesheke and then seized by the police. An apocryphal tale recounts that German governor Von Frankenberg was entertaining the English resident administrator of Northern Rhodesia (now Zambia) when a servant presented a message from British authorities in Livingstone. After reading it, the British official declared his host a prisoner of war, and thus, Schuckmannsburg fell into British hands. Whether the story is true or not, the seizure of Schuckmannsburg was the first Allied occupation of enemy territory in WWI.

Hills. The region is pockmarked with unexplored caves and sinkholes, but don't attempt to enter them unless you have extensive caving experience. The hills are also accessible from the Botswana side. A border crossing is open between Tsumkwe (though this is 30km to the west of the border) and Dobe.

Given the nearly featureless landscape that surrounds them, you may imagine that these low limestone outcrops were named when the first traveller uttered, 'Aha, some hills.' In fact, it's a rendition of the sound made by the endemic barking gecko.

Baobabs NATURAL FEATURE

The dry, crusty landscape around Tsumkwe supports several large baobab trees, some of which have grown quite huge. The imaginatively named **Grootboom** (Big Tree) is one of the largest, with a circumference of over 30m. One tree with historical significance is the **Dorslandboom**, which was visited by the Dorsland (Thirst Land) trekkers who camped here on their trek to Angola in 1891 and carved their names into the tree. Another notable tree, the immense **Holboom** (Hollow Tree), dominates the bush near the village of Tjokwe.

Panveld NATURAL SITE

Forming an arc east of Tsumkwe is a remote landscape of phosphate-rich pans. After the rains, the largest of these, Nyae Nyae, Khebi and Gautcha (all at the southern end of the arc), are transformed into superb wetlands. These ephemeral water sources attract itinerant water birds – including throngs of flamingos – but they are also breeding sites for waterfowl: ducks, spurwing geese, cranes, crakes, egrets and herons. Other commonly observed birds include teals, sandpipers and reeves, as well as the rare black-tailed godwit and the great snipe.

🛏 Sleeping

A luxury lodge, a safari camp and several campsites are the main sleeping options around Tsumkwe. Ask at the Nyae Nyae Conservancy office (p269) for information on sleeping in a San village.

The Nyae Nyae Conservancy has several campsites, the most popular being the Holboom Baobab at Tjokwe, southeast of Tsumkwe; Makuri, a few kilometres east of that; and Khebi Pan, well out in the bush south of Tsumkwe. Water is sometimes available in adjacent villages, but generally it's best to carry in all of your supplies and be entirely self-sufficient. Avoid building fires near the baobabs – it damages the trees' roots.

Omatako Valley Rest Camp CAMPGROUND $

(☑ 067-255977; www.omatakovalley.com; camping N$90) Outside the conservancy at the junction of the C44 and D3306, this community-run camp has solar power, a water pump, hot showers and a staff of local San. It offers both hunting and gathering trips as well as traditional music presentations.

Tsumkwe Country Lodge LODGE $

(☑ 061-374750; camping N$120, s/d from N$680/1000; ❄ @ ☀) The only tourist lodge in Tsumkwe proper is an upmarket affair with a bar, restaurant, small shop and pool. Guests can base themselves here and visit surrounding villages as part of an organised tour.

Nhoma Safari Camp TENTED CAMP $$$

(☑ 081 273 4606; www.tsumkwel.iway.na; camping per adult/child N$200/100, s/d luxury tents with full board from N$3625/6000; ☀) The former owners of the Tsumkwe Country Lodge, Arno and Estelle, have lived in the area for much of their lives and are well respected by the local San communities. Their luxury tented camp is perched between a fossilised river valley and a verdant teak grove, though the main attraction continues to be their wonderful excursions into local San villages.

The camp is 280km east of Grootfontein and 80km west of Tsumkwe along the C44. You must book in advance to stay here – as mobile phone reception at the camp is unreliable (there's no landline), it's best to email them.

🛈 Getting There & Away

Note that you will need your own transport; a 4WD with good clearance is recommended. There are no sealed roads in the region, and only the C44 is passable to 2WD vehicles. Petrol is sometimes available at the Tsumkwe Country Lodge, though it's best to carry a few jerry cans with you. If you're planning to explore the bush around Tsumkwe, it is recommended that you hire a local guide and travel as part of a convoy.

The Dobe border crossing to Botswana requires a 4WD and extra fuel to reach the petrol stations at Maun or Etsha 6, which are accessed by a difficult sand track through northwestern Botswana.

NORTHWESTERN NAMIBIA

For those who like to take a walk (or even a drive) on the wild side, northwestern Namibia is a stark, desolate environment where some of the most incredible landscapes imaginable lie astride 4WD tracks. Along the Skeleton Coast, seemingly endless expanses of foggy beach are punctuated by rusting shipwrecks and flanked by wandering dunes. Here, travellers are left entirely alone to bask in this riveting isolation, bothered only by the concern of whether their vehicles can survive the journey unscathed.

Not to be outdone by the barren coastline, the Kaokoveld is a photographer's dreamscape of wide-open vistas, lonely desert roads and hardly another person around to ruin your shot. A vast repository of desert mountains, this is one of the least developed regions of the country, and arguably Namibia at its most primeval. The Kaokoveld is also the ancestral home of the Himba people, a culturally rich tribal group that has retained its striking appearance and dress. And then there's Damaraland, home to the Brandberg Massif, Namibia's highest peak, and Twyfelfontein, which together contain some of Southern Africa's finest prehistoric rock art and engravings. A veritable window into the past, these two sites help to illuminate the hidden inner workings of our collective forebears, who roamed the African savannah so many eons ago.

Damaraland

From the glorious rock formations of Spitzkoppe, Erongo and the Brandberg in the south to the equally glorious red-rock, wild-desert mountains around Palmwag in the north, Damaraland is one of Namibia's most dramatic collections of landscapes. Hidden in the rocky clefts is Twyfelfontein, which along with Brandberg contains some of Southern Africa's finest prehistoric rock art and engravings, and there's even a petrified forest nearby, as well as palm-fringed, oasis-like valleys. Damaraland is also one of Southern Africa's most underrated wildlife-watching areas, one of Namibia's last 'unofficial' wildlife regions with critically endangered black rhinos, desert adapted lions and elephants, as well as the full range of Namibia specialties such as gemsbok, zebra, giraffe and spotted hyena.

This combination of wild landscapes and wild creatures is Damaraland at its best. Plan to stay here as long as you can.

The Spitzkoppe

✓ 064

One of Namibia's most recognisable landmarks, the 1728m-high **Spitzkoppe** (Groot Spitzkoppe village; per person/car N$50/20; ☉ sunrise-sunset) rises mirage-like above the dusty pro-Namib plains of southern Damaraland. Its dramatic shape has inspired its nickname, the Matterhorn of Africa, but similarities between this ancient volcanic remnant and the glaciated Swiss alp begin and end with its sharp peak. First summited in 1946, the Spitzkoppe continues to attract hard-core rock climbers bent on tackling Namibia's most challenging peak.

🏃 Activities

Beside the Spitzkoppe rise the equally impressive Pondoks, which are composed of enormous granite domes. At the eastern end of this rocky jumble, a wire cable climbs the granite slopes to a vegetated hollow known as Bushman's Paradise, where an overhang shelters a vandalised panel of ancient rhino paintings.

🛏 Sleeping

Sptitzkoppe Campsites CAMPGROUND $
(✓ 064-464144; www.spitzkoppe.com; camping N$135) These wonderful campsites in the nooks and crannies that surround the Spitzkoppe massif perfectly capture the area's otherworldly landscapes. Run by the same people as those at Spitzkoppen Lodge, this is a professionally run place with carefully chosen sites and good facilities.

Spitzkoppe Rest Camp CAMPGROUND $
(✓ 064-530879; Groot Spitzkoppe village; camping N$110) The sites at this camp are dotted around the base of the Spitzkoppe and surrounding outcrops. Most are set in magical rock hollows and provide a sense of real isolation and oneness with the bouldered surrounds. Facilities at the entrance include a reception office, ecofriendly ablutions blocks and braai (barbecue) stands, plus a bar and restaurant.

Spitzkoppe Mountain Tented Camp TENTED CAMP $$
(✓ 081 805 3178; www.spitzkoppemountain-camp.com; off D3716; r N$1220) These simple

NAMIBIA DAMARALAND

Meru-style en-suite canvas tents on stilts have fine views of the Spitzkoppe and an attractive location close to a dry riverbed. It offers Spitzkoppe excursions, Bushmen walks and other activities in the area.

★ **Spitzkoppen Lodge**   LODGE $$$
(www.spitzkoppenlodge.com; s/d N$2900/5000; 🛜 🏊) Due to open not long after our visit, this place promises to be the pick of the Spitzkoppe choices. Run by the same people that brought you Kalahari Bush Breaks (p233), the lodge consists of 15 wonderfully secluded chalets with gorgeous views all connected by an elevated walkway. The design in places evokes the Spitzkoppe mountain and there is an enduring sense of isolation and luxury.

ⓘ Getting There & Away

Under normal dry conditions, a 2WD is sufficient to reach the mountain. Turn northwest off the B2 onto the D1918 towards Henties Bay. After 18km, turn north onto the D3716.

The Brandberg

♫ 064

Driving around this massive pink granite bulge and marvelling at the ethereal light during sunset, is a highlight of the region. But inside lies the real treasure – one of the finest remnants of prehistoric art on the African continent.

The Brandberg (Fire Mountain) is named for the effect created by the setting sun on its western face, which causes this granite massif to resemble a burning slag heap. Its summit, Königstein, is Namibia's highest peak at 2573m.

The Brandberg is a conservancy and the entry fee for admission is N$50 per person and N$20 per car. Note that this includes being allocated a compulsory guide – you cannot just walk around these fragile treasures by yourself. It's good to tip the guide afterwards if you're happy with their service.

⦿ Sights

Numas Ravine   ROCK ART
Numas Ravine, slicing through the western face of the Brandberg, is a little-known treasure house of ancient paintings. Most people ask their guide to take them to the rock facing the southern bank of the riverbed, which bears paintings of a snake, a giraffe and an antelope. It lies about 30 minutes' walk up the ravine. After another half-hour you'll reach an oasis-like freshwater spring and several more paintings in the immediate surroundings.

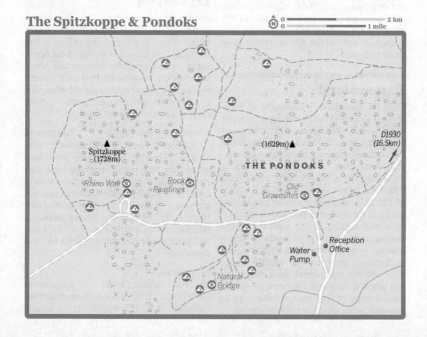

The Spitzkoppe & Pondoks

0 ——— 2 km
0 ——— 1 mile

Spitzkoppe (1728m)

(1629m)▲

D1930 (16.5km)

THE PONDOKS

Rhino Wall

Rock Paintings

Old Gravesites

Reception Office

Water Pump

Natural Bridge

Tsisab Ravine   ROCK ART

Tsisab Ravine is the epicentre of the Brandberg's rock-art magic. The most famous figure in the ravine is the White Lady of the Brandberg, in Maack's Shelter. The figure, which isn't necessarily a lady (it's still open to interpretation), stands about 40cm high and is part of a larger painting that depicts a bizarre hunting procession. In one hand the figure is carrying what appears to be a flower or possibly a feather. In the other, the figure is carrying bow and arrows.

While doubts remain as to the subject's gender, the painting is distinctive because 'her' hair is straight and light-coloured – distinctly un-African – and the body is painted white from the chest down. The first assessment of the painting was in 1948, when Abbé Henri Breuil speculated that the work had Egyptian or Cretan origins, based on similar ancient art he'd seen around the Mediterranean. However, this claim was eventually dismissed, and recent scholars now believe the white lady may in fact be a San boy, who is covered in white clay as part of an initiation ceremony.

🛏 Sleeping

There are unofficial campsites near the mouths of both the Numas and Tsisab Ravines, but neither has water or facilities and you'll need to be fully self-sufficient. There aren't many places to stay, which makes booking ahead essential, but there is something to suit most budgets.

Ugab Wilderness Camp   CAMPGROUND $
(camping N$100) Facilities are basic here, though the camp is well-run and a good base for organising guided Brandberg hikes or climbs. The turn-off is signposted from the D2359 and the camp is 10km from there. It's a good base for Messum Crater, Brandberg excursions and to watch for desert elephants in the area.

Brandberg White Lady Lodge   LODGE $$
(☑ 081 791 3117, 064-684004; www.brandbergwllodge.com; D2359; camping N$110, s/d luxury tents N$550/770, s/tw with half board N$1075/1846) The Brandberg White Lady has something for just about every kind of traveller. Campers can pitch a tent along the riverine valley, all the while taking advantage of the lodge's upmarket facilities, while lovers of their creature comforts can choose from rustic bungalows and chalets that are highlighted by their stone interi-

ors and wraparound patios. There are also luxury tents.

The lodge does wildlife drives where oryx, springboks, zebras and (if you're *really* lucky) mountain cheetahs can be seen, along with desert elephants (from August to December).

❶ Getting There & Away

To reach Tsisab Ravine from Uis, head 15km north and turn west on the D2359, which leads 26km to the Tsisab car park. To reach Numas Ravine, head 14km south of Uis and follow the D2342 for 55km, where you'll see a rough track turning eastwards. After about 10km, you'll reach a fork; the 4WD track on the right leads to the Numas Ravine car park.

Twyfelfontein Area

Unesco World Heritage–listed Twyfelfontein (Doubtful Spring), at the head of the grassy Aba Huab Valley, is one of the most extensive rock-art galleries on the continent. To date over 2500 engravings have been discovered. Guides are compulsory; note that tips are their only source of income.

❖ Sights

Burnt Mountain   MOUNTAIN
Southeast of Twyfelfontein rises a barren 12km-long volcanic ridge, at the foot of which lies the hill known as Burnt Mountain,

---

❶ SPITZKOPPE PRACTICALITIES

The Spitzkoppe is administered by the Ministry of Environment & Tourism (MET), and attended to by the local community. Local guides are also available for a negotiable price, and they provide some illuminating context to this rich cultural site.

Although you do not need technical equipment and expertise to go scrambling, climbing to the top of the Spitzkoppe is a serious and potentially dangerous endeavour. For starters, you must be fully self-sufficient in terms of climbing gear, food and water, and preferably be part of a large expedition. Before climbing the Spitzkoppe, seek local advice and be sure to inform others of your intentions. Also be advised that it can get extremely hot during the day and surprisingly cold at night and at higher elevations – bring proper protection.

an expanse of volcanic clinker that appears to have been literally exposed to fire. Virtually nothing grows in this eerie panorama of desolation. Burnt Mountain lies beside the D3254, 3km south of the Twyfelfontein turn-off.

Petrified Forest   LANDMARK

(Versteende Woud; adult/child/car N$80/free/10; ☺sunrise-sunset) The petrified forest is an area of open veld scattered with petrified tree trunks up to 34m long and 6m in circumference, which are estimated to be around 260 million years old. The original trees belonged to an ancient group of cone-bearing plants that are known as *Gymnospermae*, which includes such modern plants as conifers, cycads and welwitschias. Because of the lack of root or branch remnants, it's thought that the trunks were transported to the site in a flood.

About 50 individual trees are visible, some half buried in sandstone and many perfectly petrified in silica – complete with bark and tree rings. In 1950, after souvenir hunters had begun to take their toll, the site was declared a national monument, and it's now strictly forbidden to carry off even a small scrap of petrified wood. Guides are compulsory.

The Petrified Forest, signposted 'Versteende Woud', lies 40km west of Khorixas on the C39.

Organ Pipes   LANDMARK

Over the road from Burnt Mountain, you can follow an obvious path into a small gorge that contains a 100m stretch of unusual 4m-high dolerite (coarse-grained basalt) columns known as the Organ Pipes.

Wondergat   NATURAL FEATURE

Wondergat is an enormous sinkhole with daunting views into the subterranean world. Turn west off the D3254, 4km north of the D2612 junction. It's about 500m further on to Wondergat.

🛏 Sleeping

Abu Huab Rest Camp   CAMPGROUND $

(camping N$120) Well-shaded, close to the Twyfelfontein rock art and often visited by desert elephants, Abu Huab is an appealing choice for self-drivers, at least at first glance. There's also a small bar, but service at the whole place definitely needs a rethink and facilities (such as the nonexistent electricity) need an overhaul.

★ Camp Kipwe   LODGE $$$

(✆061-232009; www.kipwe.com; s/d with half board low season N$2800/4100, high season N$2490/5280; ❄🛜🏊) Brilliantly located amongst the boulders and rocks littered throughout its premises, Kipwe is languidly draped over the stunning landscape in very unobtrusive large rondavels (round huts) with thatched roofs that blend in beautifully with their surrounds and have lovely views. There are nine standard rooms and one honeymoon suite (rooms 3 and 4 are family rooms with kids' tents); all come with outdoor bathrooms so you can stargaze while you wash.

TWYFELFONTEIN'S ROCK ENGRAVINGS

Mostly dating back at least 6000 years to the early Stone Age, Twyfelfontein's **rock engravings** (adult/child/car N$80/free/10; ☺sunrise-sunset) were probably the work of ancient San hunters, and were made by cutting through the hard patina covering the local sandstone. In time, this skin reformed over the engravings, protecting them from erosion. From colour differentiation and weathering, researchers have identified at least six distinct phases, but some are clearly the work of copycat artists and are thought to date from the 19th century.

In the ancient past, this perennial spring most likely attracted wildlife, creating a paradise for the hunters who eventually left their marks on the surrounding rocks. Animals, animal tracks and geometric designs are well represented here, though there are surprisingly few human figures. Many of the engravings depict animals that are no longer found in the area – elephants, rhinos, giraffes and lions – and an engraving of a sea lion indicates contact with the coast more than 100km away.

Twyfelfontein became a national monument in 1952. Unfortunately, the site did not receive formal protection until 1986, when it was designated a natural reserve. In the interim, many petroglyphs were damaged by vandals, and some were even removed altogether. Restoration work continues.

There are great views from the dining/lounge area – catch the breeze with your cocktail. The lodge also runs nature drives (N$650) and excursions to the rock art. The entrance to Kipwe is just across the road (D2612) from the entrance to Mowani Mountain Camp.

★ **Doro Nawas Camp** LODGE $$$
(☑061-225178; www.wilderness-safaris.com; s/d Jun-Oct N$6510/11,270, rates vary rest of year; ⚏⚏) Part of the elite Wilderness Safari portfolio, Doro Nawas is a magnificent place. The thatched rooms are massive and luxurious, the terraces open on to vast views and there's a great mix of excursions, from Twyfelfontein rock art to wildlife drives in search of desert-adapted elephants and lions. Prices are high by Namibian standards, but the quality and service are unimpeachable.

Mowani Mountain Camp LODGE $$$
(☑061-232009; www.mowani.com; s/d with half board low season from N$3130/4760, high season from N$3830/5960; @⚏) There's little to prepare you for this beautiful lodge – hidden among a jumble of boulders, its domed buildings seem to disappear into the landscape and you don't see it until you're there. The main buildings all enjoy an ingenious natural air-conditioning system, and the accommodation nestles out of sight amid the boulders. The mountain camp is located 5km north of the Twyfelfontein turn-off from the D2612.

You pay extra for the best views from your room – worth every Namibian dollar.

Twyfelfontein Country Lodge LODGE $$$
(www.twyfelfonteinlodge.com; s/d from N$1580/2200; ✹@⚏) Over the hill from Twyfelfontein, this architectural wonder is embedded in the red rock. On your way in, be sure not to miss the ancient rock engravings, as well as the swimming pool with its incongruous desert waterfall. The lodge boasts stylish if dated rooms and a good variety of excursions. It lacks the polish of other Twyfelfontein lodges and maintenance can be an issue.

It's very close to Twyfelfontein and the rock art, fairly well signposted and easy to find.

❶ Getting There & Away

There's no public transport in the area and little traffic. Turn off the C39, 73km west of Khorixas, turn south on the D3254 and continue 15km to a

WORTH A TRIP

MESSUM CRATER

One of Damaraland's most remote natural attractions is the mysterious-looking **Messum Crater**, which comprises two concentric circles of hills created by a collapsed volcano in the Goboboseb Mountains. The crater measures more than 20km in diameter, creating a vast lost world that you may have all to yourself.

Camping is prohibited inside the crater and the crater is best visited as a day trip from the Brandberg area, where you'll find a handful of accommodation choices. Of its three main entrances, Messum is best accessed along the Messum River from the D2342 west of the Brandberg. Note that you must stick to the tracks at all times, especially if you choose either route involving the fragile lichen plains of the Dorob National Park. If you are driving in this area, you will require the relevant topographic sheets, which are available from the **Office of the Surveyor General** (p230) in Windhoek.

right turning signposted Twyfelfontein. It's 5km to the petroglyph site.

Kamanjab
POP 6010 / ☑067
Flanked by lovely low rock formations, tiny Kamanjab functions as a minor service centre for northern Damaraland, and provides an appealing stopover (and fuel stop) en route between Damaraland, Kaokoveld and Etosha National Park's western gate.

🛏 Sleeping

Oase Garni Guest House GUESTHOUSE $
(☑067-330032; s/d N$560/800; ⚏) This guesthouse in the heart of Kamanjab features small rooms with questionable plumbing and a bar-restaurant which is the centre of nightlife in town. New management in 2016 promises to improve things and even if you're not staying here, it's worth stopping by for a cold beer and a fresh cut of kudu, zebra or gemsbok. The owners can also arrange tours to a nearby Himba village.

Porcupine Camp CAMPGROUND $
(☑067-330274; www.porcupine-camp.com; camping N$80, s/d N$275/550) Around 8km

from Kamanjab along the C40 to Palmwag, Porcupine Camp is a simple, friendly place. The accommodation is in basic domed tents – we prefer the lovely, secluded campsites. The real highlight is the evening porcupine viewing (N$70 per person). No credit cards.

Oppi-Koppi Rest Camp CAMPGROUND, CHALET $$
(☑ 067-330040; www.oppi-koppi-kamanjab.com; s/d from N$700/1240) A decent Kamanjab choice, Oppi-Koppi has rather basic, brick-walled family rooms, much nicer luxury chalets and well-kept campsites.

Otjitotongwe
Cheetah Guest Farm LODGE $$$
(☑ 067-687056; www.cheetahparknamibia.com; camping incl cheetah tour N$320, s/d with full board N$1100/2100; ☀) Otjitotongwe is run by cheetah aficionados Tollie and Roeleen Nel, who keep tame cheetahs around their home and have set up a 40-hectare enclosure for wilder specimens, which they feed every afternoon at 4pm in summer, an hour earlier in winter. The no-frills thatched bungalows are simple but well-maintained. Otjitotongwe is 24km south of Kamanjab on the C40.

The project started when the Nels trapped several wild cheetahs that were poaching their livestock, in the hopes of releasing them in Etosha National Park. After learning that the government was opposed to the idea, they released the animals into the wild, though they kept a litter of cubs born in captivity. Since then, the Nels have taken in a number of recovered cheetahs and operate the wildlife farm in the hope of increasing awareness of the plight of these endangered predators.

❶ Getting There & Away
The good road north to Ruacana is open to 2WD vehicles, though you need to exercise caution once you cross the Red Line. Just north of Etosha, this veterinary cordon fence marks the boundary between commercial ranching and subsistence herding, and wandering livestock can be a driving hazard.

Palmwag
☑ 061
The 5000-sq-km Palmwag Concession and the surrounding areas together make up a rich wildlife area amid stark red hills and plains, surrounded by a bizarre landscape of uniformly sized red stones. It serves as something of a buffer zone between Etosha

in the north and the Skeleton Coast, with a reasonable chance that you'll see black rhinos (most of the camps offer rhino-tracking), desert elephants and lions, as well as spotted hyenas, giraffes, gemsboks and other antelope. The area is home to a handful of luxury lodges, and also serves as a study centre for the Save the Rhino Trust (SRT; p281), making it a good mix of great wildlife watching and serious conservation, quite apart from being stunningly beautiful country.

🛏 Sleeping
Some of Namibia's best lodges are found around Palmwag. The majority must be prebooked and rates usually include all meals and activities. Transfers by 4WD and air charters are available through the operator. There's also camping at Palmwag Lodge.

Hoada Campsite CAMPGROUND $
(☑ 081 289 0982, 061-228104; www.grootberg.com/hoada-campsite; camping N$185; ☀) Run by Grootberg Lodge, this superb campsite sits among towering boulders with excellent facilities including a fine swimming pool, flush toilets and outdoor showers).

★ Desert Rhino Camp TENTED CAMP $$$
(☑ 061-225178; www.wilderness-safaris.com; s/d with full board high season N$11,600/17,010; ☀) The safari-style tents in a remote corner of Damaraland are certainly luxurious and a worthy member of the elite Wilderness Safaris classic collection. But even more than the rooms, it's the ethos of this place – the camp has been at the centre of efforts to save Namibia's black rhino population – that impresses. Rhino tracking, and the chance to see desert lions and elephants, are other highlights.

Damaraland Camp LODGE $$$
(☑ 061-225178; www.wilderness-safaris.com; s/d with full board high season N$9030/13,120; ☀) This solar-powered desert outpost 60km south of Palmwag has all-encompassing views of stark, truncated hills and is an oasis of luxury amid a truly feral and outlandish setting. When you're not living out your end-of-the-world fantasies in your luxury tent with wood floors, adobe walls and outdoor showers, you can do a few laps in the novel pool that occupies a rocky gorge formed by past lava flows.

Wildlife drives could include rhinos, elephants and lions if you're lucky.

Grootberg Lodge LODGE **$$$**
(☑ 067-333212, 061-228104; www.grootberg.com; s/d with half board N$1950/2930) This place has best views we witnessed on our most recent research trip in Namibia, and the valley of this stunning setting is where you can track black rhino – yes, you get to drive down into that valley! An extraordinary location brought home by the very steep approach track, this is a genuinely wild, open space – there are no fences. Rooms are large and luxurious, but it's the views that you'll remember most.

The rhino are elusive, however, and much of the tracking is spent in the vehicle, or on foot either following the trackers or waiting around for them to get a new lead. But the prize is a chance to see one of Africa's most endangered animals in the wild. Other animals you may see are desert elephants, mountain cheetahs, lions, antelope (such as steenboks, klipspringers, springboks and gemsboks), as well as zebras. After a hard day tracking wildlife, the massage centre is just the ticket.

Grootberg lies 25km east of Palmwag and 90km west of Kamanjab – take the C40.

Etendeka Mountain Camp TENTED CAMP **$$$**
(☑ 061-239199; www.etendeka-namibia.com; s/d N$3300/5260; ☒) ✿ The focus of Etendeka, an ecofriendly tented camp set beneath the foothills of the Grootberg Mountains, is on conservation, not luxury. Guests usually check out with an in-depth understanding of the Damaraland environment. Expansive views of this splendid corner of the country, as well as good wildlife possibilities make this a good choice between the uber-luxurious camps and independent camping.

Palmwag Lodge LODGE **$$$**
(☑ 081 620 6887; www.palmwaglodge.com; camping N$180, s/d with half board from N$1875/2960; ☒) The oldest accommodation in the Palmwag area sits on a private concession adjacent to the Uniab River. Rooms are acceptable for the price, if unexciting, but the campsites are a welcome addition – numbers two to five have fabulous views, while the remainder are a little claustrophobic. The property contains several excellent hiking routes, and a local bull elephant, Jimbo, sometimes wanders through the camp.

Activities include rhino-tracking (half/full day N$1595/2145) in the neighbouring Torra Conservancy, as well as wildlife drives (N$550) where lion, elephant, spotted hyena, gemsbok, giraffe and zebra are all possible.

❶ Getting There & Away

Palmwag is on the D3706, 157km from Khorixas and 105km from Sesfontein. Coming from the south, you'll cross the Red Line, 1km south of Palmwag Lodge – you can carry meat heading north, but not south.

Sesfontein
POP 7360 / ☑ 065
Damaraland's most northerly outpost is almost entirely encircled by the Kaokoveld, and is somewhat reminiscent of a remote oasis in the middle of the Sahara.

History
Fed by six springs (hence its name), Sesfontein was established as a military outpost in 1896 following a rinderpest outbreak. A barracks was added in 1901, and four years later a fort was constructed to control cattle disease, arms smuggling and poaching. This arrangement lasted until 1909, when the fort appeared to be redundant and was requisitioned by the police, who used it until the outbreak of WWI. In 1987 the fort was restored by the Damara Administration (regional government) and converted into a comfortable lodge, which is now one of the most unusual accommodation options in the whole of Namibia.

❶ Sights
For adventurers who dream of uncharted territory, the spectacular and little-known Otjitaimo Canyon lurks about 10km north of the main road, along the western flanks of the north–south mountain range east of Sesfontein. To get here would involve a major expedition on foot, but if you're up for it, pick up the topographic sheets from the Office of the Surveyor General (p230) in Windhoek, pack lots of water (at least 4L per person per day), and expect stirring scenery and solitude.

🛏 Sleeping
Khowarib Lodge LODGE **$$**
(☑ 081 219 3291; www.khowarib.com; per person with half board N$1470-1845) The rooms here are original with their rough-hewn stone walls, but its the activities that we like here – wildlife drives in search of desert elephants, rhino tracking, nature walks in the Hoanib

Valley and excursions to rock-art sites and Himba villages are all possible. It's 20km southeast of Sesfontein.

Fort Sesfontein   HOTEL $$$
(☑ 065-685034; www.fort-sesfontein.com; s/d with half board N$1570/2520; 🛜🍽️) Ever fancy spending the night in a colonial fort out in the middle of the desert? At Fort Sesfontein you and 43 other guests can live out all your *Lawrence of Arabia* fantasies. Accommodation is basic but incredibly atmospheric (we love the original alcoves and niches in the rooms), and there's a good restaurant that serves German-inspired dishes.

It also offers tours to Himba villages, local rock art and other excursions.

ℹ️ Getting There & Away

The road between Palmwag and Sesfontein is good gravel, and you'll only have problems if the Hoanib River is flowing. If it hasn't been raining, the gravel road from Sesfontein to Opuwo is accessible to all vehicles.

The Kaokoveld

The Kaokoveld is a photographer's dreamscape of wide-open vistas, lonely desert roads and hardly another person around to ruin your shot. A vast repository of desert mountains, this is one of the least developed regions of the country, and arguably Namibia at its most primeval. The Kaokoveld is also the ancestral home of the Himba people, a culturally rich tribal group that has retained their striking appearance and dress.

The Kaokoveld is largely devoid of roads and is crossed only by sandy tracks laid down by the South African Defence Force (SADF) decades ago. In this harsh wilderness of dry and arid conditions, wildlife has been forced to adapt in miraculous ways – consider the critically endangered desert elephant, which has especially spindly legs suited for long walks in search of precious water.

It's that sort of place, where a sense of mystery and scenes of singular beauty are your companions while travelling out here.

Opuwo

POP 7660 / ☑ 065
In the Herero language, Opuwo means 'the end', which is certainly a fitting name for this dusty collection of concrete commercial buildings ringed by traditional rondavels (round huts with conical roofs) and huts. While first impressions are unlikely to be very positive, a visit to Opuwo is one of the cultural highlights of Namibia, particularly for anyone interested in interacting with the Himba people. As the unofficial capital of Himbaland, Opuwo serves as a convenient jumping-off point for excursions into the nearby villages, and there is a good assortment of lodges and campsites to choose from.

⦿ Sights

Tourism is booming in Himbaland, as evidenced by the paving of the road all the way up to Opuwo (but not to the border with Angola!), and the inauguration of the Opuwo Country Hotel by the Namibian president himself. Ever-so-photogenic shots of Himba women appear on just about every Namibian tourism brochure, and busloads of tourists can be seen whizzing through Opuwo's dusty streets virtually every day.

Throughout Opuwo you will see Himba wherever you go – they will be walking the streets, shopping in the stores and even waiting in line behind you at the supermarket. However tempting it might be, please do not sneak a quick picture of them, as no one appreciates having a camera waved in front of their face.

🛏️ Sleeping

There may be two excellent hotels, but as Opuwo is now very much on the tourist trail, advance bookings (months ahead in high season) are highly recommended.

Ohakane Lodge   LODGE $
(☑ 081 295 9024, 065-273031; ohakane@iway.na; s/d N$620/1030; ❄️🍽️) This well-established and centrally located lodge sits along the main drag in Opuwo and does good business with tour groups. Fairly standard but fully modern rooms are comfortable enough, but if it's in your budget, it's worth shelling out a bit more for a bungalow at the Opuwo Country Lodge.

True to its name – Ohakane means 'African wild dog' – it supports a number of World Wildlife Fund (WWF) projects to protect the species, although they haven't been seen in the area for decades.

★ Opuwo Country Lodge   HOTEL $$$
(☑ 064-418661, 065-273461; www.opuwolodge.com; camping N$160, s/d standard rooms incl breakfast N$1260/1800, s/d luxury rooms incl breakfast

SAVE THE RHINO TRUST

The **Save the Rhino Trust** (SRT; www.savetherhino.org) is dedicated to stopping illegal poaching. Since the trust was formed, it has collaborated with both the Namibian government and local communities in order to provide security and monitor population size of the only free-ranging black-rhino population in the world. To date SRT has successfully protected these rhinos and allowed the rhino group to expand in number. Census results have revealed that the population of 1130 rhinos has been preserved, with an annual growth rate of 5%. In fact, the International Union for Conservation of Nature (IUCN) has identified the population as the fastest growing in Africa.

SRT operates in Damaraland, a sparsely populated region that is lacking in resources and deficient in employment opportunities. As a result, it has worked to include locals in conservation efforts in the hope that they will benefit from the preservation of the species. This is especially important as Damaraland does not have a formal conservation status and thus does not receive government funding.

Although the organisation has been successful in stabilising rhino populations, SRT still faces challenges, such as poaching for rhino horn and the increasing demand in Namibia for arable farmland. According to SRT, the future of the rhino is dependent on the effective resolution of these two issues, and they argue that government policy must include the establishment of stable rhino populations in parks, reserves and private lands throughout the country.

For visitors interested in tracking black rhinos through the bush, SRT operates the exclusive **Desert Rhino Camp** (p278), a joint venture with Wilderness Safaris. This is probably the best place to go rhino tracking, although other Damaraland lodges offer excellent tracking as well.

NAMIBIA THE KAOKOVELD

N\$1820/2560; ✿ @ ✿) Far and away the area's swankiest accommodation option with lovely rooms, the hilltop Opuwo Country Lodge is an enormous thatched building (reportedly the largest in Namibia) that elegantly lords it over the town below. The hotel faces across a valley towards the Angolan foothills, and most of your time here will be spent soaking your cares away in the infinity-edge pool.

If the standard rooms are taken and you can't afford a luxury version, consider pitching a tent in the secluded campsite, which grants you complete access to the lodge's amenities, including a fully stocked wine bar and a regal dining hall. The turn-off leading up to the lodge is a bit tricky to find, but there are signs posted throughout the town. Activities include excursions to Himba villages and/or the Epupa Falls.

🛍 Shopping

Kunene Craft Centre ARTS & CRAFTS
(☉8am-5pm Mon-Fri, 9am-1pm Sat) Opuwo's brightly painted self-help curio shop sells local arts and crafts on consignment. You'll find all sorts of Himba adornments smeared with ochre: conch-shell pendants, wrist bands, chest pieces and even the headdresses worn by Himba brides. There's also a range of origi-nal jewellery, appliqué pillowslips, Himba and Herero dolls, drums and wooden carvings.

ℹ Information

Kaoko Information Centre (☑ 081 284 3681, 065-273420; ☉8am-6pm) KK and Kemuu, the friendly guys at this information centre (look for the tiny, tiny yellow shack), can arrange visits to local Himba villages in addition to providing useful information for your trip through the Kaokoveld region.

ℹ Getting There & Away

The paved C41 runs from Outjo to Opuwo, which makes Himbaland accessible even to 2WD vehicles. Although there is a temptation to speed along this long and lonely highway, keep your lead foot off the pedal north of the veterinary control fence, as herds of cattle commonly stray across the road. If you're heading deeper into the Kaokoveld, be advised that Opuwo is the last opportunity to buy petrol before Kamanjab, Ruacana or Sesfontein.

Swartbooi's Drift
☑ 065

From Ruacana, a rough track heads west along the Kunene to Swartbooi's Drift, where a monument commemorates the Dorsland trekkers who passed en route to their future homesteads in Angola. The town is a good place to break up the drive to Epupa Falls, and it's also a good base to go white-water rafting on the Kunene River.

🛏 Sleeping

Kunene River Lodge   LODGE **$$**
(☎ 065-274300; www.kuneneriverlodge.com; camping N$160, s/d chalets N$720/1440, r N$950/1900; ☒) The very friendly Kunene River Lodge, approximately 5km east of Swartbooi's Drift, makes an idyllic riverside stop. Campsites are sheltered beneath towering trees, and the appealing rooms and thatched A-frame chalets enjoy a pleasant garden setting. Guests can hire canoes, mountain bikes and fishing rods, as well as go on birdwatching excursions, white-water rafting trips and booze cruises.

With a minimum of two participants, the lodge also operates half-day, full-day and multiday white-water rafting trips, starting at N$420 per person, from the class IV Ondarusu rapids (upstream from Swartbooi's Drift) to Epupa Falls.

❶ Getting There & Away

At Otjikeze/Epembe, 73km northwest of Opuwo, an eastward turning onto the D3701 leads 60km to Swartbooi's Drift. This is the easiest access route, and it's open to 2WD vehicles. The river road from Ruacana is extremely rough, but in dry conditions it can be negotiated by high-clearance 2WD vehicles. On the other hand, the 93km river road to Epupa Falls – along the lovely 'Namibian riviera' – is extremely challenging even with a 4WD and can take several days.

Epupa Falls

☎ 061

Although you'd think this remote corner of the Kaokoveld would be off the tourist trail, Epupa Falls is a popular detour for overland trucks and organised safaris, and can get swamped with tourists. But if you're passing through the area, the falls is certainly worth the detour - the sight of so much water in the middle of the dry Kaokoveld is miraculous to say the least, and if the pools are free from crocs, a dip is a possibility.

🛏 Sleeping

Epupa Camp   LODGE, CAMGROUND **$$$**
(☎ 061-237294; www.epupa.com.na; camping N$120, s/d with full board N$1800/2800; ☒) Located 800m upstream from the falls and with a lovely riverside setting, Epupa Camp offers beautifully situated accommodation among a grove of towering baobab and palm trees. There are nine luxury tents filled to the brim with curios, and a slew of

---

THE HIMBA, ETIQUETTE & TAKING PICS

In the past, rural Himba people were willing models for photography. These days, however, you are likely to encounter traditionally dressed Himba people who will wave you down and ask for tips in exchange for having their photograph taken. Naturally, whether you accept is up to you, but bear in mind that encouraging this trade works to draw people away from their traditional lifestyle, and propels them towards a cash economy that undermines long-standing values and community cooperation.

It's recommended that instead you trade basic commodities for photographs. In times of plenty, Himba grow maize to supplement their largely meat- and milk-based diet, though rain is highly unpredictable in Namibia. Pap (corn meal) is a very desirable gift for the Himba, as is rice, bread, potatoes and other starches. Try to resist giving sugar, soft drinks and other sweets, as the majority of Himba may never meet a dentist in their lifetime.

If you would like to have free rein with the camera, visiting a traditional village – if done in the proper fashion – can yield some truly amazing shots. Needless to say, a guide who speaks both English and the Himba language is essential to the experience. You can either join an organised tour through your accommodation, or stop by the Kaoko Information Centre (p281) in Opuwo.

Before arriving in the village, please do spend some time shopping for gifts – entering a village with food items will garner a warm welcome from the villagers, who will subsequently be more willing to tolerate photography. At the end of your time in the village, buying small bracelets and trinkets directly from the artisan is also a greatly appreciated gesture.

EXPLORING THE KAOKOVELD

Even if you're undaunted by extreme 4WD exploration, you still must make careful preparations for any trip off the Sesfontein–Opuwo and the Ruacana–Opuwo–Epupa Falls routes. To summarise, you will need a robust 4WD vehicle, plenty of time and enough supplies to see you through the journey. It's also useful to take a guide who knows the region, and to travel in a convoy of at least two vehicles.

Poor conditions on some tracks may limit your progress to 5km/h, but after rains, streams and mud can stop a vehicle in its tracks. Allow a full day to travel between Opuwo and Epupa Falls, and several days each way from Opuwo to Hartmann's Valley and Otjinjange (Marienflüss) Valley. Note that Van Zyl's Pass may be crossed only from east to west. Alternative access is through the Rooidrum road junction north of Orupembe (via Otjihaa Pass).

Camping in the Kaokoveld requires awareness of the environment and people.

activities on offer, including Himba visits, boat trips, sundowner hikes, birdwatching walks and trips to rock-art sites. Five campsites are also available.

Omarunga Lodge　　　LODGE, CAMPGROUND $$$
(☑064-403096; www.natron.net/omarunga-camp/main.html; camping N$100, single/double chalets with full board N$2458/3916; ☒) This German-run camp operates through a concession granted by a local chief, and has a well-groomed campsite beneath the palm trees with modern facilities as well as a dozen luxury chalets. It's a very attractive spot, but it can't hold a candle to the slightly more upmarket Epupa Camp. Don't be tempted to swim in the river – crocodiles lurk!

⊙ Getting There & Away

The road from Okongwati is accessible to high-clearance 2WD vehicles, but it's still quite rough. As the rugged 93km 4WD river route from Swartbooi's Drift may take several days, it's far quicker to make the trip via Otjiveze/Epembe.

The Northwest Corner

☑064

West of Epupa Falls is the Kaokoveld of travellers' dreams: stark, rugged desert peaks, vast landscapes, sparse, scrubby vegetation, drought-resistant wildlife, and nomadic bands of Himba people and their tiny settlements of beehive huts. This region, which is contiguous with the Skeleton Coast Wilderness, has been designated the Kaokoveld Conservation Area and it's one of Namibia's true gems. It's also a pretty rough ride on bad tracks – getting here and around is part of the adventure.

⊙ Sights

**Otjinjange &
Hartmann's Valleys**　　　NATURAL SITE
Allow plenty of time to explore the wild and magical Otjinjange (better known as Marienflüss) and Hartmann's Valleys – broad sandy and grassy expanses descending gently to the Kunene River. Note that camping outside campsites is prohibited at both valleys.

Van Zyl's Pass　　　NATURAL SITE
The beautiful, but frightfully steep and challenging, Van Zyl's Pass forms a dramatic transition between the Kaokoveld plateaus and the vast, grassy expanses of Otjinjange Valley (Marienflüss). This winding 13km stretch isn't suitable for trailers and may only be passed from east to west, which means you'll have to return via Otjihaa Pass or through Purros.

⊨ Sleeping

**Ngatutunge
Pamwe Camp Site**　　　CAMPGROUND $
(Purros Campsite; camping N$60; ☒) Community-run Ngatutunge campsite is perched along the Hoarusib River 2km from Purros village, and surprisingly has hot showers, flush toilets, well-appointed bungalows, a communal kitchen and (believe it or not!) a swimming pool. It's also a good spot for hiring guides to visit nearby Himba villages or observing desert-adapted wildlife.

Elephant Song Camp　　　CAMPGROUND $
(☑064-403829; camping N$100) Community-run Elephant Song is located in the Palmwag Concession, a very rough 25km down the Hoanib River from Sesfontein. This camp caters to outdoorsy types, with

NAMIBIA THE KAOKOVELD

great views, hiking, birdwatching and the chance to see rare desert elephants. Sites are simple with braai (barbecue) pits and a little shade.

Okarohombo Camp Site   CAMPGROUND $
(camping N$70) This community-run campsite is located at the mouth of the Otjinjange Valley. Facilities include flushable toilets, showers and a communal kitchen.

★ **Serra Cafema Camp**   TENTED CAMP $$$
(www.wilderness-safaris.com; s/d high season N$16,320/25,140; ▣) One of Namibia's most opulent and remote safari experiences, Serra Cafema is a breathtaking place. Stunning desert scenery, combined with a special riverside location and excellent cultural immersion opportunities with the local Himba are big selling points here. The public areas open onto some gorgeous views, while the rooms, each with a private terrace overlooking the river, are large and lovely.

Quad biking is another possibility here.

❶ Getting There & Away

From Okongwati, the westward route through Etengwa leads to either Van Zyl's Pass or Otjihaa Pass. From Okauwa (with a landmark broken windmill) to the road fork at Otjitanda; which is a Himba chief's *kraal* (hut), the journey is extremely rough and slow going. Along the way, stop off for a swim at beautiful Ovivero Dam. From Otjitanda, you must decide whether you're heading west over Van Zyl's Pass (which may only be traversed from east to west!) into Otjinjange (Marienflüss) and Hartmann's Valleys, or south over the equally beautiful, but much easier, Otjihaa Pass towards Orupembe.

You can also access Otjinjange (Marienflüss) and Hartmann's Valleys without crossing Van Zyl's Pass by turning north at the three-way junction in the middle of the Onjuva Plains, 12km north of Orupembe. At the T-junction in Rooidrum (Red Drum), you can decide which valley you want. Turn right for Otjinjange (Marienflüss) and left for Hartmann's. West of this junction, 17km from Rooidrum, you can also turn south along the fairly good route to Orupembe, Purros (provided that the Hoarusib River isn't flowing) and on to Sesfontein.

Alternatively, you can head west from Opuwo on the D3703, which leads 105km to Etanga; 19km beyond Etanga, you'll reach a road junction marked by a stone sign painted with white birds. At this point, you can turn north toward Otjitanda (27km away) or south towards Otjihaa Pass and Orupembe.

The Skeleton Coast

This treacherous coast – a foggy region with rocky and sandy coastal shallows, rusting shipwrecks and soaring dunes – has long been a graveyard for unwary ships and their crews, hence its forbidding name. Early Portuguese sailors called it *As Areias do Inferno* (The Sands of Hell), as once a ship washed ashore, the fate of the crew was sealed. This protected area stretches from Sandwich Harbour, south of Swakopmund, to the Kunene River, taking in around 20,000 sq km of dunes and gravel plains to form one of the world's most inhospitable waterless areas in the world's oldest desert.

Dorob National Park

Declared a national park in December 2010, Dorob extends beyond the Swakop River and down to Sandwich Harbour in the south, while its northern border is the Ugab River. Its undoubted highlight is the Cape Cross Seal Reserve. It's also extremely popular among fisherfolk. The most interesting area for visitors is a 200km-long and 25km-wide strip that extends from Swakopmund to the Ugab River.

At the time of writing, there were no entrance fees for Dorob.

◉ Sights

★ **Sandwich Harbour**   HARBOUR
Sandwich Harbour, 56km south of Walvis Bay in Dorob National Park, is one of the most dramatic sights in Namibia – dunes up to 100m-high plunge into the Atlantic, which washes into the picturesque lagoon. The harbour is now deserted and a stirring wilderness devoid of any human settlement. Birdwatchers will have a field day and Sandwich Harbour 4x4 (p306) facilitate half- and full-day trips down here.

Sandwich Harbour historically served as a commercial fishing and trading port. Some historians suggest that the name may be derived from an English whaler, the *Sandwich*, whose captain produced the first map of this coastline. Still, others contend that the name may also be a corruption of the German word *sandfische*, a type of shark often found here.

🏃 Activities

The area is extremely popular with South Africans on fishing expeditions, who flock here to tackle such saltwater species as galjoens, steenbras, kabeljous and blacktails. In fact, between Swakopmund and the Ugab River are hundreds of concrete buildings, spaced at intervals of just hundreds of metres. Although these appear to be coastal bunkers guarding against an offshore attack, they're actually toilet blocks for people fishing and camping.

ℹ️ Getting There & Away

There's no public transport along this coast – you'll need your own wheels. The coastal C34 road is in part built from salt but is in generally excellent condition. If you're coming from the north, take the C43 road south from Palmwag, then west along the C39.

Henties Bay
🎣 064

At Henties Bay, 80km north of Swakopmund, the relatively reliable Omaruru River issues into the Atlantic (don't miss the novel golf course in the riverbed!). It was named for Hentie van der Merwe, who visited its spring in 1929. Today it consists mainly of holiday homes, and refuelling and provisioning businesses for anglers headed up the coast. As such, it's more a mildly interesting outpost or way station on your way along the coast than anything worth lingering over.

🛏️ Sleeping

Buck's Camping Lodge   LODGE, CAMPGROUND **$**
(🎣 064-501039; Nickey Iyambo Rd; camping N$270) Buck's Camping Lodge, near the police station in town, is expensive but for the extra dollars you get a campsite with your own private bathroom. Look for the caravan sign just off the road.

De Duine Country Hotel   HOTEL **$**
(🎣 081 124 1181, 064-500001; www.deduinehotel. com; Duine Rd; s/d N$480/700; ❄️✖️) The De Duine Country Hotel, the most established hotel in Henties Bay, sits on the coast, though not a single room has a sea view – go figure! The German colonial-style property does feature rooms with swimming pool and garden views, though.

ℹ️ Information

Tourist Information Office (🎣 064-501143; www.hentiesbaytourism.com; Nickey Iyambo Rd; ☺8am-1pm & 2-5pm Mon-Fri)

ℹ️ Getting There & Away

The C34 salt road, which begins in Swakopmund and ends 70km north of Terrace Bay, provides access to Dorob National Park and the southern half of the Skeleton Coast Park. The park is also accessible via the C39 gravel road that links Khorixas with Torra Bay. Henties Bay lies at the junction of the coastal salt road and the C35, which turns inland towards Damaraland.

Note that motorcycles are not permitted in Skeleton Coast Park. Permits (which are free and can be obtained at the two gates to the park along the road) are required to transit the area, and the salt road from Swakopmund is passable year-round with a 2WD.

Cape Cross Seal Reserve

The best-known breeding colony of Cape fur seals along the Namib coast is at this **reserve** (per person/car N$80/10; ☺10am-5pm), where the population has grown large and fat by taking advantage of the rich concentrations of fish in the cold Benguela Current. The sight of more than 100,000 seals basking on the beach and frolicking in the surf is impressive to behold, though you're going to have to contend with the overwhelming odoriferousness of piles and piles of stinky seal poo. Bring a handkerchief or bandana to cover your nose – seriously, you'll thank us for the recommendation.

No pets or motorcycles are permitted, and visitors may not cross the low barrier between the seal-viewing area and the rocks where the colony lounges.

History

Although it's primarily known for the seals, Cape Cross has a long and illustrious history. In 1485 Portuguese explorer Diego Cão, the first European to set foot in Namibia, planted a 2m-high, 360kg *padrão* (a tribute to Portuguese king João II) at Cape Cross.

In 1893, however, a German sailor Captain Becker of the Falke removed the cross and hauled it off to Germany. The following year, Kaiser Wilhelm II ordered that a replica be made with the original inscriptions in Latin and Portuguese, as well as a commemorative inscription in German. This cross remains at the site, in addition to a second cross, made of dolerite, which was erected in 1980 on the site of Cão's original cross.

🛏 Sleeping

Campsites CAMPGROUND **$**
(camping N$100) There are campsites on the water's edge 1.7km back along the coast from the seal colony. They're far enough away from the stink and have uninterrupted sea views, but facilities are basic and they only open from November to July. They operate on a first-come, first-served basis – ask at the entry to the reserve.

★ **Cape Cross Lodge** LODGE, CAMPGROUND **$$$**
(☑ 064-694012, 064-461677; www.capecross.org; camping per adult/child N$100/50, s/d N$1600/2450; ✳🕿) Cape Cross Lodge has an odd but strangely appealing architecture, which is self-described as a cross between Cape Dutch and fishing village style. The nicer rooms have spacious outdoor patios that overlook the coastline, though you really can't choose a bad room at this all-around

stunner of a lodge, conveniently located just before the official reserve entrance.

It's a superb, isolated spot right on a sweeping bend of the bay overlooking blue seas and rollers lolling in and crashing over white-sand beaches. There are also 20 excellent campsites, although they're separated from the seafront by the main lodge building.

There's even a nice little museum which focuses on the seafaring history of this stretch of coast. The restaurant (mains N$60 to N$110) dishes out plenty of seafood including a fish sandwich (with admittedly weird mayo) and a seafood platter for N$215.

ℹ Getting There & Away

Cape Cross lies 46km north of Henties Bay along the coastal salt road. There's no public transport here, but a 2WD is all you'll need to get here from the south.

CAPE FUR SEALS

There are seven seal species in Southern African waters, but except for very occasional vagrants from the Antarctic and sub-Antarctic islands, the only mainland species is the Cape fur seal. Communal to the extreme, this massive population is divided between only about 25 colonies; a few of them, like Cape Cross on Namibia's western coast, number more than 100,000.

Despite their gregariousness, Cape fur seals are not especially sociable; colony living makes sense for breeding opportunities, and to reduce the chance of predators sneaking up, but individual seals are essentially loners on land, and they constantly quarrel over their own little patch. Except for pups playing with each other in crèche-like 'playgrounds', virtually every other interaction in the colony is hostile, creating extraordinary opportunities for watching behaviour.

Cape fur seals have a thick layer of short fur beneath the coarser guard hairs, which remain dry and trap air for insulation. This enables the animals to maintain an internal body temperature of 37°C and spend long periods in cold waters.

Male Cape fur seals weigh less than 200kg on average, but during the breeding season they take on a particularly thick accumulation of blubber and balloon out to more than 360kg. Females are much smaller, averaging 75kg, and give birth to a single, blue-eyed pup during late November or early December. About 90% of the colony's pups are born within just over a month.

Pups begin to suckle less than an hour after birth but are soon left in communal nurseries while their mothers leave to forage for food. When the mothers return to the colony, they identify their own pup by a combination of scent and call.

The pups moult at the age of four to five months, turning from a dark grey to olive brown. Mortality rates in the colony are high, and up to a quarter of the pups fail to survive their first year, with the bulk of deaths occurring during the first week after birth. The main predators are the brown hyena and the black-backed jackal, which account for 25% of pup deaths. Those pups that do survive may remain with their mothers for up to a year.

Cape fur seals eat about 8% of their body weight each day, and the colonies along the western coast of Southern Africa annually consume more than 1 million tonnes of fish and other marine life (mainly shoaling fish and squid). That's about 300,000 tonnes more than is taken by the fishing industries of Namibia and South Africa put together!

Skeleton Coast Park

🎵 064

At Ugabmund, 110km north of Cape Cross, the salt road passes through the entry gate to the Skeleton Coast Park, where rolling fogs and dusty sandstorms encapsulate its eerie, remote and wild feel. Despite the enduring fame of this coastline, surprisingly few travellers ever reach points north of Cape Cross. In order to preserve this incredibly fragile environment, Namibian Wildlife Resorts (NWR) imposes strict regulations on individual travellers seeking to do more than transit through the park. If you plan to linger, visit the NWR offices in Windhoek (p230) or Swakopmund (p303).

You can get a free transit permit to pass between Ugabmund and Springbokwater, which can be obtained at the gates. To transit the park, you must pass the entry gate before 1pm and exit through the other gate before 3pm the same day. Note that transit permits aren't valid for Torra Bay or Terrace Bay.

🏃 Activities

Ugab River Guided Hiking Route HIKING
This 50km-long route begins by crossing the coastal plain, then climbs into the hills and follows a double loop through lichen fields and past caves, natural springs and unusual geological formations. It's open to groups of between six and eight people on the second and fourth Thursday of each month from April to October, and must be booked through Namibia Wildlife Resorts (p303).

Hikes start at 9am from Ugabmund and finish on Saturday afternoon. Most hikers stay Wednesday night at the Mile 108 Camp Site, 40km south of Ugabmund, which allows you to arrive at Ugabmund in time for the hike. Hikers must provide and carry their own food and camping equipment.

🛏 Sleeping

Ugab River Rhino Camp CAMPGROUND $
(www.rhino-trust.org.na; GPS: S 20°57.44', E 14°08.01'; camping N$60) Outside the Skeleton Coast Park, this campsite is administered by the Save the Rhino Trust (p281). This remote landscape is truly enigmatic, and those who've visited have only glowing comments. To get there, turn east onto the D2303, 40km north of Cape Cross; it's then 70km to the camp. Watch out for black rhinos!

Torra Bay Camping Ground CAMPGROUND $
(camping N$145; ⊙ Dec & Jan) This campsite, which opens during the Namibian school holidays, is flanked by a textbook field of barchan dunes. These dunes are actually the southernmost extension of a vast sand sea that stretches all the way to the Curoca River in Angola. Petrol, water, firewood and basic supplies are available, and campers may use the restaurant at Terrace Bay Resort. Torra Bay is 215km north of Cape Cross.

Terrace Bay Resort CHALET $$$
(camping N$145; s/d N$990/1600, 4- to 10-person beach chalets per person N$610) Open year-round, this resort is a luxurious alternative to camping at Torra Bay. Around the camp you may spot black-backed jackals or brown hyenas, and the scenery of sparse coastal vegetation and lonely dunes is the Skeleton Coast at its finest. The site has a restaurant, a shop and a petrol station. Terrace Bay is 49km north of Torra Bay.

ℹ Getting There & Away

The Skeleton Coast Park is accessed via the salt road from Swakopmund, which ends 70km north of Terrace Bay. The park is also accessible via the C39 gravel road which runs between Khorixas and Torra Bay. Note that motorcycles are not permitted in the Skeleton Coast Park.

Skeleton Coast Wilderness Area

The Skeleton Coast Wilderness Area, stretching between the Hoanib and Kunene Rivers, makes up the northern third of the Skeleton Coast and is a part of the Skeleton Coast Park. This section of coastline is among the most remote and inaccessible areas in Namibia, though it's here in the wilderness that you can truly live out your Skeleton Coast fantasies. Since the entire area is a private concession and your only option for visiting is staying in the luxury lodge, you're going to have to part with some serious cash to visit.

History

In the early 1960s, Windhoek lawyer Louw Schoemann began bringing business clients to the region, and became involved in a consortium to construct a harbour at Möwe Bay, at the southern end of the present-day Skeleton Coast Wilderness Area. In 1969, however, the South African government dropped the project, and in 1971 it declared the region a protected reserve. Five years

SKELETONS ON THE COAST

Despite prominent images of rusting ships embedded in the hostile sands of the Skeleton Coast, the most famous shipwrecks have long since disappeared. The harsh winds and dense fog that roll off the South Atlantic are strong forces of erosion, and today there are little more than traces of the countless ships that were swept ashore during the height of the mercantile era. In addition, the few remaining vessels are often in remote and inaccessible locations.

One such example is the *Dunedin Star,* which was deliberately run aground in 1942 just south of the Angolan border after hitting some offshore rocks. The ship was en route from Britain around the Cape of Good Hope to the Middle East war zone, and was carrying more than 100 passengers, a military crew and cargo.

When a rescue ship arrived two days later, getting the castaways off the beach proved an impossible task. At first, the rescuers attempted to haul the castaways onto their vessel by using a line through the surf. However, as the surge grew stronger, the rescue vessel was swept onto the rocks and wrecked alongside the *Dunedin Star.* Meanwhile, a rescue aircraft, which managed to land on the beach alongside the castaways, became bogged in the sand. Eventually all the passengers were rescued, though they were evacuated with the help of an overland truck convoy. The journey back to civilisation was two weeks of hard slog across 1000km of desert.

Further south on the Skeleton Coast – and nearly as difficult to reach – are several more intact wrecks. The *Eduard Bohlen* ran aground south of Walvis Bay in 1909 while carrying equipment to the diamond fields in the far south. Over the past century, the shoreline has changed so much that the ship now lies beached in a dune nearly 1km from the shore.

On picturesque Spencer Bay, 200km further south and just north of the abandoned mining town of Saddle Hill, is the dramatic wreck of the *Otavi.* This cargo ship beached in 1945 following a strong storm, and is now dramatically perched on Dolphin's Head, the highest point on the coast between Cape Town's Table Mountain and the Angolan border. Spencer Bay also claimed the Korean cargo ship *Tong Taw* in 1972, which is currently one of the most intact vessels along the entirety of the Skeleton Coast.

More accessible wrecks include *South West Seal* (1976), just south of Toscanini and north of Henties Bay, and the *Zeila* (2008), 14km south of Henties Bay; the latter is close enough to the towns to attract touts and hangers-on.

later, when the government decided to permit limited tourism, the concession was put up for bid, and Schoemann's was the only tender.

For the next 18 years, his company led small group tours and practised ecotourism long before it became a buzz word. Louw Schoemann died in 1993, but his sons have since carried on the business.

🛏 Sleeping

⭐ **Hoanib Skeleton Coast Camp** LODGE $$$
(☏ 061-225178; www.wilderness-safaris.com; s/d all-inclusive high season N$16,350/26,100, rates vary rest of year; 🌐) Now here's something special. So far from the nearest publicly accessible road, and built in a splendid amalgam of canopied canvas and light woods, this uber-luxurious tented camp is one of the most beautiful places to stay in Namibia. With a more contemporary look than many safari camps in the region, and all the better

for it, Hoanib exudes light and space and end-of-the-earth romance.

Desert elephants, lions, gemsboks, giraffes, ostriches. They're all here, but the landscape is every bit as memorable as the wildlife.

ℹ Getting There & Away

The Skeleton Coast Wilderness Area is closed to private vehicles. Access is restricted to fly-in trips.

CENTRAL NAMIBIA

Central Namibia zeroes in on the tourist trade but it does so Namibian-style offering epic road journeys, big skies and mesmerising landscapes. In that sense it's not unlike other parts of the country – except here it is home to two large cities and a spectacular desert.

Walvis Bay and Swakopmund were originally established as port towns during the colonial era. The drive into them defines their surreal nature as desert wildernesses, which is magically replaced by (in the case of Swakopmund) a Germanic urban landscape that would be a colonial relic if it weren't for the life and energy brought to bear by a thriving tourist industry.

The region is defined by the Namib Desert, a barren and desolate landscape of undulating apricot-coloured dunes interspersed with dry pans. Indeed, the Nama word 'Namib', which inspired the name of the entire country, rather prosaically means 'vast dry plain'. Nowhere is this truer than at Sossusvlei, Namibia's most famous strip of sand, where gargantuan dunes tower more than 300m above the underlying strata.

Swakopmund

POP 44,730 / ☏ 064

Sandwiched between Atlantic rollers and the Namib Desert, Swakopmund is one of those great traveller way stations along the African road. At once Namibia's adventure capital and a surreal colonial remnant, part destination in its own right and part launch pad for an exploration of the Skeleton Coast and Namib Desert, this is a city with as much personality as it has sea frontage. Like Lüderitz on the south coast, the half-timbered German architecture, seaside promenades and the town's pervasive Gemütlichkeit, a distinctively German appreciation of comfort and hospitality, Swakopmund, especially out of season, can feel like a holiday town along Germany's North Sea and Baltic coasts transplanted onto African soil. But the city is also thoroughly African and its multi-dimensional appeal means that most people end up staying longer than they planned.

History

Small bands of Nama people have occupied the Swakop River mouth from time immemorial. The first permanent European settlers were Germans who didn't arrive until early 1892. Because nearby Walvis Bay had been annexed by the British-controlled Cape Colony in 1878, Swakopmund remained German South West Africa's only harbour, and consequently rose to greater prominence than its poor harbour conditions would have

otherwise warranted. Early passengers were landed in small dories, but after the pier was constructed, they were winched over from the ships in basket-like cages.

Construction began on the first building, the Alte Kaserne (Old Barracks), in September 1892. By the following year it housed 120 Schutztruppe (German Imperial Army) soldiers, and ordinary settlers arrived soon after to put down roots. The first civilian homes were prefabricated in Germany and then transported by ship. By 1909, Swakopmund had officially become a municipality.

The port emerged as the leading trade funnel for all of German South West Africa and attracted government agencies and transport companies. During WWI however, South West Africa was taken over by South Africa, and the harbour was allowed to silt up as maritime operations moved to nearby Walvis Bay. Strangely enough, this ultimately turned Swakopmund into a holiday resort, which is why the city is generally more pleasant on the eye than the industrial-looking Walvis Bay.

◉ Sights

Alte Gefängnis (Old Prison) HISTORIC BUILDING
(Nordring St) This impressive 1909 structure, on Nordring St, was built as a prison, but if you didn't know this, you'd swear it was either an early train station or a health-spa hotel. The main building was used only for staff housing, while the prisoners were relegated to much less opulent quarters on one side.

Bahnhof (Railway Station) HISTORIC BUILDING
This ornate railway station, built in 1901 as the terminal for the Kaiserliche Eisenbahn Verwaltung (Imperial Railway Authority), connected Swakopmund to Windhoek. In 1910, when the railway closed down, the building assumed the role as main station for the narrow-gauge mine railway between Swakopmund and Otavi.

Deutsche-Afrika Bank Building ARCHITECTURE
(near cnr Woermann & Moltke Sts) Swakopmund brims with numerous historic examples of traditional German architecture. The handsome neo-classical Deutsche-Afrika Bank Building was opened in 1909 as a branch office of the Deutsche-Afrika Bank. It's now a functioning Bank of Windhoek branch.

Swakopmund

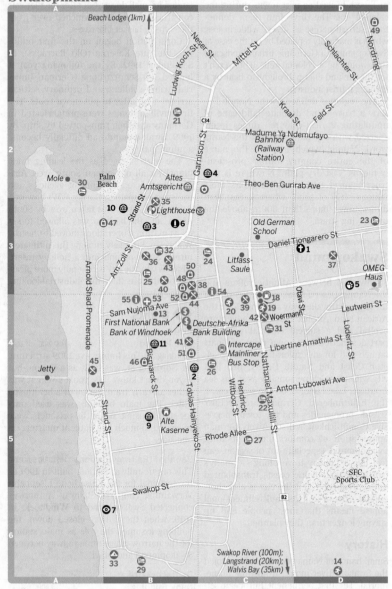

Beach Lodge (1km)

Neser St

Ludwig Koch St

Mittel St

Schlachter St

Nordring

49

Kraal St

Feld St

Garnison St

C34

21

Madume Ya Ndemufayo
Bahnhof
(Railway
Station)

Theo-Ben Gurirab Ave

Mole

30

Palm
Beach

Strand St

Altes
Amtsgericht

4

10

35

Lighthouse

Old German
School

23

47

3

6

Am Zoll St

Daniel Tjongarero St

1

Arnold Shad Promenade

32

36

43

25

40

48

50

24

Litfass-
Saule

37

OMEG
Haus

5

55

53

52

38

54

16

18

19

Otavi St

Leutwein St

Sam Nujoma Ave

13

First National Bank
Bank of Windhoek

20

39

42

Woermann
St

31

Luderitz St

Deutsche-Afrika
Bank Building

Libertine Amathila St

Jetty

45

11

41

51

46

Intercape
Mainliner
Bus Stop

26

2

Bismarck St

Tobias Hainyeko St

Hendrick
Witbooi St

Nathaniel Maxuilili St

Anton Lubowski Ave

17

22

9

Alte
Kaserne

Rhode Allee

27

Strand St

SFC
Sports
Club

B2

Swakop St

7

33

29

Swakop River (100m);
Langstrand (20km);
Walvis Bay (35km)

14

NAMIBIA SWAKOPMUND

Hohenzollern Building HISTORIC BUILDING
(Libertine Amathila St) This imposing baroque-
style building was constructed in 1906 to
serve as a hotel. Its rather outlandish decor is
crowned by a fibreglass cast of Atlas supporting the world, which replaced the precarious
cement version that graced the roof prior to
renovations in 1988.

★ **Jetty** LANDMARK
In 1905 the need for a good cargo- and
passenger-landing site led Swakopmund's

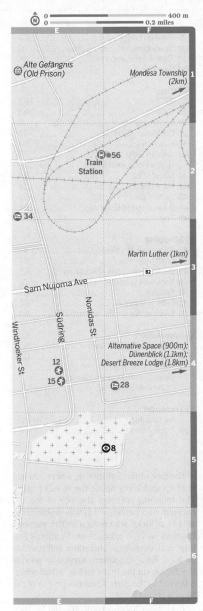

founders to construct the original wooden pier. In the years that followed, it was battered by the high seas and damaged by woodworm, and in 1911 construction began on a 500m iron jetty. When the South African forces occupied Swakopmund, the port became redundant (they already controlled Walvis Bay), so the old wooden pier was removed in 1916, and the unfinished iron pier – a starkly beautiful thing – was left to the elements.

Kaiserliches Bezirksgericht
(State House) HISTORIC BUILDING
(Daniel Tjongarero St) This rather stately building was constructed in 1902 to serve as the district magistrates' court. It was extended in 1905, and again in 1945 when a tower was added. After WWI it was converted into the official holiday home of the territorial administrator. In keeping with that tradition, it's now the official Swakopmund residence of the president.

Kristall Galerie GALLERY
(☑ 064-406080; cnr Garnison St & Theo-Ben Gurirab Ave; N$30; ☺9am-5pm Mon-Sat) This architecturally astute gallery features some of the planet's most incredible crystal formations, including the largest quartz crystal that has ever been found. The adjacent shop sells lovely mineral samples, crystal jewellery, and intriguing plates, cups and wine glasses that are carved from local stone.

Marine Memorial MONUMENT
(Marine Denkmal; Daniel Tjongarero St) Often known by its German name, Marine Denkmal, this memorial was commissioned in 1907 by the Marine Infantry in Kiel, Germany, and designed by sculptor AM Wolff. It commemorates the German First Marine Expedition Corps that helped beat back the Herero uprisings of 1904. As a national historical monument, it will continue to stand, but one has to wonder how long it will be before the Herero erect a memorial of their own.

Moon Landscape VIEWPOINT
If you're on a quest to see weltwitschias, continue east along the Weltwitschia Drive to the Moon Landscape, a vista across eroded hills and valleys carved by the Swakop River. Here you may want to take a quick 12km return side-trip north to the farm and oasis of **Goanikontes**, which dates from 1848. It lies beside the Swakop River amid fabulous desert mountains, and serves as an excellent picnic site.

★National Marine Aquarium AQUARIUM
(☑064-4101214; Strand St; adult/child N$40/20; ☺10am-4pm Tue-Sun) This recently overhauled waterfront aquarium provides an

Swakopmund

excellent introduction to the cold offshore world in the South Atlantic Ocean. Most impressive is the tunnel through the largest aquarium, which allows close-up views of graceful rays, toothy sharks (you can literally count the teeth!) and other little marine beasties.

Old German Cemetery CEMETERY

It's worth having a quick wander past the historical cemeteries beside the Swakop River. The neatly manicured Old German Cemetery dates from the colonial era, and the tombstones, which are still maintained by resident families, tell countless stories.

Swakopmund Museum MUSEUM

(☎ 064-402046; Strand St; adult/student N$30/15; ☉ 8am-1pm & 3-5pm Mon-Fri, 10am-noon Sat) When ill winds blow, head for this museum

at the foot of the lighthouse, where you can hole up and learn about the town's history. The museum occupies the site of the old harbour warehouse, which was destroyed in 1914 by a 'lucky' shot from a British warship. Displays include exhibits on Namibia's history and ethnology, including information on local flora and fauna. Especially good is the display on the !nara melon, a fruit which was vital to the early Khoikhoi people of the Namib region.

It also harbours a reconstructed colonial home interior, Emil Kiewittand's apothecary shop and an informative display on the Rössing Mine. Military buffs will appreciate the stifling uniforms of the Camel Corps and the Shell furniture, so called because it was homemade from 1930s depression-era petrol and paraffin tins.

Woermannhaus HISTORIC BUILDING
(Bismarck St) From the shore, the delightful German-style Woermannhaus stands out above surrounding buildings. Built in 1905 as the main offices of the Damara & Namaqua Trading Company, it was taken over four years later by the Woermann & Brock Trading Company, which supplied the current name. In the 1920s, it was used as a school dormitory and later served as a merchant sailors' hostel. It eventually fell into disrepair, but was declared a national monument and restored in 1976.

Alte Kaserne FORTRESS
(Anton Lubowski Ave) The imposing, fort-like Alte Kaserne was built in 1906 by the railway company, and now houses the Hostelling International Youth Hostel.

Altes Amtsgericht HISTORIC BUILDING
This gabled building, on the corner of Garnison and Bahnhof Sts, was constructed in 1908 as a private school. When the funds ran out, the government took over the project and requisitioned it as a magistrates' court. In the 1960s it functioned as a school dormitory, and now houses municipal offices. Just so no one can doubt its identity, the words 'Altes Amtsgericht' (German for 'Old Magistrates' Court') are painted across the front.

German Evangelical
Lutheran Church CHURCH
(Daniel Tjongarero Av) This neo-baroque church was built in 1906 to accommodate the growing Lutheran congregation of Dr Heinrich Vedde – it still holds regular services.

Lighthouse LIGHTHOUSE
(Strand St) This operational lighthouse, an endearing Swakopmund landmark just off Strand St, was constructed in 1902. It was originally built 11m high, but an additional 10m was added in 1910.

Litfass-Saule ARCHITECTURE
(cnr Daniel Tjongarero & Nathaniel Maxulili Sts) In 1855, the Berlin printer Litfass came up with the notion of erecting advertising pillars on German street corners. For the citizens of early Swakopmund, they became a common source of information and advertising. The remaining example of this local curiosity, Litfass-Saule, sits on the corner of Daniel Tjongarero and Nathaniel Maxulili Sts.

Living Desert Snake Park ZOO
(☑064-405100; Sam Nujoma Ave; N$30; ⊘8am-5pm Mon-Fri, 9am-1pm Sat) This park houses an array of serpentine sorts. The owner knows everything you'd ever want to know – or not know – about snakes, scorpions, spiders and other widely misunderstood creatures.

Mole LANDMARK
In 1899, architect FW Ortloff's sea wall (better known as the Mole) was intended to enhance Swakopmund's poor harbour and create a mooring place for large cargo vessels. But Mr Ortloff was unfamiliar with the Benguela Current, which sweeps northwards along the coast, carrying with it a load of sand from the southern deserts. Within less than five years, the harbour entrance was choked off by a sand bank.

Two years later the harbour itself had been invaded by sand to create what is now called Palm Beach. The Mole is currently used as a mooring for pleasure boats.

OMEG Haus HISTORIC BUILDING
(Sam Nujoma Ave) Thanks to the narrow-gauge railway to the coast, the colonial company Otavi Minen und Eisenbahn Gesellschaft (OMEG), which oversaw the rich Otavi and Tsumeb mines, also maintained their office in Swakopmund. Known as OMEG Haus, it is a historic example of traditional German architecture.

Old German School ARCHITECTURE
(Post St) The 1912 baroque-style Old German School was the result of a 1912 competition, which was won by budding German architect Emil Krause.

Prinzessin Rupprecht Heim HISTORIC BUILDING
(Lazarett St) The single-storey Prinzessin Rupprecht Heim, on Lazarett St, was constructed in 1902 as a military hospital. In 1914 it was transferred to the Bavarian Women's Red Cross, which named it after its patron, Princess Rupprecht, wife of the Bavarian crown prince. The idea was to expose convalescents to the healthy effects of the sea breeze. The building currently operates as a hotel.

🏃 Activities
Adventure sports and Swakopmund go hand in hand. From quad biking up the crest of a soaring seaside dune to jumping out of a plane at 3000m, Swakop is one of the top destinations in Southern Africa for extreme-sports enthusiasts. Although filling your days with adrenaline-soaked activities is certainly not cheap, there are few places in the world where you can climb

up, sandboard down and soar over towering sand dunes.

Most activity operators don't have offices in town, which means that you need to arrange all of your activities through either your accommodation or the Namib-i (p303) tourist information centre.

★ **Alter Action**   ADVENTURE SPORTS
(☑ 064-402737; www.alter-action.info; lie down/stand up US$40/55) Sandboarding with Alter Action is certain to increase your heart rate. If you have any experience snowboarding or surfing, it's highly recommended that you have a go at the stand-up option. You will be given a snowboard, gloves, goggles and enough polish to ensure a smooth ride.

While you can't expect the same speeds as you would on the mountain, you can't beat the experience of carving a dune face, and falling on sands hurts a lot less than ice! The lie-down option (which makes use of a greased-up sheet of Masonite) requires much less finesse but is equally fun. The highlight is an 80km/h 'schuss' down a 120m mountain of sand, which finishes with a big jump at the end. Slogging up the dunes can be rather taxing work, so you need to be physically fit and healthy.

Trips depart in the morning and last for approximately four hours. The price includes the equipment rental, pick-up, transport to and from the dunes, instruction, lunch and either a beer or soft drink upon completion.

★ **Ground
Rush Adventures**   ADVENTURE SPORTS
(☑ 064-402841; www.skydiveswakop.com.na; tandem jumps N$2500, handycam/professional video N$500/900) Ground Rush Adventures provides the ultimate rush, and skydiving in Swakopmund is sweetened by the outstanding dune and ocean backdrop. The crew at Ground Rush has an impeccable safety record to date, and they make even the most nervous participant feel comfortable about jumping out of a plane at 3000m and freefalling for 30 seconds at 220km/h.

The price also includes a 25-minute scenic flight in a tiny Cessna aircraft, which provides striking views of the coastline between Swakop and Walvis Bay to the south. It is worth pointing out that the ascent can often be the scariest part, especially if you're afraid of flying (though it certainly makes the jump that much easier!). If you want physical evidence of your momentary lapse of reason,

there are two photo/video options available: one is a handycam strapped to your tandem master, while the other is a professional photographer jumping out of the plane alongside you and filming the entire descent. Have a light breakfast – you'll thank us later!

Living Desert Tours   WILDLIFE
(☑ 081 127 5070, 064-405070; www.livingdesert namibia.com; half-day tours N$650) Get up close and personal with the Namib's fascinating wildlife on this excellent 4WD excursion. You'll go in search of the transparent Namib dune gecko, legless lizards, sidewinder snakes and other desert-adapted species.

Okakambe Horse Stables   HORSE RIDING
(☑ 064-405258, 081 124 6626; www.okakambe.iway. na; 1-/2-hr ride N$650/820) Meaning 'horse' in the local Herero and Oshivambo languages, Okakambe specialises in horse riding and trekking through the desert. The German owner cares immensely for her horses, so you can be assured that they're well fed and looked after. Discounts are available for larger groups and longer outings, while more experienced riders can organise multiday treks. You'll find it 12km east of Swakopmund on the D1901.

★ **Pleasure Flights**   SCENIC FLIGHTS
(☑ 064-404500; www.pleasureflights.com.na; prices vary) One of the most reputable light-plane operators in Namibia, Pleasure Flights has been offering scenic aerial cruises for almost 20 years. Given so much of Namibia's South Atlantic coastline is inaccessible on the ground, this is a fabulous way to get a glimpse. Destinations include the Salt Works, Sandwich Harbour, Welwitschia Drive, the Brandberg Mountains, Sossusvlei, the Skeleton Coast and beyond.

Prices start at around N$900 per person for a one-hour circuit, though prices are dependent on the length of the flight and the number of passengers on board, as well as the fluctuating price of aviation fuel. Generally speaking, if you can put together a large group, and you spring for the longer flight, you will get much better value for your dollars. Regardless, chartering a private plane is a privileged experience that is well worth the splurge, and there are few places in the world that can rival the beauty and grandeur of Central Namibia.

Swakop Cycle Tours   CYCLING
(☑ 081 251 5916; www.swakopcycletours.com; bicycle/walking tours from N$380/285, bicycle

rental per half-/full day N$195/255; ⊙9am & 2pm) Visit the local Mondesa township to see how locals live as part of this 3½-hour cycle tour. Prices include a guide, bike and helmet rental, and local food tasting. It also arranges 2½-hour city walking tours and bicycle rental.

Batis Birding Safaris   BIRDWATCHING
(☑081 639 1775, 064-404908; www.batisbirding safaris.com; prices vary) Full- and half-day birding safaris into the surrounding desert are what Batis do best; they also run night wildlife walks and other eco-excursions. They're the people to help you track down the elusive dune lark, Karoo eremomela and other local specialties; there's a detailed list of possible sightings for each tour on their website.

Desert Explorers   ADVENTURE SPORTS
(☑064-406096;   www.namibiadesertexplorers. com; prices vary) They can organise just about anything here, but the specialty is quad biking in the dunes.

Outback Orange   ADVENTURE SPORTS
(☑064-400968;   www.outback-orange.com;   42 Nathaniel Maxuilili St; quad bikes 1-/2-hr N$400/600) Outback Orange offers stomach-dropping tours on quad bikes through the enormous dune field adjacent to Swakop. If you've ever wanted to re-create the *Star Wars* experience of riding a speeder through the deserts of Tatooine, this is your chance! In two hours, you'll travel over 60km and race up and down countless dunes, all the while enjoying panoramic views of sand and sea.

These tours are definitely not for the weak-hearted as you can pick up some serious speed on these bikes, and there are plenty of hairpin turns and sheer drops to contend with throughout the trip.

Swakopmund Camel Farm   ADVENTURE SPORTS
(☑064-400363; www.swakopmundcamelfarm.com; adult/teenager/child per 20min ride N$150/100/75) If you want to live out all of your *Lawrence of Arabia*–inspired desert fantasies, visit this camel farm, off the D1901,12km east of Swakopmund. After donning the necessary amount of Bedouin kitsch, you can mount your dromedary and make haste for the horizon.

While camels run the gamut from uncouth to downright mean-tempered, don't underestimate their speed and grace! A camel galloping in full stride can cover an enormous distance, and their unique physiology

---

TREKKOPJE MILITARY CEMETERY

In January 1915, after Swakopmund was occupied by South African forces, the Germans retreated and cut off supplies to the city by damaging the Otavi and State railway lines. However, the South Africans had already begun to replace the narrow-gauge track with a standard-gauge one, and at Trekkopje, their crew met German forces. When the Germans attacked their camp on 26 April 1915, the South Africans defended themselves with guns mounted on armoured vehicles and won easily. All fatalities of this battle are buried in the Trekkopje cemetery – 112km northeast of Swakopmund along the B2 – which is immediately north of the railway line, near the old train station.

justifiably earns them the nickname 'ships of the deserts'.

☞ Tours

If you've arrived in Swakopmund by public transport, and don't have access to a private vehicle, then consider booking a tour through a recommended operator. Central Swakop is compact and easily walkable, but you need to escape the city confines if you really want to explore the area.

Prices are variable depending on the size of your party and the length of tour. As with activities in Swakop, money stretches further if you get together with a few friends and combine a few destinations to make a longer outing.

Possible tours include the Cape Cross seal colony, Rössing Mine gem tours, Welwitschia Drive, Walvis Bay Lagoon, and various destinations in the Namib Desert and Naukluft Mountains.

The most popular operators are Charly's Desert Tours (p296), Namib Tours and Safaris (p296) and Turnstone Tours (p297). With the exception of Charly's, most operators do not have central offices, so it's best to make arrangements through your accommodation.

If you're interested in arranging a visit to the Mondesa township, Hafeni Cultural Tours (p296) runs a variety of different excursions that provide insight into how the other half of Swakopmunders live.

Charly's Desert Tours ADVENTURE
(☑ 064-404341; www.charlysdeserttours.com; Sam Nujoma Ave) One of the most popular (and reputable) of the day- and multi-day tour operators. It offers sundowners on the dunes and excursions to the Cape Cross seal colony, Rössing Mine, the Welwitschia Drive, Walvis Bay Lagoon and the Namib Desert.

★ **Hata Angu Cultural Tours** CULTURAL
(☑ 081 124 6111; www.culturalactivities.in.na; tours from N$400; ☉ 10am & 3pm) These four-hour tours are a refreshing change from your typical Swakop adventure. Here you'll meet an African herbalist, try home-made local dishes, drink at a local shebeen in a Swakop township and even shake hands with a chief. They can also organise sandboarding.

Swakop Tour Company TOURS
(☑ 081 124 2906; www.swakoptour.com; 3-/5-hr tours N$650/900) George Erb runs these excellent natural-history excursions with an emphasis on photography. Possibilities include the five-hour Klipspringer Canyon Tour or three-hour Dunes Tour with other excursions further afield.

Swakopmund Walking Tours WALKING
(☑ 064-461647; www.swakopmund-stadtfuhrungen. com; per person N$300) Billed as 'a walk through Swakopmund's history', these excellent two-hour walking tours run by Angelica Flamm-Schneeweiss give an overview of the city's history and bring it alive with colourful stories. Swakopmund Museum is the meeting point.

★ **Tommy's Living Desert Tours** WILDLIFE
(☑ 081 128 1038; www.livingdeserttours.com.na; half/full day N$700/1350) We like this half-day tour into the nearby sand dunes in search of desert wildlife – it gives a much more intimate picture of the desert than is possible while sandboarding or quad biking. Tommy, who picks you up from your hotel, is an engaging host. If you're lucky, you'll see the Namaqua chamaeleon, Peringuey's adder (sidewinder), the sand-diving lizard and all manner of scorpions and reptiles.

Tommy also does a full-day tour.

Hafeni Cultural Tours CULTURAL TOUR
(☑ 081 146 6222, 064-400731; hafenictours@ gmail.com; 4hr tour N$450) If you're interested in arranging a visit to the Mondesa township, Hafeni Cultural Tours runs a variety of different excursions that provide insight into how the other half of Swakopmunders live. It also offers Himba cultural tours, and day excursions to Cape Cross, Spitzkoppe and the flamingos of Walvis Bay.

Namib Tours & Safaris SAFARI, ADVENTURE
(☑ 064-406038; www.namibia-tours-safaris.com; cnr Sam Nujoma Ave & Nathaniel Maxuilili St) Organises tours and safaris across southern Africa.

Ocean Adventures WILDLIFE
(☑ 081 240 6290; www.swakopadventures.com; off Strand St) Catamaran tours to see dolphins, as well as the Cape fur seals of Pelican Point. The tours are a nice alternative to all that land-based adrenaline action.

THE MARTIN LUTHER

In the desert 4km east of Swakopmund, a lonely and forlorn steam locomotive languished for several years. The 14,000kg machine was imported to Walvis Bay from Halberstadt in Germany in 1896 to replace the ox wagons used to transport freight between Swakopmund and the interior. However, its inauguration into service was delayed by the outbreak of the Nama-Herero wars, and in the interim its locomotive engineer returned to Germany without having revealed the secret of its operation.

A US prospector eventually got it running, but it consumed enormous quantities of locally precious water. It took three months to complete its initial trip from Walvis Bay to Swakopmund, and subsequently survived just a couple of short trips before grinding to a halt just east of town. Clearly this particular technology wasn't making life easier for anyone, and it was abandoned and dubbed the *Martin Luther*, in reference to the great reformer's famous words to the Diet of Reichstag in 1521: 'Here I stand. May God help me, I cannot do otherwise.'

Although the *Martin Luther* was partially restored in 1975, and concurrently declared a national monument, it continued to suffer from the ravages of nature. Fortunately, in 2005 students from the Namibian Institute of Mining and Technology restored the locomotive to its former grandeur. They also built a protective encasement that should keep the *Martin Luther* around at least for another century.

Open Space Tours TOURS
(📞 081 273 5330; norcoast@yahoo.com; Nathaniel Maxuilili St) Recommended half- and full-day tours to Cape Cross and the Skeleton Coast, as well as exploration of Weltwitschia.

Rössing Mine TOURS
(📞 064-402046; mine tours N$60) This mine, 55km east of Swakopmund, is the world's largest open-cast uranium mine. Three-hour mine tours leave at 10am on the first and third Friday of each month; book at least one day in advance at the Swakopmund Museum (tours depart from here). You can also arrange a visit through most tour companies.

Uranium was first discovered here in the 1920s by Peter Louw, though his attempts at developing the mine quickly failed. In 1965, the concession was transferred to Rio Tinto-Zinc, and comprehensive surveys determined that the formation measured 3km long and 1km wide. Ore extraction came on line in 1970, but didn't reach capacity for another eight years.

Rössing, with 2500 employees, is currently a major player in Swakopmund's economy. The affiliated Rössing Foundation provides an educational and training centre in Arandis, northeast of the mine, as well as medical facilities and housing for its Swakopmund-based workers. It has promised that the eventual decommissioning of the site will entail a massive clean-up, but environmentalists are tempering their enthusiasm about its environmental commitments until something is actually forthcoming.

Turnstone Tours ADVENTURE
(📞 064-403123; www.turnstone-tours.com; day tours from N$1550) Turnstone runs 4WD camping tours around Swakopmund, as well as day trips to Messum Crater, Cape Cross, Sandwich Harbour and elsewhere.

🛏 Sleeping

Swakopmund has a number of budget hotels and hostels that are of a high standard, as well as family-run guesthouses and B&Bs. There are also a handful of attractive mid-range and top-end hotels that are definitely worth the splurge.

Given Swakopmund's chilly climate, air-conditioning is absent at most hotels, though you won't miss it once the sea air starts blowing through your room. On the contrary, a heater is a requirement in the winter months when the mercury drops along the coast.

During the school holidays in December and January, accommodation books up well in advance – make reservations as early as possible.

Desert Sky Backpackers HOSTEL $
(📞 064-402339; www.desertskylodging.com; Anton Lubowski Ave; camping/dm N$160/200, d N$650, with shared bathroom N$600; @) This centrally located backpackers haunt is an excellent place to drop anchor in Swakopmund. The indoor lounge is simple and homey, while the outdoor picnic tables are a nice spot for a cold beer and warm conversation. Free coffee is available all day, and you're within stumbling distance of the pubs if you want something stronger.

Swakop Lodge HOSTEL $
(📞 064-402030; 42 Nathaniel Maxuilili St; dm/s/d N$150/450/650; ❄@🛜) This backpacker-orientated hotel is the epicentre of the action in Swakopmund, especially since this is where many of the adrenaline activities depart from and return to, and where many of the videos are screened each night. The hotel is extremely popular with overland trucks, so it's a safe bet that the attached bar is probably bumping and grinding most nights of the week.

Tiger Reef Campsite CAMPGROUND $
(📞 064-400935, 081 380 6014; camping per site N$250, plus per person N$100) This campsite sits right on the sand at the beach front, sheltered from the wind by lovely tamarisk trees. It's convenient to the city centre.

Alternative Space GUESTHOUSE $
(📞 064-402713; www.thealternativespace.com; 167 Anton-Lubowski St; s/d incl breakfast from N$600/900; @) Out on the desert fringe, 800m east of town, this delightfully alternative place is run by Frenus and Sybille Rorich. The main attractions are the castle-like architecture (or 'erotic architecture' as they call it...), saturation artwork and an industrial scrap-recycling theme. Be advised that this is most definitely not a party place.

Villa Wiese B&B $
(📞 064-407105; www.villawiese.com; cnr Theo-Ben Gurirab Ave & Windhoeker St; dm/s/d N$185/450/650; @) Villa Wiese is a friendly and funky guest lodge occupying a historic colonial mansion complete with vaulted ceilings, rock gardens and period furniture. It draws

an eclectic mix of overlanders, backpackers and independent travellers, and serves as a slightly more sophisticated alternative to other budget-oriented options in town. The nearby Dunedin Star is its overflow property, and has similar costs and atmosphere.

Dunedin Star Guest House GUESTHOUSE $

(☑064-407105; www.dunedinstar.com; cnr Daniel Tjongarero & Windhoeker Sts; s/d N$490/670) The overflow property for Villa Wiese.

Hotel Pension Rapmund GUESTHOUSE $

(☑064-402035; www.hotelpensionrapmund.com; 6-8 Bismarck St; s/d N$702/960, luxury r N$1404; 🛜) Overlooking the park promenade and much better than it looks from the outside, this long-standing hotel pension has light and airy rooms that are adorned with rich woods and plenty of African and German-inspired flourishing to create an attractive accommodation spot. The location is on the money and some rooms have terrific views.

Hotel-Pension d'Avignon GUESTHOUSE $

(☑064-405821; www.natron.net/tour/davignon/main.html; 25 Libertine Amathila St; s/d incl breakfast N$390/560; 🛜🍽) A great option close to town that won't break the budget, d'Avignon is a smart, well-run guesthouse that has been recommended by travellers. Triple rooms are also available and there's a TV lounge to collapse into in the evenings.

Sophiadale Base Camp CAMPGROUND, CHALET $

(☑064-403264; www.sophiadale.org; camping N$130, 2-person rondavels N$600; d incl breakfast N$700) Campsites here have large, shady trees and there are even sunroofs around the camping ground. Fireplaces and electrical powerpoints are big ticks, and the amenities block is scrubbed clean on a regular basis. Or if you feel like a roof over your head, upgrade to a large, solid rondavels which is basic, good value and comes with a braai area.

The camp is 12km east of town, take the turn off from the road to Windhoek.

★ Sea Breeze Guesthouse GUESTHOUSE $$

(☑064-463348; www.seabreeze.com.na; Turmalin St; s/d incl breakfast N$900/1285; @) This upmarket guesthouse is right on the beach about 4.5km north of town, and is an excellent option if you're looking for a secluded retreat. Ask to see a few of the rooms as several of them have spectacular sea views; and there's a great family room. There's plenty of advice available on what to see and do around town. Follow the Strand north and keep an eye out for signs.

Stiltz LODGE $$

(☑064-400771; www.thestiltz.com; Am Zoll; s/d from N$1260/1680) Balanced atop 3.5m-high stilts with a bird's-eye view over the coast and town, the Stiltz is unlike anywhere else in Swakopmund. The rooms vary in size and design – some are slightly cavernous, others are warm and perfectly proportioned – but it's the views that will live longest in the memory.

Swakopmund Luxury Suites HOTEL $$

(☑064-463298; www.swakopmundluxurysuites.com; Tobias Hainyeko St; s/d N$975/1500; 🛜) Classy, contemporary rooms dominate this fine, newish suites-only hotel just over a block back from the waterfront. The rooms are large and the white-linen, steely-grey aesthetic adds a sense of sophistication lacking in many other Swakopmund hotels.

Dünenblick APARTMENT $$

(☑064-463979; www.selfcatering-swakopmund.com; Riverside Ave; s/d N$1000/1200; 🛜) Ideal for families, these split-level apartments overlooking the sand and sea have kitchens, ample space and, at the very least, partial views of the sand dunes.

Prinzessin Rupprecht Residenz HOTEL $$

(☑064-412540; http://en.hotel-prinzessin-rupprecht.com; 15 Anton Lubowski Ave; s/d from N$660/1080, s with shared bathroom N$370) This place has 24 rooms, so you have a good chance of snagging accommodation here if you haven't booked ahead. Housed in the former colonial military hospital, the hotel appeals to history buffs looking to catch a glimpse of the Swakopmund of old. The interior has been largely retained, and you can still stroll along the hospital corridors and try to picture the building's former life.

★ Atlantic Villa BOUTIQUE HOTEL $$

(☑064-463511; www.atlantic-villa.com; Plover St; s/d N$980/1380, with sea view N$1200/1720, ste N$2100/2940) Styling itself as a boutique guesthouse, Atlantic Villa is a stylish place. Expect clean-lined rooms decked all in white and Nespresso coffee machines; many rooms have ocean views. In the northern part of town, it's also blissfully quiet.

★ Sam's Giardino Hotel HOTEL $$

(☑064-403210; www.giardinonamibia.com; 89 Anton Lubowski Ave; s/d from N$1000/1500;

🖕✉) Sam's Giardino Hotel is a wonderfully personal place in the backstreets emphasising superb wines, fine cigars and relaxing in the rose garden with a friendly dog named Beethoven. There's a lovely front garden and a lot of common areas with books, and a grotto with stacks of wine bottles. The rooms are simple but very comfortable. Book ahead for the five-course dinner (N$280) and some wine tasting (N$190).

Sam, the Swiss owner, is a delight and a mine of local information.

Hansa Hotel   HOTEL $$
(📞064-414200; www.hansahotel.com.na; 3 Hendrick Witbooi St; s/d from N$1280/1810; 🖕✉)
Swakopmund's most established upmarket hotel bills itself as 'luxury in the desert'. Individually decorated rooms with lofty ceilings and picture windows are tasteful and elegant, though the highlight of the property is its classic dining hall with white-glove service, bone china, sterling silver and fine crystal stemware.

THE WONDERFUL WORLD OF WELTWITSCHIA

Among Namibia's many botanical curiosities, the extraordinary *Welwitschia mirabilis*, which exists only on the gravel plains of the northern Namib Desert from the Kuiseb River to southern Angola, is probably the strangest of all. It was first noted in 1859, when Austrian botanist and medical doctor Friedrich Welwitsch stumbled upon a large specimen east of Swakopmund.

Welwitschias

Despite their dishevelled appearance, welwitschias actually have only two long and leathery leaves, which grow from opposite sides of the cork-like stem. Over the years, these leaves are darkened in the sun and torn by the wind into tattered strips, causing the plant to resemble a giant wilted lettuce. Pores in the leaves trap moisture, and longer leaves actually water the plant's own roots by channelling droplets onto the surrounding sand.

Welwitschias have a slow growth rate, and it's believed that the largest ones, whose tangled masses of leaf strips can measure up to 2m across, may have been growing for up to 2000 years! However, most midsized plants are less than 1000 years old. The plants don't even flower until they've been growing for at least 20 years. This longevity is probably only possible because they contain some compounds that are unpalatable to grazing animals, although black rhinos have been known to enjoy the odd plant.

The plants' most prominent inhabitant is the yellow and black pyrrhocorid bug, which lives by sucking sap from the plant. It's commonly called the push-me-pull-you bug, due to its almost continuous back-to-back mating.

Welwitschia Drive

This worthwhile excursion by vehicle or organised tour is recommended if you want to see one of Namibia's most unusual desert plants, the welwitschia. Welwitschias reach their greatest concentrations on the Welwitschia Plains east of Swakopmund, near the confluence of the Khan and Swakop Rivers, where they're the dominant plant species.

In addition to this wilted wonder itself, Welwitschia Drive also takes in grey and black lichen fields, which were featured in the BBC production *The Private Life of Plants*. It was here that David Attenborough pointed out these delightful examples of plant-animal symbiosis, which burst into 'bloom' with the addition of fog droplets. If you're not visiting during a fog, sprinkle a few drops of water on them and watch the magic.

Further east is the **Moon Landscape** (p291), a vista across eroded hills and valleys carved by the Swakop River. Here you may want to take a quick 12km return side-trip north to the farm and oasis of **Goanikontes** (p291), which dates from 1848. It lies beside the Swakop River amid fabulous desert mountains, and serves as an excellent picnic site.

The Welwitschia Drive, which turns off the Bosua Pass route east of Swakopmund, lies inside the Dorob National Park. Most often visited as a day trip from Swakopmund, the drive can be completed in two hours, but allow more time to experience this other-worldly landscape.

For an alternative take on the experience, pick up the pamphlet 'The Weltwitschia Plains – A Scenic Drive' from the **NWR office** (p303) in Swakopmund.

Organic Square
Guest House   BOUTIQUE HOTEL **$$**
(www.guesthouse-swakopmund.com; Rhode Allee;
s/d N$965/1565; 🖎) Very much part of the new
wave of contemporary-styled boutique hotels
sweeping Swakopmund, Organic Square is
close to the city centre and gets that whole
minimalist sense of style down pat.

Beach Lodge   HOTEL **$$**
(🖳 064-414500; www.beachlodge.com.na; Stint St;
s/d from N$1190/1750; 🖎) This boat-shaped
place, which sits right on the sand about
1km north of town, allows you to watch the
sea through your very own personal port-
hole; not all rooms have sea views. Rooms
vary in size and amenities and some come
complete with windowside bath-tubs.

Brigadoon Bed & Breakfast   B&B **$$**
(🖳 064-406064; www.brigadoonswakopmund.
com; 16 Ludwig Koch St; s/d N$1105/1680; 🖎🞨)
This Scottish-run B&B occupies a pleasant
garden setting opposite Palm Beach. It re-
cently underwent a major refurbishment,
giving it stylish, contemporary rooms boast-
ing flat-screen TVs, minibars and brand
spanking new bathrooms. Each room also
has its own private patio area.

Schweizerhaus Hotel   HOTEL **$$**
(🖳 064-400331; www.schweizerhaus.net; 1 Bis-
marck St; s/d from N$840/1360; 🖎) Although
it's best known for the landmark institution
that is Cafe Anton, the Schweizerhaus Hotel
itself is also a class act. Standard but comfortable rooms benefit from fine views of the
beach and the adjacent lighthouse, which
lights up the sky when the heavy fog rolls
in from sea.

★**Desert Breeze Lodge**   LODGE **$$$**
(🖳 064-406236, 064-400771; www.desertbreeze
swakopmund.com; off B2; s/d from N$1570/2140)
The 12 luxury bungalows here are lovely,
modern and comfortable but it's the views
you come here for – set on Swakopmund's
southern outskirts but still close to the
centre, Desert Breeze has sweeping views
of the sand dunes from its perch above the
Swakop riverbed. The views are, quite sim-
ply, sublime.

Strand Hotel   HOTEL **$$$**
(🖳 064-411 4308; www.strandhotelswakopmund.
com; Strand St; r/ste per person from 1600/2200;
🖎) Overlooking Palm Beach, the new Strand
is the kind of upmarket hotel that the
Swakopmund waterfront has been crying

out for for decades; modern and professional with good service and attractive rooms.
It's not that the rooms are particularly original. But they are supremely comfortable,
most have sea views from their balconies
and it ticks most of the boxes for business
and leisure travellers alike.

✖ Eating

True to its Teutonic roots, Swakopmund's
restaurants have a heavy German influence,
though there's certainly no shortage of local
seafood and traditional Namibian favourites, as well as a surprising offering of truly cosmopolitan fare. While Windhoekers
might disagree, Swakopmund can easily
contend for the title of Namibia's culinary
capital.

Self-caterers can head for the well-
stocked supermarket on Sam Nujoma Ave
near the corner with Hendrick Witbooi St.
Most backpacker spots have kitchens on the
premises.

Die Muschel Art Cafe   CAFE **$**
(🖳 081 849 5984; off Tobias Hainyeko St, Brauhaus
Arcade; snacks & light meals N$26-50; ⊙ 9am-6pm
Mon-Fri, 8.30am-5pm Sat, 10am-5pm Sun) The
size of a postage stamp and cute as a button,
this fine little cafe next to the bookshop of
the same name does great coffee to go with
its oven-baked rolls and cupcakes. Enjoy it
all at one of the tables on the pedestrianised
street outside.

Raith's Gourmet   CAFE **$**
(Tobias Hainyeko St; snacks & mains N$20-
50; ⊙ 7am-5pm Mon-Fri, to 2pm Sat & Sun)
Very central and convenient and open all
weekend, this is a self-proclaimed bakery-
deli-bistro-gelateria (though 'bistro' might
be stretching it...) It's mainly a bakery with
fresh-made rolls and sandwiches for lunch,
and pies and pasties. Indulge in a croissant
and scrambled eggs for breakfast. There's
a good selection of meats and cheeses too
if you're self-catering or just planning a
picnic.

Cafe Anton   CAFE **$**
(🖳 064-400331; 1 Bismarck St; light meals
N$40-70; ⊙ 7am-7pm) This much-loved lo-
cal institution, located in Schweizerhaus
Hotel, serves superb coffee, *Apfelstrudel*,
Kugelhopf (cake with nuts and raisins),
Mohnkuchen (poppy seed cake), *Linzer-
torte* (cake flavoured with almond meal,
lemon and spices, and spread with jam)

and other European delights. The outdoor seating is inviting for afternoon snacks in the sun.

Garden Cafe
CAFE $

(off Tobias Hainyeko St; mains N$35-80; ☺8am-6pm Mon-Fri, to 3pm Sat, 11am-3pm Sun) Set in a nice little garden away from the main street, Garden Cafe has open-air tables and chairs, changing specials and freshly prepared cafe food including salads, wraps and burgers (desserts are yummy too). It's pleasantly topped off by friendly and efficient service. In winter the cafe is still in full swing with patrons huddled around tables basking in skinny shafts of sunlight.

Knitters among you will love the attached wool shop, but there's also a more standard craft shop as well.

Napolitana
ITALIAN $

(☑064-402773; 33 Nathaniel Maxuilili St; mains from N$45; ☺noon-2.30pm & 5-10pm) It's nothing special and the decor is where a mock Via Veneto meets the American Wild West, but Napolitana serves up surprisingly good pizza, pasta and desserts. A good, informal choice for families.

★22° South
ITALIAN $$

(☑064-400380; Strand St; mains N$80-190; ☺noon-2.30pm & 6-9.30pm Tue-Sun) Inside the ground floor of the lighthouse, this atmospheric place is run by an Italian-Namibian couple who prepare Swakopmund's best (and homemade) Italian food. It's a slightly more formal option than the many pizzerias around town, and the quality of the food is similarly elevated.

★Kücki's Pub
PUB FOOD $$

(☑064-402407; www.kuckispub.com; Tobias Hainyeko St; mains N$95-160) A Swakopmund institution, Kücki's has been in the bar and restaurant biz for a couple of decades. The menu is full of seafood and meat dishes alongside comfort food, and everything is well prepared. The warm and congenial atmosphere is a welcome complement to the food.

Fish Deli
SEAFOOD $$

(☑064-462979; www.fishdeli-swakopmund.com; 29 Sam Nujoma Ave; mains N$88-145; ☺9.30am-9.30pm Mon-Fri, 9.30am-1.30pm & 6-9.30pm Sat) Recommended by some locals as the best place for a seafood meal in town. It's a simple but clean setup inside and importantly the fish comes straight from the water to

your plate – no frozen stuff here. It also has a sushi menu.

Swakopmund Brauhaus
GERMAN $$

(☑064-402214; www.swakopmundbrauhaus.com; 22 Sam Nujoma Ave; mains N$75-125; ☺11am-2.30pm & 5-9.30pm Mon-Sat) This excellent restaurant and boutique brewery offers one of Swakopmund's most sought-after commodities, namely authentic German-style beer. And, so as not to break with tradition, feel free to accompany your frothy brew with a plate of mixed sausages, piled sauerkraut and a healthy dollop of spicy mustard.

Hansa Hotel Restaurant
INTERNATIONAL $$$

(☑064-400311; www.hansahotel.com.na; 3 Hendrick Witbooi St; mains N$100-245; ☺8am-9pm) It's hard to top history, and the Hansa Hotel is steeped in it. In the main dining hall at this classic colonial spot, you can indulge in culinary excesses and wash them down with a bottle from the extensive wine list. Lunch is served on the outside terrace while seafood and game meats are the specialities.

Tug
SEAFOOD $$$

(☑064-402356; www.the-tug.com; off Strand St; mains N$75-315; ☺5-10pm Mon-Thu, 6-10pm Fri, noon-3pm & 6-10pm Sat & Sun) Housed in the beached tugboat *Danie Hugo* near the jetty, the Tug is something of an obligatory destination for any restaurant-goer in Swakopmund. Regarded by many as the best restaurant in town, the Tug is an atmospheric, upmarket choice for meat and seafood, though a sundowner cocktail with the Angelfish burger in North African spices will do just fine.

Due its extreme popularity and small size, advance bookings are recommended.

Deutsches Haus
GERMAN $$$

(☑064-404896; www.hotel.na; 13 Luderitz St; mains lunch N$70-110, dinner N$90-160; ☺noon-10pm) The fine dining at Deutsches Haus takes place in the well-organised, upmarket country dining room or the bench seating out the front of the building. It's one of the best-run restaurants in town, as evidenced by the attentive and professional service. German dishes are freshly prepared and quickly served.

🛍 Shopping

Street stalls sell Zimbabwean crafts on the waterfront by the steps below Cafe Anton on Bismarck St.

Cosdef Arts & Crafts Centre ARTS & CRAFTS
(☑064-406122; www.cosdef.org.na; ⊘9am-5pm)
This worthy project supports local artisans and unemployed people by providing a shopfront for their work. The quality is high and the overall message, one of building sustainability in local communities, is one that deserves support. For an idea of what's available, check out https://namibiacraft-collections.wordpress.com or its Facebook page. Opening hours were in a state of flux at the time of writing, at least on weekends.

Die Muschel Book & Art Shop BOOKS
(☑064-402874; Hendrick Witbooi St; ⊘8.30am-6pm Mon-Fri, 8.30am-1pm & 4-6pm Sat, 10am-6pm Sun) Swakopmund's best bookshop, with German- and English-language books. Great for guides and maps. Esoteric works on art and local history are also available here.

Peter's Antiques ANTIQUES
(☑064-405624; www.peters-antiques.com; 24 Tobias Hainyeko St; ⊘9am-1pm & 3-6pm Mon-Fri, 9am-1pm & 4-6pm Sat, 4-6pm Sun) This place is an Ali Baba's cave of treasures, specialising in colonial relics, historic literature, West African art, politically incorrect German paraphernalia and genuine West African fetishes and other artefacts from around the continent.

Baraka Le Afrique ARTS & CRAFTS
(☑064-405081; cnr Bismarck & Libertine Amathila Sts; ⊘9am-6pm) Baraka has a quirky portfolio that ranges from pith helmets and a handful of antique African maps to *Tintin in the Congo* clocks and modern versions of colonial nostalgia homewares.

Karakulia Weavers HOMEWARES
(☑064-461415; www.karakulia.com.na; 2 Rakotoka St; ⊘9am-1pm & 2-5pm Mon-Fri, 9am-1pm Sat) This local carpet factory produces original and beautiful African rugs, carpets and wall hangings in karakul wool and offers tours of the spinning, dyeing and weaving processes.

Kirikara ARTS & CRAFTS
(☑064-463146; www.kirikara.com; Am Ankerplatz; ⊘9am-1pm & 2.30-5.30pm Mon-Sat) Handicrafts and homewares from across Africa make this shop a modern-day Aladdin's Cave of pottery, fabrics, jewellery, baskets, masks and statues and just about anything else that takes the owners' fancy. Not everything may be from Namibia, but it's guaranteed to be very desirable.

A TERN FOR THE WORSE

Around 90% of the world population of the tiny Damara tern, of which less than 2000 breeding pairs remain, are endemic to the open shores and sandy bays of the Namib coast from South Africa to Angola. Adult Damara terns, which have a grey back and wings, a black head and white breast, measure just 22cm long, and are more similar in appearance to swallows than to other terns.

Damara terns nest on the Namib gravel flats well away from jackals, hyenas and other predators, though their small size renders them incapable of carrying food for long distances. As a result, they must always remain near a food source, which usually consists of prawns and larval fishes.

When alarmed, Damara terns try to divert the threat by flying off screaming. Since the nest is usually sufficiently well camouflaged to escape detection, this is an effective behaviour. However, if the breeding place is in any way disturbed, the parent tern abandons the nest and sacrifices the egg or chick to the elements. The following year, it seeks out a new nesting site, but more often than not, it discovers that potential alternatives are already overpopulated by other species, which it instinctively spurns.

Over the past few seasons, this has been a serious problem along the Namib coast, mainly due to the proliferation of unregulated off-road driving along the shoreline between Swakopmund and Terrace Bay. This problem is further compounded by the fact that Damara terns usually hatch only a single chick each year. In recent years, the terns have failed to breed successfully, and if the current situation continues, they may well be extinct within just a few years.

Although the biggest risk to the Damara tern continues to be off-road drivers, the increase in tourist activities on the dunes is also taking its toll. One way of reducing the environmental impact of activities is for a company to operate in a confined area. When you're booking through a company, inquire about its conservation policies.

Craft Market
MARKET
(◷9am-5pm) Swakopmund's artisans and souvenir sellers have gathered together here all in the one place. It's worth a wander, although the quality varies, and there are an awful lot of carved-wood giraffes.

Swakopmunder Buchhandlung
BOOKS
(☏064-402613; Sam Nujoma Ave; ◷8.30am-5.30pm Mon-Fri, 8.30am-1pm Sat, 9.30am-12.30pm Sun) A wide selection of literature from various genres.

ⓘ Information

DANGERS & ANNOYANCES
Although the palm-fringed streets and cool sea breezes in Swakopmund are unlikely to make you tense, you should always keep your guard up in town. Regardless of how relaxed the ambience might be, petty crime unfortunately occurs.

If you have a private vehicle, be sure that you leave it all locked up with no possessions inside visible during the day. At night, you need to make sure you're parked in a gated parking lot and not on the street. Also, when you're choosing a hotel or hostel, be sure that the security precautions (ie an electric fence and/or a guard) are up to your standards. Finally, although Swakopmund is generally safe at night, it's best to stay in a group, and when possible, take a taxi to and from your accommodation.

EMERGENCY
Police (☏10111, 402431)

MEDICAL SERVICES
Bismarck Medical Centre (☏064-405000; cnr Bismarck St & Sam Nujoma Ave) To visit a doctor, go to this recommended centre.

MONEY
There are plenty of banks in the centre of town with ATMs; try around the corner of Tobias Hainyeko St and Sam Nujoma Ave.

POST
Main post office (Garnison St) Also sells telephone cards and offers fax services.

TOURIST INFORMATION
Namib-i (☏064-404827; Sam Nujoma Ave; ◷8am-1pm & 2-5pm Mon-Fri, 9am-1pm & 3-5pm Sat, 9am-1pm Sun) This tourist information centre is a very helpful resource. In addition to helping you get your bearings, it can also act as a booking agent for any activities and tours that happen to take your fancy.

NWR (NWR; ☏064-402172; www.nwr.com.na; Woermannhaus, Bismarck St; ◷8am-1pm & 2-5pm Mon-Fri, park permits only 8am-1pm Sat

& Sun) Like its big brother in Windhoek, this office sells Namib-Naukluft Park and Skeleton Coast permits, and can also make reservations for other NWR-administered properties around the country.

ⓘ Getting There & Away

AIR
Air Namibia (☏064-405123; www.airnamibia.com.na) has several flights a week between Windhoek's Eros Airport and Walvis Bay, from where you can easily catch a bus or taxi to Swakopmund.

BUS
There are twice weekly buses between Windhoek and Swakopmund (from N$200, five hours) on the **Intercape Mainliner** (p375) from the company's bus stop. You can easily book your tickets in advance online.

Also consider **Town Hopper** (☏064-407223; www.namibiashuttle.com), which runs private shuttle buses between Windhoek and Swakopmund (N$270), and also offers door-to-door pick-up and drop-off service.

Finally, combis (minibuses) run this route fairly regularly, and a ride between Windhoek and Swakopmund shouldn't cost more than N$120. Swakopmund is also a minor public-transport hub, serving various regional destinations, including Walvis Bay by combi, with fares averaging between N$25 and N$50.

CAR
Swakopmund is about 400km west of Windhoek on the B2, the country's main east–west highway. Paved roads connect Windhoek to Swakopmund and continue south to Walvis Bay, from where a predominantly gravel road continues to Sesriem, the base town for Sossusvlei. All of the above is accessible in a 2WD.

TRAIN
Very few travellers use **Trans-Namib** (☏061-298 1111; www.transnamib.com.na) trains, especially given the ease of bus travel and the fact that the trains take much longer.

The plush *Desert Express* (p378) 'rail cruise' runs to and from Windhoek.

Walvis Bay
POP 100,000 / ☏064
Walvis Bay (vahl-fis bay), 30km south of Swakopmund, is pleasant enough, particularly around the new waterfront development and along the esplanade. The town proper is not so compact and your own wheels make life a lot easier. It's a good

Walvis Bay

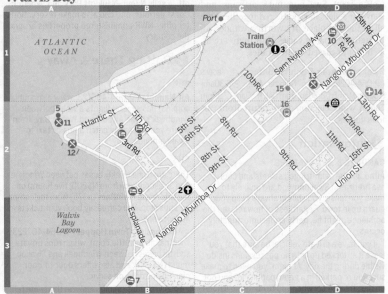

NAMIBIA WALVIS BAY

alternative to staying in Swakopmund if that city is too much of a scene for you – Walvis Bay has a far more relaxed feel to it. And the accommodation options and food choices are excellent.

Unlike Swakopmund, Walvis Bay was snatched by the British years before the German colonists could get their hands on it. As a result, Walvis Bay is architecturally uninspiring, and lacks the Old World ambience of its northerly neighbour. In marked contrast, the area around Walvis Bay is home to a number of unique natural attractions, including one of the largest flocks of flamingos in the whole of Southern Africa.

And this is the only real port between Lüderitz and Luanda (Angola). The natural harbour at Walvis Bay is the result of the sand spit Pelican Point, which forms a natural breakwater and shelters the city from the strong ocean surge.

History

Although Walvis Bay was claimed by the British Cape Colony in 1795, it was not formally annexed by Britain until 1878 when it was realised that the Germans were eyeing the harbour. In 1910 Britain relinquished its hold on Walvis Bay, and it became part of the newly formed Union of South Africa.

After the end of WWI, South African was given the UN madate to administer all of German South West Africa as well as the Walvis Bay enclave. This stood until 1977, when South Africa unilaterally decided to return it to the Cape Province. The UN was not impressed by this unauthorised act, and insisted that the enclave be returned to the mandate immediately. In response, South Africa steadfastly refused to bow.

When Namibia achieved its independence in 1990, Namibians laid claim to Walvis Bay. Given the strategic value of the natural harbour, plus the salt works (which produced 40,000 tonnes annually – some 90% of South Africa's salt), the offshore guano platforms and the rich fishery, gaining control over Walvis Bay became a matter of great importance for Namibia.

In 1992, after it had become apparent that white rule in South Africa was ending, the two countries agreed that South Africa would remove its border crossings, and that both countries would jointly administer the enclave. Finally, facing growing domestic troubles and its first democratic elections, South Africa gave in, and at midnight on 28 February 1994, the Namibian flag was raised over Walvis Bay for the first time.

Walvis Bay

◎ Sights
1	Bird Paradise	F2
2	Rhenish Mission Church	B2
3	The Hope	C1
4	Walvis Bay Museum	D2

◔ Activities, Courses & Tours
	Mola Mola Safaris	(see 11)
5	Sandwich Harbour 4x4	A2

⊟ Sleeping
6	Courtyard Hotel Garni	B2
7	Lagoon Lodge	B3
8	Langholm Hotel	B2
9	Oyster Box Guesthouse	B2
10	Remax	D1

⊗ Eating
11	Anchor @ The Jetty	A2
12	Raft	A2
13	Willi Probst Bakery & Cafe	D1

ⓘ Information
14	Welwitschia Medical Centre	D1

ⓘ Transport
15	Air Namibia	C1
16	Intercape Mainliner Bus Stop	C2

◎ Sights

Salt Works   BIRD SANCTUARY
Southwest of the lagoon is this 3500-hectare salt-pan complex, which currently supplies over 90% of South Africa's salt. As with the one in Swakopmund, these pans concentrate salt from seawater with the aid of evaporation. They are also a rich feeding ground for shrimp and larval fish. It's one of the three wetlands around Walvis Bay (along with the lagoon and Bird Island), which together form Southern Africa's single most important coastal wetland for migratory birds.

Bird Island   BIRD SANCTUARY
Along the Swakopmund road, 10km north of Walvis Bay, take a look at the offshore wooden platform known as Bird Island. It was built to provide a roost and nesting site for seabirds and a source of guano for use as fertiliser. The annual yield is around 1000 tonnes, and the smell from the island is truly unforgettable.

Bird Paradise   BIRD SANCTUARY
Immediately east of town at the municipal sewage-purification works is this nature sanctuary, which consists of a series of shallow artificial pools, fringed by reeds. An observation tower and a short nature walk

afford excellent birdwatching. It lies 500m east of town, off the C14 towards Rooikop airport. As with both other local wetlands, you can expect to see flamingos.

Dune 7   LANDMARK
In the bleak expanse just off the C14, 6km by road from town, Dune 7 is popular with locals as a slope for sandboarding and skiing. The picnic site, which is now engulfed by sand, has several shady palm trees tucked away in the lee of the dune.

Lagoon   LAGOON
The shallow and sheltered 45,000-hectare lagoon, southwest of town and west of the Kuiseb River mouth, attracts a range of coastal water birds and enormous flocks of lesser and greater flamingos. It also supports chestnut banded plovers and curlew sandpipers, as well as the rare Damara tern (p302).

Rhenish Mission Church   CHURCH
(5th Rd) Walvis Bay's oldest remaining building, the Rhenish Mission Church was prefabricated in Hamburg, Germany, reconstructed beside the harbour in 1880 and consecrated the following year. Because of machinery sprawl in the harbour area, it was relocated to its present site in

the mid-20th century, and functioned as a church until 1966.

The Hope
MONUMENT

During the winter, rail services between Swakopmund and Walvis Bay are often plagued by windblown sand, which covers the tracks and undermines the trackbed and sleepers. This isn't a new problem – 5km east of town on the C14, notice the embankment which has buried a section of narrow-gauge track from the last century. In front of the train station are the remains of the *Hope*, an old locomotive that once ran on the original narrow-gauge railway.

Both were abandoned after the line was repeatedly buried beneath 10m sand drifts. The *Hope* is now a national monument and stands on 6th St in front of the train station.

Lookout
VIEWPOINT

A good spot for getting an overview of the bird-rich ponds.

Port
HARBOUR

(☑064-208320) With permission from the public-relations officer of the Portnet or from the Railway Police – beside the train station near the end of 13th Rd – you can visit the fishing harbour and commercial port, and see the heavy machinery that keeps Namibia's import-export business ticking. Trust us, it's more interesting than it sounds. Don't forget to bring your passport.

Walvis Bay Museum
MUSEUM

(Nangolo Mbumba Dr; ⊙9am-5pm Mon-Thu, to 4.30pm Fri) The town museum is located in the library. It concentrates on the history and maritime background of Walvis Bay, but also has archaeological exhibits, a mineral collection and natural-history displays on the Namib Desert and the Atlantic Coast.

🏃 Activities

Sea-kayaking, boat trips, birdwatching and excursions to Sandwich Harbour (56km south) are all highlights of a visit to Walvis Bay. If that's not enough action for you, try Swakopmund to the north.

Mola Mola Safaris
BOATING

(☑081 127 2522, 064-205511; www.mola-namibia. com; Waterfront) This professional marine safari company offers fully customisable boating trips around the Walvis Bay and Swakopmund coastal areas, where you can expect to see dolphins, seals and countless birds. Prices are dependent on your group size and length of voyage, but the standard three-hour Marine Dolphin Cruise starts at N$620/420 per adult/child.

Sandwich Harbour 4x4
TOUR

(☑064-207663; www.sandwich-harbour.com; Waterfront; adult/child half-day N$1100/850, full day N$1300/1050) Sandwich Harbour 4x4 operates half- and full-day trips down to

---

FLAMINGOS AT WALVIS

Lesser and greater flamingos flock in large numbers to pools along the Namib Desert coast, particularly around Walvis Bay and Lüderitz. They're excellent fliers, and have been known to migrate up to 500km overnight in search of proliferations of algae and crustaceans.

The lesser flamingo filters algae and diatoms (microscopic organisms) from the water by sucking in and vigorously expelling water from its bill. The minute particles are caught on fine hairlike protrusions, which line the inside of the mandibles. The suction is created by the thick fleshy tongue, which rests in a groove in the lower mandible and pumps back and forth like a piston. It has been estimated that a million lesser flamingos can consume over 180 tonnes of algae and diatoms daily.

While lesser flamingos obtain food by filtration, the greater flamingo supplements its algae diet with small molluscs, crustaceans and other organic particles from the mud. When feeding, it will rotate in a circle while stamping its feet in an effort to scare up a tasty potential meal.

The greater and lesser flamingos are best distinguished by their colouration. Greater flamingos are white to light pink, and their beaks are whitish with a black tip. Lesser flamingos are a deeper pink – often reddish – colour, with dark-red beaks.

Located near Walvis Bay are three diverse wetland areas; the **lagoon** (p305), the **salt works** (p305) and the **Bird Paradise** (p305) at the sewage works.

Together they form Southern Africa's single most important coastal wetland for migratory birds, with up to 150,000 transient avian visitors stopping by annually, including massive flocks of both lesser and greater flamingos.

spectacular Sandwich Harbour. It also runs an excellent full-day Sandwich Harbour and sea-kayaking combo for N$1850/1350 per adult/child.

Eco Marine Kayak Tours   KAYAKING
(☑064-203144; www.emkayak.iway.na) Sea-kayaking trips around the beautiful Walvis Bay wetlands and beyond are conducted by this outfit. Note that there is no central office, though bookings can be made over the phone or through your accommodation.

🛏 Sleeping

Accommodation options are located either in the city centre, on the waterfront or at Langstrand (Long Beach), which is 10km north of Walvis Bay on the road to Swakopmund.

Self-catering is a good option in Walvis Bay with houses and apartments available both on the coast and in the city. A two-bedroom place can be found for around N$750; contact **Remax** (☑064-212451; www.remax.co.za; Sam Nujoma Ave).

Courtyard Hotel Garni   HOTEL $
(☑064-206252, 064-213600; 16 3rd Rd; s/d from N$450/550; @🛜🏊) This low-rise place in a quiet neighbourhood near the water has generous rooms that are a bit beaten around the edges – it's comfortable enough and there are nice common areas, but it's probably a tad overpriced in peak season (when rates are known to double) and the beds are quite small. Kitchenette useful for self-caterers. Guests can access the indoor heated pool and sauna.

Burning Shore   RESORT $$
(☑064-207568; www.marriott.com; 152 4th St; s/d from N$1100/1800; ✳🏊) At the Burning Shore, a secluded retreat (managed by the Protea/Marriott Hotel chain) with only a dozen rooms, you can soak up the beauty and serenity of the adjacent dunes and the ocean. Rooms are luxurious without being pretentious, which lends a relaxed elegance and cool sophistication to the entire property. It's 15km from Walvis Bay at Longbeach/Langstrand.

⭐Langholm Hotel   HOTEL $$
(☑064-209230; www.langholmhotel.com; 2nd St W; s/d from N$1070/1228) Getting consistently good reviews from travellers, the excellent Langholm sits on a quiet street a couple of blocks back from the water and satisfies both business and leisure travellers with professional service and stylish rooms

with strong colours and a contemporary aesthetic.

⭐Oyster Box Guesthouse   GUESTHOUSE $$
(☑064-202247, 061-249597; www.oysterboxhouse.com; cnr Esplanade & 2nd West; s N$865-1109, d N$1374-1730; ✳🛜) More like a classy boutique hotel, this guesthouse is a stylish affair right on the waterfront, a short walk from Raft restaurant. Rooms are very contemporary and bedding includes crisp sheets and fluffy pillows. Helpful staff can book activities for you around town and arrange transport. A lovely choice.

Lagoon Lodge   HOTEL $$
(☑064-200850; www.lagoonlodge.com.na; 2 Nangolo Mbumba Dr; s/d N$1090/1860; 🛜🏊) A garish yellow facade greets visitors to this French-run lodge which commands a magnificent location next to the lagoon, and features individually decorated rooms with private terraces facing out towards the sand and sea. As well as the heartfelt welcome, the free wireless and unbroken views over the water are highlights. The location on the promenade is handy for an evening/early morning walk along the waterfront.

🍴 Eating

The Waterfront area is a development claiming a cluster of bars and restaurants right on the water overlooking the harbour and the big machinery of the port not far away. It has a very genuine feel, unlike some of its counterparts in South Africa that have suffered from over-development. There's a small but classy selection of places to sit outside on the water's edge and enjoy a cold drink and a meal.

Willi Probst Bakery & Cafe   CAFE $
(☑064-202744; http://williprobstbakery.webs.com; cnr 12th Rd & 9th St; light meals N$25-60; ⏱6.30am-3pm Mon-Sat) If you're feeling nostalgic for Swakopmund (or Deutschland for that matter), take comfort in knowing that Probst specialises in stodgy German fare: pork, meatballs, schnitzel and the like, while pies and breakfast pizzas mix things up a little. A range of sweet treats ensures that it is everyone's friend.

⭐Anchor @ The Jetty   INTERNATIONAL $$
(☑064-205762; Esplanade, Waterfront; breakfast/mains from N$45/75; ⏱7.30am-10pm Tue-Sat, to 3pm Sun & Mon) The food is good at the Anchor but the real attraction is the location overlooking the water. It makes a particularly

lovely spot for breakfast, and if you're tired of eating stodgy food, it does a pretty mean fruit salad. Later on, seafood dominates things. Sit at a table right on the water and watch the morning cruise boats slink out of the bay.

★ **Raft**   SEAFOOD $$
(☑ 064-204877; theraftrestaurant.com; Esplanade; mains N$77-227; ☺ 11am-11pm Mon-Sat, to 2pm Sun) This Walvis Bay landmark sits on stilts offshore, and has a great front-row view of the ducks, pelicans and flamingos. Here you can expect high-quality meats and seafood in addition to spectacular sunsets and ocean views. The seafood extravaganza is well worth the extravagant N$367 price tag.

ⓘ Information

EMERGENCY
Police (☑ 10111; cnr 11th St & 13th Rd)

MEDICAL SERVICES
Welwitschia Medical Centre (13th Rd; ☺ 24hr).

POST
Post office (Sam Nujoma Ave) Provides public telephones and fax services.

ⓘ Getting There & Away

Air Namibia (☑ 064-203102; www.airnamibia. com.na) has around seven flights a week between Windhoek's Eros Airport and Walvis Bay's Rooikop Airport, located 10km southeast of town on the C14.

All buses and combis to Walvis Bay run via Swakopmund. The **Intercape Mainliner stop** is at the Spur Restaurant on Ben Gurirab St. There are also other private bus services running between Windhoek and Walvis Bay.

Hitching isn't difficult between Walvis Bay and Swakopmund, but weather conditions can be rough if heading for Namib-Naukluft Park or the Skeleton Coast.

Namib-Naukluft Park

Welcome to the Namib, the oldest desert on earth and certainly one of the most beautiful and accessible desert regions on the planet. This is sand-dune country par excellence, silent, constantly shifting and ageless, and an undoubted highlight of any visit to Namibia. The epicentre of its appeal is at Sossusvlei, Namibia's most famous strip of sand, where gargantuan dunes tower more than 300m above the underlying strata. Elsewhere, the land lives up to its name: the Nama word 'Namib' inspired the name of the entire

country and rather prosaically means 'Vast Dry Plain'. And then there are the Naukluft Mountains – barren and beautiful and filled with an appeal all of their own.

The **Namib-Naukluft National Park** (per person per day N$80, per vehicle N$10; ☺ sunrise-sunset) takes in around 23,000 sq km of arid and semi-arid land, and protects various areas of vast ecological importance in the Namib and the Naukluft. The park also abuts the NamibRand Nature Reserve, the largest privately owned property in Southern Africa, forming a massive wildlife corridor that promotes migratory movement.

Namib Section

While most people associate the Namib solely with Sossusvlei, the desert sweeps across most of Central Namibia, and is characterised by a large array of geological formations. Given the extremes of temperature and environment, you will need a 4WD vehicle and good navigation skills in order to properly explore the Namib. Truly, this is one place where the journey itself is worth as much, if not more, than the destination.

◉ Sights

Kuiseb Canyon   CANYON
On the Gamsberg Pass route west of the Khomas Hochland, Kuiseb Canyon contains the ephemeral Kuiseb River, which is no more than a broad sandy riverbed for most of the year. Although it may flow for two or three weeks during the rainy season, it only gets as far as Gobabeb before seeping into the sand. At Rooibank, drinking water for Walvis Bay is pumped from this subterranean supply.

It was in Kuiseb Canyon that the famous geologists Henno Martin and Hermann Korn went into hiding for more than two years during WWII, as recounted in Martin's book *The Sheltering Desert*. Today, the canyon's upper reaches remain uninhabited, though there are scattered Topnaar Khoikhoi villages where the valley broadens out near the north river bank.

Hamilton Hills   HILLS
The range of limestone hills known as the Hamilton Hills, south of Vogelfederberg campsite, rises 600m above the surrounding desert plains. It provides lovely desert hikes, and the fog-borne moisture supports an amazing range of succulents and other botanical wonders.

🛏 Sleeping

The Namib-Naukluft Park has eight exclusive camps, some of which have multiple but widely spaced campsites. Sites have tables, toilets and braai pits, but no washing facilities. Brackish water is available for cooking and washing but not drinking – bring enough water. All sites must be prebooked through Namibia Wildlife Resorts (NWR) in Windhoek (p230) or Swakopmund (p303). Camping costs N$170 per person (maximum of eight people) plus N$80/10 per person/car per day in park fees; fees are payable when the park permit is issued.

Bloedkoppie   CAMPGROUND $

(Blood Hill; camping N$170) These spots are among the most beautiful and popular sites in the park. If you're coming from Swakopmund, they lie 55km northeast of the C28, along a signposted track. The northern sites may be accessed with 2WD, but they tend to be more crowded. The southern sites are quieter and more secluded, but can be reached only by 4WD.

The surrounding area offers some pleasant walking, and at Klein Tinkas, 5km east of Bloedkoppie, you'll see the ruins of a colonial police station (basically a ruined hut) and the graves of two German police officers dating back to 1895.

Groot Tinkas   CAMPGROUND $

(camping N$170) Groot Tinkas must be accessed with 4WD and rarely sees much traffic. It enjoys a lovely setting beneath shady rocks and the surroundings are super for nature walks. During rainy periods, the brackish water in the nearby dam attracts a variety of birdlife.

Homeb   CAMPGROUND $

(camping N$170) Homeb is located in a scenic spot upstream from the most accessible set of dunes in the Namib-Naukluft Park, and can accommodate several groups. Residents of the nearby Topnaar Khoikhoi village dig wells in the Kuiseb riverbed to access water beneath the surface, and one of their dietary staples is the !nara melon (p319), which obtains moisture from the water table through a long taproot.

This hidden water also supports a good stand of trees, including camel thorn acacia and ebony.

Kuiseb Canyon   CAMPGROUND $

(camping N$170) Kuiseb Canyon is a shady site at the Kuiseb River crossing along the C14 and is also a convenient place to break up a trip between Windhoek and Walvis Bay. The location is scenic enough, but the dust and noise from passing vehicles makes it less appealing than other campsites.

There are pleasant short canyon walks, but during heavy rains in the mountains the site can be flooded; in the summer months, keep tabs on the weather to make sure you don't overheat or get caught in a downpour.

Mirabib   CAMPGROUND $

(camping N$170) Mirabib is a pleasant facility that accommodates two parties at separate sites, and is comfortably placed beneath rock overhangs along a large granite escarpment. There's evidence that these shelters were used by nomadic peoples as early as 9000 years ago, and also by nomadic shepherds in the 4th or 5th century.

Vogelfederberg   CAMPGROUND $

(camping N$170) Vogelfederberg is a small facility, 2km south of the C14, and makes a convenient overnight camp. Located just 51km from Walvis Bay, it's more popular for picnics or short walks. It's worth looking at the intermittent pools on the summit that shelter a species of brine prawn whose eggs hatch only when the pools are filled with rainwater.

The only shade is provided by a small overhang where there are two picnic tables and braai pits.

Ganab   CAMPGROUND $

(camping N$170) Ganab is a dusty, exposed facility, translating to 'Camelthorn Acacia', that sits beside a shallow stream bed on the gravel plains. It's shaded by hardy acacia trees, and a nearby bore hole provides water for antelopes.

Kriess-se-Rus   CAMPGROUND $

(camping N$170) Kriess-se-Rus is a rather ordinary site in a dry stream bank on the gravel plains, 107km east of Walvis Bay on the Gamsberg Pass Route. It is shaded, but isn't terribly prepossessing, and is best used simply as a convenient stop en route between Windhoek and Walvis Bay.

ℹ Getting There & Away

The main park transit routes, the C28, C14, D1982 and D1998, are all open to 2WD traffic. However, the use of minor roads requires a park permit (N$80 per day plus N$10 per vehicle), which can either be picked up at any of the park gates or arranged in advance through NWR.

NAMIBIA NAMIB-NAUKLUFT PARK

Namib-Naukluft Park

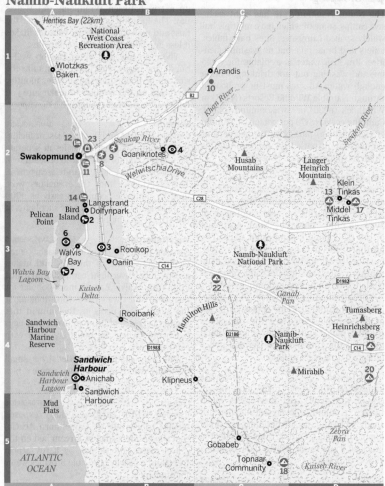

While some minor roads in the park are accessible to high-clearance 2WD vehicles, a 4WD is highly recommended.

Naukluft Mountains

♪ 063 / ELEVATION 1973M

The Naukluft Mountains, which rise steeply from the gravel plains of the central Namib, are characterised by a high plateau bounded by gorges, caves and springs cut deeply from dolomite formations. The Tsondab, Tsams and Tsauchab Rivers all rise in the massif, and the relative abundance of water creates an ideal habitat for mountain zebras, kudus,

leopards, springboks and klipspringers. In addition to wildlife watching, the Naukluft is home to a couple of challenging treks that open up this largely inaccessible terrain.

History

In the early 1890s, the Naukluft was the site of heated battle between the German colonial forces and the Nama. In January 1893 a contingent of Schutztruppe soldiers estimated that they could force the Nama to flee their settlement at Hoornkrans in three days. However, due to their unfamiliarity with the terrain, and their lack of

Namib-Naukluft Park

◎ Top Sights
1 Sandwich Harbour A4

◎ Sights
2 Bird Island..A3
3 Dune 7 ....B3
4 Goanikontes B2
5 Kuiseb Canyon E4
6 Lagoon...A3
Moon Landscape ....(see 4)
7 Salt Works...A3

⊕ Activities, Courses & Tours
8 Batis Birding Safaris............................B2
9 Okakambe Horse Stables....................B2
10 Rössing Mine C1
Swakopmund Camel Farm.........(see 9)

⊟ Sleeping
11 Alternative Space A2
12 Atlantic Villa..A2
Beach Lodge............................... (see 12)
13 Bloedkoppie..D2
14 Burning Shore A2
15 Camp Gecko F5
Desert Breeze Lodge.................. (see 11)
Dünenblick .... (see 11)
16 Ganab E3
17 Groot Tinkas..D3
18 Homeb..C5
19 Kriess-se-Rus D4
Kuiseb Canyon ....(see 5)
20 Mirabib D4
21 Rostock Ritz E5
Sea Breeze Guesthouse .... (see 12)
Sophiadale Base Camp.............. (see 9)
22 Vogelfederberg C3

⊞ Shopping
23 Cosdef Arts & Crafts Centre A2

experience in guerrilla warfare, the battle waged for months, resulting in heavy losses on both sides. Eventually, the Nama offered to accept German sovereignty if they could retain their lands and weapons. The Germans accepted, thus ending the Battle of the Naukluft.

🏃 Activities

Naukluft 4WD Trail Off-Road   SCENIC DRIVE
Off-road enthusiasts will love the 73km, two-day Naukluft 4WD Trail. It begins near the start of the Olive Trail and follows a loop near the northeastern corner of the Naukluft area. Accommodation is provided in one of the stone-walled A-frames at the 28km point. Facilities include shared toilets, showers and braai pits. Up to four vehicles/16 people are permitted here at a time.

Book through the NWR office in Windhoek; the route (including accommodation) costs N$280 per vehicle plus an additional N$80 per person per day.

Olive Trail   HIKING
The 11km Olive Trail, named for the wild olives that grow alongside it, is one of Namibia's most popular hikes and deservedly so. It begins at the car park 4km northeast of the park headquarters. The walk runs clockwise around the triangular loop and takes four to five hours.

Naukluft Mountains

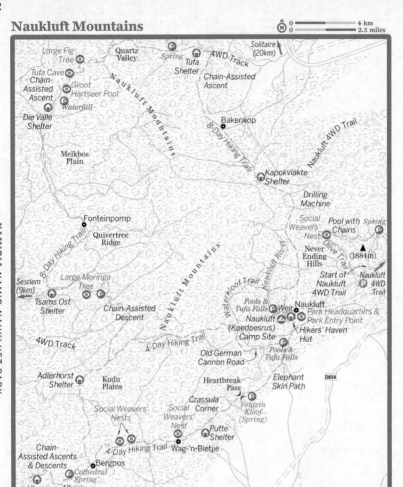

Map labels:
Large Fig Tree, Quartz Valley, Spring, 4WD Track, Solitaire (20km), Tufa Cave, Chain-Assisted Ascent, Tufa Shelter, Chain-Assisted Ascent, Groot Hartseer Pool, Waterfall, Naukluft Mountains, Die Valle Shelter, Bakenkop, Melkbos Plain, 8-Day Hiking Trail, Kapokvlakte Shelter, Naukluft 4WD Trail, Drilling Machine, Fonteinpomp, Social Weavers' Nest, Pool with Chains, Spring, Quivertree Ridge, Never Ending Hills, (1884m), Sesriem (9km), 8-Day Hiking Trail, Large Moringa Tree, Naukluft Mountains, Waterkloof Trail, Naukluft River, Olive Trail, Start of Naukluft 4WD Trail, Naukluft 4WD Trail, Tsams Ost Shelter, Chain-Assisted Descent, Pools & Tufa Falls, Weir, Naukluft, Park Headquarters & Park Entry Point, 4WD Track, Naukluft (Koedoesrus) Camp Site, Hikers' Haven Hut, 4-Day Hiking Trail, Old German Cannon Road, Pools & Tufa Falls, Adlerhorst Shelter, Kudu Plains, Heartbreak Pass, Elephant Skin Path, D854, Crassula Corner, Fontein Kloof (Spring), Social Weavers' Nests, Social Weavers' Nest, Putte Shelter, Chain-Assisted Ascents & Descents, 4-Day Hiking Trail, Wag-'n-Bietjie, Bergpos, Cathedral Spring, Ubusis Canyon Hut, Ubusis Canyon, Maltahöhe-Sesriem Road (39km)

N 0 —— 4 km
   0 —— 2.5 miles

The route begins with a steep climb onto the plateau, affording good views of the Naukluft Valley. It then turns sharply east and descends a constricted river valley, which becomes deeper and steeper and makes a couple of perfect U-turns before it reaches a point where hikers must traverse a canyon wall – past a pool – using anchored chains. In several places along this stretch, the dramatic geology presents an astonishing gallery of natural artwork. Near the end of the route, the trail strikes the Naukluft 4WD route and swings sharply south, where it makes a beeline back to the car park.

Waterkloof Trail
HIKING

This lovely 17km anticlockwise loop takes about seven hours to complete, and begins at the Naukluft (Koedoesrus) campsite, located 2km west of the park headquarters. The trail traverses a lovely range of landscapes and habitats, from riverbank to canyon, plateau to rocky ridge.

It climbs the Naukluft River and past a frog-infested weir (don't miss the amazing reed tunnel!) and a series of pools, which offer cool and refreshing drinking and swimming. About 1km beyond the last pool, the trail then turns west, away from the Naukluft River and up a kloof (ravine). From there to the halfway point, the route traverses an increasingly open plateau.

Shortly after the halfway mark, the trail climbs steeply to a broad 1910m ridge, which is the highest point on the route. Here you'll have fabulous desert views before you begin a long, steep descent into the Gororosib Valley. Along the way, you'll pass several inviting pools full of reeds and tadpoles, and climb down an especially impressive waterfall before meeting up with the Naukluft River. Here, the route turns left and follows the 4WD track back to the park headquarters.

FOUR- & EIGHT-DAY LOOPS

The two big loops through the massif can be hiked in four and eight days. For many people the Naukluft is a magical place, but its charm is more subtle than that of Fish River Canyon in southern Namibia. For example, some parts are undeniably spectacular, such as the Zebra Highway, Ubusis Canyon and Die Valle (look for the fantastic stallion profile on the rock beside the falls). However, a couple of days involve walking in relatively open country or along some maddeningly rocky riverbeds.

The four-day 60km loop is actually just the first third of the eight-day 120km loop, combined with a 22km cross-country jaunt across the plateau back to park headquarters. It joins up with the Waterkloof Trail at its halfway point, and follows it the rest of the way back to park headquarters. Alternatively, you can finish the four-day route at Tsams Ost Shelter, midway through the eight-day loop, where a road leads out to the Sesriem-Solitaire Rd. However, you must prearrange to leave a vehicle there before setting off from park headquarters. Note that hikers may not begin from Tsams Ost without special permission from the rangers at Naukluft.

These straightforward hikes are marked by white footprints (except those sections that coincide with the Waterkloof Trail, which is marked with yellow footprints). Conditions are typically hot and dry, and water is only reliably available at overnight stops (at Putte, it's 400m from the shelter).

To shorten the eight-day hike to seven days, it's possible to skip Ubusis Canyon by turning north at Bergpos and staying the second night at Adlerhorst. Alternatively, very fit hikers combine the seventh and eighth days.

In four places – Ubusis Canyon, above Tsams Ost, Die Valle and just beyond Tufa Shelter – hikers must negotiate dry waterfalls, boulder-blocked kloofs and steep tufa formations with the aid of chains. Some people find this off-putting, so be sure you're up to it.

🛏 Sleeping

⭐ **Tsauchab River Camp** CAMPGROUND **$**
(☑ 063-293416; www.tsauchab.com; campsites N$150, plus per adult/child N$110/65, chalets s/d N$760/1400; 🐾🌊) If you're an avid hiker (or just love excellent settings!), you're in for a treat. The scattered campsites here sit beside the Tsauchab riverbed – one occupies a huge hollow tree – and each has a private shower block, a sink and braai area. The stone-built chalets grow in number with each passing year; also down in the riverbed, they're lovely and quiet.

HIKING PRACTICALITIES

Most Naukluft visitors come to hike either the Waterkloof or Olive Trails (p311). These hikes are open to day visitors, but most hikers want to camp at Naukluft (Koedoesrus), which must be prebooked.

The four-day and eight-day loops have more restrictions attached. Thanks to stifling summer temperatures and potentially heavy rains, these two are only open from 1 March to the third Friday in October. Officially, you can only begin these hikes on the Tuesday, Thursday and Saturday of the first three weeks of each month. The price of N$100 per person includes accommodation at the Hikers' Haven hut on the night before and after the hike, as well as camping at trailside shelters and the Ubusis Canyon Hut. In addition, you'll have to pay N$80 per person per day and another N$10 per day for each vehicle you leave parked. Groups must comprise three to 12 people.

Due to the typically hot, dry conditions and the lack of reliable natural water sources, you must carry at least 3L to 4L of water per person per day, as well as food and emergency supplies.

Johan and Nicky are warm and welcoming hosts and Johan's eclectic sculptures, mostly from old car engine parts, are a real feature of this place. Activities include self-guided hikes and 4WD trails. The 6km Kudu Hiking Trail climbs to the summit of Rooikop. Beside a spring 11km away from the main site is the 4WD exclusive site, which is the starting point for the wonderful 21km Mountain Zebra Hiking Trail.

★ **Zebra River Lodge**   LODGE $$
(☑ 061-301934; www.zebra-river-lodge.com; s/d with full board from N$1275/1610; ☎ ⊠) Occupying a magical setting in the Tsaris Mountains, this is Rob and Marianne Field's private Grand Canyon. Go for one of the more expansive rock chalets – you'll feel like you're sleeping inside the mountain and they're some of Namibia's more original rooms.

The surrounding wonderland of desert mountains, plateaus, valleys and natural springs is accessible on a network of hiking trails and 4WD tracks. If you take it very slowly, the lodge road is accessible by 2WD vehicles.

Büllsport Guest Farm   FARMSTAY $$$
(☑ 063-693371; www.buellsport.com/main.html; s/d with half board from N$1780/3150) This scenic farm, owned by Ernst and Johanna Sauber, occupies a lovely, austere setting below the Naukluft Massif, and features a ruined colonial police station, the Bogenfels arch and several resident mountain zebras. A highlight is the 4WD excursion up to the plateau and the hike back down the gorge, past several idyllic natural swimming pools. There are also horse-riding trails.

❶ Getting There & Away

The Naukluft is best reached via the C24 from Rehoboth and the D1206 from Rietoog; petrol is available at Büllsport and Rietoog. From Sesriem, 103km away, the nearest access is via the dip-ridden D854.

Sesriem & Sossusvlei

☑ 063

Appropriate for this vast country with its epic landscapes – its number one tourist attraction – Sossusvlei still manages to feel isolated. The dunes, appearing other-worldly at times, especially when the light hits them just so near sunrise, are part of the 32,000-sq-km sand sea that covers much of the region. The dunes reach as high as 325m, and are part of one of the oldest and driest ecosystems on

earth. However, the landscape here is constantly changing – wind forever alters the shape of the dunes, while colours shift with the changing light, reaching the peak of their brilliance just after sunrise.

The gateway to Sossusvlei is Sesriem (Six Thongs), which was the number of joined leather ox-wagon thongs necessary to draw water from the bottom of the nearby gorge. Sesriem remains a lonely and far-flung outpost, home to little more than a petrol station and a handful of tourist hotels and lodges.

🏃 Activities

Namib Sky Balloon Safaris   BALLOONING
(☑ 081 304 2205, 063-683188; www.namibsky. com; per person from N$5950) Floating over the dunes in a hot air balloon (prices include a champagne breakfast) is a breathtaking way to appreciate the stunning landscape. Pickups a half-hour before sunrise are arranged at many accommodation places in the area.

❍ Sights

★ **Sossusvlei**   PAN
(round trip N$100) Sossusvlei, a large ephemeral pan, is set amid red sand dunes that tower up to 325m above the valley floor. It rarely contains any water, but when the Tsauchab River has gathered enough volume and momentum to push beyond the thirsty plains to the sand sea, it's completely transformed. The normally cracked dry mud gives way to an ethereal blue-green lake, surrounded by greenery and attended by aquatic birdlife, as well as the usual sand-loving gemsbok and ostriches.

This sand probably originated in the Kalahari between three and five million years ago. It was washed down the Orange River and out to sea, where it was swept northward with the Benguela Current to be deposited along the coast. The best way to get the measure of this sandy sprawl is to climb a dune, as most people do. And of course, if you experience a sense of déjà vu here, don't be surprised – Sossusvlei has appeared in many films and advertisements worldwide, and every story ever written about Namibia features a photo of it.

At the end of the 65km 2WD road from Sesriem is the 2WD car park; only 4WDs can drive the last 4km into the Sossusvlei Pan itself. Visitors with lesser vehicles park at the 2WD car park and walk, hitch or catch the shuttle to cover the remaining distance. If you choose to walk, allot about 90 minutes,

Sesriem & Sossusvlei

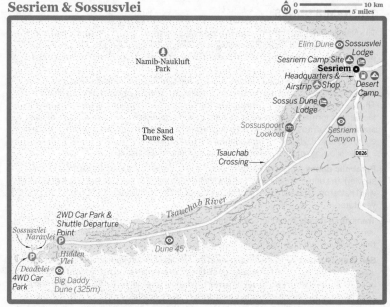

NAMIBIA NAMIB-NAUKLUFT PARK

and carry enough water for a hot, sandy slog in the sun.

★ Deadvlei   NATURAL FEATURE

Although it's much less famous than its neighbour Sossusvlei, Deadvlei is actually the most alluring pan in the Namib-Naukluft National Park – it's arguably one of Southern Africa's greatest sights. Sprouting from the pan are seemingly petrified trees, with their parched limbs casting stark shadows across the baked, bleached white canvas. The juxtaposition of this scene with the cobalt-blue skies and the towering orange sands of Big Daddy, the area's tallest dune (325m), is simply spellbinding.

It's an easy 3km return walk from the Deadvlei/Big Daddy Dune 4WD parking area – follow the waymarker posts.

★ Hidden Vlei   NATURAL FEATURE

This unearthly dry vlei (low, open landscape) amid lonely dunes makes a rewarding excursion. It's a 4km return hike from the 2WD car park. The route is marked by white-painted posts. It's most intriguing in the afternoon, when you're unlikely to see another person.

★ Sesriem Canyon   CANYON

The 3km-long, 30m-deep Sesriem Canyon, 4km south of the Sesriem headquarters,

was carved by the Tsauchab River through the 15-million-year-old deposits of sand and gravel conglomerate. There are two pleasant walks: you can hike upstream to the brackish pool at its head or 2.5km downstream to its lower end. Check out the natural sphinx-like formation on the northern flank near the canyon mouth.

Dune 45   VIEWPOINT

The most accessible of the large red dunes along the Sossusvlei road is Dune 45, so-called because it's 45km from Sesriem. It rises over 150m above the surrounding plains, and is flanked by several scraggly and often photographed trees.

Elim Dune   VIEWPOINT

This often visited red dune, 5km north from the Sesriem Camp Site, can be reached with 2WD vehicles, but also makes a pleasant morning or afternoon walk. The park authorities suggest that this is the best place to watch the sunset – for the views of the actual sunset, rather than the surrounding dunes.

🛏 Sleeping

Advanced reservations are essential, especially during the high season, school holidays and busy weekends. For an overview of accommodation options in the area, visit

THE NAMIB DUNES

The Namib dunes stretch from the Orange to the Kuiseb Rivers in the south, and from Torra Bay in Skeleton Coast Park to Angola's Curoca River in the north. They're composed of colourful quartz sand and come in varying hues – from cream to orange and red to violet.

Unlike the ancient Kalahari dunes, those of the Namib are dynamic, which means that they shift with wind, and are continuously sculpted into a variety of distinctive shapes. The top portion of the dune, which faces the direction of migrations, is known as the slipface, and is formed as the sand spills from the crest and slips down. Various bits of plant and animal detritus also collect here and provide a meagre food source for dune-dwelling creatures, and it's here that most dune life is concentrated.

The following major types of dunes can be found in the Namib:

Parabolic dunes Along the eastern area of the dune sea (including those around Sossusvlei), the dunes are classified as parabolic or multicyclic, and are the result of variable wind patterns. These are the most stable dunes in the Namib, and therefore the most vegetated.

Transverse dunes The long, linear dunes along the coast south of Walvis Bay are transverse dunes, which lie perpendicular to the prevailing southwesterly winds. As a result, their slipfaces are oriented towards the north and northeast.

Seif dunes Around the Homeb campsite in the Namib-Naukluft Park are the prominent linear or seif dunes, which are enormous all-direction-oriented sand ripples. With heights of up to 100m, they're spaced about 1km apart and show up plainly on satellite photographs. They're formed by seasonal winds; during the prevailing southerly winds of summer, the slipfaces lie on the northeastern face. In the winter the wind blows in the opposite direction, which causes slipfaces to build up on the southern-western faces.

Star dunes In areas where individual dunes are exposed to winds from all directions, a formation known as a star dune appears. These dunes have multiple ridges, and when seen from above may appear to have a star shape.

Barchan dunes These dunes prevail around the northern end of the Skeleton Coast and south of Lüderitz, and are the most mobile as they are created by unidirectional winds. When shifting, barchan dunes take on a crescent shape, with the horns of the crescent aimed in the direction of migration. In fact, it is barchan dunes that are slowly devouring the ghost town of Kolmanskop near Lüderitz.

Hump dunes Typically forming in clusters near water sources, hump dunes are considerably smaller than other dune types. They are formed when sand builds up around vegetation (such as a tuft of grass), and is held in place by the roots of the plant, forming a sandy tussock. Generally, hump dunes rise less than 3m from the surface.

Sossusvlei Accommodation (www.sossusvlei.org/accommodation).

Sossus Oasis Campsite CAMPGROUND $
(☑ 063-293632; www.sossus-oasis.com; camping N$180) Nicer than the main Sesriem Camp Site but outside the main gate, Sossus Oasis has an on-site petrol station, kiosk, restaurant and decent if dusty sights with good shade and a private ablutions block for each site.

Sesriem Camp Site CAMPGROUND $
(☑ 061-2857200; www.nwr.com.na/resorts/sesriem-camp; camping N$200) With the exception of the upmarket Sossus Dune Lodge, this is the only accommodation inside the park gates –

staying here guarantees that you will be able to arrive at Sossusvlei in time for sunrise. The campsite is rudimentary – sandy sites with bins, taps, and trees for shade – and expensive for what you get. It can also get really noisy which defeats the purpose of why you came out here.

But you pay for the location inside the park. Given its popularity, you must book in advance at the NWR office in Windhoek, and arrive by sunset or the camp staff will reassign your site on a standby basis. A small shop at the office here sells snacks and cold drinks, and the campsite bar provides music and alcohol nightly.

Desert Camp
TENTED CAMP **$$**
(☑ 063-683205; www.desertcamp.com; s with half board N$1482-1695, d with half board N$2224-2508; ⊠) The sister property of the Sossusvlei Lodge, located 3km outside the park gate, targets midrange travellers who want the comforts of a lodge without having to part with too much cash. Desert Camp consists of 20 East African–style canvas tents, complete with private bathrooms, kitchenettes and braai pits, which fan out from the central communal area.

Desert Quiver Camp
LODGE **$$**
(☑ 081 330 6655; www.desertquivercamp.com; s with half board N$1419-1587, d with half board N$2142-2364) Lined up across the desert 5km from the park entrance off the road in from Solitaire, Desert Quiver Camp has striking A-frame chalets that are nicely turned out, but they could benefit from a few more windows to really make you feel a part of the desert. Meals are at the nearby Sossusvlei Lodge, but self-catering rates are also available.

★ Little Kulala
LODGE **$$$**
(☑ 061-225178; www.wilderness-safaris.com; s/d all-inclusive Jun-Oct N$13,480/20,750, rates vary rest of year) Part of Wilderness Safaris' Classic portfolio, Little Kulala is simply stunning. Expansive rooms, each with their own plunge pools, watch over rippling sands and silhouetted desert trees with the sand sea dominating the view not far away. Meals are outstanding, there's a well-stocked wine cellar, the public areas are gorgeous and the whole effect is of a near-perfect sophisticated oasis.

Activities include excursions into the sand sea, but this is one place where we recommend leaving enough time to simply enjoy the surrounds. And by night, the stars out here are utterly extraordinary.

Kulala Desert Lodge
LODGE **$$$**
(☑ 061-225178; www.wilderness-safaris.com; s/d all-inclusive Jun-Oct N$6510/11,270, rates vary rest of year) If you've stayed in a Wilderness Safaris lodge before, you know the deal. If you haven't, you're in for a treat. Semi-luxurious canvas tents and great food are just the start, as the whole property faces off towards the sand dunes in the middle distance. It's close enough to the park entrance for a quick arrival but far enough away to feel like you're kilometres from anywhere.

Le Mirage Desert Lodge
HOTEL **$$$**
(☑ 063-693019; www.mirage-lodge.com; s/d with half board N$2950/4500; 🖧⊠) Some places like to blend in with their surroundings. Then there's La Mirage... This extravagent stone mock-castle does indeed rise like a mirage out of the desert. The whole affair is over the top, but it's a very comfortable place to stay, with pool, grass and sunbeds set around a bar area, a restaurant and large rooms sumptuously furnished. It's on the C27, 21 km from Sesriem.

It's worth paying a little extra for one of the Oasis Rooms in the castle annex – the camel thorn rooms in the main reception building are lovely but lack the wow factor. And don't miss the sundowner spot out the back for a cocktail at day's end, or the spa. There's also quad biking for guests.

Sossus Dune Lodge
LODGE **$$$**
(☑ 061-2857200; www.nwr.com.na/resorts/sossus-dune-lodge; s/d chalets with half board N$3190/5940; ⊠) Splash out at this ultraexclusive lodge, which is administered by NWR, and is one of only two properties located inside the park gates. Constructed entirely of local materials, the lodge consists of elevated bungalows that run alongside a curving promenade, and face out towards the silent desert plains.

In the morning, you can roll out of your plush queen-sized bed, take a hot and steamy shower, sit down to a light breakfast of filter coffee and fresh fruits, and then be one of the first people to watch the morning light wash over Sossusvlei.

Sossusvlei Lodge
LODGE **$$$**
(☑ 063-293636; www.sossusvleilodge.com; campsites per 2 people N$300, s with full board N$2466-3433, d with full board N$3640-4930; ⊠) People either love this curious place or hate it, but it does make a statement. Accommodation is in self-contained chalets with private verandas, and guests can mingle with one another in the swimming pool, bar-restaurant and observatory. Walk-in rates are often cheaper.

There's an adventure centre here that organises scenic flights, hot-air ballooning, quad biking and many other activities.

❶ Information
Sesriem Canyon and Sossusvlei are part of the Namib-Naukluft National Park and are open year-round. If you want to see the sunrise over Sossusvlei, you must stay inside the park, either at the Sesriem Camp Site or the Sossus Dune Lodge. From both places, you

NAMIBIA NAMIB-NAUKLUFT PARK

are allowed to start driving to Sossusvlei before the general public is allowed through the main gates. If you're content with simply enjoying the morning light, however, you can stay in Sesriem or Solitaire and simply pass through the park gate once the sun rises above the horizon – be prepared for queues at the park gate, however.

All visitors headed for Sossusvlei must check in at the park office and secure a park entry permit.

Namib-Naukluft park entry at Sossusvlei is N$80 per adult, N$10 per car.

ℹ Getting There & Away

Sesriem is reached via a signposted turn-off from the C14, and petrol is available in town. There is no public transport leading into the park, though hotels can arrange tours if you don't have your own vehicle.

The road leading from the park gate to the 2WD car park is paved, though the speed limit remains 60km/h. Although the road is conducive to higher speeds, there are oryx and springbok dashing about, so drive with extreme care.

Solitaire Area
🗂 062, 063 & 064

Solitaire is a lonely and aptly named settlement of just a few buildings about 80km north of Sesriem along the A46. Although the town is nothing more than an open spot in the desert, the surrounding area is home to several guest farms and lodges, which can serve as an alternative base for exploring Sossusvlei. Otherwise, the town is little more than a place to refuel.

🛏 Sleeping

Solitaire Country Lodge LODGE $
(🗂 061-305173; www.sossusvlei.org/accommodation/solitaire-country-lodge/; C19; camping per person N$100, s/d N$495/805; @ 🏊) Despite its relative youth, the property was designed to evoke images of a colonial-era farmhouse, albeit one with a large swimming pool in the backyard! Serviceable rooms are fairly sparse, a decent size and set around a large, grassed square.

Solitaire Guest Farm FARMSTAY $$
(🗂 061-305173; camping N$150, s/d with half board from N$1000/1600; 🏊) This inviting guest farm, located 6km east of Solitaire on the C14, is a peaceful oasis situated between the Namib plains and the Naukluft Massif.

Bright rooms, home-cooked meals and relaxing surroundings make it a good choice.

Camp Gecko TENTED CAMP $$
(🗂 062-572017; www.campgecko.net; s/d with half board N$1018/1778) East of Solitaire, original Camp Gecko has Meru-style safari tents and unusual, two-storey tents known as Bush Hideaways. It's an excellent choice at a price a little lower than most in the area.

★ **Agama River Camp** LODGE, CAMPGROUND $$$
(🗂 063-683245; www.agamarivercamp.com; camping N$150, s/d chalet N$1700/2680) This relatively new lodge is in a handy spot between Solitaire and Sesriem (34km from Sesriem). The chalets are supremely comfortable and have rooftop decks so you can sleep under the stars. There's also an excellent campsite, while in the main lodge there's a sundowner deck and lounge; meals only available if booked well in advance.

★ **Moon Mountain** TENTED CAMP $$$
(🗂 061-305176; www.moonmountain.biz; s/d from N$2210/4000; 🏊) Off the C19 between Sesriem and Solitaire, this extraordinary tented camp clings to a steep hillside and the result is vertigo-inducing, sunset-facing views. The wood-floored tents open up to maximise the sense of flying above the desert but even so you'll just want to sit on your balcony (or in your private splash pool) all evening. Stunning bathrooms round out a wonderful package. The suites are even more decadent.

Rostock Ritz LODGE $$$
(🗂 081 258 5722, 064-694000; www.rostock-ritz-desert-lodge.com; camping from N$150, s/d chalets from N$1590/2544; 🏊) This unique accommodation is known for its bizarre water gardens and cool and cave-like cement-domed chalets. The Rostock Campsite is a peaceful 7km from the lodge itself. The staff can arrange a number of activities, including hiking, a visit to the nearby hot springs and the obligatory trip to Sossusvlei. The Ritz lies east of the C14, just south of the C26 junction.

ℹ Getting There & Away

Solitaire is connected to Sesriem by the unpaved C19, and petrol is available in town.

Check to see if the shuttle service is still running from Solitaire petrol station to Sousslevi for N$150 return; check with the station for the times the service runs. We reckon you're better off getting there under your own steam, but it does provide another option.

!NARA MELONS

Historically, human existence in the Namib Desert has been made possible by an unusual spiny plant, the !nara melon. It was first described taxonomically by the same Friedrich Welwitsch who gave his name to the welwitschia plant.

Although the !nara bush lives and grows in the desert, it is not a desert plant since it lacks the ability to prevent water loss through transpiration. So it must take in moisture from the groundwater table via a long taproot. As a result, !nara melons are an effective way of monitoring underground water tables: when the plants are healthy, so is the water supply. Its lack of leaves also protects it from grazing animals, although ostriches do nip off its tender growing shoots.

As with the welwitschia, the male and female sex organs in the !nara melon exist in separate plants. Male plants flower throughout the year, but it's the female plant that produces the 15cm melon each summer, providing a favourite meal for jackals, insects and humans. In fact, it remains a primary food of the Topnaar Khoekhoen people, and has also become a local commercial enterprise. Each year at harvest time, the Topnaar erect camps around the Kuiseb Delta to collect the fruits. Although melons can be eaten raw, most people prefer to dry them for later use, or prepare, package and ship them to urban markets.

NamibRand Nature Reserve

🗹 061

Bordering the Namib-Naukluft Park, this reserve (www.namibrand.org) is essentially a collection of private farms that together protect over 200,000 hectares of dunes, desert grasslands and wild, isolated mountain ranges. Currently, several concessionaires operate on the reserve, offering a range of experiences amid one of Namibia's most stunning and colourful landscapes. A surprising amount of wildlife can be seen here, including large herds of gemsboks, springboks and zebras, as well as kudus, klipspringers, spotted hyenas, jackals, and Cape and bat-eared foxes.

🛏 Sleeping

NamibRand Family Hideout   FARMSTAY **$**
(🗹 061-226803; www.nrfhideout.com; camping N$150, farm rates vary with the number of people) Run on solar energy and making a virtue of its remoteness, NamibRand's hosts Andreas and Mandy offer a warm welcome, two wonderfully isolated campsites and accommodation in the farmhouse (sleeps 10); much of the old farm infrastructure, now defunct, has been left in situ to evoke the property's sheep-farming days

★ Sossusvlei Desert Lodge   LODGE **$$$**
(🗹 in South Africa 27-11-809 4300; www.andbeyond.com; per person all-inclusive high/low season N$10,185/6345; ❇ 🛜 ☲) This stunning place frequently appears in *Condé Nast* as one of the top lodges in the world, and we're

inclined to agree. The property contains 10 chalets, which are constructed from locally quarried stone, and appear to blend effortlessly into the surrounding landscape. The interiors showcase contemporary flair with lovely earth tones, and feature personal fireplaces, marble baths and linen-covered patios.

As always with &Beyond properties, exemplary service is a feature. Of special interest is the on-site observatory, which boasts a high-powered telescope and local star charts.

Wolwedans Boulders Camp   LODGE **$$$**
(🗹 061-230616; www.wolwedans.com/lodges-camps/boulders-safari-camp/; s/d all-inclusive N$8750/12,500) A stunning Wolwedans property, Boulders Lodge puts its back hard up against a protrusion of bouldered hills, which gives a sense of refuge from the great emptiness of the land all around, but with splendid views of the desert in all its immensity. The rooms are stunning, with extraordinary views without even leaving your bed.

Wolwedans Dune Lodge   LODGE **$$$**
(🗹 061-230616; www.wolwedans.com; s/d all-inclusive from N$6930/9900; ❇ ☲) One of the more affordable lodges in the NamibRand, Wolwedans Dune Lodge features an architecturally arresting collection of raised wooden chalets that are scattered amid towering red sand dunes. Service is impeccable, and the atmosphere is overwhelmingly elegant, yet you can indulge your wild side at any time with chauffeured 4WD dune drives and guided safaris.

ℹ️ Getting There & Away

Access by private vehicle is restricted in order to maintain the delicate balance of the reserve. Accommodation prices are also extremely high, which seeks to limit the tourist footprint. As a result, you must book in advance through a lodge, and then arrange either a 4WD transfer or a chartered fly-in.

SOUTHERN NAMIBIA

If you're beginning a regional odyssey in South Africa, one of the best ways to approach Namibia is from South Africa's vast Northern Cape, crossing the border into the infinite, desert-rich south of the country. Once in Namibia, the landscape, noticeably starker than its southern neighbour, is tinged with a lunar feel from the scattered rocky debris, and is marked from the irrepressible movement of the oldest sand dunes on the planet.

Although the tourist trail in Namibia firmly swings north towards Etosha National Park, the deserts of southern Namibia sparkle beneath the sun – quite literally – as they're filled with millions of carats of diamonds.

The port of Lüderitz has long been a traveller's favourite. A surreal colonial relic that has largely disregarded the 21st century, Lüderitz clings fiercely to its European roots, with traditional German architecture set against a backdrop of fiery sand dunes and deep blue seas.

Your first sight of Fish River Canyon will, more than any place in Namibia, leave you with feelings of awe and grandeur – it is mother earth at her very finest. One of the largest canyons in the world, it's also one of the most spectacular

The Central Plateau

The central plateau is probably not where you'll spend most of your time in Namibia. Most travellers encounter the region on their way elsewhere – the plateau is bisected by the B1, which is the country's main north–south route, stretching from the South African border to Otjiwarongo. What this means is that, for most drivers, this excellent road is little more than a mesmerising broken white line stretching towards a receding horizon – a paradise for lead-foot drivers and cruise-control potatoes.

Even so, with most of the central plateau's towns on or just off the main B1 route, there are numerous places to break up the journey, whether as a base for exploring the region's natural attractions, for fuel stops, or even as detour destinations in their own right. Of the latter, Bethanie, Gondwana Cañon Park, Keetmanshoop and Seeheim are probably the pick.

Dordabis

POP 1500 / ☎ 062

The lonely ranching area around Dordabis is the heart of Namibia's karakul (sheep) country, and supports several sheep farms and weaveries.

⊙ Sights

Farm Ibenstein Weavery ARTS CENTRE

(☎ 062-573524; www.ibenstein-weavers.com.na; ⊙ by appointment) At the Farm Ibenstein Weavery, located 4km down the C15 from Dordabis, you can learn about spinning, dyeing and weaving, as well as purchase hand-woven rugs and carpets.

🛏️ Sleeping

Eningu Clayhouse Lodge LODGE $$$

(☎ 062-581880, 064-464144; www.eningulodge.com; Nina Rd, Peperkorrel Farm; s/d with half board N$1460/2720) Yes, the name Eningu Clayhouse Lodge sounds a lot like the title of a children's book, but appropriately enough, this place is a bit of a fantasy. It was painstakingly designed and constructed by Volker and Stephanie Hümmer, whose efforts with sun-dried adobe have resulted in an appealing African-Amerindian architectural cross – the large and lovely rooms have hand-painted floors, earth hues and handwoven rugs.

It really is visually arresting, and activities here include wonderful hiking trails (with a mountain hut en route), wildlife viewing, archery, and stargazing through their telescope. To get here, follow the D1458 for 63km southeast of Chief Hosea Kutako International Airport and then turn west on the D1471; travel for 1km to the Eningu gate.

ℹ️ Getting There & Away

To reach Dordabis, head east from Windhoek on the B6 and turn right onto the C23, 20km east of town; the town centre is 66km down this road.

Arnhem Cave

With a subterranean length of 4.5km, Arnhem Cave is the longest cave system in Namibia. Formed in a layer of limestone and dolomite, Arnhem was sandwiched between folds of stratified quartzite and shale, and discovered in 1930 by farmer DN Bekker. Shortly thereafter, mining operations began extracting the deposits of lucrative bat guano, which were commonly used at the time as fertiliser.

◉ Sights

Guided tours (one hour/two hours N$100/120) dive into darkness, beyond the reach of sunlight. Because it's dry, there are few stalagmites or stalactites, but it's possible you could see up to six bat species: the giant leaf-nosed bat, the leaf-nosed bat, the long-fingered bat, Geoffroy's horseshoe bat, Denti's horseshoe bat and the Egyptian slit-faced bat. It's also inhabited by a variety of insects, worms, shrews and prawns. The grand finale is the indescribable first view of the blue-cast natural light as you emerge from the depths.

🛏 Sleeping

Arnhem Cave & Lodge   LODGE $$
(📞 062-581885; camping N$110, chalets per person from N$525) This place lies within an hour's walk of Arnhem Cave, and is located on the same farm. Day visitors can arrange guided tours here, while overnight visitors are treated to a bucolic retreat lying just beyond the lights of the capital.

❶ Getting There & Away

To get to the cave head first for the guesthouse. Turn south 3km east of Chief Hosea Kutako International Airport on the D1458. After 66km, turn northeast on the D1506 and continue for 11km to the T-junction, where you turn south on the D180. The guesthouse is 6km down this road.

Mariental

POP 12,480 / 📞 063

The small administrative and commercial centre of Mariental is home to the large-scale Hardap irrigation scheme, which allows citrus-growing and ostrich farming. For most travellers, however, Mariental is little more than a petrol stop before heading out west to Sesriem and Sossusvlei.

🛏 Sleeping

Mariental Hotel   HOTEL $
(📞 063-242466; www.marientalhotel.com; cnr Hendrik Witbooi Ave & Charney Rd; s/d N$480/780; ❋ 🛜 🏊) If you get stuck for the night, the well-established Mariental Hotel has basic carpeted rooms with modern amenities, if a rather drab colour scheme, as well as a dining room serving Namibian standards.

★ Kalahari Red Dunes Lodge   LODGE $$$
(📞 063-264003; www.redduneslodge.com; off B1; s/d with full board N$2500/4200; ❋ 🛜 🏊) Off the B1 a few clicks southeast of Kalkrand and around halfway between Mariental and Rehoboth, Red Dunes Lodge has a lovely collection of thatch-and-canvas guestrooms with teak floors, stone tiling, wood fires, private terraces and outdoor showers. They're nicely spaced to ensure privacy and the swaying Kalahari grasslands that envelop this 10,000-acre property add a real sense of bush isolation despite its accessibility.

Bagatelle Kalahari Game Ranch   LODGE $$$
(📞 063-240982; www.bagatelle-kalahari-game ranch.com; D1268; s/d with half board N$2635/3960; ❋ 🛜 🏊) Wooden chalets on elevated stilts facing the setting sun from atop a sand dune... The rooms here have a range of styles with soothing earth tones, high ceilings and stylish throws. Activities include stargazing, night drives (watch for the elusive aardwolf), feeding of the rescued cheetahs, searching for meerkats and a Bushman walk. It's a lovely place. It's northeast of Mariental; take the C20 east then north on the D1268.

Kalahari Anib Lodge & Campsite   CAMPGROUND $$$
(📞 061-427200, 063-204529; www.gondwana-collection.com; C20; camping N$175, s/d from N$1333/2138; ❀ ❋ 🛜 🏊) Gorgeous wood-floored rooms here have a more contemporary look than your average safari lodge and we love it all the more for it. There are also three excellent campsites, an equally excellent restaurant and palm-strewn grounds, all adding up to an entirely agreeable Kalahari experience. It's around 30km northeast of Mariental, just north of the C20.

❶ Getting There & Away

Intercape Mainliner (p375) buses travelling from Windhoek (from N$495, three hours, four weekly) to Keetmanshoop (from N$459, 2½ hours) pass through Mariental.

Hardap Dam Game Reserve

✔ 063

This **reserve** (per person N$30, plus per vehicle N$15; ☺ sunrise-6pm), 15km northwest of Mariental, is a 25,000-hectare wildlife park with 80km of gravel roads and a 15km hiking loop. Hardap is Nama for 'Nipple'; it was named after the conical hills topped by dolerite knobs that dot the area. The highlights here are fishing and birdwatching around the lake.

There are several picnic sites east of the lake, and between sunrise and sunset you can walk anywhere in the reserve. Note that swimming isn't permitted in the dam.

Most travellers come for the blue lake, which breaks up the arid plateau landscape and provides anglers with carp, barbel, mudfish and blue karpers. The lake also supports countless species of water bird, including flamingos, fish eagles, pelicans, spoonbills and Goliath herons.

🛏 Sleeping

Hardap Resort   HOTEL $$

(✆ 063-240286, 061-2857200; www.nwr.com.na/resorts/hardap-resort; camping/dm N$120/250, s incl breakfast N$800-1500, d incl breakfast N$900-1600; ☒) Attractive rooms, many with balconies overlooking the lake, are an excellent place to spend the night. The higher the rate, the better the view; the cheaper rooms (apart from the five-bed dorms) are bush chalets. Camping is also possible. Bookings must be made through the NWR (p230) in Windhoek.

ℹ Getting There & Away

To get to the reserve, you will need your own vehicle; take the signposted turning off the B1, 15km north of Mariental, and continue 6km to the entrance gate.

Brukkaros

With a 2km-wide crater, this extinct volcano (1586m) dominates the skyline between Mariental and Keetmanshoop. It was formed some 80 million years ago when a magma pipe encountered ground water about 1km below the earth's surface and caused a series of violent volcanic explosions.

From the car park, it's a 3.5km hike to the crater's southern entrance; along the way, watch for the remarkable **quartz formations** embedded in the rock. From here, you can head for the other-worldly **crater floor**, or turn left and follow the southern rim up to the abandoned sunspot research centre, which was established by the US Smithsonian Institute in the 1930s.

🛏 Sleeping

Brukkaros Campsite   CAMPGROUND $

(camping N$70) The basic Brukkaros Campsite has sites with toilets and a bush shower, but you must supply your own drinking water. Half of the campsites are literally carved out of the volcano and offer some truly stunning views across the valley.

ℹ Getting There & Away

Brukkaros rises 35km west of Tses on the B1. Follow the C98 west for 40km and then turn north on to the D3904 about 1km east of Berseba. It's then 8km to the car park. Note that a 4WD is required to access some of the higher campsites at Brukkaros Campsite.

Rehoboth

POP 28,840 / ✔ 062

Rehoboth lies 85km south of Windhoek and just a stone's throw north of the Tropic of Capricorn.

◉ Sights

Town Museum   MUSEUM

(✆ 062-522954; www.rehobothmuseum.com; N$25; ☺ 9am-noon & 2-4pm Mon-Fri, 9am-noon Sat) The town museum, housed in the 1903 residence of the settlement's first colonial postmaster, recounts the historical roots of Rehoboth from 1844.

🛏 Sleeping

Lake Oanob Resort   RESORT $$

(✆ 062-522370; www.oanob.com.na; camping N$70-140, s/d from N$860/1134, 6-bed chalets N$2880; ☒) If you're looking to rehabilitate your travel-worn body and mind, a surprisingly relaxing retreat is the Lake Oanob Resort, located alongside the Oanob Dam, just west of Rehoboth. The resort is centred on a stunningly calm and tranquil blue lake. Amenities include a shaded camping area, a thatched bar and restaurant, and beautiful stone self-catering bungalows on the lake's shores.

ℹ Getting There & Away

Intercape Mainliner (p375) buses running from Windhoek to Keetmanshoop pass through Rehoboth (from N$468, one hour, four weekly).

Keetmanshoop

POP 20,980 / ☎ 063

Keetmanshoop (*kayt*-mahns-*hoo*-up) sits at the main crossroads of southern Namibia, and this is why you may end up here. More of a place to overnight than spend any time, it's nonetheless a friendly enough little town.

There are a few examples of German colonial architecture, including the 1910 Kaiserliches Postampt, and the town museum, which is housed in the 1895 Rhenish Mission Church, which itself is arguably more interesting than the contents of the museum inside. The ramshackle bits and pieces on display are good for killing an hour or so.

◎ Sights

Town Museum   CHURCH, MUSEUM
(cnr Kaiser St & 7th Ave; ☉ 7.30am-4.30pm Mon-Fri) **FREE** The town museum occupies the 1895 Rhenish Mission Church, which itself is arguably more interesting than the contents of the museum inside. The ramshackle bits and pieces on display are good for killing an hour or so.

Kaiserliches Postampt   HISTORIC BUILDING
(Imperial Post Office; cnr 5th Ave & Fenschel St) The 1910 Kaiserliches Postampt used to house the post office. There's an information office inside where you can arrange local tours.

⊨ Sleeping

Bernice B&B   GUESTHOUSE $
(☎ 063-224851; bernicebeds@iway.na; 129 10th St; s/d N$240/360) Although down a side road, Bernice B&B is extremely well signed from any direction that you approach town – just follow the signs! Book ahead as it does get busy. There are family options, DSTV and good-size rooms which are a little dated but otherwise well kept and nice enough.

Quivertree
Forest Rest Camp   CAMPGROUND, BUNGALOWS $
(☎ 063-683421; www.quivertreeforest.com; camping N$120, s/d/tr/q bungalows from N$620/965/1260/1950; ☀) About 14km east of town, the Quivertree Forest Rest Camp proudly boasts Namibia's largest stand of kokerboom (quiver trees). Day rates (per person N$60) include use of picnic facilities and entry to the Giant's Playground, a bizarre natural rock garden 5km away. Accommodation is simple but adequate.

Pension Gessert   GUESTHOUSE $
(☎ 063-223892, 081 4347379; www.natron.net/gessert/main.html; 138 13th St; s/d N$600/1000, s with shared bathroom N$450; ☎ ☀) In the quiet Westdene neighbourhood of town, Pension Gessert offers quaint and homey rooms with modern touches, a beautiful cooling green garden to relax in and a swimming pool.

❶ Getting There & Away

Intercape Mainliner (p375) runs buses between Windhoek and Keetmanshoop (from N$522, 5½ hours, four weekly). Book your tickets in advance online as this service continues on to Cape Town, South Africa and fills up quickly.

Combis (minibuses) also run up and down the B1 with fairly regular frequency, and a ride between Windhoek and Keetmanshoop shouldn't cost more than N$180. Less regular combis connect Keetmanshoop to Lüderitz, with fares averaging around N$250.

Trans-Namib (p378) operates a night train between Windhoek and Keetmanshoop (from N$160, 12 hours, daily except Saturday).

Naute Dam

Naute Dam is an attractive spot that is surrounded by low truncated hills, and attracts large numbers of water birds.

◎ Sights

Naute Kristall   DISTILLERY
(☎ 063-683810, 081 127 7485; www.nautekristall. com; ☉ by appointment) Call ahead for directions and a one-hour tour of this innovative distillery thats produce NamGin, Namibia's very own, home-grown gin. It's overseen by Michael and Katrin, who still play an important role in Kristall Kellerei Winery (p236) in Omaruru.

❶ Getting There & Away

To get to the dam, drive 30km west of Keetmanshoop on the B4 and turn south on the D545.

Seeheim

POP 20 / ☎ 063

It's a long and lonely drive southwest to Lüderitz, which is why you might want to consider stopping for the night at the Seeheim rail halt, 48km southwest of Keetmanshoop. Although the tiny town is home to little more than petrol stations and small shops, about 13km west on the B4 is the

Naiams farm, where a signpost indicates a 15-minute walk to the remains of a 1906 **German fort**. The fort was raised to prevent Nama attacks on German travellers and Lüderitz-bound freight.

🛏 Sleeping

Seeheim Hotel   HOTEL **$$**
(☑ 081 128 0349, 063-683643; www.seeheimhotel.com; s/d/f N$750/1160/1400) The historic Seeheim Hotel features an atmospheric old bar as well as period furniture. Rooms are simple, clean affairs with mosquito nets (upstairs rooms are better).

ⓘ Getting There & Away

The tarred B4 highway connects Keetmanshoop with Lüderitz, though you're going to need your own vehicle if you want to access this stretch of highway.

Duwisib Castle

☑ 063

A curious neobaroque structure located about 70km south of Maltahöhe smackdab in the middle of the barren desert, this European **castle** (N$70; ⊙8am-1pm & 2-5pm) is smaller than some grandiose descriptions suggest and really worth a stop only if you're passing by. The portraits and scant furniture certainly give it a European feel though and the pleasant courtyard is a good place to relax in the shade of some majestic trees.

History

The castle was built in 1909 by Baron Captain Hans Heinrich von Wolf. After the German-Nama wars, the loyal baron commissioned architect Willie Sander to design a castle that would reflect his commitment to the German military cause. He also married the stepdaughter of the US consul to Dresden, Miss Jayta Humphreys, and planned on ruling over his personal corner of German South West Africa.

Although the stone for the castle was quarried nearby, much of the raw material was imported from Germany, and required 20 ox wagons to transport it across the 330km of desert from Lüderitz. Artisans and masons were hired from countries as far away as Ireland, Denmark, Sweden and Italy. The result was a U-shaped castle with 22 rooms, all suitably fortified and decorated with family portraits and military paraphernalia. Rather than windows, most rooms have embrasures, which emphasise Von Wolf's apparent obsession with security.

As history would have it, WWI broke out, and the Baron reenlisted in the Schutzruppe (German Imperial Army), only to be killed two weeks later at the Battle of the Somme. The baroness never returned to Namibia, though some people claim that the descendants of her thoroughbred horses still roam the desert. In the late 1970s, ownership of the Duwisib Castle and its surrounding 50 hectares was transferred to the State, and is now administered by NWR.

🛏 Sleeping

Betta Camp Site   CAMPGROUND **$**
(☑ 081 477 3992; www.bettacamp.net; cnr C27 & D826; camping N$100, chalets per person N$300, with full board N$500) A welcoming stop on the road in these parts is Betta Camp Site, roughly 20km past Duwisib. Apart from petrol and campsites if you want to crash the night, make a beeline for the kiosk where you can stock up on supplies and indulge in the most delicious homemade goodies. Snaffle down freshly baked farm bread, apple pie, pancakes and other sweet treats. There is even firewood and BBQ packs.

Duwisib Castle Rest Camp   CAMPGROUND **$**
(camping N$110) This very amenable camp (with a sparkling amenities block) occupies one corner of the castle grounds and is well set up with campsites containing bin, braai and bench seating. The adjoining kiosk sells snacks, coffee and cool drinks. Book through the NWR office (p230) in Windhoek.

Duwisib Guest Farm   GUESTHOUSE **$$**
(☑ 063-293344; www.farmduwisib.com; camping N$110, s/d with half board N$980/1720) Located 300m from the castle, this pleasant guest farm has rooms with views of the main attraction, and self-catering family units that sleep up to eight people. While you're there, be sure to check out the historic blacksmith shop up the hill.

ⓘ Getting There & Away

There isn't any public transport to Duwisib Castle. If you're coming from Helmeringhausen, head north on the C14 for 62km and turn northwest on to the D831. Continue for 27km, then turn west onto the D826 and travel a further 15km to the castle.

NAMIBIA & ITS METEORS

A meteorite is an extraterrestrial body that survives its impact with the earth's surface without being destroyed. Although it's estimated that about 500 meteorites land each year, only a handful are typically recovered. However, in a single meteor shower sometime in the dim and distant past, more than 21 tonnes of 90% ferrous extraterrestrial boulders crashed to earth in southern Namibia. It's rare for so many meteorites to fall at once, and these are thought to have been remnants of an explosion in space, which were held together as they were drawn in by the earth's gravitational field.

Thus far, at least 77 meteorite chunks have been found within a 2500-sq-km area around the former Rhenish mission station of Gibeon, 60km south of Mariental. The largest chunk, which weighs 650kg, is housed in Cape Town Museum, South Africa, while other bits have wound up as far away as Anchorage, Alaska. Between 1911 and 1913, soon after their discovery, 33 chunks were brought to Windhoek for safekeeping. Over the years, they've been displayed in Zoo Park and at Alte Feste in Windhoek, but have now found a home on Post Street Mall.

Maltahöhe

POP 6000 / ☑ 063

Maltahöhe, lying at the heart of a commercial ranching area, is a convenient stopover along the back route between Namib-Naukluft Park and Lüderitz.

🛌 Sleeping

Hotel Maltahöhe   HOTEL $
(☑ 063-293013; s/d N$550/825) In town, you can bed down for the night at the Hotel Maltahöhe, which has won several national awards for its amenable, spic-and-span accommodation. It also has a restaurant and bar offering Continental cuisine.

ℹ Getting There & Away

Maltahöhe lies at the junction of the C19 and C14; you're most likely to pass through here on your way between Sesriem and Mariental. There's no public transport along this route.

Helmeringhausen

☑ 063

Helmeringhausen is little more than a homestead, hotel and petrol station, and has been the property of the Hester family since 1919.

◉ Sights

Agricultural Museum   MUSEUM
(Main St; ⊙ on request from hotel) FREE The highlight of Helmeringhausen is the idiosyncratic Agricultural Museum, established in 1984 by the Helmeringhausen Farming Association. It displays all sorts of interesting old furniture and farming implements collected from local properties, as well as an antique fire engine.

🛌 Sleeping

Helmeringhausen Hotel   HOTEL $$
(☑ 063-283307; www.helmeringhausennamibia.com; s/d N$650/1100; ☀) A surprisingly swish hotel with elegant rooms in addition to a very popular restaurant and bar. The menu is limited, but the beer is cold and it has a well-stocked wine cellar. Those who like eating game meat may feel uncomfortable being watched by all those accusing trophies. There's also a great courtyard area for soaking up the sun and enjoying a cold drink.

It gets busy with tour groups – book ahead in high season.

ℹ Getting There & Away

Helmeringhausen is 130km south of Maltahöhe on the C14.

Bethanie

POP 2000

One of Namibia's oldest settlements, Bethanie was founded in 1814 by the London Missionary Society. After seven years the mission was abandoned due to tribal squabbling and although a German missionary, Heinrich Schmelen, attempted to revive it several times, he was thwarted by drought.

Schmelen's original 1814 mission station, **Schmelenhaus**, occupied a one-storey cottage. It was burnt to the ground when he left Bethanie in 1828, and later rebuilt in 1842 by the first Rhenish missionary, Reverend Hans Knudsen. The building now sits on the grounds of the Evangelical Lutheran Church and houses a museum full of old photos of the mission. If it's locked, a notice on the door will tell you where to pick up a key.

Also worth a look is the 1883 **home** of Captain Joseph Fredericks, the Nama chief who signed a treaty with the representatives of Adolf Lüderitz on 1 May 1883 for the transfer of Angra Pequena (present-day Lüderitz). It was here in October 1884 that Captain Fredericks and the German Consul General, Dr Friedrich Nachtigal, signed a treaty of German protection over the entire territory.

🛌 Sleeping

Bethanie Guesthouse GUESTHOUSE **$**
(☏ 063-283013; Main St; s/d from N$450/850; 🛜🏊) Bethanie Guesthouse, one of Namibia's oldest hotels and under newish management, inhabits a personality-steeped building with good facilities including camping and modern, if unexciting rooms. It's a welcoming place.

ⓘ Getting There & Away

The Bethanie turn-off is signposted on the B4, 140km west of Keetmanshoop.

The South Coast

Call that wilderness? *This* is wilderness. From Walvis Bay to Lüderitz, Namibia disappears into an almost-trackless waste dominated by enormous linear dunes, which roll back from the sea towards the inland gravel plains that are occasionally interrupted by isolated mountain ranges. Welcome to the Sperrgebiet (Forbidden Area), which plays host to the country's highly lucrative and highly secure diamond-mining efforts, and which can be visited only as part of an organised tour.

A strange blip on this largely uninhabited desert region, the town of Lüderitz is rich in German colonial architecture, and occupies an other-worldly setting between the dunes and sea. It's a lovely if anachronistic place to spend a few days.

Aus

POP 300 / ☏ 063

A stop on the long drive west to Lüderitz, Aus is home to a former prison camp and also boasts two highly recommendable guest farms where you can slow down and

---

WILD HORSES

On the desert plains west of Aus live some of the world's only wild desert-dwelling horses. The origin of these eccentric equines is unclear, though several theories abound. One theory suggests that the horses descended from Schutztruppe (German Imperial Army) cavalry horses abandoned during the South African invasion in 1915, while others claim they were brought in by Nama raiders moving north from beyond the Orange River. Yet another theory asserts that they descended from a load of shipwrecked horses en route from Europe to Australia. Still others maintain that the horses descended from the stud stock of Baron Captain Hans-Heinrich von Wolf, the original owner of the **Duwisib Castle** (p324).

These horses, whose bony and scruffy appearance belies their probable high-bred ancestry and apparent adaptation to the harsh conditions, are protected inside the Diamond Area 1. In years of good rain, they grow fat and their numbers increase to several hundred. Their only source of water is Garub Pan, which is fed by an artificial borehole.

If not for the efforts of a few concerned individuals, the horses would probably have been wiped out long ago. These individuals, led by security officer Jan Coetzer of Consolidated Diamond Mines (CDM), recognised that the horses were unique, and managed to secure funding to install the borehole at Garub Pan. At one stage, the Ministry of Environment & Tourism (MET) considered taming the horses for use on patrols in Etosha National Park, though the proposal fell through. There have also been calls to exterminate the horses by individuals citing possible damage to the desert environment and gemsbok herds. So far, however, the tourism value of the horses has swept aside all counterarguments.

The horses may also be valuable for scientific purposes. For instance, they urinate less than domestic horses, and are smaller than their supposed ancestors. The horses are also able to go without water for up to five days at a time. These adaptations may be valuable in helping scientists understand how animals cope with changing climatic conditions.

About 10km from Aus on the road to Lüderitz, start watching out for feral desert horses. About 20km west of Aus, turn north at the sign 'Feral Horses' and follow the track for 1.5km to Garub Pan, which is home to an artificial water hole where the horses often visit.

spend some time soaking up the desolate beauty of the shifting sands.

🛏 Sleeping

Desert Horse Inn   LODGE $$

(☑ 063-258021; www.klein-aus-vista.com; camping N$120, r per person from N$990; ✿ ⚙ ⚙) This 10,000-hectare ranch, 3km west of Aus, is a hiker's paradise with six different trails you can do, from 4km to 20km in length. Accommodation is provided in the main lodge, which is cast in soothing earth tones and with lovely large rooms. Meals are available at the main lodge. Apart from the wonderful hiking, activities include horse riding and 4WD tours of the ranch's vast desert concession.

The excellent campsites sit beneath camel thorn shade and make the most of the big-sky views.

Bahnhof Hotel   HOTEL $$

(☑ 063-258091;   www.bahnhof-hotel-aus.com; 20 Lüderitz Strasse; s/d N$890/1520) One of the better in-town hotels along the B1, the Bahnhof has rooms with wood floors, white walls and splashes of colour and character. Smallish windows make some a little claustrophobic, but they're an excellent if pricey option for those keen not to stray too far from the main highway. There's a reasonable on-site restaurant with an appealing outdoor terrace and international dishes.

Namtib Desret Lodge   LODGE $$

(☑ 063-683055; www.namtib.net; camping N$130, s/d N$1050/1640) 🌿 In the beautiful Tirasberge, the private Namtib Biosphere Reserve is run by ecologically conscious owners who've created a self-sustaining farm in a narrow valley, with distant views of the Namib plains and dune sea. The rooms are tastefully turned out and comfortable. To reach the reserve, take the C13 north of Aus for 55km, then turn west on the D707; after 48km, turn east onto the 12km farm road to the lodge.

There is an incredible wealth of nature on display here, and it's certainly worth spending a night or two getting acquainted with all the empty space.

Eagle's Nest Chalets   CHALET $$$

(www.klein-aus-vista.com; chalet per person N$1325) These two- to four-person self-catering chalets get the mix of deliciously remote with proximity to the affiliated Desert Horse Inn facilities 7km away; if you don't feel like

WARTIME AUS

After the Germans surrendered to the South African forces in 1915, Aus became one of two internment camps for German military personnel (military police and officers were sent to Okahandja in the north while noncommissioned officers went to Aus). Since the camp quickly grew to 1500 prisoners and 600 South African guards, residents were forced to seek shelter in flimsy tents. However, the resourceful inmates turned to brick-making and constructed houses for themselves – they even sold the excess bricks to the guards for 10 shillings per 1000. The houses weren't opulent – roofs were tiled with unrolled food tins – but they did provide protection from the elements. The prisoners also built several wood stoves and even sank boreholes.

After the Treaty of Versailles the camp was dismantled, and by May 1919 it was closed. Virtually nothing remains, though several of the brick houses have been reconstructed. The former camp is 4km east of the village of Aus, down a gravel road, then to the right; there's now a national plaque commemorating it.

cooking, you can eat at the lodge restaurant. Built in stone and glass and with the backs to the barren mountains, this fine place offer sweeping views and a glorious sense of space and light.

ⓘ Information

Aus Information Centre (☑ 063-258151; ⊙ 8am-5pm Mon-Fri, to 2pm Sat & Sun) has a cafe, internet and lots of information on nature, war and wild horses of the area. Ask here about the Aus Walking Trail which begins at the info centre.

ⓘ Getting There & Away

Aus is 125km east of Lüderitz on the B4. Travel in this region typically requires a private vehicle.

Lüderitz

POP 12,540 / ☑ 063

Before travelling to Lüderitz, pause for a moment to study the country map and how the town is sandwiched between the barren Namib Desert and the windswept South Atlantic coast. As if Lüderitz' unique

Lüderitz

0 ———— 400 m
0 ———— 0.2 miles

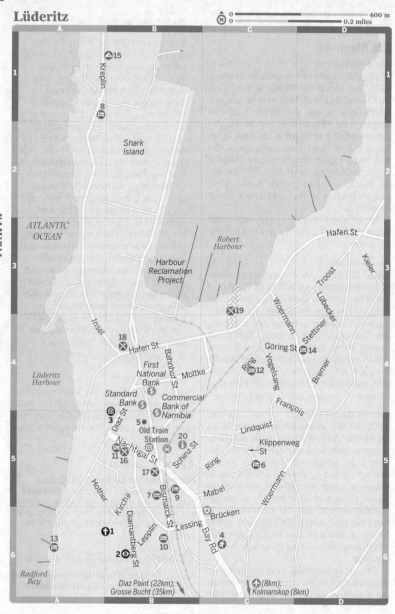

NAMIBIA

ATLANTIC
OCEAN

Shark
Island

Kreplin

Robert
Harbour

Harbour
Reclamation
Project

Hafen St

Kieler

Troost

Lübecker

Stettiner

Bremer

Lüderitz
Harbour

Insel

Göring St

Ring

Vogelsang

Woermann

Hafen St

Bahnhof St

First
National
Bank

Moltke

François

Standard
Bank

Commercial
Bank of
Namibia

Diaz St

Lindquist

Klippenweg
St

Old Train
Station

Nachtigal St

Schinz St

Ring

Woermann

Hother

Kirche

Diamantberg St

Lepplin

Bismarck St

Mabel

Lessing

Brücken

Bay Rd

Radford
Bay

Diaz Point (22km);
Grosse Bucht (35km)

(8km);
Kolmanskop (8km)

geographical setting wasn't impressive
enough, its surreal German art nouveau
architecture will seal the deal. A colonial
relic scarcely touched by the 21st century,
Lüderitz recalls a Bavarian *dorfchen* (small
village), with churches, bakeries and cafes.

Unlike its more well-heeled Teutonic rival
Swakopmund, Lüderitz feels stuck in a
time warp, a perception that delivers both
gloom and a certain charm (at least for visitors). In short, it's one of the most incongruous places in Africa.

Lüderitz

But it's the natural environment surrounding the town where southern Namibia really comes alive. The rocky coastline of the Lüderitz peninsula harbours flamingo flocks and penguin colonies, while the adjacent Sperrgebiet National Park is arguably the country's wildest and most pristine landscape.

History

In April 1883 Heinrich Vogelsang, under orders from Bremen merchant Adolf Lüderitz, entered into a treaty with Nama chief Joseph Fredericks and secured lands within an 8km radius of Angra Pequeña (Little Bay). Later that year Lüderitz made an appearance in Little Bay, and following his recommendation, the German chancellor Otto von Bismarck designated South Western Africa a protectorate of the German empire. Following the discovery of diamonds in the Sperrgebiet in 1908, the town of Lüderitz was officially founded, and quickly prospered from the gem trade.

Indeed, the history of diamond mining in Namibia parallels the history of Lüderitz. Although diamonds were discovered along the Orange River in South Africa, and among the guano workings on the offshore islands as early as 1866, it apparently didn't occur to anyone that the desert sands might also harbour a bit of crystal carbon. In 1908, however, railway worker Zacharias Lewala found a shiny stone along the railway line near Grasplatz and gave it to his employer, August Stauch. Stauch took immediate interest and, to his elation, the state geologist confirmed that it was indeed a diamond. Stauch applied for a prospecting licence from the Deutsche Koloniale Gesellschaft (German Colonial Society) and set up his own mining company, the Deutsche Diamanten Gesellschaft (German Diamond Company), to begin exploiting the presumed windfall.

In the years that followed, hordes of prospectors descended upon the town of Lüderitz with dreams of finding wealth buried in the sands. Lüderitz became a boom town as service facilities sprang up to accommodate the growing population. By September 1908, however, diamond madness was threatening to escalate out of control, which influenced the German government to intervene by establishing the Sperrgebiet. This 'Forbidden Zone' extended from 26°S latitude southward to the Orange River mouth, and stretched inland for 100km. Independent prospecting was henceforth verboten, and those who'd already staked their claims were forced to form mining companies.

In February 1909 a diamond board was created to broker all diamond sales and thereby control prices. However, after WWI ended, the world diamond market was so depressed that in 1920, Ernst Oppenheimer of the Anglo-American Corporation was able to purchase Stauch's company, along with eight other diamond-producing companies. This ambitious move led to the formation of Consolidated Diamond Mines (CDM), which was administered by De Beers South Africa and headquartered in Kolmanskop.

In 1928 rich diamond fields were discovered around the mouth of the Orange River, and in 1944 CDM decided to relocate to the purpose-built company town of Oranjemund. Kolmanskop's last inhabitants left in 1956, and the sand dunes have been encroaching on the town ever since.

In 1994 CDM gave way to Namdeb Diamond Corporation Limited (Namdeb), which is owned in equal shares by the government of Namibia and the De Beers Group. De Beers is a Johannesburg- and London-based diamond-mining and trading corporation that has held a virtual monopoly over the diamond trade for much of its corporate history. Today, diamonds are still Lüderitz' best friend, though it's also home to several maritime industries, including the harvesting of crayfish, seaweed and seagrass, as well as experimental oyster, mussel and prawn farms.

⊙ Sights

LÜDERITZ TOWN

Felsenkirche CHURCH
(Kirche St; ☺ 4-5pm Mon-Sat) FREE The prominent Evangelical Lutheran church dominates Lüderitz from high on Diamond Hill. It was designed by Albert Bause, who implemented the Victorian influences he'd seen in the Cape. With assistance from private donors in Germany, construction of the church began in late 1911 and was completed the following year. The brilliant stained-glass panel situated over the altar was donated by Kaiser Wilhelm II, while the Bible was a gift from his wife. Come for the views over the water and the town.

Goerke Haus HISTORIC SITE
(Diamantberg St; N$35; ☺ guided tour 2-4pm Mon-Fri, 4-5pm Sat & Sun) The sheer scale of Goerke Haus and the way it blends into the rock face is very impressive. Originally the home of Lieutenant Hans Goerke, and designed by architect Otto Ertl and constructed in 1910 on Diamond Hill, it was one of the town's most extravagant properties. The house has undergone an admirable renovation job and is certainly worth a look.

Lüderitz Museum MUSEUM
(☏ 063-202582; Diaz St; N$20; ☺ 3.30-5pm Mon-Fri) This museum contains information on the town's history, including displays on natural history, local indigenous groups and the diamond-mining industry. Phone to arrange a visit outside standard opening hours.

LÜDERITZ PENINSULA

The Lüderitz Peninsula, much of which lies outside the Sperrgebiet, makes an interesting half-day excursion from town.

Agate Bay, just north of Lüderitz, is made of tailings from the diamond workings. There aren't many agates these days, but you'll find fine sand partially consisting of tiny grey mica chips.

The picturesque and relatively calm bay, **Sturmvogelbucht**, is a pleasant place for a braai (barbecue), though the water temperature would be amenable only to a penguin or polar bear. The rusty ruin in the bay is the remains of a 1914 Norwegian whaling station; the salty pan just inland attracts flamingos and merits a quick stop.

At **Diaz Point**, 22km by road from Lüderitz, is a classic lighthouse and a replica of the cross erected in July 1488 by Portuguese navigator Bartolomeu Dias on his return from the Cape of Good Hope. Portions of the original have been dispersed as far as Lisbon, Berlin and Cape Town. From the point, there's a view of a nearby seal colony and you can also see cormorants, flamingos, wading birds and even the occasional pod of dolphins.

Also at the point is a **coffee shop** serving hot/cold drinks, toasties, oysters, beer and great chocolate cake. It's possible to **camp** out here as well (campsite N$95, per person N$55) on rocky, flat ground roped off between the lighthouse and water. There are decent amenities although the site is more exposed to the wind than Shark Island.

Halifax Island, a short distance offshore south of Diaz Point, is home to Namibia's best-known jackass-penguin colony. Jackass or Cape penguins live in colonies on rocky offshore islets off the Atlantic Coast. With binoculars, you can often see them gathering on the sandy beach opposite the car park.

Grosse Bucht (Big Bay), at the southern end of Lüderitz Peninsula, is a wild and scenic beach favoured by flocks of flamingos, which feed in the tidal pools. It's also the site of a small but picturesque shipwreck on the beach.

Just a few kilometres up the coast is **Klein Bogenfels**, a small rock arch beside the sea. When the wind isn't blowing a gale, it makes a pleasant picnic spot.

☞ Tours

With the exception of the Kolmanskop ghost town (p334), allow at least five days to plan any excursion into the Sperrgebiet as tour companies need time to fill out all of the paperwork and acquire all of the necessary permits.

INTERNATIONAL TRADE

The international trade in diamonds as gemstones is unique in comparison to precious metals like gold and platinum since diamonds are not traded as a commodity. As a result, the price of diamonds is artificially inflated by a few key players, and there exists virtually no secondary market. For example, wholesale trade and diamond cutting was historically limited to a few locations, including New York, Antwerp, London, Tel Aviv and Amsterdam, though recently centres have been established in China, India and Thailand.

Since its establishment in 1888, De Beers has maintained a virtual monopoly on the world's diamond mines and distribution channels for gem-quality stones. At one time it was estimated that over 80% of the world's uncut diamonds were controlled by the subsidiaries of De Beers, though this percentage has dropped below 50% in more recent years. However, De Beers continues to take advantage of its market position by establishing strict price controls, and marketing diamonds directly to preferential consumers (known as sight holders) in world markets.

Once purchased by sight holders, diamonds are then cut and polished to sell as gemstones, though these activities are limited to the select locations mentioned earlier. Once they have been prepared, diamonds are then sold on one of 24 diamond exchanges known as bourses. This is the final tightly controlled step in the diamond supply chain, as retailers are only permitted to buy relatively small amounts of diamonds before preparing them for final sale to the consumer.

In recent years, the diamond industry has come under increasing criticism regarding the buying and selling of conflict or 'blood' diamonds, those diamonds mined in war zones and sold to finance the ongoing conflict. In response to increasing public concern, the Kimberley Process was instituted in 2002, which was aimed at preventing the trade of conflict diamonds on the international market. The main mechanism by which the Kimberley Process operates is by documenting and certifying diamond exports from producing countries in order to ensure that proceeds are not being used to fund criminal or revolutionary activities.

NAMIBIA THE SOUTH COAST

Coastways Tours Lüderitz　DRIVING
(☑063-202002; www.coastways.com.na) This highly reputable company runs multiday self-catering 4WD trips deep into the Sperrgebiet (from Lüderitz to Walvis Bay, for example). Note that the cost of the permit is included in the price of the relevant tour.

Lüderitz Safaris & Tours　ADVENTURE
(☑063-202719;　ludsaf@africaonline.com.na; Bismarck St) Provides useful tourist information, organises visitor permits for the Kolmanskop ghost town, books seats on the schooner *Sedina* (N$375 per person), which sails past the Cape fur seal sanctuary at Diaz Point and the penguin colony on Halifax Island. It also conducts guided oyster tours with time for tastings and generally it's a great information service with very knowledgeable staff.

🛏 Sleeping

Lüderitz has plenty of accommodation to choose from but book ahead to ensure that your first choice has space.

Lüderitz Backpackers Lodge　HOSTEL $
(☑063-202000; www.namibweb.com/backpackers.htm; 2 Ring St; camping N$90, dm/d/f N$120/300/450) Housed in a historic colonial mansion, this is the only true backpackers spot in town with rudimentary accommodation. The vibe is congenial and low-key, and the friendly management is helpful in sorting out your onward travels. And of course, the usual backpacker amenities are on offer here, including a communal kitchen, braai pit, TV lounge and laundry facilities. Prices may increase when it's busy.

Shark Island Campsite　CAMPGROUND $
(www.nwrnamibia.com/shark-island.htm; camping N$150, lighthouse per person N$330) This is a beautifully situated but aggravatingly windy locale. Shark Island is connected to the town by a causeway but is no longer an island, thanks to the harbour reclamation project that attached it to the mainland. The centrepiece of the island is a historic lighthouse that caps the central rock, and features two bedrooms, a living room and a kitchen – perfect for self-caterers!

Book accommodation through the NWR office in Windhoek; bookings can also be made at the entrance.

⭐ Hansa Haus Guesthouse   GUESTHOUSE $

(☑ 063-203699; www.hansahausluderitz.co.za; 85 Mabel St; s/d from N$552/650; 🛜) This family-run guesthouse in an early 20th-century German-style house is one of the better places in town. The wood floors, white-linen look and the sea breezes (especially on the upstairs terrace) round out a lovely package.

⭐ Haus Sandrose   APARTMENT $

(☑ 063-202630; www.haussandrose.com; 15 Bismarck St; s/d from N$530/760) Haus Sandrose is comprised of uniquely decorated self-catering rooms surrounding a sheltered garden. The bright rooms are good value and exude a cheerful and roomy feel; note some rooms are bigger than others. It's a great location and very friendly.

⭐ Kairos B&B   B&B $

(☑ 063-203080, 081 650 5598; http://kairos cottage.com/; Shark Island; s/d N$480/680) This brand spanking new, cheerful, whitewashed building houses a promising new guesthouse and overlooks the water just before Shark Island. It's in a lovely location and is just a few minutes' drive from the town centre. Also here is a coffee shop serving breakfast and lunch.

Kapps Hotel   HOTEL $

(☑ 063-202345; www.kappshotel.com; Bay Rd; s/d N$350/560) This is the town's oldest hotel, dating back to 1907, which has managed to retain a certain faded grandeur while adding a touch of modernity. Darkish downstairs rooms have huge bathrooms. The attached Rumour's Grill is a great place to drop into for either a cold beer at the end of a long drive or a strong nightcap on the way up to bed.

Krabbenhoft une Lampe   APARTMENT $

(☑ 081 127 7131, 063-202674; http://klguesthouse. com; 25 Bismarck St; s/d apt from N$330/400) One of the more unusual sleeping options in town, the Krabbenhoft is a converted carpet factory that now offers a number of self-catering flats upstairs from a furniture shop and Avis car-rental office. Accommodation has loads of character, floor-to-ceiling bookshelves, high ceilings, lots of natural light, good shared kitchen facilities and the novelty factor can't be beat.

Kratzplatz   B&B $

(☑ 063-202458; www.kratzplatz.com; 5 Nachtigal St; s/d incl breakfast from N$440/800) Housed in a converted church complete with vaulted ceilings, this centrally located B&B offers a variety of different rooms to choose from set amid a patch of greenery. Rooms are in varying condition – some are a little worn but comfortable and the upstairs ones come with outside chair and table on the balcony. The attached Barrels restaurant has a lively beer garden and a wonderful German kitchen.

Protea Sea-View
Hotel Zum Sperrgebiet   HOTEL $

(☑ 063-203411; www.marriott.com; cnr Woermann & Göring Sts; r from N$833; ❄ 🛜 🏊) In a town defined by its colonial heritage, the Protea bucks the trend with a modern offering of polished steel and sparkling glass. There are only 22 sun-blessed rooms here, each accented by a sweeping terrace facing out towards the sea. Despite being part of the Marriott's portfolio, prices are reasonable and the atmosphere unpretentious.

Lüderitz Nest Hotel   HOTEL $$$

(☑ 063-204000; www.nesthotel.com; 820 Diaz St; s/d from N$1320/2100; ❄ 🏊) Lüderitz' oldest upmarket hotel occupies a jutting peninsula in the southwest corner of town, complete with its own private beach. Each room is stylishly appointed with modern furnishings and faces out towards the sea. Amenities include a pool, sauna, kids playground, car hire, terraced bar and a collection of gourmet restaurants. This hotel is what you would expect: decent service, clean and good facilities. It's overpriced but its drawcard is the magnificent water views from the rooms.

✖ Eating

If the sea has been bountiful, various hotels serve the catch of the day, though you can always count on a long list of German specialities. If you're self-catering, there are a number of supermarkets as well as small seafood merchants in town.

⭐ Diaz Coffee Shop   CAFE $

(☑ 081-700 0475; cnr Bismarck & Nachtigal Sts; mains froim N$45; ⏱ 8am-9pm) The cappuccinos are strong, the pastries are sweet, and the ambience wouldn't at all look out of place in Munich. Patrons sit in a large room with some comfy seating and receive quick service; the food, such as hot wraps or chicken schwarma, is delicious. The coffee shop has recently broadened its horizons to become an evening oyster and wine bar – very cool. Try the speciality coffee...if you dare.

★ Garden Cafe
CAFE $

(☑ 081-124 8317; 17 Hafen St; light meals from N$25) The garden setting, white-wood furnishings, great coffee and filled rolls add up to one of our favourite little haunts in town. The baked treats, Black Forest gateau among them, are also highlights. Travellers tend to agree with our positive experience – we're yet to hear a bad word said about this place.

Seabreeze Coffee Shop
CAFE $

(Waterfront Complex; snacks & meals N$15-50; ⊘ 7.15am-4.30pm Mon-Fri, 8am-1pm Sat) This smallish waterfront cafe offers attractive sea views, so make it a double espresso and linger a bit longer than you normally would. Bratwurst sausage, boerewors (farmer's sausage) in a hotdog, burgers and toasties feature on the menu, along with breakfasts. It's a well-run place with outdoor seating.

Barrels
GERMAN $$

(☑ 063-202458; 5 Nachtigal St; mains N$50-120; ⊘ 6-10pm Mon-Fri) A wonderfully festive bar-restaurant accented by occasional live music, Barrels offers rotating daily specials highlighting fresh seafood and German staples. Portions are hefty and the buffet (N$150) is great value.

Penguin Restaurant
SEAFOOD $$

(☑ 063-204000; http://nesthotel.com/services/restaurant; 820 Diaz St; mains from N$80; ⊘ noon-2pm & 6-9pm) Part of the Nest Hotel and with a prime waterfront location, Penguin restaurant does all the usual Lüderitz seafood suspects – oysters, seafood curry, seafood platter – and they're usually excellent, but travellers give this place mixed reviews. It's a classier place than most in town

Ritzi's Seafood Restaurant
SEAFOOD $$

(☑ 063-202818; Waterfront Complex; mains from N$75; ⊘ 8am-9pm Tue-Sat, noon-9pm Mon) Occupying a choice location in the waterfront complex, Ritzi's is the town's top spot for seafood matched with fine sunset views. The food can be a little hit-or-miss, but the location is difficult to beat and outside dining catches the breeze and the views. Try the seafood curry or seafood platter; there's a decent wine selection.

ℹ Information

DANGERS & ANNOYANCES

Stay well clear of the Sperrgebiet, unless you're part of an organised tour, as much of the area remains strictly off limits despite its national-park status. The northern boundary is formed by the B4 and extends almost as far east as Aus. The boundary is patrolled by some fairly ruthless characters, and trespassers will be prosecuted (or worse).

MONEY

Several banks on Bismarck St change cash and travellers cheques.

TOURIST INFORMATION

Namibia Wildlife Resorts (☑ 063-202752; www.nwr.com.na; Schinz St; ⊘ 7.30am-1pm & 2-4pm Mon-Fri) This local office can help with national-park information.

ℹ Getting There & Away

Air Namibia (p374) travels about three times a week between Windhoek and Lüderitz. The airport is 8km southeast of town.

Somewhat irregular combis connect Lüderitz to Keetmanshoop, with fares averaging around N$250. Buses depart from the southern edge of town at informal bus stops along Bismarck St.

Lüderitz and the scenery en route are worth the 334km trip from Keetmanshoop via the tarred B4. When the wind blows – which is most of the time – the final 10km into Lüderitz may be blocked by a barchan dune field that seems bent upon crossing the road. Conditions do get hazardous, especially if it's foggy, and the drifts pile quite high before road crews clean them off. Obey local speed limits, and avoid driving at night if possible.

Sperrgebiet National Park

Although it's been off-limits to the public for most of the last century, in 2008 the Namibian government inaugurated the Sperrgebiet (Forbidden Area) as a national park. Geographically speaking, the park encompasses the northern tip of the Succulent Karoo Biorne, an area of 26,000 sq km of dunes and mountains that appear dramatically stark, but represent one of 25 outstanding global 'hot spots' of unique biodiversity.

The Sperggebiet originally consisted of two private concessions: Diamond Area 1 and Diamond Area 2. The latter, home to the Kolmanskop ghost town and Elizabeth Bay, has been open to the public for some time now. Since 2004, parts of the former have also been opened up to specialist conservation groups, though given the diamond industry's security concerns, access has been carefully controlled.

History

The 'Forbidden Area' was established in 1908 following the discovery of diamonds near Lüderitz. Although mining operations were localised along the coast, a huge swath of southern Namibia was sectioned off in the interest of security. The tight restrictions on access have helped to keep much of the area pristine. De Beers Centenary, a partner in De Beers Consolidated Diamond Mines, continues to control the entire area until the MET establishes a management plan for the park. We're still waiting...

⊙ Sights

Kolmanskop   HISTORIC SITE
(N$75; ⊘ 9.30am & 11am Mon-Sat, 10am Sun)
Named after early Afrikaner trekker Jani Kolman, whose ox wagon became bogged in the sand here, Kolmanskop was originally constructed as the CDM headquarters. Although Kolmanskop once boasted a casino, bowling alley and a theatre with fine acoustics, the slump in diamond sales after WWI and the discovery of richer pickings at

---

GEOLOGY & THE FOUR CS OF DIAMONDS

Diamonds are the best-known allotrope (form) of carbon, and are characterised by their extreme hardness (they are the hardest naturally occurring mineral) and high dispersion of light (diamonds are prismatic when exposed to white light). As a result, they are valued for industrial purposes as abrasives since they can only be scratched by other diamonds, and for ornamental purposes since they retain lustre when polished. It's estimated that 130 million carats (or 26,000kg) of diamonds are mined annually, yielding a market value of over US$9 billion.

Diamonds are formed when carbon-bearing materials are exposed to high pressures and temperatures for prolonged periods of time. With the exception of synthetically produced diamonds, favourable conditions only occur beneath the continental crust, starting at depths of about 150km. Once carbon crystallises, a diamond will then continue to grow in size so long as it is exposed to both sufficiently high temperatures and pressures. However, size is limited by the fact that diamond-bearing rock is eventually expelled towards the surface through deep-origin volcanic eruptions. Eventually they are forced to the surface by magma, and are expelled from a volcanic pipe.

Since the early 20th century the quality of a diamond has been determined by four properties, now commonly used as basic descriptors of a stone: carat, clarity, colour and cut.

Carat

Carat weight measures the mass of a diamond, with one carat equal to 200mg. Assuming all other properties are equal, the value of a diamond increases exponentially in relation to carat weight since larger diamonds are rarer.

Clarity

Clarity is a measure of internal defects known as inclusions, which are foreign materials or structural imperfections present in the stone. Higher clarity is associated with value, and it's estimated that only about 20% of all diamonds mined have a high enough clarity rating to be sold as gemstones.

Colour

Although a perfect diamond is transparent with a total absence of hue, virtually all diamonds have a discernable colour due to chemical impurities and structural defects. Depending on the hue and intensity, a diamond's colour can either detract from or enhance its value (yellow diamonds are discounted, while pink and blue diamonds are more valuable).

Cut

Finally, the cut of a diamond describes the quality of workmanship and the angles to which a diamond is cut.

Oranjemund ended its heyday. By 1956, the town was totally deserted, and left to the mercy of the shifting desert sands.

Today, Kolmanskop has been partially restored as a tourist attraction, and the sight of decrepit buildings being invaded by dunes is simply too surreal to describe. You can turn up at any time, and you're not required to arrive as part of an organised tour, though you do need to purchase a permit in advance through either the NWR office in Lüderitz (p333) or a local tour operator. Guided tours (in English and German), which are included in the price of the permit, depart from the museum in Kolmanskop. After the tour, you can return to the museum, which contains relics and information on the history of Namibian diamond mining.

Unfortunately the coffee shop and gift shop and often-large tourist numbers dampen the potentially eerie effect of this old town. If there are a lot of tourists around (likely) then you're better off skipping the organised part of the trip here and focusing instead on wandering around the decrepit buildings and piles of sand, getting a bit of a taste for this old deserted town.

Kolmanskop is only a 15-minute drive from Lüderitz, just off the main B4 highway. Tour agencies sell tours to Kolmanskop, or you can drive yourself so long as you have arranged the permit beforehand.

ⓘ Getting There & Away

Do not attempt to access the Sperrgebiet in a private vehicle as you will be inviting a whole mess of trouble. The only exception to this statement is Kolmanskop, which can be accessed if you have the necessary permits.

The Far South & Fish River Canyon

Situated within the angle between Southern Africa's two most remote quarters, Namaqualand and the Kalahari, Namibia's bleak southern tip exudes a sense of isolation from whichever direction you approach it. As you travel along the highway, the seemingly endless desert plains stretch to all horizons, only to suddenly tear asunder at the mighty Fish River Canyon. This gash across the desert landscape is one of Namibia's most stunning geological formations, luring in determined bands of trekkers each winter, bent on traipsing across its vast expanse.

Forty percent of the Sperrgebiet National Park is desert, and 30% is grassland; the rest is rocks, granite mountains and moonscape. Though the area has yet to be fully explored, initial scientific assessments have discovered 776 plant species, 230 of which are thought to be unique to the park. There are also populations of gemsbok, brown hyenas and rare, threatened reptile species, including the desert rain frog. Bird species are extremely varied, and include the dune lark, black-headed canary and the African oystercatcher.

The Namibian Nature Foundation (www.nnf.org.na) will eventually take over the planning for the park and will focus on community-based initiatives to ensure that locals benefit. The eventual development of tourism in the Sperrgebiet is expected to stimulate the economy of Lüderitz, which will serve as the main gateway to the park.

Grünau

POP 400 / ☎ 063

For most travellers, Grünau is either the first petrol station north of the South African border, or a logical overnight stop for weary drivers between Cape Town and Windhoek. We could go on, but it really doesn't get any more exciting than that...

⌖ Sleeping

White House Guest Farm GUESTHOUSE **$**
(☎ 081 285 6484, 063-262061; www.withuis.iway.na; r N$300-620) An excellent spot to rest for the night is the White House Guest Farm. Dolf and Kinna de Wet's wonderful and popular B&B (yes, it is a white house) has well-priced, self-catering accommodation. Kitchen facilities are available, though the hosts will also provide set meals and braai packs on request. Head 11km towards Keetmanshoop on the B1 and turn west at the White House signpost; it's 4km off the road. This renovated farmhouse, which dates from 1912, is architecturally stunning.

ⓘ Getting There & Away

Grünau is 144km northwest of the Velloorsdrift border crossing along the C10, and 142km north of the Noordoewer border crossing along the B1.

Fish River Canyon

☑ 063

Nowhere else in Africa will you find anything quite like **Fish River Canyon** (per person per day N$80, per vehicle N$10). Whether you're getting a taste of the sheer scale and beauty of it from one of the lookouts, or hiking for five days to immerse yourself in its multifaceted charm, Fish River Canyon is a special place.

At one level, the numbers don't lie: the canyon measures 160km in length, up to 27km in width, and the dramatic inner canyon reaches a depth of 550m. But as impressive as these numbers are, it's difficult to get a sense of perspective without actually experiencing the enormous scope of the canyon, something best done on the monumental five-day hike that traverses half the length of the canyon. The reward is nothing less than an unforgettable relationship with one of Africa's greatest natural wonders.

Fish River Canyon

History

The San have a legend that the wildly twisting Fish River Canyon was gouged out by a frantically scrambling snake, Koutein Kooru, as he was pursued into the desert by hunters. However, the geological story is a bit different...

Fish River, which joins the Orange River 110km south of the canyon, has been gouging out this gorge for aeons. Surprisingly, Fish River Canyon is actually two canyons, one inside the other, which were formed in entirely different ways. It's thought that the original sedimentary layers of shale, sandstone and loose igneous material around Fish River Canyon were laid down nearly two billion years ago, and were later metamorphosed by heat and pressure into more solid materials, such as gneiss. Just under a billion years ago, cracks in the formation admitted intrusions of igneous material, which cooled to form the dolerite dykes (which are now exposed in the inner canyon).

The surface was then eroded into a basin and covered by a shallow sea, which eventually filled with sediment – sandstone, conglomerate, quartzite, limestone and shale – washed down from the surrounding exposed lands. Around 500 million years ago, a period of tectonic activity along crustal faults caused these layers to rift and to tilt at a 45-degree angle. These forces opened a wide gap in the earth's crust and formed a large canyon.

This was what we now regard as the outer canyon, the bottom of which was the first level of terraces that are visible approximately 170m below the eastern rim and 380m below the western rim. This newly created valley naturally became a watercourse (the Fish River, oddly enough), which began eroding a meandering path along the valley floor and eventually gouged out what is now the 270m-deep inner canyon.

Fish River Canyon

⊚ **Sights**

⊕ **Activities, Courses & Tours**

⊜ **Sleeping**

⊙ Sights

The canyon, seen most clearly in the morning, is stark, very beautiful and seemingly carved into the earth by a master builder – it flaunts its other-worldliness. The exposed rock and lack of plant life is quite startling. Its rounded edges and sharp corners create a symphony in stone of gigantic and imposing proportions. If you have a viewpoint to yourself it's a perfect place to reflect on this country's unique landscape, harsh environment and immense horizons.

Main Viewpoint   VIEWPOINT
This viewpoint has probably the best – and most photographed – overall canyon outlook, with views that take in the sharp river bend known as Hell's Corner. Better still, it's accessible to everyone, not just those hiking the full five-day canyon trail.

🏃 Activities

Hiking is obviously the main event here, but following the death of an ill-prepared hiker in 2001, the NWR decided to strictly prohibit day hikes and leisure walks into Fish River Canyon.

Fish River Hiking Trail   HIKING
(per person N$250; ☾15 Apr-15 Sep) The five-day hike from Hobas to Ai-Ais is Namibia's most popular long-distance walk – and with good reason. The magical 85km route, which follows the sandy riverbed past a series of ephemeral pools, begins at Hikers' Viewpoint, and ends at the hot-spring resort of Ai-Ais.

Due to flash flooding and heat in summer months, the route is open only from 15 April to 15 September. Groups of three to 30 people may begin the hike every day of the season, though you will have to book in advance as the trail is extremely popular. Reservations can be made at the NWR office (p230) in Windhoek.

Officials may need a doctor's certificate of fitness, issued less than 40 days before your hike, though if you look young and fit, they're unlikely to ask. Hikers must arrange their own transport to and from the start and finish, as well as accommodation in Hobas and Ai-Ais.

Thanks to the typically warm, clear weather, you probably won't need a tent, but you must carry a sleeping bag and food. In Hobas, check on water availability in the canyon. In August and September, the last 15km of the walk can be completely

CROSS-BORDER PARK

Fish River Canyon is part of the **Ais- Ais Richtersveld Transfrontier Park**, one of an increasing number of 'peace' or cross-border parks in Southern Africa. Straddling southern Namibia and South Africa (and measuring 6045 sq km), it boasts one of the most species-rich arid zones in the world. It also encompasses Richtersveld National Park (in South Africa) and the Orange River valley.

dry and hikers will need several 2L water bottles to manage this hot, sandy stretch. Large, plastic soft-drink bottles normally work just fine.

➡ Hiking Route

From Hobas, it's 10km to **Hikers' Viewpoint**, which is the start of the trail – hikers must find their own transport to this point. The steep and scenic section at the beginning takes you from the canyon rim to the river, where you'll have a choice of fabulous sandy campsites beside cool, green river pools.

Although some maps show the trail following the river quite closely, it's important to note that the best route changes from year to year. This is largely due to sand and vegetation deposited by the previous year's floods. In general, the easiest hiking will be along the inside of the river bends, where you're likely to find wildlife trails and dry, nonsandy terrain that's free of vegetation tangles, slippery stones and large boulders.

After an exhausting 13km hike through the rough sand and boulders along the east bank, the **Sulphur Springs Viewpoint** track joins the main route. If you're completely exhausted at this stage and can't handle the conditions, this trail can be used as an emergency exit from the canyon. If it's any encouragement, however, the going gets easier as you move downstream, so why not head a further 2km to **Sulphur Springs**, set up camp and see how you feel in the morning?

Sulphur Springs (more commonly called Palm Springs) is an excellent campsite with thermal sulphur pools (a touch of paradise) to soothe your aching muscles. The springs, which have a stable temperature of 57°C, gush up from the underworld at an amazing

NAMIBIA THE FAR SOUTH & FISH RIVER CANYON

30L per second and contain not only sulphur, but also chloride and fluoride.

Legend has it that during WWI, two German prisoners of war hid out at Sulphur Springs to escape internment. One was apparently suffering from asthma, and the other from skin cancer, but thanks to the spring's healing powers, both were cured. It's also said that the palm trees growing here sprang up from date pips discarded by these two Germans.

The next section of the hike consists of deep sand, pebbles and gravel. The most direct route through the inside river bends requires hikers to cross the river several times. The **Table Mountain** formation lies 15km beyond Sulphur Springs, and a further 15km on is the first short cut, which avoids an area of dense thorn scrub known as Bushy Corner. Around the next river bend, just upstream from the **Three Sisters** rock formation, is a longer short cut past **Kanebis Bend** up to **Kooigoedhoogte Pass**. At the top, you'll have a superb view of **Four Finger Rock**, an impressive rock tower consisting of four thick pinnacles (though they more closely resemble a cow's udder than fingers).

After descending to the river, you'll cross to the west bank and start climbing over yet another short cut (although you can also follow the river bend). At the southern end of this pass, on the west bank of the river, lies the grave of Lieutenant Thilo von Trotha, who was killed here in a 1905 confrontation between the Germans and the Nama.

The final 25km into Ai-Ais, which can be completed in one long day, follows an easy but sandy and rocky route. South of von Trotha's grave, the canyon widens out and becomes drier. Be advised that towards the end of winter, the final 15km are normally completely dry, so you will need to carry sufficient water.

Ai-Ais Hot Springs HOT SPRINGS
(adult/child N$80/free; ☺ sunrise-sunset) The hot springs at Ai-Ais (Nama, appropriately, for 'Scalding Hot') are beneath the towering peaks at the southern end of Fish River Canyon. They're rich in chloride, fluoride and sulphur, and are reputedly therapeutic for sufferers of rheumatism or nervous disorders. The hot water is piped to a series of baths and spas as well as an outdoor swimming pool.

Although the 60°C springs have probably been known to the San for thousands of years, the legend goes that they were 'discovered' by a nomadic Nama shepherd rounding up stray sheep.

A pleasant diversion is the short scramble to the peak that rises above the opposite bank (note that the trail is not marked). It affords a superb view of Ai-Ais, and you will even see the four pinnacles of Four Finger Rock rising far to the north. The return trip takes approximately two hours.

Amenities include a shop, restaurant, petrol station, tennis courts, post office and, of course, a swimming pool, spa and mineral-bath facilities.

Be advised that during summer, there's a serious risk of flooding – Ai-Ais was destroyed by floods in both 1972 and 2000.

🛏 Sleeping

Accommodation inside the park must be prebooked through the NWR office (p230) in Windhoek. In addition to the accommodation inside and close to the park, other excellent possibilities can be found at Gondwana Cañon Park.

Hobas Camp Site CAMPGROUND $
(camping N$170, s/d N$1080/1760; ☎) Administered by NWR, this pleasant and well-shaded campground near the park's northern end is about 10km from the main viewpoints. Facilities are clean and there's a kiosk and swimming pool, but no restaurant or petrol station. Rooms in bush chalets were under construction when we last passed through.

Ai-Ais Hot Springs Spa RESORT $$
(www.nwrnamibia.com/ai-ais.htm; camping N$190, mountain/river-view d N$1330/1620; ☎) Administered by NWR, amenities here include washing blocks, braai pits and use of the resort facilities, including the hot springs. The rooms are tidy, if a touch overpriced, and there are also slightly more expensive river-view rooms. There are family chalets available and an on-site restaurant and small grocery store.

★ Fish River Lodge LODGE $$$
(☑ 061-228104, 063-683005; www.fishriverlodge-namibia.com; s/d N$1995/3056) With 20 chalets located on the western rim of the canyon, Fish River Lodge is a magical spot to enjoy the landscape. Rooms are gorgeous, modern and come with superlative views. Activities include a five-night canyon hike (85km, April to September), or a day hike for the less ambitious.

Access to the lodge is from the D463, which links the B4 in the north and the C13 to the west.

❶ Information

The main access points for Fish River Canyon are at Hobas, near the northern end of the park, and Ai-Ais, near the southern end. Both are administered by the NWR. Accommodation must be booked through the Windhoek **office** (p230). Daily park permits (N$80 per person and N$10 per vehicle) are valid for both Hobas and Ai-Ais.

The **Hobas Information Centre** (⊘7.30am-noon & 2-5pm), at the northern end of the park, is also the check-in point for the five-day canyon hike. Packaged snacks and cool drinks are available here, but little else. If you're on your way to view the canyon, use the toilets here – there are none further on.

The Fish River typically flows between March and April. Early in the tourist season, from April to June, it may diminish to a trickle, and by mid-winter, to just a chain of remnant pools along the canyon floor.

❶ Getting There & Away

There's no public transport to Hobas or Ai-Ais, and you'll really need a private vehicle to get around. The drive in from Grünau to Hobas is on a decent gravel road, accessible most of the year in a 2WD, although it can be problematic immediately after heavy rain.

Gondwana Cañon Park

🕿 061

Founded in 1996, the 100,000-hectare Gondwana Cañon Park was created by amalgamating several former sheep farms and removing the fences to restore the wilderness country immediately northeast of |Ai- |Ais Richtersveld Transfrontier Park. Water holes have been established and wildlife is returning to this wonderful, remote corner of Namibia. In the process, the park absorbed the former Augurabies-Steenbok Nature Reserve, which had been created earlier to protect not only steenboks, but also Hartmann's mountain zebras, gemsboks and klipspringers. Predators are still yet to arrive in numbers, but expect that to change as word gets out...

🏃 Activities

A wide range of activities, from 4WD excursions and guided hikes to horseback riding and scenic flights, is available through the accommodation places in the area.

🛏 Sleeping

Cañon Mountain Camp
LODGE $$

(🕿 061-244558; r N$1080; ☒) One of the more budget-orientated properties in the area, this remote mountain camp occupies a high-altitude setting amid dolerite hills. Self-caterers can take advantage of the fully equipped kitchen, braai pits and communal lounges. The whitewashed walls evoke a cross between New Mexico and the south of Spain.

Canyon Roadhouse
GUESTHOUSE $$$

(🕿 061-230066; www.gondwana-collection.com; camping N$175, s/d from N$1511/2422; 🛜☒) This wonderful (and terribly kitsch) place attempts to re-create a roadhouse out on the wildest stretches of Route 66 – at least as it exists in the collective imagination. Buffets are served on an antique motorcycle, the stunning window shades and bar stools are made from used air filters from heavy-duty vehicles. Rooms (which are all the same) are brightly coloured with low-slung roofs and modern touches.

The walk-in shower is a luxury and the cheapish furniture is offset by a Mediterranean feel. There's a well-maintained area out the back with 12 campsites, toilets and braai facilities. Its a handy place to stop for lunch during the day too -- try the Amarula cheesecake. It also offers guided excursions to Fish River Canyon viewpoints nearby as well as hiking and 4WD excursions.

★ Canyon Lodge
LODGE $$$

(🕿 063-693014, 061-427200; www.gondwana-collection.com; camping from N$120, s/d from N$2035/3256; 🏵🛜☒) This mountain retreat is one of Namibia's most stunning accommodation options and it comes at a price that is surprisingly reasonable. The whole place, but especially the luxury stone bungalows, is sympathetically integrated into its boulder-strewn backdrop. The outlook is dramatic and the bungalows, with flagstone floors, have great privacy. The restaurant, housed in a 1908 farmhouse, is tastefully decorated with historic farming implements and has rambling gardens.

It's a very friendly place, the food is first-class and we've never met a nicer barman.

Canyon Village
COTTAGE $$$

(🕿 061-427200, 063-693025; www.gondwana-collection.com; s/d from N$1425/2280; 🏵☒) Drawing inspiration from the Cape Dutch villages of yesteryear, this wonderfully

NAMIBIA THE FAR SOUTH & FISH RIVER CANYON

bucolic spot hugs a rock face on the outskirts of Fish River Canyon. Cottages are spacious and comfortable, and afford great views of the area. The centrepiece is a thatched restaurant serving traditional Afrikaner specialities.

ℹ Getting There & Away

Gondwana Cañon Park can be accessed via private vehicle along the C37, south of Seeheim.

Noordoewer

☑ 063

Noordoewer sits astride the Orange River, which has its headwaters in the Drakensberg Mountains of Natal (South Africa) and forms much of the boundary between Namibia and South Africa. Although the town primarily serves as a border crossing and a centre for viticulture, it is a good base for organising a canoeing or rafting adventure on the Orange River.

🏃 Activities

Canoe and rafting trips are normally done in stages and last three to six days. The popular trips from Noordoewer north to Aussenkehr aren't treacherous by any stretch – the white water never exceeds Class II – but they do provide access to some wonderfully wild canyon country. Other possible stages include Aussenkehr to the Fish River mouth; Fish River mouth to Nama Canyon (which has a few more serious rapids); and Nama Canyon to Selingsdrif.

Amanzi Trails   CANOEING
(☑ in South Africa 27 21-559 1573; www.amanzi trails.co.za) This well-established South African company is based in Amanzi River Camp, and specialises in four-/five-night guided canoe trips down the Orange River costing N$2990/3380 per person. It also arranges shorter self-guided trips and longer excursions up Fish River for more experienced clients.

Felix Unite   CANOEING
(☑ in South Africa 27 87 354 0578; www.felixunite. com) Another highly reputable South African operator, Felix Unite, based in Camp Provenance, specialises in five-day guided canoe and rafting trips down the Orange River costing N$3295 per person. It can also combine these excursions with lengthier trips around the Western Cape of South Africa.

🛏 Sleeping

Amanzi River Camp   CAMPGROUND $
(☑ in South Africa 27 21-559 1573; http://amanzitrails.co.za/amanzi-river-camp/; camping per adult/child N$130/80, s/d/tr/q chalets N$430/550/670/790) This well-situated camp, 15km down Orange River Rd, sits on the riverbank. It's the launch point for Amanzi Trails (p340), so you can stock up on supplies, indulge in a hot meal and get a good night's rest before embarking on your canoe trip.

Camp Provenance   CAMPGROUND $$
(☑ in South Africa 27-21-702-9400; www.felixunite. com; camping N$120, r N$965-1725) Approximately 10km west of Noordoewer is this safari-chic river camp and launch point for Felix Unite. Purists can pitch their own tent on the grassy field, while lovers of creature comforts can bed down in a permanent tent or chalet, and stockpile their reserves for the paddling ahead.

ℹ Getting There & Away

Noordoewer is located just off the B1 near the South African border, and is only accessible by private transport.

UNDERSTAND NAMIBIA

Namibia Today

As a relative newcomer to the world of nations, Namibia has mastered political stability and economic prosperity better than most African veterans. This is a country that works. Yes, many of its people live in grinding poverty and wealth disparity is a major issue, but the country's overall economic performance and social harmony continue to impress and there's nothing to suggest that these are likely to change any time soon.

Economic Progress

Namibia's economy continues to roll along nicely. Although it was affected by the global recession in 2008–09, its mineral deposits ensured its economy rebounded as uranium and diamond prices recovered. By 2015 the country was again reporting a growth rate in excess of 5%.

There is much to be excited about when it comes to the country's economic future.

Offshore oil and natural-gas exploration has thrown up some promising signals; the country is one of the world's largest producers of diamonds and uranium, with large deposits of gold, copper and zinc; while its tourism industry goes from strength to strength. In 2014, for example, the tourism sector was responsible for nearly one out of every five jobs in the country, according to the World Travel and Tourism Council. Nearly one million visitors come to Namibia every year – a lot when you remember that the country's total population is only 2.44 million people.

But like so many other countries, Namibia faces a massive challenge in ensuring that the country's prosperity benefits all Namibians. Crippling droughts have caused widespread hardship in a country that grows around half of its cereal requirements and where, according to the UN, nearly one-third of the population lives below the poverty line and roughly the same number is unemployed.

An Independent Voice

As their German and South African overlords learned through history, Namibia doesn't take kindly to being told what to do. When other African countries criticised the International Criminal Court for prosecuting more African suspects than suspects from elsewhere, Namibia joined the chorus and took it a step further, withdrawing from the ICC. When the world turned on Namibia early in 2014 when the country auctioned a hunting licence to shoot an old black rhino considered a threat to others of its kind, the government stood firm – instead of banning hunting as Botswana did in the same year, Namibia complained that the furore had resulted in lower bids by publicity-shy hunters, and that the money available for conserving black rhinos was much less as a result.

And so the pattern continues. Namibia has positioned itself so that it has strong political and economic ties to the West, but a subtle pivot in 2007 has seen the country strengthen its ties with China while continuing to do business with Europe and the US. This comes despite concern in some Western capitals about its ability to influence Namibian decision-making in economic, social and environmental fields. Namibia has also raised some eyebrows by, as recently as 2016, refusing to criticise Zimbabwean president Robert Mugabe on the grounds that to do so

would be to meddle in Zimbabwe's internal politics.

Namibia remains a responsible global citizen, but its willingness to chart its own course on the international stage suggests a genuine maturity, regardless of whether you agree with each of its individual policy positions.

Human-Wildlife Conflict

Like many countries in Southern Africa, Namibia is struggling to balance the needs of a growing population with the demands of a fragile environment.

Namibia may look like it has plenty of open spaces, and many of its large carnivores in particular – cheetahs and lions among them – may live at much lower densities here than they do in some other regions of Africa, but think how easy it is for the delicate balance between wildlife and human populations to end. A cheetah, as the story so often goes, ranges onto private farmland. It may or may not kill a lamb or young cow in its search for prey – sometimes its mere presence is enough for the owner of the land to seek revenge. In so doing, the cheetah population takes another hit it can ill afford. Multiply this to so many similar scenarios across the country and you'll see how even Africa's largest cheetah population quickly becomes vulnerable. And as the number of wildlife-rescue centres across the country attests, the problem is certainly not going away.

But there are always two sides to this story. Farmers in Namibia are usually much more tolerant of livestock losses than Western farmers are ever likely to be, but this mindset of sharing their land with wild cats does change during times of drought when they are struggling to make ends meet – the loss of a lamb or a goat can make the difference between surviving or having to jack it all in.

Namibia is finding creative solutions: struggling farms converted into more prosperous nature reserves across the country's heartland; reinforcing livestock *kraals* (huts) and teaching herders better practices to protect their livestock from predators in the Caprivi Strip; using the commercial or trophy hunting of 'problem animals' to raise money for conservation. Sometimes it works. Sometimes it doesn't. Increasingly it is a battle for survival for herders and wildlife alike.

History

Namibia's history is a familiar African story, beginning with ancient peoples and the stories they told on remote rock walls, and entering the modern world with colonial repression and a brutal war of independence. But that's not where the story ends. Instead, Namibia has emerged from such turbulence as a confident, independent country where the future looks far brighter than its past.

In the Beginning

Namibia's history extends back into the mists of time, a piece in the jigsaw that saw the evolution of the earliest human beings. The camps and stone tools of *Homo erectus* (literally 'man who stands upright') have been found scattered throughout the region. One archaeological site in the Namib Desert provides evidence that these early people were hunting the ancestors of present-day elephants, and butchering their remains with stone hand axes, as early as 750,000 years ago.

By the middle Stone Age, which lasted until 20,000 years ago, the Boskop, the presumed ancestors of the San, had developed into an organised hunting-and-gathering society. Use of fire was universal, tools (made from wood and animal products as well as stone) had become more sophisticated and natural pigments were being used for personal adornment. From around 8000 BC (the late Stone Age) they began producing pottery, and started to occupy rock shelters and caves such as those at Twyfelfontein and Brandberg, and the Tsodilo Hills in neighbouring Botswana.

The Settlement of Namibia

The archaeological connection between the late Stone Age people and the first Khoisan arrivals isn't clear, but it is generally accepted that the earliest documented inhabitants of Southern Africa were the San, a nomadic people organised into extended family groups who were able to adapt to the severe terrain.

During the early Iron Age, between 2300 and 2400 years ago, rudimentary farming techniques appeared on the plateaus of south-central Africa. However, whether or not the earliest farmers were Khoisan, who had adapted to a settled existence, or migrants from East and central Africa, remains in question. Regardless, as the centuries came and went, Bantu-speaking groups began to arrive in sporadic southward waves.

The first agriculturists and iron workers of definite Bantu origin belonged to the Gokomere culture. They settled the temperate savannah and cooler uplands of southeastern Zimbabwe, and were the first occupants of the Great Zimbabwe site. Cattle ranching became the mainstay of the community, and earlier hunting and gathering San groups retreated to the west, or were enslaved and/or absorbed.

At the same time, the San communities were also coming under pressure from the Khoekhoen (the ancestors of the Nama), who probably entered the region from south. The Khoekhoen were organised loosely into tribal groups and were distinguished by their reliance on raising livestock. They gradually displaced the San, becoming the dominant group in the region until around AD 1500.

During the 16th century, the Herero arrived in Namibia from the Zambezi Valley, and proceeded to occupy the north and west of the country. As ambitious pastoralists they inevitably came into conflict with the Khoekhoen over the best grazing lands and water sources. Eventually, given their superior strength and numbers, the Herero came to dominate nearly all of the indigenous Namibian groups. By the late 19th century a new Bantu group, the Owambo, settled in the north along the Okavango and Kunene Rivers.

European Exploration & Incursion

In 1486 the Portuguese captain Diego Cão sailed as far south as Cape Cross, where he erected a stone cross in tribute to his royal patron, João II. The following year, another cross was erected by Bartolomeu Dias at Lüderitz, but it wasn't really until the early 17th century that Dutch sailors from the Cape colonies began to explore the desert coastline, although they refrained from setting up any permanent stations.

Soon after, however, growing European commercial and territorial interests were to send ambitious men deeper into Namibia's interior, and in 1750 the Dutch elephant hunter Jacobus Coetsee became the first European to cross the Orange River. In his wake came a series of traders, hunters and missionaries, and by the early 19th century there were mission stations at Bethanie, Windhoek, Rehoboth, Keetmanshoop and various other sites. In 1844 the German Rhenish Missionary Society, under Dr Hugo Hahn, began working among the Herero. More successful were the Finnish Lutherans, who arrived in the north in 1870 and established missions among the Owambo.

By 1843 the rich coastal guano (excrement of seabirds; used to make manure and a gunpowder ingredient) deposits of the southern Namib Desert were attracting commercial attention. In 1867 the guano islands were annexed by the British, who then proceeded to take over Walvis Bay in 1878. The British also mediated the largely inconclusive Khoisan–Herero wars during this period.

The Scramble for Africa

The Germans, under Chancellor Otto von Bismarck, were late entering the European scramble for Africa. Bismarck had always been against colonies; he considered them an expensive illusion, famously stating, 'My map of Africa is here in Europe'. But he was to be pushed into an ill-starred colonial venture by the actions of a Bremen merchant called Adolf Lüderitz.

Having already set up a trading station in Lagos, Nigeria in 1881, Lüderitz convinced the Nama chief, Joseph Fredericks, to sell Angra Pequena, where he established his second station trading in guano. He then petitioned the German chancellor for protection. Bismarck, still trying to stay out of Africa, politely requested the British at Walvis Bay to say whether they had any interest in the matter, but they never bothered to reply. Subsequently, in 1884, Lüderitz was officially declared part of the German Empire.

Initially, German interests were minimal, and between 1885 and 1890 the colonial administration amounted to three public administrators. Their interests were served largely through a colonial company (along the lines of the British East India Company in India prior to the raj), but the organisation couldn't maintain law and order.

So in the 1880s, due to renewed fighting between the Nama and Herero, the German government dispatched Curt von François and 23 soldiers to restrict the supply of arms from British-administered Walvis Bay. This seemingly innocuous peacekeeping regiment slowly evolved into the more powerful Schutztruppe (German Imperial Army), which constructed forts around the country to combat growing opposition.

At this stage, Namibia became a fully fledged protectorate known as German South West Africa. The first German farmers arrived in 1892 to take up expropriated land on the central plateau, and were soon followed by merchants and other settlers. In the late 1890s the Germans, the Portuguese in Angola and the British in Bechuanaland (present-day Botswana) agreed on Namibia's boundaries.

Reaping the Whirlwind

Meanwhile, in the south, diamonds had been discovered at Grasplatz, east of Lüderitz, by South African labourer Zacharias Lewala. Despite the assessment of diamond-mining giant De Beers that the find probably wouldn't amount to much, prospectors flooded in to stake their claims. By 1910 the German authorities had granted exclusive rights to Deutsche Diamanten Gesellschaft (German Diamond Company).

For all the devastation visited upon the local populace, Germany was never to benefit from the diamond riches it found. The outbreak of WWI in 1914 was to mark the end of German colonial rule in South West Africa. By this time, however, the Germans had all but succeeded in devastating the Herero tribal structures, and had taken over all Khoikhoi and Herero lands. The more fortunate Owambo, in the north, managed to avoid German conquest, and they were only subsequently overrun during WWI by Portuguese forces fighting on the side of the Allies.

In 1914, at the beginning of WWI, Britain pressured South Africa into invading Namibia. The South Africans, under the command of Prime Minister Louis Botha and General Jan Smuts, pushed northward, forcing the outnumbered Schutztruppe to retreat. In May 1915 the Germans faced their final defeat at Khorab near Tsumeb and, a week later, a South African administration was set up in Windhoek.

By 1920 many German farms had been sold to Afrikaans-speaking settlers, and the German diamond-mining interests in the south were handed over to the South Africa–based Consolidated Diamond Mines

(CDM), which later gave way to the Namdeb Diamond Corporation Limited (Namdeb).

South African Occupation

Under the Treaty of Versailles in 1919, Germany was required to renounce all of its colonial claims, and in 1920 the League of Nations granted South Africa a formal mandate to administer Namibia as part of the Union of South Africa.

While the mandate was renewed by the UN following WWII, South Africa was more interested in annexing South West Africa as a full province in the Union, and decided to scrap the terms of the mandate and rewrite the constitution. In response, the International Court of Justice determined that South Africa had overstepped its boundaries, and the UN established the Committee on South West Africa to enforce the original terms of the mandate. In 1956 the UN further decided that South African control should be terminated.

Undeterred, the South African government tightened its grip on the territory, and in 1949 granted the white population parliamentary representation in Pretoria. The bulk of Namibia's viable farmland was parcelled into some 6000 farms for white settlers, while other ethnic groups were relegated to newly demarcated 'tribal homelands'. The official intent was ostensibly to 'channel economic development into predominantly poor rural areas', but it was all too obvious that it was simply a convenient way of retaining the majority of the country for white settlement and ranching.

As a result, a prominent line of demarcation appeared between the predominantly white ranching lands in the central and southern parts of the country, and the poorer but better-watered tribal areas to the north. This arrangement was retained until Namibian independence in 1990, and to some extent continues to the present day.

Swapo

Throughout the 1950s, despite mounting pressure from the UN, South Africa refused to release its grip on Namibia. This intransigence was based on its fears of having yet another antagonistic government on its

DARK TIMES

When the Germans took over Namibia, they faced a problem: all the best land fell within the territories of either the Herero or the Nama.

In 1904 the paramount chief of the Herero invited his Nama, Baster and Owambo counterparts to join forces with him to resist the growing German presence. This was an unlikely alliance between traditional enemies. Driven almost all the way back to Windhoek, the German Schutztruppe (German Imperial Army) brought in reinforcements, and under the ruthless hand of General von Trotha went out to meet the Herero forces at their Waterberg camp.

On 11 August 1904 the Battle of Waterberg commenced. Although casualties on the day were fairly light, the Herero fled from the scene of battle east into the forbidding Omaheke Desert. Seizing the opportunity, von Trotha ordered his troops to pursue them to their death. In the four weeks that followed, around 65,000 Herero were killed or died of heat, thirst and exhaustion. The horror only concluded when German troops themselves began to succumb to exhaustion and typhoid, but by then, some 80% of the entire Herero population had been wiped out.

From the early 1990s, traditional Herero leaders lobbied for an official apology as well as monetary compensation from the German government. Finally in 2004, on the 100th anniversary of the Battle of Waterberg, Heidemarie Wieczorek-Zeul, Germany's development aid minister, apologised for the genocide, and in 2005 Germany pledged US$28 million to Namibia over a 10-year period as a reconciliation initiative.

Still many problems remain. The Namibian government, almost exclusively made up of Owambo members, believes that any compensation should be channelled through it rather than go directly to the Herero, citing its policy of nontribalism as a key concern.

What may have been a minor episode in German colonial history was a cataclysm for the Herero nation. Demographic analysts suggest there would be 1.8 million Herero in Namibia today if not for the killings, making it, rather than the Owambo, the dominant ethnic group. And yet, today only about 120,000 Herero remain.

doorstep, and of losing the income that it derived from the mining operations there.

Forced labour had been the lot of most Namibians since the German annexation, and was one of the main factors that led to mass demonstrations and the increasingly nationalist sentiments in the late 1950s. Among the parties was the Owamboland People's Congress, founded in Cape Town under the leadership of Samuel Daniel Shafiishuna Nujoma and Herman Andimba Toivo ya Toivo.

In 1959 the party's name was changed to the Owamboland People's Organisation, and Nujoma took the issue of South African occupation to the UN in New York. By 1960 his party had gathered increased support, and it eventually coalesced into the South-West African People's Organisation (Swapo), with its headquarters in Dar es Salaam, Tanzania.

In 1966 Swapo took the issue of South African occupation to the International Court of Justice. The court upheld South Africa's right to govern South West Africa, but the UN General Assembly voted to terminate South Africa's mandate and replace it with a Council for South West Africa (renamed the Commission for Namibia in 1973) to administer the territory.

In response, on 26 August 1966 (now called Heroes' Day), Swapo launched its campaign of guerrilla warfare at Ongulumbashe in northern Namibia. The next year, one of Swapo's founders, Toivo ya Toivo, was convicted of terrorism and imprisoned in South Africa, where he would remain until 1984. Nujoma, however, stayed in Tanzania and avoided criminal prosecution. In 1972 the UN finally declared the South African occupation of South West Africa officially illegal and called for a withdrawal, proclaiming Swapo the legitimate representative of the Namibian people.

In 1975 Angola gained independence under the Cuban-backed Popular Movement for the Liberation of Angola (MPLA). Sympathetic to Swapo's struggle for independence in neighbouring Namibia, the fledgling government allowed it a safe base in the south of the country, from where it could step up its guerrilla campaign against South Africa.

South Africa responded by invading Angola in support of the opposition party, National Union for the Total Independence of Angola (Unita), an act that prompted the Cuban government to send hundreds of troops to the country to bolster up the MPLA. Although the South African invasion failed, and troops had to be withdrawn in March 1976, furious and bloody incursions into Angola continued well into the 1980s.

In the end, it was neither solely the activities of Swapo nor international sanctions that forced the South Africans to the negotiating table. On the contrary, all players were growing tired of the war, and the South African economy was suffering badly. By 1985 the war was costing R480 million (around US$250 million) per year, and conscription was widespread. Mineral exports, which once provided around 88% of the country's gross domestic product, had plummeted to just 27% by 1984.

Independence

In December 1988 a deal was finally struck between Cuba, Angola, South Africa and Swapo that provided for the withdrawal of Cuban troops from Angola and South African troops from Namibia. It also stipulated that the transition to Namibian independence would formally begin on 1 April 1989 and would be followed by UN-monitored elections held in November 1989 on the basis of universal suffrage. Although minor score settling and unrest among some Swapo troops threatened to derail the whole process, the plan went ahead, and in September, Sam Nujoma returned from his 30-year exile. In the elections, Swapo garnered two-thirds of the votes, but the numbers were insufficient to give the party the sole mandate to write the new constitution, an outcome that went some way to allaying fears that Namibia's minority groups would be excluded from the democratic process.

Following negotiations between the Constituent Assembly (soon to become the National Assembly) and international advisers, including the USA, France, Germany and the former USSR, a constitution was drafted. The new constitution established a multiparty system alongside an impressive Bill of Rights. It also limited the presidential executive to two five-year terms. The new constitution was adopted in February 1990, and independence was granted a month later, with Nujoma being sworn in as Namibia's first president.

Postindependence

In those first optimistic years of his presidency, Sam Nujoma and his Swapo party based their policies on a national reconciliation program aimed at healing the wounds left by 25 years of armed struggle. They also embarked on a reconstruction program based on the retention of a mixed economy and partnership with the private sector.

These moderate policies and the stability they afforded were well received, and in 1994 President Nujoma and his party were reelected with a 68% landslide victory over the main opposition party, the Democratic Turnhalle Alliance (DTA). Similarly in 1999, Swapo won 76.8% of the vote, although concerns arose when President Nujoma amended the constitution to allow himself a rather unconstitutional third term.

Other political problems included growing unrest in the Caprivi Strip (p261), starting in 1999 with a failed attempt by rebels to seize Katima Mulilo. Continued fighting drove Caprivians out (and kept tourists away) until the conflict ended in 2002.

In 2004 the world watched warily to see if Nujoma would cling to power for a fourth term, and an almost audible sigh of relief could be heard in Namibia when he announced that he would finally be stepping down in favour of his chosen successor, Hifikepunye Pohamba.

Like Nujoma, Pohamba is a Swapo veteran, and he swept to power with nearly 77% of the vote. In 2009 he was re-elected for a second term. He left behind the land ministry, where he presided over one of Namibia's most controversial schemes – the expropriation of land from white farmers. This policy formed part of the 'poverty agenda', which, along with Namibia's HIV/AIDS crisis, the unequal distribution of income, managing the country's resource wealth fairly, and the challenge of raising living standards for Namibia's poor, would become the defining domestic issues of his presidency.

In 2011 it was announced that Namibia had found offshore oil reserves amounting to 11 billion barrels, although it remains unclear whether the deposits will prove to be commercially viable. In the same year, the government's ongoing efforts to seek redress for colonial wrongs continued to bear fruit when the skulls of 20 Herero and Nama people were returned to Namibia from a museum in Germany.

In line with the constitution, and in keeping with Namibia's impressive postindependence record of largely peaceful transitions, President Pohamba honoured his pledge to stand aside in 2014. His successor, Hage Geingob, easily won elections in November of that year. Unusually for Namibia, political unrest marred the lead-up to the election and one protester was shot by police. Even so, international observers praised Namibia for its free and fair elections (and for its use of electronic voting, an African first). This, and the size of Swapo's electoral victory (Swapo won 87% of the vote in presidential polls and 80% of parliamentary seats), suggest that its dominance of Namibian politics is unlikely to change any time soon.

The Namibian People

Namibia's population in 2016 was estimated at 2,436,469 people, with an annual population growth rate of 1.98%. At approximately two people per square kilometre, Namibia has one of Africa's lowest population densities, while nearly 60% of the population is aged under 25.

The population of Namibia comprises 12 major ethnic groups. Half the people come from the Owambo tribe (50%), with other ethnic groups making up a relatively small percentage of the population: Kavango (9%), Herero/Himba (7%), Damara (7%), Afrikaner and German (6%), Nama (5%), Caprivian (4%), San (3%), Baster (2%) and Tswana (0.5%).

Like nearly all other sub-Saharan nations, Namibia is struggling to contain its HIV/AIDS epidemic, which is impacting heavily on average life expectancy and population growth rates. HIV/AIDS became the leading cause of death in Namibia in 1996, and in 2015 just under 9% of the population was HIV positive. Life expectancy in Namibia has dropped to 63.6, although that figure is again climbing. By 2021 it is estimated that up to a third of Namibia's children under the age of 15 could be orphaned.

San

The word San is a collective term referring to the traditional groups of hunter-gatherers that occupy sub-Saharan Africa, and whose languages belong to the Khoisan family of languages. According to archaeological evidence, San communities were present in Namibia as early as 20,000 years ago, and left behind written records in the form of rock art.

By AD 1000, however, the southward Bantu migration pushed the San into inhospitable areas, including the Kalahari. Regardless, anthropologists have dubbed the San our 'genetic Adam', stating that all living humans can ultimately trace back their lineage to this population group.

One of the most striking findings based on anthropological research is that traditional San communities were nonhierarchical and egalitarian, and grouped together based on kinship and tribal membership. Since groups were never able to build up a surplus of food, full-time leaders and bureaucrats never emerged.

Although village elders did wield a measure of influence over the mobile group, the sharpest division in status was between the sexes. Men provided for their families by hunting game, while women supplemented this diet by foraging for wild fruits, vegetables and nuts. While this was a tough and tenuous life by modern standards, more recent ethnographic data has shown that hunter-gatherers worked fewer hours and enjoyed more leisure time than members of industrial societies.

Owambo

As a sort of loose confederation, the Owambo have always been strong enough to deter outsiders, including the slavers of yore and the German invaders of the last century. They were historically an aggressive culture, which made them the obvious candidates to fight the war of independence. They also make up Namibia's largest ethnic group (about 50% of the population) and, not surprisingly, most of the ruling South West Africa People's Organisation (Swapo) party.

The Owambo traditionally inhabited the north of the country, and are subdivided into 12 distinct groups. Four of these occupy the Kunene region of southern Angola, while the other eight comprise the Owambo groups in Namibia. The most numerous group is the Kwanyama, which makes up 35% of Namibia's Owambo population and dominates the government.

NAMIBIA THE NAMIBIAN PEOPLE

THE POVERTY AGENDA

Land reform has been a contentious issue in Southern Africa (including in Namibia, where most of the arable land is owned by white farmers), with the government seeking to redistribute land to landless black Namibians. The Namibian government has been pursuing a policy of 'willing seller, willing buyer', whereby it has compensated those who have voluntarily chosen to sell their farms, though it has also expropriated a small number of properties.

The Legal Assistance Centre (LAC), a nongovernmental human rights organisation based in Windhoek, says that the government's resettlement scheme has 'placed 800 farms in black hands in the 17 years since independence'. It is the equivalent of about 12% of all farms. The Namibian Agricultural Union (NAU) puts the figure at more than 1000 farms, or the equivalent of 16%. However, there are concerns that the pace of the reform is too slow. The LAC report also states that no resettlement farms are doing well, and that black farmers get subdivided portions of previous farms to support the same numbers of livestock, giving them no chance to be profitable. Critics argue that the scheme amounts to swapping one form of poverty for another.

Despite calls for the speed of the process to be increased, the NAU says disadvantaged Namibians currently own more than nine million hectares of commercial farmland in the country, nearly two-thirds of the government's resettlement target for 2020. It argues that land reform is a process on track and needs time.

The past few years have seen politicians call for an increase in compulsory land acquisitions to increase the pace of land reform, but sceptics say there are few economic benefits to be had from such a policy. Although in principle many people support land reform, Namibia's arid environment is ill-suited to a system of smallholdings farmed by poor Namibians who have neither the economic resources nor technical experience to develop the land. The real social issue, some say, is not so much land reform, but the government's failure to provide work opportunities for ordinary Namibians.

Whatever the problems, it is clear that most Namibians have no interest in replicating the economic and social chaos in nearby Zimbabwe.

Recently, large numbers of Owambo have migrated southward to Windhoek, or to the larger towns in the north, to work as professionals, craftspeople and labourers. They have enjoyed considerable favour from the government over the years and, with the exception of white Namibians of European descent, are among the most successful of the tribal groups.

Kavango

The Kavango originated from the Wambo tribe of East Africa, who first settled on the Kwando River in Angola before moving south in the late 18th century to the northern edges of the Okavango. Since the outbreak of civil war in Angola in the 1970s, however, many Kavango have emigrated further south, swelling the local Namibian population and making them Namibia's second-largest ethnic group. They are divided into five distinct subgroups: the Mbukushu, the Sambiyu, the Kwangari, the Mbunza and the Geiriku.

The Kavango are famous for their highly skilled woodcarvers. However, as with other groups in northern Namibia, large numbers of Kavango are now migrating southward in search of employment on farms, in mines and around urban areas.

Herero/Himba

Namibia's 120,000 Herero occupy a few regions of the country, and are divided into several subgroups. The largest groups include the Tjimba and Ndamuranda in Kaokoveld, the Maherero around Okahandja, and the Zeraua, who are centred on Omaruru. The Himba of the Kaokoveld are also a Herero subgroup, as are the Mbandero, who occupy the colonially demarcated territory formerly known as Hereroland, around Gobabis in eastern Namibia.

The Herero were originally part of the early Bantu migrations south from central Africa. They arrived in present-day Namibia in the mid-16th century and, after a 200-year sojourn in the Kaokoveld, they moved southward to occupy the Swakop Valley and the central plateau. Until the colonial period, they remained as seminomadic pastoralists in this relatively rich grassland, herding and grazing cattle and sheep.

However, bloody clashes with the northward-migrating Nama, as well as with German colonial troops and settlers, led to a violent uprising in the late 19th century, which culminated in the devastating Battle of Waterberg in August 1904. In the aftermath, 80% of the country's Herero population was wiped out, and the remainder were dispersed around the country, terrified and demoralised. Large numbers fled into neighbouring Botswana, where they settled down to a life of subsistence agriculture (although they have since prospered to become the country's richest herders).

The characteristic Herero women's dress is derived from Victorian-era German missionaries. It consists of an enormous crinoline worn over a series of petticoats, with a horn-shaped hat or headdress. If you happen to be in Okahandja on the nearest weekend to 23 August, you can witness the gathering of thousands of Hereros immaculately turned out in their traditional dress, come to honour their fallen chiefs on Maherero Day.

The Himba, a tribal group numbering not more than 50,000 people, are a seminomadic pastoral people who are closely related to the Herero, yet continue to live much as they have for generations. The women in particular are famous for smearing themselves with a fragrant mixture of ochre, butter and bush herbs, which dyes their skin a burnt-orange hue and serves as a natural sunblock and insect repellent. As if this wasn't striking enough, they also use the mixture to cover their braided hair, which has an effect similar to dreadlocking. Instead of wearing Western clothes, they prefer to dress traditionally, bare-breasted, with little more than a pleated animal-skin skirt in the way of clothing.

Similar to the Masai of Kenya and Tanzania, the Himba breed and care for herds of cattle in addition to goats and sheep. Unlike the East African savannah, Himba homelands are among the most extreme environments in the world, and their survival is ultimately dependent on maintaining strong community alliances. It was this very climatic harshness and resulting seclusion from outside influences that enabled the Himba to maintain their cultural heritage over the centuries.

During the 1980s and early 1990s, the Himba were severely threatened by war and drought, though they have experienced a tremendous resurgence in recent years. At present, the population as a whole has succeeded in gaining control of their homelands, and in exerting real political power on the national stage.

Damara

The Damara resemblance to some Bantu of West Africa has led some anthropologists to believe they were among the first people to migrate into Namibia from the north, and that perhaps early trade with the Nama and San caused them to adopt Khoisan as a lingua franca.

What is known is that prior to the 1870s, the Damara occupied much of central Namibia from around the site of Rehoboth, westward to the Swakop and Kuiseb Rivers, and north to present-day Outjo and Khorixas. When the Herero and Nama began expanding their domains into traditional Damara lands, large numbers of Damara were displaced, killed or captured and enslaved. The enmity between them resulted in Damara support for the Germans against the Herero during the colonial period. As a reward, the Damara were granted an enlarged homeland, now the southern half of Kunene province.

When Europeans first arrived in the region, the Damara were described as seminomadic pastoralists, who also maintained small-scale mining, smelting and trading operations. However, during the colonial period, they settled down to relatively sedentary subsistence herding and agriculture. In the 1960s the South African administration purchased for the Damara more than 45,000 sq km of marginal European-owned ranch land in the desolate expanses of present-day Damaraland.

It has not done them much good – the soil in this region is generally poor, most of the land is communally owned, and it lacks the good grazing that prevails in central and southern Namibia. Nowadays, most of Namibia's 80,000 Damara work in urban areas and on European farms, and only about a quarter of them actually occupy Damaraland.

Namibians of European Descent

There were no European settlers in Namibia until 1884, when the Germans set up a trading depot at Lüderitz Bay. By the late 1890s, Namibia was a German colony and settlers began to arrive in ever-greater numbers. At the same time, Boers (white South Africans of Dutch origins) were migrating north from the Cape. Their numbers continued to increase after Namibia came under South African control following WWI.

Nowadays there are around 85,000 white Namibians, most of whom are of Afrikaans descent. They are concentrated in the urban, central and southern parts of the country, and are involved mainly in ranching, commerce, manufacturing and administration. Furthermore, white Namibians almost exclusively manage and control the tourism industry.

Caprivians

In the extreme northeast, along the fertile Zambezi and Kwando riverbanks, live the 80,000 Caprivians, comprising five main tribal groups: the Lozi, Mafwe, Subia, Yei and Mbukushu. Most Caprivians derive their livelihood from fishing, subsistence farming and herding cattle.

Until the late 19th century, the Caprivi Strip was under the control of the Lozi kings. Today, the lingua franca of the various Caprivian tribes is known as Rotse, which is a derivative of the Lozi language still spoken in parts of Zambia and Angola.

Nama

Sharing a similar language to the San of Botswana and South Africa, the Nama are another Khoisan group, and one of Namibia's oldest indigenous peoples.

The Nama's origins are in the southern Cape. However, during the early days of European settlement, they were either exterminated or pushed northwards by colonial farmers. They eventually came to rest in Namaqualand, around the Orange River, where they lived as seminomadic pastoralists until the mid-19th century, when their leader, Jan Jonker Afrikaner, led them to the area of present-day Windhoek.

On Namibia's central plateau, they came into conflict with the Herero, who had already occupied that area, and the two groups fought a series of bloody wars. Eventually the German government enforced the peace by confining both groups to separate reserves.

Today there are around 60,000 Nama in Namibia, and they occupy the region colonially designated as Namaqualand, which stretches from Mariental southward to Keetmanshoop. They're known especially for their traditional music, folk tales, proverbs and praise poetry, which have been handed down through the generations to form a basis for their culture today.

Topnaar

The Topnaar (or Aonin), who are technically a branch of the Nama, mainly occupy the western central Namib Desert, in and around Walvis Bay. However, unlike the Nama, who historically had a tradition of communal land ownership, the Topnaar passed their lands down through family lines.

Today the Topnaar are arguably the most marginalised group in Namibia. Historically they were dependent upon the !nara melon, which was supplemented by hunting. Now their hunting grounds are tied up in Namib-Naukluft Park. Those Topnaar that remain in the desert eke out a living growing !nara melons (p319) and raising stock (mainly goats).

Most Topnaar have migrated to Walvis Bay and settled in the township of Narraville, from where they commute to fish-canning factories. Others live around the perimeter in shanty towns. In the Topnaar community, southeast of Walvis Bay, a primary school and hostel have been provided, although only a minority of students come from the Topnaar community.

Coloureds

After the transfer of German South West Africa (as Namibia used to be known) to South African control after WWI, the South African administration began to introduce the racial laws of apartheid. Thus, at the beginning of the 1950s, cohabitation of mixed-race couples became illegal, although marriage was still allowed. On Afrikaans and German farms all over the territory, farmers married Damara and Herero women, but a few years later marriage, too, was forbidden.

This left the children of these unions in an unenviable position, shunned by black and white communities alike. There are now around 52,000 coloureds in Namibia, living mainly in Windhoek, Keetmanshoop and Lüderitz.

Basters

Although distinct from coloureds, Basters are also the result of mixed unions, specifically between the Nama and Dutch farmers in the Cape Colony. In the late 1860s, after coming under pressure from the Boer settlers in the Cape, they moved north of the Orange River and established the settlement of Rehoboth in 1871. There they established their own system of government with a headman (Kaptein) and legislative council (Volksraad). They also benefited from supporting the Germans during the colonial period, with increased privileges and recognition of their land rights.

Most of Namibia's 35,000 Basters still live around Rehoboth and either follow an urban lifestyle or raise livestock.

Tswana

Namibia's 8000 Tswana make up the country's smallest ethnic group. They are related to the Tswana of South Africa and Botswana, the Batswana, and live mainly in the eastern areas of the country, around Aminuis and Epukiro.

The Namibian Way of Life

On the whole, Namibians are a conservative and God-fearing people – an estimated 80% to 90% of the country is Christian – so modesty in dress and behaviour is considered important. Education is a crucial pillar to advancement in the country, but Namibians (especially women) still struggle to enjoy the benefits of an economy that is, for the most part, performing well.

Women in Namibia

In a culture where male power is mythologised, it's unsurprising that women's rights lag behind. Even today, it's not uncommon for men to have multiple sexual partners and, until recently, in cases where husbands abandoned their wives and their children, there was very little course for redress. Since independence, the Namibian government has been committed to improving women's rights with bills such as the Married Persons Equality Act (1996), which equalised property rights and gave women rights of custody over their children.

Even the government acknowledges that achieving gender equality is more about changing grassroots attitudes than passing laws. According to a US Department of State Human Rights Report in 2015, domestic violence was widespread, and endemic social problems such as poverty, alcoholism and

NAMIBIAN SOCIAL STRUCTURES

On a national level, Namibia is still struggling to attain a cohesive identity, and history weighs heavy on the generations who grew up during the struggle for independence. As a direct and unfortunate result, some formidable tensions still endure between various social and racial groups.

Although the vast majority of travellers will be greeted with great warmth and curiosity, some people may experience unpleasant racism or unwarranted hostility – this is not confined to black/white relations, and can affect travellers of all ethnicities as Namibia's ethnic groups are extremely varied. Acquainting yourself with Namibia's complex and often-turbulent past will hopefully alert you to potentially difficult or awkward situations. Taking care of basic etiquette like dressing appropriately, greeting people warmly and learning a few words of the local languages will also stand you in good stead.

Socially, Namibians enjoy a rock-solid sense of community thanks to the clan-based system. Members of your clan are people you can turn to in times of need. Conversely, if someone from your clan is in trouble, you are obligated to help, whether that means providing food for someone who is hungry, caring for someone who is sick, or even adopting an orphaned child in some cases. This inclusiveness also extends to others, and it is not uncommon for travellers to be asked to participate in a spontaneous game of football or a family meal.

Such an all-embracing social structure also means that the traditional family nucleus is greatly extended. Many Namibian families will include innumerable aunts and uncles, some of whom might even be referred to as mother or father. Likewise, cousins and siblings are interchangeable, and in some rural areas, men may have dozens of children, some of whom they might not even recognise. In fact, it is this fluid system that has enabled families to deal in some way with the devastation wreaked by the HIV/AIDS crisis.

the feeling of powerlessness engendered by long-term unemployment only served to increase women's vulnerability to violence. According to the US Department of State, the Namibian government has passed one of the most comprehensive legislative acts against rape in the world, however women's groups and NGOs point out that many sexual crimes against women are never reported and never reach the authorities.

Namibian women do feature prominently in local and civic life, and many a Namibian woman took a heroic stance in the struggle for independence.

In 2016 women held 43 out of 104 seats in the National Assembly, an impressive 41.35% of all MPs, while women have been increasingly appointed to ministerial roles under the ruling party's much-touted 'zebra policy', whereby every ministry must have a male and a female in the top two positions. In the private sector, however, women remain underrepresented in senior leadership positions.

Women are also undoubtedly the linchpin of the Namibian home. They shoulder a double responsibility in raising children and caring for family members as well as contributing to the family income. This load has only increased with the horrendous effects of HIV/AIDS on the family structure – in 2015 just over 13% of the adult Namibian population was living with HIV/AIDS, down from 18% in 2009.

Female literacy (84.5% in 2015) is actually higher than for men (79.2%), but maternal mortality remains high (265 per 100,000 live births, compared to 129 in Botswana and 138 in South Africa).

Religion

About 80% to 90% of Namibians profess Christianity, and German Lutheranism is the dominant sect in most of the country. As a result of early missionary activity and Portuguese influence from Angola, there is also a substantial Roman Catholic population, mainly in the central and northern areas.

Most non-Christian Namibians – mainly Himba, San and some Herero – live in the north and continue to follow animist traditions. In general, their beliefs are characterised by ancestor veneration, and most practitioners believe that deceased ancestors continue to interact with the living, and serve as messengers between their descendants and the gods.

Muslims make up just 1% to 3% of the population.

Economy

The country's economy is dominated by the extraction and processing of minerals for export. Although mining only accounts for 11.5% of the GDP, it provides more than half of foreign-exchange earnings. Most famously, Namibia's large alluvial diamond deposits have earned it the enviable reputation as one of the world's primary sources for gem-quality stones. However, the country is also regarded as a prominent producer of uranium, lead, zinc, tin, silver and tungsten.

The Namibian economy continues to perform strongly, with growth rates falling slightly in recent years, but still an extremely healthy 4.5% in 2015. Unemployment, however, remains high, with an official rate of 28.1% in 2014 – unofficially, the figure stands closer to 50%, with close to three-quarters of 15- to 19-year-olds unemployed.

The mining sector employs only about 2% of the population, while about half the population depends on subsistence agriculture for its livelihood. Namibia normally imports about 50% of its cereal requirements, and in drought years, food shortages are a major problem in rural areas. Although the fishing industry is also a large economic force, catches are typically canned and marked for export.

In recent years, tourism has grown considerably throughout the country, though white Namibians still largely control the industry.

The Namibian economy is closely linked to the regional powerhouse of South Africa, and the Namibian dollar is pegged one-to-one to the South African rand.

Arts

With its harsh environment and historically disparate and poor population, Namibia does not have a formal legacy of art and architecture. What it does have in abundance is a wealth of material arts and crafts: carvings, basketry, tapestry, beadwork and textile weaving.

There are some excellent festivals dedicated to the arts – for one of Namibia's newest, most exciting arts events head to Omaruru in September for the Artist Trail (p236).

Literature

Dogged by centuries of oppression, isolation, lack of education and poverty, it is hardly surprising that prior to independence there was a complete absence of written literature in Namibia, though there was a rich tradition of oral literature. What written literature there was boils down to a few German colonial novels – most importantly Gustav Frenssen's *Peter Moor's Journey to Southwest Africa* (original 1905, English translation 1908) – and some Afrikaans writing. The best-known work from the colonial period is undoubtedly Henno Martin's *The Sheltering Desert* (1956, English edition 1957), which records two and a half years spent by the geologist author and his friend Hermann Korn avoiding internment as prisoners of war during WWII.

Only with the independence struggle did an indigenous literature begin to take root. One of contemporary Namibia's most significant writers is Joseph Diescho (b 1955), whose first novel, *Born of the Sun,* was published in 1988, when he was living in the USA. To date, this refreshingly unpretentious work remains the most renowned Namibian effort. As with most African literature, it's largely autobiographical, describing the protagonist's early life in a tribal village, his coming of age and his first contact with Christianity. It then follows his path through the South African mines and his ultimate political awakening. Diescho's second novel, *Troubled Waters* (1993), focuses on a white South African protagonist, who is sent to Namibia on military duty and develops a political conscience.

Namibia also has a strong culture of women writers. Literature written by Namibian women after independence deals primarily with their experiences as women during the liberation struggle and in exile, as well as with the social conditions in the country after independence. Thus, the writing of Ellen Namhila (*The Price of Freedom;* 1998), Kaleni Hiyalwa (*Meekulu's Children;* 2000) and Neshani Andreas (*The Purple Violet of Oshaantu;* 2001) gives us a great insight into the sociopolitical world of postcolonial Namibia.

A New Initiation Song (1994) is a collection of poetry and short fiction published by the Sister Namibia collective. This volume's seven sections cover memories of girlhood, body image and heterosexual and lesbian relationships. Among the best works are those of Liz Frank and Elizabeth !Khaxas. The most outstanding short stories include 'Uerieta' by Jane Katjavivi, which describes a white woman's coming to terms with African life, and 'When the Rains Came' by Marialena van Tonder, in which a farm couple narrowly survives a drought. One contributor, Nepeti Nicanor, along with Marjorie Orford, also edited another volume, *Coming on Strong* (1996).

Those who read German will appreciate the works of Giselher Hoffmann (b 1958), which address historical and current Namibian issues. His first novel, *Im Bunde der Dritte* (Three's Company; 1984), is about poaching. *Die Erstgeboren* (The Firstborn; 1991) is told from the perspective of a San group that finds itself pitted against German settlers. Similarly, the Nama-Herero conflict of the late 19th century is described from the Nama perspective in *Die Schweigenden Feuer* (The Silent Fires; 1994). It's also concerned with the impact of modernisation on indigenous cultures.

Cinema

Since 2002, the Namibian Film Commission has been encouraging local film production and promoting the country as a film location. In the same year, a little-known film called *Beyond Borders,* about the Ethiopian famine in 1984, was shot in the country – and the film's star, Angelina Jolie, returned in 2006 to give birth to her daughter. On a more serious note, the annual Wild Cinema Festival (p223) is gaining impressive ground, attracting thousands of theatregoers every autumn.

After a few hiccups, the story of Namibia's first president, Sam Nujoma, was turned into a film in the form of *Namibia: The Struggle for Liberation*, which received mixed critical acclaim. In July 2011 the filming of the on-again-off-again fourth *Mad Max* movie was moved to Namibia, after unexpected rain turned the Australian desert into a very un–*Mad Max* carpet of flowers.

Music

Namibia's earliest musicians were the San, whose music probably emulated the sounds of animals, and was sung to accompany dances and storytelling. The early Nama, who had a more developed musical technique, used drums, flutes and basic stringed instruments, also to accompany dances. Some of these were adopted and adapted by the later-arriving Bantu, who added marimbas, gourd rattles and animal-horn trumpets to the range. Nowadays drums, marimbas and rattles are still popular, and it isn't unusual to see dancers wearing belts of soft-drink (soda) cans filled with pebbles to provide rhythmic accompaniment to their steps.

A prominent European contribution to Namibian music is the choir. Early in the colonial period, missionaries established religious choral groups among local people, and both school and church choirs still perform regularly. Namibia's most renowned ensembles are the Cantare Audire

NAMIBIA ARTS

GREETINGS

The Namibia greeting is practically an art form and goes something like this: *Did you get up well? Yes. Are you fine? Yes. Did you get up well? Yes. Are you fine? Yes.*

This is an example of just the most minimal greeting; in some cases greetings can continue at great length with repeated enquiries about your health, your crops and your family, which will demand great patience if you are in a hurry.

However, it is absolutely essential that you greet everyone you meet, from the most casual encounter in the corner store, to an important first meeting with a business associate. Failure to greet people is considered extremely rude, and it is without a doubt the most common mistake made by outsiders.

Learn the local words for 'hello' and 'goodbye' (p000), and use them unsparingly. If you have the time and inclination, consider broadening your lexicon to include longer and more complex phrases.

Even if you find yourself tongue-tied, handshakes are also a crucial icebreaker. The African handshake consists of three parts: the normal Western handshake, followed by the linking of bent fingers while touching the ends of upward-pointing thumbs, and then a repeat of the conventional handshake.

VILLAGE VS URBAN LIFE

Most Namibians still live in homesteads in rural areas – less than half of the population lives in urban areas, although the figure inches higher with each passing year – and lead typical village lives. Villages tend to be family- and clan-based and are presided over by an elected *elenga* (headman). The *elenga* is responsible for local affairs – everything from settling disputes to determining how communal lands are managed. Even those who have moved to the cities often maintain strong ties to their villages.

The sad reality, however, is that life is a struggle for the vast majority of Namibians, particularly in urban areas – on many town fringes you'll see ramshackle settlements without even the most basic services.

Choir and the Mascato Coastal Youth Choir (www.mascatoyouthchoir.com), the country's national youth choir. The German colonists also introduced their traditional 'oompah' bands, which feature mainly at Oktoberfest (p223) and other German-oriented festivals.

If you need some music to keep you company on those long, lonely Namibian roads, check out the soulful tunes of Hishishi Papa, a storyteller musician whose *Aantu Aantu* album is perfect driving music.

Architecture

While most visitors to Namibia have already set their sights on the country's natural wonders, there are a surprising number of architectural attractions to discover as well. Striking German colonial structures continue to stand as testament to the former European occupation of Namibia.

While most of Windhoek has modernised with the chock-a-block concrete structures that typify most African cities, there are a few remaining colonial gems. Towering over the city is the German Lutheran Christuskirche (p218), which masterfully uses local sandstone in its European-leaning neo-Gothic construction. Another notable structure is the Alte Fest (Old Fort), which was constructed in 1890 by Curt von François and his men to serve as the barracks for the German army. It remains the oldest surviving building in

the city, and now serves a much more peaceful function as the National Museum (p220).

If you truly want to experience the shining jewels in Namibia's architectural crown, you're going to need to head out to the coast. Here, improbably squeezed between the icy waters of the South Atlantic and the overbearing heat of the Namib Desert, are the surreal colonial relics of Swakopmund (p289) and Lüderitz (p327). Walking the streets of either town, you'd be easily forgiven for thinking that you were in a Bavarian *dorfchen* (small village) transplanted onto the shores of southwestern Africa. Somewhat forgotten by time and history, both towns are characterised by a handsome blend of German imperial and art nouveau styles, which become all the more bizarre when viewed against the backdrop of soaring dunes and raging seas.

Dance

Each group in Namibia has its own dances, but common threads run through most of them. First, all dances are intended to express social values to some extent, and many dances reflect the environment in which they're performed.

Dances of the Ju/'hoansi (!Kung) men (a San group in northeastern Namibia) tend to mimic the animals they hunt, or involve other elements that are important to them. For example, the 'melon dance' involves tossing and catching a *tsama* melon according to a fixed rhythm. The Himba dance *ondjongo* must be performed by a cattle owner, and involves representing care and ownership.

Specific dances are also used for various rituals, including rites of passage, political events, social gatherings and spiritual ceremonies. For example, the Ju/'hoansi male initiation dance, the *tcòcmà,* may not even be viewed by women. In the Kavango and Caprivi region, dances performed by traditional healers require the dancer to constantly shake rattles held in both hands. Most festive dances, such as the animated Kavango *epera* and *dipera,* have roles for both men and women, but are performed in lines with the genders separated.

Visual Arts

The majority of Namibia's established modern painters and photographers are of European origin, and concentrate largely on the country's colourful landscapes, bewitching light, native wildlife and, more recently, its diverse peoples. Well-known names include François de Necker, Axel Eriksson, Fritz Krampe and Adolph Jentsch. The well-known colonial landscape artists Carl Ossman and Ernst Vollbehr are exhibited in Germany. The work of many of these artists is exhibited in the permanent collection of the National Art Gallery (p221) in Windhoek, which also hosts changing exhibitions of local and international artists.

Non-European Namibians who have concentrated on three-dimensional and material arts have been developing their own traditions. Township art – largely sculpture made out of reclaimed materials such as drink cans and galvanised wire – develops sober themes in an expressive and colourful manner. It first appeared in the townships of South Africa during the apartheid years. Over the past decade or two, it has taken hold in Namibia, and is developing into a popular art form.

In an effort to raise the standard and awareness of the visual arts in Namibia, a working group of artists, including Joseph Madesia and François Necker, established the Tulipamwe International Artists' Workshop in 1994. Since then they have held a long list of workshops in farms and wildlife lodges around Namibia where Namibian, African and international artists can come together and share ideas and develop their skills base.

Namibian Cuisine

Food in Namibia, for the black population at least, has always been more about survival than inspiration, although you're unlikely to encounter the basic food eaten by most Namibians on most tourist menus. Instead, you'll find predominantly international dishes on most menus, with a couple of local variations – German dishes (particularly cakes and pastries) are a highlight, as are the widely available game meats (eg eland, oryx or kudu).

Staples & Specialities

Traditional Namibian food consists of a few staples, the most common of which is *oshifima*, a doughlike paste made from millet, usually served with a stew of vegetables or meat. Other common dishes include *oshiwambo*, a tasty combination of spinach and

beef, and *mealie pap*, an extremely basic porridge.

As a foreigner you'll rarely find such dishes on the menu. Most Namibian restaurants in big towns such as Windhoek, Swakopmund and Lüderitz serve a variation on European-style foods, such as Italian or French, alongside an abundance of seafood dishes. Outside these towns you'll rapidly become familiar with fried-food joints.

Whatever the sign above the door, you'll find that most menus are meat-oriented, although you might be lucky to find a few vegetarian side dishes. The reason for this is pretty obvious – Namibia is a vast desert, and the country imports much of its fresh fruit and vegetables from South Africa. What is available locally is the delicious gem squash and varieties of pumpkin such as butternut squash. In season, Namibian oranges are delicious; in the Kavango region, papayas are served with a squeeze of lemon or lime.

More than anything else, German influences can be found in Namibia's *konditoreien* (cake shops), where you can pig out on *Apfelstrudel* (apple strudel), *Sachertorte* (a rich chocolate cake layered with apricot jam), *Schwartzwälder Kirschtorte* (Black Forest cake) and other delicious pastries and cakes. Several places in Windhoek and Swakopmund are national institutions. You may also want to try Afrikaners' sticky-sweet *koeksesters* (small doughnuts dripping with honey) and *melktart* (milk tart).

Cooked breakfasts include bacon and boerewors (farmer's sausage), and don't be surprised to find something bizarre – curried kidneys, for example – alongside your eggs. Beef in varying forms also makes an occasional appearance at breakfast time.

Evening meals feature meat, normally beef or game. A huge beef fillet steak or a kudu cutlet will set you back no more than N$100. In some lodges, expect to find eland and oryx (gemsbok) on the menu. Fish and seafood are best represented by kingklip, kabeljou and several types of shellfish. These are available all over Namibia, but are best at finer restaurants in Windhoek, Swakopmund and Lüderitz, where they'll normally be fresh from the sea.

Drinks

In the rural Owambo areas, people socialise in tiny makeshift bars, enjoying local brews such as *oshikundu* (beer made from mahango–millet), mataku (watermelon wine), tambo (fermented millet and sugar) or mushokolo (a beer made from a small local seed) and walende, which is distilled from the makalani palm and tastes similar to vodka. All of these concoctions, except walende, are brewed in the morning and drunk the same day, and they're all dirt cheap.

For more conventional palates, Namibia is awash with locally brewed lagers. The most popular drop is the light and refreshing Windhoek Lager, but the brewery also produces Tafel Lager, the stronger and more bitter Windhoek Export and the slightly rough Windhoek Special. Windhoek Light and DAS Pilsener are both drunk as soft drinks (DAS is often called 'breakfast beer'!), and in winter Namibia Breweries also brews a 7% stout known as Urbock. South African beers such as Lion, Castle and Black Label are also widely available.

Although beer is the drink of choice for most Namibians, the country also has a few wineries, including the Kristall Kellerei (p236), 3km east of Omaruru. It produces Paradise Flycatcher, which is a red blend of ruby cabernet, cabernet sauvignon and tinta barocca, as well as colombard and a prickly-pear-cactus schnapps (a good blast). South African wines are also widely available. Among the best are the cabernet and pinot varieties grown in the Stellenbosch region of Western Cape province. A good bottle of wine will set you back between N$100 and N$250.

Environment

Namibia's natural world is a grand epic of extraordinary landforms (from sand-dune deserts that reach the coast to the haunting, barren mountain ranges of the interior) and these shelter a wonderful array of wildlife, especially in the country's north. But this is also one of the driest countries on earth and issues of desertification and water scarcity loom large over the country's future. And unlike neighbouring Botswana, Namibia allows commercial or trophy hunting.

The Landscape

The Namib, the desert of southwestern Africa that so appropriately gives its name to the driest country south of the Sahara, is the oldest desert on the planet. It is a scorched earth of burned and blackened-red basalt that spilled from beneath the earth 130 million years ago, hardening to form what we now know as Namibia. Precious little can grow or thrive in this merciless environment. That anything survives out here owes everything to the sheer ingenuity of the natural world and the resilience of its human population.

NORTHEASTERN NAMIBIA

Known as the Land of Rivers, northern Namibia is bounded by the Kunene and Okavango Rivers along the Angolan border, and in the east by the Zambezi and the Kwando/Mashe/Linyanti/Chobe river-systems, all of which flow year-round. In the northeast, the gently rolling Kavango region is dominated by the Okavango River. East of Kavango is the spindly Caprivi Strip, a flat, unexceptional landscape that is characterised by expanses of acacia forest. In wild contrast to the bleached-blue skies and vast, open expanses of most of the country, the Kavango and Caprivi regions are a well-watered paradise. Further south, in Namibia's northeastern interior along the border with Botswana, is the Otjozondjupa region, a wild and thinly populated strip of scrub forest that is home to several scattered San villages.

THE SKELETON COAST

Northwestern Namibia is synonymous with the Skeleton Coast, a formidable desert coastline engulfed by icy breakers. As you move inland, the sinister fogs give way to the wondrous desert wilderness of Damaraland and the Kaokoveld. The former is known for its unique geological features, including volcanic mounds, petrified forests, red-rock mesas and petroglyph-engraved sandstone slabs. The latter is known as one of the last great wildernesses in Southern Africa. Despite their unimaginably harsh conditions, both regions are also rich in wildlife, which has adapted to the arid environment and subsequently thrived.

The Namib Desert extends along the country's entire Atlantic coast, and is scored by a number of rivers, which rise in the central plateau, but often run dry. Some, like the ephemeral Tsauchab, once reached the sea, but now end in calcrete pans. Others flow only during the summer rainy season, but at some former stage carried huge volumes of water and carved out dramatic canyons such as Fish River (p336) and Kuiseb (p308), where Henno Martin and Hermann Korn struggled to survive WWII. Much of the surface between Walvis Bay and Lüderitz is covered by enormous linear dunes, which roll back from the sea towards the inland gravel plains that are occasionally interrupted by isolated mountain ranges.

SOUTHERN NAMIBIA

Southern Namibia takes in everything from Rehoboth in the north to the Orange River along the South African border, and westward from the Botswana border to the Forbidden Coast. The south's central plateau is characterised by wide open country, and the area's widely spaced rural towns function mainly as commercial and market centres. Further south, the landscape opens up into seemingly endless plains, ranges and far horizons. In the far south of the region, the Fish River Canyon forms a spectacular gash across the otherwise-flat landscape.

The country's far southeast, along the borders with Botswana and South Africa, is dominated by the Kalahari Desert, the largest expanse of sand on the planet.

Wildlife

If you're here to see wildlife, you'll want to spend most of your time in the north, in the country's three main wildlife areas: Kaokoveld, where elusive desert elephants and black rhinos follow the river courses running to the Skeleton Coast; the Caprivi Strip and Khaudum National Park, where Namibia's last African wild dogs find refuge and lions are making a comeback; and, best of all, Etosha National Park, one of the world's finest wildlife reserves.

Further south is one of the largest wildlife reserves in Africa, the Namib-Naukluft Park, which covers an astonishing 6% of Namibian territory. Much of it is true desert, and large mammals occur in extremely low densities, though local species include Hartmann's mountain zebras as well as more widespread Southern African endemics such as springboks and gemsboks. For aficionados of smaller life, the Namib is an endemism hot spot – on the dunes, desert-adapted birdlife flickers into view, alongside reptiles and desert-specialist insects.

The severe Namibian coast is no place to expect abundant big wildlife, although it's the only spot in the world where massive fur-seal colonies are patrolled by hunting brown hyenas and black-backed jackals.

The coast also hosts flamingos and massive flocks of summer waders, including sanderlings, turnstones and grey plovers, while Heaviside's and dusky dolphins can often be seen in the shallow offshore waters.

In 2009 the Namibian government opened Sperrgebiet National Park, a vast 16,000-sq-km expanse of land home to the threatened desert rain frog, dramatic rock formations and disused diamond mines. The area's haunting beauty, which is highlighted by shimmering salt pans and saffron-coloured sand dunes, provides one of the world's most dramatic backdrops for adventurous wildlife watchers. The Sperrgebiet fringe is also home to one of Africa's only populations of wild horses.

MAMMALS

Northern Namibia is one of Southern Africa's most rewarding wildlife-watching destinations.

The greatest prizes here are desert elephants, black rhinos, lions, leopards, cheetahs and, if you're really lucky, African wild dogs. Other unusual sightings include the elusive Hartmann's mountain zebra.

More commonly sighted species include ostriches, zebras, warthogs, greater kudus, giraffes, gemsboks, springboks, steenboks, mongoose, ground squirrels and small numbers of other animals, such as black-backed jackals and bat-eared foxes. If you're *really* lucky, you might encounter caracals, aardwolfs, pangolins (go on, dream a little...) and brown hyenas.

Along the country's desert coasts you can see jackass penguins, flamingos and Cape fur seals.

REPTILES

The dry lands of Namibia boast more than 70 species of snake, including three species of spitting cobra. It is actually the African puff adder that causes the most problems for humans, since it inhabits dry, sandy riverbeds. Horned adders and sand snakes inhabit the gravel plains of the Namib, and the sidewinder adder lives in the Namib dune sea. Other venomous snakes include the slender green vine snake, both the green and black mamba, the dangerous zebra snake and the boomslang (Afrikaans for 'tree snake'), a slender 2m aquamarine affair with black-tipped scales. Despite such a formidable list, few travellers even see any of the country's snake species, let alone encounter any difficulties with them.

NAMIBIA ENVIRONMENT

NAMIBIA ENVIRONMENT

Lizards, too, are ubiquitous. The largest of these is the *leguaan* (water monitor), a docile creature that reaches over 2m in length, swims and spends a lot of time laying around water holes, probably dreaming of becoming a crocodile. A smaller version, the savannah *leguaan*, inhabits kopjes (small hills) and drier areas. Also present in large numbers are geckos, chameleons, legless lizards, rock-plated lizards and a host of others.

The Namib Desert supports a wide range of lizards, including a large vegetarian species, *Angolosaurus skoogi*, and the sand-diving lizard, *Aprosaura achietae*, known for its 'thermal dance'. The unusual bug-eyed palmato gecko inhabits the high dunes and there's a species of chameleon.

In the watery marshes and rivers of the north of the country, you'll find Namibia's reptile extraordinaire, the Nile crocodile. It is one of the largest species of crocodile on the planet, and can reach 5m to 6m in length. It has a reputation as a man eater, but this is probably because it lives in close proximity to human populations – just in case, always seek local advice before going for a swim in a Namibian river. In the past there have been concerns over excessive hunting of the crocodile, but these days numbers are well up, and it's more at risk from pollution and accidental entanglement in fishing nets.

INSECTS & SPIDERS

Although Namibia doesn't enjoy the profusion of bug life found in countries further north, a few interesting specimens buzz, creep and crawl around the place. Over 500 species of colourful butterfly, including the African monarch, the commodore and the citrus swallowtail, are resident, as well as many fly-by-night moths.

Interesting buggy types include the large and rarely noticed stick insects and the ubiquitous and leggy *shongololo* (millipede), which can be up to 30cm long. The dunes are also known for their extraordinary variety of tenebrionid (known as *toktokkie*) beetles.

The Namib Desert has several wonderful species of spider. One to avoid is the poisonous, large (and frighteningly hairy) baboon spider. The tarantula-like 'white lady of the dunes' is a white, hairy affair attracted to light. There's also a rare 'false' spider known as a *solifluge* (sun spider). You can see its circulatory system through its light-coloured translucent outer skeleton.

Common insects such as ants, stink bugs, grasshoppers, mopane worms and locusts sometimes find their way into frying pans for snacks. Among travellers, it takes something of a culinary daredevil to dive into a newspaper-wrapped ball of fried bugs, though for locals the practice provides essential protein supplements.

BIRDS

Despite Namibia's harsh and inhospitable desert landscape, more than 700 bird species have been recorded in the country. The richest pickings for birders are in the lush, green Caprivi Strip, which borders the Okavango Delta. Here, particularly in the Mahango Game Reserve, you'll find the same exotic range of species as in Botswana's Okavango Panhandle, Okavango Delta and Linyanti regions. Wetland species include the African jacana, snakebird, ibis, stork, egret, shrike, kingfisher, great white

---

WHERE TO WATCH WILDLIFE

Undoubtedly Namibia's most prolific wildlife populations are in Etosha National Park (p250), one of Africa's premier wildlife reserves. Its name means 'Place of Mirages', for the dusty salt pan that sits at its centre. During the dry season, huge herds of elephants, zebras, antelope and giraffes, as well as rare black rhinos, congregate here against an eerie, bleached-white backdrop. Predators, too, are commonly sighted here.

Namibia's other major parks for good wildlife viewing are Bwabwata National Park (p261) and Nkasa Rupara National Park (p267) in the Caprivi Strip.

Along the coast, penguins and seals thrive in the chilly Atlantic currents; the colony of Cape fur seals at **Cape Cross Seal Reserve** (p285) is one of the country's premier wildlife-watching attractions.

Not all of Namibia's wildlife is confined to national parks. Unprotected Damaraland (p273), in the northwest, is home to numerous antelope species and other ungulates, and is also a haven for desert rhinos, elephants, lions, spotted hyenas and other specially adapted subspecies.

heron and purple and green-backed heron. Birds of prey include Pel's fishing owl (which is much prized among birders), goshawk, several species of vulture, and both the bateleur and African fish eagle.

The coastal wildfowl reserves support an especially wide range of birdlife: white pelicans, flamingos, cormorants and hundreds of other wetland birds. Further south, around Walvis Bay and Lüderitz, flamingos (p306) and jackass penguins share the same desert shoreline.

Situated on a key migration route, Namibia also hosts a range of migratory birds, especially raptors, which arrive around September and October and remain until April. The canyons and riverbeds slicing across the central Namib Desert are home to nine species of raptor. Throughout the desert regions, you'll also see the intriguing social weaver, which builds an enormous nest that's the avian equivalent of a 10-storey block of flats. Central Namibia also boasts bird species found nowhere else, such as the Namaqua sand-grouse and Grey's lark.

Other iconic species that birders may want to build their trips around include Hartlaub's francolin (in the rocky uplands of central and northern Namibia), Rüppell's bustard (on the Namib Desert fringe), Barlow's lark (the far south, around Sperrgebiet), Rüppell's parrot (acacia woodlands and dry riverbeds), Monteiro's hornbill (arid woodlands in the interior), dune lark (dry riverbeds of the Namib), Herero chat (arid interior in the centre and north), rockrunner (arid interior in the centre and north) and Carp's tit (northern woodlands).

FISH

The Namibian coastal waters are considered some of the world's richest, mainly thanks to the cold Benguela Current, which flows northward from the Antarctic. It's exceptionally rich in plankton, which accounts for the abundance of anchovies, pilchards, mackerel and other whitefish. But the limited offshore fishing rights have caused problems, and there is resentment that such countries as Spain and Russia have legal access to offshore fish stocks. Namibia has now declared a 200-nautical-mile exclusive economic zone to make Namibian fisheries competitive.

Fishing is an extremely popular activity for visitors, particularly along the Skeleton Coast north of Swakopmund.

ENDANGERED SPECIES

Namibia has a number of endangered species, among them the black rhino, desert elephant, lion and African wild dog. It is also considered a key battleground in the fight to save the cheetah. Poaching continues to take its toll on a number of flagship species, especially the rhino.

In the eastern reaches of the Caprivi Strip, and across the border in Botswana's Chobe National Park, a small population of puku antelope survives, the last of its kind in Southern Africa (although healthy, if declining, populations survive in Tanzania and northern Zambia).

Overfishing and the 1993–94 outbreak of 'red tide' along the Skeleton Coast have decimated the sea-lion population, both through starvation and commercially inspired culling.

The stability of some bird and plant species, such as the lichen fields, the welwitschia plant, the Damara tern, the Cape vulture and numerous lesser-known species, has been undoubtedly compromised by human activities (including tourism and recreation) in formerly remote areas. However, awareness of the perils faced by these species is increasing among operators and tourists alike, which adds a glimmer of hope to the prospects of their future survival.

ELEPHANTS

Sadly, Namibia elected not to participate in the landmark 2016 Great Elephant Census (www.greatelephantcensus.com), which found 352,271 elephants across 18 countries. As a consequence, no one really knows how many elephants live within the country's borders. The government estimates a figure of 22,711 elephants in total, with 13,136 in the country's northeast. Namibia's government also continues to advocate for permission to trade in ivory, claiming that its elephant population is stable and growing.

LIONS

After a difficult few decades, Namibia's lions are making something of a comeback. According to Dr Paul Funston, director of the lion program with Panthera (www.panthera.org), Namibia is home to as many as 800 lions, which is up considerably from even a few years ago.

Etosha National Park is the main stronghold in Namibia, with an estimated population of 450 to 500 lions. This population within park boundaries is part of

NAMIBIA ENVIRONMENT

a broader Etosha-Kunene population that takes in private farms, conservancies and unprotected areas across Namibia's north, including Kaokoveld and Damaraland.

The desert lion, which roams the Skeleton Coast and is part of the Etosha-Kunene population, has also made a spectacular recovery, and now numbers between 180 and 200. These desert lions, which were thought to have been wiped out in the 1980s, shot to fame in the recent National Geographic film *Vanishing Kings: Lions of the Namib*, which focused on five male lions in the Gomatum valley in the Kunene region. In a sad footnote that says much about the perils faced by lions in Namibia, four of the five protagonists in the film were killed in 2016 – one was shot and three were poisoned. The Desert Lion Conservation Foundation (www.desertlion.org) is an excellent resource on Namibia's desert lions.

A further lion population stretches from Khaudum National Park into the parks and reserves of the Caprivi Strip (Bwabwata, Mudum and Nkasa Rupara) and numbers around 70 to 80 lions. While numerically small, this population's importance is due to its location – it provides an additional dispersal zone for lions in northern Botswana, but also a link to lion populations and habitats across international borders in Angola and Zambia. As a whole, this greater transfrontier area, which also extends into Zimbabwe, is home to perhaps 3500 lions, making the Khaudum-Caprivi population part of one of the most important lion areas on earth.

Beyond that, isolated populations of lions may occur elsewhere in Namibia, such as with a small spillover population from Botswana and South Africa's Kgalagadi Transfrontier Park along Namibia's far southeast. But for the most part, once lions leave protected areas, it's only a matter of time before they're shot by ranchers to protect their cattle.

BLACK RHINOS

As many as 100,000 black rhinos lived in Africa as recently as 1960. Now, fewer than 5000 are thought to remain, with over 96% of them in Namibia, South Africa, Zimbabwe and Kenya. As such, Namibia is a priceless stronghold for this critically endangered species. According to some estimates, half of the remaining black rhinos live in Namibia.

Although the poaching statistics for black rhinos in Namibia have yet to rival those in South Africa, there remains considerable cause for concern. According to Save the Rhino Trust (www.savetherhinotrust.org), which watches over what it claims to be Africa's largest free-roaming populations of black rhino in Damaraland, 24 black rhinos were poached in Namibia in 2015. Halfway through 2016, that number had increased alarmingly to more than 60. Namibia's government puts the figure even higher – 162 rhinos poached in the 18 months to August 2016. Most of the poaching has taken place in Etosha National Park and the northern Kunene region.

For all of this, your chances of seeing Namibia's rhinos are surprisingly good. The water holes of Etosha National Park, immortalised in the memorable footage of solitary rhinos mingling under the cover of darkness in BBC Earth's *Africa* series, are brilliant places to catch a glimpse; the water holes adjacent to Olifantsrus (p252) and Okaukuejo (p253) camping areas are fairly reliable rhino hot spots after sunset.

Rhino tracking in the surrounding conservancies is also a major reason to stay at Desert Rhino Camp (p278) or Palmwag Lodge (p279) in Damaraland – these are among Namibia's most rewarding wildlife excursions. Other possibilities include the Kunene region, Waterberg plateau and Erongo.

AFRICAN WILD DOGS

Namibia sits at the southwestern range of the endangered African wild dog, and, save for isolated (and probably unsustainable) populations elsewhere in the country, its Namibian range is restricted to the country's far northeast. Your best chance of seeing wild populations are at Khaudum National Park, or in the parks of the Caprivi Strip, such as Bwabwata National Park. This northeastern population received a boost by the discovery by Panthera of a small but significant wild dog population in southwestern Angola.

At the time of writing, Okonjima Nature Reserve had two rescued wild dogs roaming within its boundaries, with the possibility of more, although the medium-term plan for this pack-in-the-making was for its resettlement to an appropriate protected area elsewhere. Etosha National Park, which currently has no wild dogs, is often touted as a place where conservationists would like to reestablish a population, although there are no concrete plans in place.

There is also a captive African wild dog population of around 20 at Harnas Wildlife Foundation (p232), northwest of Gobabis.

CONSERVATION ORGANISATIONS

Anyone with a genuine interest in a specific ecological issue should contact one or more of the following organisations. These organisations do not, however, provide tourist information or offer organised tours (unless stated otherwise). Some do, however, have centres where you can visit and learn more.

Afri-Cat Foundation (www.africat.org) A nonprofit organisation focusing on research and the reintroduction of large cats into the wild. There's also an on-site education centre and a specialist veterinary clinic.

Cheetah Conservation Fund (www.cheetah.org) A centre of research and education on cheetah populations and how they are conserved. It's possible to volunteer with this organisation.

Integrated Rural Development & Nature Conservation (www.irdnc.org.na) IRDNC aims to improve the lives of rural people by diversifying their economic opportunities to include wildlife management and other valuable natural resources. Its two main projects are in the Kunene region and the Caprivi Strip.

Panthera (www.panthera.org) The world's premier wild-cat-conservation NGO with programs in place to support leopards, cheetahs and lions. Its work in the Caprivi Strip with local lion and human populations has played a significant role in turning things around.

Save the Rhino Trust (www.savetherhino.org) SRT has worked to implement community-based conservation since the early 1980s. By 2030 it hopes that its efforts will have succeeded in reestablishing the black rhino in Namibia in healthy breeding populations.

NAMIBIA ENVIRONMENT

HARTMANN'S MOUNTAIN ZEBRAS

Although some scientists argue that the Hartmann's Mountain zebra should be considered a separate species, it remains a subspecies of the Cape Mountain zebra, which is the world's smallest zebra species and is listed as vulnerable on the International Union for Conservation of Nature's (IUCN) Red List of Threatened Species.

Agile and shy in the arid, rocky mountain country it inhabits, the Hartmann's Mountain zebra has narrower stripes on the torso, no stripes on the underbelly, and wider black stripes on the back haunches when compared to better-known plains or common zebra. In addition to northwestern South Africa and southwestern Angola, the Hartmann's Mountain zebra is found in Namibia's rocky interior, including Kunene province in the north, the Erongo Mountains, the Naukluft Mountains and Fish River Canyon.

CHEETAHS

According to an estimate by the IUCN, the world's cheetah population stands at just 6700 adult and adolescent cheetahs spread across 29 populations and they inhabit just 10% of their former range. Almost two-thirds of the world's surviving cheetahs are in Southern Africa, with Namibia home to Africa's largest population.

Although Namibia's cheetahs live at quite low densities, shrinking habitats and human encroachment on former wilderness areas have resulted in increasing conflict between cheetahs and farmers. In such cases, the cheetah rarely wins. Organisations such as the Cheetah Conservation Fund (CCF; www.cheetah.org) are at the forefront of efforts to mitigate this conflict.

Cheetahs can be difficult to see, although chance encounters are always possible. Your best chance is probably Etosha National Park, although sightings are also on the increase in Bwabwata National Park and Nkasa Rupara National Park. Another excellent option is to go cheetah tracking at Okonjima Nature Reserve, where radio collars have been placed on cheetahs reintroduced to the wild.

To watch the feeding of captive cheetahs that have been rescued from the wild, visit Harnas Wildlife Foundation (p232) or Otjitotongwe Cheetah Guest Farm (p278).

Environmental Issues

As you might expect in a country that is the driest in sub-Saharan Africa, Namibia faces some of the most pressing environmental challenges of our time.

According to the United Nations Environmental Program (UNEP), 99% of Namibia's land mass is at risk of desertification. Cattle outnumber people in Namibia and overgrazing is considered a driving force behind the desertification process, which can result in soil erosion, declining groundwater reserves, reduced soil fertility and deforestation. The related issue of water scarcity is another massive concern, both in terms of the country's agricultural output and in the provision of drinking water to a growing population.

HUNTING

Unlike in neighbouring Botswana, hunting is legal in Namibia, although it is strictly regulated and licensed. The Ministry of the Environment and Tourism along with the Namibia Professional Hunting Association (www.napha-namibia.com) regulate hunting, which accounts for 5% of the country's revenue from wildlife.

The Namibian government views its hunting laws as a practical form of wildlife management and conservation. Many foreign hunters are willing to pay handsomely for big wildlife trophies, and farmers and ranchers frequently complain about the ravages of wildlife on their stock. The idea is to provide farmers with financial incentives to protect free-ranging wildlife. Management strategies include encouraging hunting of older animals, evaluating the condition of trophies and setting bag limits in accordance with population fluctuations.

In addition, quite a few private farms are set aside for hunting. The owners stock these farms with wildlife bred by suppliers – mainly in South Africa – and turn them loose into the farm environment. Although community-based hunting concessions have appeared in the Otjozondjupa area, these still aren't widespread.

Plants

Because Namibia is mostly arid, much of the flora is typical African dryland vegetation: scrub brush and succulents, such as euphorbia. Along the coastal plain around Swakopmund are the world's most extensive and diverse fields of lichen. They remain dormant during dry periods, but with the addition of water they burst into colourful bloom.

Most of the country is covered by tree-dotted, scrub-savannah grasses of the genera *Stipagrostis, Eragrostis* and *Aristida*. In the south, the grass is interrupted by ephemeral watercourses lined with tamarisks, buffalo thorn and camelthorn. Unique floral oddities here include the *kokerboom* (quiver tree), a species of aloe that grows only in southern Namibia.

In the sandy plains of southeastern Namibia, raisin bushes *(Grewia)* and candlethorn grow among the scrubby trees, while hillsides are blanketed with green-flowered *Aloe viridiflora* and camphor bush.

The eastern fringes of Namib-Naukluft Park are dominated by semidesert scrub-savannah vegetation, including some rare aloe species *(Aloe karasbergensis* and *Aloe sladeniana)*. On the gravel plains east of the Skeleton Coast grows the bizarre *Welwitschia mirabilis,* a slow-growing, ground-hugging conifer that lives for more than 1000 years.

In areas with higher rainfall, the characteristic grass savannah gives way to acacia woodlands, and Etosha National Park enjoys two distinct environments: the wooded savannah in the east and thorn-scrub savannah in the west. The higher rainfall of Caprivi and Kavango sustains extensive mopane woodland, and the riverine areas support scattered wetland vegetation, grasslands and stands of acacias. The area around Katima Mulilo is dominated by mixed subtropical woodland containing copalwood, Zambezi teak and leadwood, among other hardwood species.

National Parks & Reserves

Despite its harsh climate, Namibia has some of Southern Africa's grandest national parks, ranging from the world-famous, wildlife-rich Etosha National Park to the immense Namib-Naukluft Park, which protects vast dune fields, desert plains, wild mountains and unique flora. There are also the smaller (but ecologically significant) reserves of the Caprivi region, the renowned Skeleton Coast and the awe-inspiring Fish River Canyon in |Ai- |Ais Richtersveld Transfrontier Park, which ranks among Africa's most spectacular natural wonders.

Around 15% of Namibia is designated as national park or conservancy.

VISITING THE NATIONAL PARKS IN NAMIBIA

Access to most wildlife parks is limited to closed vehicles only. A 2WD is sufficient for most parks, but for Nkasa Rupara National Park, Khaudum National Park and parts of

Bwabwata National Park, you need a sturdy 4WD with high clearance.

Entry permits are available on arrival at park entrances, but campsites and resorts should be booked in advance, although it is possible to make a booking on arrival, subject to availability.

FOREIGNERS	COST PER DAY
adult	N$80 (Etosha, Cape Cross, |Ai-|Ais/Fish River, Skeleton Coast, Naukluft Park, Waterberg); N$40 all other parks
child (under 16)	free
camping	cost varies
vehicles	N$10

NAMIBIA WILDLIFE RESORTS (NWR)

The semiprivate Namibia Wildlife Resorts (p230) in Windhoek manages a large number of rest camps, campsites and resorts within the national parks. If you haven't prebooked (ie if you're pulling into a national park area on a whim), there's a good chance you'll find something available on the spot, but have a contingency plan in case things don't work out. This is not advised for Etosha or Sossusvlei, which are perennially busy.

CONSERVANCIES & PRIVATE GAME RESERVES

In Namibia a conservancy is an amalgamation of private farms, or an area of communal land where farmers and/or local residents agree to combine resources for the benefit of wildlife, the local community and tourism. These conservancies and

NAMIBIA ENVIRONMENT

NATIONAL PARKS & RESERVES

PARK	FEATURES	ACTIVITIES	BEST TIME
Dorob National Park	stretches from the Ugab River in the north down to Sandwich Harbour in the south (it consumes the old National West Coast Tourist Recreation Area); coastal dune belt; desert plants; sand dunes; vast gravel plains; prolific birdlife; major river systems	Fishing; birdwatching	Jun-Nov
Etosha National Park	22,275 sq km; semi-arid savannah surrounding a salt pan; 114 mammal species	Wildlife viewing; birdwatching; night drives	May-Sep
Fish River Canyon (part of |Ai- |Ais Richtersveld Transfrontier Park)	Africa's longest canyon (161km); hot springs; rock strata of multiple colours	Hiking; bathing	May-Nov
Khaudum National Park	3840 sq km; bushveld landscape crossed by fossilised river valleys	Wildlife viewing; hiking; 4WD exploration	Jun-Oct
Namib-Naukluft Park	50,000 sq km; Namibia's largest protected area; rare Hartmann's zebras	Wildlife watching; walking	year-round
Nkasa Rupara National Park	320 sq km; mini-Okavango; 430 bird species; canoe trails through park	Wildlife viewing; birdwatching; canoe trips	Sep-Apr
Mudumu National Park	850 sq km; lush riverine environment; 400 bird species	Wildlife watching; birdwatching; guided trails	May-Sep
Skeleton Coast National Park	20,000 sq km; wild, foggy wilderness; desert-adapted animals	Wildlife viewing; walking; fly-in safaris	year-round
Waterberg Plateau Park	400 sq km; table mountain; refuge for black and white rhinos and rare antelope	Wildlife viewing; rhino tracking; hiking	May-Sep

similar set-ups nicely complement the national park system, can create important income for community development, and account for more than 17% of Namibia. They are immense sanctuaries free from fencing, allowing wildlife to roam at will, and are often located in some of the country's most stunning landscapes. Lodges and community campsites offer great opportunities to experience these wild places and, unlike in national parks, night drives are sometimes possible.

Another sort of protected area is the private game reserve, of which there are now more than 180 in Namibia. The largest of these, by far, are the 2000-sq-km NamibRand Nature Reserve (p319), adjoining the Namib-Naukluft Park, and the 1020-sq-km Gondwana Cañon Park (p339), bordering Fish River Canyon. Another excellent example is Okonjima Nature Reserve (p239). In all three, concessionaires provide accommodation and activities for visitors. Most of the smaller game reserves are either private game reserves or hunting farms, which sustain endemic animal species rather than livestock.

SURVIVAL GUIDE

 **Directory A–Z**

ACCOMMODATION

Accommodation in Namibia is some of the best priced and most well kept in Southern Africa, and covers a huge range of options.

B&Bs and guesthouses These are found all across Namibia and are often simple but welcoming and well priced.

Rest camps, campsites and caravan parks Most are fenced, and may have a small kiosk and even a swimming pool.

Guest farms Often in remote areas with rustic accommodation and activities.

Hotels and hostels Backpacker hostels inhabit Windhoek, Swakopmund and elsewhere. Hotels are everywhere, with a vast range in quality.

Safari lodges From well priced and relatively simple to opulent with sky's-the-limit prices.

Price Ranges

Price ranges refer to a high-season double room with bathroom:

$	less than N$1050 (US$75)
$$	N$1050–2100 (US$75-150)
$$$	more than N$2100 (US$150)

B&Bs

B&Bs are mushrooming all around the country. As private homes, the standard, atmosphere and welcome tends to vary a great deal. Generally speaking, B&Bs are a pleasure to frequent and can be one of the highlights of any trip to Namibia. Some places don't actually provide breakfast (!), so it pays to ask when booking.

For listings, pick up the *Namibia B&B Guide* or contact the Accommodation Association of Namibia (www.accommodation-association. com), which also lists a number of self-catering flats and guest farms.

Camping

Namibia is campers' heaven, and wherever you go in the country you'll find a campsite nearby. These can vary from a patch of scrubland with basic facilities to well-kitted-out sites with concrete ablution blocks with hot and cold running water and a kiosk.

In many of the national parks, campsites are administered by **Namibia Wildlife Resorts** (p230) and need to be booked beforehand online or through its offices in Windhoek, Swakopmund and Cape Town. These sites are all well maintained, and many of them also offer accommodation in bungalows. Unlike in Botswana, most campsites, at least in national parks, are fenced.

To camp on private land, you'll need to secure permission from the landowner. On communal land – unless you're well away from human habitation – it's a courtesy to make your presence known to the leaders in the nearest community.

Most towns also have caravan parks with bungalows or rondavels (round huts), as well as a pool, restaurant and shop. Prices are normally per site, with a maximum of eight people and two vehicles per site; there's normally an additional charge per vehicle. In addition, a growing number of private rest camps, with rooms and campsites and well-appointed facilities, are springing up in rural areas and along major tourist routes.

Guest Farms

Farmstays are a peculiarly Namibian phenomenon, whereby tourists can spend the night on one of the country's huge private farms. They give an intriguing insight into the rural white lifestyle, although, as with B&Bs, the level of hospitality and the standard of rooms and facilities can vary enormously. The emphasis is on personal service and quaint rural luxury, and bedding down on a huge rural estate in the middle of the bush can be a uniquely Namibian experience.

As an added bonus, many of these farms have designated blocks of land as wildlife reserves, and offer excellent wildlife viewing and photographic opportunities. With that said, many also serve as hunting reserves, so bear this in mind when booking if you don't relish the thought of trading trophy stories over dinner.

For all farmstays, advance bookings are essential.

Hostels

In Windhoek, Swakopmund, Lüderitz and other places, you'll find private backpacker hostels, which provide inexpensive dorm accommodation, shared ablutions and cooking facilities. Most offer a very agreeable atmosphere, and they are extremely popular with budget travellers. On average, you can expect to pay around N$100 per person per night. Some also offer private doubles, which cost around N$250 to N$400.

Hotels

Hotels in Namibia are much like hotels anywhere else, ranging from tired old has-beens to palaces of luxury and indulgence. Rarely, though, will you find a dirty or unsafe hotel in Namibia given the relatively strict classification system, which rates everything from small guesthouses to four-star hotels.

One-star hotels must have a specific ratio of rooms with private and shared facilities. They tend to be quite simple, but most are locally owned and managed and provide clean, comfortable accommodation with adequate beds and towels. Rates range from around N$350 to N$500 for a double room, including breakfast. They always have a small dining room and bar, but only few offer frills such as air-conditioning.

Hotels with two- and three-star ratings are generally more comfortable, and are often used by local business people. Rates start at around N$450 for a double, and climb to N$650 for the more elegant places.

There aren't really many four-star hotels in the usual sense, though most high-end lodges could qualify for a four-star rating. To qualify for such a rating, a hotel needs to be an air-conditioned palace with a salon, valet service and a range of ancillary services for business and diplomatic travellers.

Safari Lodges

Over the last decade the Namibian luxury safari lodge has come along in leaps and bounds, offering the kind of colonial luxury that has been associated with Botswana.

Most of the lodges are set on large private ranches or in concession areas. Some are quite affordable family-run places with standard meals or self-catering options. In general they are still more affordable than comparable places in Botswana or the Victoria Falls area, yet more expensive than similar lodges in South Africa.

ACTIVITIES

Given its stunning landscapes, Namibia provides a photogenic arena for the multitude of outdoor activities that are on offer. These range from the more conventional hiking and 4WD trails to sandboarding down mountainous dunes, quad biking, paragliding, ballooning and camel riding. Most of these activities can be arranged very easily locally, and are relatively well priced.

4WD Trails

Traditionally, 4WD trips were limited to rugged wilderness tracks through the Kaokoveld, Damaraland and Otjozondjupa, but recent years have seen the rise of fixed-route 4WD trails established for 4WD enthusiasts. Participants must pay a daily fee, and are obligated to travel a certain distance each day and stay at prespecified campsites. You'll need to book at least a few weeks in advance through **Namibian Wildlife Resorts** (p230). Contact it to see which trails are currently available. You could also try www.namibian.org/travel/adventure/4x4_action.htm, which includes a booking service; and www.drivesouthafrica.co.za/blog/best-4x4-trails-in-namibia for more information.

Canoeing & Rafting

Along the Orange River, in the south of the country, canoeing and rafting trips are growing in popularity. Several operators in Noordoewer (p340) offer good-value descents through the spectacular canyons of the Orange River, along the South African border. White-water rafting on the Kunene River is available through the inexpensive **Kunene River Lodge** (p282) at Swartbooi's Drift, and also through several more upmarket operators.

Fishing

Namibia draws anglers from all over Southern Africa. The Benguela Current along the Skeleton Coast brings kabeljou, steenbras, galjoen, blacktails and copper sharks close to shore. Favoured spots include the various beaches north of

Swakopmund, as well as more isolated spots further north.

In the dams, especially Hardap and Von Bach, you can expect to catch tilapia, carp, yellowfish, mullet and barbel. Fly-fishing is possible in the Chobe and Zambezi Rivers in the Caprivi region; here you'll find barbel, bream, pike and Africa's famed fighting tiger fish, which can grow up to 9kg.

Hiking

Hiking is a highlight in Namibia, and a growing number of private ranches have established wonderful hiking routes for their guests.

You'll also find superb routes in several national parks. Multiday walks are available at Waterberg Plateau, (four- and eight-day Naukluft Mountains loops), the Ugab River, Daan Viljoen Game Park and Fish River Canyon, but departures are limited, so book as far in advance as possible.

Hiking groups on most national-park routes must consist of at least three but no more than 10 people, and each hiker needs a doctor's certificate of fitness (forms are available from the Windhoek Namibia Wildlife Resorts office) issued no more than 40 days before the start of the hike. If you're young and you look fit, this requirement might be waived on most trails, with the exception of the demanding 85km hike in Fish River Canyon. The NWR can recommend doctors, but again, in most cases this requirement is waived.

While this might seem restrictive to folks who are accustomed to strapping on a pack and taking off, it does protect the environment from unrestrained tourism, and it ensures that you'll have the trail to yourself – you'll certainly never see another group.

If you prefer guided hiking, get in touch with **Trail Hopper** (☎ 061-264521; www.namibweb.com/trailhopper.htm), which offers hikes all over the country, including Fish River Canyon, a five-day Brandberg Ascent and a Naukluft Mountain Trek. Prices depend on the size of the group.

Rock Climbing

Rock climbing is popular on the red rocks of Damaraland, particularly the Spitzkoppe and the Brandberg, but participants need their own gear and transport. For less experienced climbers it's a dangerous endeavour in the desert heat, so seek local advice beforehand, and never attempt a climb on your own.

Sandboarding

A popular activity is sandboarding, which is commercially available in Swakopmund and Walvis Bay. You can choose between sled-style sandboarding, in which you lay on a Masonite board and slide down the dunes at very high speeds, or the stand-up version, in which you schuss down on a snowboard.

CHILDREN

Many parents regard Africa as just too dangerous for travel with children, but in reality Namibia presents few problems to families travelling with children. We travelled with our own children in the country and not only survived unscathed but had a wonderful time.

As a destination Namibia is relatively safe healthwise, largely due to its dry climate and good medical services. There's a good network of affordable accommodation and an excellent infrastructure of well-maintained roads. In addition, foreigners who visit Namibia with children are usually treated with great kindness, and a widespread local affection for the younger set opens up all sorts of social interaction.

The greatest difficulty is likely to be the temperature (it can get *very* hot) and distances can be vast.

For invaluable general advice on taking the family abroad, see Lonely Planet's *Travel with Children*.

Essential Documents for Parents

Travellers with children should be aware of recent changes regarding the documents you must carry while travelling through the region. The law requires that all parents arriving, transiting and departing South Africa, Namibia and Botswana *must* produce an unabridged birth certificate for their children, and the birth certificate must state the names of both parents. Families not in possession of these documents will be refused to travel.

If one parent is travelling alone with their children, the travelling parent must carry with them an affidavit from the other (ie non-travelling) parent who is listed on the birth certificate granting their consent for the travel to take place in their absence. Where this is not possible, either a court order granting full parental responsibilities and rights or a death certificate of the other parent must be produced.

We have travelled across the borders of all three countries with our children on numerous occasions and although we were not always asked for these documents, we were asked for each of these documents at least once. Travel without them at your peril.

Practicalities

While there are few attractions or facilities designed specifically for children, Namibian food and lodgings are mostly quite familiar and manageable. Family rooms and chalets are normally available for only slightly more than double rooms. These normally consist of one double bed and two single beds. Otherwise, it's usually easy to arrange more beds in a standard double room for a minimal extra charge.

Camping can be exciting, but you'll need to be extra vigilant so your kids don't just wander off unsupervised, and you'll also need to be alert to potential hazards such as mosquitoes and campfires. Most mosquito repellents with high levels of DEET may be unsuitable for young children. They should also wear sturdy enclosed shoes to protect them from thorns, bees and scorpion stings.

If you're travelling with kids, you should always invest in a hire car, unless you want to be stuck for hours on public transport. Functional seatbelts are rare even in taxis, and accidents are common – a child seat brought from home is a good idea if you're hiring a car or going on safari. Even with your own car, distances between towns and parks can be long, so parents will need to provide essential supplemental entertainment (toys, books, games, a Nintendo DS etc).

Canned baby foods, powdered milk, disposable nappies and the like are available in most large supermarkets.

Sights & Activities

Travelling by campervan and camping, or staying in luxury tented lodges, are thrilling experiences for young and old alike, while attractions such as the wildlife of Etosha National Park or the world's biggest sandbox at Sossusvlei provide ample family entertainment.

Full-scale safaris are generally suited to older children. Be aware that some upmarket lodges and safari companies won't accept children under a certain age and those that do may require you to book separate game drives. Endless hours of driving and animal viewing can be an eternity for small children, so you'll need to break up your trip with lots of pit stops and picnics, and plenty of time spent poolside where possible.

Older children are well catered for with a whole host of exciting activities. Swakopmund is an excellent base for these. They include everything from horse riding and sandboarding to ballooning and paragliding. Less demanding activities might include looking for interesting rocks (and Namibia has some truly incredible rocks!); beachcombing along the Skeleton Coast; or running and rolling in the dunes at Lüderitz, Sossusvlei, Swakopmund and elsewhere along the coast.

CUSTOMS REGULATIONS

Most items from elsewhere in the Southern African Customs Union – Botswana, South Africa, Lesotho and Swaziland – may be imported duty-free. From elsewhere, visitors can import duty-free 400 cigarettes or 250g of tobacco, 2L of wine, 1L of spirits and 250mL of eau de cologne. Those aged under 18 do not qualify for the tobacco or alcohol allowances. There are no limits on currency import, but entry and departure forms ask how much you intend to spend or have spent in the country – we have left this blank every time we've entered the country and have never been questioned on it.

Vehicles may not be sold in Namibia without payment of duty. For pets, you need a health certificate and full veterinary documentation (note that pets aren't permitted in national parks or reserves).

DISCOUNT CARDS

Travellers with student cards score a 15% discount on Intercape Mainliner buses, and occasionally receive discounts on museum admissions. Seniors over 60, with proof of age, also receive a 15% discount on Intercape Mainliner buses, and good discounts on domestic Air Namibia fares.

EMBASSIES & CONSULATES

It's important to realise what your own embassy (the embassy of the country of which you are a citizen) can and can't do to help you if you get into trouble. Generally speaking, it won't be much help in emergencies if the trouble you're in is remotely your own fault. Remember that you are bound by the laws of the country you are in. Your embassy will not be sympathetic if you end up in jail after committing a crime locally, even if such actions are legal in your own country. The embassies listed here are all in Windhoek.

Angola (Map p222; ☑ 061-227535; 3 Dr Agostino Neto St; ⊙ 9am-4pm)

Botswana (Map p219; ☑ 061-221941; 101 Nelson Mandela Ave; ⊙ 8am-1pm & 2-5pm)

Finland (Map p222; ☑ 061-221355; www.finland.org.na; 2 Crohn St, cnr Bahnhof St; ⊙ 9am-noon Mon, Wed & Thu)

France (Map p219; ☑ 061-276700; www.ambafrance-na.org; 1 Goethe St; ⊙ 8am-12.30pm & 2-5.45pm Mon-Thu, 8am-1pm Fri)

Germany (Map p222; ☑ 061-273100; www.windhuk.diplo.de; 6th fl, Sanlam Centre, 154 Independence Ave; ⊙ 9am-noon Mon-Fri, plus 2-4pm Wed)

Kenya (Map p222; ☑ 061-226836; www.khcwindhoek.com; 5th fl, Kenya House, 134 Robert Mugabe Ave; ⊙ 8.30am-1pm & 2-4.30pm Mon-Thu, to 3pm Fri)

Malawi (Map p222; ☑ 061-221391; 56 Bismarck St, Windhoek West; ⊙ 8am-noon & 2-5pm Mon-Fri)

South Africa (Map p219; ☑ 061-2057111; www.dirco.gov.za/windhoek; cnr Jan Jonker St & Nelson Mandela Dr, Klein Windhoek; ⊙ 8.15am-12.15pm)

UK (Map p222; ☑ 061-274800; www.gov.uk/government/world/organisations/british-high-commission-windhoek; 116 Robert Mugabe Ave; ⊘8am-noon Mon-Thu)

USA (Map p222; ☏061-2958500; https://na.usembassy.gov; 14 Lossen St; ⊘8.30am-noon Mon-Thu)

Zambia (Map p222; ☏061-237610; www.za-hico.iway.na; 22 Sam Nujoma Dr, cnr Mandume Ndemufeyo Ave; ⊘9am-1pm & 2-4pm)

Zimbabwe (Map p222; ☏061-228134; www.zimwhk.com; Gamsberg Bldg, cnr Independence Ave & Grimm St; ⊘8.30am-1pm & 2-4.45pm Mon-Thu, 8.30am-2pm Fri)

EATING PRICE RANGES

The following price ranges refer to a main course.

$	less than N$75
$$	N$75–150
$$$	more than N$150

LGBT TRAVELLERS

As in many African countries, homosexuality is illegal in Namibia, based on the common-law offence of sodomy or committing 'an unnatural sex crime'. Namibia is also very conservative in its attitudes, given the strongly held Christian beliefs of the majority. In view of this, discretion is certainly the better part of valour, as treatment of gay men and lesbians can range from simple social ostracism to physical attack. In 1996 Namibia's president, Sam Nujoma, continued his very public campaign against homosexuals, recommending that all foreign gays and lesbians be deported or excluded from the country. One minister called homosexuality a 'behavioural disorder which is alien to African culture', while in 2005 the Deputy Minister of Home Affairs and Immigration, Teopolina Mushelenga, claimed that lesbians and gays had caused the HIV/AIDS pandemic and were 'an insult to African culture'.

The climate for gays and lesbians in Namibia has, however, eased somewhat in recent years. With no prosecutions recorded under the sodomy law since independence, the United Nations Human Rights Committee called in 2016 for the law against sodomy to be abolished and for laws to be introduced prohibiting discrimination on the grounds of sexual orientation. The call received the public support of Namibia's ombudsman and stirred little public debate. In the same year, an Afrobarometer opinion poll found that 55% of Namibians would welcome, or would not be bothered by, having a homosexual neighbor. Namibia was one of only four African countries countries polled to have a majority in favour of the proposition.

Useful Resources

Afriboyz (www.afriboyz.com/Homosexuality-in-Africa.html) Links to gay topics in an African context.

African Horizons (www.africanhorizons.com) Gay-friendly tour operator that offers trips to Southern Africa, including Botswana.

Global Gayz (www.globalgayz.com/africa/namibia) Links to gay issues in Namibia and other African countries.

Organisations

A number of advocacy groups operate openly (if discreetly) in Windhoek. Among these, OutRight Namibia (http://outrightnamibia.org) is a human-rights organisation based in Windhoek that was formed by gay and lesbian activists to challenge homophobia and advocate for equal rights. Namibian lesbians (and other women's interests) are also represented by Sister Namibia (www.sisternamibia.org).

INSURANCE

Travel insurance to cover theft, loss and medical treatment is strongly recommended. Some policies specifically exclude 'dangerous activities', which can include scuba diving, motorcycling and even trekking. If 'risky' activities are on your agenda, as they may well be, you'll need the most comprehensive policy.

You may prefer to have an insurance policy that pays doctors or hospitals directly rather than you having to pay on the spot and claim later. If you have to claim later, make sure you keep all documentation. Some policies ask you to call back (reverse charges) to a centre in your home country, where an immediate assessment of your problem is made. Check that the policy covers ambulances or an emergency flight home.

Worldwide travel insurance is available at www.lonelyplanet.com/travel-insurance. You can buy, extend and claim online anytime, even if you're already on the road.

INTERNET ACCESS

Internet access is firmly established and widespread in Namibia, and connection speeds are fairly stable. Most larger or tourist-oriented towns have at least one internet cafe. Plan on spending around N$50 per hour online. An increasing number of backpacker hostels, hotels in larger towns and some lodges and guesthouses also offer wi-fi internet access, although this rarely extends beyond the hotel reception area.

LEGAL MATTERS

All drugs are illegal in Namibia, penalties are stiff and prisons are deeply unpleasant. So don't think about bringing anything over the border, or buying it while you're here. The police are also allowed to use entrapment techniques, such as posing as dealers, to catch criminals, so don't be tempted.

Police, military and veterinary officials are generally polite and on their best behaviour. In your dealings with officialdom, you should always make every effort to be patient and polite in return.

MAPS
Country Maps

The best paper map of Botswana is the *Namibia* (1:1,000,000) map published by Tracks4Africa (www.tracks4africa.co.za). Updated every couple of years using detailed traveller feedback, the map is printed on tear-free, waterproof paper and includes distances and estimated travel times. Used in conjunction with Tracks4Africa's unrivalled GPS maps, it's far and away the best mapping product on the market.

If for some reason you are unable to get hold of the Tracks4Africa map, other options include the Namibia map produced by Reise-Know-How-Verlag (1:250,000) or the Freytag & Berndt map (1:200,000). *Shell Roadmap – Namibia* or *InfoMap Namibia* are good references for remote routes. InfoMap contains GPS coordinates and both companies produce maps of remote areas such as Namibia's far northwest and the Caprivi Strip.

Good for an overview rather than serious navigation is the *Namibia Map* endorsed by the Roads Authority, which shows major routes and lists accommodation. Even the Globetrotter *Namibia* map is easy to read and quite detailed. Also consider Nelles Vertag's *Namibia* (1:1,500,000), and Map Studio, which also publishes a *Namibia* map (1:1,550,000) and a road atlas (1:500,000).

Regional Maps

InfoMap publishes a number of detailed maps to Namibia's regions. Its copious use of GPS coordinates for towns, attractions, accommodation and road junctions greatly aids the maps' usefulness. Maps in the series include *Damaraland – Western Namibia* (1:430,000) and *Kaokoland – North Western Namibia* (1:600,000).

National-Park Maps

You'll find maps of Etosha National Park across the country. NWR's reliable English-German *Map of Etosha* (from N$40) is the pick and also most widely available. It has the added bonus of park information and quite extensive mammal and bird identification sheets.

A welcome recent addition to Namibia's mapping portfolio is the simple but handy *Kavango-Zambezi National Parks* map, which includes high-level overviews of Namibia's far northeastern parks: Khaudum, Mahango, Bwabwata, Mudumu and Nkasa Rupara. It's

available at some lodges or online at www.thinkafricadesign.com.

MONEY

Money can be exchanged in banks and exchange offices. Banks generally offer the best rates.

ATMs

Credit cards can be used in ATMs displaying the appropriate sign or to obtain cash advances over the counter in many banks; Visa and MasterCard are among the most widely recognised. You'll find ATMs at all the main bank branches throughout Namibia, and this is undoubtedly the simplest (and safest) way to handle your money while travelling.

Cash

While most major currencies are accepted in Windhoek and Swakopmund, once away from these two centres you'll run into problems with currencies other than US dollars, euros, UK pounds and South African rand (and you may even struggle with pounds). Play it safe and carry US dollars – it'll make your life much simpler.

When changing money, you may be given either South African rand or Namibian dollars; if you think you'll need to change any leftover currency outside Namibia, the rand is a better choice.

There is no currency black market, so beware of street changers offering unrealistic rates.

Credit/Debit Cards

Credit cards and debit cards are accepted in most shops, restaurants and hotels, and credit- and debit-card cash advances are available from ATMs. Check charges with your bank.

Credit-card (but not debit-card) cash advances are available at foreign-exchange desks in most major banks, but set aside at least an hour or two to complete the rather tedious transaction.

Keep the card supplier's emergency number handy in case your card is lost or stolen.

Tipping

Tipping is welcomed everywhere, but is expected only in upmarket tourist restaurants, where it's normal to leave a tip of 10% to 15% of the bill. Some restaurants add a service charge as a matter of course. As a rule, taxi drivers aren't tipped, but it is customary to give N$2 to N$5 to petrol-station attendants who clean your windows and/or check the oil and water. Note that tipping is officially prohibited in national parks and reserves.

At safari lodges, guides and drivers of safari vehicles will also expect a tip, especially if you've spent a number of days in their care.

Most safari companies suggest the following as a rule of thumb:

→ guides/drivers – US$10 per person per day
→ camp or lodge staff – US$10 per guest per day (usually placed in a communal box)
→ transfer drivers and porters – US$3

Travellers Cheques

Travellers cheques can be cashed (normally fetching a better rate than cash) at most banks and exchange offices. American Express (Amex), Thomas Cook and Visa are the most widely accepted brands.

It's preferable to buy travellers cheques in US dollars, UK pounds or euros rather than another currency, as these are most widely accepted. Get most of the cheques in largish denominations to save on per-cheque rates. Travellers cheques may also be exchanged for US dollars cash – if the cash is available – but banks charge a hefty commission.

You must take your passport with you when cashing cheques.

OPENING HOURS

Banks 8am or 9am-3pm Monday to Friday, 8am-12.30pm Saturday

Drinking and entertainment 5pm to close (midnight-3am) Monday to Saturday

Eating breakfast 8 to 10am, lunch 11am to 3pm, dinner 6 to 10pm; some places open 8am to 10pm Monday to Saturday

Information 8am or 9am-5pm or 6pm Monday to Friday

Petrol stations Only a few open 24 hours; in outlying areas fuel hard to find after hours or Sunday.

Post offices 8am to 4.30pm Monday to Friday, 8.30-11am Saturday

Shopping 8am or 9am-5pm or 6pm Monday to Friday, 9am-1pm or 5pm Saturday; late-night shopping to 9pm Thursday or Friday

PHOTOGRAPHY

While many Namibians enjoy being photographed, others do not. You should always ask where possible. The main point is that you should always respect the wishes of the person in question, and don't snap a picture if permission is denied.

Officials in Namibia aren't as sensitive about photography as in some other African countries, but it still isn't a good idea to photograph borders, airports, communications equipment or military installations without first asking permission from any uniformed personnel that might be present.

Memory cards for digital cameras are widely available in Windhoek and Swakopmund.

For pointers on taking pictures in Africa, look out for Lonely Planet's *Travel Photography* book.

POST

Domestic post generally moves slowly; it can take weeks for a letter to travel from Lüderitz to Katima Mulilo, for example. Overseas airmail post is normally more efficient.

PUBLIC HOLIDAYS

Banks, government offices and most shops are closed on public holidays; when a public holiday falls on a Sunday, the following day also becomes a holiday.

New Year's Day 1 January
Good Friday March or April
Easter Sunday March or April
Easter Monday March or April
Independence Day 21 March

ⓘ PRACTICALITIES

Newspapers There are a decent number of commercial newspapers, of which the *Namibian* and the *Windhoek Advertiser* are probably the best. The *Windhoek Observer*, published on Saturday, is also good. The two main German-language newspapers are *Allgemeine Zeitung* and *Namibia Nachrichten*.

Radio The Namibian Broadcasting Corporation (NBC) operates a dozen-or-so radio stations in nine languages. The two main stations in Windhoek are Radio Energy (100FM) and Radio Kudu (103.5FM); the best pop station is Radio Wave, at 96.7FM in Windhoek.

TV The NBC broadcasts government-vetted TV programs in English and Afrikaans. News is broadcast at 10pm nightly. Most top-end hotels and lodges with televisions provide access to satellite-supported DSTV, which broadcasts NBC and a cocktail of cable channels.

Weights & Measures Namibia uses the metric system.

Electricity Electrical plugs are three round pins (like South Africa).

Smoking Smoking is banned in all public places in Namibia. Penalties range from N$500 to one month in jail (!). The definition of 'public places' has yet to be tested in court, so be discreet when lighting up.

Ascension Day April or May
Workers' Day 1 May
Cassinga Day 4 May
Africa Day 25 May
Heroes' Day 26 August
Human Rights Day 10 December
Christmas Day 25 December
Family/Boxing Day 26 December

SAFE TRAVEL

Namibia is one of the safest countries in Africa. It's also a huge country with a very sparse population, and even the capital, Windhoek, is more like a provincial town than an urban jungle. Unfortunately, however, crime is on the rise in the larger cities, in particular Windhoek, but a little street sense will go a long way here.

Scams

A common scam you might encounter in Namibia is the pretty innocuous palm-ivory nut scam practiced at various petrol stations. It starts with a friendly approach from a couple of young men, who ask your name. Without you seeing it they then carve your name onto a palm-ivory nut and then offer it to you for sale for anything up to N$70, hoping that you'll feel obligated to buy the personalised item. You can obtain the same sort of thing at any curio shop for around N$20. It's hardly the crime of the century, but it pays to be aware.

A more serious trick is for one guy to distract a parked motorist while their accomplice opens a door and grabs your bags from the back seat or from the front passenger seat. Always keep the doors of your vehicle locked, and be aware of distractions. It's rare but it does happen – Walvis Bay has been something of a hot spot for this scam in the past.

The Sperrgebiet

En route to Lüderitz from the east, keep well clear of the Sperrgebiet (Forbidden Zone), the prohibited diamond area. Well-armed patrols can be overly zealous. The area begins immediately south of the A4 Lüderitz–Keetmanshoop road and continues to just west of Aus, where the off-limits boundary turns south towards the Orange River. It's best to have a healthy respect for boundaries.

Theft

Theft isn't rife in Namibia, but Windhoek, Swakopmund, Walvis Bay, Tsumeb and Grootfontein have problems with petty theft and muggings, so it's sensible to conceal your valuables, not leave anything in your car and avoid walking alone at night. It's also prudent to avoid walking around cities and towns bedecked in expensive jewellery, watches and cameras. Most hotels provide a safe or secure place for valuables, although you should be cautious of the security at some budget places.

Never leave a safari-packed vehicle anywhere in Windhoek or Swakopmund, other than in a guarded car park or private parking lot.

Theft from campsites can also be a problem, particularly near urban areas. Locking up your tent may help, but anything left unattended is still at risk.

Vegetation

An unusual natural hazard is the euphorbia plant. Its dried branches should never be used in fires as they release a deadly toxin when burnt. It can be fatal to inhale the smoke or eat food cooked on a fire containing it. If you're in doubt about any wood you've collected, leave it out of the fire. Caretakers at campsites do a good job of removing these plants from around pitches and fire pits, so you needn't worry excessively. As a precaution, try to only use bundles of wood that you've purchased in a store to start fires. If you're bush camping, best to familiarise yourself with the plant's appearance. There are several members of the family, and you can check out their pictures either online or at the tourist information centres in Windhoek.

SHOPPING

Namibia's range of inexpensive souvenirs includes all sorts of things, from kitsch African curios and batik paintings to superb Owambo basketry and Kavango woodcarvings. Most of the items sold along Post St Mall in Windhoek are cheap curios imported from Zimbabwe. Along the highways around the country, roadside stalls sometimes appear, selling locally produced items, from baskets and simple pottery jars to the appealing woven mats and wooden aeroplanes that are a Kavango speciality. In Rundu and other areas of the northeast, you'll find distinctive San material arts – bows and arrows, ostrich-egg beads and leather pouches. An excellent place to browse a whole range of craftwork is the **Namibia Crafts Centre** (p229) in Windhoek.

The pastel colours of the Namib provide inspiration for a number of local artists, and lots of galleries in Windhoek and Swakopmund feature local paintings and sculpture. Some lovely items are also produced in conjunction with the karakul wool industry, such as rugs, wall hangings and textiles. The better weaving outlets are found in Dordabis, Swakopmund and Windhoek.

Windhoek is the centre of the upmarket leather industry, and there you'll find high-quality products, from belts and handbags to made-to-measure leather jackets. Beware, however, of items made from crocodile or other protected species, and note that those comfortable shoes known as Swakopmunders

NAMIBIA DIRECTORY A–Z

are made from kudu leather. Several shops have now stopped selling them.

Minerals and gemstones are popular purchases. Malachite, amethyst, chalcedony, aquamarine, tourmaline, jasper and rose quartz are among the most beautiful. You'll find the best jewellery shops in Windhoek and Swakopmund; the most reputable of these is **House of Gems** (p229) in Windhoek.

Bargaining

Bargaining is only acceptable when purchasing handicrafts and arts directly from the producer or artist, but in remote areas the prices asked normally represent close to the market value. The exception is crafts imported from Zimbabwe, which are generally sold at large craft markets for inflated prices that are always negotiable.

TELEPHONE

The Namibian fixed-line phone system, run by Telecom Namibia (www.telecom.na), is very efficient, and getting through to fixed-line numbers is extremely easy. However, as in the rest of Africa, the fixed-line system is rapidly being overtaken by the massive popularity of mobile phones.

Fixed-line calls to the UK/US and Europe cost around N$3.60 to N$5 per minute at peak times; to neighbouring countries it's around N$2.40 to N$4.14 per minute. Click on 'Tariffs' and then 'International Services' on the website for exact charges.

Given the increasing number of wi-fi hot spots in the country, using Skype is also becoming a more common (and much cheaper) alternative.

Mobile Phones

MTC (www.mtc.com.na) is the largest mobile service provider in Namibia, operating on the GSM 900/1800 frequency, which is compatible with Europe and Australia but not with North America (GSM 1900) or Japan. The other provider is Telecom Namibia. (www.telecom.na).

There is supposedly comprehensive coverage across the country, although in reality it's hard to get a signal outside the major towns and along the major highways – the more remote you are, the less likely you'll get coverage, which is why a satellite phone is an attractive backup proposition if you're travelling extensively away from population areas.

Both providers offers prepaid services. For visitors to the country, you're better off paying a one-off SIM-card fee then buying prepaid vouchers at the ubiquitous stores across Namibia.

You can easily buy a handset in any major town in Namibia, which will set you back from N$600.

Most Namibian mobile-phone numbers begin with ☑ 081, which is followed by a seven-digit number.

Phone Codes

When phoning Namibia from abroad, dial your international access code (usually ☑ 00, but ☑ 011 from the USA), followed by Namibia's country code ☑ 264, the area code without the leading zero and, finally, the required number. To phone out of Namibia, dial ☑ 00 followed by the desired country code, area code (if applicable) and the number.

When phoning long distance within Namibia, dial the three-digit regional area code, including the leading zero, followed by the six- or seven-digit number.

Phonecards

Telecom Namibia phonecards are sold at post offices to the value of N$20, N$50 and N$100. They are also available at most shops and a number of hotels. Public telephone boxes are available at most post offices and can also be found scattered around towns.

TOURIST INFORMATION

The level of service in Namibia's tourist offices is generally high, and everyone speaks impeccable English, German and Afrikaans.

Namibia's national tourist office, **Namibia Tourism** (p230), is in Windhoek, where you'll also find the local **Windhoek Information & Publicity Office** (p231).

Also in Windhoek is the office of **Namibia Wildlife Resorts** (p230), where you can pick up information on national parks and make reservations at any NWR campsite.

Other useful tourist offices include **Lüderitz Safaris & Tours** (p331) in Lüderitz and **Namib-i** (p303) in Swakopmund.

TRAVELLERS WITH DISABILITIES

There are very few special facilities, and people with limited mobility will not have an easy time in Namibia. All is not lost, however – with an able-bodied travelling companion, wheelchair travellers will manage here. This is mainly because Namibia has some advantages over other parts of the developing world: footpaths and public areas are often surfaced with tar or concrete; many buildings (including safari lodges and national-park cabins) are single-storey; car hire is easy and hire cars can be taken into neighbouring countries; and assistance is usually available on internal and regional flights. In addition, most safari companies in Namibia, including budget operators, are happy to 'make a plan' to accommodate travellers with special needs.

VISAS

Nationals of many countries, including Australia, the EU, USA and most Commonwealth countries, do not need a visa to visit Namibia. Citizens of most Eastern European countries do require visas.

Tourists are granted an initial 90 days, although most immigration officials will ask how long you plan to stay in the country and tailor your visa duration accordingly.

Visas may be extended at the **Ministry of Home Affairs** (p230) in Windhoek. For the best results, be there when the office opens at 8am and submit your application at the 3rd-floor offices (as opposed to the desk on the ground floor).

VOLUNTEERING

Namibia has a good track record for grassroots projects and community-based tourism. However, it's seldom possible to find any volunteering work in-country due to visa restrictions and restricted budgets. Any organisations that do offer volunteer positions will need to be approached well in advance of your departure date. Many conservation outfits look for volunteers with specific skills that might be useful in the field.

WOMEN TRAVELLERS

On the whole Namibia is a safe destination for women travellers, and we receive few complaints from women about any sort of harassment. Having said that, Namibia is still a conservative society. Many bars are men only (by either policy or convention), but even in places that welcome women, you may be more comfortable in a group or with a male companion. Note that accepting a drink from a local man is usually construed as a come-on.

The threat of sexual assault isn't any greater in Namibia than in Europe, but it's best to avoid walking alone in parks and backstreets, especially at night. Hitching alone is not recommended. Never hitch at night and, if possible, find a companion for trips through sparsely populated areas.

In Windhoek and other urban areas, wearing shorts and sleeveless dresses or shirts is fine. However, if you're visiting rural areas, wear knee-length skirts or loose trousers and shirts with sleeves. If you're poolside in a resort or lodge where the clientele is largely foreign, then revealing swimwear is acceptable; otherwise err on the side of caution and see what other women are wearing.

ℹ Getting There & Away

Unless you are travelling overland, most likely from Botswana or South Africa, flying is by far the most convenient way to get to Namibia. Namibia isn't exactly a hub of international travel, nor is it an obvious transit point along major international routes, but it does have an increasing number of routes, including to Frankfurt and Amsterdam. Otherwise, you're most likely to fly via South Africa.

ENTERING THE COUNTRY

Entering Namibia is straightforward and hassle-free: upon arrival and departure, you must fill out an immigration card. If arriving by air, queues can be long, particularly when a couple of planes arrive at the same time (fill out the arrival cards while in the queue to save time), but once you finally reach the counter it's usually straightforward. If you are entering Namibia across one of its land borders, the process is similarly painless: you will need to have all the necessary documentation and insurance for your vehicle. Most nationalities (including nationals from the UK, USA, Australia, Japan and all the Western European countries) don't even require a visa.

If travelling with children, parents should be aware of the need to carry birth certificates and may require other documents (p366).

Passports

All visitors entering Namibia must hold a passport that is valid for at least six months after their intended departure date from Namibia. Also, allow a few empty pages for stamp-happy immigration officials, especially if you'll be crossing over to see Victoria Falls in Zambia and Zimbabwe. In theory, you should also hold proof of departure, either in the form of a return or onward ticket. In practice, this is rarely asked for.

AIR

Most international airlines stop at Johannesburg or Cape Town in South Africa, where you'll typically switch to a **South African Airways** (Map p222; ☑ 061-273340; www.flysaa.com; Independence Ave) flight for your final leg to Windhoek. South African Airways has daily flights connecting Cape Town and Johannesburg to Windhoek. Johannesburg is also the main hub for connecting flights to other African cities.

For North American travellers, it's worth checking the price of a flight via Frankfurt, as this may be cheaper than a direct flight to South Africa.

Book well in advance for flights from the following neighbouring countries.

Botswana Air Namibia runs several flights a week between Windhoek and Maun.

Zimbabwe Air Namibia flies to Victoria Falls a few times a week.

Zambia You will need to transit through Jo'burg for flights to Lusaka or Livingstone.

ℹ️ GOVERNMENT TRAVEL ADVICE

The following government websites offer travel advisories and information for travellers.

Australian Department of Foreign Affairs & Trade (www.smartraveller. gov.au)

Canadian Department of Foreign Affairs & International Trade (www. voyage.gc.ca)

French Ministère des Affaires Étrangères et Européennes (www. diplomatie.gouv.fr/fr/conseils-aux-voyageurs)

Italian Ministero degli Affari Esteri (www.viaggiaresicuri.mae.aci.it)

New Zealand Ministry of Foreign Affairs & Trade (www.safetravel.govt.nz)

UK Foreign & Commonwealth Office (www.gov.uk/foreign-travel-advice)

US Department of State (www.travel. state.gov)

Airports & Airlines

Chief Hosea Kutako International Airport (WDH; ☎ 061-2996602; www.airports.com.na) is the destination airport for most international flights into Namibia. It's located 42km east of the capital.

Eros Airport (ERS; ☎ 061-2955500; www.airports.com.na) in Windhoek is mainly for small charter flights, although **Air Namibia** (☎ 061-2996333, 061-2996600; www.airnamibia. com.na; Chief Hosea Kutako International Airport) also runs flights to Katima Mulilo, Ondangwa and Walvis Bay from here.

Air Namibia (www.airnamibia.com.na) is the main domestic carrier and flies routes to other parts of Southern Africa as well as long-haul flights to Frankfurt.

LAND

Thanks to the Southern African Customs Union, you can drive through Namibia, Botswana, South Africa and Swaziland with a minimum of ado. To travel further north requires a *carnet de passage*, which can amount to heavy expenditure.

If you're driving a hire car to/from Namibia you will need to present a letter of permission from the rental company saying the car is allowed to cross the border.

Border Crossings

Namibia has a well-developed road network with easy access from neighbouring countries. The main border crossings into Namibia are as follows:

Angola Oshikango, Ruacana, Rundu

Botswana Buitepos, Mahango and Ngoma

South Africa Noordoewer, Ariamsvlei

Zambia Katima Mulilo

All borders are open daily, and the main crossings from South Africa (Noordoewer and Ariamsvlei) are open 24 hours. Otherwise, border crossings are generally open at least between 8am and 5pm, although most open from 6am to 6pm. Immigration posts at some smaller border crossings close for lunch between 12.30pm and 1.45pm. It is always advisable to reach the crossings as early in the day as possible to allow time for any potential delays. For more information on opening hours, check out the website www.namibweb.com/border.htm.

Angola To enter Namibia overland, you'll need an Angolan visa permitting overland entry. At Ruacana Falls, you can enter the border area temporarily without a visa to visit the falls by signing the immigration register.

Botswana The most commonly used crossing is at Buitepos/Mamuno, between Windhoek and Ghanzi, although the Caprivi border posts at Mohembo/Mahango and Ngoma (the latter is a short drive from Kasane in Botswana) are also popular. The Mpalila Island/Kasane border is only available to guests who have prebooked accommodation at upmarket lodges on the island.

The Mohembo/Mahango crossing connects northeastern Namibia with Shakawe, Maun and the Okavango Panhandle. Drivers crossing here pass through Mahango Game Reserve at Popa Falls. Entry is free if you're transiting, or US$5 per person per day plus US$5 per vehicle per day if you want to drive around the reserve (which is possible in a 2WD). No motorbikes are permitted in the reserve.

There is also a little-used border crossing at Gcangwa–Tsumkwe along a 4WD-only track close to Botswana's Tsodilo Hills.

South Africa Namibia's border crossings with South Africa are among the country's busiest, but they're generally hassle-free. The crossings at Noordoewer and Ariamsvlei are open 24 hours (although we advise against driving at night on either side of the border). There is an additional border post along the coast, between Alexander Bay and Oranjemund (6am to 10pm), but it's closed to tourists and anyone without permission from the diamond company Namdeb.

Zambia The border crossing between Zambia and Namibia is at Katima Mulilo in Namibia's Caprivi Strip. The Namibian side of things is generally quick and easy, but Zambian formalities can take a little longer.

Visas into Zambia cost US$50 per person for most nationalities, while you'll also have to pay the Zambian road toll (US$48), carbon tax (ZMK150), third party vehicle insurance (ZMK487, valid for one month and payable even if you already have insurance) if you're bringing in a vehicle. There is a bank next to the border crossing. Changing money at the bank is preferable to the young men who will approach your vehicle with wads of kwacha. If you arrive outside banking hours and are left with no choice, make sure you know the current exchange rates, count your money carefully and don't let them hurry you into a quick exchange that will rarely be to your benefit.

If you're heading to Liuwa National Park and other places in Zambia's far west, an excellent sealed road (so new it wasn't even on Tracks4Africa's GPS system when we drove it) runs from the border all the way to Mongu and Kalabo, at the entrance to Liuwa National Park.

If you're on your way to Livingstone, the road is sealed but not in great condition. It is, however, accessible in a 2WD.

Zimbabwe There's no direct border crossing between Namibia and Zimbabwe. To get there you must take the Chobe National Park transit route from Ngoma Bridge through northern Botswana to Kasane/Kazungula, and from there to Victoria Falls.

Bus

There's only really one main inter-regional bus service connecting cities in Namibia with Botswana and South Africa. **Intercape Mainliner** (☑ 061-227847; www.intercape.co.za) has services between Windhoek and Johannesburg and Cape Town (South Africa). It also travels northeast to Victoria Falls, and between larger towns within Namibia. There are also long-distance Intercape Mainliner services running between Windhoek and Livingstone.

Tok Tokkie Shuttle (☑ 061-300743; www.shuttlesnamibia.com) makes the 12-hour Windhoek–Gaborone run, departing Windhoek at 6pm on Wednesday and Friday, and from Gaborone at 1pm on Thursday and Saturday. One-way fares are N$500 and there's free wi-fi and air-con on board.

Otherwise, you may need to hitch from Gobabis to the border, cross the border on foot (bearing in mind that this crossing is about 1km long) then probably hitch from the border to Ghanzi, unless you happen to coincide with the daily minibus between the Mamuno border crossing and Ghanzi.

Car & Motorcycle

Crossing borders with your own vehicle or a hire car is generally straightforward, as long as you have the necessary paperwork: the vehicle

registration documents if you own the car, or a letter from the hire company stating that you have permission to take the car over the border, and proof of insurance. The hire company should provide you with a letter that includes the engine and chassis numbers, as you may be asked for these.

Note that Namibia implements a road tax, known as the Cross-Border Charge (CBC) for foreign-registered vehicles entering the country. Passenger vehicles carrying fewer than 25 passengers are charged N$140 per entry, and N$90 for motorbikes. It is very important that you keep this receipt as you may be asked to produce it at police roadblocks, and fines will ensue if you can't.

Driving To & From South Africa

You can drive to Namibia along good, sealed roads from South Africa, either from Cape Town (1490km) in the south, crossing the border at Noordoewer, or from Jo'burg (1970km) in the east, in which case the border crossing is at Nakop.

Renting a car in South Africa sometimes works out cheaper than renting one in Namibia, although these days most Namibian car-rental companies (especially those of the 4WD variety) are outposts of South African companies anyway. While per-day rental is usually cheaper in South Africa, you'll also have to factor in the cost of driving to/from South Africa and/or the cost of dropping off the car in Namibia.

The cheapest 2WD will end up costing the rand equivalent of about US$50 per day, and a 4WD will cost in the region of US$100 per day.

❶ Getting Around

Namibia is a sparsely populated country, and distances between towns can be vast. However, there is an excellent infrastructure of sealed

> **❶ WHERE TO BUY MAPS**
>
> The best place to purchase maps in Namibia is at petrol stations, although you can get your hands on more general maps at local bookshops. We found InfoMap's regional maps in both supermarkets and petrol stations across the north.
>
> There's a good selection in the bookshops at Johannesburg's OR Tambo International Airport.
>
> In the USA, Trek Tools (www.trektools.com) is an excellent and exhaustive source for maps of Namibia. A similarly extensive selection of maps is available in the UK from Stanfords (www.stanfords.co.uk).

roads, and to more remote locations there are well-maintained gravel and even salt roads. With such a low population density, it's hardly surprising that the public-transport network is limited. Public buses do serve the main towns, but they won't take you to the country's major sights. By far the best way to experience Namibia is in the comfort of your own hire car.

AIR

Air Namibia (www.airnamibia.com.na) has an extensive network of local flights operating out of Windhoek's **Eros Airport** (p374). There are six flights per week to Rundu, Katima Mulilo and Ondangwa.

From Windhoek's **Hosea Kutako International Airport** (p231), domestic destinations include Lüderitz and Oranjemund (three times per week) and Walvis Bay (daily).

BICYCLE

Namibia is a desert country, and makes for a tough cycling holiday. Distances are great and horizons are vast; the climate and landscapes are hot and very dry; the sun is intense; and, even along major routes, water is scarce and villages are widely spaced. If all of this wasn't enough of a deterrent, also bear in mind that bicycles are not permitted in any national parks.

Loads of Namibians do get around by bicycle, and cycling around small cities and large towns is much easier than a cross-country excursion. With that said, be wary of cycling on dirt roads as punctures from thorn trees are a major problem. Fortunately, many local people operate small repair shops, which are fairly common along populated roadsides.

BUS

Namibia's bus services aren't extensive. Luxury services are limited to the **Intercape Mainliner** (p375), which has scheduled services from Windhoek to Swakopmund, Walvis Bay, Grootfontein, Rundu, Katima Mulilo, Keetmanshoop and Oshikango. Fares include meals on the bus.

There are also local combis (minibuses), which depart when full and follow main routes around the country. From Windhoek's Rhino Park petrol station they depart for dozens of destinations.

CAR & MOTORCYCLE

The easiest way to get around Namibia is in your own car, and an excellent system of sealed roads runs the length of the country, from the South African border at Noordoewer to Ngoma Bridge on the Botswana border and Ruacana in the northwest. Similarly, sealed spur roads connect the main north–south routes to Buitepos, Lüderitz, Swakopmund and Walvis Bay. Elsewhere, towns and most sites of interest

are accessible on good gravel roads. Most C-numbered highways are well maintained and passable to all vehicles, and D-numbered roads, although a bit rougher, are mostly (but not always) passable to 2WD vehicles. In the Kaokoveld, however, most D-numbered roads can only be negotiated with a 4WD.

Nearly all the main car-rental agencies have offices at Hosea Kutako International Airport.

Motorcycle holidays in Namibia are also popular due to the exciting off-road riding on offer. Unfortunately, however, it's difficult to rent a bike in Namibia, though the bigger car companies generally have a couple in their fleet. Note that motorcycles aren't permitted in the national parks, with the exception of the main highway routes through Namib-Naukluft Park.

Automobile Associations

The **Automobile Association of Namibia** (AAN; 061-224201; www.aa-namibia.com) is part of the international AA. It provides highway information and you can also acquire maps from it if you produce your membership card from your home country.

Driving Licence

Foreigners can drive in Namibia on their home driving licence for up to 90 days, and most (if not all) car-rental companies will accept foreign driving licences for car hire. If your home licence isn't written in English, you'd be better off getting an International Driving Permit (IDP) before you arrive in Namibia.

Fuel & Spare Parts

The network of petrol stations in Namibia is good, and most small towns have a station. Mostly diesel, unleaded and super (leaded) are available, and prices vary according to the remoteness of the petrol station. Although the odd petrol station is open 24 hours, most are open 7am to 7pm.

All stations are fully serviced (there is no self-service), and a small tip of a couple of Namibian dollars is appropriate, especially if the attendant has washed your windscreen.

As a general road-safety rule, you should never pass a service station without filling up, and it is advisable to carry an additional 100L of fuel (either in long-range tanks or jerrycans) if you're planning on driving in more remote areas. Petrol stations do run out of fuel in Namibia, so you can't always drain the tank and expect a fill-up at the next station. In more remote areas, payment may only be possible in cash.

Spare parts are readily available in most major towns, but not elsewhere. If you're planning on some 4WD touring, it is advisable to carry the following: two spare tyres, jump leads, fan belt, tow rope and cable, a few litres of oil, wheel spanner and a complete tool kit. A sturdy roll of duct tape will also do in a pinch.

If you're hiring a car make sure you check you have a working jack (and know how to use it!) and a spare tyre. As an extra precaution, double-check that your spare tyre is fully pressurised as you don't want to get stuck out in the desert with only three good wheels.

Hire

Whatever kind of vehicle you decide to rent, you should always check the paperwork carefully, and thoroughly examine the vehicle before accepting it. Car-rental agencies in Namibia have some very high excesses due to the general risks involved in driving on the country's gravel roads. You should also carefully check the condition of your car and never *ever* compromise if you don't feel totally happy with its state of repair.

Always give yourself plenty of time when dropping off your hire car to ensure that the vehicle can be checked over properly for damage etc. The car-rental firm should then issue you with your final invoice before you leave the office.

Insurance

No matter who you hire your car from, make sure you understand what is included in the price (unlimited kilometres, tax, insurance, collision waiver and so on) and what your liabilities are. Most local insurance policies do not cover damage to windscreens and tyres.

Third-party motor insurance is a minimum requirement in Namibia. However, it is also advisable to take damage (collision) waiver, which costs around US$25 extra per day for a 2WD, and about US$50 per day for a 4WD. Loss (theft) waiver is also an extra worth having.

For both types of insurance, the excess liability is about US$1500 for a 2WD and US$3000 for a 4WD. If you're only going for a short period of time, it may be worth taking out the super collision waiver, which covers absolutely everything, albeit at a price.

Road Hazards

Namibia has one of the highest rates of road accidents in the world – always drive within speed limits, take account of road conditions and be prepared for other vehicles travelling at high speed. Avoid driving at night when speeding vehicles and faulty headlights can make things perilous. Both domestic and wild animals can also be a hazard, even along the main highways. And remember that the chances of hitting a wild or domestic animal is far, far greater after dark.

In addition to its good system of sealed roads, Namibia has everything from high-speed gravel roads to badly maintained secondary roads, farm roads, bush tracks, sand tracks, salt roads and challenging 4WD routes. Driving under these conditions requires special techniques, appropriate vehicle preparation, a bit of practice and a heavy dose of caution.

Around Swakopmund and Lüderitz, watch out for sand on the road. It's very slippery and can easily cause a car to flip over if you're driving too fast. Early-morning fog along Skeleton Coast roads is also a hazard, so keep within the prescribed speed limits.

Road Rules

To drive a car in Namibia, you must be at least 21 years old. Like most other Southern African countries, traffic keeps to the left side of the road. The national speed limit is 120km/h on sealed roads out of settlements, 80km/h on gravel roads and 40km/h to 60km/h in all national parks and reserves. When passing through towns and villages, assume a speed limit of 60km/h, even in the absence of any signs.

Highway police use radar, and love to fine motorists (officially about N$70 for every 10km you exceed the limit, but often far more – much seems to be at the discretion of the police officer in question…) for speeding. Sitting on the roof of a moving vehicle is illegal, and wearing seatbelts (where installed) is compulsory in the front (but not back) seats. Drunk-driving is also against the law, and your insurance policy will be invalid if you have an accident while drunk. The legal blood-alcohol limit in Namibia is 0.05%. Driving without a licence is also a serious offence.

If you have an accident causing injury, it must be reported to the authorities within 48 hours. If vehicles have sustained only minor damage, and there are no injuries – and all parties agree – you can exchange names and addresses and sort it out later through your insurance companies.

In theory, owners are responsible for keeping their livestock off the road, but in practice animals wander wherever they want. If you hit a domestic animal, your distress (and possible vehicle damage) will be compounded by the effort involved in finding the owner and the red tape involved when filing a claim.

HITCHING

Although hitching is possible in Namibia (and is quite common among locals), it's illegal in national parks, and even main highways receive relatively little traffic. On a positive note, it isn't unusual to get a lift of 1000km in the same car. Truck drivers generally expect to be paid, so agree on a price beforehand; the standard charge is N$15 per 100km.

Lifts wanted and offered are advertised daily at **Cardboard Box Backpackers** (p225) and **Chameleon Backpackers Lodge** (p225) in Windhoek. At the Namibia Wildlife Resorts office, also

NAMIBIA GETTING AROUND

in Windhoek, there's a noticeboard with shared car hire and lifts offered and wanted.

Hitching is never entirely safe in any country. If you decide to hitch, understand that you are taking a small but potentially serious risk. Travel in pairs and let someone know where you're planning to go if possible.

LOCAL TRANSPORT

Public transport in Namibia is geared towards the needs of the local populace, and is confined to main roads between major population centres. Although cheap and reliable, it is of little use to the traveller, as most of Namibia's tourist attractions lie off the beaten track.

TRAIN

Trans-Namib Railways (☑ 061-298 2032; www.transnamib.com.na) connects some major towns, but trains are extremely slow – as one reader remarked, they move 'at the pace of an energetic donkey cart'. In addition, passenger and freight cars are mixed on the same train, and trains tend to stop at every post, which means that rail travel isn't popular and services are rarely fully booked.

Windhoek is Namibia's rail hub, with services south to Keetmanshoop, west to Swakopmund and east to Gobabis. Trains carry economy and business-class seats, but although most services operate overnight, sleepers are not available. Book at train stations or through the Windhoek booking office at the train station; tickets must be collected before 4pm on the day of departure.

Tourist Trains

Namibia has two tourist trains, which are up-market private charters that aim to re-create the wondrous yesteryear of rail travel. The relatively plush 'rail cruise' aboard the **Desert Express** (☑ 061-298 2600; www.transnamib.com.na/services/passenger-service) offers a popular overnight trip between Windhoek and Swakopmund (single/double from N$6500/10,500) weekly in either direction. En suite cabins with proper beds and furniture are fully heated and air-conditioned, and have large picture windows for gazing out at the passing terrain. It also offers a special seven-day package combining Swakopmund and Etosha National Park, complete with wildlife drives, picnic bush lunches and plenty of long and glorious rail journeys to savour.

The **Shongololo Dune Express** (☑ in South Africa 27-861-777 014; www.shongololo.com), which journeys between Pretoria and Swakopmund via Fish River Canyon, Lüderitz, Kolmanskop, Keetmanshoop, Windhoek and Etosha, does 12-day trips taking in Namibia's main sites. All-inclusive fares range from R59,800 to R75,000 per person, depending on the type of cabin. Regardless of which level you choose, the Shongololo is akin to a five-star hotel on wheels. Guests are wined and dined to their stomach's content, and you can expect fine linen, hot showers, ample lounge space and a permeating sense of railway nostalgia.

Survival
Guide

Health

As long as you stay up to date with your vaccinations and take basic preventive measures, you're unlikely to succumb to most serious health hazards. While Botswana and Namibia do offer an impressive selection of tropical diseases, it's more likely you'll get a bout of diarrhoea or a cold than an exotic malady. The main exception to this is malaria, which is a real risk in lower-lying areas.

BEFORE YOU GO

A little predeparture planning will save you trouble later. Get a check-up from your dentist and from your doctor if you have any regular medication or chronic illness, eg high blood pressure or asthma. You should also organise spare contact lenses and glasses (and take your optical prescription with you); get a first-aid and medical kit together; and arrange necessary vaccinations.

Travellers can register with the International Association for Medical Advice to Travellers (www.iamat.org), which provides directories of certified doctors in-country. If you'll be spending much time in more remote areas, consider doing a first-aid course (contact the Red Cross or St John's Ambulance), or attending a remote medicine first-aid course, such as that offered by Wilderness Medical Training (www.wildernessmedical-training.co.uk).

If you are bringing medications with you, carry them in their original containers, clearly labelled. A signed and dated letter from your physician describing all medical conditions and medications, including generic names, is also a good idea. If carrying syringes or needles, be sure to have a physician's letter documenting their medical necessity.

Insurance

In Botswana and Namibia, most doctors expect payment in cash. Find out in advance whether your insurance plan will make payments directly to providers, or will reimburse you later for overseas health expenditures. It's also vital to ensure that your travel insurance will cover any emergency transport required to get you to a hospital in a major city, or all the way home, by air and with a medical attendant if necessary. Not all insurance covers this, so check the contract carefully. If you need medical assistance, your insurance company might be able to help locate the nearest hospital or clinic, or you can ask at your hotel. In an emergency, contact your embassy or consulate.

RECOMMENDED VACCINATIONS

The World Health Organization (www.who.int/en) recommends that all travellers be covered for diphtheria, tetanus, measles, mumps, rubella and polio, as well as for hepatitis B, regardless of their destination. The consequences of these diseases can be severe, and outbreaks do occur.

According to the Centers for Disease Control & Prevention (www.cdc.gov), the following vaccinations are recommended for Botswana and Namibia: hepatitis A, hepatitis B, rabies and typhoid, and boosters for tetanus, diphtheria and measles. Despite an outbreak in Angola in 2016 and a single case along the Angola–Namibia border at the time, yellow fever was not a risk in the region at the time of writing, but the certificate is an entry requirement if you're coming from an infected region.

Medical Checklist

It's a very good idea to carry a medical and first-aid kit with you, to help yourself in the case of minor illness or injury. Following is a list of items to consider packing:

➡ antibiotics (prescription only), eg ciprofloxacin (Ciproxin) or norfloxacin (Utinor)

➡ antidiarrhoeal drugs (eg loperamide)

➡ acetaminophen (paracetamol) or aspirin

➡ anti-inflammatory drugs (eg ibuprofen)

➡ antihistamines (for hay fever and allergic reactions)

➡ antibacterial ointment (eg Bactroban) for cuts and abrasions (prescription only)

➡ antimalaria pills, if you'll be in malarial areas

➡ bandages, gauze

➡ scissors, safety pins, tweezers, pocket knife

➡ DEET-containing insect repellent

➡ permethrin-containing insect spray for clothing, tents and bed nets

➡ prickly-heat powder for heat rashes

➡ sun screen

➡ oral rehydration salts

➡ iodine tablets (for water purification)

➡ sterile needles, syringes and fluids if travelling to remote areas.

Websites

There is a wealth of travel-health advice on the internet. The Lonely Planet website at www.lonely-planet.com is a good place to start. The World Health Organization publishes the helpful *International Travel and Health,* available free at www.who.int/ith/. Other useful websites include MD Travel Health (www.mdtravelhealth.com) and Fit for Travel (www.fitfortravel.scot.nhs.uk).

Official government travel-health websites:

Australia http://smarttraveller.gov.au/guide/all-travellers/health/Pages/default.aspx

Canada www.hc-sc.gc.ca/index_e.html

UK www.gov.uk/foreign-travel-advice

USA wwwnc.cdc.gov/travel

Further Reading

➡ *A Comprehensive Guide to Wilderness and Travel Medicine* (1998) Eric A Weiss

➡ *The Essential Guide to Travel Health* (2009) Jane Wilson-Howarth

➡ *Healthy Travel Africa* (2000) Isabelle Young

➡ *How to Stay Healthy Abroad* (2002) Richard Dawood

➡ *Travel in Health* (1994) Graham Fry

➡ *Travel with Children* (2015) Sophie Caupeil et al

IN BOTSWANA & NAMIBIA

Availability & Cost of Health Care

Good-quality health care is available in all major urban areas in Botswana and Namibia, and private hospitals are generally of excellent standard. Public hospitals, by contrast, are often under-funded and overcrowded, and reliable medical facilities are rare in off-the-beaten-track areas.

Prescriptions are generally required in Botswana and Namibia. Drugs for chronic diseases should be brought from home. There is a high risk of contracting HIV from infected blood transfusions. To minimise this, seek out treatment in reputable clinics. The BloodCare Foundation (www.bloodcare.org.uk) is a useful source of safe, screened blood, which can be transported to any part of the world within 24 hours.

Infectious Diseases

Following are some of the diseases that are found in Botswana and Namibia, though with a few basic preventative measures, it's unlikely that you'll succumb to any of these.

Cholera

Cholera is caused by a bacteria and spread via contaminated drinking water. You should avoid tap water and unpeeled or uncooked fruits and vegetables, although tap water, especially in Namibia, is sometimes safe. The main symptom is profuse watery diarrhoea, which causes debilitation if fluids are not replaced quickly. An oral cholera vaccine is available in the USA, but it is not particularly effective. Most cases of cholera can be avoided by close attention to drinking water and by avoiding potentially contaminated food. Treatment is by fluid replacement (orally or via a drip), but sometimes antibiotics are needed. Self-treatment is not advised.

Dengue Fever

Dengue fever, spread through the bite of the mosquito, causes a feverish illness with headaches and muscle pains similar to those experienced with a bad, prolonged attack of influenza. There might be a rash. Mosquito bites should be avoided whenever possible. Self-treatment: paracetamol and rest.

Filariasis

Filariasis is caused by tiny worms migrating in the lymphatic system, and is spread by the bite of an infected mosquito. Symptoms include localised itching and swelling of the legs and/or genitalia. Treatment is available. Self-treatment: none.

Hepatitis A

Hepatitis A, which occurs in both countries, is spread through contaminated food (particularly shellfish) and water. It causes jaundice and, although it is rarely fatal, it can cause prolonged lethargy and delayed recovery. If you've had hepatitis A, you shouldn't drink alcohol for up to six months afterwards, but once you've recovered there won't be any long-term problems. The first symptoms include dark urine and a yellow colour to the whites of the eyes. Sometimes a fever and abdominal pain might be present. Hepatitis A vaccine (Avaxim, VAQTA, Havrix) is given as an injection: a single dose will give protection for up to a year, and a booster after a year gives 10-year protection. Hepatitis A and typhoid vaccines can also be given as a single-dose vaccine, known as hepatyrix or viatim. Self-treatment: none.

Hepatitis B

Hepatitis B, found in both countries, is spread through infected blood, contaminated needles and sexual intercourse. It can also be spread from an infected mother to the baby during childbirth. It affects the liver, causing jaundice and occasionally liver failure. Most people recover completely, but some people might be chronic carriers of the virus, which could lead eventually to cirrhosis or liver cancer. Those visiting high-risk areas for long periods or those with increased social or occupational risk should be immunised. Many countries now routinely give hepatitis B as part of the childhood vaccination program. It is given singly or can be given at the same time as hepatitis A (hepatyrix). A course will give protection for at least five years. It can be given over four weeks or six months. Self-treatment: none.

HIV & AIDS

HIV, the virus that causes AIDS, is an enormous problem in Botswana and Namibia, with a devastating impact on local health systems and community structures. Botswana in particular has one of the highest rates of infection on the continent, with an HIV-positive incidence of 25.16%, second only to nearby Swaziland. The rate is more than 15.97% in Namibia. The virus is spread through infected blood and blood products, by sexual intercourse with an infected partner, and from an infected mother to her baby during childbirth and breastfeeding. It can be spread through 'blood to blood' contacts, such as with contaminated instruments during medical, dental, acupuncture and other body-piercing procedures, and through sharing used intravenous needles.

At present there is no cure, but medication that might keep the disease under control is available. In 2002 the Botswana government elected to make antiretroviral drugs available to all citizens free of charge, becoming the first country in the world to offer this treatment for free. Still, for people living in remote areas of the country access to such treatment is a problem, as is the continuing stigma attached to 'owning up' to having the infection. In Namibia, antiretroviral drugs are still largely unavailable, or too expensive for the majority of Namibians.

If you think you might have been infected with HIV, a blood test is necessary; a three-month gap after exposure and before testing is required to allow antibodies to appear in the blood. Self-treatment: none.

Malaria

Apart from road accidents, malaria is probably the only major health risk that you face while travelling in this area, and precautions should be taken. At the time of writing, the northern half of both Botswana and Namibia were considered areas of medium to high malaria risk. The disease is caused by a parasite in the bloodstream spread via the bite of the female Anopheles mosquito. There are several types of malaria; falciparum malaria is the most dangerous type and the predominant form in Botswana and Namibia. Infection rates vary with season and climate, so check out the situation before departure. Several different drugs are used to prevent malaria and new ones are in the pipeline. Up-to-date advice from a travel-health clinic is essential, as some medication is more suitable for some travellers than others (eg people with epilepsy should avoid mefloquine, and doxycycline should not be taken by pregnant women or children aged under 12).

The early stages of malaria include headaches, fevers, generalised aches and pains, and malaise, which could be mistaken for flu. Other symptoms can include abdominal pain, diarrhoea and a cough. Anyone who develops a fever in a malarial area should assume malarial infection until a blood test proves negative, even if you have been taking antimalarial medication. If not treated, the next stage could develop within 24 hours, particularly if falciparum malaria is the parasite: jaundice, then reduced consciousness and coma (also known as cerebral malaria) followed by death. Treatment in hospital is essential, and the death rate might still be as high as 10%, even in the best intensive-care facilities.

Many travellers think that malaria is a mild illness, and that taking antimalarial drugs causes more illness through side effects than actually getting malaria. This is unfortunately not true. If you decide against antimalarial drugs, you must understand the risks, and be obsessive about avoiding mosquito bites. Use nets and insect repellent, and report any fever or flu-like symptoms to a doctor as soon as possible. Some people advocate homeo-pathic preparations against malaria, such as Demal200, but there is no evidence that this is effective, and many homeopaths do not recom-mend their use.

Malaria in pregnancy frequently results in miscar-riage or premature labour, and the risks to both mother and foetus during pregnan-cy are considerable. Travel throughout the region when pregnant should be carefully considered. Adults who have survived multiple bouts of early childhood malaria will have developed immunity and usually only develop mild cases of malaria; most Western travellers have no immunity at all, thus the need for precautions. Even if you've recently had malaria you are still vulnerable to a serious infection, so don't think that you are immune.

ANTIMALARIAL A TO D

A – Awareness of the Risk No medication is totally effective, but protection of up to 95% is achievable with most drugs, as long as other measures have been taken.

B – Bites To be avoided at all costs. Sleep in a screened room, use a mosquito spray or coils, sleep under a permethrin-impregnated net at night. Cover up at night with long trousers and long sleeves, preferably with permethrin-treated clothing. Apply appropriate repellent to all areas of exposed skin in the evenings.

C – Chemical prevention (ie antimalarial drugs) Usually needed in malarial areas. Expert advice is needed as resistance patterns can change, and new drugs are in development. Not all antimalarial drugs are suitable for everyone. Most antimalarial drugs need to be started at least a week before, and continued for four weeks after, possible exposure to malaria.

D – Diagnosis If you have a fever or flu-like illness within a year of travel to a malarial area, malaria is a possibility, and immediate medical attention is necessary.

Rabies

Rabies is spread by receiv-ing bites or licks from an infected animal on broken skin. Few human cases are reported in Botswana and Namibia, with the risks high-est in rural areas. It is always fatal once the clinical symp-toms start (which might be up to several months after an infected bite), so postbite vaccination should be given as soon as possible. Post-bite vaccination (whether or not you've been vaccinated before the bite) prevents the virus from spreading to the central nervous system. Animal handlers should be vaccinated, as should those travelling to remote areas where a reliable source of postbite vaccine is not available within 24 hours. Three preventive injections are needed over a month. If you have not been vacci-nated, you'll need a course of five injections starting 24 hours or as soon as possible after the injury. If you have been vaccinated, you'll need fewer postbite injections, and have more time to seek medical help. Self-treat-ment: none.

Schistosomiasis (Bilharzia)

This disease is a risk in parts of Botswana and Namibia. It's spread by flukes (minute worms) that are carried

by a species of freshwater snail, which then sheds them into slow-moving or still water. The parasites penetrate human skin during swimming and then migrate to the bladder or bowel. They are excreted via stool or urine and could contaminate fresh water, where the cycle starts again. Swimming in suspect fresh-water lakes or slow-running rivers should be avoided. Symptoms range from none, to transient fever and rash, and advanced cases might have blood in the stool or in the urine. A blood test can detect antibodies if you might have been exposed, and treatment is readily available. If not treated the infection can cause kidney failure or permanent bowel damage. It's not possible for you to infect others. Self-treatment: none.

Tuberculosis (TB)

Tuberculosis is spread through close respiratory contact and occasionally through infected milk or milk products. BCG vacci-nation is recommended if you'll be mixing closely with the local population, espe-cially on long-term stays, although it gives only mod-erate protection against the disease. TB can be asymp-tomatic, only being picked up on a routine chest X-ray. Alternatively, it can cause a cough, weight loss or fe-ver, sometimes months or even years after exposure. Self-treatment: none.

Typhoid

This is spread through food or water contaminated by infected human faeces. The first symptom is usually a fever or a pink rash on the abdomen. Sometimes sep-ticaemia (blood poisoning) can occur. A typhoid vaccine (typhim Vi, typherix) will give protection for three years. In some countries, the oral vac-cine Vivotif is also available. Antibiotics are usually given as treatment, and death is

Yellow Fever

Although not a problem within Botswana and Namibia at the time of writing, you'll need to carry a certificate of vaccination if arriving from an infected country. For a list of countries with a high rate of infection, see the website of the World Health Organization (www.who.int/en/) or the Centers for Disease Control & Prevention (wwwnc.cdc.gov/travel).

Traveller's Diarrhoea

This is a common travel-related illness. It's possible that you'll succumb, especially if you're spending a lot of time in rural areas or eating at inexpensive local-food stalls. Sometimes dietary changes, such as increased spices or oils, are the cause. To help prevent diarrhoea, avoid tap water unless you're sure it's safe to drink, only eat fresh fruits or vegetables that have been cooked or peeled, and be wary of dairy products that might contain unpasteurised milk. Although freshly cooked food can often be a safe option, plates or serving utensils might be dirty, so be selective when eating food from street vendors (make sure that cooked food is piping hot all the way through). If you develop diarrhoea, be sure to drink plenty of fluids, preferably an oral rehydration solution containing lots of water and some salt and sugar. A few loose stools

WATER

Stick to bottled water, and purify any river water before drinking it.

don't require treatment but if you start having more than four or five stools a day you should start taking an antibiotic (usually a quinoline drug, such as ciprofloxacin or norfloxacin) and an antidiarrhoeal agent (such as loperamide) if you're not within easy reach of a toilet. If diarrhoea is bloody, persists for more than 72 hours or is accompanied by fever, shaking chills or severe abdominal pain, you should seek medical attention.

Amoebic Dysentery

Contracted by eating contaminated food and water, amoebic dysentery causes blood and mucus in the faeces. It can be relatively mild and tends to come on gradually, but seek medical advice if you think you have the illness. It won't clear up without treatment (which is with specific antibiotics).

Giardiasis

This, like amoebic dysentery, is also caused by ingesting contaminated food or water. The illness usually appears a week or more after you have been exposed to the offending parasite. Giardiasis might cause only a short-lived bout of typical traveller's diarrhoea, but it can also cause persistent diarrhoea. Ideally, seek medical advice if you suspect you have giardiasis, but if you are in a remote area you could start a course of antibiotics.

Environmental Hazards

Heat Exhaustion

This condition occurs if heavy sweating and excessive fluid loss are followed by inadequate replacement of fluids and salt, and it's primarily a risk in hot climates when taking unaccustomed exercise before full acclimatisation. Symptoms include headaches, dizziness and

tiredness. Dehydration is already happening by the time you feel thirsty – aim to drink sufficient water to produce pale, diluted urine. Self-treatment: fluid replacement with water and/or fruit juice, and cooling by cold water and fans. The treatment of the salt-loss component consists of consuming salty fluids (as in soup), and adding a little more table salt to foods than usual.

Heatstroke

Heat exhaustion is a precursor to the much more serious condition of heatstroke. In this case there is damage to the sweating mechanism, with an excessive rise in body temperature, irrational and hyperactive behaviour, and eventually loss of consciousness and death. Rapid cooling by spraying the body with water and fanning is ideal. Emergency fluid and electrolyte replacement by intravenous drip is usually also required.

Insect Bites & Stings

Mosquitoes might not always carry malaria or dengue fever, but they (and other insects) can cause irritation and infected bites. To avoid these, take the same precautions as you would for avoiding malaria. Use DEET-based insect repellents. Excellent clothing treatments are also available; mosquitos that land on treated clothing will die.

Bee and wasp stings cause real problems only to those who have a severe allergy to the stings (anaphylaxis). If you are one of these people, make sure to carry an EpiPen – an adrenaline (epinephrine) injection, especially when travelling in remote areas. This could save your life.

Scorpions are found in arid areas. They can cause a painful bite that is sometimes life-threatening. If bitten by a scorpion, seek immediate medical assistance. Medical treatment should be sought if collapse occurs.

Ticks are always a risk if away from urban areas. If you do get bitten, press down around the tick's head with tweezers, grab the head and gently pull upwards. Avoid pulling the rear of the body as this may squeeze the tick's gut contents through the attached mouthparts into the skin, increasing the risk of both infection and disease. Smearing chemicals on the tick will not make it let go and is not recommended.

Bedbugs are found in hostels and cheap hotels and lead to itchy, lumpy bites. Spraying the mattress with crawling-insect killer after changing bedding will get rid of them. Scabies are also found in cheap accommodation. These tiny mites live in the skin, often between the fingers, and they cause an intensely itchy rash. The itch is easily treated with malathion and permethrin lotion from a pharmacy; other members of the household also need treating to avoid spreading scabies, even if they do not show any symptoms.

Snake Bites

Basically, avoid getting bitten! Don't walk barefoot, or stick your hand into holes or cracks. Boomslangs (venomous Southern African tree snakes) tend to hang out in trees, especially on overhanging limbs, so also exercise caution when walking in forests. However, about half of those bitten by venomous snakes are not actually injected with poison (envenomed). If bitten by a snake, do not panic. Immobilise the bitten limb with a splint (such as a stick) and apply a bandage over the site with firm pressure, similar to bandaging a sprain. Do not apply a tourniquet, or cut or suck the bite. Get medical help as soon as possible. It will help get you the correct antivenene if you can identify the snake (although antivenene has some potentially serious side effects and may not always be given); try to take note of the snake's appearance just in case.

Traditional Medicine

According to estimates, as many as 85% of residents of Botswana and Namibia rely in part, or wholly, on traditional medicine. Given the high costs and unavailability of Western medicine in many rural areas, traditional healers are the first contact for many when falling ill. The *sangoma* (traditional healer) and *inyanga* (herbalist) hold revered positions in many communities, and traditional medicinal products are widely available in local markets. Unfortunately, some traditional medicines are made from endangered or threatened species like aardvarks, cheetahs and leopards.

Language

English is the official language of Botswana, but the most common language is Setswana (Tswana). The second most common Bantu language is Sekalanga, a derivative of the Shona language spoken by the Bakalanga people who are centred around Francistown.

English is the official language of Namibia, but the lingua franca is Afrikaans. Only in the Caprivi is English preferred over Afrikaans. As their first language, most Namibians speak one of the many Bantu or Khoisan languages. The Bantu group includes Owambo, Kavango, Herero and Caprivian. Khoisan dialects include Khoikhoi (Nama), Damara and San dialects such as !Kung San. Many native Khoisan speakers also speak at least one Bantu and one European language, normally Afrikaans. Thanks to Namibia's colonial past, German is also widely spoken, while in the far north you'll also hear a lot of Portuguese.

AFRIKAANS

Afrikaans developed from the dialect spoken by the Dutch settlers in South Africa from the 17th century. Today, it's the first language of around six million people and the first language of over 150,000 Namibians.

If you read our coloured pronunciation guides as if they were English, you'll be understood. The stressed syllables are in italics. Note that aw is pronounced as in 'law', eu as the 'u' in 'nurse', ew as the 'ee' in 'see' with rounded lips, oh as the 'o' in 'cold', uh as the 'a' in 'ago', kh as the 'ch' in the the Scottish *loch,* zh as the 's' in 'pleasure', and r is trilled.

WANT MORE?

For in-depth language information and handy phrases, check out Lonely Planet's *Africa Phrasebook*. You'll find it at **shop. lonelyplanet.com**, or you can buy Lonely Planet's iPhone phrasebooks at the Apple App Store.

Basics

Hello.	Hallo.	ha-*loh*
Goodbye.	Totsiens.	tot-*seens*
Yes.	Ja.	yaa
No.	Nee.	ney
Please.	Asseblief.	a-si-*bleef*
Thank you.	Dankie.	dang-kee
Sorry.	Jammer.	ya-min

How are you?
Hoe gaan dit?   hu khaan dit

Fine, and you?
Goed dankie, en jy?   khut dang-kee en yay

What's your name?
Wat's jou naam?   vats yoh naam

My name is ...
My naam is ...   may naam is ...

Do you speak English?
Praat jy Engels?   praat yay eng-ils

I don't understand.
Ek verstaan nie.   ek vir-*staan* nee

Accommodation

Where's a ...?	Waar's 'n ...?	vaars i ...
campsite	kampeerplek	kam-*peyr*-plek
guesthouse	gastehuis	khas-ti-hays
hotel	hotel	hu-*tel*

Do you have a single/double room?
Het jy 'n enkel/   het yay i eng-kil/
dubbel kamer?   di-bil kaa-mir

How much is it per night/person?
Hoeveel kos dit per nag/   hu-fil kos dit pir nakh/
persoon?   pir-soon

Directions

How much is it to ...?
Hoeveel kos dit na ...?   *hu*·fil kos dit naa ...

Please take me to (this address).
Neem my asseblief na   neym may a·si·*bleef* naa
(hierdie adres).   (*heer*·dee a·*dres*)

Is this the road to ...?
Is dit die pad na ...?   is dit dee pat naa ...

Where's the (nearest) ...?
Waar's die (naaste) ...?   vaars dee (*naas*·ti) ...

Can you show me (on the map)?
Kan jy my   kan yay may
(op die kaart) wys?   (op dee kaart) vays

What's the address?
Wat is die adres?   vat is dee a·*dres*

How far is it?
Hoe ver is dit?   hu fer is dit

How do I get there?
Hoe kom ek daar?   hu kom ek daar

Eating & Drinking

Can you recommend a ...?	*Kan jy 'n ... aanbeveel?*	kan yay i ... *aan*·bi·feyl
bar	*kroeg*	krukh
dish	*gereg*	khi·*rekh*
place to eat	*eetplek*	*eyt*·plek

I'd like ..., please.	*Ek wil asseblief ... hê.*	ek vil a·si·*bleef* ... he
a table for two	*'n tafel vir twee*	i *taa*·fil fir twey
the bill	*die rekening*	dee *rey*·ki·ning
the menu	*die spyskaart*	dee *spays*·kaart

Do you have vegetarian food?
Het julle vegetariese   het *yi*·li fe·gee·*taa*·ree·si
kos?   kos

beer	*bier*	beer
breakfast	*ontbyt*	awnt·*bayt*
coffee	*koffie*	*ko*·fee
dairy products	*suiwelprodukte*	*soy*·vil·pru·dik·ti
dinner	*aandete*	*aant*·ey·ti
drink	*drankie*	*drang*·kee
eggs	*eiers*	*ay*·irs
fish	*vis*	fis
fruit	*vrugte*	*frikh*·ti

lunch	*middagete*	*mi*·dakh·ey·ti
market	*mark*	mark
meat	*vleis*	vlays
milk	*melk*	melk
nuts	*neute*	*ney*·ti
restaurant	*restaurant*	*res*·toh·rant
seafood	*seekos*	*sey*·kaws
sugar	*suiker*	*say*·kir
tea	*tee*	tey
vegetable	*groente*	*khrun*·ti
water	*water*	*vaa*·tir
wine	*wyn*	vayn

Emergencies

Help!   *Help!*   help

Call a doctor!   *Kry 'n dokter!*   kray i *dok*·tir

Call the police!
Kry die polisie!   kray dee pu·*lee*·see

I'm lost.
Ek is verdwaal.   ek is fir·*dwaal*

Where are the toilets?
Waar is die toilette?   vaar is dee toy·*le*·ti

I need a doctor.
Ek het 'n dokter nodig.   ek het i *dok*·tir noo·dikh

It hurts here.
Dis hier seer.   dis heer seyr

I'm allergic to (penicillin).
Ek's allergies vir   eks a·*ler*·khees fir
(penisillien).   (pi·ni·si·*leen*)

Shopping & Services

I'm looking for ...
Ek soek na ...   ek suk naa ...

How much is it?
Hoeveel kos dit?   *hu*·fil kos dit

What's your lowest price?
Wat is jou laagste prys?   vat is yoh *laakh*·sti prays

There's a mistake in the bill.
Daar's 'n fout op   daars i foht op
die rekening.   dee *rey*·ki·ning

I want to buy a phonecard.
Ek wil asseblief   ek vil a·si·*bleef*
'n foonkaart koop.   i *foon*·kaart koop

I'd like to change money.
Ek wil asseblief   ek vil a·si·*bleef*
geld ruil.   khelt rayl

I want to use the internet.
Ek wil asseblief die   ek vil a·si·*bleef* dee
Internet gebruik.   *in*·tir·net khi·*brayk*

Time & Dates

What time is it?
Hoe laat is dit?   hu laat is dit

It's (two) o'clock.
Dis (twee-)uur.   dis (twey·)ewr

Half past (one).
Half (twee).   half (twey)

yesterday	*gister*	khis·tir
today	*vandag*	fin·dakh
tomorrow	*môre*	mo·ri
Monday	*Maandag*	maan·dakh
Tuesday	*Dinsdag*	dins·dakh
Wednesday	*Woensdag*	wuns·dakh
Thursday	*Donderdag*	don·ir·dakh
Friday	*Vrydag*	vray·dakh
Saturday	*Saterdag*	sa·tir·dakh
Sunday	*Sondag*	son·dakh
1	*een*	eyn
2	*twee*	twey
3	*drie*	dree
4	*vier*	feer
5	*vyf*	fayf
6	*ses*	ses
7	*sewe*	see·vi
8	*agt*	akht
9	*nege*	ney·khi
10	*tien*	teen
20	*twintig*	twin·tikh
30	*dertig*	der·tikh
40	*veertig*	feyr·tikh
50	*vyftig*	fayf·tikh
60	*sestig*	ses·tikh
70	*sewentig*	sey·vin·tikh
80	*tagtig*	takh·tikh
90	*negentig*	ney·khin·tikh
100	*honderd*	hon·dirt
1000	*duisend*	day·sint

Transport

boat	*boot*	boot
bus	*bus*	bis
plane	*vliegtuig*	flikh·tayg
train	*trein*	trayn

A ... ticket, please.	*Een ... kaartjie, asseblief.*	eyn ... kaar·kee a·si·bleef
one-way	*eenrigting*	eyn·rikh·ting
return	*retoer*	ri·tur

DAMARA/NAMA

The very similar dialects of the Damara and Nama peoples, whose traditional lands take in most of Namibia's wildest desert regions, belong to the Khoisan group of languages.

As with the San dialects, they feature several 'click' sounds, created by slapping the tongue against the teeth, palate or side of the mouth. These are normally represented by exclamation points (!), single or double slashes (/, //) and a vertical line crossed by two horizontal lines (‡).

Basics

Hello.	!Gâi tses.
Good morning.	!Gâi-//oas.
Good evening.	!Gâi-!oes.
Goodbye. (said by person leaving)	!Gâise hâre.
Goodbye. (said by person staying)	!Gâise !gûre.
Yes.	Î.
No.	Hâ-â.
Please.	Toxoba.
Thank you.	Aio.
Excuse me.	‡Anba tere.
Sorry.	Mati.
How are you?	Matisa?
I'm well.	!Gâi a.
Do you speak English?	Engels !khoa idu ra?
What is your name?	Mati du/onhâ?
My name is ...	Ti/ons ge a ...

EMERGENCIES DAMARA/NAMA

Help!	Huitere!
Call a doctor!	Laedi aoba ‡gaire!
Call the police!	Lapa !nama ‡gaire!
Leave me alone.	//Naxu te.
I'm lost.	Ka tage hâi.

Where is the ...?	Mapa ... hâ?
Go straight.	‡Khanuse ire.
Turn left.	//Are /khab ai ire.
Turn right.	//Am /khab ai ire.
far	!nu a
near	/gu a

I'd like ...	Tage ra ‡khaba ...
How much?	Mati ko?
market	‡kharugu
shop	!khaib
small	‡khariro
large	kai

baboon	//arub
dog	arib
elephant	‡khoab
giraffe	!naib
goat	piri
horse	hab
hyena	‡khira
leopard	/garub
lion	xami
monkey	/norab
rabbit	!oâs
rhino	!nabas
warthog	gairib
zebra	!goreb
What time is it?	Mati ko /laexa i?
today	nets
tomorrow	//ari

1	/gui
2	/gam
3	!nona
4	haka
5	kore
6	!nani
7	hû
8	//khaisa
9	khoese
10	disi
50	koro disi
100	/oa disi
1000	/gui /oa disi

GERMAN

German (spoken in Namibia) is easy for English speakers to pronounce because almost all of its sounds are also found in English. If you read our coloured pronunciation guides as if they were English, you'll have no problems being understood. The stressed syllables are indicated with italics. Note that kh is like the 'ch' in 'Bach' or the Scottish 'loch' (pronounced at the back of the throat), r is also pronounced at the back of the throat (almost like a g, but with some friction), zh is pronounced as the 's' in 'measure', and ü as the 'ee' in 'see' but with rounded lips.

Basics

Hello.	Guten Tag.	goo·ten tahk
Goodbye.	Auf Wiedersehen.	owf vee·der·zay·en
Yes.	Ja.	yah
No.	Nein.	nain
Please.	Bitte.	bi·te
Thank you.	Danke.	dang·ke
You're welcome.	Bitte.	bi·te
Excuse me./ Sorry.	Entschuldigung.	ent·shul·di·gung

How are you?
Wie geht es Ihnen/dir? (pol/inf) — vee gayt es ee·nen/deer

Fine. And you?
Danke, gut. — dang·ke goot
Und Ihnen/dir? (pol/inf) — unt ee·nen/deer

What's your name?
Wie ist Ihr Name? (pol) — vee ist eer nah·me
Wie heißt du? (inf) — vee haist doo

My name is ...
Mein Name ist ... (pol) — main nah·me ist ...
Ich heiße ... (inf) — ikh hai·se ...

Do you speak English?
Sprechen Sie Englisch? (pol) — shpre·khen zee eng·lish
Sprichst du Englisch? (inf) — shprikhst doo eng·lish

I don't understand.
Ich verstehe nicht. — ikh fer·shtay·e nikht

Accommodation

campsite	Campingplatz	kem·ping·plats
guesthouse	Pension	pahng·zyawn
hotel	Hotel	ho·tel
room in a private home	Privatzimmer	pri·vaht·tsi·mer

Do you have a ... room?	Haben Sie ein ...?	hah·ben zee ain ...
double	Doppelzimmer	do·pel·tsi·mer
single	Einzelzimmer	ain·tsel·tsi·mer

How much is it per ...?	Wie viel kostet es pro ...?	vee feel kos·tet es praw ...
night	Nacht	nakht
person	Person	per·zawn

Is breakfast included?
Ist das Frühstück inklusive? — ist das *frü*·shtük in·kloo·*zee*·ve

Eating & Drinking

I'd like the menu, please.
Ich hätte gern die Speisekarte, bitte. — ikh *he*·te gern dee *shpai*·ze·kar·te *bi*·te

What would you recommend?
Was empfehlen Sie? — vas emp·*fay*·len zee

I'm a vegetarian.
Ich bin Vegetarier/ Vegetarierin. (m/f) — ikh bin ve·ge·*tah*·ri·er/ ve·ge·*tah*·ri·e·rin

Please bring the bill.
Bitte bringen Sie die Rechnung. — *bi*·te *bring*·en zee dee *rekh*·nung

beer	Bier	beer
bread	Brot	brawt
breakfast	Frühstück	frü·shtük
cheese	Käse	kay·ze
coffee	Kaffee	ka·fay
dinner	Abendessen	ah·bent·e·sen
egg/eggs	Ei/Eier	ai/ai·er
fruit	Frucht/Obst	frukht/awpst
grocery store	Lebensmittel-laden	lay·bens·mi·tel·lah·den
juice	Saft	zaft
lunch	Mittagessen	mi·tahk·e·sen
market	Markt	markt
meat	Fleisch	flaish
milk	Milch	milkh
restaurant	Restaurant	res·to·rahng
salt	Salz	zalts
seafood	Meeresfrüchte	mair·res·frükh·te
sugar	Zucker	tsu·ker
tea	Tee	tay
vegetable	Gemüse	ge·mü·ze
water	Wasser	va·ser
wine	Wein	vain

Emergencies

Help!
Hilfe! — hil·fe

Go away!
Gehen Sie weg! — gay·en zee vek

Call the police!
Rufen Sie die Polizei! — roo·fen zee dee po·li·tsai

Call a doctor!
Rufen Sie einen Arzt! — roo·fen zee ai·nen artst

Where are the toilets?
Wo ist die Toilette? — vo ist dee to·a·le·te

I'm lost.
Ich habe mich verirrt. — ikh hah·be mikh fer·irt

I'm sick.
Ich bin krank. — ikh bin krangk

Time, Dates & Numbers

What time is it?
Wie spät ist es? — vee shpayt ist es

It's (10) o'clock.
Es ist (zehn) Uhr. — es ist (tsayn) oor

At what time?
Um wie viel Uhr? — um vee feel oor

At ...
Um ... — um ...

morning	Morgen	mor·gen
afternoon	Nachmittag	nahkh·mi·tahk
evening	Abend	ah·bent
yesterday	gestern	ges·tern
today	heute	hoy·te
tomorrow	morgen	mor·gen

Monday	Montag	mawn·tahk
Tuesday	Dienstag	deens·tahk
Wednesday	Mittwoch	mit·vokh
Thursday	Donnerstag	do·ners·tahk
Friday	Freitag	frai·tahk
Saturday	Samstag	zams·tahk
Sunday	Sonntag	zon·tahk

1	eins	ains
2	zwei	tsvai
3	drei	drai
4	vier	feer
5	fünf	fünf
6	sechs	zeks

7	sieben	zee·ben
8	acht	akht
9	neun	noyn
10	zehn	tsayn
20	zwanzig	tsvan·tsikh
30	dreißig	drai·tsikh
40	vierzig	feer·tsikh
50	fünfzig	fünf·tsikh
60	sechzig	zekh·tsikh
70	siebzig	zeep·tsikh
80	achtzig	akht·tsikh
90	neunzig	noyn·tsikh
100	hundert	hun·dert
1000	tausend	tow·sent

Transport & Directions

boat	Boot	bawt
bus	Bus	bus
plane	Flugzeug	flook·tsoyk
train	Zug	tsook

At what time's the ... bus?	Wann fährt der ... Bus?	van fairt dair... bus
first	erste	ers·te
last	letzte	lets·te

1st-class ticket	Fahrkarte erster Klasse	fahr·kar·te ers·ter kla·se
2nd-class ticket	Fahrkarte zweiter Klasse	fahr·kar·te tsvai·ter kla·se
one-way ticket	einfache Fahrkarte	ain·fa·khe fahr·kar·te
return ticket	Rückfahrkarte	rük·fahr·kar·te

At what time does it arrive?
Wann kommt es an?   van komt es an

Does it stop at ...?
Hält es in ...?   helt es in ...

What station is this?
Welcher Bahnhof   vel·kher bahn·hawf
ist das?   ist das

What's the next stop?
Welches ist der   vel·khes ist dair
nächste Halt?   naykh·ste halt

I want to get off here.
Ich möchte hier   ikh merkh·te heer
aussteigen.   ows·shtai·gen

Where's ...?
Wo ist ...?   vaw ist ...

What's the address?

Wie ist die Adresse?   vee ist dee a·dre·se

How far is it?
Wie weit ist es?   vee vait ist es

Can you show me (on the map)?
Können Sie es mir   ker·nen zee es meer
(auf der Karte) zeigen?   (owf dair kar·te) tsai·gen
Es ist (zehn) Uhr.   es ist (tsayn) oor

At what time?
Um wie viel Uhr?   um vee feel oor

At ...
Um ...   um ...

Shopping & Services

I'd like to buy ...
Ich möchte ... kaufen.   ikh merkh·te ... kow·fen

Can I look at it?
Können Sie es mir   ker·nen zee es meer
zeigen?   tsai·gen

How much is this?
Wie viel kostet das?   vee feel kos·tet das

That's too expensive.
Das ist zu teuer.   das ist tsoo toy·er

Can you lower the price?
Können Sie mit dem   ker·nen zee mit dem
Preis heruntergehen?   prais he·run·ter·gay·en

ATM	Geldautomat	gelt·ow·to·maht
post office	Postamt	post·amt
tourist office	Fremdenverkehrsbüro	frem·den·fer·kairs·bü·raw

HERERO/HIMBA

The Herero and Himba languages are quite similar, and are especially useful if travelling around remote areas of North-Central Namibia and particularly the Kaokoveld, where Afrikaans remains a lingua franca and few people speak English.

Herero is a rolling, melodious language, rich in colourful words. Most Namibian place names that begin with 'O' (eg Okahandja, Omaruru and Otjiwarongo) are derived from the Herero language.

Basics

Hello.	Tjike.
Good morning.	Wa penduka.
Good afternoon.	Wa uhara.
Good evening.	Wa tokerua.
Good night.	Ongurova ombua.

Yes./No.	Ii./Kako.
Please.	Arikana.
Thank you.	Okuhepa.
How are you?	Kora?
Well, thank you.	Mbiri naua, okuhepa.
Pardon.	Makuvi.
Do you speak Afrikaans/English?	U hungira Otjimburu/Otjingirisa?
How many?	Vi ngapi?
When?	Rune?
Where?	Pi?
arrival	omeero
departure	omairo
from	okuza
one way (single)	ourike
return	omakotokero
ticket	okatekete
to	ko
travel	ouyenda
caravan park	omasuviro uo zo karavana
game reserve	orumbo ro vipuka
(short/long) hiking trail	okaira komakaendro uo pehi (okasupi/okare)
marsh	eheke
mountain	ondundu
point	onde
river (channel)	omuramba
today	ndinondi
tomorrow	muhuka
yesterday	erero
Monday	Omandaha
Tuesday	Oritjaveri
Wednesday	Oritjatatu
Thursday	Oritjaine
Friday	Oritjatano

EMERGENCIES HERERO/HIMBA

Help!	Vatera!
Call a doctor!	Isana onganga!
Call the police!	Isana oporise!
I'm lost.	Ami mba pandjara.

Saturday	Oroviungura
Sunday	Osondaha
1	iimue
2	imbari
3	indatu
4	iine
5	indano
6	hamboumue
7	hambomabari
8	hambondatu
9	imuvyu
10	omurongo

!KUNG SAN

The languages of Namibia's several San groups are characterised by 'click' elements. Perhaps the most useful dialect for the traveller is that of the !Kung people, who are concentrated in Northern Namibia.

Clicks are made by compressing the tongue against different parts of the mouth to produce sounds. Names that include an exclamation mark are of Khoisan origin and should be rendered as a sideways click sound, similar to the sound one would make when encouraging a horse, but with a hollow tone (like the sound made when pulling a cork from a bottle).

In normal speech, the language features four different clicks (lateral, palatal, dental and labial), which are usually represented in Namibia by the symbols '//', '‡', '/' and '!', respectively. However, other orthographies are used around the region, and clicks may be represented as 'nx', 'ny', 'c', 'q', 'x', '!x', '!q', 'k', 'zh', and so on. To simplify matters, in the following list of basic phrases all clicks are represented by '!k' (locals will usually forgive you for pronouncing the clicks as a 'k' sound or for simplifying the four clicks to one).

Basics

Hello.	!Kao.
Good morning.	Tuwa.
Goodbye, go well.	!King se !kau.
How are you?	!Ka tseya? (to a man) !Ka tsiya? (to a woman)
Thank you (very much).	(!Kin)!Ka.
What is your name?	!Kang ya tsedia? (to a man) !Kang ya tsidia? (to a woman)
My name is ...	!Kang ya tse/tsi ... (m/f)

LOZI

Lozi (also known as Rotsi) is the most common Caprivian dialect, spoken throughout the Caprivi region, especially around Katima Mulilo. It originates from Barotseland in Zambia. As you can see from the list of options in the following phrases, social status is strongly reflected in spoken Lozi.

Basics

Hello.	Eeni, sha. (to anybody)
	Lumela. (to a peer)
	Mu lumeleng' sha. (to one or more persons of higher social standing)
Goodbye.	Siala foo/hande/sinde. (to a peer)
	Musiale foo/hande/sinde. (to more than one peer or one or more persons of higher social standing)
Good morning.	U zuhile. (to a peer)
	Mu zuhile. (to more than one peer or one or more persons of higher social standing)
Good evening/ afternoon.	Ki manzibuana. (to anybody)
	U tozi. (to a peer)
	Mu tozi. (to one or more persons of higher social standing)
Good night.	Ki busihu. (to anybody)
Please.	Sha. (only to people of higher social standing)
Thank you (very much).	N'i tumezi (hahulu).
Excuse me.	Ni swalele. (inf)
	Mu ni swalele. (pol)
Yes.	Ee. (to a peer)
	Eeni. (to more than one peer or one or more persons of higher social standing)
No.	Awa. (to a peer or peers)
	Batili. (to one or more persons of higher social standing)
Do you speak English?	Wa bulela sikuwa? (to peers)
	W'a utwa sikuwa? (to more than one peer or one or more persons of higher standing)
	Mw'a bulela sikuwa?
	Mw'a utwa sikuwa?
I don't understand.	Ha ni utwi.
What is your name?	Libizo la hao ki wena mang'? (to a peer)
	Libizo la mina ki mina bo mang'? (to a person of higher social standing)
What is that?	S'ale king'? (near)
	Ki sika mang' s'ale? (far)

Where?	Kai?
Here.	Fa./Kafa./Kwanu.
(Over) There.	F'ale./Kw'ale.
How much?	Ki bukai?
Enough.	Ku felile.
What time is it?	Ki nako mang'?
today	kachenu
tomorrow	kamuso
yesterday	mabani

1	il'ingw'i
2	z'e peli or bubeli
3	z'e t'alu or bulalu
4	z'e ne or bune
5	z'e keta-lizoho
6	z'e keta-lizoho ka ka li kang'wi
7	supile
10	lishumi
20	mashumi a mabeli
1000	likiti

OWAMBO

There are eight dialects of Owambo; Kwanyama and Ndonga are the official Owambo languages. Owambo (or Oshiwambo) – specifically the Kwanyama dialect – is the first language of more Namibians than any other, and it's a second language for many non-Owambo Namibians of both Bantu and Khoisan origin.

Basics

Good morning.	Wa lalapo.
Good evening.	Wa tokelwapo.
How are you?	Owu li po ngiini?
I'm fine.	Ondi li nawa.
Yes.	Eeno.
No.	Aawe.
Please.	Ombili.
Thank you.	Tangi.
Excuse me.	Ombili manga.
I'm sorry.	Onde shi panda.
Do you speak English?	Oho popi Oshiingilisa?
Can you please help me?	Eto vuluwu pukulule ndje?
How much is this?	Ingapi tashi kotha?
I'm lost.	Ombili, onda puka.
Where is the ...?	Openi pu na ...?

here/there	mpaka/hwii
near/far	popepi/kokule
that way	ondjila
this way	no onkondo
Turn right.	Uka kohulyo.
Turn left.	Uka kolumoho.

today	nena
tomorrow	ungula
yesterday	ohela
Monday	Omaandaha
Tuesday	Etiyali
Wednesday	Etitatu
Thursday	Etine
Friday	Etitano
Saturday	Olyomakaya
Sunday	Osoondaha

1	yimwe
2	mbali
3	ndatu
4	ne
5	ntano
6	hamano
7	heyali
8	hetatu
9	omugoyi
10	omulongo

SETSWANA

Setswana (also commonly known as Tswana) is a Bantu language in the Sotho-Tswana language group that is understood by around 90% of Botswana's population. It is the language of the dominant ethnic group, the Batswana.

Setswana is pronounced more or less as it is written, except for *g*, which is pronounced as an English 'h' (or, more accurately, a strongly aspirated 'g') and *th*, which is pronounced as a slightly aspirated 't'.

Basics

Hello.	Dumêla rra/mma. (to a man/woman) Dumêlang. (to a group)
Hello!	Ko ko! (announcing arrival outside a yard or house)
Goodbye.	Tsamaya sentle. (said by person staying) Sala sentle. (said by person leaving)
Yes.	Ee.
No.	Nnyaa.
Please.	Tsweetswee.
Thank you.	Kea leboga.
Excuse me./Sorry.	Intshwarele.
Pardon me.	Ke kopa tsela.
No problem.	Go siame.
How are you?	A o tsogile? (in the morning)
How are you?	O tlhotse jang? (in the afternoon/evening)
I'm fine.	Ke tlhotse sentle. (pol) Ke teng. (inf)
How's it going?	O kae?
Are you well?	A o sa tsogile sentle?
Yes, I'm well.	Ee, ke tsogile sentle.
What's your name?	Leina la gago ke mang?
My name is ...	Leina la me ke ...
Where are you from?	O tswa kae?
I'm from ...	Ke tswa kwa ...
Where do you live?	O nna kae?
I live in ...	Ke nna kwa ...
Where are you going?	O ya kae?
Do you speak English?	A o bua Sekgoa?
Does anyone here speak English?	A go na le o o bua Sekgoa?
I don't understand.	Ga ke tlhaloganye.
Could you speak more slowly, please?	A o ka bua ka bonya tswee-tswee?

Accommodation

campsite	lefelo la go robala mo tenteng
guesthouse	matlo a baeng
hotel	hotele
youth hostel	matlo a banana

Where is a ... hotel?	Hotele e e ... ko gae?
cheap	go tlase ka di tlotlwa
good	siame
Do you have any rooms available?	A go na le matlo?

I'd like ...	Ke batla ...
a double room	kamore tse pedi
a room with a bathroom	kamore e e nang le ntlwana ya go tlhapela
a single room	kamore e le mongwe
to share a dorm	go tlhakanela kamore

How much is it ...?	Ke bokae ...?
for one night	bosigo bo le bongwe
for two nights	masego a mated
per person	motho a le mongwe

Eating & Drinking

What would you like?	O batla eng?
I'd like ...	Ke batla ...
I'm vegetarian.	Ke ja merogo fela.
Cheers!	Pula!
breakfast	sefitlholo
dinner	selaelo
lunch	dijo tsa motshegare
meals	dijo
menu	karate tsa dijo

beef	nama ya kgomo
bread	borotho
butter	mafura
chicken	koko
coffee	kofi
egg	mai
fish	tlhapi
fruit	leungo
goat	pudi
meat	nama
milk	mashi
mutton	nku
rice	raese
soft drink	sene tsididi
sugar	sukiri
tea	tee
vegetables	merogo
(boiled) water	metsi (a a bedileng)

Emergencies

| Help! | Nthusa! |
| Leave me alone! | Ntlhogela! |

Call a doctor!	Bitsa ngaka!
Call the police!	Bitsa mapodisi!
I'm lost.	Ke la tlhegile.
I'm ill.	Ke a lwala.
My friend is ill.	Tsala yame e a lwala.

Where is the ...?	E ko kae ...?
dentist	ngaka ya meno
doctor	ngaka
hospital	sepatela
pharmacy	khemesiti
aspirin	pilisi
condoms	dikausu
diarrhoea	letshololo
medicine	molemo
nausea	go feroga sebete
stomachache	mala a a botlhoko
syringe	mokento

Shopping & Services

I'm looking for a/the ...	Ke batla ...
bank	ntlo ya polokelo
city centre	toropo
market	mmaraka
museum	ntlo ya ditso
post office	poso
public toilet	matlwana a boitiketso
tourist office	ntlo ya bajanala

What time does it open/close?	Ke nako mang bula/tswala?
How much is it?	Ke bokae?
It's too expensive.	E a dura.
Can you lower the price?	Fokotsa tlhwatlhwa?

Time, Dates & Numbers

What time is it?	Ke nako mang?
afternoon	tshogololo
next week	beke e e tlang
night	bosigo
today	gompieno
tomorrow	ka moso
yesterday	maabane

Monday	mosupologo
Tuesday	labobedi
Wednesday	laboraro
Thursday	labone
Friday	latlhano
Saturday	matlhatso
Sunday	tshipi
1	bongwe
2	bobedi
3	borara
4	bone
5	botlhano
6	borataro
7	bosupa
8	borobabobedi
9	boroba bongwe
10	lesome
20	masome a mabedi
30	masome a mararo
40	masome a mane
50	masome a matlhano
60	masome amarataro
70	masome a supa
80	masome a a robang bobedi
90	masome a a robang bongwe
100	lekgolo
1000	sekete

Transport & Directions

Where is the ...?	E ko kae ...?
bus stop	maemelo a di bese
train station	maemelo a terena
When is the ...?	E ... goroga nako mung?
boat	sekepe
bus	bese
canoe	mokoro
train	terena
I'd like ...	Ke batla ...
a one-way ticket	karata ya go tsamaya fela
a return ticket	karata ya go boa
the first class	ya ntlha
the second class	ya bobedi
Which way is ...?	Tsela ... e kae?
Where is the station/hotel?	Seteseine/hotele se kae?
Can you show me on the map ...?	A o mpotshe mo mepeng?
Could you write the address?	Nkwalele aterese?
Is it far?	A go kgala?
Go straight ahead.	Thlamalala.
Turn left.	Chikela mo molemong.
Turn right.	Chikela mo mojeng.
near	gaufi
far	kgakala

GLOSSARY

ablutions block – camping-ground building with toilets, showers and a washing-up area

Afrikaans – language spoken in South Africa, which is a derivative of Dutch

ANC – African National Congress; ruling party in South Africa

apartheid – literally 'separate development of the races'; a political system in which people are officially segregated according to their race

ATVs – all-terrain vehicles

Bantu – the name used to describe over 400 ethnic groups in Africa united by a common language

barchan dunes – migrating crescent-shaped sand dunes

Basarwa – Batswana term for the San people; it means 'people of the sticks' and is considered pejorative

Batswana – Setswana name for the people of Botswana; adjective referring to anything of or from Botswana; also (confusingly) refers to people from the Batswana tribe; plural of *Motswana*

BDF – Botswana Defence Force; the Botswanan army

BDP – Botswana Democratic Party

Bechuanaland – the name given by the British to describe the Crown Colony they established in Botswana in 1885

Benguela current – the frigid current that flows northwards along the west African coast as far as Angola from Antarctica

boerewors – Afrikaner farmer's sausage

Boers – the Dutch word for 'farmer' which came to denote Afrikaans-speaking people

bogobe – sorghum porridge; a staple food

bojalwa – a popular and inexpensive sprouted-sorghum beer

bojazz – Botswana jazz

boomslang – dangerous and venomous tree-dwelling 2m-long snake

borankana – Setswana word meaning traditional entertainment

borehole – a deep well shaft in the ground used for the abstraction of water, oil or gas

braai – Afrikaans term for a barbecue featuring lots of meat grilled on a special stand called a braaivleis

BSAC – British South Africa Company; late-19th-century company led by Cecil Rhodes

bushveld – flat grassy plain covered in thorn scrub

CDM – Consolidated Diamond Mines

Chibuku – bojalwa that is brewed commercially; the 'beer of good cheer' drunk in Zimbabwe and also in Botswana

CKGR – Central Kalahari Game Reserve

combi – usual term for 'minibus'

conflict diamonds – diamonds mined in conflict areas which are then sold illicitly

cuca shops – small bush shops of Northern Namibia; named for an Angolan beer that was once sold there

Debswana – De Beers Botswana Mining Company Ltd, partly owned by the Botswanan government, which mines, sorts and markets diamonds from Botswana

difaqane – forced migration or exodus by several Southern African tribes in the face of Zulu aggression in the 19th century

Ditshwanelo – the Botswana Centre for Human Rights

drift – river ford, mostly dry

DTA – Democratic Turnhalle Alliance

DWNP – Department of Wildlife and National Parks, which runs the Botswana government-owned national parks/reserves

elenga – village headman

euphorbia – several species of cactuslike succulents

FPK – First People of the Kalahari, a local advocacy organisation working for the right of San who have been forcibly resettled

from the Central Kalahari Game Reserve in the town of New Xade

Gemütlichkeit – a distinctively German atmosphere of comfort and hospitality

Gondwanaland – the prehistoric supercontinent which included most of the land masses in today's southern hemisphere

GPS – Global Positioning System

Great Zimbabwe – an ancient Southern African city located in modern Zimbabwe that was once the centre of a vast empire known as Monomotapa

guano – droppings from seabirds or bats which is harvested as a fertiliser

inselberg – isolated range or hill typical of the pro- Namib and Damaraland plains

karakul – variety of central Asian sheep, which produces high-grade wool and pelts

karata – phonecard; also ticket

kgosi – Setswana word for 'chief'

kgotla – traditionally constructed Batswana community affairs hall or open area used for meetings of the dikgotla

Khoisan – language grouping taking in all Southern African indigenous languages

kloof – ravine or small valley

koeksesters – small, gooey Afrikaner doughnuts, dripping in honey or sugar syrup

kokerboom – quiver tree; grows mainly in southern Namibia

konditorei – German pastry shop; found in larger Namibian towns

kopje – also kopie; small hill

kraal – Afrikaans version of the Portuguese word 'curral'; an enclosure for livestock or a hut village

lapa – circular area with a firepit, used for socialising

lediba – Setswana word for 'lagoon'; the singular of madiba

lekgapho – a unique Batswana design used to decorate ntlo

location – Namibian and South African name for township

GLOSSARY

mabele – Setswana word for sorghum, used to make bogobe

madiba – Setswana word for 'lagoons', plural of lediba

mahango – millet; a staple of the Owambo diet and used for brewing a favourite alcoholic beverage

marimba – African xylophone, made from strips of resonant wood with various-sized gourds for sound boxes

mbira – see thumb piano

mealie pap – Afrikaans name for maize-meal porridge; a staple food for most Namibians

MET – Namibia's Ministry of Environment & Tourism

Modimo – supreme being and creator of early Batswana tribal religion

mokolane – Setswana name for the palm Hyphaene petersiana

mokoro – traditional dugout canoe used in the Okavango Delta; plural mekoro

morama – an immense tuber, the pulp of which contains large quantities of water and serves as a source of liquid for desert dwellers

Motswana – one Tswana person, ie the singular of Batswana

!nara – type of melon that grows in the Namib Desert

NDF – Namibian Defence Forces, the Namibian military

Ndjambi – supernatural Herero being who represents good

ngashi – a pole made from the mogonono tree and used on a mokoro

NGO – nongovernmental organisation

N!odima – supernatural San being who represents good

n!oresi – traditional San lands; 'lands where one's heart is'

ntlo – round hut found in Batswana villages

NWR – Namibian Wildlife Resorts; semiprivate overseer of visitor facilities in Namibia's national parks

omiramba – fossil river channels in north and west Botswana; singular omuramba

oshana – dry river channel in Northern Namibia and Northwestern Botswana

oshikundu – alcoholic beverage made from mahango; popular throughout areas of Northern Namibia

pan – dry flat area of grassland or salt deposits, often a seasonal lake bed

panhandle – an informal geographic term used to describe an elongated protrusion of a geopolitical entity similar in shape to a peninsula and usually created by arbitrarily drawn international boundaries; in the case of Botswana and Namibia, this refers to the area of the Caprivi Strip

panveld – area containing many pans

pap – see *mealie pap*

participation safari – an inexpensive safari in which clients pitch their own tents, pack the vehicle and share cooking duties

pronking – four-legged leaping, as done by some antelopes (particularly springboks)

pula – the Botswana currency; 100 *thebe*; also Setswana word for 'rain'

quad bike – four-wheeled motorcycle often called an ATV (all-terrain vehicle)

robot – a traffic light

rondavel – a round hut which is often thatched

SACU – Southern African Customs Union, comprised of Botswana, South Africa, Lesotho, Namibia and Swaziland

San – a tribal group, which has inhabited Botswana for at least 30,000 years

sangoma – traditional Batswana doctor who believes that he/she is inhabited by spirits

savannah – grasslands with widely spaced trees

seif dunes – prominent linear sand dunes, as found in the Central Namib Desert

Setswana – language of the Batswana; the predominant language of Botswana

shebeen – illegal drinking establishment

shongololo – ubiquitous giant millipede

Sperrgebiet – 'forbidden area'; alluvial diamond region of southwestern Namibia

strandwolf – the Afrikaans name given to the Namib Desert brown hyena

Swapo – South-West Africa People's Organization; Namibia's liberation army and the ruling political party

thebe – one-hundredth of a *pula*; Setswana word for 'shield'

thumb piano – consists of narrow iron keys mounted in rows on a wooden sound board; the player plucks the ends of the keys with the thumbs; known as mbira in Tswana.

toktokkie – Afrikaans for the fog-basking tenebrionid beetle

township – indigenous suburb; generally a high-density black residential area

tsama – a desert melon historically eaten by the San people, and by livestock

Tswana – another word for *Batswana* or *Setswana*

Unita – National Union for the Total Independence of Angola

veld – open grassland, normally in plateau regions

Veterinary Cordon Fence a series of 1.5m-high, wire fences aimed at segregating wild and domestic animals

vlei – low-lying, marshy ground, covered with water during the rainy season

welwitschia – cone-bearing shrub native to the northern Namib plains

wildlife drive – a trip to spot wildlife, also known as a 'game drive'

WMA – Wildlife Management Area

Behind the Scenes

SEND US YOUR FEEDBACK

We love to hear from travellers – your comments keep us on our toes and help make our books better. Our well-travelled team reads every word on what you loved or loathed about this book. Although we cannot reply individually to your submissions, we always guarantee that your feedback goes straight to the appropriate authors, in time for the next edition. Each person who sends us information is thanked in the next edition – the most useful submissions are rewarded with a selection of digital PDF chapters.

Visit **lonelyplanet.com/contact** to submit your updates and suggestions or to ask for help. Our award-winning website also features inspirational travel stories, news and discussions.

Note: We may edit, reproduce and incorporate your comments in Lonely Planet products such as guidebooks, websites and digital products, so let us know if you don't want your comments reproduced or your name acknowledged. For a copy of our privacy policy visit lonelyplanet.com/privacy.

OUR READERS

Many thanks to the travellers who used the last edition and wrote to us with helpful hints, useful advice and interesting anecdotes:

Linda Baker, Marie & Kristof Bertram, Thomas Charteris, Ty Chieu, Sonja Dale, Arno & Margriet van Eijl, Magalie Jooren, Tim Kavulla, Aura de Marimon, Merle Pape, Pawel Gluza, Ashleigh Grant, Franziska Isliker, Henry Hogger, Jakub Schwedler, Javier Vieira, Martin Weinans

WRITER THANKS

Anthony Ham

So many people helped me along the way and brought such wisdom and insight to this book. Special thanks as always to Andy Raggett at Drive Botswana, and to Paul Funston, Lise Hansson, Luke Hunter, Charlotte Pollard, Rob Reid, Eva Meurs, Daan Smit, Jacob Tembo, Induna Mundandwe, Kasia Sliwa, Lara Good, Ying Yi Ho, and to Frank, Juliane, Tim and Ann-Sophie. At Lonely Planet, heartfelt thanks to my editor Matt Phillips – no-one knows Africa like him. And to Marina, Carlota and Valentina – I loved sharing some of my favourite corners of Africa with you.

Trent Holden

First up thanks to Matt Phillips for commissioning me on this amazing part of the world, as well as all the production staff for putting this together. A huge thanks to Kim from Livingstone and Joy from Victoria Falls in Zimbabwe for all their assistance and time in ensuring info is correct. Finally lots of love to my family, especially my partner, Kate, who allows me to travel to such far flung, exotic places.

ACKNOWLEDGEMENTS

Climate map data adapted from Peel MC, Finlayson BL & McMahon TA (2007) 'Updated World Map of the Köppen-Geiger Climate Classification', Hydrology and Earth System Sciences, 11, 163344.

Cover photograph: Leopard, Chobe National Park, Botswana; Richard Du Toit/Getty©

THIS BOOK

This 4th edition of Lonely Planet's *Botswana & Namibia* guidebook was researched and written by Anthony Ham and Trent Holden. The previous edition was written by Alan Murphy, Anthony Ham, Trent Holden, Kate Morgan and David Lukas. This guidebook was produced by the following:

Destination Editor
Matt Phillips

Product Editors
Jessica Ryan, Genna Patterson

Senior Cartographers Diana Von Holdt, Corey Hutchinson

Book Designer Gwen Cotter

Assisting Editors Andrew Bain, Judith Bamber, Imogen Bannister, Carly Hall, Jodie Martire, Louise McGregor, Charlotte Orr

Cartographer Rachel Imeson

Cover Researcher
Naomi Parker

Thanks to Ronan Abayawickrema, Jennifer Carey, David Carroll, Daniel Corbett, Sandie Kestell, Claire Naylor, Karyn Noble, Lauren O'Connell, Angela Tinson, Tony Wheeler

Index

LONELY PLANET IN THE WILD

Send your 'Lonely Planet in the Wild' photos to social@lonelyplanet.com
We share the best on our Facebook page every week!